Pittsburgh Series in Social and Labor History

The Battle for Homestead
1880–1892

Politics, Culture, and Steel

PAUL KRAUSE

University of Pittsburgh Press

PITTSBURGH AND LONDON

Published by the University of Pittsburgh Press, Pittsburgh Pa. 15260
Copyright © 1992, University of Pittsburgh Press
Eurospan, London

Manufactured in the United States of America

Library of Congress Cataloging-in-Publication Data

Krause, Paul.
    The battle for Homestead, 1880–1892 : politics, culture, and steel
/ Paul Krause.
        p.   cm. — (Pittsburgh series in social and labor history)
    Includes bibliographical references and index.
    ISBN 0-8229-3702-6. — ISBN 0-8229-5466-4 (pbk.)
    1. Homestead Strike, 1892.   2. Steel industry and trade—
Pennsylvania—History—19th century.   3. Iron and steel workers—
Pennsylvania—History—19th century.   4. Working class—
Pennsylvania—History—19th century.   I. Title.   II. Series.
HD5325.I5 1892.H53   1992
331.89'2869142'0974885—dc20   91-50760
                                                                  CIP

A CIP catalog record for this title is available from the British Library.

Civilization has been an intermittent phenomenon; to this truth we have allowed ourselves to be blinded by the insolence of material success. Many late societies have displayed a pyrotechnic brilliance and a capacity for refined sensation far beyond anything seen in their days of vigor. That such things may exist and yet work against that state of character concerned with choice, which is the anchor of society, is the great lesson to be learned.

—RICHARD M. WEAVER, *Ideas Have Consequences*

For Belle and Gigs

Contents

PART FOUR
"Tried and Found Faithful":
Homestead Defies the Assault

PART FIVE
Labor in Greater Pittsburgh During the 1880s

PART SIX
1892 and Beyond: Legacies of Homestead

Preface

I grew up in Pittsburgh in the 1950s, and the landscape of my childhood, like that of my parents before me, was dominated by the great steel mills of the Monongahela Valley. Although not steelworkers themselves, my family depended for its livelihood—as did so many in Greater Pittsburgh—on the constant activity of those mills and the people who made them run.

Both my father and his father worked in Braddock, Pennsylvania. I remember, as a boy, standing outside my grandfather's clothing store and watching the crowds on the busy main avenue hurry past my father's office, past the imposing red brick library, toward the mill gate of the awesome Edgar Thomson Steel Works that loomed at the end of the street. More immediately, I recall as a young man witnessing the effects of the slow and eerie death of the mills up and down the Monongahela—the thinning of the crowds on Braddock Avenue to a trickle of ghosts, the boarded-up storefronts, the closing of the Carnegie Library, and the straggling parades of ex-steelworkers in front of the locked Edgar Thomson gates.

When, years later, as an aspiring historian in the American South, I tried to make sense of what America had become in my own lifetime, it was the lasting impression of these images that drove me, unwitting perhaps, to return to the steel mills of Greater Pittsburgh. The study of what America had become in the twentieth century sent me back to what America had tried to become in the nineteenth; and wanting to understand the many things America had tried to become in the nineteenth century sent me back to steel. Or, more precisely, to the romance of steel—with all its varied plots and subplots, discourses and counterdiscourses. The industry of America in the nineteenth century, in the broadest sense of activity and zeal, was, in fact, the steel industry. And Pittsburgh, of course, was the Steel City.

While Pittsburgh was the Steel City, it was at the Homestead Steel Works, six miles up the river, that the story of nineteenth-century steelmaking unfolded most dramatically. I therefore went back to Homestead. There, at the site of the Lockout of 1892, I recognized, in the great disputes over the meaning of steel, the articulation of still greater disputes over the meanings of America, progress, and the nature of democracy with which I had been grappling. And at that site, coincidentally, I also found myself facing, geographically and symbolically, the very blast furnaces of Braddock that had presided over my imagination some thirty years earlier.

For nearly a decade, many people have taken an interest in the research upon which this book is based and have helped me sort through it. Perhaps my largest professional thanks is owed to five very different historians who offered encouragement, understanding, and valuable criticism at crucial junctures: Melvyn Dubofsky, Eugene Genovese, Lawrence Goodwyn, the late Herbert G. Gutman, and Charles S. Maier. I would like to think that some of the pages that follow would please some members of this very eclectic group some of the time. I also wish to acknowledge the assistance of another historian, Richard Oestreicher, whose insightful critique of an earlier draft encouraged me to explore contradictions and ambiguities where I had first seen simple explanations.

At Duke University, where this study first took shape, I was fortunate to find many colleagues to challenge and guide me through the initial stages of my research. In particular, I would like to thank Bill Chafe, Robert Durden, and Bill Reddy. In Susan Levine, Leon Fink, Warren Lerner, and Tom Wartenberg, I also found faithful friends. I trust they know just how much their support and criticism has meant to me.

More recently, friends and colleagues in Vancouver and at the University of British Columbia have offered assistance with a variety of research and bibliographic problems. I am especially grateful to Edward Hundert, Steve Straker, and Heather Frankson for their time and advice, and to the Interlibrary Loan staff at the University of British Columbia library for their patience. Similarly, for their tireless efforts over the years, I would like to thank the staff of Perkins Library at Duke University, and especially Ken Berger, Bessie Carrington, Emerson Ford, Anna O'Brian, Linda Purnell, and Clifford Sanderson.

Paul Berman, Frank Couvares, Dirk Hoerder, and Mark Stolarik offered essential assistance in the early going and, in several instances, shared important material with me. Doubtless, these individuals disagree with my treatment of certain matters; in fundamental ways, however, *The Battle for Homestead* grew out of their work. Likewise, I remain deeply indebted to the distinguished scholarship of David Brody and of Joseph Frazier Wall, whose biography of *Andrew Carnegie* stands as a monumental achievement in American letters.

In Homestead and Pittsburgh my research would have been impossible without the aid of Rev. Bernard Costello, Maria Grodsky, Randy Harris, Charles Hill, Rev. Edward Kunco, Dennis Lambert, Rev. Edward

McSweeney, Irwin Marcus, Kelly C. Park, Paul Roberts, David Rosenberg, Frank Zabrosky, and Rev. Richard Zula—all of whom kindly
shared archival material with me or directed me to it. In granting access
to Andrew Carnegie's early business records, the USX Corporation provided me with important materials that proved crucial to this study. For
this, I thank in particular William E. Keslar and J.M. Mindek.

Two other Pittsburghers, Frederick A. Hetzel and Maurine Weiner
Greenwald, both of the University of Pittsburgh Press, more years ago
than I care to remember, gave me the kind of boost about which young
historians can only dream. My thanks as well to Catherine Marshall and
Irma Garlick, managing editor and copy editor, who cheerfully minded a
daunting number of p's and q's.

For support of a different, but no less appreciated, nature, I wish to
acknowledge the Graduate School of Arts and Sciences, Duke University, the Andrew W. Mellon Foundation, the University of British Columbia, and the Social Sciences and Humanities Research Council of Can-
ada. Finally, the National Endowment for the Humanities provided a
year's fellowship that allowed me to complete the research and revise
the manuscript.

The steady encouragement of my family—particularly Seymoure
Krause, Joseph Godfrey, Rose Godfrey, Judy Bennett, Trudy Kapner, and
above all Corinne Azen Krause—made it possible for me to keep on. In
many ways, however, my most profound thanks belong to my late parents, Belle Lewin Krause and Gilbert Krause, who, because they always
took pride in my work, made the work on this book so much easier.

Most of all, I am grateful to my children, Benjamin and Louisa, for
waiting patiently until "all the letters were done," and to my wife, Sima
Godfrey, who, in reading nearly all of the letters, helped arrange them in
better ways. Throughout, she has been the most demanding, and most
loving, critic; without her, neither this book nor its author would be
complete.

Introduction

Up the index of night, granite and steel—
Transparent meshes—feckless the gleaming staves—
Sibylline voices flicker, waveringly stream
As though a god were issue of the strings

—HART CRANE, *The Bridge*

Thousands of people came to New York City on 24 May 1883 to observe the formal opening of the Brooklyn Bridge. The ceremonies were called "The People's Day." It was a day that proclaimed, the speakers noted, a victory over the dark forces of history. It was a day to celebrate Progress.[1]

Among the dignitaries who attended were President Chester A. Arthur and Governor Grover Cleveland of New York. The main speaker was Congressman Abram S. Hewitt, a leader of the Democratic party and a wealthy, innovative ironmaster.

Hewitt declared that the bridge signified the triumph of technology over nature and the crowning achievement of a peculiarly American genius: it "stands before us today as the sum and epitome of human knowledge; as the very heir of the ages; as the latest glory of centuries of . . . accumulated skill . . . in the never-ending struggle of man to subdue the forces of nature to his control and use."

Americans had won the struggle, Hewitt maintained, because of the great advance toward progress upon which they had embarked in 1776, the year that witnessed the writing of the Declaration of Independence, the birth of political economy in the publication of *The Wealth of Nations,* and, in James Watt's steam engine, the onset of the Industrial Revolution. The Brooklyn Bridge now stood as the latest symbol of that undaunted advance: "In no previous period of the world's history could this bridge have been built."

The Brooklyn Bridge was made of steel, a fact important to Hewitt and to the Reverend Richard Storrs, the other keynote speaker of the day. Steel, said Storrs, was "the chiefest of modern instruments . . .

xiii

[and] the kingliest instrument of peoples for subduing the earth." The use of steel instead of iron indicated the "new supremacy of man, . . . the readiness to attempt unparalleled works, [and] the disdain of difficulties." The bridge, he claimed, was "a durable monument to Democracy itself."

The structural material used in the beams, braces, and plates of the bridge was manufactured in the Pittsburgh steel mills owned by Andrew Carnegie, himself a staunch believer in the "triumph of democracy." Like Storrs and Hewitt, who was vice president of the construction company that built the bridge, Carnegie was a committed admirer of Herbert Spencer, the era's grand preacher of progress and mindless optimism. And like Storrs and Hewitt, Carnegie too believed that steel was at once the instrument of universal progress and its most impressive symbol.

But, Hewitt said, the bridge was "more than an embodiment of the scientific knowledge of physical laws or a symbol of social tendencies" pointing inexorably toward a perfectly harmonious social order. It was "equally a monument to the moral qualities of the human soul." The man who pronounced this tribute to moral monuments had reason to gloat: the construction contracts he engineered for the bridge had netted him thousands of dollars in personal kickbacks.

Ironically, Hewitt was right about the meaning of the bridge. In ways that he and his friend Andrew Carnegie could not imagine, in ways that far surpassed their personal venality, this monument in steel, which involved a complex set of political decisions and embodied salient qualities of "high" and "low" American culture, did indeed represent a moral measure of the times.

The present study is devoted to an examination of those times. Specifically, it explores the politics, culture, and morality of steelmaking in late nineteenth-century America by tracing the circuitous path that led businessmen, engineers, political leaders, and metalworkers to Homestead, Pennsylvania—site of the world's largest and most "progressive" steel mill and of America's most infamous debate over the politics, culture, and morality of steelmaking.

PART ONE
The Battle for Homestead

Andrew Carnegie is trying to break the backbone of the Amalgamated Association, and the present lockout at Homestead is but
the sequel to his attitude towards organized labor in the past. It is
not a sentiment with Mr. Carnegie; it is nothing he has ever written a pamphlet about. On the contrary, his public utterances have
contained . . . many platitudes about the rights of workingmen to
organize and the benefits to be derived from such organization. . . . But actions speak to the workmen at Homestead very
much louder than words. They realize now that Mr. Carnegie is a
businessman, not a theorist.

> — *New York World*,
> 3 July 1892

We do not propose that Andrew Carnegie's representatives shall
bulldoze us. We have our homes in this town, we have our
churches here, our societies and our cemeteries. We are bound to
Homestead by all the ties that men hold dearest and most sacred.

> — JOHN McLUCKIE,
> burgess of Homestead,
> 3 July 1892

The question at issue is a very grave one. It is whether the Carnegie Company or the Amalgamated Association shall have absolute
control of our plant and business at Homestead. We have decided . . . to operate the plant ourselves.

> — HENRY CLAY FRICK,
> 7 July 1892

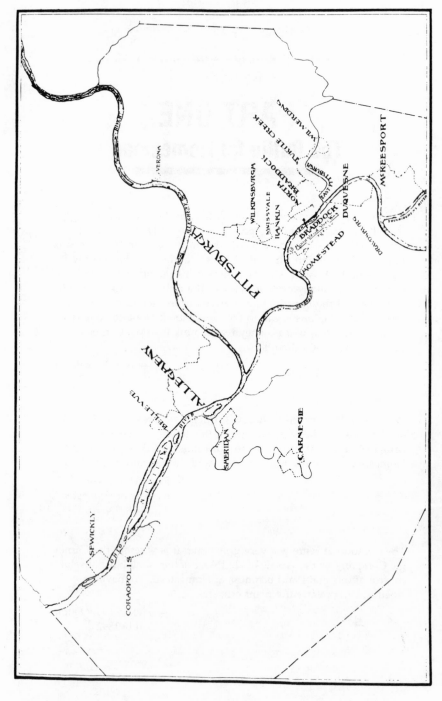

Pittsburgh and Vicinity. Adapted from John A. Fitch, *The Steel Workers* (New York: Russell Sage Foundation, 1910).

Chapter 1

Homestead and the American Republic in the Gilded Age

A CENTURY HAS passed since the lockout of 1892 at Andrew Carnegie's Homestead Steel Works, located on the Monongahela River just six miles upstream from Pittsburgh. The dramatic events of the lockout—in particular, the pitched battle between the steelworkers and the Pinkertons—are among the most familiar of American history. For many people, the story of the Homestead Lockout is as famous for the violent events that punctuated it as for the way it ended—with a resounding defeat for unionism in the steel industry. Many also understand that Homestead always has held a special fascination because it was America's greatest philanthropist, Carnegie, who, in direct contradiction of his public support for trade unions, precipitated this most "savage and significant chapter" in the history of American labor.[1]

Homestead attracted national attention well before Carnegie's chief of operations, Henry Clay Frick, a notorious opponent of unions, inaugurated the dispute on 29 June by closing down the giant mill and locking out 3,800 men. For weeks newspapers had predicted that there would be a momentous battle between the nation's most powerful steelmen, Carnegie and Frick, and the workers, led by the country's largest trade union, the Amalgamated Association of Iron and Steel Workers (AAISW). The expectations for drama were fulfilled when, on 1 July, the workers seized the mill and sealed off the town to prevent scabs from resuming operations. In the infamous battle of 6 July, 300 Pinkerton "detectives," dispatched to the mill by darkened river barge under an arrangement with the county sheriff, fought virtually the entire town; 3 Pinkertons and 7 workers were killed.[2] Four days later, 8,500 national guardsmen were called out at the request of Frick to retake the town and the mill. On 23 July, Alexander Berkman, a Russian Jewish anarchist, attempted to assassinate Frick but missed his mark. Soon after, guardsman W. L. Iams was hung by his thumbs for having jumped to his feet and shouted, "Three cheers for the man who shot Frick!"[3]

In succeeding weeks state authorities, acting in cooperation with the

3

Carnegie Steel Company and its chief lawyer, Philander C. Knox (who later would serve as U.S. attorney general and secretary of state) brought more than one hundred indictments against the leading steelworkers on charges of aggravated riot, conspiracy, murder, and treason. Only a few were tried, and none was convicted, but the combined authority of the state and one of the largest manufacturing establishments in the world proved too much for the workers. The AAISW held out until November; with its final defeat in Homestead, unionism in the national steel industry came to a virtual halt for four decades. For the workers who had led the resistance—most notably "Honest" John McLuckie, the burgess (mayor) of Homestead—Carnegie's victory meant permanent banishment from employment in steelmaking. For McLuckie it effectively meant banishment from the country: he was last seen in 1901 in Mexico, where he worked as a miner and well driver.[4]

Even before it ended, the Homestead Lockout became part of the folklore of industrial America. It entered popular culture as a quasi-mythical epic that pitted the aspirations of organized labor against the heartless rule of greedy tyrants. All over the country poets and lyricists commemorated it in verse that was often more melodramatic than the events themselves. The following angry song, widely known across America, was composed by William W. Delaney, a prominent New York songwriter.

FATHER WAS KILLED BY THE PINKERTON MEN

'Twas in Pennsylvania town not very long ago
Men struck against reduction of their pay
Their millionaire employer with philanthropic show
Had closed the works till starved they would obey
They fought for home and right to live where they had toiled so long
But ere the sun had set some were laid low
There're hearts now sadly grieving by that sad and bitter wrong
God help them for it was a cruel blow.

Chorus:

God help them tonight in their hour of affliction
Praying for him whom they'll ne'er see again
Hear the orphans tell their sad story
"Father was killed by the Pinkerton men."

Ye prating politicians, who boast protection creed,
Go to Homestead and stop the orphans' cry.
Protection for the rich man ye pander to his greed,
His workmen they are cattle and may die.
The freedom of the city in Scotland far away
'Tis presented to the millionaire suave,
But here in Free America with protection in full sway
His workmen get the freedom of the grave.[5]

As familiar as the events of July 1892 are—perhaps, indeed, because of their very familiarity—few historians have adequately addressed the larger events that preceded and the larger questions that shaped the Homestead Lockout. For the most part, scholars have been so blinded by the melodrama that they continue to perpetuate received versions as a caricatured battle between labor and capital over wages and work conditions. And yet even the most reductive, sentimental, popular accounts at the time show more sensitivity to the complex issues that determined this episode. "Reduction of their pay," according to Delaney's song, was just one of the provocations that stirred workers; they were fighting for their jobs and for rights they had every reason to expect "here in Free America."

Indeed, since the publication some eighty years ago of that pioneering effort in urban sociology, the Pittsburgh Survey, Homestead has generated surprisingly little scholarship. The industrial studies research team assembled for the Survey by the labor economist John R. Commons—notably John A. Fitch and Margaret F. Byington—effectively enshrined Homestead in an academic hall of fame. And as the historian Herbert Gutman pointed out twenty-five years ago, the best available popular narrative we have, Leon Wolff's *Lockout*, is marred by glaring conceptual and bibliographic shortcomings: Wolff's failure to consult a single labor source left formidable explanatory gaps in his rendering of Homestead.[6]

Though there has been some renewal of interest in the Homestead Lockout, Gutman's judgment stands. Yet the conventional wisdom among scholars and lay readers alike continues to be that Homestead represents, as the sociologist Steven R. Cohen asserts, "one of the most . . . thoroughly researched strikes in American history."[7] If one were to tally the number of texts and monographs that include a section or chapter on Homestead and then point to this total as evidence of how much scholarly attention the lockout has received, Cohen's assertion might be on target. The truth is, however, that virtually all secondary accounts focus rather narrowly on the summer of 1892 and therefore fail to address the outstanding question raised by Gutman: How do the particular events of the lockout relate to the "larger context" of American politics and culture in the Gilded Age?[8]

The incidents and themes that have been itemized in standard accounts are important, to be sure. However, it is not simply a story about one violent and bloody conflict between unions and management. Nor is it a story whose outcome can be explained by simple textbook references to the political shabbiness of the times, times that allowed ruthless capitalists to ride roughshod over their employees. Nor, indeed, is it a story that begins in 1892.

The story of Homestead dramatizes the broadest issues and problems of nineteenth-century industrial America. It is about the endless conflict between the pursuit of private interest and the defense of the common good. It is about the right of individuals to accumulate unlimited wealth and privilege versus the right of individuals to enjoy security in their jobs and dignity in their homes. It is about the aspirations and the frustrations of Americans who wanted their country to be a republic in fact and not merely in name. In short, as the nineteenth century was drawing to a close, Homestead posed the urgent question that remains with us still: Can—or how can—the new land of industry and technological innovation continue to be "the land of the free"? That is, how does one reconcile the undeniable attractions of material progress, implying as they invariably do a host of social and economic inequities, with the American commitment to democracy for all?

Twentieth-century history has demonstrated all too clearly the intensity of these dilemmas and the difficulties inherent in any putative solutions. That Homestead does not answer all the questions it raises, therefore, by no means limits its impact or importance. On the contrary, it is the very fact of having articulated these vital issues in an unforgettable manner that renders Homestead emblematic of an entire age of transition in America, one to which we are still very much heirs. And it is these issues, with their long and intricate history, in Homestead in particular and in post–Civil War America in general, that this book seeks to untangle and address.

At the broadest level, Homestead enacts a nationwide debate on the meaning of democracy and republican values in an age of rapid technological transformation; more locally, it dramatizes the specific social and political changes that ushered in the Age of Steel in Western Pennsylvania. From six miles up the Monongahela, Homestead tells the story of the redefinition of Pittsburgh from a city of workers and engaged citizens into one ruled by the greatest steelmakers and industrialists of the era. Homestead is also about the efforts of a notable group of immigrant workers—from the British Isles and Eastern Europe—to halt the advance of these industrial barons and to rescue and recast the most sacred political traditions of America.[9]

Received wisdom has interpreted Homestead as an isolated community subject to a discrete series of events in the early 1890s. The truth is that it was not isolated but fell squarely within the influential orbit of Pittsburgh—with all of its industrial and political upheavals. Similarly, the industrial and political redefinition of Pittsburgh was in good measure a significant by-product of the radical changes in metalmaking technology that transformed it from the Iron City into the Steel City. Indeed, it was the productive effects of these new techniques that ultimately thrust the United States into its position of economic dominance in the modern world. Like all technological advances, however, these innovations were neither politically nor morally neutral. Just as technical changes in the metal industry would alter the social and political structure of Pittsburgh, and ultimately America, so too, these innovations were themselves informed by a specific set of ideological presuppositions that had shaped Western culture since the Industrial Revolution.[10]

The chapters that follow chronicle important changes in Gilded Age America that mark its history in the inter-related spheres of industry and technological development, labor and labor organization, and political thought and discourse. The technological innovations that transformed American industry in the 1860s and 1870s—in particular the Bessemer process of steelmaking—elicited a wide variety of responses. These ranged from the unqualified enthusiasm of men such as Andrew Carnegie, Abram Hewitt, and Alexander Holley (the engineer who, in creating the Bessemer steel industry, also pointed the way to "scientific management") to the determined revolt of thousands of workers who, like John McLuckie, saw frightening signs of their own displacement and disenfranchisement in the march of technological progress. Between these two polarized responses, most workers reacted with a mixture of hope and trepidation appropriate to a period of great social indeterminacy.

Hesitations about the impact of the new technologies invading the workplace were compounded by the broader uncertainties bequeathed to workers, and all Americans, by the Civil War. Among the most troubling of these was the place of labor, white and black, within the new social order. In the view of many Americans, the "free" enterprise system—the very system that promoted technological innovation and industrial efficiency—rather than ensuring their freedom, had effectively locked them into an insidious form of wage slavery. Thousands of working Americans responded to these circumstances by demanding a new kind of abolitionism.[11]

In Pittsburgh this demand was met by efforts to build unions and create an independent workers' movement; the ensuing experience of industrial conflict shaped a political project for thousands of Pittsburghers from the late 1860s to the early 1880s. To end wage slavery and halt the drift toward permanent "dependence," labor leaders in greater Pittsburgh knew that the workers' movement had to cope with two specific challenges. Not surprisingly, the first was that posed by technological innovation in the struggle for control of the workplace. Just when businessmen and their allies were hailing American technical genius at the Philadelphia Centennial Exposition of 1876, the *National Labor Tribune,* the voice of the Pittsburgh labor movement, identified "machinery" as "the Grand Problem" of the era. In the view of the newspaper and many of its readers, new technologies, most notably of steelmaking, posed a question that addressed the democratic principles from which the labor movement drew its inspiration: How could workers convert the grand problem of machinery into a grand opportunity for building a cooperative society? The second challenge, which labor leaders saw as inextricably bound to the first, lay outside the shop floor, in the political arena. Here the question was how to mobilize the workers of Pittsburgh to wrest the reins of government from the supporters of "organized capital."[12]

The Pittsburgh workers who joined the labor movement did not stand alone. Across the country they had thousands of counterparts—in rural villages, in small towns, and in the largest cities—all determined to build an alternative to industrial capitalism. The efforts of these workers met with equally determined opposition; from Reconstruction until the 1890s, hundreds of thousands of Americans fought a war over the future definition of their country.[13]

Despite the diversity of their backgrounds and work experience, and despite what the historian Isaac Kramnick has characterized as America's "profusion and confusion of political tongues," the opponents of organized capital all looked to the legacy of republican thought to help define and legitimize their criticisms and aspirations. However colloquial their version of popular republicanism may seem, it derived nonetheless from the classical republican tradition that had been recast during the Renaissance by Machiavelli and subsequently embellished by British political theorists of the seventeenth and eighteenth centuries. Briefly, it was built upon four premises: (1) that the goal of society should be to preserve the common good, or commonwealth; (2) that in order to do so, citizens had to be virtuous, that is, able to subordinate their private wants to public needs; (3) that the virtue of all citizens was contingent upon their independence from the control of others; and (4) that to guard against "tyrants" (as well as for individuals to realize full selfhood), all citizens had to participate in public life. Failure to stave off the encroachments of tyrants in the common realm would lead inevitably to corruption. To these four premises Americans in the Revolutionary Era added a fifth: the idea of equality, that is, the idea that all citizens are entitled to natural, inalienable rights under a representative system of government.[14]

Like all interpreters of the republican tradition, critics of organized capital in the late nineteenth century produced their own functional version of these principles to defend. Stressing the ideas of the common good, virtue, and independence all the while, they rejected neither the idea of private property nor that of material prosperity achieved through the kind of individual effort that republican thought itself had helped to unleash. They did, however, challenge the emerging inequalities of power—"vices"—that arose from unchecked accumulation; and they did search for ways to translate their customary notions of nonmarket justice and mutual obligation into tactics that would place the interests of the common good above those of individuals.[15]

Yet those who defended capitalism also looked to the republican tradition to define and legitimize their beliefs in the sanctity of property and the virtue of accumulation. Publicly there was no more visible defender of republicanism during that period than Andrew Carnegie himself; he repeatedly endorsed the principles of individual rights against the injustices of the "feudal" social system from which he had escaped as a youthful idealist. In his eyes, private "vices"—the pursuit of individual advancement that America offered him—became the chief means of ensuring the public good. For people such as Carnegie and his friend Abram S. Hewitt, the accumulation of capital was the civilizing force that guaranteed the stability of the commonwealth; the preservation of an untrammeled right to accumulate was the main purpose of American democracy. Indeed, by the 1870s, Carnegie and his colleagues had squarely attached the ethos of accumulation and self-interest to the definition of democracy itself. In their eyes the preeminent natural right that Americans enjoyed was the right to limitless appropriation and property.[16]

In the view of labor reformers of the time, there existed no natural right to unlimited accumulation; a social system predicated on such a notion of right was false and therefore needed to be transformed. As Thomas Armstrong, the editor of Pittsburgh's *National Labor Tribune* wrote in the mid 1870s, the workers' movement had drawn a "bill of indictment against the civilization of the nineteenth century" which "challenges the very framework of society and declares it to be based on false principles. . . . The supremacy of the principles which labor is seeking to establish undermines the foundation of the existing order . . . [and] would ignore the present and accepted theories of value."[17]

The principles labor sought to establish, according to the *Tribune*, were grounded in notions of right and justice markedly different from the belief that self-interest is the universal, beneficent arbiter of human relations. The campaigns for "amalgamation" that punctuated Pittsburgh's labor history arose from the sense that industrial capitalism ignored "natural justice" by denying workers "a certain degree of comfort and measure of happiness which they should enjoy regardless of the empirical and cruel law of supply and demand." A shared desire to ensure such happiness by securing what American workers since the Revolutionary Era had called a "competence"—a sufficiency of means for living comfortably—provided the raw material out of which skilled industrial craftsmen and their less skilled colleagues tried to forge the requisite solidarity to attack the "unnatural" wage system.[18]

In criticizing the wealthy and staking out a claim to a competence (which typically included the ownership of a small house), workers assigned to property rights an instrumental and subordinate position. To workers, having a competence was a means to an end, and the end was a dignified life. To live with dignity meant having a modicum of material security and, therefore, a job that guaranteed security. While labor reformers rejected the hypothesis that there was a natural right to limitless amounts of private property, they accepted the argument that labor—work itself—was the property of the laborer. To deprive the worker of his work, as employers often did, was thus to deprive him of both his right to property and his right to a competence. The introduction of new technologies, along with the hard-line market ethos of industrial managers, threatened both of these.

Here, then, was the undergirding of a politics that did indeed indict nineteenth-century industrial civilization: a notion of right that ensured a competence. For the very idea of a competence presupposed that the unchecked pursuit of self-interest, a pursuit sanctioned by John Locke's apparent endorsement of the right to unlimited appropriation, would, by virtue of the marketplace laws of supply and demand, render meaningless the natural justice under which workers should enjoy "a certain degree of comfort and measure of happiness." The idea of a competence did not merely challenge the putative right to unlimited appropriation, however: it also asserted an important moral and political distinction between property for use and property for accumulation. Locke seemed to have removed the distinction. Labor reformers understood that it existed. However, in the end, they lacked a coherent strategy that would: (1) provide all citizens with sufficient property for a competence; (2) check unlimited property accumulation; and (3) ensure the individual pursuit of happiness that stood at the center of their cherished republicanism.[19]

The late nineteenth-century conflicts between organized capital and organizing labor thus embodied, to no insignificant degree, a contest over the meaning of republicanism in modern America. The defenders of capitalism privileged the rights of property and translated the republican emphasis on the development of moral personality into a quantitative process measured by the calculus of the market. The adversaries of capitalism saw a discrepancy between republican ideals and daily experience and sought to stave off the "corrupt" encroachments of a new tyranny of capital. At stake in this contest over the meaning of republicanism and the control of instruments of power and production was the very definition of public culture and the public interpretation of reality.[20]

These, then, were the issues and challenges that generally shaped the struggles between labor and capital in America in the Gilded Age and specifically underwrote both the initial growth and the eventual defeat of the labor reform movement in Pittsburgh. From the late 1860s onward, miners, metalworkers, and glassworkers in Pittsburgh actively sought to challenge the "morality of improvement" that informed the discourse of their employers by promoting the virtues of "amalgamation" and "labor republicanism." Their efforts were guided by the dedication of labor leaders such as Thomas Armstrong, John McLuckie, and Thomas W. "Beeswax" Taylor, an English immigrant whose long career as a labor activist was punctuated by a seemingly contradictory blend of radical Chartism and personal ambition. By the 1880s, however, workers in Pittsburgh had met only limited success; plagued by internal dissension and external assault, the labor movement there abandoned its original hopes for political insurgency. As possibilities for constructing an alternative political agenda narrowed and the concerted attacks from business interests intensified, more and more Pittsburgh workers made their accommodation and retreated to what the *National Labor Tribune* itself called a "healthy conservatism."[21]

Next door in Homestead, however, the fortunes of labor in the 1880s took a distinctively different, defiant turn, one that has not been adequately appreciated by historians of this era. The standard version of Homestead we have inherited is a tale of yet another—perhaps the most dramatic and resounding—defeat of labor in America in the late nineteenth century, a Homestead summed up by the outcome of the lockout of 1892. Homestead in the 1880s, however, was very different: worker solidarity and political empowerment withstood the forces that were crushing labor throughout the country, not to mention a mere six miles away. Whereas workers in Pittsburgh were unable to sustain an organized resistance to assaults from without and tensions within the labor movement, Homesteaders succeeded in consolidating the disparate strains and discourses of labor into a united community strong enough to check the nation's mightiest steelmasters. Twice, in 1882 and 1889, the Homestead steelworkers defied the immeasurable resources of men such as Andrew Carnegie to defend their "American" rights. When they were challenged yet again in 1892, the entire nation looked at Homestead, knowing that the outcome of this third confrontation might well foretell the future of all steelworkers.

How and why the Homestead steelworkers succeeded, for one bold decade, in achieving the solidarity that Pittsburgh workers could not are questions that have not been addressed by scholars of Homestead's "failure" in 1892. The story of Homestead's pursuit of a "workers' republic" urges us to rethink the meaning of labor insurgency beyond the simple plot of its rise and fall.

Chapter 2

6 July 1892: "A Carnival of Revenge"

We contend that we have a legal right to the enjoyment of our property, and to operate it and control it as we please. . . . But for years our works have been managed . . . by men who do not own a dollar in them. This will stop right here. The Carnegie Steel Company will hereafter control their works in the employment of labor.

> — The Carnegie Steel Company,
> 6 July 1892

The fight between centralized capital and organized labor may as well be pushed to the finish here at Homestead, and unless I am badly mistaken, it will be fought out here.

> — A Homestead steelworker,
> 6 July 1892

The dictates of law and humanity were alike suspended on that July day—the most unfortunate day in the history of organized labor in the United States.

> — Arthur G. Burgoyne,
> *The Homestead Strike* (1893)

On 5 JULY 1892 the labor disputes in the small town of Homestead were of intense concern to a handful of steel magnates and to thousands of American steelworkers. By the following day, the lockout in Homestead had become the most famous industrial conflict in American history, an "honor" it arguably retains to this day.

The violent events that brought Homestead national distinction on 6 July 1892 have occupied a prominent place in American history ever since the first shots were fired in the morning fog of that day a century

12

ago. Even in an era marked by decidedly tempestuous industrial relations, the fierceness of the lockout at Andrew Carnegie's prized steel mill alarmed the public in the United States and abroad. It generated two congressional investigations, an outpouring of editorial invective directed at both Carnegie and his employees, and a signal to all citizens of the Republic that America had not escaped the bitter social divisiveness of industrialization that so many of them had hoped to avoid. As one journal put it just after the workers capitulated to Carnegie in November 1892, the dispute might well have ended, but "its soul goes marching on. The shots fired that July morning at the Pinkerton barges, like the shots fired at Lexington . . . were 'heard around the world.' "[1]

For steelworkers in particular, the memory of Homestead has been especially poignant. The lockout crushed the largest trade union in America, the AAISW, and it wrecked the lives of its most devoted members. Marking the end to what John Fitch described in the Pittsburgh Survey as a decades-long struggle for control of the city's steel mills, the victory at Homestead gave Carnegie and his fellow steelmasters carte blanche in the administration of their works. The lockout put "the employers in the saddle"—precisely where they would remain, without union interference, for four decades.[2]

For the American public in general, the memory of Homestead is colored by a few unforgettably dramatic moments—the suspenseful "battle of the barges," the shooting of Henry Clay Frick, and the brutal punishment of W. L. Iams, the young soldier who cheered Alexander Berkman, Frick's would-be assassin. But, as an examination of contemporary newspapers and magazines suggests, one episode seems to stand out above all others: the sensational—and sensationalized—surrender of the Pinkerton agents and their running of the gauntlet through lines formed by thousands of enraged townspeople. The staid House committee that investigated the lockout was aghast at this incident: "The character of the injuries inflicted upon the Pinkertons in some cases were too indecent and brutal to describe. . . . The indignities to which they were subjected . . . is not only disgraceful to that town, but to civilization as well."[3]

Virtually all subsequent writing about the events of 6 July 1892 has drawn attention to details of the Pinkerton surrender, reinforcing the portrayal of that event as an abominable barbarism perpetrated by the residents of Homestead. Even the most prudent of scholars has repeated this interpretation. John Fitch, a passionate defender of organized labor, called the treatment of the Pinkertons "disgraceful in the extreme" to the cause of trade unionism. J. Bernard Hogg, himself a sympathetic labor commentator, in his study of the lockout labeled the assault "one of the blackest scenes in American labor history." And no less dispassionate an observer than Joseph Frazier Wall, Carnegie's distinguished biographer,

characterized the surrender as a horrible episode, enacted by "screaming, cursing lunatics," which to the present day "has haunted the memory of Homestead."[4]

To glean the received commentaries on 6 July, one might well get the
impression that the Pinkerton detectives were the major characters in
the Homestead Lockout. Curiously, the emphasis on their surrender and
retreat in disgrace has reduced the meaning of the *lockout* to an unruly
confrontation between workers and supposed law enforcers. Certainly,
the incident was by no means a minor one in the history of the Homestead lockout, nor can its drama be ignored. But to focus exclusively on it
deflects attention from the larger forces and issues that had determined
this moment, from the broader confrontation between steelworkers and
steelmasters that it symbolized. Moreover, such a gesture eclipses the
impact of a still larger clash of political and cultural values that shook
Homestead and all of American society in the Gilded Age.

In fact, while the Pinkerton agents were preparing to enforce the
authority putatively designated to them by Henry Clay Frick, the principal actors in the lockout were engaged in a variety of activities—some
unusual, some quite routine—that did not allow for the kind of dramatic
entries or exits that catch the public eye. Having given up on months of
lengthy negotiations, weary, frustrated workers and managers were
busily caught up in last-minute union meetings and business conferences respectively.

Some of the actors central to the events of 6 July 1892 were not even
in Homestead on that important day—steel magnates, engineers, politicians. Invisible to the eyewitnesses, the interventions of these people
had introduced another level of violence to the conflict, a violence less
localized—and therefore less easily represented—than the assault on
the Pinkertons, but broader in impact and far longer lasting. Nevertheless, in many ways, Joseph Wall's assertion remains correct: it is the
assault on the Pinkertons, along with the other bloody events of the day,
that has haunted the memory of Homestead. Ironically, it is that haunting memory of these few, brief, vivid moments that has not only ob-
scured the shadowy events but has also distracted commentators from
the complicated historical processes that shaped these events.

Both scholarly and more popular accounts of the Homestead Lockout
of 1892 have in common a fetishization of the physical violence. Titillat-
ing details have been sketched so graphically and so often that most
writers assume not only a general familiarity with the events of the day
but also a general agreement about their causes. And yet these detailed
descriptions of physical outrage are themselves only partial or inaccurate
at best, even in their presentation of the Pinkerton surrender.

Nevertheless, the constant depiction of the same select scenes of
violence, with their few grisly details, has assured scholars that they

have the facts. Joseph Wall, himself haunted by the memory of the violence at Homestead, could boldly state, "The details of that bloody 6 July on the Monongahela have been told so often that they need no elaboration here." Here Wall was only repeating the wisdom of the most authoritative student of the steel industry before him, John Fitch: "It is not necessary to give here a detailed account of the various aspects and developments of the strike of 1892. That has been done until everyone who is interested in the labor movement in United States is somewhat familiar with the story." And yet a full century later, we still do not possess an adequate account of the sequence of events—including the infamous assault on the Pinkertons. As the historian Henry David noted some forty years ago, only the highlights of the lockout have been indicated. There remains the challenge of trying to do "justice to the events of July 6, which catapulted Homestead into fame."[5]

Daunting as that task may be, one must begin, therefore, by asking the deceptively simple question: What happened in Homestead on 6 July, 1892?[6]

In point of fact, the sequence of events began the night before, when, at precisely 10:30, three hundred employees of the Pinkerton National Detective Agency hired by the Carnegie Steel Company arrived by rail in Bellevue, near Davis Island Dam, about five miles down the Ohio River from Pittsburgh. The Pinkertons were greeted by Joseph H. Gray, chief deputy to Allegheny County Sheriff William H. McCleary, John Alfred Potter, the superintendent of the Homestead Steel Works, and several of his foremen. Gray and Potter, who had been negotiating with the steelworkers since early January, promptly escorted the Pinkertons inside the two specially equipped barges purchased by Carnegie Steel for the mission to Homestead. One of the barges, the *Iron Mountain*, had been outfitted as a dormitory; the other, the *Monongahela*, housed a fully equipped kitchen and a dining room that required a corps of twenty waiters. Most of the agents did not know where they were headed when the *Little Bill* and the *Tide*, two river tugs, pulled alongside to begin the journey upriver to Homestead. (The *Tide* was soon disabled, and the *Little Bill* was left to tow both barges.)[7]

The Pinkerton agents, most of whom had enlisted for their work at the offices of the agency in New York, Philadelphia, and Chicago, were under the command of Frederick H. Heinde, 42, aboard the *Iron Mountain*, and his deputy, Charles Nordrum, 35, who led the men on the *Monongahela*. On board each of the barges were dozens of cases of provisions, ammunition, and armaments, including 300 pistols and 250 high-powered Winchester rifles. There were also cartons filled with Pinkerton uniforms—slouch, banded hats, white blouses with silver buttons emblazoned with the letter *P*, and dark blue trousers with navy stripes. As the barges made their way toward the mouth of the Monongahela in the serenity of the late-night mists, and as the men opened the cartons and changed into their "work clothes," many of them may well have been pondering the Pinkerton motto: "We Never Sleep."[8]

Unbeknown to the agents, Deputy Sheriff Gray, and Superintendent Potter, the Homestead steelworkers had established a sophisticated warning system capable of detecting company initiatives on land or water. Accordingly, when the flotilla passed the Smithfield Street bridge near downtown Pittsburgh, a union scout immediately telegraphed the headquarters of the AAISW in Homestead: "Watch the river. Steamer with barges left here." The telegram reached headquarters at 2:30 A.M. on 6 July; ten minutes later, the workers sounded a preliminary warning signal.[9]

The private army commanded by Superintendent Potter and Captain Heinde soon began to comprehend the nature of the task at hand, for the steelworkers had dispatched their own steam launch, the *Edna*, to engage the approaching enemy. When the crew members of the *Edna* spotted the barges, they fired a few stray shots and then signaled back to shore by blowing the whistle. A lookout at the Homestead light works yanked the giant whistle there, and soon every engine in town sounded the alarm; meanwhile, a horseman galloped through the streets to make certain everyone knew an attack was imminent. Immediately the residents of Homestead set off en masse for the steelworks and the river. As the *Little Bill* drew close to the Homestead shore, the first shots rang out from the riverbank. Several rounds hit the tug, and one bullet shattered windows in the pilothouse. Inside the barges the Pinkertons were becoming increasingly nervous.

Homestead's elaborate defense system was under the control of the workers' Advisory Committee, aptly described by the *New York Herald* as comprised of the town's leading union men, "amateur lawyers who had guided the lockout" in these, its earliest moments. But in the frenzy of the Pinkertons' imminent landing, the committee—at this point directed by Hugh O'Donnell, a heater in the 119-inch plate mill—lost control, and the responsibility for Homestead's defense passed to the townspeople in general. O'Donnell and the other leaders of the committee cautioned against violence, but no one listened. Among the residents there seemed to be a perfect, unspoken agreement about how to proceed. "There was no organization, but suddenly the cry arose, 'Charge on them,'" the *Chicago Tribune* reported. "There was no method, no leadership apparent in response to the blast from the light works. It was an uprising of a population."[10]

Thousands of men, women, and children rushed past the leaders of the Advisory Committee to stave off the Pinkertons: one phalanx headed for the shore, another for the Homestead Steel Works itself. William Foy, a middle-aged English immigrant who worked as a common laborer in the

mill, Anthony Soulier, a skilled helper in one of the open-hearth departments, and Margaret Finch, a steelworker's widow who ran the popular
Rolling Mill House saloon, led the dash for the riverbank. It was this
phalanx, reporters recognized, that meant business, and it was Mrs.
Finch who took charge. Described by one reporter as "a white-haired old
beldam who has seen forty strikes in her long life," Mrs. Finch quickly
"strode to the front, and brandishing the hand-billy which she always
keeps about her house for just such emergencies, shrieked aloud: 'The
dirty black sheep, the dirty black sheep. Let me get at them. Let me get at
them.' " The crowd roared its approval of Mrs. Finch; like her, many
Homesteaders believed that one of the barges contained hated black
sheep workers—scabs—who had been dispatched by the Carnegie Company to take the jobs of union laborers.[11]

By the time the crowd reached the riverbank, it was 4:00 A.M., and
day was breaking. Inside the barges, which continued to make their way
upstream to Munhall, the actual site of the steelworks, Superintendent
Potter and Deputy Sheriff Gray ordered the Pinkertons to fire only in
self-defense. But many of them, particularly in the *Iron Mountain*, were
frenzied: "What chance was there for self-defense as long as they were
cooped up within four walls?" Everyone inside the barges could hear the
growing clamor from the shore; they understood that the crowd was
keeping pace as they stemmed past the town and began the approach to
the wharf of the Carnegie Steel Company. By this time, Captain Heinde
and Captain Nordrum had armed about fifty agents with heavy billy
clubs and had distributed ammunition and all of the Winchesters and
pistols.[12]

On shore the charging procession of townspeople—including hundreds of girls and women, some carrying babies as well as guns—came
to an abrupt halt at a barbed wire fence that demarcated company
grounds from Homestead proper. The fence, which Frick had ordered
installed earlier in the summer, extended all the way down to the low
water mark of the Monongahela in order to deny land access to the
wharf. When the crowd saw that the *Little Bill* was preparing to run the
Iron Mountain and the *Monongahela* aground at the company landing
place, the strongest men ran to the fore and dismantled the barrier. It
was precisely at this point that, in swarming across the mill yard and
onto the wharf, Homesteaders crossed an important legal boundary, for
until now, they had followed the Advisory Committee's stricture against
trespassing on company land to avoid any suggestion of an assault on
property rights.[13]

The rush onto the riverbank seemed to galvanize the crowd, and
several rounds of gunfire cracked through the air. At 4:30 A.M., however,
once the *Little Bill* had pushed the *Iron Mountain* and the *Monongahela*
onto the bank, the gunfire stopped and the crowd became ominously

silent. All eyes were fixed on a tall, brawny Pinkerton who was pacing the deck of the *Monongahela*. High above him on the shore, hundreds of women, most of them the wives of East European steelworkers, broke the momentary silence: they hurled invectives, brandished fists, and threw stones at the hated Pinkerton agents.[14]

As the crowd grew more and more agitated, Hugh O'Donnell and other leaders of the Advisory Committee counseled restraint: under no circumstances, O'Donnell ordered, should the townspeople open fire. Meanwhile, scores of armed Homesteaders shouted out desperate warnings of their own to the Pinkertons: "Don't you land, you must not land." "Go back, go back, or we'll not answer for your lives." "Don't come on land or we'll brain you." O'Donnell then made an impassioned plea to the Pinkertons:

> On behalf of five thousand men, I beg of you to leave here at once. I don't know who you are nor from whence you came, but I do know that you have no business here, and if you remain there will be more bloodshed. We, the workers in these mills, are peaceably inclined. We have not damaged any property, and we do not intend to. If you will send a committee with us, we will take them through the works, carefully explain to them the details of this trouble, and promise them a safe return to their boats. But in the name of God and humanity, don't attempt to land! Don't attempt to enter these works by force!"[15]

Captain Heinde, stepping onto the deck of the *Iron Mountain* with several colleagues, replied by identifying himself and his men as agents of the Pinkerton Agency and by explaining the nature of their mission. "We were sent here to take possession of this property and to guard it for this company. . . . We don't wish to shed blood, but we are determined to go up there and shall do so. If you men don't withdraw, we will mow every one of you down and enter in spite of you. You had better disperse, for land we will!" Heinde's threat met with stony silence. Then O'Donnell spoke. He was flanked by five other steelworkers who, with backs turned away from the Pinkertons, were trying to restrain the crowd. "I have no more to say," O'Donnell shouted. "What you do here is at the risk of many lives. Before you enter those mills, you will trample over the dead bodies of three thousand honest workingmen."

For a moment the Pinkerton men stood motionless; "the scene before them was one to appall the bravest." Hundreds of armed men and women guarded the steep embankment overlooking the landing site, and hundreds more were at this very minute on their way. Already scores of Homesteaders had taken up positions on the tracks of the Pennsylvania, McKeesport, and Youghigheny Railroad ("Pmickey") bridge just upstream from the company wharf, and other workers had gathered on the opposite shore of the Monongahela.

Captain Heinde, true to his word, decided to press on with the operation. Several agents lowered a gangplank to the shore. William Foy, who had led Homesteaders to the landing, now stepped forward to the foot of the plank. Behind him were five other steelworkers, three of whom can be conclusively identified: Anthony Soulier, who had helped lead the charge to the wharf; Martin Murray, a skilled heater and union helmsman who had worked in the mill for more than a decade and served on the Advisory Committee; and Joseph Sotak, a leader of the East European steelworkers. "Now, men, we are coming ashore to guard these works, and we want to come without bloodshed," Heinde told them. "There are three hundred men behind me and you cannot stop us."[16]

Undaunted, Foy, known for his feverish sensibility, shouted back in a high-pitched, excited voice, "Come on, and you'll come over my carcass." He then threw himself face down on the gangplank and waited, revolver cocked, for Heinde and the other Pinkertons to advance. Heinde replied by raising his billy-club and slashing at Foy's head. Amid shouts from the official leaders of the Homestead workers to keep back, Heinde ordered his men forward and then stepped toward the shore. Instantly, he slipped on an oar, sending one end of it upward toward a nearby worker, identified only as an East European immigrant, who was hit in the face and knocked down.[17]

At this point the battle was joined: another East European rushed forward, swung a huge club at Heinde, and knocked him off his feet. Eyewitnesses could not agree about the subsequent sequence of events, but this much is clear: two distinct shots rang out, and both Foy and Heinde were wounded. According to reporters for the *New York Tribune*, the *New York World*, the *Homestead Local News*, the *Pittsburgh Commercial Gazette*, and several other papers, it was Foy who was hit first; even the conservative *Commercial Gazette* reported that a Pinkerton took aim at Foy and fired the initial shot. However, Deputy Gray, who was aboard the *Little Bill* at the time, later told congressional investigators that the first shot came from the riverbank. Not surprisingly, Heinde himself also testified that a worker fired the first round. The story was corroborated by Pinkerton Captain J. W. Cooper during the murder trial of one of the Homestead steelworkers, as well as by William B. Rodgers, the captain of the *Little Bill*. Arthur Burgoyne, himself an eyewitness, as well as the reporters for the *New York Sun* and the *Pittsburgh Post*, said it was impossible to determine who fired first—"a mystery." But a steelworker who participated in the skirmish and who was interviewed by the historian Bernard Hogg in the early 1940s avowed that it was, in fact, a colleague who opened fire.[18]

Whoever was responsible for the first shot, Captain Cooper took it as a signal to open fire. When he shouted the command, a score of Winchester rifles answered, sending volley after volley into the crowd of workers. They responded with a furious barrage of their own: for ten minutes they exchanged fire with the Pinkertons, bombarding the *Little Bill*, the *Monongahela*, and the *Iron Mountain* with an array of weapons that included shotguns, revolvers, and Civil War muskets and rifles.[19]

The effects of this first engagement were deadly for both sides. Three steelworkers, Martin Murray, Anthony Soulier, and George W. Rutter, were among the first who went down. Rutter, aged 46, was shot in the thigh and stomach by a Pinkerton sharpshooter. A Union veteran who had been wounded at Gettysburg and a long-time member of the AAISW, Rutter died eleven days later in a hospital bed next to the one occupied by Captain Heinde. Though Murray's wounds did not prove fatal, he was unable to retreat up the embankment with his associates. Lying semiconscious and bleeding profusely near the water's edge, he was picked up by his colleague Joseph Sotak, who had escaped injury in the Pinkertons' initial salvo. In an effort to carry him to safety, Sotak "stood over Murray's prostrate body, . . . and as he was raising him, he staggered and an instant later fell by his comrade." Sotak had been shot in the mouth; he died instantly. Hugh O'Donnell, also in the line of fire, was only slightly wounded: a bullet grazed his thumb.

As other Homesteaders dashed to their aid and then rushed up the hill overlooking the shore, at least nine more, including six East European workers, were wounded: Andrew Cudia, Charles Daeska, Joseph Loyo, Stephen Osmunger, Antoni Palatka, Henry Rusiski, Richard Durham, Harry Hughes, and John Kane. For the Pinkertons, the toll was likewise heavy: J. W. Kline was mortally wounded, and a dozen other detectives were badly shot. One of them, Edward A. R. Speer, died of his wounds on 17 July.[20]

The battle had lasted less than ten minutes; now each side held a council of war, Superintendent Potter and the Pinkertons in the barges, and the workers in the makeshift ramparts they had built from the pig and scrap iron lying about the mill yard. Potter, under pressure from the Pinkertons to mount another assault, refused to authorize any initiative until Sheriff McCleary arrived on the scene. "I will not take the responsibility for any more bloodshed," he said. Apparently Potter believed that the quiet that had descended on the mill yard meant that the leaders of the Advisory Committee would be able to control the crowd and allow the Pinkertons to assume possession of the steelworks. In the meantime, Captain Rodgers, accompanied by Deputy Sheriff Gray, would take the *Little Bill* across the river to Port Perry and put Captain Heinde and several other wounded agents aboard a train bound for Pittsburgh hospitals. The *Monongahela* and the *Iron Mountain* were to remain at their mooring; from the embankment, workers could see Pinkertons frantically cutting holes in the barges so they could ward off an attack with their Winchesters.[21]

The workers were busy preparing defenses of their own. Members of the Advisory Committee established an arsenal in union headquarters on the third floor of the Bost Building, at Eighth Avenue and Heisel Street; workers combed the town for weapons, brought them to headquarters, and then the committee distributed them to anyone willing to fight. In the mill yard, where at least five hundred women had congregated during the battle—many of them imploring the men to "kill the Pinkertons"—O'Donnell and his associates were trying to restore some semblance of order. The immediate task was to remove the wounded and persuade the women to move to safer ground; this was accomplished, but only with the utmost difficulty. Next, the workers piled steel beams into a long fortification above the riverbank, assuming strategic positions behind it in the mill and at the pump house. They then armed themselves with ammunition donated by a Homestead hardware merchant. Much of this work was accomplished without guidance from any ostensible leader: as Cornelius Atkinson, a 17-year-old laborer active in the events of the day later recalled, there was in fact "no leader, just a crazy mob."[22]

Despite Atkinson's assertion, virtually all contemporary observers agree that "Hughey" O'Donnell did help direct "the government of the crowd," to the extent that such direction was possible. However, O'Donnell's claim to uncontested leadership—substantiated to a great degree by a selective reading of Burgoyne's account—is hardly beyond dispute. Hugh Ross, a skilled worker in the 33-inch beam mill, and Jack Clifford, a shear helper in the 119-inch mill, both of whom were described by Burgoyne as pugnacious associates of O'Donnell on the Advisory Committee, took the lead in guiding the quasi-military operations of the residents. Indeed, Burgoyne himself noted that O'Donnell shared supervisory responsibilities with Ross and Clifford and was principally concerned with trying to restore order and make peace with the Pinkertons. Clifford, "with a strong trace of the daredevil in his deposition," was in all likelihood the tall, broad-chested, mustachioed worker singled out by the *New York World* as the "leader of the active warfare" in the first hours of the battle.[23]

During these first hours another steelworker, John McLuckie, a close associate of the wounded Martin Murray, also played an important role in the initiative to repulse the Pinkertons. McLuckie, an ardent trade unionist who worked in the Bessemer converting mill, was burgess of Homestead; in this position he officialy called upon all residents "to help him in preserving the peace." By this, all Homesteaders readily understood, McLuckie meant that they should unite "to make short work of the Pinkertons."[24]

McLuckie issued this proclamation, along with another that closed all of Homestead's saloons, during the lull that followed the initial encounter between the Pinkertons and the workers. By 6:00 A.M., when the news of the battle reached Pittsburgh, more than five thousand persons had congregated on the hills that rose above the steelworks and the town of Homestead. The early morning fog had lifted, and, from their relatively safe vantage point, the townspeople had a clear view of what was happening on the riverbank and on the other side of the Mononga-hela: a few of the workers had boarded skiffs and were sporadically firing at the *Iron Mountain* and *Monongahela;* some of their colleagues who had borrowed a twenty-pound cannon from General Griffin Post 207 of the Grand Army of the Republic (GAR) in Homestead were prepar-ing to fire from the opposite shore. Meanwhile, six miles downstream in Pittsburgh, thousands of mill hands who had learned of the standoff in Homestead were gathering in the streets; soon hundreds of them, many armed with guns and revolvers, began the trek upriver.[25]

It was nearly 8:00 A.M. when the Pinkertons mounted a second effort to disembark and move up the embankment to the seize the steelworks. One of the captains announced his intentions to the three workers posi-tioned closest to the barges; the workers remained silent when suddenly a shot was fired from the ramparts behind them. The Pinkertons quickly returned fire, and in the ensuing gunfight, Homestead workers suffered what proved to be their heaviest casualties of the day: four died.[26]

First to fall was John E. Morris, 28-year-old immigrant from Wales and a popular, upstanding union mainstay who did skilled work in the blooming mill. Morris was among those workers who had taken a posi-tion on the pump house that overlooked the wharf; from there he had been firing on the barges and, he believed, had laid low one of the Pinkertons. During a momentary pause in the battle, Morris tried to "sneak a look." He himself was then laid low, a single bullet piercing his forehead and knocking him off the pump house into a ditch sixty feet below. Morris cried out as he fell to his death. The sight of his mangled body horrified his companions, who immediately carried him back to his home on Ninth Avenue. It was the death of Morris and the procession to his house, where his widow and children received him, that catapulted the rage of the townspeople to new heights. "The killing of Morris seemed to craze the people, and men, women, and children ran through the streets crying revenge and for blood."

The shooting of Silas Wain, 23, a common laborer in the Bessemer mill, also shocked and angered the town. Wain, who had recently immi-grated from England, was among the hundreds of workers who had run to the mill yard when the Pinkertons arrived. From where he stood, however, he was not exposed to their gunfire; tragically, it was the friendly cannon fire from the workers across the Monongahela that ended his life. Their first shot had ripped a hole in one of the Pinkerton barges; the second exploded next to Wain, sending a piece of iron into his head. His brother, William, who was standing next to him but some-how escaped injury, watched him die. Immediately word was dispatched to cease firing, and the cannon was taken back to the south side of the Monongahela, where, along with another also borrowed from the GAR, it proved ineffectual. Meanwhile, back in town, the death of Wain triggered an especially poignant scene. He and his fiancée, Mary Jones, like him, an English immigrant, had planned to wed within weeks. When Jones learned of Wain's death, she collapsed, and she remained delirious for hours in her home on Eighth Avenue.[27]

The deaths of Henry Striegel and Peter Fares were similarly marked by irony and pathos. Striegel, 19, a teamster for a small Homestead company, had run to the mill yard along with hundreds of other non-steelworkers in the effort to thwart the Pinkertons. As he was preparing to fire, Striegel wounded himself with his own gun; when he fell, writhing, to the ground, an agent sent a bullet through his neck, killing him instantly. Members of the German Catholic community in Homestead found Striegel's death particularly upsetting even though he was a lapsed churchgoer and apparently considered something of a rake.[28]

Fares, 28, a semiskilled helper in the open-hearth department, was, on the contrary, a religious man. A Slovak immigrant from Šariš Province, in the northern part of the Austro-Hungarian Empire, he attended St. Michael's Church in Braddock; indeed, from their quarters in the heart of Homestead's Slovak colony between Dickson and Heisel streets (not far from the steelworks), he and his brother crossed the river to go to church each Sunday. On 6 July, Fares left home about 7 A.M., armed only with a loaf of bread, to join his co-workers and fellow members of the Homestead lodges of the AAISW in the mill yard. A Pinkerton sharpshooter sighted him and gunned him down shortly after 8:00 A.M.; the bullet that entered his skull above his lip blew his head off. At 8:30 Fares's brother and cousin, Imrich Stefancin, a leader of the Slovak community and an eleven-year resident of Homestead, received his remains from the co-workers who had carried him home in their arms.[29]

The loss of Morris, Wain, Striegel, Fares, and Sotak and the wounding of their colleagues touched all of the principal ethnic and occupational groups in Homestead and underscored their unity. The list of the most serious casualties suffered in the first four hours of battle constituted no less than a cross section of the town's male population. John Morris and Martin Murray were skilled Welsh steelworkers; William Foy and Silas Wain, English mill hands; Henry Striegel, a German teamster; Peter Fares and Joseph Sotak, Slovak immigrants; and George Rutter, a native-born American. Whereas the misfortunes that befell these Homesteaders seemed to fortify and further consolidate the workers' determination to resist the Pinkertons, morale plummeted inside the *Iron Mountain* and the *Monongahela* over the course of the morning of 6 July.

Even during the first confrontation with the workers, many of the Pinkertons had decided that fighting was not part of their job. Of the 300 who were transported to Homestead, only about 40 were regular employees of the Pinkerton National Detective Agency; the remaining 260 had signed up in late June for an unspecified job. When Heinde, Cooper, and Nordrum, among others, had ordered their charges to open fire, many simply refused and took shelter in the recesses of the two barges. "They were the worst sort of cowards I ever saw," Nordrum later testified. The departure of the *Little Bill,* which effectively stranded the barges at the Carnegie wharf, and a second effort, at 8:00 A.M., to establish a beachhead heightened tensions. Many of the Pinkerton recruits again refused to engage the workers and hid under bunks and tables, donned life jackets, and in general lost their self-control. When the workers fired the GAR cannon toward the barges, panic set in; only with the greatest difficulty did the regular agents manage to keep the recruits from jumping into the Monongahela.[30]

Intermittent gunshots were fired from both sides throughout the morning until about 10:50 A.M., when the return of the *Little Bill* from Port Perry signaled a renewed intensity to the battle. Still under the command of Captain Rodgers, the *Little Bill* began to approach the mill landing in an effort to tow away the *Monongahela* and the *Iron Mountain.* Captain Rodgers hoisted the Stars and Stripes in the belief that the workers would not fire on a vessel flying the American flag. "The captain's mind was speedily disabused of this idea": the workers responded with a furious volley that narrowly missed Captain Rodgers, forced his pilot from the wheel, and wounded another crew member in the groin. Rodgers had no choice but to allow the *Little Bill* to drift downstream. As it disappeared around a bend in the river, the Pinkertons realized that there would be no immediate rescue.[31]

It was at this point that the workers embarked upon a series of unsuccessful, though terrifying, efforts to sink the *Iron Mountain* and the *Monongahela.* First, they commandeered a raft, loaded it with oil-soaked lumber, set fire to it, and then sent it downriver toward the barges. The sight of the oncoming raft elicited desperate groans, and many of the agents again considered jumping overboard. (They were dissuaded by a captain who threatened to shoot anyone who did so.) Fortunately for them, however, the fire burned itself out before the raft collided with the barges. The Pinkertons soon faced another fireball: a burning railroad flatcar, loaded with barrels of oil, was sent hurtling down the railroad track that ran from the mill to the wharf. At the water's edge, however, the car came to an abrupt stop—and the agents were saved again. The workers were no more successful when they turned to explosives: they tried in vain to dynamite the barges and then to surround them with a burning oil slick.[32]

Throughout all these initiatives, the workers kept up a steady barrage of gunfire and, in late morning, killed a second Pinkerton agent, Thomas J. Connors. Connors was among those trying to hide from the battle; he was sitting under cover with his head buried in his hands when a shot severed the main artery in his right arm. Connors's slow death agony persuaded the detectives to request a formal surrender, but repeated efforts to hoist a white flag were met only with hostility from the Homestead workers. On at least two occasions, the agents did succeed in raising a banner, but each time the workers shot it down; they had heard that the Pennsylvania militia was to be mobilized, and they wanted to dispose of the Pinkertons before public authorities intervened.

As it turned out, the state militia had not yet been called out. However, the most powerful politicians in Allegheny County and the state of Pennsylvania were locked in a series of meetings and conferences that threatened to do just that. Sheriff McCleary, who had welcomed the Pinkertons when they disembarked at Davis Island Dam, arrived at his office in the early morning to confer with his closest advisers—chief among whom were "Boss" Christopher L. Magee and his junior partner in the management of municipal politics, William Flinn. At 9:00 A.M., William Weihe, the national president of the AAISW rushed to McCleary's office upon learning of the first casualties at Homestead; Weihe told the assembled officials that the only way to avoid further bloodshed was for Frick and the workers to meet. McCleary and his advisers then sent an emissary to Frick, who refused to negotiate.[33]

The workers learned of this decision from Francis Lovejoy, secretary of Carnegie Steel: "Our works are now in the hands of the sheriff, and it is his official duty to protect the property from destruction or damage. If it is necessary in his judgment to call out troops, he is the proper authority to do so. Everything is in his hands." Frick himself spoke to the press later in the day, maintaining that the company was "not taking any active part in the matter at present, as we cannot interfere with the Sheriff in the discharge of his duty, and are now awaiting his further action." The Pinkertons had been prevented from landing and were now "awaiting orders from the authorities before undertaking any further action."

On the surface, the pronouncements of Lovejoy and Frick signaled that the owners of Carnegie Steel were prepared, Burgoyne noted, to see that "the entire force of Pinkertons would be destroyed like rats in a trap." But Burgoyne and other observers also recognized that Frick and Lovejoy had been counting on the ultimate authority of the state from the outset; they knew that the more chaotic Homestead became, the more likely it was that Governor Robert E. Pattison would order out the militia, thereby clearing the way for nonunion laborers to enter the steelworks. It was for this reason that Lovejoy and Frick declared that it was the sheriff, and not the Pinkertons or the company, whose hand (theoretically) ruled at Homestead. Should the sheriff deem the situation out of control, it was up to him to petition the governor for military assistance.

In truth, there was substantial reason for Frick and Lovejoy to assert that the duly constituted civil authority of Sheriff McCleary was being flouted by the workers in their efforts to resist the Pinkertons. Responding to a request from Frick, McCleary himself had visited Homestead on the morning of 5 July to tell the workers, who already had sealed off the town and the mill from outside laborers, that he intended to restore "the rightful use and enjoyment" of the mill to its owner, the Carnegie Steel Company. That afternoon, McCleary sent a posse of twelve deputies to Homestead; in handbills posted throughout the town, he commanded that "all persons . . . abstain from assembling or congregating" at the works and "from interfering with the workmen, business or operation of said works," and that everyone should "return to their respective homes or places of residence" to ensure that the owners of the works could resume operations.[34]

The workers responded by tearing down the handbills and informing the deputies that neither they nor anyone else would be allowed to bring nonunion workers into the mill. Three thousand steelworkers and their wives, led by O'Donnell and McLuckie, then escorted the deputies out of town. "It was all most politely done," the *New York Herald* reported. Nevertheless, Homesteaders had defied the law: "The Commonwealth of Pennsylvania, in the person of 11 special deputy sheriffs, . . . has been ignominiously though politely placed upon a flat-bottomed stern-wheel boat by the locked-out steelworkers of Homestead and sent down the river to recover its astonished dignity in the city of Pittsburgh." It was this undertaking that later would earn Advisory Committee members the charge of treason.

Homestead's resolute defiance of McCleary's deputies, undertaken with the full support of the town's chief official, John McLuckie, publicly demonstrated that the sheriff could not furnish the Carnegie Company with the protection it required to open the mill and enjoy the rightful use of its own property. In truth, it was a demonstration of this very sort that Frick and other Carnegie officials were seeking. If the authority of the sheriff were inadequate, the company most assuredly would be justified in calling for assistance from the Pinkertons; and if the Pinkertons were thwarted, the only remaining step would be to mobilize the state militia. As the *Wheeling Daily Intelligencer* observed, Frick's "application . . . for assistance of the sheriff was merely for the purpose of covering what was intended to be the *coup de main* on the part of the Carnegie Company in clandestinely introducing a body of Pinkerton detectives." The *New York World*, even before the Pinkertons' attempted landing, suggested that the "ridiculously small force" McCleary had dispatched to Homestead on 5 July was part of a deliberate move to force the calling out of troops—what the paper called Andrew Carnegie's trump card.[35]

Whether Carnegie officials did in fact conceive of the state militia as their trump card remains problematic. This much, however, is certain: Frick went to great lengths to ensure that if such a mobilization proved necessary, it would be presented to the public at large as the logical, legal response to a brazen revolt of insubordinate workers. For this reason, Frick and Philander C. Knox, chief lawyer for Carnegie Steel, had sought to deputize the Pinkertons prior to their arrival in Homestead.[36]

Knox, on instructions from Frick, had met with McCleary on 26 June, shortly after Frick had concluded the agreement with the Pinkerton Agency that specified that three hundred agents would be sent to Homestead on the evening of 5 July in anticipation of opening the mill on the succeeding day. At this meeting, Knox informed McCleary of the company's plans to engage the agents and asked that the sheriff accept them as his posse to guard the works. Knox met with McCleary again on 4 and 5 July, each time requesting that the Pinkertons be sworn in; each time, McCleary declined to do so. He did say, however, that if "there was liable to be destruction of property or loss of life" to the agents, he would swear them in. In his final meeting with Knox on 5 July—a meeting attended by a representative of the Pinkerton Agency—McCleary complied with Knox's request that a deputy sheriff accompany the agents. But he once again refused to deputize the agents in advance: when Knox dictated a letter introducing Gray to Superintendent Potter as the deputy sheriff, McCleary appended a note stating only that Gray was "to have control of all action in case of trouble."

Regarding these equivocations, the historian J. Bernard Hogg found more than fifty years ago that "no reason can be assigned for the ambiguous action of McCleary." Hogg himself speculated, not without reason, that McCleary might simply have disliked the methods of the Pinkerton National Detective Agency. More likely—and this was the explanation offered by Frick himself and his good friend Judge Thomas Mellon—it may have been that McCleary was afraid to offend the large number of voters in Allegheny County who, as workers, held the Pinkertons in extreme contempt. Indeed, at the urging of McLuckie and other union leaders, a mass meeting of Homestead steelworkers in May 1891 had unanimously urged the state legislature to ban the use of Pinkertons. And it was to many such workers that McCleary owed his political life. Furthermore, he also maintained personal ties with many "ordinary" residents of Allegheny County: he had in fact served in the same company of the Union army as George Rutter.[37]

McCleary's equivocation cost him dearly. He was roundly criticized for it, as well as for his "inefficiency," by the House committee that investigated the lockout and by the daily press. Perhaps most notable among McCleary's critics was Burgoyne. "There was no obligation on this official to keep Mr. Frick's operations secret. On the contrary, he was under a strong moral obligation to prevent the execution of those operations at all hazards by giving them prompt publicity and enabling the exhaustion of all available legal means of stopping an invasion of the county by armed mercenaries. . . . Decidedly a weak an inefficient man, this sheriff . . . had abdicated in favor of Frick and the Pinkertons."

Contrary to the conclusions of both Burgoyne and Hogg, McCleary in point of fact possessed a handful of weighty obligations that required him to ensure that the battle plans of Carnegie Steel were executed and that county officials cooperated with Frick, his emissary and chief strategist, Knox, and the Pinkerton hirelings they brought to Homestead. The reason was that McCleary, as Burgoyne himself noted, stood in profound debt to a certain "gentleman prominent in Republican politics," one "Chris L. Magee," McCleary's political patron and "bondsman." What Burgoyne did not choose to reveal, however, was that this same Magee, who plotted McCleary's career, was a close friend of Carnegie and Frick and was the latter's business partner as well.[38]

Burgoyne offered his characterization of the relationship between McCleary and Magee in discussing the politically charged question of what was to happen to the Pinkertons after their infamous surrender to the workers of Homestead; nowhere else did he suggest that McCleary deferred to Magee on any issue of importance. From other accounts, however, we do know that throughout 6 July, and then continuing on into the tense early morning hours of 7 July, McCleary and Magee were in continuous consultation. In fact, Magee was in McCleary's office virtually all day on 6 July; he never left McCleary's side. We also know that Magee's rule over politics in Greater Pittsburgh was absolute; the great muckraker Lincoln Steffens noted that Magee owned municipal government and every politician who worked in it. With regard to McCleary, one prominent Homestead steelworker was therefore merely repeating conventional wisdom when, in complaining about the tremendous influence exercised by Magee over "some officers of the Amalgamated Association," he confided to a reporter for the *New York World* that they "seem to be as much under the influence of Chris Magee as Sheriff McCleary has been."[39]

Why Burgoyne chose to depict McCleary as the chief villain in the Homestead story—independently capitulating to the dark schemes of Frick and Knox, later endeavoring, again in isolation, to force Governor Pattison to dispatch the state militia to Homestead—poses an important question about what the historian David Montgomery recently termed Burgoyne's "splendid" account of the Homestead Lockout. Indeed, the omissions in Burgoyne's text regarding the interventions of "Boss"

Magee raise doubts about virtually all accounts of the lockout, for practically all have been built on Burgoyne, and all evade the role of Magee in the events of 6 July.[40]

Even before Sheriff McCleary, under Magee's watchful eye, sent the initial request for state assistance to Governor Pattison at 10:00 A.M. on 6 July, events at Andrew Carnegie's steelworks in Homestead had already implicated an impressive cast of powerful political figures. And before the fateful day ended, these men would demonstrate their remarkable power to shape events—both in and beyond the town of Homestead.[41]

McCleary's first telegram described the situation at Homestead as very grave; only prompt measures, he told the governor, could restore order and prevent "further bloodshed and great destruction of property." McCleary explained that his deputies had been driven from the town—a reference to the events of 5 July—and that "watchmen" hired by Carnegie Steel had been attacked by the workers. "The striking workmen and their friends . . . number at least 5,000, and the civil authorities are utterly unable to cope with them. Wish you would send instructions at once."

Within an hour, amid reports of unabated violence sent from Homestead to McCleary, Magee, and Flinn, Governor Pattison responded with a single, terse sentence: "Local authorities must exhaust every means at their command for the preservation of the peace." This was hardly the reply that McCleary and his advisers, particularly Magee, had expected: although Pattison was a staunch Democrat, he was at least as much in debt to Magee as was McCleary. Magee, a leader of the Republican party who had played a key role in securing the 1888 presidential nomination for Benjamin Harrison, had proudly swung the Allegheny County vote, and thereby the 1890 Pennsylvania gubernatorial election, to Pattison. In sabotaging the candidacy of the Republican standard-bearer, George W. Delamater, Magee had fulfilled a personal goal of utmost importance: thwarting the plans of his chief nemesis in the Pennsylvania GOP, Senator Matt Quay, who had backed Delamater for the Governor's Mansion. Though Magee was never to succeed in supplanting Quay in the state GOP, the 1890 election provided most impressive evidence of just how powerful Magee was in Greater Pittsburgh. As one city paper observed on the occasion of his death, "Probably no better demonstration of his great influence in city politics was ever given than the manner in which republican votes were swung to Pattison because it was known that Mr. Magee desired it."[42]

On the morning of 6 July, Magee—the steelworks of his friends and business partner under attack—no doubt harbored a new desire, and he had every reason to expect that Pattison would recognize that it was time to return a favor by immediately calling out the state militia. The governor, however, stood in roughly the same position as McCleary. To be sure, Pattison wielded notably more power; however, like McCleary, he owed his job not only to Magee but to thousands of working Pennsylvanians who had cast ballots for him. Pattison therefore quickly realized that the 1890 election returns in Homestead (427 for him, 406 for Delamater) had, with McCleary's telegram, taken on added significance that reached well beyond Homestead and into the larger arena of Pennsylvania politics.[43]

In this arena, Pattison understood, those who sanctioned the deployment of Pinkerton "myrmidons," as Burgoyne labeled them, might well be facing early retirement. Thus, when McCleary's second telegram reached Harrisburg shortly after noon ("I have no means at my command to meet the emergency. . . . A large force will be required. . . . You are, therefore, urged to act at once"), it was afforded an unequivocally cool response. The governor's message, once again, was pointed: "How many deputies have you sworn in and what means have you taken to enforce order and protect property?" McCleary and his "bondsman" were, again, dismayed by the governor's stance; they adjourned to a private room for further consultations. Meanwhile, in Homestead, the Advisory Committee received a telegram of its own from Harrisburg: this one, stating that Pattison had refused to mobilize the state militia, elicited the gratification of all residents.[44]

While the townspeople were pleased to learn of Pattison's decision not to call out the militia, many of them—women, in particular—were growing increasingly restless about developments at the "front." The women, by this time officially barred from the mill yard by the Advisory Committee, had filled the streets, "weeping, wailing and wringing their hands and begging for news of husbands, sons and brothers." At lunchtime there was a brief lull in the fighting: a squad of men carried bologna sausages, canned corn, and sardines to colleagues nearest the embankment, and officials of the AAISW's national office visited the town only to express solemnly their "regret that things had reached such a lamentable extremity."[45]

At 2:00 P.M. the workers undertook initiatives that, from the point of view of the Pinkertons, threatened to make the situation even more lamentable. In a renewed effort to set fire to the *Iron Mountain* and the *Monongahela*, some asked for, and received, hoses and a hand pump from the Homestead fire station, a long-standing center of worker politics and sociability; the plan was to pump oil onto the barges and then set fire to them. Others kept a watchful eye on the Pinkertons: from under the "Pmickey" bridge, worker-sharpshooters fired whenever a Pinkerton momentarily became visible, and three hundred additional sharpshooters, now in position near Open Hearth Furnace no. 1, maintained a steady fire. One of the sticks of dynamite thrown by the workers found its mark on a barge but did little damage beyond further terrorizing the agents. The workers were, by this time, stumped by their inability to dislodge them: an observer who visited the Homestead lines after lunch, in addition to reporting that the workers' military organization rivaled that of the best Union regiments in the Civil War, found that the men were then considering "every possible scheme for the annihilation and destruction" of the Pinkertons.[46]

In Pittsburgh, McCleary, acting on Magee's advice, sent a third telegram to the governor. This time he described the workers as an armed mob that had violated the property rights of Carnegie Steel by taking down the fence near the works and then seizing the landing site. One Pinkerton had already died, and "an armed and disciplined force is needed at once to prevent further loss of life. I therefore urge immediate action on your part." McCleary, Magee, and other officials told the press that they now were confident the governor would respond positively— but an hour later, that is, at roughly 3:00 P.M., they were still waiting for an answer. "Nothing short of the militia will, I believe, quell the disturbance," McCleary said. "What would even a thousand deputies do among so many determined men?" He concluded his mini–press conference with a blatant lie: "I don't know anything about where the Pinkerton men came from or who sent them."[47]

For McCleary and his advisers, the ongoing silence of Pattison became of greater concern the longer he maintained it. Evening was approaching, and no resolution was in sight. What would happen to the Pinkertons? Would the Homestead workers succeed in "annihilating" them? McCleary and Magee summoned William Weihe, the national president of the AAISW, in what they felt certain was their final effort to defuse the situation. The plan was to send Weihe to Homestead, ask him to address the workers, and implore him to use his influence to convince the men that the agents should be allowed to leave town without further molestation. If the workers agreed to this plan, McCleary would guarantee that the Pinkertons would not return to Homestead. Weihe promised to do his best and left for Homestead.[48]

Shortly thereafter, as McCleary was chatting with several county officials just outside his office, Magee, telegram in hand, returned from a brief absence. The "boss" was in a hurry, and he escorted McCleary and the other officials into the sheriff's office for a brief meeting. A few minutes later, a dismayed Sheriff McCleary announced to the press that Pattison had again refused to mobilize the militia. Pattison's telegram stated that because McCleary had "not made any attempt to execute the law to enforce order," no troops would be forthcoming. "I must insist upon you calling upon all citizens for an adequate number of deputies."[49]

Later, in Harrisburg, Pattison elaborated on his reasons for refusing to call out the militia.

> There is no information received from Homestead to warrant any interference on the part of the State. The sheriff must exhaust all of his authority before the state will interfere. The state lends its aid when the local authorities are overborne. The sheriff has employed but twelve deputies up to the present time, his ordinary force. If the emergency is as great as alleged, he should have employed a thousand. It is not the purpose of the military to act as police officers. The citizens of Homestead are industrious, hard-working, intelligent people. Most of them, if not all, own their own homes. In such a community, there ought to be no difficulty as to adjustments of their troubles: certainly no question as to the preservation of the peace by local authorities. The civil authorities must in the end settle the differences. I look for a speedy adjustment.[50]

However flattering and reassuring these words may have sounded to Homesteaders, there remained disquieting reports about the governor's next move. Indeed, even as Pattison's speech was flashing across the telegraph lines of Pennsylvania, he was preparing to mobilize the state militia should the "speedy adjustment" he anticipated prove elusive. In fact, by late afternoon, according to the *New York Herald,* arrangements had already been made for the arrival of troops in Pittsburgh.

To ensure that troops would in fact be needed—to fulfill formally the outstanding precondition for mobilization set by the governor—McCleary and Magee concocted a plan for "suppressing the riot now in progress at Homestead." The sheriff, in consultation with Magee and other advisers, issued a series of subpoenas requiring 105 of the most prominent residents of Allegheny County, including Magee and Flinn, to report to his office at 9:00 A.M. the following day; they would be required to go to Homestead as members of the sheriff's posse, equipped with their own arms and food. "The papers were delivered early in the morning, but the results were far from satisfactory." Small wonder: "some of the editors, bankers, merchants, manufacturers, and political leaders addressed were far too advanced in years to be physically fit for active service, at least one of the number being over 80 years of age."[51]

While McCleary's plan was drawing guffaws from the press in downtown Pittsburgh, the logic of events in Homestead indicated that a denouement was close at hand. At union headquarters the men were cheered by scores of encouraging telegrams sent by workers from across the country. The workers in Homestead sensed "that they were fighting not only their own battle, . . . but the battle of organized labor as a whole, and that the eyes of workingmen all over the continent were upon them." By 4:00 P.M., a few minutes before Weihe would tell the 3,800 Homestead workers of Sheriff McCleary's plan to remove the Pinkertons, 5,000 additional men, most of them mill hands from the South Side, Braddock, and Duquesne, and many of them armed, had arrived as reinforcements. At the embankment, some were priming the hand pump from the Homestead fire station in another effort to burn the barges; others were preparing to launch yet another dynamite attack.[52]

At the very instant when the men began pumping oil into the Monongahela, they received word that Weihe and other national officials of the AAISW had arrived and wanted to address them. In the mill yard a crowd surrounded Weihe and followed him into one of the buildings. He climbed atop a boiler and began to speak. From the start he made it clear that he had come to Homestead to endorse Sheriff McCleary's plan that the Pinkertons be allowed to surrender with the understanding that they would not return. There had already been too much bloodshed. "Stop and think," Weihe urged. But the Homestead workers would have none of his advice or McCleary's plan. "Shouts of 'No, No' rang upon all sides," and Weihe was hooted down. M. M. Garland, the president elect of the union, met with an equally hostile response when he entreated: "Men, for God's sake and your families sake, and for your own sake, listen to the pleadings of cool-headed men. We have positive assurance that these deputies will be sent away, and all we want is a statement that you will not do any more firing."[53]

As Weihe, Garland, and other national officers tried desperately to hold their audience, the proceedings were interrupted by a series of deafening blasts from the embankment: the workers were heaving fireworks, left over from the recent Forth of July celebrations, at the *Iron Mountain* and *Monongahela*. At the same time, a company of three hundred armed men from the nearby South Side ironworks owned by B. F. Jones marched into the mill yard to the beat of a military drum. At the front of the procession someone proudly carried the American flag. When Homestead workers rushed to greet their colleagues from the city, Hugh O'Donnell grabbed the flag, climbed on a pile of steel beams, and asked for silence. Hundreds of men took off their hats and shouted a lusty hurrah as he began his speech.[54]

O'Donnell proceeded cautiously. He explained that Weihe had asked him to suggest again that the Pinkertons be allowed to leave; perhaps a barge should take them away. But the workers shouted down this suggestion. Instead, a chorus of voices from the crowd declared, the agents should be required to lay down their arms and surrender to the men. Then one unidentified man in the crowd rose to speak: "We will hold them in the boats until the sheriff comes and we will have warrants sworn out for every man for murder. The sheriff will then have to take them in charge." This plan drew a loud, univocal shout of approval; O'Donnell, confident that the end was in sight, stepped down from the beams and headed outside for the Pinkerton barges, where he intended to negotiate for peace.

Arthur Burgoyne, among other observers, was puzzled by the speed and enthusiasm with which the plan for surrender was accepted by the Homestead workers, "considering the mood in which the men had been a few minutes before." Burgoyne called the plan a "comparatively mild proposal"; he did not speculate why this plan, as opposed to the one put forward by Weihe on behalf of the sheriff and his cronies, instantly appealed to the steelworkers. The key difference between the two, of course, was that the Weihe-McCleary plan said nothing about what would happen to the Pinkertons after they left town, other than that they would not return. On the other hand, the proposal that came forth from the crowd envisioned their prosecution for murder. To Burgoyne such an idea may well have been "comparatively mild"; however, to the men and women who had charged the riverbank on 6 July in defense of their jobs and homes, and who had watched their co-workers die, it was the essence of American justice—a justice that required the Pinkerton "invaders" to be treated as criminals.[55]

The Pinkertons, at the very time when the steelworkers were effecting an agreement on surrender terms, had been conducting a canvass of their own. Not surprisingly, most favored surrender, and, over the objection of their commanders, at 5:00 P.M. they raised a white flag atop the *Iron Mountain*. Then two agents walked onto the narrow deck of the barge and held up their hands. "A great shout arose from a thousand throats," and O'Donnell, accompanied by Jack Clifford and another member of the Advisory Committee, ran down to the riverbank. It was O'Donnell who did most of the talking for the steelworkers. He assured the Pinkertons that they would be given safe passage from Homestead, but he told them nothing about the agreement his own constituents had reached on what they considered the most important condition of surrender. Both O'Donnell and Clifford personally guaranteed the safety of the agents and then walked down the gangplank to escort them to shore. Behind them, angry members of the crowd were shouting, "Kill the detectives." Clifford tried to restrain the rush, but he was pushed aside; scores of workers poured onto the barges. One of them, Thomas Weldon, a skilled AAISW man of Irish descent, became the second steelworker to wound himself when he grabbed an agent's Winchester and slammed it to the ground in an effort to break it; the gun discharged into his stomach, and he died a few minutes later.[56]

As Weldon's body was carried home to his pregnant widow and five children, inside the barges each detective was "taken charge by a workman and marched tremblingly out on the gang plank." Thousands of men, women, and children had gathered to witness the surrender, and they greeted the Pinkertons with vengeful hoots and calls. The agents immediately recognized that O'Donnell's reassuring words now meant nothing. Reporters witnessing the events tried to capture the growing fury of the crowd. As the Pinkertons "scrambled up the steep bank, they were tripped and jostled about, . . . sand thrown over them, and all sorts of indignities heaped upon them. They were unmercifully guyed and badgered." The Pinkertons, Arthur Burgoyne wrote, "had to run the gauntlet, and if the experience before them was not destined to be almost as trying as that attributed to the victims of the gauntlet torture in tales of Indian life, it was not because the mob did not show all the signs of thirsting for a fierce carnival of revenge."[57]

The "carnival" began immediately "as if by a preconcerted plan," when the crowd formed itself "into two lines, 600 yards long, between which the men from the barges had to pass." At the head of the procession a steelworker carried the American flag; he was followed by one hundred of his colleagues carrying rifles and marching four abreast. The Pinkertons, walking behind the armed Homesteaders, were initially met only with more jeers and epithets. Then one of the crowd struck an agent with his open hand, and wholesale physical assaults against them began: many were knocked into insensibility by the men and women who had gathered to watch. The press was universally aghast at the turn of events. "The most shocking and dastardly deeds," one reporter observed, were committed; he was especially shocked when he saw a woman punch out the eye of an agent with her umbrella.[58]

The description provided by the *Pittsburgh Post* of the agents' march up the river embankment is typical of the reporting in the popular press:

> As the Pinkertons neared the top of the bank, they were helped along with kicks and cuffs. One man received a slap from a woman and attempted to strike back. He was at once hit on the head with a stick and the blood flowed freely. Other women punched the fellows in the ribs with parasols and belabored them with switches. The Pinkertons followed each other closely. Many of them were bald headed, others were well dressed, but most of them were tough looking. No mercy was shown them. . . . The men . . . were punched by every man that could get a lick at them. The Hungarians were particularly vicious and belted the men right and left. They were knocked on the head and struck in the face. The men plunged wildly onward, begging for the mercy which they received not. No distinction was made. They were hit on the heads with hand-billies and clubs and sticks and stricken to the ground. Onward they plunged, bleeding and dazed.[59]

Burgoyne, carried away with his own excited prose, wrote that the women of Homestead, "converted for the nonce into veritable furies, belabored Mr. Frick's janizaries with bludgeons, stoned them, kicked them and spat upon them." Like other journalists who covered the surrender, he called the episode an "exhibition of barbarism." O'Donnell and some of his colleagues tried to intervene; in Burgoyne's view, their pleas for order went unheeded because most of the mob owed no allegiance to the AAISW. "In fact, several of the men who made up the hastily-formed escort [for the Pinkertons] were themselves struck and reviled for their humanity."[60]

As the agents trudged upward toward the mill, hundreds of women and boys began to dismantle the barges. They removed quilts, sheets, pillows, cooking utensils, and cots—everything they could. The crowd then set fire to the barges. "The delight of the onlookers at this finale to the tragic events of the day knew no bounds. They cheered, clapped their hands and even danced with glee while the dry wood blazed and crackled, and two huge columns of smoke rose lazily toward the sky and formed clouds overhead. Not until the vessels had burned to the surface of the water and the last hissing embers disappeared beneath the placid bosom of the Monongahela did the enthusiasm abate."[61]

News of the surrender traveled quickly into Homestead proper, and the residents rushed to the mill. The crowd, predominantly of women and children, made its way past union headquarters in the Bost Building and then on toward the main entrance of the steelworks in Munhall. "Men, women and children in one confused mass surged rapidly toward the works," one exhilarated reporter noted. "Many of the women carried brooms and whips. One old woman [doubtless, Margaret Finch] who has figured before in many troubles of this kind tottered along carrying a huge black jack in her hands, all the time yelling: 'Oh, the dirty black sheep, just let me get my hands on them, the dirty, dirty black sheep,' Young women who were mild and gentle-looking stood in their gateways and cried to the men as they rushed by: 'Give it to the black sheep, kill them all.' "[62]

At precisely 5:45 P.M., the Pinkertons, who by then had been marched through the whole length of the steelworks, emerged from the main gate as part of yet another procession. Once again they were preceded by a man carrying the flag. He was followed by "a battalion of sons of steelworkers," the mill men from the South Side, and then a contingent of Homestead steelworkers, who had re-formed and were now marching two abreast, each carrying on his shoulder a captured Winchester; between them, locked in their arms, were the agents.[63]

Swept away by the excitement of the moment, reporters capitalized on the sensational details of the Pinkerton retreat in passionate, lurid, saleable prose. The aggrieved Homesteaders were quickly transformed into a "living, seething mass" no longer acting "like human beings"; they had forgotten the rules of civilized warfare and jumped upon each agent "like a pack of wolves." All along Eighth Avenue from the mill into Homestead proper, the agents were beaten again. Even the "best people" of Homestead did not shy away. "Well bred and well dressed women stood on front steps and laughed aloud at the sight of the miserable creatures staggering along the road," a reporter for the *New York Herald* noted. "The thirst for blood had possessed these women, too, as surely as it ever did the Roman maids and matrons in the Coliseum, and there they stood in the doorways of their homes and laughed at sights at which on any other day they would have fainted." For these women too, as the reporter saw it, Homestead had become a carnival.[64]

As the procession reached the Bost Building, the detectives were instructed to take off their hats and salute the American flag that hung from a window in union headquarters. They obliged, whereupon the townspeople could not contain their anger: "Men and women hit them with umbrellas and sticks and abused them in every way imaginable." Near the Homestead Opera House on Fifth Avenue, suitcases were torn out of the hands of the few agents who had been able to hold on to them, and the underclothes were ceremoniously tossed in the air.[65]

The Opera House, it had been decided by the Advisory Committee, would serve as a temporary jail; the Pinkertons would remain there until Sheriff McCleary picked them up and served them with the murder charges that the Homestead workers understood to be the precondition for surrender. As the procession approached the building, many of the onlookers seemed to recognize that here was their final opportunity to settle accounts. Thus it was just outside the Opera House where, from the viewpoint of Burgess McLuckie and other members of the Advisory Committee, the most serious trouble of the day occurred.[66]

The incident began when one of the Pinkertons tried to break away in a desperate effort to avoid incarceration. As he escaped from his guards, a heavy-set woman ran him down, threw him to the ground, stamped on him, punched him and then threw sand in his eyes. After this agent was corralled, order was restored, and the agents resumed their march into the Opera House. Just as the final one approached, however, the widow of one of the dead steelworkers, emboldened by grief, threw herself at him and started pummeling him.

Among the watchful observers was a large group of East European immigrants who, like the widow beating the Pinkertons, had come to the Opera House to avenge the death of a loved one. The friends and relatives of Joseph Sotak and Peter Fares believed, with good reason, that they too would be given a chance to do just that. Two immigrants jumped one of the agents: a man grabbed him by the throat and hit him in the face while a woman smashed his head with a club. So intense was the beating that a guard appointed by the Advisory Committee was forced to intervene. Leveling his gun at the "Huns," as Burgoyne called them, the guard shouted: "Stand back, or by [God] I'll shoot the next man or woman that raises a hand against them. We have promised to protect them, and we'll do it, even if we have to use our guns." The crowd responded, "Kill the murderers." More guards aimed rifles at the crowd and prepared to fire. "Disaster might have followed, had not Burgess McLuckie come forward, commanded peace and assured the crowd that the Pinkertons would be locked up and held for murder."

With McLuckie's command and his assurance that murder charges would be brought, the violence ended at about 6:15 P.M. "and no further trouble was experienced in getting the bruised and battered prisoners into their temporary quarters." While all three hundred of the Pinkertons had been terrorized over the course of their march through the steelworks and the town, fewer than half had suffered painful physical wounds. Contrary to some secondary accounts, however, none lost his life.[67]

Soon after order was restored, most of the townspeople went home to celebrate their victory: "When the parade had been dismissed, Homestead went wild with delight." The proud and festive mood was captured by "The Homestead Strike," a poem that told the story of the day:

> 'Twas on the Sixth, July, '92, just at the dawn of day,
> the Pinkerton marauders tried to land at Fort Frick Bay.
> But there they met there Waterloo from Vulcan's brawny sons,
> who repulsed them in a moment and stifled all their guns.[68]

While this "stifling" was being celebrated by most of Homestead, McLuckie and the other members of the Advisory Committee faced the important job of transferring custody of the Pinkertons to Sheriff McCleary. The decision to hand over the prisoners was made at a mass meeting of the Homestead steelworkers. Nonetheless, the Advisory Committee had previously been empowered to negotiate on behalf of the men, and it was in this capacity that it met with the ten-man Homestead Borough Council, the formal municipal authority, to consider the transfer proposal.

Collective decision making between town and union officials came easily enough. McLuckie, a leader of the Advisory Committee—some accounts held that he was in fact its director—was also the chief municipal officer. With steelworkers such as David Lynch, who served on the Advisory Committee with McLuckie, and John Rattigan, John Dierken, T. H. Williamson, and William Lloyd as members, the council was certain to reflect the interests of Andrew Carnegie's employees. It therefore took only a short time for the two bodies to endorse the release of the Pinkertons to McCleary on the condition that they be charged—and that McCleary collect them with no more than one deputy. The steelworkers did not want to open any avenue through which county law enforcement officials might introduce new workers into the mill.[69]

At the very time when McLuckie and other leaders of Homestead were consolidating their stance on the release, however, the national officers of the AAISW were making their own arrangements about this matter with Sheriff McCleary and Christopher Magee. Weihe, the president, Garland, the president elect, Stephen Madden, the secretary, and William J. Brennen, the union's attorney, arrived at McCleary's office sometime after 6:00 P.M. to begin consideration of what they knew was a most delicate matter. The session lasted for two hours, at which point Magee led the way out "for a bit of supper and further discussion of peace measures." By 10:15, Magee's dinner guests had agreed on the measures to be taken, and he accompanied them on board a special train for Homestead.[70]

Once the train had left, the national press carried reports that McCleary was on his way to Homestead to arrest the Pinkertons on the charges brought by the men. The *New York World* went so far as to report that he had already charged them, and the *Chicago Tribune* carried a story that he had taken them to the Allegheny County Jail. At 11:00 P.M. in Homestead, according to the *New York Herald*, the steelworkers were "jubilant over this official action. . . . If correctly reported," such action "places the law on their [the workers'] side."

In truth, by 11:00 P.M. the Pinkertons had not yet been arrested: they remained in the Opera House, under the guard of the steelworkers, awaiting the arrival of the special train that would bear them away. When the train finally did arrive at 12:30 A.M. on 7 July, the prisoners were in a sorry state. Their demeanor, one reporter observed, resembled that of the lowest immigrant laborer who had just arrived at Ellis Island. As they boarded the train to Pittsburgh—and presumably to jail—one leading steelworker shouted, "Good bye, boys, don't try it again." Then about fifty of the Homestead workers joined Magee, McCleary, Brennen, and other officials for the short trip to Pittsburgh.[71]

Ironically, a few minutes before the train left, Secretary Lovejoy of the Carnegie Steel Company was issuing a rather different farewell of his own in Pittsburgh. This one, directed to the steelworkers of Homestead, carried with it a number of other messages. For one thing, Lovejoy said, he was certain that the day's events would signal the "deathblow" for the AAISW in Homestead and all across the country. Moreover, it was the Homestead workers, not the Pinkertons, who would be arrested and tried for murder. "The Amalgamated people who committed these recent overt acts will probably find themselves in a very bad hole, for when the proper time arrives, a number of them will be arrested on a charge of murder, and I need scarcely say there will be no lack of evidence." Lovejoy concluded with what proved to be a prescient valedictory to the union era in the American steel industry: "This outbreak settles one matter forever, and that is that the Homestead mill hereafter

will be run non-union and the Carnegie company will never again recognize the Amalgamated Association nor any other labor organization. The
Homestead trouble will doubtless also have the effect of influencing
other mills heretofore union to become non-union and thus free their
owners from the arbitrary dictation of labor unions."

As Lovejoy's words were being telegraphed across the country and
set in type, the train carrying Magee and his Pinkerton charges arrived at
the Fourth Avenue station in Pittsburgh. Magee, together with Sheriff
McCleary, the attorney Brennen and national officers of the union, disembarked at 1:30 A.M. to confer with the superintendent of the Pittsburgh police and a number of local railroad officials. Judging from the
intensity of the conversation, a reporter for the *Pittsburgh Post* noted,
"the question of what to do with the Pinkertons seemed to be difficult to
solve." The solution for the moment was to send the train on to the
Pennsylvania Railroad yards on Eighteenth Street in Pittsburgh.[72]

The choice of the Pennsylvania was most apposite: for years, Magee
had been the railroad's chief representative in Pittsburgh, cultivating
friends, procuring contracts, winning (and paying for) favors on its behalf. In the Pennsylvania Railroad yards, Magee knew, the agents would
be safe until he and his associates decided what to do with them. The
train pulled into the yards sometime between 2:00 and 2:15 A.M.; a short
time later, Magee and McCleary, after consulting with the highest officials of the railroad, announced to the press that the agents would simply be taken away, that, contrary to the expressed desire of the municipal authorities in Homestead and the workers' Advisory Committee,
they would not be arrested and charged.[73]

William Brennen, who had begun his working life as an 11-year-old
mill hand in the American Iron Works, was one of the AAISW officials
on the platform when word came from Magee and McCleary that the
Pinkertons would be set free. Though he was a staunch Democrat (he
would go on to head the county party for nearly two decades), he had
already embarked upon the path that would distinguish his career in
that office: cooperation with the Republican machine. Brennen therefore
had no difficulty in voicing his approval of Magee's plan for clearing the
agents out of town. Indicting them would be totally inappropriate, he
said. After all, how could anyone determine which was responsible for
any of the Homestead deaths? "What else can be done except let these
fellows go? The men up at Homestead made no stipulation as to what
was to be done with the Pinkertons. All they wanted was to get them
here." Doubtless the Homestead steelworker who was complaining
about Magee's undue influence over Sheriff McCleary and certain officials of the AAISW had Brennen uppermost in mind.[74]

As for Magee, he maintained a cautious silence until the Pinkerton
agents had left Pittsburgh on another Pennsylvania Railroad "special."

Shortly after their 10:00 A.M. departure on 7 July, Magee consented to a brief interview with the press. He explained that "common human instinct dictated that the guards should be removed as soon as possible." With this "human motive in view," he "had rendered what assistance he thought necessary"; beyond this he "was at a loss to say what ultimate disposition of the men had been made." In point of fact, the train carrying the agents was headed for Philadelphia and New York. Citing "the strong feeling against the Pinkertons among the working people of Pittsburgh," Burgoyne concluded that their departure "was, no doubt, the best thing that could be done under the circumstances." He did not say for whom it was best. But, like Magee, he knew full well that the agents' hastily arranged exit effectively suppressed any possibility of legal action against them or, perhaps more important, their employer, the Carnegie Steel Company.[75]

One person remains curiously invisible on this important day in American history. Just where was the chief officer of Carnegie Steel while his Pinkertons and his steelworkers were locked in battle on the banks of the Monongahela?

On 5 July, as the Pinkerton detectives were making their way to Homestead, Andrew Carnegie, far from the din of his steelworks, was being happily cheered in Aberdeen, Scotland, where he had come to open formally the library he was bestowing on that municipality. In appreciation of this latest installment in Carnegie's burgeoning empire of philanthropy, he received the freedom of the city and was lavishly hailed by local officials.[76]

Carnegie spent the night in Aberdeen at the Haddo House hotel, where he received a telegram from Pittsburgh notifying him of the battle at Homestead. Undeterred by the news, he proceeded with his vacation plans and left on 6 July for Rannoch Lodge, a retreat in the central highlands, so isolated that it could be reached only by private carriage. Loch Rannoch and the nearby streams provided Carnegie with an idyllic setting to pursue a favorite pastime, fishing. While vacationing at the lodge, he received a number of urgent telegrams from America, and he also received a welcome letter and a few trout flies from a certain William Isherwood, whom he had met at Haddo House. "They are fastened in such a way that they seldom come to pieces, both ends of the feathers are tied along the shaft of the wire, a way that is never adopted by tackle makers. . . . I should be pleased to hear if you find them successful. They are most adapted for stream fishing."[77]

On 8 July, the day after Isherwood penned this note, Carnegie was finally located by a newspaperman. Carnegie's partners had grown increasingly concerned about his propensity to speak his mind, uncensored, and had cabled him with pointed advice to maintain silence. On this day, he complied, and the intrepid reporter who had tracked him down could report only that he refused to talk and appeared agitated, and that his wife had tried to calm him. Carnegie could not be quiet for long, however. On the following day, in what proved to be the first of a decades-long effort to distance himself from responsibility for the Homestead Lockout, he told the *New York Herald*: "The strike is most deplorable, and the news of the disaster, which reached me at Aberdeen, grieved me more than I can tell you. It came on me like a thunderbolt in a clear sky. I must positively decline to enter into any discussion as to the merits or demerits of the case. All I will say is that the strike did not take place in the old Carnegie works, but the difficulty has been entirely in the recently acquired works."[78]

In truth, the Homestead Steel Works was hardly a recent acquisition. Carnegie had owned it for nearly a decade; moreover, he had pursued a vigorous policy of antiunionism there, as elsewhere throughout his empire of steel. To be sure, in April 1892, well before leaving the United States for his vacation in Scotland, he had sent Frick the draft of a notice meant for the Homestead workers which stated that the company would no longer recognize any union upon expiration of the contract on 30 June. In a subsequent letter to Frick, dated 4 May, Carnegie reaffirmed this plan and also, on behalf of the senior partners of the firm, granted his chief of operations full authority to proceed as he saw fit: "We all approve of anything you do, not stopping short of a contest. We are with you to the end." On 10 June he issued explicit orders to Frick not to negotiate: "Of course, you will be asked to confer, and I know you will decline all conferences, as you have taken your stand and have nothing more to say."[79]

It is this ruthless, autocratic tone, not the public posture of benevolence, ignorance and remorse, that resonates in the cable Carnegie sent to Frick in response to the first news from Homestead: "All anxiety gone since you stand firm. Never employ one of these rioters. Let grass grow over works. Must not fail now." For those who would have called him on his direct responsibility in the violent episode at Homestead, however, Carnegie hung an invisible sign on his door that read simply "Gone fishin'."

Years later, in his *Autobiography*, Carnegie provided the following gloss on 6 July. Until the unfortunate events at Homestead, relations with his employees had always been "delightfully satisfactory." In fact, the only thing that prevented his immediate return from Scotland—trout fishing notwithstanding—was the impassioned plea of his partners, who feared that he would capitulate because he "was always disposed to yield to the demands of the men."[80]

Given his physical distance from the events and a convincing attitude of shock and dismay, Carnegie could claim somewhat credibly that he had no direct role in the violence that shook Homestead. It was, after all, Frick who, in Carnegie's absence, had called in the Pinkertons. (In this he was following a precedent established by Carnegie in a dispute at Braddock in 1888.) However, in creating and fortifying the system that had, over the years, produced the conditions for this violence, Carnegie's role cannot be denied. What provoked the apparently "barbaric" and "thankless" workers of Homestead was not, as an account limited to that day might indicate, the sudden intrusion of Pinkerton agents into their dispute but the slow and steady erosion of their rights and their power, over which Carnegie and his associates in steel and politics had presided for years, invisibly but no less violently.[81]

Commenting in his autobiography on the aftermath, Carnegie, as if he himself had run the gauntlet, wailed: "Nothing I have ever had to meet in all my life, before or since, wounded me so deeply. No pangs remain of any wound received in my business career save that of Homestead. It was so unnecessary." In the pages that follow, we examine the technology and changing morality of steelmaking in Gilded Age America that made the events in Homestead on 6 July 1892 not only necessary but perhaps inevitable.[82]

PART TWO
Captains of Steel, Captains of Culture

The consumption of iron is the social barometer by which to estimate the relative height of civilization among nations.

— Abram S. Hewitt

Engineers are not proud; they simply cannot help it that they are
the way, the vehicle, the power of civilization.

— Alexander L. Holley

A perfect mill is the road to wealth.

— Andrew Carnegie to his partner,
W. P. Shinn, April 1876

Chapter 3

The "Mechanical Habit of Mind"

PROBLEMS IN IRON PRODUCTION IN THE MID 1800S

FREDERICK OVERMAN, the author of the most widely read treatise on American iron production in the mid nineteenth century, concluded the 1854 edition of his book with a guarded assessment of the metals industry. Although American ironmasters enjoyed unmatched resources in ore, timber, and coal, in Overman's view they faced two large problems: the relatively high price of labor and—an issue for European ironmasters as well—a lag in the mechanization of iron production. "The application of science and machinery in the manufacture of iron does not exhibit so high a state of cultivation as we find in . . . the manufacture of calico prints and silks." He warned that "the only condition upon which we can rationally base any hope for the future relative to iron manufacture . . . consists in the union of [our] natural advantages with skill, activity, and intellectual cultivation."[1]

Overman singled out three interrelated tasks to which American ironmasters needed to devote themselves if they were to secure "victory in a close contest of competition." The first was to develop mechanical processes that would cheapen and accelerate the production of large quantities of malleable metal. The second was to acquire enough knowledge about the chemical requirements of production to "liberate" ironmasters from reliance upon on the high-priced expertise of skilled workers. And the third, which Overman considered the most important, was to improve overall managerial techniques. "Perhaps in no manufacture is rational and skillful management so indispensable an element of success as in that of iron."

Overman's treatise codified the agenda of American ironmasters for the remainder of the century. Had he been alive in 1901 to witness the creation of the United States Steel Corporation, the world's first billion-dollar company, he would no doubt have marveled at the technical, managerial, and financial ingenuity of American metalmasters, in par-

47

ticular, Andrew Carnegie, whose vast holdings in the steel industry provided the foundation for J. P. Morgan's corporate behemoth. When Overman wrote the first edition of his book, though, the prospects for a "victory" of such magnitude were not promising. At that time iron-masters were confronting what appeared to be an insurmountable obstacle in the production process. The bottleneck was in the refining sector of iron manufacture, where highly skilled and handsomely paid puddlers slowly "cooked" iron and exercised, by twentieth-century standards, a remarkable degree of control over the conditions of their labor. The self-regulation these men enjoyed amounted to a highly disagreeable fact of life for Overman and his colleagues.[2]

Just what was puddling, and why did Overman and his readers want to supplant it? Puddling was a delicate, complicated, and time-consuming procedure that transformed pig iron, the crude product of blast furnaces, into wrought iron, a material that could be used for rails and other commercial purposes.

As Frederick Overman well knew, the puddler required great physical strength and an extraordinary knowledge of practical metallurgy to perform his job. He had to know, for example, how to regulate the temperature of the furnace, when to start and stop stirring the iron, how much scrap to add, and precisely when to add it. Some of the difficulties faced by puddlers stemmed from wide variations in the characteristics of the pig iron they used. These variations caused unexpected chemical reactions and temperature changes; years of accumulated wisdom were required to assess the specific qualities peculiar to any one batch of pig iron. "None of us ever went to school and learned the chemistry of it from books," recalled a puddler, James J. Davis. "We learned the trick by doing it, standing with our faces in the scorching heat while our hands puddled the metal in its glaring bath."[3]

Specifically, puddling involved nine steps. First, the puddler prepared the furnace by "lining the hearth" with scrap iron, which he melted in order to create a smooth working bottom in the hollowed-out hearth of the brick furnace. Then he "charged" the furnace with about six hundred pounds of pig iron; during the third stage of the process, called "melting," the puddler melted and stirred the pig with his long iron "paddle" in order to purify the metal by burning off impurities. In "clearing," he picked up a "rabble," inserted it in the furnace, and stirred the iron until it became congealed. The puddler then lowered the furnace temperature and added more scrap so that the metal would "rise on the boil." As the carbon in the pig iron oxidized and "boiled," he continued stirring until the metal "came to nature." Next he began "turning and balling" the mass to divide it into three "balls," which he "drew" from the furnace. Then he prepared for the next "heat."

Although puddling, which had been developed in the 1780s, was a great improvement over earlier methods of producing wrought iron, it did not yield a perfect product. Impurities invariably remained in the balls, and they had to be "squeezed." For this puddlers used a machine that worked on the same principle as a coffee mill. The process of making wrought iron did not end, however, when a "bloom" emerged from the squeezer. Further refining was done in rolling mills, where workers as skilled as puddlers manipulated the blooms through powerful metal rolls that worked like clothes wringers.[4]

Frederick Overman and other iron manufacturers regarded puddling and the many procedures involved in rolling as problems principally because they were slow and costly. Moreover, the skilled laborers who produced wrought iron and the products made from it enjoyed great flexibility in setting their work schedules. Ironmasters did not contract with skilled workers for a certain number of hours, nor did they direct them how or how quickly to do their jobs. Rather, skilled workers were paid on the basis of what they produced, and the workers ultimately determined how much was produced.[5]

It was to these circumstances that Overman alluded when he spoke of the urgent need to transform the manufacture of iron into a "rational" enterprise. As a loyal son of the Industrial Revolution, he was determined to apply to the metals industry the same rational principles of work and machinery that had transformed the English textile trade and had brought entrepreneurial distinction to the mill owners of Lowell, Massachusetts. Preeminent among these principles was widening the division of labor in order to increase the speed of work and the quantity of product. For, as Adam Smith had demonstrated, manufacturing processes could be quickened by breaking them down into discrete tasks and subtasks. Any increase in the specialization of work, Smith observed, would: increase the pace of all workers insofar as each could concentrate on one task instead of many; save the time lost when a worker completed one task and then moved to another; and ease the introduction of machinery that could perform the simpler tasks and thus allow one worker to complete the labor formerly done by many.[6]

In their efforts to alter the production process by expanding the division of labor by task, European and American factory masters often looked to Smith for guidance. But it was left to the political economists of the early nineteenth century, and chiefly to Charles Babbage, to identify what has remained the most compelling attraction of the division of labor by task. Babbage explained that if a manufacturing process is parceled out to a number of workers, each of whom possesses the skill requisite to perform only a single task, then the overall labor cost is necessarily less than if workers skilled in various aspects of the process are employed to produce an equivalent amount.[7]

By the mid 1800s, Overman and other American manufacturers

clearly understood that the labor needed to produce an item can always be purchased for less when it is subdivided by task. Moreover, they believed that efforts to maximize their profits by applying the Babbage principle, as it came to be called, served the common good and therefore aided the progress of civilization. The emergence of this belief, legitimized by what the critic Raymond Williams called the morality of improvement, signaled an important transformation in Western political culture: the triumph of strictly economic appetites over a moral code that condemned acquisitiveness and held that no person should take advantage of a neighbor's necessity. This new morality certified the pursuit of individual economic advantage as universally beneficent and "rational," and it legitmized efforts to organize work, and indeed all public and private life, toward the achievement of maximum productivity and profit.[8]

The rise of the morality of improvement coincided with the technological innovations of the Industrial Revolution that Frederick Overman admired and so urgently wanted to apply to the iron industry. To men such as Overman, the mechanization of iron manufacturing offered far more than just the promise of greater productivity and profits; it became an obligatory pursuit in itself; invention, like acquisition, became a duty. As Lewis Mumford has commented, machines were seen as "the true embodiment of everything that was excellent." The search for mechanical innovation took on a religious fervor; mechanics and capital accumulation, both putatively linked to natural law, became mutually validating. If, as Adam Smith's metaphor of the invisible hand had suggested, rationally ordered human society was but a reflection of the immutable laws of matter and motion, what objects could better represent value than machines, machines designed in accord with those same laws of the universe and of rational profit making? Mumford elaborates: "The application of power to motion, and the application of motion to production, and of production to money-making, and so the further increase of power—this was the worthiest object . . . put before men." Accordingly, he labeled this ethic that cojoined the pursuit of technics and of wealth the "mechanical habit of mind."[9]

The first American textile masters represented the proud embodiment of the mechanical habit of mind. In their hands machinery became the chief means of fulfilling the grand goal of rational enterprise. Following Adam Smith, the early factory masters saw the introduction of "labor-saving" machinery as the principal means of achieving this goal. Industrialists who came of age later in the nineteenth century understood that efficient manufacturing was more complicated: taking their cue from Babbage, they recognized that success also depended upon deliberate efforts to manage the activity of workers. Indeed, the introduction of machinery and the pursuit of managerial initiatives aimed at

controlling "the domestic economy" of the factory were of equal importance. "The *economical principles* which regulate the application of machinery, and which govern the interior of all our great factories are quite as
essential to the prosperity of a great commercial country as are [purely]
mechanical principles."[10]

Frederick Overman had no doubt read Adam Smith, and he was familiar with the Babbage principle even if he did not call it by name. He also
appreciated the importance in the factory of a well-managed domestic
economy. But in 1854, Overman and his colleagues in iron manufacture
could still do little to install the rational principles of political and machine
science in their industrial establishments, for the labor-intensive technics
of metal manufacture stood in the way of "improvement."

Yet Overman was confident of ultimate success. In what proved a
prescient observation, he wrote that by dint of their "energy and perse-
verance," American ironmasters would eventually reduce production
costs, speed the process, minimize the importance of the workers' expertise, and rationalize management by applying to metalmaking the same
principles of factory production that had revolutionized the textile industry. His predictions were, in fact, realized with startling rapidity. Just two
years later, in 1856, Henry Bessemer astounded the world with a radically new metallurgical process that seemed to promise to end puddling
and once and for all establish inexpensive and rational procedures in
metalmaking.[11]

Bessemer was an Englishman, but the impact his invention made was
nowhere as revolutionary as in America. Shortly after he announced his
discovery of a new process, leadership in metalmaking passed from British to American factory masters and to the technical and managerial experts they consulted and employed. These iron and steel entrepreneurs,
these engineers and factory managers were, like Overman, already fully
wedded to the propositions that the reduction of labor costs, the introduction of mechanical improvements, the "rational and skillful management"
of industrial enterprises, and the acquisition of the workers' specialized
knowledge were essential to "victory in a close contest of competition."
Unlike Overman, however, the first generation of American steelmakers
had at their disposal, thanks to the Bessemer process, the means to separate workers from the work process and then to reintegrate the two along
lines more favorable to management.

One might well argue that in the end, then, it was these very captains
of steel—not the leaders of the chemical and electrical industries, as the
historian David Noble has argued—who were the first industrialists to
appreciate thoroughly Babbage's insight that technical and managerial
initiatives are intertwined. It was they who were the first to expropriate
systematically the workers' knowledge of and control over production;
moreover, it was they who were the first to disseminate technical and

managerial information through newly created professional societies that brought together engineers and entrepreneurs in shared pursuits. In short, it was the captains of steel, taking their ideological cues from Smith, Babbage, and Overman and their practical model from Bessemer, who transformed the mechanical habit of mind into "the mechanical mode of action" that we have come to know as scientific management.[12]

THE BESSEMER PROCESS

Henry Bessemer chose a provocative title for the paper he read to the Mechanical Section of the British Association for the Advancement of Science when, on 11 August 1856, he announced the discovery of a new metalmaking process. Bessemer called his paper "The Manufacture of Iron without Fuel," and the staid members of the association braced themselves for a day of fatuousness when they learned that title. To them the idea of making iron without fuel seemed no less absurd than a proposal to "Make Ice without Cold."[13]

However, the members of the association responded enthusiastically when they heard Bessemer's paper, for he revealed that he had indeed succeeded in producing malleable metal from pig iron without using coal. Even more exciting to the members, though, was another promise of Bessemer's new process: it would shorten and cheapen the manufacture of malleable iron by entirely eliminating puddling. Unlike puddling, the new process, Bessemer told his audience, demanded "no manipulation or particular skill." Moreover, it required "only one workman."[14]

Bessemer's claims of reducing the skill requirement and the number of workers proved to be exaggerations. In truth, his metalmaking required considerable skill and more than one worker. However, it did demand far fewer skilled workers than did puddling; as Bessemer claimed, it would "save a great deal of labor" per unit of metal produced.[15]

Indeed, the new process met all the criteria implied in the injunction "Save labor," which stood at the heart of nineteenth-century political economy. As the myriad of contemporary hagiographic accounts testify, Bessemer's invention also gave the century's most concrete expression to the mechanical habit of mind: in describing the invention and practice of the process, virtually all commentators proclaimed that it was divinely inspired and promised universal good.[16]

 Charles Babbage, for one, certainly would have rejoiced at the invention, for, according to Bessemer, the new process promised to "rescue" iron manufacture "from the trammels which have so long surrounded it." By this he meant that by eliminating puddlers, his technique would mechanize and expand the division of labor and shift control of the production process toward factory masters. Because the new process assured that the puddlers' trade secrets would be buried as vestiges of a bygone era, and because enormous licensing fees and construction costs ensured that only the wealthy could establish a Bessemer mill, the invention gave to ironmasters a long-awaited prize. They could now break the puddlers' monopoly of knowledge; they could now separate and then reintegrate workers and the work process in a "rational" way.[17]

Bessemer claimed sole credit for the new process. But he had in fact followed the well-traveled path later outlined by the sociologist S. C. Gilfillan, who suggested that technological innovation invariably stems from "a perpetual *accretion* of little details" and not from the insights of a single, isolated, genius. In truth, the Bessemer process was anticipated virtually in its entirety by William Kelly, an American ironmaster, almost a decade earlier. That Bessemer, Kelly, and other ironmasters were working on similar problems at the same time means, as the historian Peter Temin has suggested, that there clearly was "some kind of 'pressure' for the discovery of a new process." However, this pressure was more than an ill-defined force at work in the minds of those individuals who wanted merely to eliminate production bottlenecks or, as Gilfillan would have it, advance the cause of science. The pressure to invent a new process grew directly from two interrelated desires: to speed up and reduce the cost of production and to alter relations between workers and employers.[18]

Thus, in his paper before the British Association, Bessemer avowed that he had discovered the means to ensure what Frederick Overman had called "victory in a close contest of competition," for his process would cheapen and accelerate the production of malleable metal and "liberate" ironmasters from their employees' high-priced expertise. And although Bessemer did not explicitly claim that the new process would make management more rational and skillful, no one in his audience could avoid drawing such a conclusion. If Overman had attended the meeting, he too would have joined in the hearty applause.

Although Bessemer eliminated the bottleneck of puddling, he did not make the breakthrough by mechanizing puddling. Rather, he succeeded, where other inventors and ironmasters had failed, by inventing an altogether new process—and an altogether new metal. The new metal, Bessemer steel, supplanted puddled iron as the dominant commodity in American metalmaking only in the late 1880s. The eclipse of puddling was slow, and well into the 1890s thousands of puddlers continued to practice their craft. Yet ironmasters and ironworkers understood from the outset that Bessemer's converter promised the ultimate demise of puddling.[19]

The product of the Bessemer converter was not, strictly speaking, steel, and Bessemer and his metalmaking colleagues called it malleable iron until they recognized the commercial value of a name change. They wanted to adopt the name *steel* because that metal, as defined on the eve of the invention, was vastly superior to and more expensive than wrought iron. By using the name *steel* the manufacturers and engineers engaged in Bessemer metalmaking hoped to hasten the acceptance of their product and legitimize their claims that it was superior to puddled iron.[20]

Bessemer's first step along the path that led to a new kind of malleable metal and the demise of puddling began with his invention during the Crimean War of a special artillery shell that could be fired from a smooth-bore gun. The French government was interested in the new weapon but doubted that an ordinary gun, made from brittle cast iron, could withstand the strain of firing the heavy projectile. "The real question," Bessemer wrote, "was, could any guns be made to stand such long projectiles?"[21]

Though this question was real, it reflected only part of the reality that Bessemer described as having informed his subsequent efforts to develop a metal suitable for guns that would fire the new artillery shell: they could have been made from high-quality shear steel, but that was the product of a long and very expensive process. The chief problem that Bessemer faced, therefore, was to find a metal that could be used in artillery and was sufficiently inexpensive to be practicable. He thus set out to find a metal as strong as cast iron and as malleable as shear steel that could be made without a lengthy refining process. To do so, he knew, he had to invent a metal that, like cast iron, could be cast into molds and therefore did not require skilled labor for refining. Unlike cast iron, though, it could not be brittle.[22]

The development of such a metal, Bessemer understood, would have enormous implications. "I began to appreciate fully the fact that if I could improve cast iron and render it malleable and still retain its fluid state, apart from its use in artillery, it would be of [the] greatest commercial value." At stake was the future of puddling, for a cast metal that was strong and malleable might supplant not only shear steel, which was made from wrought iron, but also wrought iron itself.[23]

Bessemer made his key discovery while experimenting with a concoction of steel and pig iron. By accident he noticed that cold air blown over heated pig iron decarburized the pig and thus converted it "into malleable iron without puddling or any other manipulation." The chemistry of the conversion was, he explained, astoundingly simple: oxygen in the air combined with carbon in the pig iron. The result was a rapid explosion that, by virtue of its great heat, consumed the carbon and most of the other impurities in the pig iron and transformed it into a decarburized, malleable metal. The principle of the Bessemer process thus amounted to refining pig iron by harnessing the heat produced by the interaction of oxygen and carbon instead of by generating heat through the addition of coal, as was done in the puddler's furnace.[24]

To accomplish the transformation of pig into malleable metal, Bessemer used an egg-shaped vessel with a heat-resistant lining. Into the vessel he poured molten pig iron and also pumped cold air through six tuyeres, or nozzles, connected to an air compressor. All remained quiet for about ten minutes, according to Bessemer's account of his first "blow." Then the fireworks began: "Sparks, . . . accompanied by hot gases, ascended through the opening at the top of the converter, . . . the apparatus becoming a veritable volcano in a state of active eruption." When the flames died down, Bessemer terminated the process.[25]

Though Bessemer initially succeeded in producing a malleable metal in his experimental converter, his work soon turned to "utter failure." Why? "My knowledge . . . was at that time very limited," he later acknowledged, in a comment that amounted to an understatement of overwhelming proportions.[26]

In the months immediately following the reading of his paper, Bessemer had little luck in producing his new metal. In fact, most of it proved virtually useless. When cooled, it crumbled into small fragments under the slightest pressure. Moreover, because the metal also was weak and brittle when hot, it could not be rolled. A third problem was that Bessemer did not know precisely when to stop the blow in the converter. As a result, the carbon content of the converted metal varied from batch to batch. And because carbon is the principal determinant in the characteristics possessed by metal, he initially could produce metal only of uneven quality.

Though Bessemer engaged a team of three chemists to investigate, he failed to solve the problems. The discovery that had been "a brilliant meteor that had flitted across the metallurgical horizon, . . . [soon] vanished into darkness." Light returned when Robert Mushet, a professional metallurgist, discovered that the addition of a manganese-based ore called spiegeleisen would remove excess oxygen and sulphur from the molten metal after it was blown in the converter. The removal of these two offending elements solved the problems of crumbling and weakness. Moreover, Mushet suggested that each blow be allowed to continue through to its chemical conclusion, when all the carbon is eliminated. Then the desired amount of carbon could be added to the blown metal to achieve the appropriate level of, say, hardness or malleability.[27]

Mushet succeeded in producing ingots of superior quality within months of Bessemer's announcement to the British Association. However, neither Mushet nor Bessemer, who quarreled for years over the relative importance of their metallurgical contributions, succeeded in solving what proved to be an even greater difficulty: to succeed, the Bessemer process required the use of nonphosphoric pig iron. Luckily, both Mushet and Bessemer had used pig that had a low phosphorus content in their initial experiments. But until 1878, when metallurgists invented a method to purify phosphoric ores, the Bessemer process remained unpopular in Europe, where there were only small deposits of nonphosphoric ore.[28]

In the late 1860s, however, American ironmasters began to exploit the iron deposits of the Lake Superior region. There they found vast quantities of high-quality, nonphosphoric iron ore. The combination, then, of a technical process that could refine pig iron without puddling and an ample supply of suitable raw materials helped set the stage for America's second industrial revolution.[29]

The revolution began in earnest when American entrepreneurs, engineers, and factory managers, themselves steeped in the ethos of improvement and wedded to the mechanical habit of mind, developed practical applications for the technological insights of Bessemer and Mushet. Though the product of the Bessemer converter was inferior to wrought iron for some purposes, it could be manufactured on a mass scale. Most important, the knowledge needed to use the converter belonged to metalmasters, and not workers. Thus the Bessemer process created the opportunity to break the monopoly of skill exercised by puddlers and to reinvent the production process in ways that allowed employers to administer the domestic economy of their manufacturing establishments more efficiently.

The results were the first modern steel mills and the emergence of scientific management. The most advanced of these mills, Andrew Carnegie's Edgar Thomson Steel Works, and some of the earliest advances in modern management, materlialized in Western Pennsylvania on the Monongahela River in Braddock, almost directly opposite what was then the quiet farming village of Homestead.

Chapter 4

Captains of Steel

THE MEN WHO financed, designed, and supervised American steelworks between the mid 1860s and the early 1890s shared Frederick Overman's desires to reduce labor costs, introduce new production techniques, and manage factories in a rational manner. To be sure, these desires were rooted in the propositions that self-interest and the accumulation of wealth constituted the good, and that machinery was to be used along with labor to pursue the good. For the captains of steel, however, the pursuit of these goals was not simply a selfish endeavor; in their eyes, the creation of modern civilization—a peculiarly American civilization—was contingent upon their success.[1]

Alexander L. Holley, the preeminent architect of the new steel industry, spoke for all of his colleagues in the business of Bessemer steelmaking: "Engineers are not proud; they simply cannot help it that they are the way, the vehicle, the power of civilization." Thousands of new professionals and the hundreds of societies they created in the late nineteenth century saw themselves as sharing in this mission of civilization. But Holley's fellow engineers, as well as his entrepreneurial colleagues, made a special claim to the calling, for it was they who were creating the very materials to build modern American civilization: rails that stretched for thousands of miles; girders that spanned the great rivers of the continent; beams for the colossal new skyscrapers; boiler plates for locomotives and ships.[2]

The captains of steel believed that the project of building a modern America was impossible to complete so long as wrought iron remained the dominant product of the metals industry and metalworkers remained powerful enough to resist technical and managerial initiatives. Consequently, soon after Henry Bessemer delivered his paper on the manufacture of malleable metal without fuel, the owners of some of the largest ironworks in the United States began to experiment with his process. By the end of the 1860s, the leading ironmasters, engineers, and plant supervisors were convinced that the triumph of the new steelmaking was close at hand. An article in one of their trade journals in 1867 declared: "There is everything to indicate that within a moderate period, and possibly within a few years, malleable iron will become an obsolete material, . . . [and] steel will be yet found to be perfectly adapted, and to possess in a far higher degree of those qualities, not only of hardness and of durability, but of pliability and malleability also, which now render iron the nobler metal of our age."[3]

The men whose efforts in the United States gave substance to the predicted obsolescence of iron comprised a very small group that possessed expertise in the technical requirements of production. They were also particularly skilled in the management of large work forces and in finance and accounting. Among them were representatives of the first generation of engineers trained in American universities—men such as Alexander Holley. But there were also "practical" workers who had acquired their engineering expertise on the shop floor and then joined managerial ranks—men such as W. R. Jones, the manager of Andrew Carnegie's Edgar Thomson Steel Works in Braddock. And of course there were the great entrepreneurs of the era—men such as Carnegie himself.

From the end of the Civil War into the 1890s, these steel engineers, managers, and entrepreneurs shared a common purpose. All of them, especially the engineers, claimed an extraordinary authority that, they believed, derived from their respect for and possession of difficult and esoteric knowledge. Whereas the puddler and other craftsmen had learned their skills in a purely practical way, by following customs of the trade, the steelman was a true professional: his knowledge was based on superior theories, and he learned and worked by the "laws of science." As the historian Burton Bledstein explains with reference to the new class of positivist professionals, these men firmly believed that the study of scientific laws singled them out for the highest human calling: "to free the power of nature within every worldly sphere." Like other professionals, the steelman saw himself as a self-governing individual in the exercise of this pursuit, one embarked upon not in the name of self-interest but in the service of all mankind. It was by virtue of this full-blown claim, linked to his scientific expertise, that the steelman of the late nineteenth century towered over industrial America as a cultural authority and prophet of progress.[4]

This authority found institutional expression in the American Institute of Mining Engineers (AIME), founded in 1871, and the American Society of Mechanical Engineers (ASME), founded in 1880. Neither organization ever pretended to represent only the engineering profession. Members of both saw them as serving the needs of mining and metalmaking businesses as well as representing the best ambitions of American culture and society. Unlike the American Society of Civil Engineers, which was committed to the idea that engineering should be an independent profession, the AIME had membership standards that allowed anyone "practically engaged in mining, metallurgy, or metallurgical engineering" to join. Thus it was as much a trade association as a professional society—one whose self-declared object was "the economical production of useful minerals and metals."[5]

The ASME and AIME had much in common. Many men held membership in both organizations, and some were officers in both. In fact, the key organizers of the ASME were the most prominent members of the AIME. Among them were Holley and his good friend Robert Henry Thurston. These two led the way in cementing the relationships of engineers and financiers. Noting "the advantages of the association of businessmen with engineers" in the AIME and in the British Iron and Steel Institute, Holley told his colleagues at the initial meeting of the ASME that he fully expected the new organization to nurture similar relations. It would build on "the direct business results of bringing professional knowledge, capital, and business talent together under the most favorable circumstances." Thurston, a pioneer in engineering education, proudly boasted in 1881 that ASME members employed three million workers, possessed assets of $2.5 billion, and met an aggregate payroll of $1 billion. Indeed, no other association had so many members "tied to business." A few years later, Thurston sounded what was to become a major theme in the public pronouncements of his colleagues: that all Americans should look to engineers for a proper "adjustment" of the relations of workers and employers and that engineers would settle the "labor problem" once and for all.[6]

Resolving this problem was, for men like Thurston, part of the project to build a new social order. In this endeavor the captains of the steel regarded the Bessemer converter as their most important tool. They believed that civilization could be carried to new heights only insofar as its undergirding was cast, literally, in molten—though malleable—metal and in the social relations of factory life and urban politics that made its production possible. Creating the new metal and shaping the new social relations, the captains of steel understood, involved a struggle. Men such as Holley, Carnegie, and his fellow ironmaster Abram S. Hewitt proved more than equal to the task. With the "skill, activity, and intellectual cultivation" that Frederick Overman had prescribed, they and their colleagues in plant management helped catapult the technique of metalmaking and the organization of its production to the most sophisticated levels attained by any industry in the nineteenth century.

Holley, Carnegie, and Hewitt also articulated the most compelling justifications for the undertakings of the captains of steel. Hewitt, who pioneered the development of open-hearth steelmaking, translated workplace initiatives of men such as himself into the larger political

arena, where he became one of the most forceful defenders of the emerging corporate order. Holley, who invented the Bessemer steel mill, was
instrumental in defining the aspirations and educational needs of engineers, the talented new race, as he defined them, of privileged men.
And Carnegie, who built the world's largest industrial empire and cultivated close ties with leading politicians, helped redefine American success in his writings and in the example of his amassed fortune.[7]

Beyond their symbolic roles in expounding a new ethos for the steel
era, Holley, Carnegie, and, to a lesser extent, Hewitt played very real
roles in the construction of the metalmaking facilities that would reorient
the political culture of the Pittsburgh district and indeed the nation. It
was Holley who designed the world's most advanced steelworks at the
time in Braddock, Pennsylvania; he also participated in the planning of
the Pittsburgh Bessemer Steel Works (PBSW) in Homestead. Holley,
along with Hewitt, the engineer and the entrepreneur, were thus among
the first to define the new monumental world of steelmaking that would
culminate in Andrew Carnegie's Homestead Steel Works.

The effects of the new technological advances in metalmaking were
by no means limited to the immediate worlds of engineers, entrepreneurs, and steel producers. On the contrary, the new pyrotechnics produced a profound impact on the American psyche epitomized best,
perhaps, by a readymade mythology of the Bessemer converter that
captured the imagination of a broad public. Writing in *Scribner's* in 1872,
for instance, James Richardson likened the Bessemer process, with its
huge blasts of air, to Aeolus, divine keeper of the winds, and described
the attendant tasks in the process as "Cyclopean"—beyond the range of
mere mortals. Contemporary graphic images of the converter similarly
emphasized its awesome size and otherworldly force, which were
evoked in sublime and fantastic terms.[8]

Like the captains of steel, many contemporary writers, journalists,
and graphic artists regarded the mighty converter enthusiastically as no
less than the harbinger of a new and better way of life. For some it
became an eloquent metaphor for modern America itself. The converter,
wrote one engineer-businessman-historian in 1891, had produced "a
fabric of national prosperity and happiness that shall wear through the
ages and continue to clothe this people while time endures." This claim,
however—modest by comparison with most that appeared in professional and popular journals—ran counter to the experience of thousands
of iron- and steelworkers. Their experience, far less euphoric or mythologized than the accounts summarized here, tells a very different story of
steel, one to which I shall turn shortly. Nevertheless, for all these men—
engineers, entrepreneurs, authors, and metalworkers—there was no
escaping the impact of the Bessemer converter and all that it stood for.
As the literary critic Alfred Kazin has asserted, for better or for worse the

new America of the Gilded Age was indeed "baptized by the Bessemer process."[9]

ABRAM S. HEWITT AND THE PROMISE
OF THE OPEN HEARTH

In 1890 the leading iron and steel manufacturers and engineers of Great Britain, all members of the British Iron and Steel Institute, visited the United States along with some of their colleagues from Germany. The ostensible purpose of the visit, made at the invitation of the AIME and cosponsored by the ASME, was to acquaint British and German iron- and steelmasters with the latest in American production techniques. After a series of meetings in New York, the Europeans toured the most important mining and manufacturing districts in the United States. Along the way, the entourage was feted by prominent industrialists and politicians, including President Benjamin Harrison.

Sir James Kitson, a wealthy ironmaster who was president of the British Iron and Steel Institute, captured the celebratory mood of the visit: "Everything possible was done by our American friends to make our visit pleasant. . . . Special trains and carriages were placed at our service. Brilliant receptions and the most sumptuous banquets were held in our honor. . . . Towns competed for our presence, and vied with each other in the grandeur and cordiality of their receptions."[10]

Since the 1860s, American and European metal manufacturers and engineers had enjoyed a cordial relationship. They shared the results of their investigations of new production methods in the publications of their professional societies and trade organizations. The owners, managers, and design and operating engineers of European and American metalworks had also made a practice of exchanging information at industrial expositions and professional meetings. As was indicated by the "lavish" attention showered upon the European visitors, however, the meetings of 1890 were special, for, in crossing the Atlantic to accept an invitation of nearly twenty years' standing, British and German iron- and steelmasters acknowledged American metalmaking supremacy. Appropriately, the visit occurred in the first year in which American iron and steel mills outproduced those in Great Britain, thereby fulfilling the charge bequeathed them by Frederick Overman. The members of the British Iron and Steel Institute recognized the achievement of their colleagues by presenting the Bessemer Gold Medal, the institute's highest honor, "for distinguished services to the iron and steel trade" to an American. The recipient was Abram S. Hewitt.[11]

Hewitt in 1890 was in the twilight of a successful career in industry and politics. A former congressman, mayor of New York, and national leader of the Democratic party, he played a key role in the introduction of new techniques of steel production in the United States. As the principal owner of the Trenton Iron Company and the New Jersey Steel and Iron Company, Hewitt was the first American ironmaster to experiment with a Bessemer converter and to operate an open-hearth furnace. Although his efforts to produce both Bessemer and open-hearth steel ended in commercial failure, he continued to be a leading manufacturer of iron. His prominence among metalmaking entrepreneurs was underscored by his election, in 1876 and again in 1890, as president of the AIME.[12]

Hewitt's close ties to European metalmakers went back to 1867, when he served as a U.S. commissioner to the Paris Exposition. In this role he wrote a glowing report on continental and British metalmaking that was based on inspections of the largest European mills as well as on the Paris exhibit. The report, entitled "The Production of Iron and Steel in Its Economic and Social Relations," constituted more than a description of metalmaking techniques, however. Though he did survey new production methods, Hewitt also drew connections between the domestic economy of the workplace and political developments outside the factory gates. Chief among such developments in the late 1860s was the rising discontent shared by European and American workers. Hewitt, like other ironmasters, was deeply troubled by the initiatives of workers to alter their relations with employers. In fact, his report amounted to a strategic guide to counter the workers' movement on both sides of the Atlantic.[13]

Hewitt's overview of the new methods of metalmaking and of the accompanying changes in work relations and political culture has lent itself to a peculiar interpretation—first offered by the historian Allan Nevins—that places him on the cutting edge of enlightened reform, if not outright advocacy of workers' rights. In truth, Hewitt's views reflected above all the intelligent self-interest of a factory owner. His report on European metalmaking, like much of his writing, translated this self-interest into the pursuit of a higher civilization. Tellingly, Hewitt observed that the measure of civilization was how much metal could be produced and used: "The consumption of iron is the social barometer by which to estimate the relative height of civilization among nations." In his eyes, as in the eyes of his fellow entrepreneurs, engineers, and factory managers, raising the level of civilization became an injunction to quicken, cheapen, and increase production. Hewitt recognized, though, that this injunction led directly to the great social upheaval of the late nineteenth century and to what he characterized as workers' efforts aimed at "the reorganization of the relations of capital and labor" and of the "fundamental principles of social order."[14]

The "fundamental principles" meant for Hewitt "the security of capital, the security of person, and the right of free discussion." These principles were in grave danger because trade unions mistakenly believed that increases in production should herald "a corresponding rearrangement of the laws of distribution of the proceeds." This line of reasoning, he warned, indicated that trade unions were determined to destroy society.[15]

Hewitt's proposal for ending what he regarded as a war between workers and employers was to introduce more machinery and "improve" overall production techniques so as to secure the position of capital, to create a "governing class . . . of engineers and conductors of industry," and to effect minor adjustments in work relations that, though they might give workers a larger share of the proceeds, would not alter the hierarchy upon which he and his colleagues believed the factory to be naturally based.

Hewitt gave voice to this deeply held commitment to hierarchy in his 1867 report on iron and steel production and in two rounds of testimony before a parliamentary commission investigating Britain's labor problem that very year. His disparaging remarks about American puddlers, in particular, infuriated the workers. "A puddlers' strike is a very familiar thing with us," Hewitt told the commission. "They are the most ignorant men that we have." In fact, puddlers and other ironworkers were so ignorant that it was inappropriate for any of them to dare to think. "I do not say it in derogation of [the worker]. But it is for the master to do the thinking."[16]

According to the Sons of Vulcan, the union of American puddlers, Hewitt's slander against "those who sweat for bread" constituted an assault against the moral standing of the union and a "base calumny upon . . . free American citizens." They saw Hewitt as a "low, unprincipled, and contemptible man." The puddlers reacted strongly to Hewitt's words because they understood that he was determined to launch an assault that went beyond mere rhetoric. Like all ironmasters, he wanted to dispense altogether with the labor of puddlers.[17]

Hewitt moved quickly. Only months after Henry Bessemer read his paper to the British Association for the Advancement of Science, Hewitt became the first American ironmaster to construct a Bessemer converter. His initial efforts with Bessemer steelmaking were unsuccessful, however, and he became convinced that the new process would never supplant puddling. Instead, he looked to the open-hearth furnace to achieve this coveted goal.[18]

Open-hearth steelmaking, developed primarily by William Siemens and Pierre Martin, caught Hewitt's eye at the Paris Exposition. He concluded that open-hearth metal lent itself to a wide variety of uses, was relatively inexpensive to produce, required less skilled labor than puddling, and, once the American patent rights were secured, promised handsome royalties. Hewitt, who succeeded in securing these rights, correctly observed that open-hearth steelmaking was essentially a "modification" of puddling: the process dramatically increased the furnace temperatures to which pig iron was subjected and so removed the excess carbon in it without requiring a puddler.[19]

As Hewitt saw it practiced in France, the open-hearth process consisted of loading pig iron into the hearth of a furnace heated by a gas fire. The extraordinary intensity of the heat was produced by Siemens's development of the "regenerative principle." In effect, Siemens—who, like Bessemer, saw puddling as the chief target of his invention—used the waste gases emitted by the iron as it was heated to create more heat. Heat was "regenerated" by placing fires at both sides of the hearth, passing heated currents of air and gas alternately from each fire over the molten pig iron, allowing the waste gas produced by the heated pig to pass into a chamber above one of the two fires, and then trapping the heat of the waste gas in special firebrick. Then the firebrick imparted the heat it retained to the next flow of gas that would pass back over the hearth.

The first attempts to make metal with Siemens's regenerative furnace produced mixed results largely because the furnace could not withstand the high temperatures required to melt pig iron. This problem and some others associated with Siemens's first ventures were solved by Martin, who found that by adding relatively small quantities of scrap iron and steel to the molten bath, he could maintain the integrity of the furnace and produce high-quality metal. Nonetheless, problems remained, and Hewitt underestimated just how intractable they would prove.

The most troublesome problem for Hewitt, and indeed for all metalmakers, was that because iron and fuel of such widely varying character was used, only a tedious process of trial and error could yield the proper mix of ingredients. "The quality can be regulated with perfect certainty," Hewitt wrote in a letter written from Paris. "The time is six hours, and the quantity produced is six tons, which is one ton per hour. . . . No work is required, and just one man to watch the process and make the charges." As Hewitt learned, though, open-hearth steelmaking was neither so simple nor so fast; it required more skilled labor than he anticipated. Indeed, within two years of the initial heat at his Trenton mill, he abandoned the new method and continued to rely on puddled iron and cast steel. With the advance of Bessemer practice and a westward shift in the metalmaking industry, Hewitt's mills were soon eclipsed by those in Johnstown, Pittsburgh, Cleveland, and Chicago.[20]

Though Hewitt was shrewd enough to sense the promise of the open-hearth process, he and his engineers lacked the technical expertise to make it work efficiently and inexpensively. Not until the 1880s, when the introduction of the basic process allowed phosphoric iron to be used, did open-hearth steelmaking begin to supplant the Bessemer method.

The first important steps in this direction were taken at the Homestead Steel Works, where Hewitt's dreams of mass quantities of inexpensively produced, high-quality steel were realized in the open-hearth furnaces of Andrew Carnegie.

While Hewitt's manufacturing enterprises in New Jersey grew less prosperous, his political star ascended. He ran successfully for Congress in 1874 and, except for the 1879–81 term, represented the Lower East side until his election as mayor of New York in 1886. In that campaign, Hewitt defeated Henry George, arguably the most popular labor activist of his day, thereby critically wounding any national effort to establish an independent labor party. Hewitt also served as national chairman of the Democratic party and as one of its chief spokesmen; he in fact served as the party's resident theoretician on the labor problem, and in this capacity, he was selected as chairman of the House committee established to investigate the causes of the depression of the 1870s and the labor uprising of 1877.[21]

The line of questioning pursued by Hewitt, his remarks to key witnesses who appeared before the committee, and his overview of the relations of labor and capital delivered to a church congress in 1878 reveal a sensibility keenly attuned to the difficulties confronting those committed to upholding the wage system. Indeed, Hewitt's thinking in some respects proved prescient on the matter of how to contain social unrest.[22]

Hewitt's experience on the House committee and as an ironmaster convinced him that he and his colleagues in business and politics faced a dilemma that required resolution in order to avoid even greater disturbances than those of 1877. "The problem . . . is to make men who are equal in liberty—that is, in political rights and therefore entitled to the ownership of property—content with that inequality in its distribution which must inevitably result from the application of the law of justice." The way out of the predicament, according to Hewitt, was to make the distribution of property less unequal without disturbing the question of ultimate ownership. He suggested that selling shares to workers would create a true "partnership" of labor and capital and spur production and consumption.[23]

Hewitt, following the philosopher Herbert Spencer, asserted that his vision of a "harmonious" future was predicated on the inevitable evolution toward perfection that found concrete expression in the corporation. "To attack corporations, therefore, . . . is . . . to attack that phase of human organization which offers the best promise for the advancement of the working classes," for "the corporate principle" provided an "association of labor and capital upon the basis of an ownership distributed among those who contribute either capital or labor." Such ownership "is indispensable not merely to harmony, but to the achievement of the largest possible results and the equitable distribution of the products of human industry." Hewitt neglected to say how this equitable distribution would occur, nor did he note that at other times he had found unequal distribution to be an "inevitable" result of "the law of justice." Thus the association of labor and capital that he foresaw was, as he himself acknowledged, aimed at preserving untrammeled the right to accumulate.[24]

This right, Hewitt professed, was the inevitable outcome of the "Christian scheme as it has been developing for eighteen centuries." Like other businessmen, though, he understood that the preservation of property rights could not be ensured by faith alone. The growth of what he called "communism" was a "discouraging omen" that required decisive action. And few industrialists or politicians of the era took more decisive action against the workers' movement than did Hewitt. He saw more clearly than most of his colleagues the interconnections of employers' initiatives in the factory, in politics, and in the broader cultural arena. He deftly juggled his roles as an innovative factory master and entrepreneur, a standard-bearer for mainstream politics, and a tireless propagandist for the creed that deemed rising outputs and uncensored acquisitiveness as the hallmarks of a higher civilization. It was true that Hewitt, like Andrew Carnegie, expressed occasional twinges of concern that acquisitiveness had become the guiding motivation of the era: "It cannot be that the aim of society is only to produce riches. There must be moral limits within which the production of wealth is to be carried on." In his own practice, however, he observed no limits, and he saw entrepreneurial acumen as the supreme moral attribute.[25]

Success in his many roles won for Hewitt the Bessemer Gold Medal in 1890. His acceptance speech stands as a monument of his contributions to the enduring legacy of the captains of steel. In proudly declaring that greater machinery held the promise of greater justice, Hewitt judiciously overlooked the relationships between those who owned machines and those who made them work. Only the invention of printing, the discovery of America, the construction of the magnetic compass, and the introduction of the steam engine, he noted, were comparable in importance to the invention of the Bessemer converter. "The face of society has been transformed by these discoveries and inventions; . . . it is quite certain that if we were deprived of the results of these inventions, the greater portion of the human race would perish by starvation and the remainder would relapse into barbarism." Hewitt concluded that the Bessemer converter, above all other inventions and discoveries, was most "potent in preparing the way for the higher civilization which awaits the coming century."[26]

The importance of the Bessemer converter and of the open-hearth furnace to progress and the growth of civilization was a recurring theme in many of the steelmasters' public utterances. In fact, it also informed a paper delivered by the engineer Henry A. Howe that immediately followed Hewitt's acceptance speech.

Howe, like Hewitt, linked the flowering of Western civilization to great production outputs. But Howe explored the mechanical processes and managerial techniques by which greater outputs were achieved much more carefully than did Hewitt. Echoing Charles Babbage, Howe advised his colleagues to push the division of labor to its limits so that each worker "should become more skilled in a smaller range of operations to which his work is restricted." The result would be to allow steelmasters "to employ less intelligent and costly men." Most important, the pace of each man's labor should be quickened. "Proof that the pace was such as to shorten his years of physical vigor, and thus lessen the amount which he can accomplish in his lifetime, would, I apprehend, count for little with directors and managers. The workman is paid not for his lifetime, but for the number of days he actually works." "As humanitarians," Howe and his colleagues might regret such conditions of employment in the steel industry. But "as managers, hired by others to make money for them by metallurgy," they were obliged to enhance the employer's profits.[27]

Here, then, was the underside of the civilization that engineers and entrepreneurs such as Howe and Hewitt strove to erect. Progress in their eyes meant larger outputs and larger profits, which, as all steelmasters knew, were possible only insofar as labor was treated as a factor of production that was sold and bought and then directed to work as long and as fast as possible. In the "higher" civilization envisioned by men such as Hewitt, it was indeed up to the master to do the thinking.

It was against such thinking that the labor movement of the Gilded Age directed itself. And it was in directly challenging such thinking, in places such as Homestead, that workers scored important if fleeting successes.

ALEXANDER HOLLEY, BESSEMER ENGINEERING, AND THE ORIGINS OF SCIENTIFIC MANAGEMENT

The American, British, and German engineers and steelmasters who gathered in New York City on 2 October 1890 to review their achievements and to share their insights had a busy day. The men, who according to the *New York Times* represented "hundreds of millions in invested wealth," met in Chickering Hall, where they heard a series of speeches on the entrepreneurial and technical accomplishments of nineteenth-century metalmakers.

The engineers and steelmasters were in a celebratory mood and responded enthusiastically to Abram S. Hewitt's acceptance of the Bessemer Gold Medal. Later they listened to and discussed the observations of Henry Howe on "the striking features of American Bessemer practice," above all the large output and rapid production of Bessemer steel mills. According to Howe, the "uncommon man" most responsible for the distinctively American successes in volume and speed was the greatest engineer-entrepreneur of the era, Alexander Lyman Holley.[28]

Shortly after the discussion of Howe's paper, a memorial service in honor of Holley was held. In his eulogy, the principal speaker echoed Howe's enthusiastic assessment of Holley's accomplishments. The audience then adjourned to Greenwich Village, where they dedicated a monument in Washington Square. The inscription beneath the bronze bust read: "In honor of Alexander Lyman Holley, foremost among those whose genius and energy established in America, and improved throughout the world, the manufacture of Bessemer steel, this memorial is erected by engineers of two hemispheres."[29]

The memorial service and the monument were not the first tributes paid to Holley. Just after his death in 1882, the British Iron and Steel Institute had posthumously awarded him the Bessemer Gold Medal, and the engineering societies whose spirit he animated held special meetings to honor him. The AIME published a book of speeches praising Holley's achievements, and encomiums to him found their way into papers published by the AIME and the ASME well into the 1890s. Indeed, from the late 1870s to the present, all steelmen have held Holley's name in reverence. Mill owners have pointed to him as the godfather of the Bessemer process, managerial experts have claimed him as the author of scientific management and engineers and engineering educators have looked to his writings for guidance and inspiration.[30]

Holley himself saw his technical accomplishments in steelmaking as linked indissolubly to new and more careful managment practices. And he thought that the best way to ensure continued success in technics proper, as well as in mangement's efforts to control the production process, was to educate a new "class" or "race" or men. Such men, professional engineers, would be trained in the best universities, where they would study "science." They would also be trained in the most up-to-date industrial enterprises, where they could acquire "practical" skills—what Holley called the "art" of production.

In a narrow sense, Holley saw the work of engineers as serving the needs of capital, which, he once noted, was the parent of both science and art and would bless their union insofar as engineering proceeded along the course he envisioned. But Holley's understanding of capital, engineering, and the dissemination of textbook and shop floor knowledge was bound up in a larger and more compelling vision that sought to embrace the whole realm of human endeavor: he maintained that the building and management of industrial works, the science and practice of technics, and the training of men to push output to new heights constituted no less than the very "enginery of civilization."

The engineer and his associates, in Holley's view, were quite simply responsible for building the engine and ensuring that it operated more and more efficiently. Profit making, then, fell back ultimately on the engineer; engineering was the very cornerstone of material progress, and aiding the cause of progress was a quintessentially moral task. "Commerce, banking, jurisprudence, political economy, government are more or less useful systems, [but] for what?" He answered: "For formulating and realizing the potentiality of engineering. And so the noble art—stimulating labor, promoting comfort, founding prosperity, diffusing happiness, establishing knowledge . . . leads on to universal health, equity and virtue." Holley's assertion expressed the credo of a generation of engineers: in technology lay the key to universal happiness.[31]

The ideas that material and moral progress were identical and that the engine of this progress was provided by technology permeated American high culture in the late nineteenth century. Some of the most influential men of the era helped articulate these ideas. None, however, was as forceful as Holley in stating the nobility of purpose and the righteousness of cause that he linked to the endeavors of engineers and businessmen. Holley's preeminence as an advocate of the morality of improvement was not, however, limited to merely rhetorical skills, for he was, as the steelmasters never ceased to point out, deeply engaged in working out the practical details of how to make society conform to their values.[32]

Holley approached the technical and managerial problems of steelmaking as a crusader against ignorance and superstition. His less talented colleagues, who thought of themselves in similar terms, looked to him as a patron saint; that he peppered his public addresses with quotations from Goethe or remarks about the beauty of an Italian sunset only served to underscore the authoritative quality of his cultured voice. In truth, Holley did possess the greatest combination of practical and theoretical skills among the men who, in their efforts to transform the American metals industry, saw the promise of a new America. This promise, the steelmasters believed, came closer to realization with each Bessemer plant that Holley, the era's foremost fetishist of machine progress, designed or helped build and manage.[33]

Holley's involvement in Bessemer steelmaking began in 1862 when he visited Henry Bessemer's steelworks in Sheffield. He studied engineering in college and designed and wrote about locomotives, then traveled to Europe to study ordnance. For two reasons, Bessemer's converter quickly became the chief object of Holley's interest. First, he plainly recognized that it promised "the most favorable results" in terms of profits. Second, it was grounded in science and therefore promised to supplant the traditional practices and powers of puddlers. "The new treatment of iron is based on chemical laws," Holley wrote. Like Abram Hewitt, he was quick to discredit puddlers as a group of hack laborers: "The old treatment was a matter of tradition, trial, failure, and guesswork." Shortly after he returned to the United States, he persuaded two prominent ironmasters in Troy, New York, to join him in an effort to buy the American patent rights to Bessemer's process, and by 1864 he was building his first Bessemer works. He had thus embarked upon the "enlightened" path that would unite profit making and science.[34]

Though Holley was the architect of this union, the first Bessemer steel works in the United States was built and operated by a company in competition with the enterprise at Troy. However, in 1866 the owners of the competing mill joined with the owners of the Troy works to form the Pneumatic Steel Association, and the various conflicting patent claims to the Bessemer process were all resolved. Under license from the association and its successor, the Bessemer Steel Company, Holley by 1880 had designed six of the eleven Bessemer plants in operation in the United States. He was the consulting engineer for three other plants, and his designs directly inspired the remaining two. In effect, until his death in 1882, he stayed in continuous contact with the engineers and managers of all American Bessemer plants.

Holley and the other supervisory personnel who helped design and manage the first generation of American Bessemer plants constituted a small, close-knit fraternity whose members moved from one mill to another. Holley, recognized as the leader of the group, met frequently with his fellow engineers and managers to obtain up-to-date knowledge on technical and managerial problems. He used this information to design new steelworks for his clients, most prominent among whom was Andrew Carnegie. For him, Holley designed the premier Bessemer mill of the era, the Edgar Thomson Steel Works in Braddock, in 1872.[35]

The plan of the "ET," as it was called, grew out of Holley's work on and inspections of the first ten Bessemer works in the United States. Most of these had been built upon existing puddling mills. By contrast, the Edgar Thomson was an entirely new edifice; Holley was thus free for the first time to design a plant from start to finish in order to fulfill his great ambition: "to increase the output of a unit of capital and of a unit of working expense." He looked to efficient management, in addition to the quality of machinery and its arrangement within the plant, as providing the foundation for the speedy flow of materials and increased output. And for Holley, as for his friend Hewitt, efficiency meant above all that management would brook no "interference" from workers' organizations.

As Holley remarked in discussing another one of his Bessemer mills, only a combination of the latest machinery, the best layout, and the most intelligent management would yield the desired goal. A good design that ensured "a very large and regular output" would place machinery "in an arrangment which provides large and unhampered spaces for all the principal operations of manufacture and maintenance, while at the same time concentrat[ing] these operations." Interchangeable parts were also important, since they reduced the amount of time lost when equipment failed. However, it was ultimately good management that would hold the key to larger and less costly outputs: as the capacity of steel mills grew by virtue of better equipment and design, "better organization and more readiness, vigilance, and technical knowledge on the part of management have been required to run works up to their capacity."[36]

Holley understood, then, that increasing the output depended on technical and managerial initiatives and that success in one realm depended on success in the other. Though he never wrote a detailed assessment of the managerial techniques he considered most effective, he shared with the other pioneers of mass factory production[37] an agenda for success that saw "the grimy workman" and his organizations as a principal obstacle to be overcome. Accordingly, from the very outset of operations at the Edgar Thomson, management took steps to eliminate workers' organizations.

Holley's views on engineering education underscored his animus toward labor and his vision of management's role in solving the labor problem. The course of study for future engineers would begin by transferring knowledge from workers to a managerial elite, which would then be in a position to combat the "baser elements of disunion" in the factory and in society at large. Chief among these baser elements was "trades-unionism," which, in Holley's view, tended to "repress improvement" and "often violently defeats the works of progressive thinkers and sometimes destroys their authors."[38]

Holley's views on labor were shared by other members of the steelmaking fraternity and, in fact, amounted to quasi-official policy for the AIME and the ASME. Among Holley's colleagues in these organizations, William R. Jones was the most astute manager of men; when Holley began work on the Edgar Thomson, he named Jones his chief assistant. Later he recommended that Carnegie hire Jones as the general superintendent of the works. Jones, who invented a number of steelmaking devices, served in that capacity until his death in 1889. Well before then, the combined mechanical and managerial wisdom of Holley and Jones yielded production outputs that astounded the metalmaking world.[39]

The impressive record of the Edgar Thomson, Holley and Jones understood, owed as much to the management of its domestic economy as to its advanced equipment and layout. That there was a need for "improved" management as the iron era gave way to the Age of Steel was a proposition accepted, at this time, by all iron- and steelmasters. Indeed, as the second industrial revolution crested in the 1880s, the president of the ASME, Robert Thurston, tellingly selected the labor problem as the outstanding issue then confronting his constituency. "The relations of the employers to the working classes, . . . [have] more importance to us and to the world, and . . . [have] a more direct and controlling influence upon material prosperity and the happiness of the nation than any modern invention or than any discovery in science." It was from the membership of the ASME, "if from any body of men, that the world should expect a complete and thorough[ly] satisfactory practical solution of the . . . 'labor problem.' "[40]

One solution, in the view of the men who belonged to the ASME and the AIME, was to eliminate labor unions altogether. The tactic of choice was scientific management. Indeed, it was not at all fortuitous that Henry R. Towne presented the ASME with what is generally regarded as the first significant articulation of the scientific management movement in 1886, the year marked by labor's Great Upheaval. In reality, Holley and Jones had been practicing some principles of scientific management since the 1860s. Towne's speech, which he called "The Engineer as an Economist," was thus more a codification of such practice than a call to new action.[41]

In his speech, Towne collapsed the categories of mechanical engineering and shop management into each other more explicitly than Holley or Thurston had done. Engineering and managing were directed toward the same end: "the organization of productive labor." And labor "must be directed and controlled by persons having not only practical familiarity" with production techniques "but having also, and equally, a practical knowledge of how to observe, analyze, and compare essential facts in relation to wages, supplies, expense accounts and all else that enters into or affects the economy of production and the cost of the product." Only mechanical engineers, Towne concluded, were prepared to perform such a wide range of tasks.[42]

Towne's speech was important because he explicitly linked the need for new management techniques with the development of new production techniques, which went hand-in-hand with more aggressive methods of personnel management. And the cutting edge of innovation for both was in the metals industries beginning in the 1860s. Later, as David Noble has argued, engineers in the chemical and electrical industries directed technical education, university research, and management science. But it was the mechanical engineers in the steel industry who in fact first consummated what Noble has called "the wedding of science to the useful arts."[43]

By 1872, when Carnegie hired Holley to design a new Bessemer works and supervise its construction in Braddock, Holley stood on the brink of this achievement. Indeed, he already had envisioned the means of overcoming most of the key technical problems that stood in the way of "economical" Bessemer steelmaking. These problems stemmed from a variety of sources: the steelmasters' ignorance of the chemical processes of the new method; an absence of materials that could withstand the high heat generated by the converter; machinery that was ill suited to factory production; and, finally, a poor grasp both of how to arrange the cumbersome Bessemer machinery and of how to move the heavy materials required and produced by the process.

Holley's efforts to speed production and increase outputs addressed each of these four problem areas. But his outstanding contributions involved the design and arrangement of the Bessemer machinery. In effect, Holley invented a factory where Bessemer steel could be handled and produced rapidly.[44]

At the time of Holley's visit to Henry Bessemer's steelworks in England, the floor plan of the standard British plant consisted of two Bessemer converters facing each other across a casting pit that contained molds to receive the molten metal after it had been converted. The converters were only three or four feet above the floor, and the casting pit was as deep as nine feet. The arrangement was cramped, and workers had little space to maneuver the cranes they used to move the exceedingly heavy materials of production. The linings of the converters and the openings into them that carried the blast of air necessary for conversion often burned out after only a few blows. And the machinery that tipped the converter on its side after the blow ended, so that the metal could be poured into a huge ladle, was poorly designed. The result was that sometimes the contents of the converter would spill out uncontrollably. The ladle itself was prone to a burn-through from the molten metal.[45]

The two most important of Holley's innovations were his removable bottom for the converter and his new floor plan. The latter, which came to be called the American floor plan, increased the speed of the converting process by making it easier for workers and machines to handle production materials. Holley placed the two converters side by side and raised them about nine feet off the ground. He also raised the casting pit to approximately two feet beneath floor level. The new plan thus opened up the work area and among other things made possible the addition of another crane to remove ingot molds from the casting pit. Holley also consolidated the control levers for converters, ladles, and cranes so that they could be manipulated from a single location. And he brought a cupola furnace into the converting mill that allowed pig iron to be rapidly melted prior to being poured into the converters.[46]

It was, however, the invention of the "Holley vessel bottom" that was most responsible for increasing the pace of production and the profits of Bessemer steelmaking. As Robert Hunt noted in 1876, the Holley bottom "has rendered possible, as much as any other one thing, the present immense production" of Bessemer mills. Prior to its introduction, the converter lining had to be repaired while it remained in the shell of the converter. Workers had to wait until the shell cooled enough to allow them to climb inside to fix or replace the lining; the wait could be long. The Holley bottom, on the other hand, could be removed or put inside a converter without waiting for it to cool.

The results stemming from the adoption of removable bottoms and Holley's floor plan were spectacular in the eyes of mill owners. Men and machines now could be kept at work continuously. And the gains were indeed impressive: as Holley pointed out, his improvements more than tripled daily outputs. "The same engine and boiler capacity, the same vessels and accessories, the same quality and nearly the same extent of hydraulic machinery, melting apparatus and buildings . . . required . . . to make six five-ton heats per day" would, in a plant designed by Holley, "make sixteen five-ton heats."[47]

Following Holley's overhaul of American Bessemer practice, the scale of production rose dramatically as iron manufacture gave way to steel. Where puddling furnaces held six hundred pounds of pig, the first American converters could hold two and one half tons. By the mid 1870s, seven-ton converters were the rule. And by 1892, almost half of the forty-one American converters in use produced more than ten tons per heat.[48]

To carry out production on a scale of such magnitude required machinery and jobs that in most instances differed radically from those associated with iron manufacture. Most of the work in a Holley style Bessemer mill demanded less skill than did ironwork. However, the new Bessemer jobs demanded no less stamina.

As practiced in the Edgar Thomson and in other Bessemer mills, the process began with workers melting down pig iron in small furnaces, called cupolas. They tapped the cupola, poured its contents into ladles, and, by manipulating hydraulic cranes, dumped the molten pig into the converters, thereby charging them. A worker called the charger directed operations up to this point. Next, the blower and the regulators stepped in. The regulators positioned the converter by moving another set of levers so that it was horizontal during charging and tapping and vertical during the blow. The blower was in charge of controlling the blast of air pumped into the converter. He had to know when to stop the blast and how much spiegeleisen to add. His job thus presupposed a solid understanding of the properties of the pig iron with which he worked. Other workers were responsible for melting the "spiegel," for moving the ladles that dumped the converted steel into the ingot molds in the pit, for taking the molds to another area where additional work was done, and for building and installing replacement bottoms and tuyeres.

Each step in the process of making Bessemer steel demanded large numbers of workers. But they needed less aggregate skill than that possessed by puddlers and their colleagues to produce an equivalent amount of unfinished metal. And with few exceptions, each Bessemer worker required less knowledge about the total process. Furthermore, those few workers who needed to know as much as or perhaps even more than did puddlers about the characteristics of pig iron were usually trained by management, and not by fellow workers. As practiced in Holley's plants, Bessemer steelmaking thus allowed management to exercise greater control over the stages of production.

The steelmasters consequently saw the Bessemer process as a key tool in their efforts to solve the labor problem and thereby raise outputs to an acceptable level at an acceptable cost. Robert Hunt, a close associate of Holley who served as the superintendent of the Bessemer mill in Johnstown, Pennsylvania, was one of many steelmasters who emphasized the importance of Bessemer steelmaking's diminished skill requirements. In discussing his great successes at the Cambria Iron Works, he took note of how the new process had fulfilled the promise of its inventor to break free from of the "trammels" of the trade:

> I think one thing which had a strong bearing on the increased production was the labor organization of the Cambria works. In compliance with the policy decided upon, I started the converting works without a single man who had ever seen the outside of [a] Bessemer works, and, with a very few exceptions, they were not even skilled rolling-mill men, but on the contrary were selected from intelligent laborers. The result was that we had willing pupils with no prejudices, and without any reminiscences of what they had done in the old country or at any other works.[49]

In addition to guaranteeing the willing efforts of utter novices in the steelmaking process, Hunt succeeded in fragmenting the collective labor force within the mill by training workers only in the limited aspect of production to which they were assigned. The total picture, like the total process, was available only to a select few at the top.

Not surprisingly, the Edgar Thomson engaged in similar hiring policies when it began producing Bessemer steel on 26 August 1875. The first heats of the two five-ton converters and the overall operation of the mill were conspicuous successes. One reason, according to the *Bulletin* of the American Iron and Steel Association, was that "many of the workmen then saw the Bessemer process for the first time." In general, the *Bulletin* attributed the mill's success to the managerial and technical prowess of William R. Jones, who had also been a supervisor in Johnstown, and to Holley, who laid out the works "with reference to the least and cheapest internal transportation." Moreover, it was Holley who had possessed the wisdom to hire Jones as his assistant and then persuade Carnegie to retain him as chief of operations. Holley believed that in Jones he had found a man who could properly control the domestic economy of the plant.

Until his death in the works fourteen years later, however, Jones found that directing the domestic economy of the Edgar Thomson constituted a perpetual challenge requiring more than a careful selection and "judicious" ethnic mix of workers to create, as he once put it, the most "tractable" work force. Many of the ethnically diverse workers at the works found ways to overcome their differences at the workplace—and in politics—and often saw a dark undercurrent of paternalistic control in Jones' professed desire to make the works "a pleasant place" by avoiding "all haughty and disdainful treatment of men." Some workers responded to Jones by joining the Noble and Holy Order of the Knights of Labor and the AAISW, and Jones often countered by introducing new technologies that would better unify production and divide the men. Thus, at a session of the ASME in 1884 on the use of natural gas in steelmaking, Jones stated:

> Another question is suggested by Mr. Metcalf's inquiring into the commercial value of the gas. If Mr. Metcalf had been working, like myself, among eighty-two coal heavers, one half of whom belonged to the Amalgamated Association, and the other half to the Knights of Labor, each striving to show how much better labor agitators they were than the other gang, he would appreciate the value of gas. In fact, whenever I approached the boiler house I felt I was going into the walls of a penitentiary. Every one looked at me as much to say, 'Have you got permission to come in here?" Ever since I used natural gas and got rid of those eighty-two coal heavers, I felt like saying, 'God bless the discoverer of natural gas."[50]

In publicly applauding the use of a technical innovation to solve a managerial problem, Jones reaffirmed the stalwart principles of his mentor, Holley, who had died two years earlier. From his place in managerial heaven, Holley would nevertheless surely have joined his colleague in asking God to bless the discoverer of natural gas, for he, like Jones, had clashed with workers for control over the workplace. And like Jones, Holley also reveled in the the power of technology as a weapon in the clash.

Alexander Holley always perceived that the most "gigantic difficulty" he faced, the most "precipitous" mountain he had to climb, the most "pestilential swamp" he had to traverse amounted in reality to an "uncompromising struggle" not with nature but with American workers. The struggle was waged not only over the control of the great industrial plants of the era but over the very issue of who would direct the "enginery of civilization." Inevitably, the Pittsburgh district, with its concentration of steelworks, became the arena for some of the most heated battles in this struggle. And, as we shall see, the contest for control of the Edgar Thomson Steel Works in Braddock and of the Bessemer mill across the river in Homestead figured most prominently in the outcome.[51]

PART THREE
Labor Reform in Pittsburgh, 1867–1881: From "Amalgamation" to the Brink of Collapse

Existing relations produce slavery on one side and opulence on the other. They destroy republicanism and create a monarchy of capital and a serfdom of labor.

> — *National Labor Tribune,*
> August, 1875

Men have for years been hugging the delusive phantom of party politics as though relief or cure was to be found therein. No words that we can utter are likely to dispel that insane belief and hope. The masses cling tenaciously to party, and will . . . continue until all parties organized to perpetuate the control of capital have ground them beneath their feet.

> — *National Labor Tribune,*
> July, 1876

The days of capitalistic rule are numbered. Private capital and private ownership cannot exist in a republic. One or the other must fall. Prepare, O workingmen of America, to enter into the promised land which is near us, if we be but true.

> — *National Labor Tribune,*
> January, 1877

Chapter 5

Indicting and Embracing the Civilization of the Nineteenth Century

THE TECHNOLOGICAL INNOVATIONS that transformed industrial production in the post–Civil War years, together with the restructuring of opportunities for working Americans, elicited a wide variety of responses. These ranged from the absolute enthusiasm of entrepreneurs and engineers such as Abram Hewitt and Alexander Holley, who helped refashion the steel industry, to the angry revolt of workers who read in technical advances unmistakable signs of their own displacement and retreat. Staking their position somewhere in between those two polarized responses, most workers reacted to the rapid redefinition of industrial society with a mixture of hope and trepidation.

In this chapter on the labor movement in Pittsburgh, we begin with that wide range of responses by singling out a number of exemplary individuals whose lives and careers were intimately bound up with developments in the steel industry. Whereas some of these men already bear the status of historical celebrities—predictably, the enthusiastic, prosperous, and notorious steelmen such as Andrew Carnegie and Henry Clay Frick—others have never had their story told: men such as Thomas Armstrong, John McLuckie, Thomas W. "Old Beeswax" Taylor, and Pavel Olšav, labor leaders, steelworkers, and immigrants. This unlikely team of individuals, for all their differences and disputes, characterizes at the broadest level the political and cultural conflicts that divided industrial America in the late nineteenth century. And it is by matching the personal chronicles of such very different people against one another that we can best derive a sense of the complexities that informed the successes and failures of Pittsburgh's labor movement into the 1880s.

The two decades that followed the Civil War were to a large degree a period of social indeterminacy. Like Americans elsewhere, citizens of Pennsylvania had not yet fully come to grips with the uncertainties of urban expansion and mass factory production bequeathed them by the war. The war had also left the country perplexed about the place of labor, white and black, within the new social order.[1]

In truth, many Americans had begun to question the relationship between labor and the larger social order even before the Civil War. "There is no permanent class of hired laborers among us," Abraham Lincoln had declared in the 1850s. The reason, he said, was that the free labor system provided unending opportunities for everyone. As evidence he cited the trajectory of his own life. "Twenty-five years ago, I was a hired laborer." But no more. And what was true for him pointed to the grand truth for all white Northerners: "The hired laborer of yesterday labors on his own account today, and will hire others to labor for him tomorrow. Advancement—improvement in condition—is the order of things in a society of equals."[2]

By the mid 1870s, a similar declaration would have provoked hoots of laughter from thousands of workers in depression-ravaged Pittsburgh. For them the promise of advancement had been destroyed by the hardships of eking out a living, and Lincoln's description of the North as "a society of equals" held little relevance in light of the growing power of what workers called organized capital. Thousands of workers in the Pittsburgh district, as well as in other industrial centers, had abandoned the idea that the American labor system was "free." In their eyes, the wage system celebrated by the "great emancipator" had become wage slavery.

But even before the Great Depression commenced in 1873, the metamorphosis of free labor into wage slavery was far advanced. A reporter for the *New York Times* noted in 1869 that changes in factory organization had already dramatically altered Northern society. Self-employed, independent "mechanics" who labored in small workshops were "far less common than they were before the war, . . . the small manufacturers thus swallowed up have become workmen on wages in the greater establishments." This transformation was a startling development that heralded deeper change: "a system of slavery as absolute if not as degrading as that which lately prevailed in the South." The only difference between slavery in the South and the new Northern slavery, the reporter concluded, was that in the South "agriculture was the field, landed proprietors were the masters, and Negroes were the slaves; while in the North manufacturers is [sic] the field, manufacturing capitalists threaten to become the masters, and it is the white laborers who are to be slaves."[3]

Needless to say, Hewitt, Carnegie, and the other great entrepreneurs of the era disagreed. Such men saw only the promise of a nobler civilization in the phenomenal growth of manufacturing output that had begun in the 1850s and in the narrowing circle of businessmen who owned factories. In the eyes of hundreds of thousands of Americans whose livelihood derived from working for others, however, the reporter for the *New York Times* had hit upon a most troubling paradox: in the wake of the victory of republican free labor over chattel slavery—a victory gained largely through the efforts of workers—a new system of oppression had arisen.[4]

As the reporter recognized, growing numbers of workers equated the wage system with wage slavery because working for wages constituted an assault on republican notions of independence and liberty. The republican canon held that no one who depended on another for his livelihood, and who therefore did not command his own productive property, could be considered free. Thousands who spent their lives working as hirelings, and whose security in employment was therefore based on the needs of their employers, were afraid that they had indeed become slaves. In the view of many working Americans, such circumstances demanded a new kind of abolitionism.[5]

"The complete emancipation of the wealth producers from the thraldom and loss of wage slavery" was how Uriah Stephens, a founder and the first grand master workman of the Knights of Labor, understood labor's task in 1871. Like other Knights, he believed that this task constituted a moral crusade. "Civil and religious liberty and theoretical equality before the law we already have in America. That was achieved for us by our revolutionary forefathers, and bequeathed by them as a sacred legacy to us, their descendants and successors." But as the labor movement swelled to more than two hundred thousand union members in the early 1870s, this sacred legacy seemed to be in jeopardy. The republican heritage was under siege by acquisitive man, "the great Anti-Christ of civilization." Only the workers' movement, Stephens affirmed, could save American society from the Devil. Another national leader of the Knights, a shoemaker named George McNeill, captured their critical spirit when he maintained that the wage system and republicanism were incompatible: "The foundation of the Republic is equality, . . . [and] we declare that there is an inevitable and irresistible conflict between the wage system of labor and the republican system of government."[6]

No individual did more to nurture this critical sense among Pittsburgh workers and to build their connections with the national labor movement than Thomas A. Armstrong. Born in Steubenville, Ohio, Armstrong came to the Iron City in 1857 as a boy of 17 who, having learned the "art typographical" while working as a newsboy, was determined "to seek his fortune" as a printer. Hired by the *Pittsburgh Chronicle-Telegraph*, he soon after left the pursuit of wealth to study "the relations existing between capital and labor" as a member of the local printers' union. The Civil War interrupted his career as a printer and trade unionist: Armstrong enlisted in the 139th Pennsylvania Volunteers Regiment in 1862, was soon promoted to sergeant, and sustained serious wounds as a company commander when he led a charge at the Battle of Cedar Creek. Armstrong subsequently stated that he had joined the

Union army to defend freedom in a fight that would ennoble not only American laborers but all humanity.[7]

For Armstrong, as for so many other labor reformers, the righteous cause to preserve the Republic by protecting the Union became in the postwar years the righteous cause to preserve the Republic by protecting labor. Armstrong first rose to prominence in this respect in 1866 by coauthoring the National Labor Union's *Address . . . to the Workingmen of the United States*. But it was not until the 1870s that Armstrong, who stood at center stage of the national labor movement until his death in 1887, found the appropriate forum for his skills. This forum, the *National Labor Tribune*, was arguably the most important labor newspaper in the United States during the two decades of his stewardship. Under him the paper became the official organ of the Knights of Labor, the AAISW, and other important unions in the upper Ohio Valley.

From the paper's initial issue in 1872, Armstrong shaped his editorial positions out of the Civil War and trade union experience he shared with so many of the thirty thousand workers who read the *Tribune* each week. The newspaper "must drill our soldier's from the corporal's squad up to the division drill" so that the "Vicksburgs of Labor's enemies" might be stormed and taken. The drilling was designed to promote unions and their amalgamation into organizations that embraced workers of a given trade and, ultimately, into "one big union" of all workers. From 1873 until the early 1880s, the *Tribune* consistently argued that such amalgamation was the key to making fundamental social change—to replacing "the present accepted theories of value" with labor's own cooperative idea. The labor movement, Armstrong proclaimed, "challenges the very framework of society and declares it to be based on false premises." Indeed, the newspaper avowed that the workers' movement had "drawn [a] bill of indictment against the civilization of the nineteenth century."[8]

While Armstrong and many of his readers pointed to the growing inequities of nineteenth-century America, other residents of Pittsburgh and vicinity became progressively more confident in the justness of the emerging order. Their personal experience seemed to confirm that there were endless possibilities for personal advancement. And for men such as Carnegie and Frick, there were.

Carnegie, for example, took the first steps toward amassing his colossal fortune during the Civil War by investing in oil, telegraphy, and bridge building. In 1863 alone, the twenty-eight-year-old Carnegie earned more than $42,000—"a phenomenal record," according to his biographer, "for in terms of interest upon principal, it came close to representing the income of a millionaire." Indeed, Carnegie himself was impressed. "I'm rich, I'm rich," he proudly told a friend. Unlike Armstrong, the young Carnegie did not allow the Civil War to deter him from private goals: drafted in 1864, the year Armstrong was wounded, Carnegie paid $850 to find a substitute conscript. Four years later, he held assets of $400,000 and his income surpassed $56,000. By the mid 1870s, in the midst of the Great Depression, he was able to spend roughly $1.25 million to build the Edgar Thomson Steel Works, which by 1880 was generating in excess of $1.6 million in annual profits.[9]

Like Carnegie, Frick also expanded his commercial interests in the 1870s and emerged from the depression with a fortune. Born to a well-to-do family in 1849, he always seemed to know precisely what he wanted. And as Joseph Frazier Wall has put it, what Frick "wanted from the time he was a child could be stated in one word—money." In fact, the young Frick vowed to become a millionaire, and with the help of a family friend, Judge Thomas Mellon, who provided Frick with his first significant loan, he succeeded on 19 December 1879, his thirtieth birthday.[10]

For every Carnegie and Frick, there were dozens of individuals in the Pittsburgh district who accumulated less spectacularly but in their own day achieved considerable recognition for their financial achievements. Some of these, like Carnegie and Frick themselves, forged intimate ties with Homestead and its steelworks. Consider, for example, William Clark and William Brown Dickson.

Clark, born in 1830 in England, emigrated as a young man and, like Carnegie, settled in Pittsburgh. He began his working career as an unskilled ironworker but soon advanced through the ranks. By 1869 he owned one of the city's largest mills, the Solar Iron Works, and went on to build and personally manage the PBSW in Homestead, which Carnegie bought from him and his partners in 1883. The career of Clark, who also served on the Pittsburgh City Council, conforms to the myth of the self-made man no less than that of his more famous rival: he was known for his intelligence, ambition, and what may be politely called an unwavering commitment to individualism in the world of work.[11]

William Brown Dickson, like Frick, was raised in Western Pennsylvania. Although Dickson belonged to a younger generation—he was born in 1865—his career in steelmaking began in the very year, 1881, that Frick himself formally entered the industry by establishing a partnership with Carnegie. Dickson's start was rather less auspicious: he worked as a common laborer in the Homestead converting mill. Unlike most of his co-workers, he eschewed the collective initiatives of trade unionism and from the outset stood tall as a company man. The individualist choice served him well; he rose steadily, and Carnegie eventually named him a junior partner. By the time he was thirty-six, Dickson had accumulated hundreds of thousands of dollars in stocks and bonds, was sitting on the board of the U.S. Steel Corporation, and served as a corporate vice president and special assistant to President Charles M. Schwab, another self-made steelman who supervised the Homestead works in the late 1880s.[12]

Confronting Carnegie, Frick, Clark, Dickson, and Schwab all the while was a host of men who remained ordinary workers; a surprising number of them shared a common past with the steelmasters, but their convictions and careers took them down very different paths. Some of these committed labor reformers had come to America, just as Carnegie and Clark had, in search of new opportunities; others ("Honest" John McLuckie, for example) had grown up within sight of Carnegie's mill in Braddock. Until the Homestead Lockout of 1892, McLuckie did not achieve the power or recognition of a Thomas Armstrong. A miner-turned-unskilled-steelworker, he was, rather, a mid-level leader, organizing at the point of production, canvassing for labor parties in union sanctuaries and open-air meetings, running for—and occasionally winning—minor elective office.[13]

Throughout his fifteen-year career in the Ohio Valley labor movement, McLuckie never wavered in the face of physical or political intimidation. Born in 1852 in the Monongahela River town of Elizabeth, he entered electoral politics in 1876, running for the state legislature on an independent labor ticket. One Friday night while McLuckie was addressing a meeting of his fellow Turtle Creek miners, an arsonist torched his home in an apparent effort to force him out of the campaign. McLuckie lost all of his possessions and was subsequently defeated in the election, but in Braddock he went on to become a leader of both the Knights of Labor and the AAISW. It was in Braddock, in fact, that he helped lead the AAISW against Carnegie in 1882 when the union took him on at the Edgar Thomson Steel Works. Defeated again, McLuckie moved to Bellaire, Ohio, where he served on the city council and achieved a certain notoriety in business and conservative labor circles for his unsuccessful efforts to mediate a critically important dispute between the Knights and the AAISW.

In a most important respect, the attempt to maintain labor solidarity at Bellaire captures the essence of McLuckie the union man. In that town, and subsequently in Homestead, where he settled in 1887, he remained true to the vision of amalgamation that Armstrong and other Knights of Labor had first enunciated in the mid 1870s: that all workers should unite to ward off the encroachments of organized capital. Moreover, whereas Armstrong sanctioned the *National Labor Tribune*'s virulently racist attacks against blacks and East European and Chinese immigrants, McLuckie's election as burgess of Homestead in 1890 represented an overwhelming defeat of the town's nativist constituencies. Two years later, a hostile reporter who had followed his exploits in the Bellaire conflict and the Homestead Lockout paid him what he most certainly considered a high compliment: "He is not a low, vulgar, fighting striker; he is a bright, smart, intelligent, oil-tongued man—an agitator, and one of the kind that is bad for workmen and for a community."[14]

To be sure, the community of Homestead realized that McLuckie was "a man of considerable ability." But there were few residents who felt that he was in any manner "bad" for the town. Reelected burgess in 1892, he also helped lead the town's unofficial government during the lockout of that year, the workers' Advisory Committee. His role in the conflict earned him charges of murder, conspiracy, and treason, and he was eventually hounded out of that state. Blacklisted by Carnegie, McLuckie never again found work in the steel industry.

In Homestead there were dozens of men who shared McLuckie's vision and pride. Some of them were highly skilled steelworkers such as John Elias Jones, a Welsh immigrant who settled in Homestead in 1881, and Thomas Crawford, an Englishman who arrived soon after. Jones led the union men in the Homestead strike of 1882 and the lockout of 1889, and he served three terms on the town council. And it was Crawford—not, as received historical wisdom would have it, Hugh O'Donnell—who managed the Advisory Committee during the 1892 lockout and was responsible for the overall coordination of the workers' activities.[15]

One of Crawford's most important lieutenants was Pavel Olšav, a Slovak immigrant who had arrived in Homestead in 1881. Olšav, a laborer in the steelworks, became the most important leader of the East European community and in the 1892 lockout organized a special lodge of the AAISW that was crucial to maintaining interethnic solidarity. Like thousands of other Slovaks who came to the Pittsburgh district beginning in the early 1880s, Olšav grew up in a region of the Hapsburg Empire where a variety of economic, political, and demographic forces had created large numbers of landless laborers and had triggered mass migration to North America. Zemplín Province, his birthplace, was far removed from the world of Homestead. But the aspirations of Olšav and many of his fellow East European immigrants were not so remote as some would assume from the goals of native-born Americans such as John McLuckie and British immigrants such as Thomas Crawford and John Elias Jones. For all the differences in background and experience, these men shared a common purpose in their determination to transform the wage system.[16]

Somewhere between dedicated labor leaders and their great antagonists—men such as Carnegie and Frick—were many who wavered. They were the workers who sought justice for themselves and their colleagues in the workplace but also hankered after the opportunity for advancement. The careers of David R. Jones, R. D. Layton, and Thomas W. "Old Beeswax" Taylor point to the compelling and contradictory callings that vied for workers' allegiances in the postwar years.

Jones was born in 1853 near Swansea, Wales. He emigrated as a young man and initially settled near Wilkes-Barre, Pennsylvania, where he worked as an anthracite miner. He later attended college in Ohio and moved to Six Mile Ferry, a mining settlement just downstream from Homestead. There he became a schoolteacher and lent his support to the local miners. In the late 1870s miners all along the lower Monongahela chose Jones, by then a law student, to lead their districtwide organization and to serve as their chief negotiator. In this capacity, and as a zealous organizer for the Knights of Labor, Jones achieved national recognition. He helped win important concessions from Western Pennsylvania mine owners and, for his trouble, was tried and convicted on charges of criminal conspiracy. Tellingly, these charges were brought by a good friend and business associate of both Carnegie and Frick, Thomas Mellon.[17]

By the mid 1880s, however, Jones was leading a thoroughly proper life in keeping with the standards of the emerging middle class. As a Knight of Labor, he had once counseled all workers to bury their differences of "creed, color, or race" in order to avoid "vassalage and practical slavery." But Jones left the workers' movement once he was admitted to the bar. His legal practice flourished, and soon he purchased a house in Homestead for the handsome sum of $1,500. Jones and his wife even made the grand tour of Europe, and he published a travelogue about their adventures. In 1886 he was elected burgess of Homestead. Reelected in 1887, he subsequently relinquished the job when he was elected to the state legislature in 1888.

In Harrisburg, Jones sponsored labor legislation and, in the wake of the 1892 Homestead Lockout, defended a steelworker charged with disorderly conduct. But above all, he continued to aspire to the kind of respectability enjoyed by his mentor, George Guthrie, a man destined to become Pittsburgh's leading reform mayor and a hero in the polite world of liberal Progressivism. A world of difference separated apparent reformers such as David Jones and a man such as John McLuckie; in fact, Jones seemed to have more in common with his ostensible antagonists— Mellon, Frick, Carnegie, and the like. In 1880, Thomas Armstrong wrote in a letter to Terrence V. Powderly, leader of the Knights of Labor, that Jones's activities as an organizer had to be closely monitored because of his consuming egocentrism and drive for personal gain. "He is very ambitious. . . . He is an indiscreet talker so far as saying I, 'Big I' at that, . . . [and] if he does not do right, . . . sit down on him." Even at the height of his success in the miners' union, Jones was criticized for his authoritarian tactics and the relentless pursuit of his own power.[18]

Like Jones, Robert D. Layton was known for his ambition and became an important figure in the Knights of Labor in the late 1870s and early 1880s, when the order's greatest power lay in the Pittsburgh district. Layton, born in 1847 in Butler County, was raised in Pittsburgh. At the age of seventeen he enlisted in the Union army, saw action, and near the end of the war was captured and held prisoner by Confederate forces. Soon after his escape he was discharged and took up toolmaking, a trade he pursued until 1882. That year, Layton was elected general secretary and treasurer of the Knights of Labor and editor of their official newspaper, the *Journal of United Labor*. He also served as the master workman of the Knights' District Assembly 3 in Pittsburgh and as Terrence Powderly's chief political operative in Western Pennsylvania—a job that required maintaining a close watch on Powderly's rivals, particularly Thomas Armstrong, who in 1882 ran for governor.[19]

Layton had previously run for office himself on an independent labor ticket, but he mustered little enthusiasm for Armstrong's beleaguered candidacy. Like Armstrong, however, he was committed to the grand ideas of amalgamation and cooperation, and he, too, believed that the creation of an egalitarian social order was inextricably bound to the question of who owned the factories of America. The *Journal of United Labor* held that building a just society presupposed fundamental changes in economic organization: "The remedy must be *in a change of ownership.*" In Layton's view, the creation of producers' cooperatives represented the key element in the effort to transform the wage system. And the following letter reveals that he wanted to use his job as editor to agitate on behalf of cooperation—a term, he recognized, that could mask the insurgent thrust of the Knights' project: "I will begin in a few Nos. [of the *Journal*] to give the order something more interesting in relation to co-operation. In fact write about co-operation. So far, I have been talking Socialism and called it Co-operation in order to have the members read it without fear of being led into something 'awful.' A rose smells as sweet by any other name."[20]

By the time Layton wrote this letter, he and thousands of other "co-operators" had reason to fear that they lacked a strategy to make cooperation work on a scale appropriate to their grand aspirations. Indeed, this anxiety informed Layton's proverbial joke that equated socialism and cooperation: his unwillingness to use the word *socialism* publicly signaled a momentous narrowing of American political discourse and possibilities. Indeed, the Pennsylvania elections of 1882 would demonstrate just how fearful workers might be even when they were being led into something far less "awful" than socialism.

For Layton, this demonstration was apparently convincing enough to induce him to leave the Knights, open an insurance agency, and begin to cultivate the good graces of Pennsylvania's most powerful politician, Senator Matthew Quay, in an effort to win a Republican patronage appointment. Accordingly, in the fall of 1888, Quay dispatched Layton to Indiana to help mount an intense statewide electoral campaign. Layton was rewarded the following year when President Harrison named him Pittsburgh's immigration inspector.

Except for a few years of Democratic rule and a brief posting in New York City, Layton held the immigration position in Pittsburgh until after the turn of the century. He performed his duties with such alacrity, he boasted, that by 1904 he had succeeded in deporting more Chinese nationals than the combined total of all other noncoastal immigration offices. In this astounding shift from labor reformer to immigrant-buster, Layton did not lack role models. Terrence Powderly, the outspoken general master workman of the Knights of Labor until 1893, had himself effected an identically dramatic change of career; in 1896 he campaigned vigorously for the Republican William McKinley who, following his election as president, named Powderly commissioner general of immigration. Himself a virulent critic of Chinese immigrants, Powderly would no doubt have been pleased with Layton's new acclaim as an intrepid deporter of immigrant workers.[21]

Other accomodators joined forces with Layton in his shifting of allegiances. When he traveled to Indiana in 1888 to campaign for the Republican party, he was accompanied by yet another former Knight who was trying to curry favor with Senator Quay—Thomas W. "Old Beeswax" Taylor. As a young man, Taylor had been forced to leave England because of his radical politics; in America he became, like Layton, an ardent proponent of cooperation and a dedicated advocate of an independent labor party. In 1882, Taylor wrote the most important ode of the labor movement in the Gilded Age, "Storm the Fort, Ye Knights of Labor." And in the spring of 1888, after many failures in electoral politics, Taylor finally achieved a measure of success: he was elected burgess of Homestead, a town that had already achieved considerable distinction as a workers' stronghold. At the time of his election, however, Taylor was by no means an insurgent politician. Indeed, he was finalizing his plans to enter high-profit real estate ventures and publicly boasting about his relationship with Quay, notoriously corrupt even by the shoddy political standards of the day.[22]

Like the lives of David Jones, Robert Layton, and Terrence Powderly, the trajectory of Taylor's stunningly ambiguous career presents a curious puzzle for readers trying to make sense of the competing pressures of this era. Often on the lookout for the chance to improve his prospects in life, Taylor had also tried genuinely to cultivate in himself and in his colleagues that degree of mutualism requisite to building an insurgent social movement. Like Jones, Layton, and Powderly—like hundreds of thousands of Americans—Taylor in the end abandoned the path of resistance and effected a personal adjustment to what in the late nineteenth century had become abiding realities of American life: two-party politics and the competitive wage system.

The details of this adjustment, of Taylor's adventures in labor reform and commercial enterprise, epitomize the tensions that beset an entire generation of working Americans. As such, the fuller narrative of his career is reserved for separate discussion in part 5. However, before approaching the checkerboard of Beeswax Taylor's career, in order to appreciate the apparent sellout of colleagues such as Jones, Layton, and Powderly (the metaphor of the sellout itself begs our analysis), we must consider the larger forces that were shaping and tugging at the labor movement in greater Pittsburgh from the late 1860s to the early 1880s.

Chapter 6

Roots of Labor Reform and Machine Politics

RALPH KEELER and Harry Fenn, a journalist and an artist from Britain on assignment for *Every Saturday*, a weekly magazine published in Boston, traveled to Pittsburgh in early 1871 to report on what was becoming the preminent manufacturing center of North America. On their "reconnaissance" of the area, they rode to the top of Coal Hill, now known as Mt. Washington, via the new Monongahela Incline. There they found an extraordinary view of Pittsburgh and its sister cities, Birmingham and Allegheny, and of the hills through which the Monongahela and Allegheny rivers cut on the journey to their confluence at the Ohio. "Upon the brink of a precipice that overhung the smoking chimneys of countless factories and foundries, we beheld one of the most picturesque views on this continent. . . . The meetings and windings of three broad rivers beneath us, the crowded dusky hills thrust back from the water, and . . . the densely packed houses . . . of three cities, form a scene unrivalled in the world elsewhere."[1]

The Pittsburgh that Keeler and Fenn portrayed was exceptional in many respects. The economy of the metropolitan area was thriving to a degree unmatched by any region in the United States, and the population also had grown dramatically. More than 140,000 persons lived in Pittsburgh and Allegheny when Keeler and Fenn visited—an increase of about 80 percent since 1860—and approximately 60,000 more lived within the boroughs and towns that they saw from Coal Hill. Between 1860 and 1870 the work force in greater Pittsburgh's manufacturing establishments increased from 17,500 to more than 34,000, 13,500 of whom were metalworkers. The increase in their ranks from 4,800 in 1860 reflected Pittsburgh's meteoric rise to the position of what Keeler called "the great metal manufactory of the United States."[2]

The growth in Pittsburgh's metals industry had been staggering indeed. During the 1860s the capital invested in metalmaking establishments such as rolling and puddling mills, foundries, and crucible steelworks rose by more than 300 percent; the value of their products increased by more than 500 percent. Most of the growth was in the puddling and rolling sector. In 1856 the twenty-five rolling mills operating in Pittsburgh processed 140,000 tons of iron, employed 4,600 workers, paid them close to $2.9 million, and sold their products for $10.7 million. By 1870 there were thirty-three rolling mills in the metropolitan district; together they manufactured more than $20 million in iron products, employed 7,100 workers, and paid them about $4.5 million. In addition, the city's six cast steel plants sold their goods for $3.5 million and employed about 1,000 workers.[3]

Pittsburgh's rise to manufacturing prominence in iron and steel owed at least as much to the location of the city as to the demands created by the Civil War and the initiatives of energetic entrepreneurs such as B. F. Jones, Curtis G. Hussey, and, of course, Andrew Carnegie. The city lay at the center of a vast deposit of bituminous coal that contained more than 50 billion tons of "black diamonds." Called the Great Pittsburgh Seam, it covered 8.6 million acres and ran so close to the surface that in some places coal could simply be dug up with a shovel. It was this deposit that quite literally fueled Pittsburgh's take-off, sustaining individual families such as one encountered by Keeler and Fenn on Coal Hill as well as vast industrial enterprises such as Jones's American Iron Works, which employed 2,500 men.[4]

Most of the coal consumed by the American Iron Works and other mills in the city came from the Monongahela mines upriver. These collieries yielded nearly as much bituminous coal in 1870 as the combined output of all other mines in the United States, and the bulk of the Monongahela coal came from mines in Mifflin Township, across the river near Braddock, and farther upstream near McKeesport, Elizabeth, and Monongahela City. In the early 1870s about seventy-five mines operated in this area, the largest employing about five hundred laborers and the average work force under a hundred. In 1860, when three thousand hands worked in the mines, the output had surpassed 30 million bushels; by 1870, both figures had doubled.[5]

In the manufacture of glass, too, Pittsburgh was a leader. The output of glassmaking enterprises, like that of collieries and metalmaking concerns, grew exponentially in the 1860s. By 1870 almost 4,300 hands worked in the glassworks of Allegheny County, an increase of about 200 percent since 1860. Five years later, the city's seventy-three glassworks employed more then 5,200 workers.[6]

With virtually an unlimited supply of coal close at hand, and with easy access to the impressive iron ore, natural gas, and petroleum deposits located to the north and west of the city, "Pittsburgh could not help becoming a great industrial centre," one British visitor noted. Commanding twenty thousand miles of navigable rivers, and situated at the center of an ever lengthening system of railroad lines, Pittsburgh, "the Gateway to the West," was by 1870 "the metropolis of the American iron industry." It was, however, outside the city proper where the great steelworks of the district were built: the National Tube Works in Mc-Keesport, the Edgar Thomson Steel Works in Braddock, the Allegheny Bessemer Steel Works in Duquesne, and the PBSW in Homestead. Each of these mills, utilizing the new technologies of steel and eventually employing thousands of workers, clearly signaled bold initiatives in industrial and social organization.[7]

The site of the first of the new mills, Carnegie's Edgar Thomson Steel Works, was a 107-acre tract of farmland. If Keeler and Fenn had returned to Coal Hill the evening of 26 August 1875, they might have seen glimmerings from the initial blows of the mill's Bessemer converters. Certainly they would have been impressed, for in describing the dramatic operations of a Pittsburgh blast furnace, Keeler had identified the city's metalmaking might with the very quintessence of progress. Fenn's illustrations had echoed this theme.[8]

Without a doubt, the explosions from the Bessemer converters at the Edgar Thomson augured a new era for all the inhabitants of the Pittsburgh district. But many of those who made their living in the mines and mills along the Monongahela saw in the pyrotechnics of Bessemer steelmaking more threats than opportunities. To them the production of Bessemer steel offered no guarantee of progress. In the face of such undertakings, workers understood that they had to organize; in their view, extraordinary countermeasures were required to protect their position in the regional—and national—polity.

Some of the patterns that characterized the course of industrial relations after the Civil War emerged in Pittsburgh as early as 1850. That year, puddlers and ironmasters squared off in their first major dispute. The puddlers were defeated, however, and over the course of the decade, ironmasters repeatedly reduced wages. The largest reductions came during the depression of 1857–59, which provided the catalyst for the organization of a national union of puddlers, the Sons of Vulcan.[9]

During the first years of the Civil War, the membership of the Vulcans grew steadily as leaders organized local "forges" outside Pittsburgh. But the Iron City remained the locus of the union's strength, and its grand master was Miles Humphries, a Pittsburgh puddler. In 1865, Humphries' negotiations with ironmaster B. F. Jones resulted in a document known as the "sliding scale of prices," so named because it tied the puddlers' wages to the market price of iron. Questions about the scale were to occupy center stage in the iron and steel industry until Carnegie defeated the steelworkers of Homestead in 1892.

Soon after the agreement with Jones and other ironmasters was achieved, for example, puddlers in Pittsburgh tried to win an advance on the scale by demanding more money for each ton of iron they refined. The ironmasters initially conceded, but then they staged a lockout that lasted from December 1866 to the following May. During the lockout, Carnegie joined his fellow manufacturers in trying to resume operations by "importing" puddlers from Belgium, who were hired, the Vulcans later claimed, to "crush out the very manhood of the honest toiler." But the Belgian puddlers did not possess sufficient knowledge or experience to work with the unfamiliar iron and coal of North America. The ironmasters ultimately acceded to the puddlers' sliding scale proposal and, more importantly, formally recognized the puddlers' union by signing an agreement that applied to virtually all the puddling mills in greater Pittsburgh.[10]

The iron molders of Pittsburgh also enjoyed successes during the early 1860s, when they affiliated with the International Molders Union. The union, led by William H. Sylvis, consistently won wage concessions and was able to enforce its apprenticeship rules. Not surprisingly, its victories elicited a strong response from the iron founders, and the molders became enmeshed in the most heated labor conflicts of the period: throughout the industrial North, the molders lost a series of strikes in 1866 and 1867. The most damaging and bitter of these was in Pittsburgh. When the molders struck in January 1867 in an effort to resist a 20 percent reduction in wages, foundries hired nonunion workers and called out the police. The International Molders Union collected $40,000 from its membership in support of the strikers. After a nine-month struggle, however, the strikers were defeated. Resignation from the union was a prerequisite for reinstatement, and "the union was completely broken up" as a result.[11]

The losses in Pittsburgh and elsewhere helped convince Sylvis and other labor leaders that trade unionism was not an adequate response to the wage system. "Combination, as we have been using or applying it, makes war upon the effects, leaving the cause undisturbed. . . . The cause of all these evils is the WAGES SYSTEM, . . . [and] we must adopt a system which will divide the profits of labor among those who produce them." Sylvis and the iron molders therefore turned to cooperation and established a chain of worker-owned foundries. The one established in Pittsburgh became the cornerstone of the molders' cooperative ventures. Called the International Foundry, it became Sylvis's prize undertaking. But it failed—as did the union's other cooperative foundries. And so, too, did the International Molders Union. By the late 1870s the buildings once occupied by Pittsburgh's International Foundry housed the iron mill owned by William Clark, a particularly odious nemesis of organized metalworkers and one of the initial owners of the PBSW in Homestead.[12]

The river miners in the Pittsburgh district were more successful than the molders had been. In 1859 miners created their first districtwide

union, and during the Civil War they won a series of disputes under the
banner of the American Miners' Association. Wages were a key issue,
but owners consistently resorted to a wide range of initiatives to cut
labor costs, thereby linking wages to other matters. They habitually
docked miners by "shortweighing" their daily output, penalized them
for any slate or clay mined along with coal, withheld payment for
"dead" maintenance work in the mines, price-gouged at the ubiquitous
company store while irregularly paying "scrip" redeemable only at that
store, and charged astonishingly high rents for company-owned tenements. The miners were quick to recognize that only legislative prohibi-
tions against such practices, coupled with legislative guarantees of the
right to organize, promised any hope of relief. As early as 1864, and in
the midst of a bitter strike against the mine owners, the Monongahela
miners therefore resolved to vote only for those candidates who supported the rights of miners.[13]

Like the miners, glassworkers in Greater Pittsburgh also began to
organize in the late 1850s. The window glass blowers led the way. In
1857 in Birmingham they created the Window Glass Blowers' Union,
which, until it was decimated by the depression of the 1870s, exercised
strict control over employers and enjoyed uninterrupted growth in membership. Flint glass workers, who made a variety of smaller glass products, had a less successful record. Prior to the war, the flints were united
in the Glass Blowers' Benevolent Union, which folded in 1868 after losing two important strikes.[14]

Despite the collapse of the glassblowers' union, its members played
an important role in the birth of labor reform politics in Pittsburgh. One
of the initial organizers, Isaac Cline, was recognized as a national labor
leader from the first congress of the National Labor Union in 1866
through the late 1880s, and another glassblower, Andrew Burtt, who left
the trade to become a school principal, also became a leading labor
reformer in Pittsburgh. It is telling, however, that the most prominent of
labor reform leaders, at both the local and national levels, was neither an
ironworker, nor a miner, nor a glassblower, but a typographer—Thomas
A. Armstrong, coauthor of the National Labor Union's *Address . . . to the
Workingmen of the United States*.[15]

The *Address*, published in 1867, constituted a resounding indictment
of the emerging order. Condemning long working hours, the introduction of "labor-saving machinery," unequal pay for women laborers, the
hiring of black laborers to break strikes, "a false, vicious financial system," and growing concentration in land ownership as threats to "republican institutions," it vowed that workers were "determined to destroy"
the wage system. In its place the labor movement would create an independent workers' party and go on to erect a new society predicated
upon "that equality of right which is the basis of a true democracy."[16]

In Pittsburgh, Armstrong gathered together a growing network of semiprofessional activists to mount such an effort: Burtt, a former glassworker, Miles Humphries, B. A. McGinty, and Joseph Chiverton, all of whom were puddlers and had served as grand master of the Sons of Vulcan in the 1860s, and George Baber, a journalist. These men were associated with the *Workingmen's Weekly Advocate* and the *Daily Evening Advocate*, which began to appear on the streets of Pittsburgh in 1867. Published and edited by Armstrong and Baber, both were "devoted to the interests of labor reform" and enjoyed a dedicated readership of thousands.[17]

Armstrong and his fellow activists were aided in their efforts to rally workers to the cause by the disputes of 1866–67 in Pittsburgh's metal industries as well as by a bitter conflict in the city's cotton mills. The labor reformers censured Democratic and Republican politicians alike for failing to protect the city's workers and asked them to answer the National Labor Union's call for a new kind of politics. The hopes of the labor leaders soared in September 1867 when the Allegheny County Labor Reform party convened its initial convention and proclaimed that it represented the first local response to the National Labor Union. Baber declared: "This convention [is] the most auspicious event in the history of the county. Other counties [will] follow the example and the great Labor Party [will] start out on its glorious march to victory. This convention [is] but the embodiment of the feeling which has existed in this community for fifty years, and which [is] destined to culminate in the disenthrallment of the laboring classes throughout the continent."[18]

On the whole, however, the dizzying interaction of local and national political allegiances that emerged in Pittsburgh after the Civil War undermined many initiatives of the labor reformers. The importance of the immediate postwar years in the city's long-term political development can hardly be overstated, for it was then that the dominant pattern of municipal politics—a pattern that would remain in place well into the twentieth century—began to take shape. Indeed, it was in the midst of the very challenge mounted by the labor reformers that the architect of Pittsburgh's renowned political ring, Christopher L. Magee, took his first steps toward achieving indisputable control of city hall.[19]

To be sure, much remains unknown about postwar politics in Pittsburgh. As the historian Paul Kleppner has pointed out, there are serious gaps in our understanding of the city's political history; some of the most conspicuous are in the Reconstruction Era. Yet even without access to detailed demographic analyses, it is possible to trace many of the dynamics that informed the municipal politics of Pittsburgh during the late nineteenth century. Moreover, these dynamics, as well as being important to the local understanding of Pittsburgh politics, constitute the vital backdrop to political developments and events upstream in

Homestead, the very developments and events that pushed workers, politicians, and steelmen toward the deadly skirmish of 6 July 1892.[20]

Workers in Pittsburgh scored their initial postwar victory in December 1865, when William C. McCarthy, a printing pressman and radical Republican, won the party's mayoral nomination in the city's first direct primary election. McCarthy, who belonged to the typographers' local led by Thomas A. Armstrong, narrowly defeated the incumbent, James Lowry, Jr., in a campaign that revealed deep fissures within the Republican party. Lowry, a party founder and a solid businessman, appealed to the organization's moderate constituency "and the better people of the city." McCarthy, in contrast, drew his support from saloons and volunteer firehouses—the very centers of plebeian life. In the view of Lowry's supporters, many of whom were, like him, upstanding Scots Protestants, the rowdy street celebrations that followed McCarthy's primary victory constituted an odious sign that workers—and Catholic workers, at that!—had become a political force. Worried supporters of Lowry charged fraud and then bolted the party; they drafted James Blackmore, a Democrat and wealthy businessman, to run against McCarthy in the general election in January 1866. McCarthy, again drawing heavily on support from workers, defeated Blackmore, but only by 53 out of a total of 5,819 votes. (At the time, the typical Republican plurality was approximately 1,500 votes.)[21]

McCarthy's triumph signaled the arrival of labor politics in Pittsburgh. The victory, however, was by no means unequivocal: his slim margin in the general election suggests not only that Pittsburgh workers were divided but also that this division may well have arisen from a hesitation to support radical Republicanism when the standard-bearer was Catholic. In 1867, moreover, when workers organized their own party, the contradictory nature of their insurgency became even clearer: the Democrat, Blackmore, by this time worth over $300,000, was nominated by acclamation by the Labor Reform party and also won a resounding endorsement from the former Republican mayor James Lowry, Jr. Deprived of the Republican mayoral nomination by party conservatives who decided against another direct primary, McCarthy nonetheless managed to cut a deal with them, thereby securing for himself the party's nomination for city treasurer.[22]

According to David Montgomery and other historians, it was the cancellation of the 1867 Republican primary and McCarthy's loss of the mayoral nomination that provided the impetus for the labor party. But the nomination of Blackmore by the labor reformers and then by the Democrats, Blackmore's subsequent victory in the general election, and McCarthy's own crushing defeat at the hands of labor's candidate for city treasurer imply that matters were not so simple, or labor so strong, in postwar Pittsburgh.

McCarthy, purportedly a labor candidate, had after all lost to a wealthy merchant who ran as a labor reformer and a Democrat. On the surface the victory of Blackmore might therefore suggest that labor enjoyed considerable strength. Yet when labor reform candidates ran for county and state office in 1867 in races where there was no fusion with Democrats, the reformers were trounced. Of Andrew Burtt's unsuccessful candidacy for the state senate, the *National Labor Tribune* remarked some years later that he had won "the most flattering vote ever given an opposition candidate in this county." It was, however, a very stingy kind of flattery: the victorious Republican outpolled Burtt by a margin of more than three to one, and the Democratic candidate doubled his vote. The *Pittsburgh Commercial* more accurately observed that Burtt's loss had demonstrated that no one on the labor reform ticket "at any time had the ghost of a chance of being elected."[23]

One year later, in 1868, the election results seemed to corroborate the observations of the *Commercial*. From the point of view of dedicated labor reformers such as Thomas Armstrong, the political web in greater Pittsburgh had become hopelessly tangled. In January, Blackmore was inaugurated as mayor, but the Republican-controlled state legislature quickly enacted a special "ripper" bill requiring a fall election. Blackmore was nominated again by the Labor Reform party, but this time his candidacy bitterly split the organization. For their part, the Republicans reinstituted the direct primary; they chose Jared Brush, a "comfortably wealthy" former boilermaker described by the Republican press as representing "the laboring element of society." This description no doubt drew guffaws from some labor reformers: one of Brush's most prominent supporters was James Park, Jr., an ironmaster and noted union buster who was destined to join William Clark in building the PBSW in Homestead. Whatever questions might be raised regarding Brush's allegiances, Republicans, however, could lay some claim to their "identification" with Pittsburgh labor: Miles Humphries, a puddler and the leader of the Sons of Vulcan, won the party's nomination for the state legislature and was elected in the fall. Furthermore, the party counted among its most ardent standard-bearers an active union brother, Alexander P. Callow, who was soon to be elected mayor of Allegheny. A close friend of Armstrong, (with whom he may have worked on the *National Labor Tribune*), himself a Civil War hero, and a founder and past president of the Pittsburgh Typographical Union, Callow nonetheless distanced himself from the Labor Reform party and proudly led other workers through city streets in Republican election parades.[24]

It was in fact such parades that underscored what was perhaps the most difficult obstacle labor reformers faced in 1868—or, for that matter, at any time in Pittsburgh during the Reconstruction Era. For the Republican press issued a steady barrage of invective at the labor reformers, suggesting that anyone who voted against the Republican party was a traitorous "Ku-Kluxer." The governor and other ranking Republicans from across the state traveled to Pittsburgh to inveigh against the "Democratic" workingmen, and a series of mass meetings of more than fifteen thousand people drove home the same point about these putative "Copperheads." So intense was the feeling in Pittsburgh that Republican supporters and their critics confronted each other in several street fights; Callow himself was knocked out in one such melee, and James Blackmore was injured while trying to calm the crowd.[25]

The labor reformers had little room for maneuver in this heated atmosphere. To woo Pittsburgh workers, labor party leaders imported Samuel Fenton Cary, Cincinnati's "labor Congressman," and Richard F. Trevellick, a Cornish immigrant who was known for his remarkable oratorical skills. Both appeared at rallies for Andrew Burtt, who had been nominated for a congressional seat, and they may have helped his effort: Burtt drew 10,700 votes in the general election. But his Republican opponent, a Stalwart, received 15,200 votes and roundly defeated Burtt even in worker-dominated Birmingham and Ormsby. Brush, the Republican, also shellacked Blackmore.[26]

In the end, the 1868 elections left the labor reform movement in Pittsburgh in dissarray. To many, one lesson was clear: if sympathetic candidates were to be successful, they would, like Miles Humphries and Alexander P. Callow, have to disavow independent labor politics and embrace the Republican party. While such a decision entailed an obvious departure from the agenda of labor reformers, it did carry with it the prospect for personal success down the path of electoral victory—what David Montgomery has called "the most significant avenue of social advancement open to the workingman" in postwar America. Humphries, for example, served three terms in the state house of representatives and two in the senate, won appointment as commissioner of the state Bureau of Industrial Statistics and, after the turn of the century, became fire chief of Pittsburgh.[27]

More important, however, than any individual sellout effected by trade unionists such as Humphries and Callow was the larger political rule to which these decisions pointed: namely, that in the industrial North after the Civil War, workers and their leaders were under enormous pressure to vote as they had shot. Creating exceptions to this rule, as Lawrence Goodwyn has shown, proved to be a Herculean political—and cultural—task in Gilded Age America; the Populists themselves scored only fleeting successes. And just as the Populist defeat in the 1890s sealed the political fate of the South for decades to come, so the defeat of labor insurgency in Pittsburgh in the late 1860s, while perhaps less significant for the country at large, carried with it similarly ominous consequences. Into the vacuum of labor politics left by the collapse of the Labor Reform party stepped Christopher L. Magee, the shrewd master-mind of professional party politics who, even as he made millions for himself and his business associates, ultimately succeeded in marketing his political machine as the genuine voice of Pittsburgh's workers.[28]

Despite the failure of labor reformers to effect a groundswell for radical party politics, as the 1870s began, working Pittsburghers never-theless had some reason to take solace. Whatever the outcome of specific elections, to workers and their opponents one thing was now evident: not only could the labor vote no longer be ignored, but it had to be acknowledged that labor had become a significant political force at the municipal level. On a different but related plane, Pittsburgh trade unions, conforming to a national trend, also began to enjoy new suc-cesses, not necessarily at the polls, but at the point of production.[29]

Notable in this regard, the puddlers led the way; not surprisingly, their prominence in the civic life of Pittsburgh grew in proportion to the city's increasing economic dependence upon the iron industry. As Ralph Keeler wrote after his 1871 visit, only the nighttime scene of the city's countless furnaces was more impressive than the expertise, strength, and independence of Pittsburgh's skilled workers. In the wake of the initial defeats of labor reformers in the arena of politics, it was the threats launched on the shop floor by the captains of steel against this new-found strength and independence—of skilled workers in general and of expert puddlers in particular—that would give added impetus to the workers' movement in Pittsburgh, and across the nation, in the 1870s.[30]

Chapter 7

Custom Confronts Capital: The Lockout of 1874–1875

The puddlers do not look through the same spectacles as you.
—DAVID HARRIS, puddler,
to the ironmasters of Pittsburgh

Just A FEW years after the journalists Keeler and Fenn visited Pittsburgh and found it thriving, most of the city's mills had closed down and hundreds of paupers roamed the streets. One of the causes of this dramatic downturn was the collapse of the international banking house of Jay Cooke and Company in September 1873, a collapse that destabilized the nation's credit system. American railroads were particularly hard hit, and thousands of ironworkers who made rails suddenly found themselves without employment. The "smoking chimneys of countless factories and foundries" that Keeler had seen from Coal Hill gave way to an ominously different scene. "Idle men by the scores were to be seen on every street, and the city wore a listless and woe-begone look. Men, women and children beg from house to house and besiege the doors of relief societies for the commonest necessaries of life." The "decent carnival" of Pittsburgh workers had come to an abrupt end: the Great Depression of the 1870s had begun.[1]

In spite of the hardships the depression caused, labor leaders in Pittsburgh saw it as an opportunity to energize and educate the workers' movement. The lesson to be learned, the *National Labor Tribune* maintained, was that the caprice and competitiveness of "the wages system must and will give way to cooperation," that "justice and equality will take the place of law," and that "the good of all," and not the interests of "capital," would become "the rule . . . and the end of all individual and combined effort."[2]

As the depression became more severe, growing numbers of workers in greater Pittsburgh expressed similar aspirations, often in letters published by the *Tribune*. While many workers saw the promise of union solidarity as a hopeful solution to the social and economic crisis, industrialists, for their part, in an attempt to counter the effects of the depression by reducing costs, stepped up their attacks against organized labor. To their arsenal of antilabor tactics they added a new weapon: technological innovation. The 1870s in metalmaking were the great decade of technical change—the takeoff decade for Bessemer steel—when ironmasters moved to fulfill the agenda charted by Frederick Overman: mechanizing the production of malleable metal, improving managerial techniques, and liberating themselves from the expensive expertise of skilled workers. The key to all three tasks, as Overman suggested, had been finding a process to replace puddling.[3]

When, in 1872, Andrew Carnegie decided to build a mammoth Bessemer steel mill in Braddock and hired Alexander Holley to design it, the new era in metalmaking formally began. Appropriately enough, Carnegie's initiative came just as his fellow ironmasters locked out four thousand puddlers in an effort to do away with their union, the Sons of Vulcan. The bitter dispute that followed, and the national movement for amalgamation to which it gave birth, reminded ironmasters of just how troublesome their employees could be and indicated that the insurgent vocabulary of the *National Labor Tribune* was not mere rhetoric. In the view of the ironmasters, the lockout proved that Carnegie's way of solving the puddling bottleneck represented the indisputable method of choice.

Overlooked by historians, the lockout of 1874–75 was one of the most important industrial disputes of its day. It is a critical opening chapter to the history of Pittsburgh in the Gilded Age which closes with the Homestead Lockout of 1892. Underlying the 1874–75 lockout, as with the more famous confrontation in Homestead, was a debate over the place of labor in the American Republic and the nature of the Republic itself. As we know, the lockout of 1892 killed the most powerful trade union of the era, the AAISW, and definitively arrested American trade unionism until the 1930s. It was, however, the lockout of 1874–75 that provided the impetus for creating the AAISW. Moreover, in the wake of the lockout, Pittsburgh workers helped found the Knights of Labor, the labor organization that envisioned an amalgamation of all workers. Nevertheless, as impressive as these gestures of solidarity were, in the midst of the 1874–75 lockout workers also began to confront many of the sources of disunity that would hound the labor movement into the twentieth century—foremost among which were racism and intercraft rivalry.[4]

Although the lockout of 1874–75 was to address the broadest issues of republican justice and dignity for workers, the crisis that immediately precipitated it arose from a rather intricate debate over how the wages of Pittsburgh puddlers should be set. Accordingly, the account that follows reconstructs some of the mathematical calculations that determined the adversarial positions of workers and ironmasters in the dispute. Tedious as the variations in these wage scales may appear, it was political principle, much more than mathematics, that dictated the manner by which they would be interpreted. And the conflict that arose from the interpretation dramatizes succinctly the two competing views of labor that shaped so many industrial disputes of the era.

On the one side there were the ironmasters of Pittsburgh, who saw profit making as the chief purpose of labor; labor, for them, was but a factor of production whose market value they were entitled to determine. On the other side stood the puddlers; they saw labor as the guarantor of republican fairness and material well-being. For them labor possessed an intrinsic, "customary," value that only they could set and that was separate from the calculus of the market.[5]

The immediate cause of the lockout—which threw a total of forty thousand people out of work—was the downward slide in the selling price of iron precipitated by the onset of the Great Depression of 1873–1879. The selling price of iron determined the piece rates upon which the wages of the puddlers who produced it were based. The determination was made in accordance with an agreement with the manufacturers, called the sliding scale, which had been adopted in 1867. The scale of 1867, like the iron industry's first scale, signed in 1865, provided that the puddlers' piece rates rose and fell with the price of iron.[6]

Because the scale provided for piece rates, the wages of puddlers were tied not only to the selling price of iron but also to the amount they produced. The scale, however, made no reference to the question of output, which was determined by the puddlers' customary notions of how much work to do each day, as well as by the condition of the iron market. What the scale essentially set, then, was the rate of payment for each ton of puddled iron. The rate was derived from a base, an imprecise measure that tied together the market price of iron and the piece rates embedded in the scale.

The sliding scale of 1867 fixed the puddlers' piece rates (per ton of iron they produced) to the manufacturers' "card rate," named after the manufacturers' "card of prices" (per pound of iron they sold). When iron sold for 5¢ per pound, for example, a puddler would earn $8 for each ton he puddled. When the selling price was 4.75¢, he would earn $7.75 per ton. The scale of 1867 reached its lowest card rate of 3¢ per pound and the corresponding piece rates also descended to a low of $6 per ton. Below these levels, the card rates and piece rates did not go.

What would happen when the selling price of iron fell below 3¢ a pound? This was the question for ironmasters and puddlers alike as the winter of 1874 began. From the beginning of 1873 to the autumn of 1874, the selling price had fallen from 5 to 2.5¢ per pound; some manufacturers claimed they were forced to sell iron for even less than that. The falling prices caused a rapid decline in profits, and it was this decline, manufacturers said, that forced them to reduce production costs by means of a cut in wages.

Under the scale of 1867, the manufacturers or the puddlers could break their agreement simply by serving thirty days' notice. Thus, in early November 1874, the ironmasters announced that they would terminate the scale on 7 December. Joined together in the Association of Iron Manufacturers, which represented virtually every mill owner in the Pittsburgh district, the ironmasters declared that they wanted to make a new scale more in keeping with depressed market conditions.[7]

The Association of Iron Manufacturers, chaired by B. F. Jones, the owner of the largest ironworks in Pittsburgh, proposed a new scale that would pay $5 per ton when the card rate was 3¢ per pound and $4.50 when the card rate was 2.5¢. Thus, when a pound of iron sold for 3¢, the manufacturers' proposal reduced the piece rate by $1. And because the manufacturers' scale extended downward to a card rate of 2.5¢, it could reduce piece rates by as much as $1.50. Here is how the scale of 1867 compared with the manufacturers' proposal:[8]

1867 SCALE		MANUFACTURERS' PROPOSAL	
Card Rate (per pound)	Piece Rate (per ton)	Card Rate (per pound)	Piece Rate (per ton)
5 ¢	$8.00	5 ¢	$8.00
4.5 ¢	$7.50	4.5 ¢	$7.50
4.0 ¢	$7.00	4.0 ¢	$7.00
3.5 ¢	$6.50	3.5 ¢	$6.50
3.4 ¢	$6.40	3.4 ¢	$6.40
3.3 ¢	$6.30	3.3 ¢	$6.30
3.2 ¢	$6.20	3.2 ¢	$6.20
3.1 ¢	$6.10	3.1 ¢	$6.10
3.0 ¢	$6.00	3.0 ¢	*$5.00*
	("Minimum")		
		2.9 ¢	$4.90
		2.8 ¢	$4.80
		2.7 ¢	$4.70
		2.6 ¢	$4.60
		2.5 ¢	$4.50

As the card rate for bar iron was 2.5¢ per pound when the manufacturers made their proposal, its immediate effect would indeed be to reduce puddlers' piece rates by $1.50. This drastic reduction was meant to offset the "burden" of the minimum rate that manufacturers sustained: even though the price of iron had fallen to less than 3¢ per pound, they had continued to pay the puddlers $6 a ton.

From the manufacturers' standpoint, maintaining the minimum piece rate was unacceptable for two reasons. The first was that the scale of 1867 did not explicitly state that $6 was to be a minimum. The puddlers, of course, interpreted the silence of the written scale to their liking, and for their part, the manufacturers had tacitly endorsed the minimum by paying it. The manufacturers, however, maintained that in 1867 the puddlers had orally agreed to revise the scale if card rates fell below 3¢. "It was agreed," B. F. Jones asserted, "that if iron went below three cents, the present scale should be inoperative." The second justification for reducing piece rates was that under current market conditions, the base of the scale was set too high, making it impossible to continue profitable operations.

Manufacturers and leaders of the Sons of Vulcan met several times during November 1874 in an effort to reach a new agreement. The puddlers were represented by David Harris, the president of the union, Joseph Bishop, its ranking official in the Pittsburgh district, and several other puddlers from various forges in the city. Into the third week of November, they refused to make any changes in the scale. But as the termination date and its promise of a midwinter work stoppage grew closer, the puddlers agreed to adjust the piece rates. They disagreed, however, with the manufacturers over the nature of the adjustment.[9]

Unlike the manufacturers, the puddlers found the base of the scale satisfactory, and they wished to see the revision made according to that base. In effect, their counterproposal amounted to a simple downward extension of the scale of 1867. The extension would stop at the existing card rate of 2.5¢, which at the time translated into a piece rate of $5.50, thereby constituting an immediate reduction of 50¢ per ton. The piece rate of $5.50 should be the new minimum in the puddlers' view. (Their proposal did not indicate what would occur if the price of iron fell to less than 2.5¢ a pound.) Here is how the workers' proposed revision of the scale compared to the manufacturers' proposal:

PUDDLERS' PROPOSAL		MANUFACTURERS' PROPOSAL	
Card Rate (per pound)	Piece Rate (per ton)	Card Rate (per pound)	Piece Rate (per ton)
5 ¢	$8.00	5 ¢	$8.00
4.5 ¢	$7.50	4.5 ¢	$7.50
4.0 ¢	$7.00	4.0 ¢	$7.00
3.5 ¢	$6.50	3.5 ¢	$6.50
3.4 ¢	$6.40	3.4 ¢	$6.40
3.3 ¢	$6.30	3.3 ¢	$6.30
3.2 ¢	$6.20	3.2 ¢	$6.20
3.1 ¢	$6.10	3.1 ¢	$6.10
3.0 ¢	$6.00	3.0 ¢	$5.00

2.9 ¢	$5.90	2.9 ¢	$4.90
2.8 ¢	$5.80	2.8 ¢	$4.80
2.7 ¢	$5.70	2.7 ¢	$4.70
2.6 ¢	$5.60	2.6 ¢	$4.60
2.5 ¢	$5.50	2.5 ¢	$4.50
	(New "Minimum")		

In defense of their proposal, on the other hand, the manufacturers argued that the 1867 scale prohibited successful competition against the mills of Philadelphia, Troy, and cities to the east of Pittsburgh that were not covered by the agreement. "We are surrounded by competition on all sides," said one ironmaster, James J. Bennett, at a negotiating session. "The Pittsburgh mills have run on thinking they would hold to their trade, but (they) are doing it at a heavy cost, without profit and in many instances at a heavy loss. . . . That condition of affairs cannot last much longer." Only a reduction of one dollar per ton in the piece rates "would cover the present condition of affairs and would enable the mills to work on and give employment to the men here!" In short, the ironmasters claimed that they could not compete because their labor costs were significantly greater than those in other regions.[10]

The puddlers acknowledged that the piece rates in the 1867 scale were indeed higher than those paid in other regions. But they contended that their work was more difficult than puddling in Eastern mills because inferior raw materials were used in Pittsburgh and because much of the iron made in the city was for goods other than rails and therefore demanded more "working." Moreover, the Pittsburgh puddlers produced figures, never refuted by the ironmasters, suggesting that, though their piece rates were higher than those paid, for example, in Philadelphia, with the onset of the depression the difference had in fact narrowed. In other words, they argued, the ironmasters of Pittsburgh had increased their competitive advantage in labor costs.

The puddlers therefore concluded that in deciding to terminate the scale, the Pittsburgh ironmasters were acting not to recover the competitive edge whose loss they lamented but to secure larger profits, and that it was this desire that had caused the sharp fall in iron prices in the first place. "The [price] cutting has been done by yourselves," David Harris told the ironmasters. "The competition is in your own circle, . . . the fault lies among yourselves. You have by your own system of undercutting brought the price of iron down to the low figure it is today, and therefore the hard-fisted boilers are not responsible for this condition of affairs. We have not a voice or hand in the making of the price of iron."[11]

Though the puddlers claimed that they had nothing whatever to do with setting the market price of iron, they had always looked to the sliding scale as a way of regulating the "prices" ironmasters paid for labor. By codifying the puddlers' power to restrict output, the scale provided a safeguard against the slashing of piece rates by the employers. More important, the scale also gave puddlers an assurance that, no matter how poor the market, they would continue to receive "a fair day's wages for a fair day's work." Indeed, protecting this "right" was one of the chief objects of the Sons of Vulcan. Under the scale, puddlers themselves could decide what constituted a fair day's work—typically six heats, which together lasted just over ten hours. To a large degree, however, it was the scale that determined what constituted a fair day's wage. True, in making the determination, the scale allowed a fair day's wage to change in accord with the puddlers' own production goals as well as with market variations. But the scale presupposed that the idea of "fair" was qualitative and not variable—a point crucially important in the eyes of the puddlers. Card and piece rates might fluctuate in response to the market, but in the scale there was an unchanging ratio between the two that constituted the base of the scale.[12]

Little is known about how the puddlers and ironmasters set the base of the sliding scale. But the absence of precise information about it does not obscure its meaning. To the contrary, the very fact that the base was grounded upon "common sense" demonstrates what it was—and was not.

For the puddlers, the scale was the means by which they could achieve and protect what they took to be their right to fairness. The scale was not merely an instrument that would bring the highest possible wage: after all, the base of the scale, and indeed the scale itself, was predicated upon a customary understanding of fairness. And this understanding bore little relation to the basic principle of fairness in private enterprise: maximizing one's net comparative advantage, typically at the expense of someone else. As Miles Humphries, who negotiated the first scale, recounted, market factors did not figure in the initial deliberations. "The cost of living and the cost of production did not enter into consideration at all, only a fair proportion of the profits or of the selling price." John Jarrett, a vice president of the puddlers' union in 1873, said that the puddlers, in negotiating the initial postwar scales, knew only that the ironmasters' profits "were enormous and that wages were out of proportion to profits." The puddlers "had no actual figures to determine what these profits were" but simply tried "to hit upon a reasonable and equitable proportion" of the profits.[13]

Indeed, it was a "spirit of equity" and a desire for permanence in employment, and not a search for the highest possible wage, that in 1867 had informed the puddlers' efforts to make a lasting agreement about the scale. To be sure, they had previously sought an upward adjustment on grounds that the postwar boom dictated a reassessment of the base.

But when bar iron prices seemed to stabilize at a lower level in 1867, they had agreed to a reduction in the base. From that point on, even during the extraordinary boom of 1872–73, they did not seek an increase.[14]

The puddlers, then, were satisfied with the base of the scale during the economic boom in the Pittsburgh district that lasted until September 1873. Wages were at the highest level of the nineteenth century—they averaged more than $4.60 a day—and the ironmasters' profits were very high indeed. By virtue of their agreement on a base for the scale in 1867, puddlers and ironmasters seemed to have succeeded "in devising measures calculated to harmonize the conflicting interests that . . . existed . . . between them." Significantly, the realization of this hope for harmony that the puddlers had expressed was in their eyes utterly dependent upon the maintenance of a fair and fixed base in the scale. It was the base that ensured equity in good as well as in hard times and recognized that puddlers were, at the very least, the manufacturers' junior partners, who shared in profits and losses. Perhaps more important, the base and the scale itself gave substance to the idea, so appealing to Gilded Age workers, that they were not merely wage earners, not merely factors of production paid according to how long they labored, but rather "producers" who earned in accord with how much they produced and how good their product was.[15]

Puddlers therefore had ample reason to refer to the iron industry as "our trade." The sense of proprietorship derived not only from their knowledge that their skills were absolutely essential to the production of wrought iron but also from the employers' recognition of their absolute right to a "fair day's wage." After all, the ironmasters had signed an agreement that was based upon the puddlers' customary sense of fairness and a tacit if unequal partnership between worker and employer. Thus, when the manufacturers unilaterally decided to reduce the base of the scale and set a new standard of fairness, the puddlers concluded that their partnership, their sense of justice, and their sense of themselves as producers—as opposed to hireling laborers or wage slaves—were all under attack.

For these reasons the puddlers considered the manufacturers' proposal to reduce the base an "outrageous proposition." Any alteration, even temporary, was unacceptable. "We see no necessity for a reduction," David Harris told the ironmasters. "If the scale was good enough when it was established, and it was good long since that period, it surely ought to be while we are passing through a depression and the men are actually suffering and realizing greater inconvenience than the manufacturers are." Harris also reminded the manufacturers that the puddlers were willing to accept a reduction in piece rates—but only with the current base—and he indicated how important it was to them that the base be maintained. "We have sacredly observed that contract, and we feel like observing it still, and I hope the manufacturers will not break this scale arrangement. We look upon it as an anchor, and if we cut loose from it, the Lord only knows where we will drift."[16]

The manufacturers offered a markedly different interpretation of the situation. "We are treating with the Union," James J. Bennett told his colleagues. "If the Union proposes to regulate our profits and prices, we might as well give up business. I am willing to recognize the Union so long as it confines itself to its legitimate business, but I cannot permit it to regulate my contracts. . . . That I will never recognize, and I do not believe there is a gentleman in this room who will do it."[17]

Bennett was right: the Association of Iron Manufacturers would brook no effort on the part of the puddlers to set the base. From the standpoint of the manufacturers, the base of the scale determined profits, and regulating profits was not part of the "legitimate business" of the puddlers' union. Indeed, by deciding that "the whole basis of the scale was too high," as B. F. Jones put it, the manufacturers again exposed the deep division between their views and those of the puddlers. Whereas the puddlers regarded the base as setting the standard for fairness, the manufacturers saw it chiefly as a factor shaping their profits and their costs—specifically, labor costs. For the manufacturers, the value of labor could be increased or decreased depending on the terms of its "sale."[18]

That the value of labor could vary according to a contractual agreement of course implied that labor itself was a commodity and that laborers were factors of production. "As a manufacturer, I intend to be free to buy my commodities where I please, and when I please, and sell them when I please and where I please," Bennett told the puddlers. "The puddlers do not look through the same spectacles as you," retorted David Harris. The puddlers, Harris avowed, had no objection to the manufacturers' setting the selling price of iron. "We have not a voice or hand in the making of the price of iron," he said, but the puddlers did "have a hand and voice in making [the] scale." From the puddlers' point of view, then, the manufacturers were free to sell iron howsoever they pleased, but they should have no say in setting the value of labor.[19]

This proposition was made explicit by Joseph Bishop, the leader of the Sons of Vulcan in Pittsburgh in 1874–75. (Bishop later became president of the Vulcans as well as of the AAISW.) Before a select committee of the House of Representatives that investigated the Great Depression, Bishop was asked by Abram S. Hewitt, an ironmaster and the chairman of the committee, if ironworkers would ever submit to arbitration to settle their disputes with employers. "No, sir," was the terse answer. "In other words," Hewitt asked, "you reserve to yourselves the final and absolute right to decide whether you are right or not?" Bishop responded, "Yes, sir—for the reason that we believe that we are able to judge the merits of the case and know what our labor is worth."[20]

It was precisely this ethos that led the puddlers to reject what B. F. Jones himself called the manufacturers' ultimatum. The decision did not come easily. "Every man's bread and butter is at stake," declared the union's column in the *National Labor Tribune*. "The fate of thousands for this winter hangs on the wise decision of this question." At a districtwide meeting of delegates from all the forges, the Sons of Vulcan decided that thousands, many of whom indeed were to walk the streets of Pittsburgh that winter begging for food, would face a better fate if the ultimatum were rejected. For their part, the Pittsburgh ironmasters were equally determined; like their colleague Hewitt, they could not tolerate the puddlers' view of labor, and they therefore began closing their mills on 7 December. Three days later, all but two hundred of the city's eight hundred puddling furnaces were cold; by 12 December, iron was being puddled in only seventy-three furnaces.[21]

The resolve of the ironmasters and the puddlers remained strong, and the winter and spring of 1875 proved a tumultuous time in Pittsburgh. Puddlers who succeeded in finding temporary work with railroads, with other businesses, or with the city were systematically dismissed. At the urging of the employers, city authorities excluded puddlers' families from public relief. The daily press launched a spiteful campaign against them; one paper even paid a disenchanted union member to spy on his colleagues and report his findings in a column called "Local Intelligence." Moreover, the manufacturers brought in strike breakers, and the Pennsylvania National Guard and local police were mobilized. Despite the public assurances—and parades—that heralded a tenacious solidarity, divisions within the ranks of Pittsburgh ironworkers soon emerged.[22]

The most immediate problem for the puddlers was that the iron manufacturers were able to reopen many of their mills. While a handful of puddlers agreed to work under the manufacturers' terms, it was not so much the defection of these black sheep that kept the mills running. Important as they were to the iron-making process, puddlers only refined the raw material, pig iron, brought to the mills. Once that was done, their tasks were over. Work crews comprised of rollers, roll turners, roughers, catchers, and heaters—collectively knows as finishers—were in charge of working up wrought iron into marketable goods. And these finishers, who were not eligible for membership in the Sons of Vulcan and therefore not subject to their rejection of the ironmasters' scale, continued to work in the rolling mills of Pittsburgh.[23]

A story in the *National Labor Tribune* in early January 1875 called attention to a familiar problem for those ironworkers and labor reformers who had been urging an amalgamation of the separate unions in the iron industry. "ROLLERS AND HEATERS," the headline read. "You are enabling the manufacturers to fight the boilers. . . . Were we to be broken in the present lockout you would next be attacked and reduced. Your interests are with us. . . . As working men, we ought to stand together, and work together, and suffer together."[24]

Other problems confronted the Sons of Vulcan. The union did not admit helpers and helpers often stepped in for puddlers during strikes and lockouts. To minimize discord, Joseph Bishop and other leading Vulcans in Pittsburgh began an organizing campaign aimed at recruiting helpers and nonunion puddlers. In early March "a grand mass meeting" of Vulcans, nonunion puddlers, and helpers heard Bishop speak on the necessity of concerted action. He appealed "to all men of whatever department of mill labor to join together, to unite their strength, that they might not be defeated by being attacked piecemeal." Bishop urged all workers to form "one strong, broad, deep, wide organization wherein all labor would be shielded from attacks."[25]

Bishop's appeal held special meaning for the ironworkers. Not only in Pittsburgh were puddlers engaged in a bitter struggle: their colleagues at the Cambria Iron Works in Johnstown, the nation's largest, had been locked out too. Furthermore, Bishop's proposal for a union of all workers was also particularly appealing to glassblowers and miners, whose organizations had suffered badly during the depression.[26]

Accordingly, within a week of Bishop's speech, Pittsburgh workers took important organizational steps toward "a unity of Unions" and what the *National Labor Tribune* called industrial independence. It noted that a new "secret organization" in Philadelphia embracing all workers was on its way to Pittsburgh. "We heartily welcome . . . this union of unions. . . . [It] is designed to reach farther and higher and deeper and take hold of and grapple with questions and interests and difficulties which our trade unions cannot by [their] nature handle." It was, according to the *Tribune,* an organization that might well redeem the Republic. By June 1875 this new union of unions had taken hold in the Pittsburgh district and was "spreading silently, like the rising of a tide," under the banner of the Knights of Labor.[27]

Labor reformers such as Armstrong and Bishop who were committed to a "unity of unions" had only to point to the ironmasters' lockout for examples of the need to broaden the labor movement, for in addition to the divisions between the puddlers and finishers of Pittsburgh, new workers "imported" by several ironmasters also had weakened the Vulcans' cause. In fact, the Pittsburgh Bolt Company had succeeded in early March in restarting its puddling furnaces with fifty nonunion puddlers, most of them brought from Richmond, Virginia. Within weeks, these black sheep were operating twenty furnaces for the company, whose finishers had continued working in defiance of the Vulcans' request for support. The union also faced a challenge at the Black Diamond Steel Works: its owner, James Park, Jr.—a principal in the first American venture to replace all puddlers by means of the Bessemer process—had hired about a dozen black sheep of his own to puddle iron.[28]

Such developments figured prominently in the efforts of the Vulcans to press for a solidarity that embraced union and nonunion puddlers as well as finishers. There were, however, limits even to this solidarity, as Park and the owners of the Pittsburgh Bolt Company were quick to appreciate, for the black sheep they brought to their mills were, in fact, black. Precisely how large a factor race was in the subsequent actions of the Pittsburgh puddlers is uncertain. This much, however, is clear: in the view of the locked-out puddlers, the sheep who puddled iron at the Pittsburgh Bolt Company and at the Black Diamond Steel Works were clearly and regrettably, as Bishop later put it, "black in both color and principle."[29]

Accordingly, not long after the puddlers from Richmond began work, three hundred union puddlers, some threatening violence, gathered near the Pittsburgh Bolt Company. In truth, the threats were directed not only at the black puddlers, who were living in company-owned houses from which the company had evicted its white employees; they also "persuaded" the finishers, who were white, to suspend operations. Work nonetheless soon resumed: the state militia was mobilized and the sheriff dispersed the locked-out puddlers. Meanwhile, black puddlers had a difficult time in the city: there were assaults, and some were attacked on the South Side by an angry crowd of white workers.[30]

The employment of black ironworkers in order to undermine the Sons of Vulcan was a relatively new tactic. Until the lockout of 1874–75, ironmasters had hired black laborers during disputes with the Vulcans on just two other occasions. And only in the early 1880s did employers begin a more concerted effort to hire black ironworkers during disputes with the overwhelmingly white organizations of iron- and steelworkers. However, some white ironworkers recognized as early as the lockout of 1874–75 that the success of labor reform depended upon an amalgamation that extended beyond the various ironworkers' unions to inlcude, eventually, all workers, white and black. Thus, at the ironworkers' convention in 1877, some members moved that membership be opened to "colored men." The resolution was defeated, and it was not until 1881 that the union voted to accept blacks, "past experience having taught the craft that they were indispensable."[31]

This grudging nod to the contributions of black workers was made in the same spirit that had animated the *Address of the National Labor Congress to the Workingmen of the United States*. That document, coauthored by Thomas Armstrong in 1868, pointed to "the important position now assigned to the colored race" in the struggle for labor reform, "unpalatable as the truth may be to many." Armstrong and the other authors of the address concluded that white laborers would decide whether their relations with black laborers would be "an element of strength or an element of weakness" in the workers' movement. For the former condition to prevail, "the cooperation of the African race in America must be secured."[32]

As these words indicate, Armstrong himself was not immune to racism. Shortly after the black puddlers arrived from Richmond in March 1874, the *National Labor Tribune* reported, "They are working, but turning out less . . . than skilled white men." Armstrong, like his close friend William Sylvis, an iron molder, was contemptuous of black Americans. But like Sylvis and many other leading labor reformers, he understood that the attainment of full "citizenship" and industrial independence for white workers was linked to their willingness to recognize, however hesitantly and incompletely, that black workers also were struggling in the postwar years to escape "the thralldom and loss" of wage slavery. Armstrong's *Address,* speeches such as those delivered by Bishop before the ironworkers' mass meeting, and, most important, the partial fulfillment of the call for racial solidarity embodied in the Knights of Labor—these were the most enlightened expressions of a collective consciousness that typicallly could still not extend full citizenship in the republic of labor to all working Americans.[33]

At its worst, this collective consciousness was virulently racist, and the calls of white labor reformers for a solidarity embracing all workers often coincided, jarringly, with expressions of racial hatred. Only a few weeks after Bishop's endorsement of a union for all workers, the *Tribune* published an inflammatory song about the black puddlers from Richmond. Called "Sing, Brudders, Sing," and sung to the tune of "Poor Old Joe," it ridiculed the skill of the black workers and condemned them for being "slaves." Curiously, the song implied that they had chosen to be slaves and that they could be "free" only by refusing to work as scabs. "Go ahead, son of Ham, work while you can for these capital braves," one verse said, "if you don't care to be like the white man free, why do and be their slaves." The chorus echoed the sentiments of Armstrong's report in the *Tribune* regarding the allegedly poor skills of the black puddlers:

> So it's fire up, Sambo, do your best.
> We'll watch the fun for awhile.
> There's a day near at hand, when we'll let you understand,
> You can't show de white man how to boil.[34]

Though overtly racist, the song indicates that the contempt for the black puddlers was multidetermined, growing out of white America's legacy of racism as well as the Vulcans' customary loathing for black sheep workers. Affirming that the black puddlers could become, like "honorable" white laborers, "free" if they chose not to scab, the song suggests that its author did not rule out an alliance with black laborers merely because they were black. That black puddlers were working as black sheep, however, touched the deepest fears of Pittsburgh's white puddlers, who conceived of their own dispute with the Pittsburgh iron-masters as no less than a struggle to liberate themselves from the degradation of wage slavery. In their eyes no condition was worse than slavery—chattel or wage slavery. For them, the activities of the black "black sheep," whose race, white workers liked to think, had been emancipated and elevated by their sacrifices in the Civil War, constituted an unpalatable irony. "Their" Civil War, that is, the Civil War of white Northerners, had been fought not so that chattel slaves might become wage slaves, and certainly not so that those who risked their lives to free the slaves might themselves become industrial bondsmen.

The hiring of the Richmond puddlers and the reopening of the mills posed a very real threat to the Sons of Vulcan. The angry response of white puddlers to the arrival of nonunionized black workers expressed, of course, no small measure of unmediated racial hatred and prejudice, feelings that would permeate the union movement well into the twentieth century. More specifically, however, the sight of these "abject scabs" conjured up for the locked-out workers the frightening prospect of their own bondage. Behind the nervous contempt that colored the racist bonhomie of "Sing, Brudders, Sing" lay the worst fears of a community of skilled craftsmen whose independent status might at any moment be irretrievably "converted," either by the tactical machinery of the Pittsburgh ironmasters or by the real and ominous machinery of Henry Bessemer. Whereas little is known of what became of the Richmond puddlers, the effects of the introduction of the Bessemer converter on this generation of ironworkers was, in contrast, widely publicized.

An article in the *National Labor Tribune* published in September 1874 flaunted the puddlers' defiance in the face of technological advance. Puddlers, it boasted, could mock the inventors of the new technology of steel. The puddler's furnace "laughs at these crazy inventors until it almost splits it sides. It calls them fools. It says, 'go ahead, beat me if you can. I am monarch of the mill, and you can't crush me,' and then it laughs again. . . . Scientific metallurgy has declared war on [puddling], and yet it cares not."[35]

The bravado bespoke a profound unease, for the puddlers of Pittsburgh understood that while the sliding scale might preserve at least a portion of their independence, it offered no protection in the event that the work they did became redundant. Only wider amalgamation offered any hope of checking the new challenges of technology related to "the unjust demands of capital." And as the puddlers' determination grew, so too did the prospects for a union of all ironworkers and, moreover, a union of unions. By the spring of 1875 the Association of Iron Manufacturers had reason to be concerned about maintaining its own solidarity.[36]

The first sign that the association recognized that it was in danger of losing the lockout came in March, when manufacturers retracted their ultimatum to reduce the base of the scale. When the iron market underwent a brief revival, mills outside of Pittsburgh that had not closed down could now play their advantage; there were rumors among members of the manufacturers' association that some Pittsburgh ironmasters were ready to break ranks. The manufacturers thus asked if the Sons of Vulcan would submit to arbitration. The puddlers refused. Interpreting the request as a sign of weakness, they held an enthusiastic march through the city on 2 April. "With drums beating and colors flying," the puddlers proclaimed that they were close to victory.

And indeed they were. On 7 April the owners of the Keystone Rolling Mill broke from the manufacturers' association and resumed operations under the scale of 1867. Other manufacturers soon followed suit, and on 14 April the association officially capitulated: "We deem it inexpedient to longer continue the suspension of our mills." The announcement made by the association, which had signed the scale on behalf of all its members, left each manufacturer free to sign or not and thus negotiate an individual agreement with the puddlers. The latter, however, returned to work only on the condition that each manufacturer agree to the old scale by cosigning it with committees designated by each local forge. Within weeks, all the manufacturers signed. The puddlers had won.[37]

"The Union has fought its battle manfully and to it belongs the honor," declared the *National Labor Tribune*. Indeed, the Vulcans not only claimed to have preserved their honor in what Joseph Bishop called "the greatest struggle in the history of our organization" but also interpreted their victory as a republican triumph over what the union president, David Harris, called "the unnatural wages system." An anonymously authored "lockout ballad" in the *Tribune* proclaimed:

> The glorious Puddlers Union,
> I love to hear the name,
> You've heard of the "Star-Spangled Banner,"
> Well, we are just the same.

Another ballad, this one written by an ironworker in Ohio, emphasized that the puddlers' success in Pittsburgh was no less than a republican victory over tyranny. Entitled "Peter Puddler and the Mill Boy," it equates the puddlers' cause with both the ideals of the American Revolution and the Union's campaign against slavery. A mill boy thrown out of work because of the puddlers' decision to fight the ironmasters asks Peter Puddler to justify the actions of the Vulcans:

Say, Peter, will you tell me why
You keep me idle day by day?
Not earn a penny that would buy
Some bread to keep the wolf at bay?

See, I am active, young and strong,
And want for bread: you are to blame,
For suff'ring I've endured so long.
. . . .
The rich and mighty of the land,
From whom our daily bread supplied,
They hold the power in their hand,
And if you are not satisfied
With terms that they may offer you
For Labor, sir, that must be done,
You must comply—what can you do?
. . . .
So honor them, yes, all you can,
For when in want they gave us bread.
The darkest days of sixty-one,
When traitors boasted of their power,
Their gold the rich did quickly loan,
Our country in her trying hour;
And now such noble men as they
We all must honor and obey!

In response, Peter Puddler relates the "history of Capital and Labor" that he has learned "from experience":

The rich provide our food, you said,
Their tyranny we should not foil,
My little friend, our daily bread,
We earn it dearly by our toil.
You say the rich men sent their gold,
'Twas but a speculation game.
My boy, now when the truth is told,
'Twas not for honor, but for gain.
I'll strike until my latest breath,
Against our wrongs, our rights to save,
I'd rather see you cold in death,
Than live to be a tyrant's slave.
The ground we break, and plow it deep;
The seed that we shall plant today,
My boy, the harvest you shall reap
When I am dead, and passed away.
Look yonder, see the banner wave—
It is the standard of the free!
Beneath it none shall be a slave,

> Nor will it shelter tyranny!
> We ever shall uphold our cause,
> Our rights as Sons of Liberty!
> We shall uphold our country's laws,
> And only ask equality![38]

The victory of the puddlers in their fight for "a fair day's wages for a fair day's work" strengthened the Sons of Vulcans but did not end the divisiveness that surfaced during the lockout. It was to some of these sources of fragmentation that David Harris, the outgoing president of the Vulcans, alluded when he spelled out the compelling reason for an amalgamation of all ironworkers. "We are aware there does exist strong and bitter antipathies between the mill trades growing out of failures on the part of one trade to support the other. . . . These . . . must be buried in oblivion if we ever expect to realize a complete emancipation from the domination of the monopolists." Altogether skirting the unresolved issue of race that had become manifest during the lockout, Harris invoked more Civil War rhetoric in his call for "emancipation":

> Let us not deceive ourselves. We are only a small detachment in the great army of ironworkers, . . . [and] we should not underrate the power of . . . wealth and the innumerable advantages the condition of society give capitalists over men who toil for bread. . . . A combined organization among the ironworkers is [therefore] just as essential to the achievement of the high aims of labor reform as was the organization and discipline of our armies necessary in waging the recent war against rebellion.[39]

The hopes of Harris, Bishop, and other advocates of amalgamation were fulfilled in 1876 when the Vulcans joined the Roll Hands and the Associated Brotherhood of Iron and Steel Heaters, Rollers, and Roughers in creating the AAISW. In announcing the merger, Bishop, the AAISW's first president, drew upon the most cherished principles of labor reform to explain the union's charge and to rally ironworkers to its cause. "We believe that labor is noble and holy, and we shall defend it and ourselves from degradation," he wrote to the metalworkers of the country. "We hope to . . . ultimately secure to each laborer the full reward of his toil. Fellow workmen, . . . be true to your principles of right and justice." By 1881 these principles of right and justice were officially extended to black workers, however grudgingly; having subjected black fellow workers to its own brand of racial degradation, the AAISW finally agreed, in theory, to defend them from the industrial degradation it so condemned.[40]

For labor reformers such as Bishop, the creation of a single ironworkers' union was but part of the larger task of amalgamation. And while many members of the AAISW remained committed to this endeavor, it was the Knights of Labor who moved most forcefully to answer Bishop's call.

Chapter 8

Toward a Wider Amalgamation:
The Knights of Labor

In the view of Pittsburgh's labor reformers, the chief issue in the ironmasters' lockout of 1874–75 involved more than preserving the Sons of Vulcan and maintaining the integrity of the puddlers' sliding scale. To be sure, labor reformers understood that the lockout represented a lethal threat to the Vulcans, which had spearheaded the workers' movement in Pittsburgh since the Civil War. The future of the union was manifestly at risk: the Association of Iron Manufacturers had declared "that the Boilers Union must and shall be fought to its death." Yet, if the Sons of Vulcan could survive the lockout and force the ironmasters to honor the base of the sliding scale, what Joseph Bishop called "the unjust demands of capital" would be dealt a setback. Indeed, Bishop and other labor leaders were certain that the movement for labor reform, derailed in the late 1860s when the Allegheny County Labor Reform party went down to ignominious defeat, would be given a significant boost by a puddlers' victory.

Ultimately, labor reformers thus recognized that at stake in the lockout was this question: Could the workers' movement, using a victory against the ironmasters as a springboard, begin to mobilize for a grand campaign to end wage slavery and redeem the Republic? As the *National Labor Tribune* commented, the puddlers "know and feel the great responsibility resting on them. . . . Amalgamation is a temporary expedient to bridge over the chasms created in society by a false industrial and commercial system. No permanent relief will come until the system itself be removed."[1]

While some leaders of the AAISW agreed with the *Tribune*'s assessment, others were less willing or able to see beyond the immediate concerns of their craft. Indeed, skilled workers often had only themselves in mind when, in the name of all labor, they organized or went on strike. The ironmasters' lockout of 1874–75, as we have seen, exposed some of the divisions among the skilled ironworkers, and a subsequent strike of puddlers' helpers pointed to the uneasy alliances between the skilled and less skilled that were to plague the AAISW perpetually. To improve these relationships, and thereby to build toward the solidarity required to transform the "false industrial and commercial system," labor reformers turned to the Knights of Labor.

The animating spirit of the Knights, the *Tribune* explained, was to "make all toilers stand on a level" so that "one man is no better than another." Thomas Armstrong recognized that the leveling spirit embedded in these words might astonish even those industrial craftsmen most committed to trade unionism. But he, his coeditor, John M. Davis, and the other labor reformers of Pittsburgh who led the Knights in the mid 1870s believed that they had located a common thread in the order's appeal to the less skilled and in the appeal to skilled workers of trade unions such as the AAISW.[2]

In describing the purpose of the AAISW, the *National Labor Tribune* observed that it was the union's intent to ensure its members' fundamental, customary rights. "The basis of the present Amalgamated Union is the conviction that there is a certain rate of wages which men should receive for their labor, [and] a certain degree of comfort and measure of happiness which they should enjoy regardless of the empirical and cruel law of supply and demand." The paper went on to emphasize that a social order predicated on the law of supply and demand worked against the well-being of all laborers—not only that of the skilled ironworkers of the AAISW—because the calculus of the market ignored the rights of all laborers. "Political economists may ridicule and disprove the soundness of the logic behind this [position], but they cannot root out the conviction of natural justice belonging to Labor."[3]

It was this conviction, labor reformers of Pittsburgh believed, that would bring together skilled and unskilled in a single amalgamation. "The competitive system of labor disregards all rules. . . . It compels [all] men to become industrial slaves . . . [and] has reduced such large numbers of intelligent men to want, that they have begun to inquire, 'is this competitive system just?' " The answer was a resounding "NO." A shared antipathy to the "unnatural" wage system and a shared determination against becoming wage slaves, then, would provide the raw materials out of which industrial craftsmen and their less skilled colleagues would forge a single, powerful weapon for the counterattack against organized capital. Though skilled workers and professional reformers such as Armstrong and Davis first codified the agenda for amalgamation, in the Pittsburgh district the movement owed its initial strength to the miners whose communities dotted the hillsides along the Monongahela.

The first wave of the miners' organizational initiatives crested in the winter of 1875–76. "Such was the excitement in the Pittsburgh district, . . . that a man must have been dull indeed not to know that some kind of secret organization was being organized, and very rapidly, too." Though the city's first assembly of Knights had been organized in 1873, the order gained little momentum until 1875, when Davis and Armstrong called attention to it in the *National Labor Tribune*. Davis formed the Knights' districtwide organization on 8 August. Called District Assembly 3, it included local assemblies of miners as well as those organized by cabinetmakers, engineers in coal mines, and ironworkers.[4]

The renaissance of union activities in the mines of Greater Pittsburgh not only provided an important impetus for the creation of District Assembly 3. The miners' organizing campaign, which brought at least twenty-nine local assemblies into the order by 1876, helped propel District 3 into a position that challenged District 1 in Philadelphia for leadership of the Knights—a challenge that arose from what the historian Norman Ware correctly identified as the "aggressive, rough, [and] politically minded" qualities of the Pittsburgh Knights. Of more immediate importance than any competition with Philadelphia Knights, though, was that thousands of miners were joining a movement dedicated to transforming the wage system. The order was particularly successful in Mifflin Township in the small river communities near what was then the pastoral settlement of Homestead. Hundreds of miners from Dravosburg, Green Springs, and Street's Run joined.[5]

Despite these successes, the question of how and when to mount a political offensive against the wage system remained a vexing problem. While labor leaders often had supported candidates affiliated with the established parties, they also had tried to fashion an independent labor-based politics. Yet the labor movement had been unable to sustain such efforts, and in the early 1870s it had turned away entirely from electoral politics. With the creation of a single ironworkers' union and the organizational successes of the Knights, however, labor leaders in Pittsburgh again began to consider launching a new political initiative.

The institutional groundwork for a new labor-based party was created in part by John M. Davis, coeditor of the *National Labor Tribune* and the master workman of District Assembly 3 of the Knights. In 1874 he organized the Junior Sons of '76, a secret association of labor reformers dedicated to an independent workers' party. The principal achievement of the Junior Sons, which never became a mass-based organization, was to arrange for a convention of national labor organizations that met in Tyrone, Pennsylvania, in December 1875. The convention adopted a platform that joined the legacy of greenback monetary reform codified by Edward Kellogg and Alexander Campbell with demands that would appeal more directly to urban laborers and miners. And while the convention urged all workers to forsake the established parties in an effort to preserve "republican institutions," the platform did not call for the creation of an independent workers' party. Instead the delegates decided to meet in Pittsburgh in April 1876 to try again to create a "grand workingmen's Union."[6]

In the months immediately following the convention in Tyrone, the long depression reached new depths in the Pittsburgh district and the city became the locus of considerable labor agitation. The socialists P. J. McGuire and Otto Weydemeyer spoke to large gatherings in January, and in February, Davis convened a mass assembly of four thousand workers that created a Labor Council whose charge was to encourage a concerted electoral effort. However, the assembly failed to reach a consensus on the issue of independent politics.[7]

The national labor convention that met in Pittsburgh in 1876 also was divided on the issue of political action. The delegates ultimately decided that workers should use "the existing political parties . . . [as] the vehicle for the attainment of their ends . . . [until] thorough education and discipline is obtained." To achieve the requisite organization, the convention urged workers to continue their trade union initiatives. The *National Labor Tribune*, which had asserted that the Pittsburgh convention would begin rewriting the Declaration of Independence according to the "gospel of labor," understated the divisions that had emerged. Indeed, it went so far as to call the convention the most successful labor congress in American history. Clearly, if was not.[8]

The convention brought most of Pittsburgh's labor leaders together, but even in the wake of their recent trade union successes, they could not agree on a political agenda. The re-creation of an independent workers' party was thus left until the onset of more favorable circumstances—a time when, the *Tribune* suggested, workers would be eager for politics. Until such an "emergency" arose, most labor activists in the Pittsburgh district decided that an effort to nominate workers in the Republican and Democratic primaries was the best course.[9]

The immediate results of the decision were disappointing, for labor failed to nominate any of its candidates in the June primaries. Hence Thomas Armstrong, John M. Davis, John McLuckie, and Andrew Burtt, among other Pittsburgh labor leaders, chose to affiliate with the national Greenback party.[10]

The activists were attracted to the greenback banner for three reasons. First, the inflation promised by greenback monetary proposals offered some relief from the long depression. Second, by supporting the greenback cause, labor activists hoped to nurture an alliance with the Western farmers who were outspoken advocates of greenbackism. And third, despite the limited appeal that greenbackism offered to urban workers, labor leaders understood that it was the most credible oppositional set of economic doctrines in which they could anchor a critique of the emerging corporate order.

But the labor leaders of Pittsburgh also understood that greenbackism would not solve labor's problems and that some persons, notably small businessmen, were drawn to monetary reform only to gain "the same power to get rich fast out of our labor as the millionaires now possess." The greenbackers' proposals to abolish the national banking system and to lower interest rates by issuing greenbacks and "interconvertible" government bonds "ought to prevail," said the *National Labor Tribune*. However, it qualified its endorsement: "Plenty of greenbacks will not eradicate the evils which create the constant conflict between capital and labor."[11]

From the outset, then, the alliance of the labor activists of Pittsburgh with the national Greenback party was tentative. It thus was small wonder that Peter Cooper, the Greenback party candidate for president in 1876, received only 769 of the 48,872 votes cast—30,000 by workers—in Allegheny County. Nor was it surprising that John McLuckie, the only worker to run on its ticket in the county, was overwhelmed in his bid for a seat in the state legislature. The *Tribune*, however, called the results sickening and charged that the workers of Pittsburgh were slaves of the established parties. "Would it not be a strange sight to see a slave forge a chain to his feet? Yet what else did millions of labor voters do the other day? And they danced as they did it. Independence? Ha-ha! We must wait until fools become wise men."

The confusion of the *National Labor Tribune*—urging workers to eschew an independent party, then soliciting support for one, criticizing Cooper and the greenbackers, then asking workers to support them—reflected a broader frustration that was to peak in the Pittsburgh district in 1877. When the frustration exploded, and the "emergency" came, however, the *Tribune* and the activists associated with it were able to put aside their hesitations about independent political action and their criticisms of Pittsburgh laborers. The activists and laborers went to work together.

They did so in the hopes of building what the *Tribune* called a grand future. Success required "the courage of Spartans, and the devotion of Romans." The grand question before the workers of Pittsburgh was, "Is this generation equal to the tasks?" If not, the paper concluded on the eve of the last great effort of Pittsburgh's labor reformers to redeem the republic, "then it falls to the next."[12]

As the hundredth anniversary of the Declaration of Independence approached, and as the *National Labor Tribune* surveyed the condition of American labor from week to week, it often reflected on the fate of the republican heritage. "We are now in a condition very similar to what our condition was just prior to 1776. Our struggle was then for political independence. It was supposed, and believed, that if the colonies became politically independent, that all evils incident to political society could be avoided. But a century of political independence has shown us that that is one thing, [and] that industrial independence is quite another." In fact, workers were a long way indeed from being independent: they were "in industrial slavery."[13]

The bondage of the industrial era was characterized by a growing concentration of economic power. "The political 'one man power' of a century ago which we overturned is followed by a 'one man power' in our industries, . . . As this power centers in a few, the masses lose a corresponding power over their own actions, and become dependent on the will and pleasure of a few lords." While such circumstances obtained in all industries, the owners of mines, metalworks, and above all railroads posed the most serious threat to the republican aspirations of American laborers. The inevitable result, the *National Labor Tribune* noted in May 1875, was a grand confrontation with the wage system. "Just when or how the conflict will come about that will rock the whole nation to its center, no man can tell, but that it is coming we do not doubt." Armstrong was hopeful that labor would free itself and thereby redeem the republic: "Against these aggregating ills we will soon combine, and arise and strike as becomes freemen" to make "another revolution."[14]

The conflict came in July 1877, when two weeks of strikes initiated by railroad workers turned into the Great Labor Uprising, a furious rebellion against the rule of capital that began in Martinsburg, West Virginia, and spread along the major rail lines from Pennsylvania to California. Laborers in virtually all trades joined the railroad men in work stoppages and mass demonstrations, street fights against the National Guard and police, and the destruction of property owned by the railroads. More than one hundred people were killed, nearly all of them by state and federal troops dispatched to quell the disturbances. To Thomas Armstrong and other labor leaders of Pittsburgh, the uprising was a tragedy. However, it also was the "emergency" that might well "bring the labor vote together."[15]

In Pittsburgh, the hub of the Pennsylvania Railroad and its western branches, the most violent of all the disturbances began on 19 July when railroad workers refused to operate the Pennsylvania's notorious doubleheaders, trains that were twice the regular size but whose work force had been cut. Almost immediately, the railroad men were joined by miners and other workers, who gathered on the tracks of prevent trains from leaving the city. On 21 July thousands more miners, iron- and steelworkers, less skilled laborers, and women and children assembled near the depot at Twenty-Eighth Street. There a division of the National Guard comprised of men from Philadelphia was preparing to clear the tracks. This was accomplished by charging the crowd with bayonets and firing into it. At least twenty Pittsburghers were killed; about thirty were badly wounded.[16]

As the news of the killings spread, Pittsburgh "went mad." More workers rushed to the scene, forced the guardsmen to retreat to the railroad roundhouse, and then began a siege. The crowd set fire to thirty-nine buildings owned by the Pennsylvania Railroad, destroyed more than a hundred locomotives and twelve hundred freight cars, and engaged in wholesale looting. The following day, twenty more Pittsburghers were killed when a crowd clashed with the guardsmen as they marched from the roundhouse down Penn Avenue. Sobered by the bloodshed, the city began to settle down by 23 July. Yet the Roundhouse Riot, as it came to be known, left a searing mark upon the collective memory of Pittsburgh's workers—and of their employers.[17]

To the latter, the disturbances were "a communistic dance of death and destruction" and a palpable reminder that the Paris Commune might yet come to the United States. Indeed, for industrialists and their supporters the uprisings confirmed the belief not only that workers posed a threat to industrial efficiency but also that their organizations had to be eliminated once and for all. And unless they were, a committee of Pennsylvania legislators concluded, "more serious troubles than any that have yet occurred" would be the result. The legislators thus counseled all employers to embark upon a vigorous program of antiunion initiatives that would "completely undermine and destroy" labor organizations and the influence of the "demagogues" who led them.[18]

Yet to the workers of the Pittsburgh district, the disturbances became a symbol of and an opportunity for a broader solidarity that might include other groups in the city. Thus the uprising that began as a strike against the Pennsylvania Railroad and its policies of discriminatory freight rates, low wages, doubleheaders, and antiunionism took on qualities that made it resemble the revolt of an entire community. The Pennsylvania legislators who investigated it commented: "From the first commencement of the strike, the strikers had the active sympathy of a large portion of the people of Pittsburgh." Even a hostile businessman conceded that "men of respectability and wealth openly came out in sympathy with the strikers and the mob."[19]

No residents of the Pittsburgh area, however, surpassed miners and factory workers in giving substance to such sentiments. The state investigatory committee concluded that these men considered "the cause of the railroad men their cause, . . . and they were not only willing but anxious to make a common fight against the corporations." Hundreds of armed miners from the Monongahela collieries chartered a boat to Pittsburgh so that they could protect the people from the guardsmen. Indeed, the miners were so incensed that "they would like to have the strike assume the shape of a general war against all branches of business." Hundreds of miners organized parades, calling upon others to join in the march to Pittsburgh.[20]

Among others who set out for the city were scores of striking metal-workers from the National Tube Works in McKeesport. On the way the strikers stopped at the Edgar Thomson Steel Works in Braddock and "compelled a general suspension" of work there. Some of the workers from Andrew Carnegie's prized metalworks joined the march, which went on to close other mills along the Monongahela. And at Benjamin Franklin Jones's American Iron Works, hundreds of mill hands also used the trainmens' strike as a starting point to register their grievances. The mill hands walked away from their jobs, causing operations to shut down and putting two thousand men, many of them skilled puddlers and finishers, out of work. But in word and deed even the most skilled laborers made it known that they were with the less skilled railroad men and the other striking workers. Skilled metal- and glassworkers, carpenters, and engineers were among those arrested for "rioting." And at least three of the hundreds of puddlers who confronted the guardsmen were killed in the uprising.[21]

The solidarity of the skilled and less skilled also was attested to by the Committee of Safety organized by city officials. The committee, which included labor activists such as Thomas Armstrong, John M. Davis, Joseph Bishop, and Andrew Burtt, maintained that its efforts were not directed against the strikers. Rather, its charge was to prevent the introduction of more troops by helping to restore order.[22]

True, the skilled saw themselves as distinct "from thieves and similar classes of the population," who, according to the Committee of Safety, were the main perpetrators of "vandalism." But the skilled made no effort to distance themselves from the strike of the trainmen or from those staged by other workers. The *National Labor Tribune* declared that the Pennsylvania Railroad bore the "awful responsibility . . . for the disorder, the outrages, the murders, the incendiarism," and the prevailing "condition of affairs bordering upon anarchy." It went on to "indict" the state as the Pennsylvania Railroad's coconspirator, an indictment brought on grounds that went beyond the joint efforts of state authorities and businessmen to break the strike. It was brought because the state had forsaken the "republic" in favor of the interests of "moneyed capital" and because the rule of law had become an instrument of oppression. In its assessment of the uprising, the *Tribune* thus observed, "The commission of crimes against society are not always embodied in the criminal code."[23]

It was the *Tribune* that captured the essential meaning of the uprising for so many of Pittsburgh's workers: that the limits on what those in power can do—limits that accounted for the mutual obligations of workers, their employers, and the government—had been abrogated and that the employers and the government were the responsible parties. An unidentified worker blamed "the railroad officers and capitalists . . . for all this damage and expense, and for murdering and wounding hundreds of our people."[24]

That the underlying causes of the uprising and its brutal results were a violation of accepted norms points to the deep conflicts that accompanied America's transition to industrial capitalism. However, to thousands of Pittsburghers who lived through the Great Uprising and therefore were not blessed with twenty-twenty hindsight, the disturbances pointed to a transgression, not a transition. Labor leaders who had harbored doubts about the chances of making a "complete, radical [and] entire change" thus saw the troubles as a new opportunity for challenging the wage system. Indeed, the Great Uprising demonstrated that the social contract that bound together workers with employers and government was on the verge of rupture. Though Pittsburgh workers did not employ such language, their words and actions suggested that the implicit understandings that linked them with those who wielded greater economic and political power had been violated by the events of July.[25]

Among those understandings was the government's responsibility to maintain peace and order by settling disputes in a manner that is considered fair. But the government not only failed to act fairly. In the eyes of many Pittsburghers, it had also misused the instruments of violence against its own subjects. To the residents of the Iron City, such misuse constituted an egregious violation of the state's obligation to ensure peace and provide for the security of everyone.[26]

The events of July 1877 in Pittsburgh magnified with brilliant clarity the workers' sense that their way of life, built upon the thought that they were the first citizens of the community, was on the brink of extinction. In spectacular fashion the Great Uprising called into question fundamental agreements regarding political authority and social and material justice. Pittsburgh's vengeful response to the excesses of the Pennsylvania Railroad and its partner, the government, therefore constituted an expression of moral outrage against efforts to rewrite the social contract in what seemed to be an alien language.

Indeed, in arguing that government officials and businessmen were responsible for the disturbances in Pittsburgh, the *National Labor Tribune* suggested that its views were grounded upon a set of values that was at odds with the emerging order. Preeminent were those values which had to do with labor and its place in society. The uprising demonstrated that labor, which produced all social wealth, did not occupy a position in society commensurate with this most important of all callings. Because labor was "a man's all, his flesh and bones and blood and muscle—his very soul," it should have "a value beyond the dollars and cents it is worth when weighed in the balance . . . of the capitalist."

The *Tribune* and its audience understood, however, that the political economy that provided the undergirding for the wage system took the opposite view. The result, according to the newspaper, was twofold. First, the creation of "an impassable lake of unfathomable depth, breadth and length . . . between the toiling millions and those whom special legislation has enriched by their supineness or corruption." And second, the undermining of "the great principle . . . that man, by reason of his position as muscular toiler, was still a worthy member of society, to be honored and respected as of the true nobility."[27]

A workers' poem entitled "The Laborers' Strike" made some of the same points and drew similar connections between the uprising and key thoughts that had animated the workers' movement in Pittsburgh since the 1860s.

> While unprotected labor cries,
> From a thousand points we hear
> The men oppressed now striking out
> With voices loud and clear.
> The railroad men, and miners too
> 'Tis all the point we have in view,
> To get our rights . . .
> And have our jobs secure.[28]

Like the *National Labor Tribune*, the unknown author of this poem held that government should "protect" labor: "We earnestly desire that government with us agree." And like the poem, the *Tribune*'s assessment of the Great Uprising and its causes also summed up a decade's worth of experience and thought in the lives of thousands of workers. Since the late 1860s workers in Greater Pittsburgh had struggled to make the principles of labor reform the principles of an American republic, thereby protecting it from the "brutes"—as the anonymous poem had put it—allied with capital.

The most important lesson of July, however, was that workers had not been successful in their project. That they continued to harbor such aspirations was attested to not merely by "The Laborers' Strike" and the *Tribune* but by the actions of thousands of workers themselves. As James Campbell, a leading glassworker, put it, "the riot did much to solidify and organize the workingmen." Indeed, the disturbances provided the immediate impetus for the organization of local assemblies of window glass cutters, gatherers, and blowers. Together these assemblies took the crucial step toward the amalgamation of all window glass workers by forming District Assembly 8 of the Knights of Labor.[29]

Out of the uprising and its suppression also came a heightened appreciation for political action as a way to redeem the Republic. "There must be some other path found to lead the working people than that lit up by the lurid glare of the incendiary torch." The path envisioned by the labor leaders of Pittsburgh had two familiar tracks. One was to continue to

build labor's power through workers' unions. The other was summarized by the headline above the *National Labor Tribune*'s story on the
uprising: "The Ballot Our Remedy; The Bullet Our Wreck." A week later
workers began to translate the mass discontent expressed by the uprising into a political insurgency aimed at "complete, radical, entire
change."[30]

None was so forceful in the renewed effort to elevate labor to its
rightful position of "nobility" than members of the Noble and Holy Order
of the Knights of Labor. On 31 July, just three days after Governor John F.
Hartranft himself entered the city with nine thousand troops to break the
trainmens' blockade and end the railroad strike, leading Knights called an
organizational meeting in the worker-dominated forty-fifth state senato-
rial district that embraced the collieries, glass houses, and iron and steel
mills of the city's South Side. Led by a glassworker, A. C. Robertson, who
was an associate of the labor reformer Andrew Burtt, the South Side
workers christened their new organization the Greenback-Labor party
(GLP) and urged their colleagues throughout the region to mount campaigns for the fall elections.[31]

By mid-August, the initiative begun on the South Side had "grown
from a puny child to the proportions of an athlete," and workers canvassed in the city and up the Monongahela in preparation for a county
convention called for early September. The purpose of the convention
was to nominate candidates "known to be loyal to the wage worker" and
to adopt a platform that would "protect the people against the ravages of
monopolies."[32]

The convention and the politics that issued immediately from it reflected both the strengths and the weaknesses of the Pittsburgh labor
movement that were to remain with it into the early 1880s. On the one
hand, the leaders of the GLP were able to translate the grievances expressed during the railroad uprising into a political program that appealed to large numbers of workers and thus threatened the dominance
of the established parties. Yet, as the returns of the 1877 campaign were
to demonstrate, many wage earners in the Pittsburgh district declined to
forsake traditional political ties. Moreover, the campaign underscored
the great difficulty labor activists had in trying to forge a solidarity with
those critics of the emerging order who saw the redemption of American
society in monetary reform. Indeed, the allegiance of agricultural workers to monetary reform, coupled with labor's insistence that its concerns
could not be answered by mere greenbackism, made it difficult to launch
a political insurgency aimed at success on the state and national level.[33]

That workers affiliated with the Allegheny County GLP harbored
such aspirations and looked to an alliance with agrarian laborers was
shown above all by the choice of the party's name. As the *National Labor
Tribune* had pointed out during the presidential election of 1876, the

greenback cause did "not go to the bottom" of the issues before urban laborers. Yet labor leaders in Greater Pittsburgh understood that legislative redress in Harrisburg and Washington depended on close cooperation with the farmers of Pennsylvania, whose efforts to build an independent political party also were spurred by the railroad uprisings. The addition of the appellation *Greenback* to the name of the workers' party in the Pittsburgh area therefore was made in the hope of creating a coalition of farmers and urban workers. From the outset, however, the GLP in Allegheny County saw itself as a labor party.[34]

Locally the party was above all the political arm of the Knights of Labor. To be sure, leading members of the AAISW lent their support to the GLP and ran for office under its banner. And from 1877 through 1882, the party demonstrated consistent electoral strength in the city wards and outlying townships and boroughs dominated by metalworkers. But professional activists such as John M. Davis and Thomas Armstrong of District Assembly 3 of the Knights, together with the leading miners of District Assembly 9 and the leading glassworkers of District Assembly 8, provided the driving force behind the GLP.[35]

The first chairman of the party's executive committee, for example, was John Flannigan, who belonged to a local assembly in District 3 and went on to become its master workman in 1880. John McBroom, one of the party's vice presidents, served as the master workman of District 9. And Armstrong, Robertson, and some other leading glassworkers were elected to various positions at the party's first convention. Master workmen and other prominent Knights from local assemblies in Allegheny County constituted the majority of the 156 delegates who attended the first GLP convention. Among them was Frank M. Gessner, a glassworker who became master workman of Local Assembly 1785 in Homestead and, later, secretary of the Window Glass Workers' Association (Local Assembly 300). Benjamin R. Culbertson, a carpenter who was an agent for the *National Labor Tribune* and became a leading politician in Homestead in the 1880s, also was a delegate.[36]

The platform adopted by the first convention of the Allegheny County GLP, which was retained essentially intact into the early 1880s, called upon "all patriotic men to unite in the movement for industrial prosperity and financial reform." These goals could be reached at the national level through the adoption of greenback currency proposals and at the state level through enactment of legislation that would protect the rights of workers. The legislation would, among other things, repeal the anticonspiracy statute, abolish the "truck" system of payment practiced in Monongahela collieries, enforce the eight-hour working day, and prohibit employers from threatening workers who voted for a labor party.[37]

The active governmental role envisioned by labor-greenbackers in the Pittsburgh district suggests that many Knights saw the redemption of society from wage slavery not only as a project to improve their lot but also as a mission for the state. Indeed, the thrust of the political insurgency championed by the labor-greenbackers was to redeem the state. This is not to deny the appeal of self-help efforts such as worker-owned stores and factories, which many "cooperators" believed should be established without state aid. However, in light of the political agenda of Pittsburgh's Knights, the proposition that the labor movement in the Gilded Age did not adequately appreciate the role of the state is in need of some revision.[38]

Pittsburgh's labor leaders set out to solidify ties with their colleagues from Philadelphia immediately after the Allegheny County convention. Leading Knights from Pittsburgh and Philadelphia put aside their rivalry and canvassed in Harrisburg. The result was the creation of the Pennsylvania United Labor party and the nomination of several candidates for statewide office, including John M. Davis for auditor general and James L. Wright, a prominent Knight from Philadelphia, for state treasurer. The party implored workers to reject their "most abject slavery" by abandoning the Republicans and Democrats.[39]

The convention of the Pennsylvania Greenback party, which followed the conclave of labor-greenbackers, was a disappointment to many of the labor activists who had convened in Harrisburg, for the platform spoke almost exclusively to the currency problem, and the greenbackers refused to endorse the United Labor party's nomination of Davis for auditor general. Instead they chose James E. Emerson, a manufacturer from Beaver Falls who rejected labor's proposals for any relief other than that promised by currency reform. Moreover, the greenbackers chose an iron manufacturer, Frank P. Dewees of Pottsville, as chairman of their party.[40]

The greenbackers did nonetheless make certain overtures to organized labor. Terrence Powderly and Uriah Stephens, the leading Knights in Eastern Pennsylvania, and A. C. Robertson, the glassworker from Pittsburgh, served on the central committee of what Dewees labeled the United Greenback-Labor party of Pennsylvania. The party, however, existed principally in name, since urban and agrarian workers across the state formed countywide organizations whose efforts were in no way coordinated.[41]

Yet with each of the three greenback candidates for state office receiving about fifty-three thousand votes, or 10 percent of the total, the future of a third party in Pennsylvania seemed brighter than ever. The Pennsylvania Greenback party did particularly well in Allegheny County: candidates nominated by the county party carried nine wards on the city's South Side, three wards in Allegheny City, Braddock, and five other boroughs, and eight townships in addition to Mifflin. Thus the greatest successes came in those communities where miners and metal- and glassworkers predominated, and precisely where they had created local assemblies of the Knights of Labor.[42]

In assessing the 1877 election returns, the leaders of the Allegheny County GLP had reason for a certain degree of optimism. With little time to organize their effort, and in spite of a failure to mount an effective statewide campaign, the labor leaders of the Pittsburgh district were able to transform the bullets fired in the Great Uprising of July into almost nine thousand ballots. "Under the circumstances, we have done nobly," said the *National Labor Tribune*. "But . . . we must go to work at once. We must perfect our movement."[43]

The *Tribune*'s call to build on the modest successes of 1877 was pursued by the Allegheny County GLP in three directions in 1878. First, its leaders joined in the effort to create a national party of labor and currency reformers that crystallized in February at the first convention of the National Greenback-Labor party. Second, along with other worker-dominated county organizations, it tried to win control of what, after the National GLP convention, was called the National Greenback-Labor party of Pennsylvania. And third, it mounted a strong campaign in early 1878 to win ward and city offices.[44]

The 1878 spring election campaign, which saw the Pittsburgh Trades Assembly help organize greenback-labor clubs in virtually every worker-dominated section of the city and county, brought more successes to the party. Six of its candidates were elected to the city council, and a number of its nominees for ward offices such as constable, school boardsman, and elections inspector also were victorious. The successes in Allegheny County, together with the victory of Terrence Powderly in the Scranton mayoralty race, seemed to augur well for organized labor at the 1878 convention of the state National Greenback-Labor party. However, Powderly was defeated in his bid to chair the convention, and Thomas Armstrong lost the party's gubernatorial nomination to Samuel Mason, an attorney. The victory of Mason, a monetary reformer with no ties to the labor movement, came close to destroying the party's tenuous fusion of labor activists and greenbackers.[45]

Though labor and currency reformers had their differences in state politics, their uneasy alliance in the National Greenback-Labor party registered some success in the fall elections of 1878. More than one million votes were cast for "National" candidates, and fifteen congressional candidates who ran under its banner were elected. In Pennsylvania, Mason received about 12 percent of the vote, while the vote for the party's congressional candidates exceeded 14 percent of the total. And in Allegheny County, where labor leaders mounted a vigorous campaign despite their reservations about Mason, the greenback-labor vote approached eight thousand—the largest county total in the state. Among the party's most ardent supporters, again, were the steelworkers of Braddock and the miners of Mifflin Township, who organized a "Thad Stevens Greenback-Labor Club."[46]

Despite the party's impressive gains over the 1877 returns, large numbers of urban workers remained unwilling to leave the established parties. The party's eight thousand votes in Allegheny County, for example, represented only 18 percent of the total. And in Philadelphia County, the greenback-labor ticket drew under 4 percent.

By late 1878, then, labor leaders in Pittsburgh understood that the immediate future of a labor-based politics was, once again, cloudy. In what was becoming a familiar refrain, the *National Labor Tribune* concluded that electoral politics should give way to union building as the best means of enhancing labor's power. Accordingly, labor politics in greater Pittsburgh again shifted into low gear. The promised land of industrial independence remained an elusive goal.[47]

Chapter 9

Mill Owners and Machine Politicians on the Offensive

ALTHOUGH LABOR ACTIVISTS fell short of fashioning a successful electoral insurgency in the late 1870s, business leaders and mainstream politicians remained worried about the growing power of workers at the ballot box—and in the streets. Businessmen and government officials had been deeply disturbed by the implications of the 1877 uprising. The committee of Pennsylvania legislators that investigated the disturbances concluded that "more serious troubles" were certain unless decisive action was taken and counseled a program of antiunion initiatives at work. It also concluded that a military force more reliable than the state militia had proved during the 1877 disturbances was an absolute necessity. Governor Hartranft agreed: he reorganized the militia, weeded out commanders and divisions that might prove sympathetic to workers, and increased expenditures for better weapons and armories. Also, a series of legislative acts between 1878 and 1881 completely overhauled the structure of the Pennsylvania militia. The result was a well-disciplined and well-trained cadre that, over the next forty years, remained an ardent supporter of corporate rule.[1]

The efforts aimed at strengthening the military arm of government to prevent a recurrence of the events of July 1877 arose from the recognition that the disturbances had an undeniably political dimension. Even in Pittsburgh, where the daily press usually was sympathetic to labor, one newspaper joined the call for an invigorated military force capable of containing civil disturbances. Indeed, some opponents of labor pointed to the Great Uprising as evidence that in America, democracy had gone too far and that workers should not be permitted to vote. The *Indianapolis News*, for example, held that "if workingmen had no vote they might be more amenable to the teachings of the times." Senator George A. Vest of Missouri saw in universal suffrage "a standing menace to all stable and good governments" and a "twin-sister" of the Paris Commune. The *Nation* expressed similar views: universal suffrage "imparts an air of menace to many of the things civilized men hold most dear." To check future threats to the security of the Republic, the magazine suggested an increase of twenty-five thousand men in the army.[2]

The editorial comments of the *Nation*, the bulwark of liberalism in the late nineteenth century, draw attention to Max Weber's observation that "the decisive means for politics is violence." The *National Labor Tribune*, for its part, had itself remarked that the July disturbances proved as much: although the military arm of government was poorly organized and not entirely reliable, it was strong enough to rule out any possibility of restructuring society by force. To those who sided with capital, how-ever, it remained important to further augment the coercive power of the state; if the necessity of using that power were not minimized, the likely result would be an even greater crisis of authority.[3]

Thus, Pittsburgh businessmen were among the leaders of the success-ful effort in the General Assembly to "modernize" the Pennsylvania militia. But even before the July disturbances, businessmen had created a chamber of commerce and fashioned it into an influential voice for law and order. In this role, and for fear that Miles Humphries, a former puddler, would be elected, the chamber had thrown massive support in the spring mayoralty election to the Democrat, Robert Liddell. Thanks largely to its effort on his behalf, Liddell defeated Humphries, a Republi-can with close ties to the labor movement and to Thomas Armstrong and the *Tribune* in particular.[4]

While Armstrong attributed his friend's defeat to "patronage" and the "desertion of some workingmen," Liddell had impressive electoral cre-dentials: he was an English-born Protestant sympathetic to the cause of Irish independence and an officer in a brewery that operated in a workers' district. Liddell also enjoyed a reputation as one of the city's "very best citizens." Thus he was able to draw considerable support from Protestant and Catholic workers, as well as from respectable businessmen. Indeed, his ability to translate his broad associations into victory foreshadowed a troubled future for the cause of independent labor politics.

That Humphries, the former president of the puddlers' union, had again run as a Republican was even more ominous: by 1877, the local Republican party was in the hands of professional politicians who main-tained intimate ties with the business community and helped operate the corrupt statewide machine of Senator Matthew Stanley Quay. While not yet in complete control of civic affairs, Christopher L. Magee, the city treasurer, was well on his way toward dominance. The chief lieutenant of State Treasurer Robert W. Mackey, himself a banker and the owner of the influential *Pittsburgh Commercial*, Magee had been overwhelmingly elected chairmain of the Allegheny County Republican party in 1874. In this position he joined Mackey and his maternal uncle, Councilman Thomas Steel—who managed the Pittsburgh City Council—in a power-ful municipal triumvirate.[5]

Humphries was not, however, the first politician to emerge from the workers' movement and to marry his electoral career to the rising fortunes of this trio. William C. McCarthy, elected mayor in 1866 with the crucially important backing of labor reform leaders and mill workers, decided to return to mayoral politics in 1874, this time, however, as an acknowledged member of the inner ring. McCarthy won the Republican primary, the general election, and a subsequent series of heated disputes over its legality. When he finally assumed office on 1 Feburary 1875, among the first to congratulate him publicly was none other than Christopher L. Magee. Their handshake signaled that Magee and his allies had built close ties not only with the business community, but with organized labor as well. And when Miles Humphries ran for mayor in 1881 with the full backing of Magee, who was by then in command of the city machine, the cozy relationship of labor, business, and the Republican party seemed to have been consummated.[6]

Magee did not forge this relationship alone; it was, however, his leadership that made it work. And it was his determination to succeed, to seize all opportunities for advancement, that carried him to the highest echelons of power within the national Republican party—and to the pinnacles of personal wealth in Gilded Age America. Magee began his political career as a teenage municipal clerk. By 1869, when he was only twenty-one, his uncle had made him cashier of the city treasury. Two years later he was elected city treasurer. He resigned from office after two terms with a keen understanding of how the strategic handling of city funds, utility franchises, and construction contracts could win him a private fortune and the means to ensure it: the devotion of bankers and businessmen. Magee traveled to Philadelphia and New York to study the operation of political machines in those cities. On his return he remarked to a friend that in Pittsburgh a political ring "could be made as safe as a bank."[7]

Magee's optimism proved well founded. He perfected a ward-level political organization that penetrated virtually all the places of work and leisure in Pittsburgh and throughout Allegheny County. In partnership with William Flinn, the self-made owner of a large construction company who in 1882 was elected chairman of the city Republican party, Magee dispensed thousands of patronage appointments. The ability of these two to control jobs in the private sector by virtue of the selective awarding of govenment construction and utility contracts generated even more political clout. It also generated astonishing individual wealth. Flinn's company won most city construction contracts; coupled with Magee's wide-ranging investments and ventures in street railways, real estate, and electricity, their joint holdings represented $16 million in assets by the end of the century.

Magee himself operated the Duquesne Traction Company, the largest transportation line in the city, published the *Pittsburgh Times*, the leading morning daily, and had vast interests in banks and natural gas and insurance companies. Flinn's personal wealth was even greater. Magee delivered transportation franchises to his own company and construction contracts to Flinn's. As Lincoln Steffens wrote in his famous portrait of Pittsburgh under Magee's stewardship, his "idea was not to corrupt the city government, but to be it; not to hire votes in councils, but to own councilmen." The Magee-Flinn ring operated with startling efficiency, and, Steffens believed, it operated within the law. "I know of nothing like it in any other city. Tammany in comparison is a plaything."[8]

Both Magee and Flinn served in the Pennsylvania legislature, and both were powerful forces in the state and national Republican party; Magee, in fact, attained national power even before he delivered the Pennsylvania delegation at the 1888 Republican presidential convention to Benjamin Harrison. But in the city and county, both men understood the importance of rising above partisan politics as a guarantee to continued success. Indeed, at one time, almost one-fourth of the municipal workers who owed their employment to the Magee-Flinn ring were registered Democrats. Magee and Flinn could count on these appointees and their friends to elect a subservient Democrat if a "dangerous" Republican challenged the ring. To Magee and Flinn, politics was a job, and decidedly not a means to redeem the Republic. Steffens summed up the purpose of their endeavors this way: "Magee wanted power, Flinn wealth. Each got both these things; but Magee spent his wealth for more power, and Flinn spent his power for more wealth."[9]

In the eyes of these two men, then, there was no need for social transformation: after all, both had begun their careers in relative poverty and ended up as quasi patricians with their names listed in the social register. Their story embodies the myth of the self-made man as much as that of Andrew Carnegie, a close friend of Magee: "Rose from Clerk to Millionaire by Untiring Energy," was how the *Pittsburgh Leader* described Magee's life in the headline over his obituary. Flinn, known for his brusque manner, nevertheless won similar encomiums. Born in 1851 in Manchester, England, to Irish immigrants, Flinn possessed none of the familial connections that gained Magee his entry into politics. His rise, therefore, was perhaps all the more remarkable: after immigrating to America as a young boy, he began work as an apprentice brass finisher and gas and steam fitter. By the time he was 19, Flinn was running his father's small contracting business; by the age of 26, he was a Republican ward leader, and at 27 he was elected to the state house of representatives.

Throughout their careers, Magee and Flinn remained consummate professionals and embodied the alliance of business and politics that Mark Twain and Charles Dudley Warner explored in the novel that gave its title to the era. In a certain sense this alliance signaled a shift in

national politics from the genuine concerns of some Reconstruction Era
Republicans to a new agenda, one that placed a greater emphasis on the
comfortable understandings among all maintstream politicians, Democrats and Republicans alike, who were determined to expand their
spheres of influence rather than pursue any set of principles. However,
the politics of the time amounted to more than the mere triumph of the
professional politician over "the politics of ideology," more than the rise
of bureaucrats who succeeded in erecting municipal infrastructures and
exerting better administrative control over the cities of America. As the
historian Joel Tarr has suggested, Magee and Flinn did succeed in these
realms; but they also possessed an ideology and harbored principles—
namely, that entrepreneurship and politics are partners. Moreover, in
their view the politics of labor reform had no place in municipal, state, or
national affairs.[10]

Thus Magee and Flinn were able to find ready allies, only too happy
to donate monetary support, in the larger community of businessmen
and railroad officials. Indeed, Magee, himself the agent of the Pennsylvania Railroad, and Flinn were among the nation's principal executors of
the partnership between businessmen and the major political parties.

> The Pennsylvania Railroad was in the [Magee-Flinn] system from the start,
> and, as the other [rail]roads came in and found the city government bought
> up by those before them, they purchased their rights of way by outbribing
> the older roads, then joined the ring to acquire more rights for themselves
> and to keep belated rivals out. As corporations multiplied and capital
> branched out, corruption increased naturally, but the notable characteristic of
> the "Pittsburg[h] plan" of misgovernment was that it was not a haphazard
> growth, but a deliberate, intelligent organization. It was conceived in one
> mind, built up by one will, and this master spirit ruled . . . the whole town—
> financial, commercial, and political.[11]

The Pittsburgh of Christopher Magee and William Flinn was thus the
Pittsburgh of the Pennsylvania Railroad. Though the city had risen up
against the Pennsylvania in 1877, the railroad reclaimed its domain in
partnership not only with the state and national government but also
with municipal authorities. The Magee-Flinn ring, "credited with the
suppression of disorder" in Pittsburgh, was an instrument of rational,
corporate rule.[12]

Over and above the support of businessmen—and indeed one reason why they so readily offered it—was another key to the success of the
ring: Magee, in particular, learned how to present the cause of his machine to Pittsburgh's workers as the cause of Pittsburgh's workers. To be
sure, the presentation included the promise of patronage to loyalists and
the issuance of polite threats to opponents that have been a trademark of
urban politicians for a century. But Magee and his lieutenants also suc-

ceeded in selling their cause to labor on another, and more important, basis. At work, in halls where unions and fraternal orders met, at neighborhood baseball parks, in saloons, theaters, boat clubs, and volunteer fire departments, representatives of the ring convinced thousands of Pittsburgh workers that the machine was not an alien interest but truly theirs. Precisely how the Magee-Flinn ring functioned and how it succeeded in equating its cause with the cause of labor, are problems that await further study. One thing is certain: controlling patronage jobs in the city fire department, which was an important part of plebeian life in Pittsburgh, was a crucial element in the popularity of Magee and Flinn among working Pittsburghers.[13]

While the *National Labor Tribune* had always been critical of the ring, it began to sound more alarming notes in the late 1870s, in the wake of the Great Uprising and the subsequent disappointments of the GLP. Machine politicians, the newspaper warned, were the representatives of monopoly and the "money interest" who spent their time "loafing around City Hall." But as the Democratic party made more progress organizing the city's Irish and German Catholics, and as the Republican machine countered with a renewal of bloody shirt waving and a promise of economic revival based on tariff protection, the labor reformers associated with the *Tribune* found themselves in deeper and deeper trouble. "Men have for years been hugging the delusive phantom of party politics as though relief or cure was to be found therein. No words that we can utter are likely to dispel that insane belief and hope. The masses cling tenaciously to party, and will . . . continue until all parties organized to perpetuate the control of capital have ground them beneath their feet."[14]

To direct such intense railing against its own readers may have been politically unwise. But in calling attention to the growing power of Christopher L. Magee and William Flinn, the editors of the *Tribune* identified the difficult challenge that labor reformers would have to meet if their electoral efforts were ever to succeed. Despite this obstacle, and others as formidable, the labor activists of Pittsburgh did not resign themselves to defeat.

In addition to the daunting political challenge of Magee and Flinn to an independent workers' movement, there were mounting difficulties for labor reformers and dedicated trade unionists in another sphere—the workplace. "Existing [social] relations produce slavery on one side and opulence on the other," the *National Labor Tribune* declared on the eve of the centennial of American Independence. "They destroy republicanism and create a monarchy of capital and a serfdom of labor." These words summed up the workers' understanding that the prospects for "industrial independence"—garnering a competence and controlling a wide range of the conditions of their labor—diminished with each passing year. "Vast power is centering into a few . . . hands, . . . [and] one man now controls millions [of men]. . . . Men find that their labor, the source of all wealth, cannot lead them out of increasing poverty and dependence."[15]

To end wage slavery and halt the drift toward permanent "dependence," labor leaders knew that the workers' movement had to cope with two challenges. One was the familiar problem of political mobilization; the second and related problem was the challenge posed by technological innovation in the struggle for control of the workplace. Just as businessmen and their allies in politics, journalism, and the graphic arts were hailing American technical genius at the Philadelphia Centennial Exposition, the *National Labor Tribune* labeled machinery as the "Grand Problem" of the era. The challenge of machinery took the form of a question: How could the labor movement convert the "grand problem" into a grand opportunity for building a cooperative society? "As society is constituted, machinery is the handmaid of capital . . . [and] create[s] wealth through the poverty of the masses." The true purpose of technology "is [rather] to elevate and develop and ennoble humanity, to lessen manual labor," and to assist labor in effecting "that equalization of wealth" that labor itself has created.[16]

Identifying the grand problem, however, was not the same as offering a solution to it: the *Tribune*'s puzzlement about how to "dethrone" capital from its domination of technology and labor was indeed deep. Capital's "enslavement of labor cannot be maintained" because mechanization would throw more and more people out of work, thereby reducing consumption to a virtual nullity and ultimately forcing capital to turn the means of production over to labor. Although the *Tribune* affirmed that the wage system could not survive ("the history of man proclaims its impossibility") it also recognized that building a cooperative society depended upon the initiatives of its readers. Like other social critics who have envisioned broad social transformations, Armstrong, the paper's editor, drew upon the biblical metaphor of the Exodus to underscore and legitimize his message of deliverance. "The days of capitalistic rule are numbered. . . . Private capital and private ownership cannot exist in a republic. One or the other must fall. Prepare, O workingmen of America, to enter into the promised land which is near us, if we be but true."[17]

On the journey that Armstrong envisioned, some of the most consequential struggles occurred in Pittsburgh in the metalmaking industry. A key to the outcome, he had recognized, was indeed the new technology of steel. And in this regard, the centennial year of American independence did not augur at all well for the workers' movement. Indeed, developments in Braddock in 1876 set back the campaign for "industrial independence" in a way that was particularly troubling to the thousands of iron- and steelworkers who by then already belonged to the AAISW, for at the Edgar Thomson Steel Works, Andrew Carnegie and his associates thwarted the union's initial effort to organize workers in the Bessemer steel industry.

The chronicle of Carnegie's success began in late summer, when steelworkers at the Edgar Thomson organized Braddock's Lodge no. 45 of the AAISW. Soon afterward, Carnegie and his trusted superintendent, William R. Jones, ceased operations to make repairs. In early December, when Jones announced that work was to resume, he also informed the members of Lodge no. 45 that they could retain their jobs only if they signed an "ironclad" contract that prohibited union membership. In addition he told all nonunion workers that they too could resume work only by agreeing not to join a union.[18]

Predictably, the *National Labor Tribune* was outraged by the effort of Carnegie and Jones to break the union. Moreover, the ironclad contract included a clause that pegged wages to those paid at the Cambria Iron Works in Johnstown. The reputation of these works, where Jones had served his apprenticeship as a supervisor of steelworkers, was notorious among them for its virulent antiunion policies and low wages. Carnegie and Jones, the *Tribune* thus exclaimed, intended "to make another Johnstown hog hole out of Braddocks Fields." But the newspaper congratulated the workers at the Edgar Thomson for "their manly resistance" against the company's "Un-American" attempt "to pull its workingmen to such base conditions."[19]

The resistance, however manly, did not last very long. An overwhelming majority of the members of Braddock's Lodge 45 signed the contract—which prompted Joseph Bishop, the president of the AAISW, to suspend the lodge's charter and denounce all but those nine members who refused to sign. Thus Carnegie and Jones were able in 1877 to begin operations at the Edgar Thomson Steel Works, the nation's most technologically advanced Bessemer facility, without the encumbrance of a trade union.

As Bishop and his colleagues in the AAISW understood, the defeat in Braddock presaged difficult times for a union whose strength lay with skilled ironworkers. True, Bishop had been heartened by the puddlers' victory in the lockout of 1874–75 and the subsequent amalgamation of the ironworkers' unions. But the puddlers and other skilled workers in the iron industry owed a large measure of their organizational success, and indeed the preservation of their "rights," to the dependence of the ironmasters on their expertise to produce a finished product. Bessemer steelmaking had the effect of rendering obsolete much of the ironworkers' expertise and, therefore, of raising the question: Who—workers or managers—would control the production process in the new steel mills?

Indeed, two clauses of the ironclad contract presented to the Edgar Thomson workers show that the question of control was uppermost in the minds of Carnegie and Jones. Not only had they decided to crush the official organization of steelworkers that found expression in the creation of Braddock Lodge no. 45; they also sought to limit "informal" work practices that might shift the balance of power to the workers. Thus, in addition to prohibiting union membership, the contract required that workers give three days' notice before quitting. And another clause provided that if ten or more men gave notice at the same time, the company would consider the action evidence of a criminal conspiracy.

Insistence that the workers agree to these provisions does not in itself constitute hard evidence that they had engaged in the work-actions Jones and Carnegie wished to prohibit. But it seems likely that the Edgar Thomson workers did experiment with initiatives along lines suggested by the contract, for the abrupt or collective withdrawal of labor at crucial points was an obvious method of empowerment to metalworkers, whose control over the production process was now eroded. A walkout in the middle of a Bessemer blow or the surprise departure of a ten-man crew, whose knowledge of one another's work habits ensured continuous operations, may not have given steelworkers the same level of control as had the puddlers' monopoly of skill, but interrupting the Bessemer process could furnish workers with considerable leverage.[20]

Bishop and many other leaders in the AAISW remained committed to exercising this leverage despite the defeat at Braddock. But many metalworkers, Bishop included, were at a loss to explain how steelworkers might withstand additional technological assaults from "unjust capital." Thus Bishop, in an understatement of overwhelming proportion, told his colleagues at the union's convention in 1877 that "the Bessemer steel business is a question of the deepest interest to our trades." However, he offered no tactics, no plans, for the AAISW to gain a foothold in steel mills. "I hope you will give the matter due consideration," he told the delegates.

For their part, the managers and owners of the Edgar Thomson could only be delighted with the technological advances built into it. Alexander Holley, the man hired by Carnegie to design it, observed that metalmakers had only begun to develop the potential of the new technics. "Increasingly remarkable as has been the progress of iron metallurgy, . . . its possibilities are greater than ever before . . . [and] . . . hold out a higher reward to the capitalist no less than to the chemist and to the engineer." Indeed, in the two years following the AAISW's initial defeat in Braddock, the Edgar Thomson mill provided Carnegie with enormous profits: $190,000 in 1877 and $402,000 in 1878. Carnegie, well on the way to becoming one of the world's wealthiest men, was paying "Captain" Jones, the supervisor of the mill, $25,000 a year. Soon after it had opened, Carnegie proudly had told his partner, W. P. Shinn, that the Edgar Thomson "is a grand concern and sure to make us all a fortune." As usual, he was right. Yet the deeper signifiance of the "still extending" horizon of metalmaking technology, as Holley called it, was the control the new technics had given management over the production process. As the American Iron and Steel Association observed, Jones led the first operations at the Edgar Thomson with "many . . . workmen . . . [who] saw the Bessemer process for the first time."[21]

To Holley, the college-educated man of science with an intimate knowledge of shop floor technique, to Jones, the "practical" workman who was an innovative technician as well as an expert manager of men, and to Carnegie, the businessman whose fundamental dictum was to reduce costs, the implications of operating a facility as vast as the Edgar Thomson with less reliance on the skill of workers were very clear. Each knew that the mill held out the promise not only of immediate "victory in a close contest of competition," in Frederick Overman's words, but also of securing this victory under a more stable social order in and outside the mill.[22]

However, Jones and his comanagers were unable to exert unequivocal control over the production process even with the advanced technics of the Edgar Thomson. Jones told his British colleagues in a review of the mill's first years that technological innovation often drew concerted resistance from the employees. "If any changes or improvements have been made, the workmen are generally exceedingly slow to admit their usefulness, and are apt to follow their own judgments, which are generally founded on prejudice, so that instead of making an earnest effort to test the true merits of an improvement, they are apt to throw obstacles in its way. . . . Generally all the improvements introduced at these works have been condemned and opposed by the workmen." The resistance of the workers at the Edgar Thomson was so intense that Jones and his colleagues found it necessary to exercise "an almost constant personal supervision."[23]

Thus Jones learned that the technology that rendered the skills of large numbers of workers obsolete did not automatically guarantee managerial domination; at the same time, he knew that technology was indeed an important weapon in management's efforts to extend its control. Moreover, his remarks suggest that both management and labor at the Edgar Thomson understood a point that in recent years a good number of historians, sociologists, and economists—many working within the framework provided by Harry Braverman—have overlooked: that the introduction of new technology, or "labor-saving machinery," represented only a tendency to subordinate workers to the control of managers. The shop floor of the Edgar Thomson, like that at other industrial enterprises, remained contested terrain even with the technologies of the second industrial revolution. So tenuous was management's control over certain aspects of the production process at the Edgar Thomson mill that Jones once said he felt as though he was in a penitentiary when inside the boiler house.[24]

As the 1876 conflict at the Edgar Thomson suggested, both Jones and Carnegie recognized that the promise of the new technology could be fully realized only if management blocked the efforts of workers to extend their shop floor control from puddling mills to the new steel mills. The key to management's success in Bessemer steelmaking, just as it had been in ironmaking, therefore was to undermine the metalworkers' union. "If the Union proposes to regulate our profits and prices, we might as well give up business," one Pittsburgh ironmaster had said on the eve of locking out the Sons of Vulcan in 1874. "I cannot permit [the union] to regulate my contracts." *Iron Age*, the voice of American metalmasters, made similar observations in the same year, and in every year thereafter, about ironworkers in the old mills and steelworkers in the new ones.[25]

Indeed, throughout the 1870s employers and workers fought heated if sporadic battles for control of the new Bessemer industry at the point of production. In addition to the conflicts at the giant Cambria Iron Works in Johnstown and at the Edgar Thomson, Bessemer steelworkers and managers squared off in St. Louis, Missouri, and Joilet, Illinois. The disputes involved the efforts of steelworkers to organize a union; and each dispute resulted in failure for the workers. By 1878 the AAISW had not placed a lodge in a single Bessemer steel mill. In the iron industry it had a stronger hold; however, the power of the union was by no means uncontested. Only four thousand of the thirty thousand metalworkers who were eligible to join belonged to the union, and only half of all metalmaking establishments were organized.[26]

The AAISW therefore began special efforts to organize mills, particularly those to the east of Pittsburgh, where the union was weakest. The results were encouraging, and the union doubled its membership by 1880. But its organizing campaign drew feisty responses from owners. In Pennsylvania in 1879 they fired the union's leaders. A wave of strikes followed, leaving "a paralyzing influence on the movement" to organize the mills. According to union officials, the intent of the owners was to destroy the AAISW.[27]

In Pittsburgh the antiunion campaign of the mill owners began in early 1878, when James Park, Jr., attempted to hire nonunion labor at his mammoth Black Diamond Steel Works. In late 1878 puddlers employed at William Clark's Solar Iron Works went on strike under the banner of the AAISW in an effort to resist the introduction of black sheep and new work rules. The strike there was followed by one in July 1878 at the crucible mill owned by Hussey, Howe, and Company, whose decision to cut wages prompted the walkout. A similar decision was the immediate cause of a strike in 1880 at the Crescent Steel Works, owned by Reuben Miller, Jr.[28]

To the labor leaders of Pittsburgh, the most serious of these disputes involved the puddlers at the Solar Iron Works. The trouble began in early December 1878 and lasted until late March 1879. Clark and his supervisors initiated the conflict by trying to impose what the *National Labor Tribune* called "a system of injustice and oppression" that dictated to puddlers the operating rules for their furnaces. Clark required them "to work the iron according to the notions of the managers" and thus prohibited "good practical workmen" from exercising "their own judgment." The new rules and a reduction in the wages of rollers by five cents a ton prompted a walkout by the AAISW's men, and Clark retaliated by hiring nonunion workers and housing and feeding them in the mill. At stake in the dispute, said the *Tribune,* was the "manhood" and "honor" of both union and nonunion labor. Like most other disputes in the postwar metals industry, the strike at Clark's mill pointed to the intimate connections between shc'p floor practice and workers' ideas of right and justice.[29]

The strike at the Solar Iron Works ended, not long after a violent shooting incident, in a compromise. Clark rehired some of the union members and retained some of the black sheep. However, the settlement of this dispute and the agreements reached in the conflicts at the mills owned by James Park, Jr., Reuben Miller, Jr., and the Hussey family did not end the struggle between iron- and steelworkers and their employers in Greater Pittsburgh. Indeed, the struggle intensified in the 1880s in iron mills as well as the new Bessemer plants, as ironmasters pushed to expand the domain of their control.

One focal point of the struggle in the 1880s was the Edgar Thomson, where both the AAISW and the Knights of Labor made new inroads against Carnegie. Another was the second Bessemer mill built in the Pittsburgh district, the PBSW in Homestead. Park, Miller, Hussey, Clark, and two other ironmasters financed its construction and owned it. Clark also managed the mill; when he tried to change the work rules and hired black sheep, precisely what he had attempted at the Solar Iron Works, the result was another violent strike. The steelworkers of Homestead blamed Clark and his colleagues and accused them of trying to annihilate the AAISW. At stake were their "rights as free born American citizens."[30]

To the national leaders of the AAISW, union members in both Homestead and Braddock seemed unwilling to accept the inevitable. John Jarrett, elected union president in 1880, stated that the introduction of Bessemer steelmaking had resulted in "the complete subjugation of labor to the will of the employers." Moreover, Jarrett—who won a diplomatic appointment when he left the union in the late 1880s—also declared that the technologies of steelmaking represented "the unseen hand of the Almighty preparing the way for the higher industrial conditions awaiting us in the near future."[31]

While Jarrett and the other national leaders of the AAISW drifted toward accommodation, the steelworkers of Braddock and Homestead nurtured and embellished a vision of society that grew from the cause of labor reform. One such steelworker was a miner, Knight of Labor, and Greenback party candidate for the state legislature who lived within sight of the Edgar Thomson when Andrew Carnegie defeated the AAISW in 1876. His name was John McLuckie, and he believed that political organization might check the assault of capital. By the early 1880s he was working in the Edgar Thomson, helping to organize another lodge of the AAISW there and canvassing for an independent labor party. A decade later he was the burgess of Homestead as well as a leader of all union workers in town when Carnegie decided, again and finally, that he could not countenance the union.[32]

Chapter 10

Miners Amalgamate in "Late Afternoon"

Pittsburgh had made a highly favorable impression on the British journalists Ralph Keeler and Harry Fenn when they visited in the winter of 1870–71. But in assessing its industrial might they also reported the environmentally less appealing aspects of "the smoky city." The dusky emissions from the furnaces of iron and steel mills, foundries, and glassworks imparted an other-worldly quality to the city. Indeed, Keeler compared the sight of nocturnal Pittsburgh to that of "the infernal regions."[1]

To escape, increasing numbers of well-to-do Pittsburghers began building homes in the semirural suburbs east of the city. The development of neighborhoods such as Squirrel Hill, the East End, and Oakland, along with residential expansion up the Allegheny and Monongahela, set in motion forces that were to transform a "walking city" delimited by rivers and hills into a sprawling metropolis. And though these trends reached fullest expression only after the turn of the century, by the early 1870s suburbanization was well under way. As we have seen, it was also in the early 1870s that the most notable entrepreneur of the city, Andrew Carnegie, by deciding to build the Edgar Thomson Steel Works in Braddock, unleashed forces that would industrialize the outskirts of Pittsburgh.[2]

Braddock, which offered Carnegie cheap land, low taxes, a ready supply of water, and easy access to rail and river transport, was situated amid one of the richest bituminous coal deposits in the country. Indeed, when it was incorporated as a borough in 1867, most of its one thousand residents were miners. Miners also predominated in Turtle Creek (where John McLuckie lived), in other nearby towns, and in most settlements on the opposite shore of the Monongahela near Homestead. When Keeler and Fenn visited Pittsburgh, however, Homestead was a quiet village surrounded by the mining communities of Mifflin Township: Six Mile Ferry, Germantown, Amity, Green Springs, and Dravosburg.[3]

In or near these towns lived the overwhelming majority of Mifflin Township's five thousand residents. Only a few families lived in Homestead, and most of them had owned a sizable tracts of prime farmland since the eighteenth century. When Abdiel McClure and Lowry H. West, the patriarchs of two of these families, decided to divest some of their holdings and capitalize on "the tendency to suburban life" then characterizing the housing business in Pittsburgh, they found the market bullish indeed. In September 1871 the two men created a company named after the McClure homestead—the Homestead Bank and Life Insurance Company—bought 230 acres of their own land, divided it into small lots, and arranged a festive junket from Pittsburgh to promote sales. Within days, McClure and West sold almost five hundred lots to those Pittsburghers willing to spend between $385 and $496 for an opportunity to build a home away from the din and smoke of the industrial city.[4]

The city came a bit closer to Homestead in 1872 when the Pittsburgh, Virginia, and Charleston Railroad extended its lines along the south bank of the Monongahela and through the town. The direct rail link to Pittsburgh may have tarnished Homestead's reputation as being "one hundred years behind the surrounding neighborhood," as one railroad official put it. But the railroad provided easier access to the city without disturbing the semirural flavor of life in Homestead, and more than two hundred houses were erected prior to the Panic of 1873. Though a developer laid out an additional forty acres during the long depression, only one additional house was built.

Into the final year of the depression, Homestead remained an undistinguished place. One- and two-story houses stood along the railroad tracks, and a small brick factory and McClure's Homestead Planing Mill were the only businesses in town. McClure's stately residence, situated on a large tract near the center of town, dominated the landscape and commanded a view of the lazy Monongahela as it rounded a wide bend on the way to Pittsburgh. Built at the end of a winding road that rose through a neatly manicured lawn to a terraced garden, the McClure home was noteworthy enough to be called a palatial residence by the author of a contemporary history of Allegheny County. Also included in this category were the residences of other principal landowners in Mifflin Township: Abraham Hays, John Munhall, and A. H. Kenny.[5]

These men and their male children owned and operated some of the most productive collieries in the Pittsburgh area. Their holdings covered thousands of acres from the riverfront into the wooded hills along Beck's Run, Street's Run, West's Run, Munhall's Run, and other streams that flowed into the Monongahela. Roughly one thousand miners worked in the mines along these streams, and most of them lived in tenements owned by H. B. Hays and Brothers. The miners' wooden shacks stood in stark contrast to the Hays mansion and those of his friends.[6]

It was here, in the tenements of Mifflin Township, that the labor movement of Greater Pittsburgh located its main source of strength in the late 1870s. If the skilled metalworkers of the city were first to unite under the banner of amalgamation, the Monongahela miners were the earliest and most committed advocates of an amalgamation that envisioned all workers: the Knights of Labor. Indeed, as the 1870s gave way to the new decade and the AAISW struggled against the antiunion initiatives of mill owners, the miners of Mifflin Township played an increasingly important role in the workers' movement: following a series of defeats in 1877 and 1878, the Mifflin miners in fact led the way in reestablishing a districtwide organization.[7]

Their initiatives began anew in 1879. With economic recovery promising a rapid increase in the demand for coal, the miners demanded higher wages. Predictably, the operators refused: the result was yet another miners' strike. This time, however, the miners won, and the districtwide union that emerged helped pave the way for a national organization of miners. Miners in the Pittsburgh district and elsewhere credited the important victory of 1879 to the "checkweighman" at the Hays collieries in Six Mile Ferry, D. R. Jones. Jones's job was to ensure accurate weighing and "all-around justice" at the pits.[8]

Jones, who was 25 at the time, had come to the Pittsburgh area from his birthplace near Swansea, Wales, by way of the anthracite coal mines of Eastern Pennsylvania. Having left the mines in 1874 to study at Mount Union College in Ohio, he supported himself during his undergraduate years by teaching school. When he settled near Homestead in Six Mile Ferry in 1878, he pursued his teaching career at Blackburn School and also decided to study law in the city. Most of Jones's pupils were the children of the miners who worked at the collieries near his home. His relationship with the miners was always close: not long after he moved to Six Mile Ferry, he closed school and camped out with striking miners. This demonstration of solidarity, coupled with his standing as an educator and law student, prompted the miners to choose Jones as their checkweighman, to double his salary as a schoolteacher, and to welcome him as a brother in the Knights' Local Assembly 860, which they named "Victory."[9]

The districtwide victory of the miners in 1879 elevated Jones from his station as a leader in Mifflin Township to a position of unrivaled influence over the affairs of all miners in the lower Monongahela Valley. By all accounts a tremendously ambitious man, he owed his ascent to prominence to a conversation he overheard at the Pittsburgh Coal Exchange, where mine owners and coal dealers congregated to buy, sell, and discuss market conditions. Jones learned that the owners, who had a large blacklog of orders for coal, were on the verge of acceding to the demand for higher wages. His discovery came just as the miners were about to call off their strike, and his advice to continue the struggle for a few weeks ensured their triumph. Their success "emboldened them, and they at once made up their minds to put someone in the field to look after their interests."[10]

The miners chose Jones, who, as president of the Miners' Association in the Pittsburgh district, exercised for the next three years such extraordinary power over the union's affairs that even the most sympathetic observers grew concerned and expressed considerable misgivings in private. Yet they all publicly applauded him, for he led the association, which in effect was District Assembly no. 9 of the Knights, to a series of victories, and during his tenure wages rose from two-and-one-half to four cents a bushel.

That miners had two organizations to represent their interests reflected the broader debate over the relationship of unions and politics that troubled Knights and other organized workers into the 1880s. While many of the miners who belonged to District Assembly 9 took an active interest in politics, the Miners' Association was organized on the premise that in public it would pursue only the workplace interests of its members. Yet into 1881 the association was considered a local assembly within District Assembly 9 and thus subordinate to it. In truth, the distinction between District 9 and the Miners' Association always was fuzzy, and, as Jones and those who agreed with him in seeking to separate politics from union building learned, the distinction had little practical effect. In 1880, Jones was charged with conspiracy as a result of his efforts to organize miners employed by the Waverly Coal Company. Many workers saw the indictment as further evidence that only a combination of trade union and political successes could ensure their rights.[11]

To the Monongahela miners, preeminent among such rights was the right to organize, for without organization their hopes for receiving a "fair and just remuneration" for their labors would be solely in the hands of their employers. "Were the coal operators human, just, and generous," Jones told the miners, "we might with some degree of safety cast ourselves upon their benevolence, disband the Order, and allow nature to have her course." But without the protection of the union, the owners would be free to "oppress" the miners by taking "under the guise of law the profits which of right belong to [them]." Only districtwide solidarity could halt what he characterized as the suicidal, throat-cutting policy of separate pit organizations underselling one another in a crazed bid to "dig the most coal for the least money." Only districtwide solidarity could ensure sufficient earnings "to pay life expenses, . . . pay debts, and rear up children to be intelligent and respectable." In short, only solidarity could ensure the miners' right to a competence.[12]

Embedded, then, in Jones's appeal for solidarity were the very aspirations that had animated the workers' movement in the Pittsburgh district since the late 1860s. Though he understood that his audience clearly wanted higher wages, he also knew that wages alone were not the key issue. The overreaching goal of the miners was to earn enough to avoid debt and provide for a family, and Jones knew that such aspirations were bound up in a way of life that held that it is immoral to lower the value of labor to the point where these aspirations were unattainable. To reduce the value of labor beyond this ill-defined though palpably real standard of fairness therefore constituted something more than a mere reduction in wages—it was an assault upon the workers' way of life and the values that guided it. There was a wide chasm indeed between the idea that labor could be treated as a mere commodity, the value of which was subject to market fluctuations and the desire of employers to accumulate, on the one hand, and the idea that labor had an irreducible minimum worth that ought to yield to its owners the essentials of a secure and dignified material life.

Hence it was not an understatement when Jones told the Monongahela miners that their employers were ignoring "the voice of reason and the precepts of justice" and that lowered wages would reduce the miners "to the condition of the most menial peasant of Europe." In the owners' repeated efforts to lower the price of a bushel of coal, the miners saw the encroachments of an alien and tyrannical morality. Like the ironworkers who resisted the tyranny of organized capital and the efforts of its representatives to degrade labor, the Monongahela miners also saw in amalgamation their only hope to avoid what Jones called "vassalage and practical slavery." And despite his public stance against political involvement, the Monongahela miners—again, like many members of the AAISW—attached a political meaning to amalgamation by consistently supporting the GLP. Moreover, Jones himself fought to extend the meaning of amalgamation by encouraging miners to ignore differences of "creed, color, or race" and thus to "stand together by the beautiful principles" of the Knights of Labor.[13]

Within months of Jones's call for solidarity, the miners of Mifflin Township were joined there by another group of organized workers. The men came to Homestead to work in the first factory erected in the township, Bryce, Higbee, and Company's glassworks, which was built on the riverbank. The arrival of more than fifty glassworkers and their families ended Homestead's isolation as a residential suburb and also set the stage for its transformation into a factory town. Also in 1879, William Clark, the owner of the Solar Iron Works, joined six other iron- and steelmasters in deciding to build a rail mill and a Bessemer steelworks on a tract of land adjoining Homestead.[14]

The coming of a glasshouse and a steelworks to Mifflin Township were part of metropolitan Pittsburgh's steady advance up the coal-lined banks of the Monongahela. The emergence of Homestead as a factory town also coincided with changes in the direction of labor's march against the competitive wage system, for as the 1880s began, the oppositional spirit that had informed the districtwide campaigns for amalgamation lost forcefulness and the workers' movement made its first turns toward accommodation.

In Homestead, though, the story was altogether different, since the workers who settled there in the 1880s continued to nurture and embellish the insurgent legacy of labor reform. In retreat from increasingly successful businessmen and their allies in politics, Homesteaders continued to draw their leadership from the ranks of the most forceful labor reformers of the 1870s. D. R. Jones, who in 1886 and 1887 served as burgess of the town and later represented it in the state legislature, was one such leader. Another was a former Chartist, Beeswax Taylor, who was elected burgess in 1888 and whose allegiance to the principles of labor reform and worker republicanism was deeper than Jones's. A third veteran of the workers' movement of the 1870s who settled in Homestead in the 1880s was John McLuckie. Elected burgess in 1890 and 1892, and a key figure in the town's two major confrontations with Andrew Carnegie, his career as miner and steelworker, Knight and AAISW man, and politician and trade unionist qualified him to lead Homesteaders in their effort to construct a workers' version of a modern American Republic.

"Only with the falling of the dusk," though, were the contours of this a republic made clear, and by the late 1870s in the Pittsburgh area, it was already late afternoon.[15]

PART FOUR
"Tried and Found Faithful": Homestead Defies the Assault

Just think of it, my fellow workmen living in a land where not twenty years ago we had a war against slavery, in which many of our brave citizens lost their lives, wives were made widows and children orphans; in a land where freedom and independence was proclaimed, that we, as employees of the Pittsburgh Bessemer Steel Works, would go in our right minds and sober senses and sign away our rights as free-born American citizens.

— Striking steelworker,
Homestead, January, 1882

Chapter 11

Assaults on Labor

THE ROUNDHOUSE RIOT of 1877 and the Homestead Lockout of 1892 stand out as the events most emblematic of the sweeping changes that marked Pittsburgh's history in the Gilded Age. In 1877 questions about the meaning of citizenship and the rights of labor and property propelled a city of workers into revolt against the forces of organized capital. In 1892 similar questions thrust the residents of Homestead into battle. July 1877 and July 1892 sent convulsive shock waves into the ranks of the emerging middle class. But those who sat uneasily in its parlors reacted with far greater alarm in 1877 than they did in 1892.[1]

One reason that well-to-do Americans felt less frightened in 1892 was that the Homestead Lockout did not seem to threaten a national upheaval. A leading Homestead steelworker reluctantly conceded on the day of the battle with the Pinkertons that the "fight between centralized capital and organized labor" was about to "be pushed to the finish." This man understood that for Americans whose sympathies lay with the established order, there was little cause for panic in 1892. But though the "urban menace" appeared with a vengeance in that year in Homestead on 6 July, the chief response of those who felt threatened was to counsel reform—reform that might curb corporate excesses without undercutting corporate rule.[2]

In 1877 the story had been quite different. That summer, profound fears of revolutionary chaos emerged from what Pittsburgh's leading business paper called the "communistic dance of dealth and destruction" of the Great Uprising. This fear found forceful, and often hysterical, expression in the national press. The *Independent*, a widely read religious weekly, declared, for example, that when laborers coerced others into stopping work, they became criminals, rioters, and public enemies. The rule of law demanded not only that authorities compel the rioters to stop rioting but also that the latter be forcefully punished. "If the club of the policeman, knocking out the brains of the rioter, will answer, then well and good. But if it does not promptly meet the exigency, then bullets and bayonets, canister and grape . . . constitute the . . . remedy. . . . Napoleon was right when he said that the only way to deal with a mob was to exterminate it."[3]

The members of a Pennsylvania legislative commission that investigated the 1877 disturbances took a less inflammatory position. It recommended, however, that employers move to eliminate labor oganizations once and for all, for a failure to act would result in even more serious civil disturbances and damage to "the business of the country." In the view of business leaders and their political allies, the Great Uprising left in its wake an opportunity to mobilize for a final, decisive thrust against trade unionism.[4]

As we have seen, labor activists in Pittsburgh saw the uprising as an opportunity to revive independent labor politics. However, the GLP, like its predecessor, the Allegheny County Labor Reform party, achieved only marginal success in 1877 and 1878. The workers' second attempt to fashion an independent labor politics stalled, and a new breed of professional politician with strong ties to the business community emerged as the dominant power in Pittsburgh. Thus the labor activists who had regarded the ballot as their most effective weapon turned again to the task of building unions.

From the late 1870s well into the next decade, the mines and mills of Greater Pittsburgh became the principal battleground between the world of labor and the world of capital. Employers followed the suggestions of the state legislature and pursued their assault against the workers' movement with renewed vigor. Metal manufacturers, for example, fired leading members of the AAISW. In Pittsburgh factory masters such as Andrew Carnegie, William Clark, James Park, Jr., and Reuben Miller—all future owners of the Homestead mill—enjoyed considerable success in containing the organizational drives of the union. It fared no better across the nation. In the Bessemer steel industry, where the new techniques of production had obliterated the workers' monopoly of skill, it was particularly troubled. The AAISW failed to organize a single Bessemer factory before 1878.[5]

By the early 1880s in Pennsylvania, however, organized labor had to contend not only with the inroads of new production methods and the more familiar techniques of the blacklist and the ironclad contract. In addition, employers turned to the courts to attack what union leaders considered labor's most basic right: the right to organize. Moreover, Thomas Mellon, one of the leading financiers in the Pittsburgh district, sued the *National Labor Tribune* in an effort to put the region's most important labor paper out of business.[6]

It was, however, the AAISW and the Knights of Labor, particularly the miners' unions organized under the aegis of the Knights, who were the principal institutional targets of the employers' campaign. David R.

Jones, the miners' leading organizer in the Monongahela collieries, drew much of the personal fire, as did some of the Homestead steelworkers who would help elect him burgess in 1886 and 1887 and send him to the state legislature in 1888 and 1890.

Employers grounded their attack against the right to organize in a series of judicial rulings based on Pennsylvania's anticonspiracy laws and the common law tradition that defined a conspiracy as any combination of two or more persons who sought to accomplish a criminal purpose. Largely because of this tradition, unions in Pennsylvania found themselves without formal legal sanction into the 1870s. Indeed, judges often agreed with employers in viewing strikes as criminal conspiracies. True, in 1872 Pennsylvania had enacted a law that gave unions the specific right to strike without being subject to conspiracy charges, but it also provided that anyone who "hindered" others from working could be prosecuted under other statutes. In interpreting this law, courts held that any agreement to increase the price of labor—"a vendible commodity"—constituted a conspiracy. Moreover, they ruled that though unions could organize and strike, any effort to prevent new workers from taking the place of strikers also constituted a conspiracy.[7]

Though the state legislature modified the hindering provision in 1876 to affirm that "lawful" means could be used in strike actions and could not be regarded as hindering persons from working, courts soon enlarged the definition of hindering. As the conspiracy case of D. R. Jones was to prove, the effect was to call into question any protection that the 1876 statute might have given to unions.[8]

Jones and fifteen others were arrested for conspiracy on 18 March 1880 in Smithton, a mining town in Westmoreland County, just west of Pittsburgh. The Waverly Coal Company, represented by Thomas Mellon, one of its owners, argued that Jones, then serving as general secretary of the Miners' Association, and his fellow unionists had engaged in a conspiracy to hinder company employees from honoring their contracts and to prevent other miners from working for Waverly. The first charge stemmed from Jones's advice to the miners that they seek higher wages and disregard a provision in their contract requiring them to give sixty days' notice of a strike call. The second charge arose from Jones's oratory—and his enlistment of a six-piece brass band—to mobilize miners to strike and to persuade potential strikebreakers not to work for Waverly.

The trial of Jones, under whose leadership the Monongahela miners had won a number of important victories, received wide publicity in Western Pennsylvania. For workers and businessmen alike, the trial seemed to crystallize the most important issues of the day. Mellon, the self-made millionaire and politician whose sons, Andrew and Richard, were already on their way to achieving even greater political and financial successes, charged that Jones, not without considerable ambition himself, was a revolutionary "communist" and therefore should be convicted. Trade unions represented the most serious threat to modern civilization; indeed, the attraction they offered to workers indicated "a demoralized condition of public sentiment, which may require blood to purify." Jones, who had consistently dissociated himself from political insurgency and preferred arbitration to strikes, saw in the Waverly case a threat to the union movement. Affirming that his activities had involved nothing but moral suasion, and citing the 1876 statute's narrow definition of hindering (actions that used "force, threat or menace of harm to persons or property"), he held that his conviction would render illegal virtually all trade union activities. "If moral force is sufficient to constitute conspiracy under the laws, . . . then we have no legal right to use moral force. And if we have no legal right to use moral force, then the greater part of the work of the executive of any labor organization has always been and is criminal."⁹

Thomas Armstrong, the editor of the *National Labor Tribune*, who also served as the treasurer of the Miners' Association, agreed with Jones. Armstrong found the trial judge's charge to the jury particularly disturbing: Individual workers were permitted under the law to demand higher wages, but any union that struck for higher wages represented a threat to the entire community. "Combinations of workingmen for the purpose of advancing wages are unlawful." To Armstrong, Pittsburgh's leading labor reformer, the judge's finding and its implications for other unions challenged fundamental American rights. Armstrong saw the Waverly case as only the latest example of a long series of "direct attacks on personal freedom" undertaken by businessmen and their political allies. Such attacks brought into relief that vast difference between the ethos of the emerging corporate order and that of the labor movement. They were "the direct outgrowth of a miserable selfishness which regards a dollar as of greater moment than human flesh and blood" and "of perverted minds that have come to consider the teachings of Christ as very good theory for Sunday reading, but not intended for practice in the real affairs of this life." All this was happening in a country "alleged to be under a democratic republican form of government."¹⁰

Thus, for Armstrong, the men who brought, prosecuted, and tried the Waverly case, not D. R. Jones, represented the real threat to the community. Mellon and his associates, not the striking Waverly miners, had attacked the Republic. Mellon, not Jones, was the revolutionary who had turned the world upside down by subverting republican justice with an un-Christian, pecuniary ethic. Armstrong's comments on the Waverly case represented the same line of argument that had once prompted him to indict the civilization of the nineteenth century; however, the labor movement did not have at its disposal the rule of law.

Indeed, the conviction of Jones poignantly demonstrated that it was the opponents of the movement who could look to the law for ready justification of their initiatives.[11]

Jones, then studying law himself under the sponsorship of George W. Guthrie, one of Pittsburgh's more prominent attorneys, incurred only a minor penalty. Guilty on grounds that his advice to the miners was conspiratorial and that the band he had hired was a hindrance, he drew a $100 fine and a twenty-four-hour jail sentence. In imposing this nominal penalty, the judge was perhaps mindful of Jones's well-publicized plans to leave the miners' union and of his connections to a well-placed officer of the court.[12]

That Jones was not sentenced to a long term did not, however, alter the chilling effect of the anticonspiracy statute. As the *Journal of United Labor* put it: "The fact remains that working men in Pennsylvania are . . . liable to arrest and trial for simply organizing." The *Journal*'s point captured the essential meaning of the anticonspiracy law: it was a vehicle for defenders of corporate rights, and of the state, which privileged these rights, for solving the problem of coercion in the most efficient way, that is, by minimizing its use.[13]

To be sure, the defenders of corporate rule made good use of this vehicle. In 1882, Miles McPadden, the leading miners' organizer for the Knights of Labor in District Assembly no. 3, was arrested with twelve others on charges brought in connection with a strike in Clearfield County. McPadden had urged striking miners to vote for labor candidates. "As he exercised his right to criticize the old party rule and advised workingmen to vote for workingmen candidates," the *National Labor Tribune* observed, "he was regarded a dangerous man." McPadden was not, however, the only dangerous man. Between 1881 and 1884 conspiracy charges were brought against at least four other labor leaders in Pennsylvania. In 1885 a group of Monongahela miners was convicted and sentenced to eight months in prison on grounds that the gathering of workers in large numbers near a place of work, even in the absence of overt acts or malicious intent, constituted a conspiracy. Also, in 1887 and 1891 more than twenty miners from Allegheny County and the Connellsville coke region were convicted of conspiracy and sentenced to four months in prison.[14]

In the view of the *Tribune*, the conspiracy cases represented but one part of "a preconcerted movement to assail trade unions vigorously." Indeed, the prosecution of Jones, the $70,000 libel suit brought against the *Tribune* by Thomas Mellon and the Waverly Coal Company, and the efforts of Oliver Brothers and several other Pittsburgh metalmakers to dismantle lodges of the AAISW and assemblies of the Knights—all of these struck Thomas Armstrong as something more than mere coincidence in early 1882. To Armstrong, who was again trying to build support for the GLP, the consciousness of purpose shared by opponents of labor was evidence of the only real conspiracy in Pennsylvania.[15]

Among the manufacturers who were then battling metalworkers was the consortium that had just built a Bessemer steelworks in Homestead. There the owners were using the conspiracy statute, the binding force of the ironclad contract, and the armed power of the state to attack trade unionism. Armstrong asserted that the prosecution of Jones, the suit against the *National Labor Tribune,* and the struggle at Homestead indicated that employers were pursuing their alleged conspiracy "primarily by law." This observation contained an important kernel of truth. But like their colleagues all across the nation, the steelmasters of Homestead also looked to another weapon: technology. In a way that the Homestead steelmasters could not fathom, however, the advanced technics of their new mill backfired. The ironic result helped empower the first Homestead steelworkers in their effort to withstand what may not have been a conspiracy but certainly was a most determined offensive.[16]

The first struggles between the workers and managers at Homestead culminated in a violent, three-month strike in 1882. In many ways the strike prefigured the confrontations of the more famous Homestead lockouts of 1889 and 1892. In all three cases the steelworkers and their allies effectively seized control of the town and cordoned it off; they also did physical battle with their opponents and the state-sanctioned police authorities who backed them. Moreover, in 1882, 1889, and again 1892, those committed to the supremacy of corporate rights saw in the actions of Homestead's workers gestures that inverted the accepted order and, if allowed to play themselves out on a large scale, might turn the world upside down.[17]

However, the strike of 1882 was more than a symbolic "carnivalesque" gesture. The initiatives of Homestead's first steelworkers functioned as a metonym for labor's larger plans: the steelworkers' assumption of municipal authority was a rather polite enactment in miniature of the countrywide seizure of authority that would overturn the regime of property. And some of those committed to the supremacy of corporate rights likewise responded to the 1882 strike as a metonym for the great labor upheaval that they so feared. The 1882 strike was thus rich with symbolic meanings. Yet these meanings can be gleaned only through a reconstruction of specific historical processes—processes that include most notably the invention and deployment of the new techniques in metalmaking, the mobilization of Pittsburgh's workers in the 1870s, and the disturbances of 1877 and the initiatives that grew out of them. Finally, aspects of factory etiquette that developed in Homestead before the strike signaled an emerging pattern of confrontation in the steelworks. This pattern, too, ranks among the telling themes that informed the Homestead strike of 1882.[18]

THE HOMESTEAD GLASS WORKS AND
THE KNIGHTS OF LABOR

Homestead began to assume a new, industrial character in the winter of 1880–81, when workers completed the structure for the Pittsburgh Bessemer Steel Works and erected sixteen immense boilers. Management was making arrangements to install the machinery in the converting and blooming departments, and scores of workers had moved to the borough in anticipation of new jobs. Following the long depression of the 1870s, steelworkers had reason to feel optimistic about prospects for continuous employment in Homestead. And at the newly erected Homestead glassworks, operations were in full swing: a correspondent for the *National Labor Tribune* reported that he and his fellow glassworkers employed by Bryce, Higbee, and Company "were as busy as they can be just now."[19]

The arrival of industry converted Homestead into a boom town. M. P. Schooley, who settled there as the ticket agent for the Pittsburgh, Virginia, and Charleston Railroad, captured the mood of most residents in the initial issues of his weekly newspaper, the *Homestead Times*. Although some had questioned his decision to publish the *Times,* Schooley was confident that business would remain brisk: "What has brought hundreds of strangers here? We will answer again. . . . THEY also anticipated a great future for Homestead, . . . one of God's own favored spots."[20]

Schooley, who later became editor of the *Homestead Local News* and, in that capacity, served as the town's most enthusiastic booster, could not know that the nature of Homestead's future greatness was most problematic; for the town's emergence as an industrial center occurred against the backdrop of the sweeping social transformations of metropolitan Pittsburgh in the 1870s. As we have seen, the principal result of these changes was the emergence of what labor leaders called organized capital as the dominant power, on and off the factory floor. In ways that Schooley could not have guessed, the coming of industry to Homestead posed the question of who would wield power there.

In some places in Homestead, however, the question of power did not generate heightened tensions until the late 1880s. Work relations at Bryce, Higbee and Company, for example, followed the friendly standard prevailing in many family-owned glass factories, where, as one historian has put it, "the cleavage between the owner-entrepreneur and his workmen was rarely very distinct." So indistinct was it in the early 1880s at the Homestead Glass Works that the owners, Charles K. Bryce and his brother, Robert D., often joined glassworkers in the pursuit of leisure activities and common political interests.[21]

That Charles Bryce and his fellow owners had been glassworkers themselves no doubt contributed to the amicable work environment at the glass house. However, they were first and foremost entrepreneurs. While they trimmed their entrepreneurial aspirations to reflect the size of a modest factory—through 1885, the company's work force rarely exceeded one hundred—these aspirations arose from the same morality of improvement that motivated the great industrialists of the era. Indeed, among manufacturers, Bryce, Higbee and Company enjoyed a wide reputation for "enterprise" and use of "all the latest improved appliances." In 1881, for example, Charles Bryce invented a device that helped mechanize furnace operations; a few years later he became one of the first glassmakers to replace a coal-fired furnace with one that burned natural gas. The conversion meant a substantial saving in costs, largely because gas required fewers workers.[22]

The Bryces' commitment to technological innovation was rooted in the very method of production they chose—"pressing." In the view of the Bryces and fellow manufacturers of crystal tableware and other intricately shaped objects, pressing, as opposed to blowing, was the most attractive technique. The chief reason was that it reduced expenditures for raw materials, dramatically increased the pace and quantity of output, and allowed less skilled workers to make thousands of copies of the same item. Indeed, the manufacture of pressed glass was the one branch of the American glass industry that, prior to the 1890s, stepped away from a reliance upon manual processes and traditional skills and toward the lower skill requirements of mass production. Joseph D. Weeks, the glass industry's chief spokesman, explained that pressing was "a most important and valuable improvement in glassmaking . . . [because] comparatively unskilled labor can be substituted for the highly trained workmen demanded by the blowing process."[23]

The manufacture of pressed and blown glass began in the same manner. Under the instructions of the "teaser"—Jacob Miller, in the Homestead of the early 1880s—workers mixed lime or flint, silica, and other materials and then placed this batch in a furnace for "fritting." Once some of the impurities were cooked off, workers shoveled the molten frit into pots, which were then heated at about 3,500 degrees Fahrenheit for as long as sixteen hours. During this time, workers would go home. In Homestead, many of the glassworkers rented company-owned homes on Fifth Avenue; there they would wait until a boy, acting on the teaser's instructions, summoned them back to work the glass when it was ready. In the manufacture of blown glass, the next stage began when the "gatherer" collected on his blowpipe a mass of the liquefied material, rolled it, and then turned the viscous glass over to the blower. Next, the blower blew the mass into a cylinder or a globe. In a series of extraordinarily complex movements, the blower and his assistants used a variety of techniques to manipulate the mass into the desired shapes.[24]

The employees of Bryce, Higbee and Company and of other concerns that manufactured pressed glassware used many of the same methods, up to the crucial point of shaping the molten glass. In the manufacture of pressed wares, the gatherer collected glass on a rod instead of a blowpipe and then dropped the liquid glass into a mold. In Homestead, Peter Stemler, Valentine Bossert, or one of the other five "pressers" who worked for Bryce, Higbee and Company would then insert a metallic plunger into the mold. When the glass solidified, the presser withdrew the plunger, opened the mold and removed the glass, then close to its final form, so that it could be polished and annealed under the supervision of Jacob Engle, James J. McDonald, or other finishers.[25]

Although the overall skill requirements for the manufacture of pressed glass were less than for blown glass, mold makers, engravers, gatherers, pressers, finishers, and others who performed specialized tasks were well paid. Indeed, by 1880 some pressers and finishers earned as much as, and in some cases more than, glass blowers; and many skilled workers in pressed glass factories earned more than painters, carpenters, machinists, blacksmiths, and even puddlers. Joseph D. Weeks reported in the federal census of 1880, a year in which Pittsburgh puddlers earned an average of $3.50 a day, that the average daily wage was $3.55 for finishers, $3.53 for pressers, and $3.47 for blowers. Weeks found that the average for other skilled workers in pressed glass houses also was high: $3.05 for mold makers, $2.58 for engravers, and $2.35 for pot makers. Compared to blowing, then, pressing may well have been "quite a simple operation," as Weeks said. However, as the wages indicated, pressing did demand extensive skill—what Weeks himself called "considerable practice."[26]

Thus the effects of technological innovation in the glass industry in certain ways paralleled those of Bessemer steelmaking: pressing and the Bessemer process each cheapened production by eliminating old techniques that demanded great expertise. But each also created jobs that required new skills. The effects of technological innovation thus cannot be understood by way of mechanistic references to "deskilling": new techniques often create new, skilled tasks.[27]

Of course, not all labor at the Homestead Glass Works required great expertise. Indeed, most workers in pressed glass houses were unskilled, and many earned less than a dollar a day. Yet skilled workers maintained a marked presence: in Joseph Doyle's Pittsburgh concern, for example, skilled laborers had comprised more than 40 percent of the work force in the mid 1870s. At Homestead in 1880 approximately 30 percent of the glassworkers employed by Doyle and his partners in Bryce, Higbee and Company were skilled.[28]

These skilled workers exerted a wide range of influence on the shop floor. In particular, they wielded great power over the question of output by enforcing a "list" that limited the number of items each "shop"—a gatherer, presser, finisher, and several helpers—produced during a "move" of work, which normally was a half-day. No record of formal union organization at Bryce, Higbee, and Company in its initial years has been recovered, but by 1882 the Knights of Labor did have a local assembly—Local Assembly no. 1785—in Homestead; its members held skilled as well as unskilled jobs in the glass house. Given that workers in pressed glass houses typically organized on a local basis prior to affiliating with the Knights, and that Frank M. Gessner, the first master workman of Local Assembly 1785, became a leader in the Knights' national assembly of glassworkers, it seems likely that Local Assembly 1785 had its origins at Bryce, Higbee, and Company soon after production began there in 1879.[29]

In Gessner the glass- and steelworkers of Homestead had in the early 1880s a supporter with ties to the inner circle of Pittsburgh's labor reform movement. A brickmaker who supplied building materials for the Homestead Glass House and the PBSW, in 1881 he established the *Homestead Mirror,* a monthly newspaper that served as the municipal voice of the Knights of Labor. He saw the *Mirror* as a gentlemanly opponent of the entrepreneurial vision expressed by his friend M. P. Schooley, whom he criticized for "sling[ing] out . . . sweet pastorals" in the *Homestead Times* that ignored the industrial strife of the borough. As a result of his own developing alliance with the more genteel practitioners of reform, however, businessmen came to recognize Gessner, too, as a friend—one of the few "respectable" leaders of labor. The virulently antiunion *American Manufacturer* remarked, for example, that he always pleaded for reason and justice and advised against confrontation. The *Manufacturer* offered this characterization in 1887. But well before then, Gessner promised never to "overstep the boundaries of propriety" and advocated, because labor was in need of moral uplift, "decency, order, and sobriety," the very tactics of self-help that many of labor's opponents found so appealing.[30]

In the early 1880s in Homestead, however, Gessner helped lead the GLP and saw his effort to build an independent workers' party as the most important means of improvement. Like many other Knights, he also practiced self-help by way of "education": he founded Homestead's Forest Literary Society. It and its successor, the Young Men's Literary Society—organized by Gessner's brother, George, and other glassworkers—took their cue from the Franklin Literary Society in Pittsburgh. Directed by Andrew Burtt, a labor educator, it provided a forum for workers and labor leaders to give public readings and debate the great, and not-so-great, questions of the day. In Homestead the literary societies served the same purpose: "that cremation is the best method of disposing of the dead," and that women should vote, were two of the many resolutions considered by society members. The literary societies also staged "entertainments" for the entire town; nearly four hundred residents attended one that included humorous performances by Beeswax Taylor, George Gessner, and other workers.[31]

Like the skilled craftsmen of Pittsburgh, George Gessner and his coworkers extended their influence beyond both the factory gate and the realm of leisure by venturing into governmental affairs. In the Independent Fire Company, glassworkers, many of whom had belonged to volunteer fire companies in Pittsburgh, organized what in effect was Homestead's first municipal agency. Among the founders were George Gessner and three pressers, Peter Stemler, John Bossert, and John B. Jones, Sr. Their employer, Charles Bryce, became a member soon after the fire company was formed and served as its first president, though never as its captain. In addition to protecting the glass house and other structures in town, the Independent sponsored dances and baseball games; it marched together on public holidays and mourned dead members by draping the fire wagon; it forced new members through a good-natured running of the gauntlet; it serenaded them prior to marriage and afterward rode them through town. And in the mid 1880s the Independent organized its own caucus and entered electoral politics.[32]

The Independent thus served as the center of sociability for Homestead's first industrial artisans. Its structure mirrored the work relations at the Homestead Glass House: Charles Bryce was nominally in charge of affairs at work and in the firehouse, but his power derived from the men whose wages he paid. President of the Independent, but not captain, supervisor of work, but not a worker, Bryce understood the terrain of compromise on which he and the glassworkers could meet. He did not join the chorus voiced by most Gilded Age glass manufacturers—"that they were not masters in their own shops"—but this was testimony to his understanding of his own dependency. The glassworkers understood their dependency, too. And while they paid deference to Bryce and his brother, Robert, whom they included on their baseball teams, there was no room for the Bryces and their partners in the sanctuary of Local Assembly 1785.[33]

At the Pittsburgh Bessemer Steel Works the lines between worker and employer were not quite so blurred.

THE DECISION TO BUILD A STEEL MILL

The men who in 1879 decided to build a Bessemer steelworks in Homestead brought to the town decades of experience in managing the world's largest metalmaking facilities. In addition, they brought the advice and blessings of the world's premier architect of Bessemer technics,

Alexander Lyman Holley. Holley's role in the design of the PBSW, which was the name of the Homestead facility through the mid 1880s, has been overlooked by historians. Yet the story of that relationship is a key element in the unfolding drama of Homestead.[34]

Despite Holley's expert advice and the owners' own previous successes in containing the AAISW, these men were unable to defeat the union in Homestead. The reasons lay in the complex interplay between the putatively impersonal forces of technology and market fluctuations, on the one hand, and the highly personal relationships between and among competing entrepreneurs and distinct groups of steelworkers, on the other.[35]

This complex interplay produced a strange and unintended alliance between Andrew Carnegie, the principal competitor of the PBSW, and the first Homestead steelworkers. The alliance—and indeed the story of Homestead steelmaking—originated in 1875 when Bessemer steelmakers organized the Pneumatic Steel Association, whose principal object was to form a pool to divide up the market for steel rails. At the initial meeting, Carnegie became indignant when the other manufacturers gave him a smaller market share than he wanted. His threat to undersell his competitors with rails manufactured at the Edgar Thomson Steel Works won him a larger allotment. Although this pool soon collapsed, in 1877 the steel manufacturers created a more successful combination. The second pool, called the Bessemer Steel Association, hired Holley as its consultant and created the Bessemer Steel Company, Limited, which acquired the patents, many of them Holley's, necessary for efficient Bessemer production. Through the company the pool could either deny the use of the patents or charge a licensing fee to nonmembers.[36]

Confident that the new pool would secure his place in the Bessemer market, Carnegie turned his attention to the Edgar Thomson. There he found that he had a surplus of steel because the Bessemer converters were producing more ingots than could be rolled into rails. He therefore decided to enter a new sector of the steel market by selling to various finishing mills the surplus that his mill could not work up into rails. Among the principal customers who bought this surplus were six Pittsburgh concerns that converted the ingots into a variety of steel products.[37]

The owners of these mills were among the wealthiest men in Greater Pittsburgh. Each was committed to the idea of progress and technological innovation; several were experts in various production processes; all were steadfast opponents of unions. They included William G. and James Park, Jr., Curtis G. and C. Curtis Hussey, William H. Singer, Reuben Miller, William Clark, and Andrew Kloman. Clark, the nation's leading expert in the manufacture of hoop and band iron, had secured a wide reputation as a strikebreaker. As Carnegie's partner, Kloman had built in Pittsburgh the giant Lucy Furnace, the leading blast furnace in the country. He also was a pioneer in the use of the Siemens furnace and was America's preeminent technician of metal rolling. James Park, Jr., a principal in America's first Bessemer plant, had joined his brother in transforming the Black Diamond Steel Works in Pittsburgh into the world's largest crucible steel mill. Like the Park brothers, the Husseys owned a huge crucible mill. And Miller and Singer had helped make Pittsburgh the world leader in the production of high-quality cast steel.[38]

The voracious appetite for steel generated by these large concerns brought Carnegie large profits from the Edgar Thomson's surplus. However, he had not permanently forsaken the rail market. Even as he was selling his surplus Bessemer steel, he was expanding his rail mill so that it could handle the full output of the Bessemer converters. The completion of the expanded rail mill came at precisely the right moment, for as the Great Depression ended in 1879 and railroads once again began laying lines, the demand for rails shot upward. At this point, Carnegie decided to use all the ingots he produced at the Edgar Thomson to make rails. To the Pittsburgh steelmasters who had been buying his ingots, the results of his decision were potentially disastrous.[39]

Whether Carnegie took pleasure in making business more difficult for all of his former customers is problematic. At the very least, though, his decision to produce high-quality ingots from his Bessemer converters and then to halt sales—to create a demand and abruptly shut off the supply—brought him some measure of satisfaction with regard to Kloman. The reason was that Kloman, a founder of Carnegie's metal-making empire and his former partner, had committed what Carnegie called "the unpardonable sin" of disloyalty: he had secretly used his shares in the Edgar Thomson Steel Works to support other investments.* These investments ultimately soured and thus raised the prospect that outside creditors would enter Carnegie's domain.[40]

Following his forced departure from the Edgar Thomson, Kloman went into business for himself with the idea of seizing a hefty share of Carnegie's business. Kloman initially leased a rolling mill and, with ingots manufactured in another steelworks, began to produce rails and structural materials. Propelled by what one historian has called "internal demons" and "paranoiac madness" that had Carnegie as their object, Kloman soon realized that he needed a new metalmaking facility to pay back his former partner in full. What better location for a new mill might he find than Homestead? Like Braddock, the town offered all the advantages necessary for efficient production. And because it was within sight of the Edgar Thomson, a plant in Homestead would prove particularly galling to Carnegie. Kloman, however, lacked the capital to finance a complete metalmaking facility. Fortunately for him, the other steelmakers who had been buying from Carnegie also were looking for a way to replenish their supplies.[41]

In an effort to avoid the large capital outlay required by the construction of a Bessemer mill, the Parks, the Husseys, Miller, Singer, and Clark had initially countered Carnegie by buying merchant steel from a consortium that imported British metal. To compete successfully over the long term, however, they knew that they needed merchant steel that was not subject to tariff duties and whose cost might be cut still further by means of the most innovative managerial and technical practices. In their eyes the best solution was to construct their own plant. A mill that incoporated the latest in Bessemer technics would provide their steelworks in Pittsburgh with all the ingots they needed at the lowest possible cost. To build such a mill, however, they would have to circumvent Carnegie and other members of the Bessemer Steel Company, Limited, for it owned the patents for equipment that had been built into the Edgar Thomson and other technically advanced Bessemer facilities. Moreover, in its privileged relationship with Holley, the company claimed the expertise required to design and operate any new facility.[42]

For the Parks, the Husseys, Miller, Singer, and Clark, the first hedge against the possibility that Holley's expertise and the Bessemer patents would remain unavailable was to go into business with Kloman, who had something quite valuable to offer: his own mechanical expertise. He had in fact supervised the construction of the refining and finishing operations at the Edgar Thomson and had won from Carnegie his highest tribute; Carnegie called him a genius for being "the ablest of practical mechanics." Should the Husseys, the Parkes, Miller, Singer, and Clark fail to gain the services of Holley, then, they could count on Kloman for technical advice and supervision. For Kloman, entering a partnership to build a Bessemer mill offered the prospect of fulfilling his dreams of revenge against Carnegie. Indeed, when Carnegie's former customers created the Pittsburgh Bessemer Steel Company (PBSC) in October 1879 and chose Homestead as the site for their plant, they all boasted that the new company was a direct assault on Carnegie and the Edgar Thomson Steel Works.[43]

The partners understood, however, that though Kloman had tremendous technical expertise, building the most efficient Bessemer mill ultimately depended on obtaining the services of Holley. The PBSC had hopes of engaging him because, though he did have contractual obligations with the pool, he had made a practice of selling his advice to nonmembers. On behalf of at least two clients, Holley went so far as to investigate how each might build an efficient Bessemer plant without paying the pool for the use of its patents—including his. "Dear Lu," he wrote to one Pittsburgh steelmaker, "I have looked enough into the Bessemer patents to be sure that you can put in a sort of old Swedish plant without paying royalty." A letter Holley wrote in late 1879 to Julian

Kennedy, the treasurer of the Bessemer Steel Company and the supervisor of the Edgar Thomson blast furnaces, shows that he gave similar advice to the PBSC.[44]

In truth, multiple factors indicate that although Holley was not the officially designated designer of the PBSW, its converting department plainly was the product of his expertise. Despite the narrative conventions that governed the accounts of the first Bessemer mills, none of the contemporary reports on the PBSW identifies the designer by name. The omission was not gratuitous, however, and it in fact points directly to Holley as the unnamed author of the Homestead mill. Robert Hunt, one of the country's leading metallurgical engineers and a close friend of Holley, addressed the design question in discussing the PBSW. Not long after Holley died, Hunt delivered a eulogy in which he noted that the PBSW was a remarkable facility that attested to Holley's engineering talent, even as it had been designed to circumvent his patents:

> One of the finest monuments to [Holley's] ability as an engineer exists in the only Bessemer plant yet built in this country outside of his [patent]. I think my fellow Bessemer managers will unite with me in deciding it far below the standard of a Holley plant. It is very good, indeed; but compelled to avoid him, they also avoided much that was good. But in the criticism of these very works, his lovable nature was shown. I am certain to no one sooner than myself would he have freely expressed himself, but never did I hear him utter an unkind or slighting word about this, if I may so call it, rival plant. So many of its owners were his friends, . . . I suspect many a hint was given by him of dangers to be avoided.[45]

Hunt's remarks were certainly replete with ambiguities. His description of the PBSW as "one of the finest monuments" to Holley's genius and as a testimony to his "lovable nature" was bound to elicit ironic laughter: Hunt's brother engineers all knew of Holley's difficult relationship with the pool and particularly with Carnegie; they also knew of his warm regard for James Park, Jr., one of the owners of the PBSC. Hunt's audience could therefore appreciate the implication that in building the PBSW without the original Bessemer patents, Holley had nonetheless succeeded brilliantly in designing an impressive facility.[46]

In his simultaneous criticism of and praise for the PBSW, Hunt had followed the conflicting allegiances that many other Bessemer experts held. Holley was a highly esteemed, gallant colleague. But other experts had close ties to the pool; Hunt himself was a member of the inner circle of engineers and entrepreneurs who established the Bessemer industry. He therefore had reason to support the pool by publicly discouraging the construction of what Holley, in a veiled threat to the Bessemer Steel Company, Limited, had once called "improved 'Pittsburgh Bessemer' " plants. In truth, then, the new mill in Homestead was not "below the standard of a Holley plant." Rather, Hunt's comments confirm that Holley helped design it but did so by circumventing his own patent.[47]

The original steelworks at Homestead thus represented the combined expertise of Kloman and Holley. Kloman's finishing mill was to be equipped with rolls that could produce 50,000 tons of steel rails and 30,000 tons of structural material a year. The blooming mill, manufactured by the Mackintosh-Hemphill Company, was itself based on a unique prototype developed by Holley; it could turn out 60,000 tons of ingots per year. The combination of converting, blooming, and finishing mills planned by the owners of the PBSW would not, however, immediately challenge the production supremacy of the Edgar Thomson. There rail production had risen from 42,827 tons in 1877 to 100,094 tons in 1879, when the total output of Bessemer ingots of 123,303 tons astounded the metalmaking world. But Carnegie correctly understood that his competitors on the opposite side of the Monongahela did indeed pose a threat to that dominance of the marketplace: within weeks of the first blow at Homestead, the PBSC had orders for 15,000 tons of steel rails—which was almost 20 percent of the Edgar Thomson's market share.[48]

The relationships among Carnegie, Holley, and the PBSC, while interesting in their own right, illuminate more than the maneuverings of competitive businessmen; the conflict between Carnegie and the company directly affected the relations between labor and management at the steelworks in Homestead. Because the PBSC was compelled to build a Bessemer mill whose design could not include all of Holley's patents, and because it built a blooming mill unlike any other, the steelworks at Homestead was a truly singular facility. The PBSW therefore required a work force that possessed "plant-specific" skills. And, as we shall see, these skills proved to be important weaponry in the steelworkers' first major conflict with the PBSC, the Homestead strike of 1882.

Certainly neither Carnegie and his allies nor the PBSC and Holley entered into their behind-the-scenes confrontation with the knowledge that their actions would help empower the steelworkers of Homestead. Nor did they foresee that the Homestead strike of 1882 would provide an important foundation for the steelworkers' successes over the ensuing decade. The steelworks in Homestead thus ultimately gave to the owners of the PBSC and especially to Andrew Kloman, the most driven of Carnegie's opponents, what one historian has characterized as a "perverted revenge." In a way that even his most strident critics overlooked in assessing his contribution to the violence of 6 July 1892, Carnegie coauthored this revenge even before he purchased the steelworks at Homestead.[49]

WILLIAM CLARK AND
THE FIRST HOMESTEAD STEELWORKERS

William Clark, the general manager and co-owner of the Pittsburgh Bessemer Steel Works in Homestead, was a happy man at Christmas 1881. A series of technical difficulties had slowed production during December; on the twenty-fourth, however, operations ran so smoothly that workers produced more steel in one day than they had since the mill opened in February. To Clark, a mechanical expert and an aggressive businessman, the news was heartening indeed. It proved that although the PBSW had some technical problems, it could successfully compete with Andrew Carnegie's Edgar Thomson Steel Works and other advanced Bessemer facilities.[50]

Clark had another reason to celebrate. It was, after all, Christmas Eve. And when the mill closed that night, workers presented him and two of his chief assistants with handsome gifts. David Williams, the production supervisor, and George J. Humbert, the weighmaster of the Bessemer converting department, received "very valuable" gold watches of identical design. The workers gave Clark a "beautiful . . . meerschaum pipe" and a "fine gold-headed cane, appropriately inscribed."[51]

It was not uncommon for steelworkers at this time to give presents to their supervisors; however, the workers' choice of gift for Clark was uncommon, to be sure. The more typical gift for supervisory personnel, then as now, was the conventional gold watch: an elegant and practical token that symbolized the "efficient" lives of men who sought to manage the factory environment like clockwork. Unlike the watch, however, Clark's unusual Christmas gifts plainly connoted the world of leisure rather than the world of work.[52]

In the wake of Marcel Mauss's seminal essay on the meaning of gifts and gift giving (*Essai sur le don*), it is difficult to ignore the symbolic manner through which presentations of gifts replicate fundamental themes and relations in the social order. One analyst of the steel industry has argued that the general practice of the AAISW's gift giving to managers simply demonstrated the union's "bonds of solidarity with Capital" and the evident "respect [its members] felt toward those in charge." But few things are so simple or so evident. The very ironworkers who formed the AAISW were also the men who resolutely led Pittsburgh's labor insurgents against the managers from the 1860s well into the 1880s. What, then, did it mean for the steelworkers of Homestead to single out one supervisor, William Clark, by their presentation of an odd and exotic and rather idiosyncratic gift?[53]

Perhaps the presentation to Clark was merely an anomalous, fraternal interlude fostered by the Yuletide spirit. Or is it possible that the gifts in some way signaled a less jolly but more confrontational pattern of

labor relations in the Homestead mill? In order to decipher the significant codes embedded in the presentation of the meerschaum pipe and
the gold-headed cane, one must begin by reviewing the relations between the man who received and the men who gave these gifts.

William Clark was born in England in 1830. Like Beeswax Taylor and
so many before him, Clark left as a young man in search of a New World
and new opportunities. His official biographies present the outline of a
life that in every way fulfills the myth of the self-made man. Clark began
his odyssey to commercial success in Pittsburgh as an unskilled ironworker. "His quick intelligence and desire to advance himself," however, propelled him through the ranks of skilled workers to the foremost
position of roller. With his valuable skills and his reputation as "an
eminently intelligent and thorough workman," he moved swiftly across
the country in the 1850s and settled in Cincinnati, where he went into
business for himself. Clark's first ventures in the iron trade were not a
success, but he clung ever more firmly to his ambitions. He moved on to
Youngstown and eventually became senior partner of Shedd, Clark and
Company. In 1869 he returned to Pittsburgh and founded one of the
city's largest puddling and finishing mills, the Solar Iron Works; "and he
managed it successfully."[54]

At this point in his biography, Clark begins to be referred to—and no
doubt referred to himself—as a gentleman. Elected to the Pittsburgh
City Council in the early 1880s, he was admired for his "progressive"
expertise in metallurgy, code language for the ironmasters' commitment
to technological innovation and cost-efficiency. But Clark also cultivated
a new image: amateur of fine art and good reading, "a man of refined
taste and feelings," the kind of man who might well enjoy imagining
himself cushioned in an overstuffed armchair with a good book in one
hand and an exotic meerschaum pipe in the other. (Nineteenth-century
meerschaum pipes were, because of their weight, traditionally enjoyed
in an armchair. A man who smoked one was thus absent from the
factory floor.) Joseph Weeks, an admirer, wrote in Clark's obituary: "He
was during life connected with many good and many benevolent matters, but never with anything of an opposite character."

The unofficial biography of William Clark is, not surprisingly, less
mythologized and less kind. To the iron- and steelworkers who had once
been his brothers in labor and who then became his subordinates, he
was an unusually harsh taskmaster. The very ambition and tenacity that
had made him a successful worker drove him as a manager to be inflexi-
ble and relentless toward his employees. In the memory of the workers,
he remained anything but good and benevolent and refined. "I knew
him when he was a workman, and there was none more dogmatic in
regard to his rights," one acquaintance recalled. "He would cuss the

boss for mighty little and he was always touchy whenever he was inter-fered with in the least." Later in Clark's career, James Howard Bridge, the first chronicler of Andrew Carnegie's business empire, described him as follows: "A bitter opponent of labor unions; and before going to Homestead he had incurred the dislike of the men for his prowess as a 'strike-breaker,' of which he was rather proud." And in 1882, John Jarrett, the president of the AAISW, decried Clark with bitter irony: "Gentleman Clark was a working man once himself. He was then more radical than any of us. He dared anyone to blacksheep him. Now he is blacksheeping his entire mill."[55]

It was these men, the very men William Clark was "blacksheeping," who at the end of a long and difficult year of shop floor struggles offered Gentleman Clark on Christmas Eve 1881 his most unusual gift.

Who were the first Homestead steelworkers? Unfortunately, little biographical information about them remains. During Clark's tenure as general manager of the PBSW, the work force reached a maximum of about 800 men. Of these only 166 have been identified; and with few exceptions, not much more than their names and jobs has been recov-ered. What is known about the steelworkers, in particular, the skilled ones, suggests that in many respects they resembled William Clark. Like him, most had their family origins in the British Isles; and like the young Clark, the skilled men were known as staunch advocates of their factory rights.[56]

For example, John Elias Jones, a Welshman, began his rapid rise through the ranks of the unskilled by laboring on the construction of the PBSW in early 1881. Within months he advanced to a semiskilled posi-tion on the rolls, and by 1882 he was working as a roller. Just as Clark had been "dogmatic" in warding off managerial initiatives when he him-self was a roller, Jones became a steadfast union man. Like Clark, he also left the Pittsburgh district for a number of years to labor elsewhere. Jones, however, always remained a worker and in fact became one of the principal leaders of the AAISW in Homestead in the early 1880s and again after his return in 1885.[57]

Other rollers employed at the PBSW had similar backgrounds. George Barkly, who learned his trade at the Cambria Iron Works in Johnstown, came to Homestead from Allegheny City, where he had worked in the Superior Mill and helped lead the AAISW. Before coming to Homestead, Barkly had also been politically active in Allegheny City, serving on the school board in the worker-dominated ninth ward. Many of his co-workers in Allegheny City, including two rollers, Thomas L. Parry and Isaac Jones, who was a dedicated AAISW member, joined him. (In 1881 the death of Andrew Kloman left owners of the PBSW in charge of the Superior Mill, and subsequently many of the skilled work-ers were transferred to Homestead.)[58]

While the steelworks provided new opportunities for native-born and immigrant skilled workers of English, Welsh, and Irish backgrounds, scores of less skilled laborers who lived in the immediate vicinity of Homestead also found work there. Typical of these was William B. Dickson, who in 1881 entered the mill as a boy of 15; like William Clark, he would be one to find great success in the steel industry. Dickson, who lived across the Monongahela River in Swissvale, began his ascent as a laborer in the converting mill; he moved on to operating a cold saw in the rail mill and later bossed a gang of loaders in the mill yard. Eventually he rose to the rank of junior partner in the Carnegie Steel Corporation and later vice president of U.S. Steel.[59]

Small numbers of immigrants from Eastern and Northern Europe, including Swedes, Bohemians, Poles, Slovaks, and Carpatho-Rusyns, worked both inside the mill and as loaders from the beginning of operations. John Jerowiski, for example, held a position in the rail mill until August 1881, when he became the first Homesteader to die in a steelworks accident. Joseph Rosinski, who came to Homestead with his wife, Mary, brother Simon, and sister-in-law Alice, also worked in the mill.[60]

The relations between these first Homestead steelworkers and William Clark were troubled from the start. At every juncture, Clark tried to lower wages and control the work environment by thwarting the AAISW. He began operations in spring 1881 by paying wages considered unjust by workers who had belonged to AAISW lodges in Pittsburgh. In June workers in the blooming mill and the converting department retaliated by taking the first steps to organize a new AAISW lodge, Munhall Lodge no. 24, and by striking in the middle of a delicate procedure. They left Clark no alternative but ready capitulation. William Singer, one of his partners complained that the steelworkers "struck when the ingots were in the furnace and the firm was compelled to grant an increase in wages or suffer a great loss." Clark, however, countered one night not long afterward by firing the strikers and announcing that no one could work in the mill unless he agreed to four rules: not to receive advice from AAISW members; not to strike for higher wages over the next six months; not to quit in groups of three or more and before giving three-days' notice; and finally, not to join the union.[61]

The result was a sweeping victory for Clark. All but a dozen workers in the converting and blooming departments signed his ironclad contract— an event that the AAISW and the *National Labor Tribune* found most troubling. "Slavery at Homestead," the paper declared on 9 July 1881. "Talk about foreign despotism! We venture the assertion that no such rules . . . can be found anywhere in Europe, and in a free country like this it is a lasting shame and disgrace that free men tolerate it. Until the men there free themselves from it, they will be looked upon as absolute slaves." The *Tribune*'s correspondent did not know it then, but workers in the rail mill, none of whom signed Clark's ironclad contract, were already organizing to join the union.

The sparring in the works between employer and employees continued. Later in July a dispute over weighing Bessemer ingots forced Clark to replace his weighmaster. In August he had to shut down the rail mill when workers there again refused to sign an ironclad agreement. In September two heaters, Matthew Leonard and John Sullivan, quit rather than work at the PBSW for wages they considered unjust and an insult to their skill. In early October workers in the rail mill officially organized Homestead Lodge no. 11 of the AAISW. John Elias Jones and Edward Blanford, who would become increasingly active in municipal politics, were among the leaders. Later in the month, George Fitzgerald, representing workers in the converting and blooming mills, finally received from union headquarters an official charter for Munhall Lodge no. 24.[62]

Members of both lodges, Homestead 11 and Munhall 24, took their first action in mid December when, in flagrant defiance of William Clark, they passed resolutions against signing ironclad contracts. They knew that when the contract that covered the blooming and converting mills expired on 31 December, he would again press for yet another despised ironclad contract.[63]

For the workers this decision of noncompliance may well have been the most important collective event that took place before Christmas. William Clark, however, was all the while busy overseeing the stepped-up production in the mill, which soon surpassed his hopes. Accordingly, at the end of December, when production reached a year-long high, it is easy to see why Clark—like the naive and patronizing social analyst cited above—would have interpreted the presentation of his Christmas gifts as a demonstration of the AAISW's "bonds of solidarity with Capital" and a token of the workers' "respect felt toward those in charge."

No doubt Clark saw in the presentation of the cane and pipe, which he accepted enthusiastically, a sign that the steelworkers were finally prepared to make peace, a sentiment commonly associated with smoking a pipe. And yet, even while he was happily projecting his naive wish for peace onto these offerings "of comfort and joy," the workers who presented him with them clearly had a very different project for peace in mind. And it left little room for William Clark and his "tyrannical" factory regime. The opulent tokens of a far removed and romantic existence were clearly intended to flatter Clark's own pretensions to live in the armchair world of the refined and leisured. And from the perspective of the workers, the gifts did indeed signify a world far from the factory and its demands for industrial discipline: the distant world to which they would like to send William Clark. In the minds and the jargon of the workers, the cane and the pipe expressed just as surely an ironic invitation to Gentleman Clark to "go take a walk" and "put that in his pipe and smoke it."

The respective interpretations of the gifts by William Clark and the workers represent projections of two very different sets of wishes for Christmas 1881. And in the end, it was the workers who got their wish.

Just days later, before he had a decent chance to enjoy either his new meerschaum pipe or his gold-headed cane to the full, William Clark was locked in the fiercest labor dispute of his life. From this bitter confrontation, the Homestead strike of 1882, Gentleman Clark would emerge the loser.[64]

Chapter 12

The Homestead Strike of 1882

The Homestead Strike

THE HOMESTEAD STRIKE

It was on the first of January, in Eighteen Eighty-two,
The steel works they shut down, you know, for repairs they had to
    do;
But in the course of two or three days the news was very sad—
We could not go to work until we would sign the "iron-clad."

So the union boys they all said "No, we will rather at home stay;
To sign away our rights to them, we would find it would not pay."
So when the repairing it was done, and they were ready to start,
We would not sign that iron clad, and for us there was no work.

So the mill they started up to run with scabs you all do know;
You should have seem them working there, I tell you it was very slow!
But then a lesson it will them learn—they were always very
    headstrong—
To fight against the union boys they found out it was wrong.

So the union boys they gained the day, and every man got back
To work in the Homestead steel works without signing that iron-clad.
So my advice you had better take, and a union man surely be,
For if you work while men's on strike a scab you'll always be.[1]

            — JOHN MILLER, striker
            May 1882

FOR WILLIAM CLARK, Christmas 1881 had been filled with promise. Eight days later, on New Year's Day 1882, troubles at the PBSW in Homestead intensified and Clark cut his celebrations short. In response to continued protest by workers, he launched yet another assault against the formal and informal methods of shop floor control exercised by the steelworkers: he closed down the mill and told them they had to sign a new ironclad contract by 5 January. In addition to prohibiting membership in the

AAISW, Clark's new contract forbade workers from quitting in groups of three or more and from leaving without three days' notice. Those who refused to sign, he announced, would be summarily dismissed.[2]

In stunning defiance virtually the entire skilled work force of two hundred men refused to sign; and in the view of contemporary observers, the result was one of the most violent labor disputes in the history of the Pittsburgh district. At stake for both sides was the answer to a specific question: Who would control the Homestead mill and moreover the entire Bessemer industry, labor or management? Spokesmen for both sides contended that at the broadest level this conflict engaged the very meaning of democracy. The *National Labor Tribune* described Clark's iron-clad contract as "slave-binding" and "un-American"; agreeing to it, one Homestead steelworker said, would be to "sign away our rights as free-born American citizens." Management, too, saw its rights threatened and was determined to protect them. The strike raised the dangerous "question of complete and absolute submission on the part of the manufacturers to the demands of their men," one ironmaster warned. *Iron Age* interpreted the events as follows: "The strike resulted from a refusal to recognize the union as a party to the control of their own works." And the assistant manager, Frank Clark, William's son, asserted: "It has become an issue between some workmen and ourselves as to whether we shall be allowed to run our business or whether they will run it for us. We propose to run the business ourselves even if we have to call on the Secretary of War for assistance."[3]

The Clarks did not call on the secretary of war, though they did ask the governor of Pennsylvania to send in the state militia. Homestead became an armed camp from January 1882 through the end of March. New workers joined hired guards and the police in a series of Western-style brawls and shootouts with the strikers. Many on both sides were badly injured; some scabs were beaten nearly to death; and the dispute threatened to spread into Pittsburgh and to close down all of its iron and steel mills. Public safety became so precarious in Homestead that hostile commentators saw events there as precursors of another "Great Labor Uprising." Indeed, one resident sympathetic to the strikers said the town was under "a reign of terror." Although the strikers did not physically attack William Clark, they denounced him vehemently, and they did assault one of his trusted managers, John Northcraft, the immediate supervisor of the very men who had given Clark the meerschaum pipe for Christmas. The strikers also identified David Williams and George J. Humbert, the other supervisors who had received Christmas presents from the men, as dishonest union busters. Indeed, George Fitzgerald, the leader of the strikers, said that Humbert was a principal cause of problems at the mill.

In the brutal confrontations between the striking workers and those hired to replace them, in management's efforts to break the union by

enlisting the police power of the state, and in the assumption of municipal authority by the strikers, the strike of 1882 anticipated the even more
violent conflicts of 1889 and 1892 at the Homestead works. Oddly, the
1882 strike has received only passing attention from historians. And yet
its dynamics are central to any understanding of worker-management
relations at the time, for not only did it prefigure the more famous
subsequent events, but it also echoed earlier disputes that had taken
place in the PBSW, in other Bessemer steelworks, and on the floors of
Pittsburgh's old puddling mills.[4]

Here, then, is a brief outline of the major episodes of the Homestead
strike of 1882 as compiled from a variety of contemporary accounts:

The strike was technically initiated on 1 January, 1882, when William
Clark, the manager of the PBSW, notified workers that "all employees not
signing another Article of Agreement for one year on or before the 5th day
of January, 1882, may consider themselves discharged from the works."
Members of the AAISW refused to sign, and operations promptly ceased.
Tensions escalated in late January when Clark succeeded in starting up
the mill with black sheep. Despite the efforts of union leaders, there were
many sporadic outbursts of violence between strikers and the imported
scabs, many of whom were North European immigrants. In retaliation,
Clark evicted strikers from company-owned houses and also charged
them with conspiracy. He hired armed guards and requested and received
police protection from the county sheriff. Union leaders turned to the
community for support and protection; accordingly, by mid February,
twenty-four of the strikers had been sworn in by the town burgess as
municipal policemen. The responsibility for public safety now lay in the
hands of the AAISW. In addition, the union leaders formed a special
Advisory Committee to coordinate peaceful strike activities and to help
ensure civil order.

For once, the power of management seemed to be equally matched
by the organization and power of the workers. In fact, it was only a
matter of time (and money) before Clark and his partners realized that
they had been matched and outsmarted, for without the technical expertise of the skilled union men who ran the steelworks, there was no way
that the owners could meet all their contractual obligations. By March
the company had already defaulted on important orders and risked
costly lawsuits. Rather than capitulate to the demands of the strikers,
however, Clark simply made cosmetic changes to the terms of his ironclad agreement; the tensions and fighting continued. On 4 March the
Homestead dispute threatened to grow into a larger conflict when a
district wide meeting of the AAISW voted to call a sympathy strike in
neighboring Pittsburgh mills. John Jarrett, the union president, reluctantly declared the call necessary because the union considered "the
Homestead fight as a blow aimed at the whole association."[5]

There followed mass meetings and various attempts at negotiation between the strikers and management, but Clark remained intransigent. His affected strength and his inflexibility in the face of imminent crisis provoked more incidents of violence by workers; ironically, these provocations only served to underscore the real strength of the workers' organization in Homestead. Finally, late on 14 March, having acknowledged defeat, Clark and several of the other owners met with AAISW leaders to resolve the strike on terms that would be acceptable to the union. Within weeks, the AAISW had virtual possession of the mill. The technical and organizational skills of the union men had proved decisive. On 29 March, William Clark, disgusted by his defeat in the protracted struggle, resigned as manager of the works. In so doing, he may well have fulfilled the workers' Christmas wish when he walked away from the mill, gold-headed cane in hand, to engage in leisurely pipe dreams.

Viewed from a national perspective, the 1882 strike at the PBSW was a relatively small and local occurrence. Nevertheless, the specific events and confrontations of these three months dramatized the most important political and ideological debates of industrializing America. What was at stake was not just the decisive control of one factory but the decisive interpretation of the meaning of republican values.

As hostile commentators well understood, the strikers in Homestead in 1882 were plainly assaulting the rights of the corporate regime and its putative entitlement to unlimited accumulation. In laying claim to their jobs and their rights, the steelworkers challenged what William Clark and his partners considered an undisputed privilege to dispose of "their" property as they saw fit. In the view of the owners and their supporters, it was the efforts of the workers to maintain membership in the AAISW and to keep their jobs that was un-American. One Pittsburgh paper averred that the steelworkers had violated "the American doctrine that 'every man has a right to do as he chooses as long as he does not interfere with the rights of others to do the same thing.' " A partner in the PBSC, William Singer, agreed with the appraisal and, in so doing, remained blind to the fact that his actions had interfered with the rights of the steelworkers. "They talk about signing away their citizenship, . . . [but] once every year the officers of the Amalgamated Association come to us and ask us to sign the puddlers' scale. Do we refuse and make the excuse that we are signing away our citizenship?" Singer, of course, believed that his relations with workers were founded on an equal exchange of wages for labor.[6]

For decades, however, thousands of wage earners had referred to a more critical tradition within republican discourse for an understanding of this exchange. As Ira Steward had explained, the exchange of wages for labor was hardly based on equivalency; on the contrary, the real meaning of *freedom of contract* in postwar America was "wage slavery."

For the Homestead strikers the fight against Clark was in fact a fight for freedom.

True, Clark could not transform the steelworkers into chattels; but in their view he was determined to strip them of their citizenship and to turn them into wage slaves. According to Frank Gessner, the leader of Homestead's Knights of Labor, the workers saw themselves as virtuous citizens who had labored hard to amass a competence and build their "little homes" in Homestead. Clark and his partners were corrupt tyrants: "cruel greed" stood behind their effort to abridge the rights of honest workers. Gessner echoed the sentiments that had informed the puddlers' initiatives in the lockout of 1874–75: "The real question . . . is whether the [steelworks] is to be operated by the honest skilled labor of the Amalgamated Association, or whether it is to take its place as a 'scab' works, to be operated only by those who will severally sign away their rights, and become as much the property of the company as ever were the Negroes on the tobacco plantations of Virginia or the cotton fields of Louisiana?" Even John Jarrett, the cautious president of the AAISW, compared the cause of Homestead steelworkers with that of American revolutionaries—whom he characterized as "strikers" themselves.[7]

William Clark and his allies had little use for such "twisted" rhetoric. One Homesteader sympathetic to management confidently made a telling allusion to the Declaration of Independence: "When manufacturers are not permitted to employ whom they please, and when such men as they do employ are shot, wounded and beaten on their way to and from work, it certainly strikes a blow at those inalienable rights of *life, liberty and the pursuit of happiness.*" Clearly, to the owners of the PBSW these inalienable rights represented something quite different from what they meant to workers. In fact, they meant no less than the right to unchecked profit making: "The Bessemer Steel Works at Homestead are going to be run in the interests of the stockholders and independent of the Amalgamated Association. . . . The first man that comes meddling with our operations will find himself handcuffed and on his way to jail before he can realize it. We have the law and right on our side and will avail ourselves of these to the fullest extent."[8]

The owners did indeed use the harshest measures available to defend their "republican rights." Nevertheless, in Homestead in 1882 it was the workers' version of republicanism that prevailed. How did this happen?

For one thing, the workers of Homestead remained true to the spirit of labor republicanism that had animated the labor movement in Pittsburgh since the 1860s. Homestead's skilled workers, though they certainly thought of themselves as the first citizens of the borough, saw in the democratic amalgamation of the skilled and less skilled the same possibilities for a true republican victory—albeit in a much smaller arena—that had initially solidified the Gilded Age labor movement on a national level.

With roughly one-third of all workers eligible for membership in the AAISW, strike leaders looked to other organizations to ensure solidarity during the Homestead dispute of 1882. Chief among these were the Knights of Labor and the Irish National Land League. Organized in late 1881, the league's branch in Homestead was one of many across the country that grew out of the transatlantic campaign to return Ireland to the Irish and, by way of sweeping land reform, her land to the people. In the United States the movement to free and democratize Ireland appealed to thousands of workers, not all of them Irish, who joined in the league's critique of the emerging corporate order. Indeed, the league shared its constituency with trade unions in many venues. In Homestead, for example, the membership of the league's Michael Davitt Branch overlapped with that of the AAISW.[9]

While strikers repeatedly attacked Swedish immigrants who "black-sheeped" during the strike, and while the press in Pittsburgh and Homestead often printed derogatory comments about "Huns" and other East-European immigrants, leaders of the 1882 strike used the Irish National Land League to welcome immigrants who refused to scab into the house of honorable labor. To be sure, the Homestead steelworkers had nothing but contempt for those willing tools of Clark who had emigrated from Europe and who in Homestead stayed in a boarding house called, appropriately enough, Castle Garden. Yet John J. O'Donnell, president of the league in Homestead, "proudly" wrote to the *Irish World* to report that during the strike, the Michael Davitt Branch enlisted "Germans, Dutchmen, Poles, Swedes, Scotchmen, Englishmen, Welshmen as well as Irishmen . . . to battle with Capital for our rights here."[10]

The Knights of Labor, of course, resorted to similar rhetoric, and they, too, looked to an amalgamation of the skilled and unskilled. In Homestead, this found its first concrete expression during the strike of 1882 when Local Assembly 1785 was organized under the leadership of Frank Gessner. The membership included former employees of Bryce, Higbee and Company who had left the Homestead Glass Works to work in the steel mill. To their new positions as unskilled steelworkers, these former glassworkers brought their longstanding commitment to labor organization and republican virtue.[11]

But rhetorical skills and organizational skills were not enough to win this fierce dispute against such stubborn agents of corporate rights as William Clark. Ironically, it was the superior technical skills of the workers at the PBSW, which management had so carefully fostered, that gave them the real power to challenge management's claim to absolute authority.[12]

In the view of William Clark and other ironmasters, the great advantage of Bessemer steelmaking was that it increased management's control of the factory. In a Bessemer mill they need not worry about the puddlers' monopoly of skill or their work customs—including any self-imposed restrictions on output that stood in the way of "efficiency." The technics belonged to the managers: management, not labor, trained the key personnel who operated Bessemer converters. In the finishing mills that worked in conjunction with the converters, however, the story was somewhat different: industrial artisans such as rollers, heaters, and roughers performed essentially the same tasks on Bessemer steel as they had on puddled iron. Thus they were able to maintain broad discretion in directing their labor: they remained autonomous workmen even after steel had supplanted iron. But before long, workers in even the most modern of Bessemer mills, with the support of their colleagues in finishing mills, found ways to challenge their employers.[13]

Workers in Bessemer facilities certainly did not possess the same overall level of control as had ironworkers. But a walkout in the middle of a blow, when the giant Bessemer vessel was converting pig iron into steel or, later, in the middle of a heat, when the blooming or rail department was preparing steel ingots for a run through the mills, could dramatically interrupt production for days. This potential for irreversible and costly disruption gave the steelworkers considerable power—power that they had judiciously exercised at the Edgar Thomson Steel Works in 1876 and again at the PBSW in June 1881. At a time, therefore, when steelmasters were asserting their power with more and more tyranny, the AAISW understood that organizing the Bessemer mills in general, and the Homestead mill in particular, might be their greatest challenge as well as the key to their greatest success.[14]

It was against this backdrop of industrywide conflict that William Clark ordered the Homestead steelworkers to sign the ironclad contract on New Year's Day 1882. Mindful that the workers had abruptly withdrawn their labor six months earlier, Clark and his partners decided that they would risk no such further disruptions. At the same time, they recognized that issues larger than local factory production were at stake in their demand for an ironclad agreement: this was their chance to thwart larger organizational efforts by the AAISW. Like the union leaders, the owners also recognized that, because the union had "failed to gain a foothold at Bethlehem, Johnstown, Braddock, and indeed at every Bessemer works east of Pittsburgh," its campaign at Homestead was the key to its "grand effort to establish themselves" in the Bessemer industry.[15]

For its part, the AAISW clearly understood that the initiative of Clark and his partners was designed as "a threat to its very existence." As John Jarrett observed, "It is a systematic fight against the Association." The Homestead steelworkers were "determined in one thing—the rights of labor shall be recognized. . . . If they go on much further, it will be like it is at Johnstown, and we want no more towns like that. The Cambria Iron Company owns nearly all the town. It ought to be moved out of the United States."[16]

In an important sense, then, the project of the Homestead steelworkers in 1882 was to ensure the defense of republican values in Homestead. The chief tactical problem for the strikers was to prevent William Clark from resuming production with nonunion labor. Conversely, Clark had to run the mill without the skilled union men and without workers who supported it. His first step in January was to complete a series of minor repairs in the mill, maintaining a small work force but producing no steel. Meanwhile, under the direction of George Fitzgerald, John Elias Jones, and Edward Blanford, lodges 11 and 24 of the AAISW organized into groups of guards to seal off the town. In keeping with their allegiance to wartime republicanism, the guards called themselves pickets.[17]

The first encounters in Homestead in 1882 between these pickets and the workers who had signed the ironclad contract took place on 9 January. That morning, Robert P. Dickson, the brother of William Dickson, and himself an unskilled laborer who was ineligible for membership in the AAISW, tried to board a ferry on the Monongahela just opposite the steelworks. "Two pickets stopped me and warned me not to attempt to cross the river to the works," he later recalled. But he ignored the warning and asked the ferryman to start the boat. The ferryman refused, having had instructions from the sixty-five pickets who were standing nearby that he was not allowed to take anyone to work in the mill. "I protested to the ferryman that he might try to get me across anyhow, but he seemed to be afraid to try it. Then I stepped out of his door intending to see what the strikers would have to say." Thomas Gardner answered by beating him with a blackjack. Dickson said the attack was unprovoked; a Pittsburgh newspaper not known for sympathy with the strikers commented that he had invited the assault by being "boastful."[18]

Following the assault, Dickson returned to his home in Swissvale. Later he somehow managed to cross the river and enter the steelworks, where he met with William Clark. At Clark's direction, he signed a complaint against Gardner, who was subsequently arrested. At the news, a crowd of strikers and their supporters besieged the arresting officers in a house near the steelworks. In the days following, strikers extended the network of fear that they knew was necessary to win. Dickson, for example, returned to work in the mill, but he always carried a revolver. And his more famous brother, William, said that Homestead became so dangerous for the scabs that Clark was forced to feed and shelter many of them. "The workmen were housed in rough quarters provided in the various mill buildings and in temporary wooden shacks erected in the mill yard. . . . The strikers were constantly threatening to raid the mill."[19]

Throughout January, tensions remained high in Homestead. At mid-month, Clark announced that wages would be cut when the rail mill resumed operations. Like puddlers, skilled steelworkers were paid piece rates, and Clark reduced these by as much as $1.50 per one hundred tons of rails. He also announced that the rail heaters would lose their helpers even though the mill was already performing tasks equivalent to those done in the Edgar Thomson rail mill with eight fewer workers.[20]

To the steelworkers the reductions in wages and work force intensified the affront to their worth: not only did Clark intend to destroy the union, the guardian of republican justice, but he also was determined to decrease the value of their labor. Moreover, he had previously instructed the weighmaster, George Humbert, to withhold tonnage figures from workers in the Bessemer mill. "We never knew what we made except as they pleased to tell us," said George Fitzgerald, the president of AAISW Lodge no. 24. "As we worked by the ton, it was no more than right that we should know what we made." Fitzgerald also complained that management had tried to increase the pace of production to an unacceptable level. It had in fact "interfered with the workmen in innumerable ways." Humbert had been "supercilious and haughty"; the blooming mill manager, William Floyd, and the production supervisor, David Williams, who had trained and worked alongside W. R. Jones at the Cambria "hog hole," were vilified because of their willingness to carry out Clark's directives—which included an order that workers sign the ironclad contract without reading it.

Measured against labor's specific grievances in Homestead as well as the overall pattern of work relations in the iron and steel industry, Thomas Gardner's attack against Robert Dickson was not a simple "unprovoked and most unjustifiable assault," as the trial judge asserted. Gardner, a steadfast AAISW man who had faced assault charges filed in connection with an earlier strike, had indeed violated the law. "You have a perfect right to work or not work for an employer, just as you see fit," the judge told him, "but neither you nor anybody else has a right to prevent another man from working." In the view of Gardner and his brothers in the union, however, it was William Clark who was preventing men from working; it was he and his partners whose actions violated republican justice. Where some daily newspapers and the trade journals of the metals industry saw civil disorder in the initiatives of the PBSW steelworkers, these same steelworkers saw themselves as law-abiding defenders of basic American rights.[21]

The strikers were not entirely successful in keeping new workers from entering the mill. In late January, Clark stated that he was preparing to resume production under armed guard. The strikers engaged the new workers in a series of altercations. Clark responded by charging George Barkly, his son Charles, and twelve other AAISW men with assault and with violations of Pennsylvania's anticonspiracy statute. For George Barkly, whose Civil War record had earned him the rank of lieutenant and who had served as a Pittsburgh policeman, the criminal charges must have seemed painfully ironic in light of his alleged offense, sending threatening letters to a nonunion worker. To Jacob M. Gusky, a Jewish clothier whose Pittsburgh store catered to union workers, the incarceration of Barkly and the others was more than ironic: it was unacceptable. Gusky bailed them out.[22]

Despite some efforts to begin negotiations, the two sides remained far apart in February. Clark was increasingly annoyed by the strikers' incessant harassment. For example, a newsdealer, Isaac Bryan, was assaulted one morning for delivering papers to the men inside the mill. And when Frank Clark returned from Steelton, Pennsylvania, with one man willing to work in the mill, the strikers "persuaded" him to leave town. By February the strikers had reached a highly persuasive position: their numbers dominated the municipal police force and signaled their emergence as the most powerful group in the town.[23]

The AAISW lodges themselves exercised great authority in and out of the mill. Each maintained a kind of craft orientation: rail mill workers belonged to Lodge no. 11, whereas workers in the converting and blooming mill joined Lodge no. 24. Each lodge had a president, vice president, several secretaries and "guards," delegates to the National Lodge of the union, and, finally, a corresponding representative who sent announcements to the *National Labor Tribune*. Each lodge also had a mill committee to enforce union work rules in the steelworks. In addition, the two lodges sent several representatives to a joint Advisory Committee, a plantwide organization led by George Fitzgerald during the strike. This committee was powerful on a day-to-day basis: with some assistance from national officers, it was responsible for conducting negotiations, maintaining general discipline, and ensuring public safety. However, it remained at all times strictly accountable to the membership of the two lodges.[24]

Despite the solidarity among workers of different levels of skill and various ethnic groups, by the end of February, William Clark had succeeded in resuming some operations in the Homestead works. He was able to do this by seeking out workers who had little allegiance to the idea of amalgamation and who, like himself, wanted to pursue their main chance. In addition to unskilled nonunion workers, Clark thus managed to engage even a number of skilled AAISW members. Harry Gamble, for example, left the union's Invincible Lodge at the Fort Pitt Iron and Steel Works to become a scab heater in Homestead. His decision, not surprisingly, disgusted loyal union men, who saw it as an affront to their cherished republicanism. "I am sorry you have been so simple minded as to go and sign away the freedom your forefathers fought so hard to maintain," one striker wrote of Gamble. "Yet you acknowledge that you have signed it away and signed your freedom for ambition."[25]

In late February the union responded to Clark's limited success with hints that it would conduct strikes in the Pittsburgh mills operated by the owners of the PBSW. Clark and his partners retaliated by evicting more Homestead steelworkers from their rented homes. On 1 March, however, the owners suddenly decided to withdraw the ironclad agreement in the hopes of reaching a settlement. They had orders to meet and were under considerable pressure to fulfill their contractual obligations. In fact, the company already had defaulted on one order for ten thousand tons of rails and understood that it was likely to be sued for damages. Moreover, the rails it had shipped were so poorly drilled that the buyers had been unable to use them.[26]

The owners, then, had to walk a tight line: they had to fight a war of attrition against the Homestead lodges, but they also had to find a way to open the steelworks with workers who knew how to make it work. As the Homestead mill was technologically unique, the owners were at a decided disadvantage. Though some highly skilled workers—Harry Gamble, for example—helped ease the owners' predicament, the union men in Homestead were confident that their collective skill would eventually bring them victory: "We depend on our skill and energy and efficiency as workmen and believe those traits would impel Mr. Clark to take most of us back."[27]

Clark, of course, continually tried to undermine this confidence. In announcing that he had withdrawn the ironclad contract, for example, he also stated that he would rehire only those union men he considered "fit to employ." Within hours of this provocative statement, the violence at Homestead reached an unprecedented level. Strikers attacked the tenements near the mill that housed the hated scabs. The fighting spread into the town itself, and there the strikers singled out and assaulted three men who had continued to work in the mill. One of them was John Northcraft, a foreman in the converting department. Some union members who served as policemen apparently were among the assailants, for Burgess W. S. Bullock stripped eight of them of their badges.[28]

At daybreak on 2 March the fighting began anew when the scabs made their way from their tenements to the mill. The strikers had possession of the railroad tracks that stood between the tenements and the mill, and as the scabs approached across an open meadow, shots were exchanged. "The deputies, as usual, went out to bring the men in to work, and as they marched down the road toward the mill with the men in line, a large body of strikers, who had congregated near the railroad, began hooting and jeering at them." Several scabs and deputies were wounded before the strikers succeeded in turning them away. They fled, according to one reporter, in fear of their lives, as they were "pursued by the strikers firing revolvers and throwing stones with murderous intent and yelling like so many Indians."[29]

The clash persuaded Bullock to ask for more assistance from the county sheriff, who sent an additional sixteen deputies to Homestead. This brought the total force to more than fifty men, whose presence increasingly disturbed union members. "The sight of these officers seemed to have the effect of exciting rather than quieting, . . . The strikers, or Union men, kept in squads and carefully watched every newcomer or stranger that appeared in town. . . . To them, the appearance of the deputy sheriffs was a declaration of war."[30]

And indeed it was: late on the afternoon of 2 March when a party of scabs was returning home under the sheriff's escort, they were assailed by a crowd of approximately three hundred strikers and their supporters. Four deputies were the objects of particularly intense verbal abuse, and one of them, Richard Moran, was struck on the head by a stone. He responded by firing his revolver into the crowd and wounding two men—at which point the crowd descended on him with repeated shouts of "Kill the damned cop." Moran, as well as another officer who had fired into the crowd, were beaten to unconsciousness as Fitzgerald and other union leaders tried unsuccessfully to restrain the crowd. Finally, the arrival of still more officers dispersed the mob. The deputies remained in Homestead and patrolled the streets throughout the night.[31]

Fitzgerald and the other leaders of the AAISW responded by again urging all strikers to eschew violence. The union sought to renew discussions with Clark, but he refused. By 3 March, however, his work force had been greatly diminished because of "the alarm engendered by the numerous disturbances." The converting mill was shut down, and only a skeleton crew remained in the blooming and rail mills. Moreover, the strikers had "ordered" the boss machinist, William Killcrere, to close his shop. He and the blacksmiths employed in the mill agreed. Tensions remained high, and Burgess Bullock (a merchant by trade) decided to have himself sworn in as a deputy sheriff, a move that Fitzgerald and John Elias Jones roundly criticized. Public safety in Homestead was clearly the responsibility of the AAISW.[32]

With the persistence of violence, the leaders of the union grew concerned that the state militia might be called out and that Clark might as a result begin full-scale operations. Fitzgerald, Jones, and Blanford therefore pressed their initiative to reopen negotiations. Harry Gamble, the former AAISW member who was "blacksheeping," also proposed a conference with the strikers in an apparent effort to end the strike. Clark, however, intervened and halted a proposed meeting of the scabs, the union men, and borough officials. The purpose of the meeting, he recognized, was to end the strike by bringing the nonunion men into the

AAISW. Borough officials urged Clark not to intervene. "Let the borough keep its hands off our works, and we will attend to our own business," Clark replied.[33]

Homestead remained uneasy over the next few days; rumors of more attacks abounded; the sheriff sent in more deputies, most of whom remained inside the works at the request of the AAISW. In the town, union patrolmen preserved the peace. Meanwhile, at the steelworks, thirty-three nonunion men who were denied permission to attend a union meeting handed in their resignations to Clark, who was thus left even more short-handed.[34]

On Saturday 4 March, the Homestead dispute threatened to explode. A districtwide meeting of the AAISW voted to call a strike in the city mills owned by the partners of the PBSC unless they "bring about some means of settlement of the difficulties now existing at the Homestead works." Such a strike would idle five thousand to six thousand men. *Iron Age* commented on the vote, "This is an outrage. Worse than that, it is a crime."[35]

The following day, Sunday 5 March, George Fitzgerald and other union leaders convened a meeting of more than five hundred people in Homestead. Strikers, scabs, and ordinary citizens, as well as William Singer, a partner in the PBSC, listened for hours to the speeches of borough leaders, union officials, and labor activists from Homestead and across the Pittsburgh area. Beeswax Taylor and fellow Knights of Labor urged listeners to support the GLP. Frank Gessner criticized those strikers who had engaged in violence, and John Jarrett stated that the AAISW was steadfastly against resolving disputes through violent means.[36]

For the AAISW the immediate effect of the meeting was to persuade the engineers and machinists who remained in the mill to cease work. Not all responded with equal enthusiasm, however, and some divisions within the union's ranks did appear. Moreover, in a final effort to press whatever advantage they had, the owners of the Homestead works threatened to prosecute the AAISW for conspiracy in the event of a citywide strike. The threat apparently brought favorable results, for Secretary William Martin and President Jarrett of the union met with William Singer, and together they announced that a settlement was close at hand. As later press accounts revealed, their meeting did produce a tentative settlement. But the union leaders had no authority to accept it or to call off the sympathy strike without the consent of the delegates from all the Pittsburgh lodges, who were scheduled to meet on Saturday 11 March.[37]

That day several Pittsburgh papers reported that the strike was in effect over. Jarrett announced that the union would not be so "unreasonable" as to demand that all the strikers be rehired. In truth, no such demand was necessary: as the daily press reported, the strike was near conclusion because Clark had finally recognized that only the strikers could meet the skill requirements of the PBSW. "The Amalgamated members pride themselves on their skill and energy and their faithful work, and they believe that the managers of the Homestead works fully appreciate their excellence as workmen. It has been said that the force of workmen at the Homestead mill was one of the best forces in the country. The Union men feel safe in relying upon their ability . . . [to] insure the re-employment of the majority of them."[38]

The meeting of the AAISW delegates ended with a vote to accept the terms negotiated by Jarrett, Martin, and Clark, under which work was to resume on 14 March and Jarrett would sign the contract on behalf of the men—in other words, the union had won recognition. Other terms provided for no immediate reduction in wages; however, Clark and the workers were pledged to reach a new agreement on wages, within thirty days, that might include reductions. The company won the right to reinstate only as many union men as it desired. Jarrett optimistically assured union members in Homestead that despite this clause, they would all find work in the mill.[39]

The next day the Advisory Committee met with Clark and asked for a list of the men he intended to take back. Upon examining it, the committee charged that Clark had not lived up to an oral agreement: "The list of men to be taken back to the mill comprises 111 names—a number much smaller than the workers expected," one newspaper reported. Officials of the AAISW's Homestead lodges maintained that Clark had agreed to fill a full turn with their men—that is, to hire two hundred union hands in the rail, blooming, and converting mills for an entire shift of work. Clark, however, had listed only sixty-eight.[40]

Immediately after word of Clark's decision got out, the violence in Homestead resumed. A scab was beaten that evening, and early the next morning, 14 March, two guards employed by Clark were shot by a crowd of strikers. The fire was returned by nonunion men. More deputies intervened, but they were ridiculed by the strikers. "The deputy sheriffs were ordered to the scene of disorder, but the roughs merely laughed at them." About the same time, Henry Healy, a carpenter who worked in the mill, was beaten almost to the point of death, and a shoemaker who had given refuge to one of the scabs was also attacked. Strikers also assaulted Haverly Brush, a foreman in the rail mill, and they surrounded the home of a heater who had continued working in the mill. When he tried to leave for work, he was stoned.[41]

The strikers thus had succeeded in overturning the established order. This was the meaning of their laughter, for it was they, and not the legally constituted authorities, who controlled Homestead. And it was this fact that forced Clark to shut down the mill and then prompted him to request that the state militia be sent in.

The request was not answered; meanwhile, Fitzgerald and other union leaders in Homestead renewed their pleas for nonviolence. Finally, late on 14 March, Clark and several of the other owners met with AAISW leaders, and all agreed that the union men could choose who would be placed on Clark's list. The union now presented an additional demand: that the AAISW workers in Homestead be henceforth free to choose their own substitutes to stand in for them in the event of illness or absence. To the union men in Homestead, this demand was of utmost importance: it would guarantee the union's rights not just to determine who would work, but also to ensure that all would get their turn to work, albeit with reduced wages for each worker. In demanding this privilege, the Homestead steelworkers gave concrete expression to their version of a moral economy.

Clark officially refused this proposal on doubling up, as the workers called it. He soon agreed, however, that he would employ a full turn of union men, adding, "If any of the turn wished to be away for a turn, they could go and get men to fill their places." The union men claimed victory; they would "soon have full possession of the mill." Furthermore, the PBSC agreed to drop all criminal charges, and Clark also recognized the authority of the AAISW lodges in Homestead, and not merely the union president, John Jarrett, to sign contracts. On 20 March the first crew of strikers returned to work.[42]

Within weeks the AAISW did indeed have virtual possession of the mill. "Our men started up on one turn, the sheep operated the other. The sheep . . . turned out some forty tons; our men followed with 140 tons. A few days only sufficed to work most of our men in on the sheep turn, when we got a majority, and as a result most of the sheep had to go." The skill of the union men had proved decisive. Not only did they work faster, but they also produced steel of higher quality.

To be sure, the workers could take just pride in their triumph and productivity. Yet, ironically enough, the owners' submission to the demands of labor resulted in a triumph of sorts for them, too. Now that skilled union men manned the mill at all turns, production could reach unprecedented heights and generate fine-quality steel and fine profits for the company.[43]

The Homestead strike of 1882 thus constitutes an exceptional example of worker-management relations in the 1880s, for the moral and political victory of the steelworkers entailed some measure of success for the steelmasters too. In light of the successful negotiation of their contract, Homestead workers took great pride in their republican ideals, which they had not betrayed in the face of real menace. It was with just such pride that three months later these workers would parade through the streets of Pittsburgh carrying a banner that proclaimed, "Tried and Found Faithful." And yet, for all their faith in labor republicanism, their victory was not without compromise. For what were the spoils of their victory? The steelworkers had indeed legitimized their right to control conditions on the shop floor, and they had also earned respect in the arena of municipal government. But in practical terms, they had won back little more than the right to produce more steel, more efficiently, and to generate more profits for the very steelmasters who had tyrannized them from the start. This underlying paradox of labor's victory escaped the still jubilant steelworkers in 1882; it would, however, ominously rise to the surface to trouble the Homestead workers in 1889 and to torment them in 1892.[44]

Chapter 13

"Defense, Not Defiance":
Defeat in the City and the State

T HOUSANDS OF WORKERS came to downtown Pittsburgh early on 17 June 1882. Some traveled by railroad from Ohio and West Virginia; others walked from suburbs and inner-city neighborhoods. Huge crowds welcomed them with banners, Chinese lanterns, flowers, and hundreds of American flags. "From early in the day, the streets were a moving mass of men, women and children." It was a Saturday, the day on which workers customarily transformed downtown Pittsburgh into their "decent carnival." Despite chilly temperatures and heavy rain, the mood was unusually festive and warm this Saturday morning. Bands and singing groups performed on sidewalks, and workers jammed restaurants, shops, and saloons. "Every street in the central portion of the city was crowded by . . . a good-natured throng . . . ; everybody seemed to vie with everybody else in enthusiasm."[1]

The occasion for the celebration was a "Grand Labor Parade" organized by District Assembly no. 3 of the Knights of Labor, the AAISW and other trade unions. The parade—in effect the first commemoration of Labor Day in the United States—drew at least thirty thousand marchers and more than one hundred thousand observers to the city in what the Knights called "a peaceable protest against the evils that exist against the many by and through the power of wealth possessed by the few." The Knights further declared their parade a statement to support "the rights of freemen." Indeed, marchers made labor republicanism the dominant theme of the day. The banners they carried echoed the foremost ideas of the workers' movement of the 1870s: that labor was "noble and holy" and "the source of all wealth"; that "monopoly" was undermining the republic and making it impossible to win "a fair day's wages for a fair day's work" and a "competence obtained by honest labor"; and that amalgamation was the key to resisting wage slavery and reaffirming the rights of citizen workers.[2]

In keeping with the ubiquitous assertions of labor reformers that the workers' movement constituted a "Grand Army of Labor," the parade was organized along quasi-military lines with five "divisions" led by "commanders," "adjutants," and "aides." Beyond its appeal to military patriotism, the orderly formation of the parade served moreover to distinguish the organized activities of the workers from the 1877 mob rule of Pittsburgh's Roundhouse Riot. Ranking officials such as Isaac Cline, Andrew Burtt, Jr., and A. C. Rankin dressed in paramilitary attire and rode on horseback, and workers' bands played martial music. The "chief of staff" was Thomas Armstrong, the editor of the *National Labor Tribune* and the preeminent Knight in Pittsburgh; his friend Beeswax Taylor, who had recently moved to Homestead, rode in a carriage at the head of the procession.

Behind Armstrong and Taylor assemblies of the Knights followed; then came miners, glassworkers, iron molders and, finally lodges of the AAISW. Approximately seven thousand Knights and ten thousand AAISW men marched together. The miners, with roughly six thousand marchers—eleven hundred of them from collieries near Homestead—comprised the third largest contingent. They were "commanded" by their union president, D. R. Jones, then fighting conspiracy charges brought by Thomas Mellon and the Waverly Coal Company.[3]

The Braddock Glee Club, composed of AAISW men and Knights from the Edgar Thomson mill, provided one of the highlights of the parade. Their rendition of Beeswax Taylor's labor ode, "Storm the Fort, Ye Knights of Labor," elicited particularly hearty cheers along the parade route. John McLuckie, who had helped organize Braddock Lodge no. 97 of the AAISW, proudly helped to represent it, along with 800 Braddock steelworkers. Not far behind marched 385 of their brothers from Homestead, members of AAISW lodges 11 and 24, under the command of George Fitzgerald and John Elias Jones, who had successfully led the three-month challenge of the authority of William Clark. One hundred fifty additional Homesteaders, belonging to Local Assembly 1785, followed; these Knights of Labor included steelworkers who had participated in the steel strike as well as glassworkers employed at Bryce, Higbee, and Company.[4]

The banner carried by Lodge 24 summed up the recent experience of all the Homestead strikers: "Tried and Found Faithful." As the daily press reported, this banner spoke for itself: the Homestead men had been severely tested, but their allegiance to the house of labor had stood firm. Ironically, however, while the allegiance of the Homestead workers stood firm indeed in June 1882, the house of labor was beginning to teeter.

At the time of the grand parade, Homestead was not the only labor community under assault. The organizers of the parade were only too aware of similar tensions across Western Pennsylvania. In Pittsburgh itself, agents of organized capital had been attacking workers' organizations in the courts, factories, and polling places for more than a decade. In spite of the increasing pressures, the union movement had grown in size and strength during these years. District Assembly 3 of the Knights had expanded to seventy local assemblies and ten thousand members by April 1882; thousands of other workers belonged to the trade assemblies of glassworkers and miners. Moreover, workers had achieved an independent political voice in the GLP. Nevertheless, by 1882 the party had yet to overcome the traditional allegiances of most workers—and the majority of Pittsburgh's workers remained unaffiliated with a trade union. As Thomas Armstrong, a leader of the GLP, said of the Pennsylvania labor movement: "The elements of its strength and weakness are almost equal, . . . yet its enemies were never more resolute than they are at this moment. The situation is thus full of hope and at the same time fraught with peril."[5]

It is against this shifting backdrop of potential hopes and potential failures that Armstrong, along with Knights, trade unionists, Land Leaguers and labor-greenbackers, recognized the immediate need for a major public event that would consolidate the morale of workers in Greater Pittsburgh. In the spring of 1882 they began crisscrossing the region in a flurry of organizational activity, hoping to mount the most potent challenge to date against the regime of capital. And in order to do this, they sought to nurture in all wage earners the same allegiance to labor republicanism that had helped Homesteaders construct their budding workers' republic. In practical terms, this meant recruiting new union members and launching a political campaign on behalf of the GLP.[6]

The parade was conceived as a grand spectacle to promote and top off public enthusiasm for these activities. Mindful of the party's woeful showing in the 1881 elections, Beeswax Taylor, John McLuckie, and other activists began to canvass branches of the Irish National Land League, trade unions, and local assemblies of the Knights in early spring with an eye toward choosing the most appealing candidates for the fall election. Speaking for the *National Labor Tribune,* Armstrong affirmed, "We have presented to us a grand opportunity of making our party not the third, but the first, in this county if we act wisely in the coming campaign."[7]

Terrence Powderly, grand master workman of the Knights and an officer in the Land League, joined in the effort. His fellow Knights had reason to hope that his prominence and celebrity in labor circles would guarantee the successful outcome of all their campaigns. But Powderly's role in the movement was compromised from the start by personal ambitions and political ambivalence: he, too, strove for the main chance and in the end decided that his chance could be more readily secured within the safer ranks of the political establishment. Powderly's eventual defection from the cause of political insurgency emphatically weakened it at the top. More significantly however, his retreat dramatized the uncertainties and the hesitations that undermined labor's foundations in Pittsburgh, in Pennsylvania, and indeed throughout the nation. Nor could his timing have been more symbolic; for it was on the very day of the grand parade, which he had helped organize, that he chose to announce his withdrawal from independent labor politics.[8]

When Powderly first came to Pittsburgh in the spring of 1882, his advocacy of workers' rights and land nationalization elicited the enthusiastic response of hundreds of workers. The *Irish World* proudly observed that among Powderly's admirers the potential for political insurgency was great. In the eyes of the ever cautious Powderly, however, the possibility of political insurrection clearly jeopardized his career ambitions. By the time the GLP held its nominating convention on 18 May, therefore, the grand master workman was already backing away from his tentative attachment to independent labor politics and toward what the daily press called the conservative trade union position. The convention, nonetheless, nominated Armstrong for governor with Powderly as his running mate for lieutenant governor.[9]

Armstrong sensed in Powderly's ambivalence an ominous threat to the party and to the labor movement. In a desperate letter that summed up twenty years' of struggle, he implored Powderly to remain on the ticket.

> You *must not leave me*. I will not desert you nor the principles of humanity for which we have jointly battled for so many years. . . . You have doubtless read the attack on me by the *Philadelphia Telegraph?* It says that I was responsible for the Pittsburgh riots [of 1877]; that *my candidacy is an insult to every honest workingman in the State,* and by insinuation that you are too decent a man to allow your name to go on the same ticket with me. You *must not,* therefore, desert. I appeal by all that is holy in your nature to stand firm.[10]

On 17 June, the day of the grand parade, Powderly publicly rejected Armstrong's plea. "I think I can do you more good off the ticket than on it," he said, without explanation. In truth, Powderly felt an intense personal rivalry with Armstrong and also feared that a loss by the GLP would grievously injure the Knights and threaten his supremacy in the order. Moreover, he had fashioned an agreement with power brokers in Scranton that ensured his mayoralty there in return for leading the local GLP into fusion with the Democrats.[11]

At the time of the grand parade, therefore, despite all appearances of order, strength, and festivity, the labor movement faced the very real possibility of collapse from within. Nor were all the strategic faults at the top. For in the ranks of the AAISW—the most powerful labor union in Pittsburgh, if not the country—the solidarity of the workers was threatened by fractious disputes. It was with special purpose, therefore, that the thousands of members of the union who marched in the grand parade strove to reassert their unity and strength. Theirs was less a demonstration of faith in the future than an attempt to recapture the original spirit of amalgamation that had brought them together in the 1870s.

However, that spirit had never been absolute. From the start union leaders knew that their greatest organizational challenge would be to transcend the profound intercraft rivalries that divided the workers. As David Harris, the president of the old Sons of Vulcan, had explained on the eve of consolidation with the roll hands' and rollers' unions, solidarity among the various trades within the iron industry was tenuous at best: "There does exist strong and bitter antipathies between the mill trades growing out of failures on the part of one trade to support the other." Moreover, by the late 1870s union leaders recognized that the AAISW had failed to extend its power beyond the the the iron to the steel industry; technological innovations threatened to destroy the union's very base by eliminating the craft of puddling altogether.[12]

In Pittsburgh, where puddlers far outnumbered finishers, tensions between the trades had become fierce. Time and again, leaders of the AAISW in Pittsburgh cautioned puddlers against radicalism and arrogance for fear that the finishers would withdraw their support. Still, puddlers continued to stage work stoppages without "just cause" or the authorization of national union leadership. And each time this happened, the owners of the iron mills, ever intent on breaking the union, took careful note. Union leaders warily juggled the threats from within their organization with the constant assaults from without. "We know positively that while [the owners] acquiesce they do so because they must," the *National Labor Tribune* warned in 1881. "They bide their time for the grand bounce they are anxious to precipitate when an opportune occasion shall present."[13]

In the view of the owners, the occasion presented itself in April 1882 when negotiations for the yearly iron scale commenced. Puddlers, emboldened by a string of earlier successes and by the recent victory of their Homestead colleagues, decided to seek an advance. The owners retaliated by creating a secret organization requiring all members to pledge that they would not capitulate to the union. "There is a quiet firmness among the manufacturers," their journal, the *American Manufacturer* declared. "They appear to feel that they have been driven far enough during the last few years, and that now is a good time to make a stand."[14]

The puddlers interpreted the owners' bold stand as an affront to their worth and their rights. Ignoring repeated entreaties from union leaders and the firm disapproval of the finishers, the puddlers demanded an increase in the sliding scale. The owners refused. On 31 May, with internal tensions still running high, twenty-five thousand ironworkers went on strike. In the face of the "complete annihilation" of the union that the ironmasters swore, finishers, puddlers, and leaders momentarily suspended their differences to form a shaky alliance. Their collective appearance as a powerful and unshaken union at the grand parade of 17 June was thus less a demonstration of true strength than a camouflage for the grave beating they feared they would suffer.[15]

The AAISW was not the only union with a struggle on its hands at the time of the parade. The Miners' Association had gone on strike in March against a proposed wage reduction. In retaliation owners imported strikebreakers, prosecuted strikers for violation of the state conspiracy laws, evicted them from their rented homes, and suspended their credit at company stores. Nonstriking river and railroad miners had supported the two thousand strikers through April and May, and confidence had been high. But the Monongahela collieries closed for the summer and donations had virtually dried up. For the miners, too, the parade was a means to restore morale and to make a public appeal for donations.[16]

Shoring up rifts within specific trade organizations was then very much a preoccupation of the union leaders who organized the grand parade. Cooperation between unions—and between races—was also a central theme of the day. Many marchers wore "double-badges," one for their trade union and one for the local assembly of the Knights of Labor to which they belonged. The desire for "a wide amalgamation" of all workers was represented by the participation of "colored brethren" who, along with white workers, jointly carried several banners. Every attempt was thus made to mask and hopefully erase the traces of dissension that had scarred the labor movement from within; the proud celebration of workers' solidarity was designed to minimize as well the numerous assaults that labor had barely deflected from without.[17]

The intent of the organizers was not, however, merely to demonstrate that labor was unified. They also sought to redress the negative image of worker protest that had been the legacy of the Great Uprising of 1877. The *National Labor Tribune*, for one, expressed the hopes that the parade would contrast with the disorder and "mob rule" of 1877. And it did: the parade had disabused "the country . . . of many false theories" and thus shown that unionism was not "a form of socialism of the aggressive red-flag order." It was an irrefutable symbol, an outward sign, of what was going on within the labor movement: ironworkers and glassworkers, miners and molders, trade unionists and Knights, skilled and less skilled, white and black, had banded together in a "disciplined, orderly and numerous" manner so that they might "preserve the republic intact." Indeed, only organized labor could meet this monumental task of preserving the republic because, as the marchers had made explicit, labor itself constituted the very fabric of civil society.[18]

The grand parade, then, served to remind workers of the fading promises of amalgamation and labor republicanism. In its structure, moreover, the parade prefigured in miniature the formation of their model republic of labor. Workers alone had a place in this imagined state, which comprised five (roughly equal) estates: the skilled and less skilled of all trades, miners, glassworkers, molders, and iron and steelworkers. Sixteen policemen rode at the head of the procession to signify that this state was above all one of law and order. Just as the parade was headed by Chief Marshal R. H. Jones of the AAISW, Thomas Armstrong of the Knights and Miners' Association, and Beeswax Taylor and other officials from District Assembly 3, so, too, would be the workers' state led by an interlocking directorate of union officials and worker politicians.

The entire procession enacted a logic conforming to the structure and aspirations of the labor reform movement in Pittsburgh. A leader of the AAISW rode at the head of the parade, and members protected the rear; in the "iron city" that labor sought to protect and in the workers' republic they sought to build, metalworkers were the most powerful. The first division of marchers, however, were those workers who had demonstrated the deepest commitment to the idea of amalgamation: the member of the mixed trade assemblies of the Knights.[19]

It was not only the *National Labor Tribune* and the *Irish World* that were impressed by the parade and the comportment of the marchers. It was "the greatest trades union demonstration this country has seen," according to one daily. The national press joined each of Pittsburgh's papers, some of them hostile to labor, in marvel at the workers' achievement. The sight of thousands of workers, "strong and sober, testifying their faith in the principles they advocate," the *Pittsburgh Commercial-Gazette* observed, "could not be other than grand." The *Pittsburgh Post* was equally effusive in describing the chief participants: "strongly built men from the mills, broad-chested men from the glasshouses, and heavy and steep-shouldered men from the mines." That the parade was perceived as so extraordinary an event; that the workers were seen as such robust citizens; that they chose to portray their organizations as friendly, unified, and constitutive of the republic—all of this belied the disquieting truth of sustained labor strife.[20]

Within months of the parade the weaknesses and underlying divisions within this opposition came to the surface. The AAISW's effort in the Big Strike of 1882 collapsed in September amid fratricidal disagreement between the puddlers and the finishers. Both groups went so far as to consider forming separate unions. The puddlers charged that the union president, John Jarrett, had betrayed them by encouraging the defection of the finishers from the AAISW. As a result, Jarrett resigned as the union's annual convention in 1883. "The influence of this strike was very damaging, especially upon the morale of the membership," he claimed. "Internal dissensions became so rife as to put the association to the severest test." Indeed, membership fell from 16,000 in 1882 to 5,700 in 1885.[21]

While the defeat in the 1882 strike may well have been the principal cause of the decline in union membership, the AAISW also suffered cataclysmic setbacks in the steel industry during these years. Between 1882 and 1885 the union was defeated in all but one of eleven strikes in steel mills. The exception, of course, was Homestead. In the words of William Weihe, who succeeded Jarrett as president, this period of its history deserved to be known as "the non-union movement." The same designation could be applied to the 1882 record of District Assembly 3 of the Knights. In April, Master Workman A. C. Rankin reported that the district had seventy local assemblies and was growing rapidly. By the following spring, only thirty-three assemblies remained. The striking miners of District Assembly 9 also were defeated in 1882, and D. R. Jones, the president of the Miners' Association, left the union to become a lawyer.[22]

The losses suffered by the AAISW and the Pittsburgh Knights and miners were only part of labor's 1882 disaster. The political insurgency planned by Thomas Armstrong and other GLP leaders collapsed in a sorry web of private ambition and conflicting personal allegiances. In Allegheny County, workers created the United Labor party and nominated their own ticket, which stood apart from the state GLP. Within the ranks of labor reformers, Terrence Powderly was the most famous to compromise the cause by refusing to run, but there were many others. D. R. Jones, Williams Weihe, and A. C. Rankin all turned down the labor nomination; John McLuckie was one of the few labor activists who did not desert. Armstrong himself, leader of the GLP ticket and the preeminent labor reformer in the state, shocked many of his colleagues by endorsing a staunch Republican for the state legislature, his old friend Miles Humphries.[23]

The results of the November election revealed the enormous dimensions of labor's defeat. Statewide, Armstrong received 30,000 votes to 356,000 for the victorious Democratic candidate, Robert E. Pattison, and 316,000 for Republican James A. Beaver. In Philadelphia, Armstrong polled just 672 votes. Even in Allegheny County, his home base, Armstrong was badly defeated: his 4,600 votes were dwarfed by Beaver's 18,700 and Pattison's 16,800. John McLuckie also was trounced in his bid for the state senate. The only unequivocally bright spot for independent labor politics was in Homestead, where Armstrong managed to defeat all of his opponents.[24]

The campaign, which had exposed bitter divisions within the GLP, left Armstrong bitter and resigned. He wrote:

> It does not matter sufficiently for discussion just now what the cause of our defeat was. Enought to say that the endeavor to enlist organized labor in politics was a failure, and will forever remain thus so as far as the *Labor Tribune* is concerned. It is evident that whatever shall be accomplished for labor through politics must be done indirectly, by the agitation of questions in which labor may be interested with the view to compelling an established party to adopt them.

In the past, Armstrong had suggested tactical retreats along similar lines. But he had never before been so categorical in his renunciation of independent labor politics. "Defense, not defiance," summed up his new position. Other leaders joined him; their goal now was to rebuild the unions and "prudently" manage them in a spirit of what the *National Labor Tribune* called "healthy conservatism." So discouraged was Robert Layton, a ranking official in the Knights, that he publicly announced the demise of independent labor politics and his allegiance to the Republican party.[25]

Thus the workers' movement of Pittsburgh, which, as Armstrong wrote in the 1870s, had "indicted the civilization of the nineteenth century," slowly moved, with his grudging sanction, toward an uneasy accommodation with it. The retreat from insurgency was made at least as much in a spirit of resignation as in embrace of the corporate order. Indeed, given the intensity of earlier assaults on labor by management, and the omnipresent lure of the ethic of acquisitiveness, the workers' movement in Gilded Age Pittsburgh strikes us now as all the more remarkable for its resilience than for its weaknesses.[26]

And yet, as we have seen, that movement was woefully fragmented and weakened by 1882. In the face of increasing pressures from all sides, defiant workers who had marched in the parade on 17 June were reluctantly forced to change their tune. It was thus no accident that in his coverage of the procession for the *Tribune,* Thomas Armstrong began by quoting the parade banner whose message for him captured the spirit of the day: "Defense, Not Defiance." The sad irony is that America's first Labor Day parade, which was conceived to celebrate labor insurgency, also marked the beginning of its demise.[27]

The Homestead Steel Works, Carnegie, Phipps, and Company, 1890. Looking north, toward the Monongahela River. (Kelly C. Park)

Homestead steelworkers during the 1880s. Their pose is uncharacteristically relaxed for photographs of this time. (Carnegie Library of Homestead/Randolph J. Harris)

The industrial artisan: a puddler working his furnace at A. M. Byers Co., Pittsburgh. (Steel Industry Heritage Task Force)

After the revolution in metalmaking: the Bessemer converter at the Homestead Steel Works in the 1880s. (Randolph J. Harris)

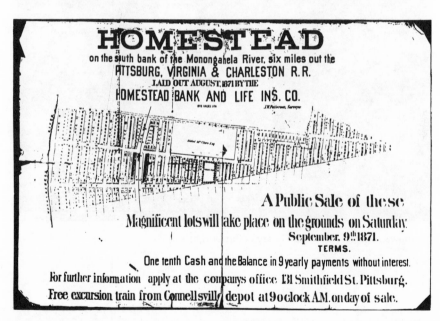

Handbill announcing the first public sale of residential lots in Homestead, 9 September 1871.

Andrew Carnegie. (Carnegie Library of Pittsburgh)

Henry Clay Frick. (Carnegie Library of Pittsburgh)

Christopher Lyman Magee, the "boss" of the city and county Republican machine and one of Frick's business partners. Along with Philander Knox, Magee helped engineer the deployment and evacuation of the Pinkerton agents on 6 and 7 July 1892. (*Notable Men of Pittsburgh, 1901*)

Philander C. C. Knox, the chief corporate lawyer for Carnegie and Frick. He served as their key strategist in 1892. Later, he became U.S. attorney general and secretary of state. (*Notable Men of Pittsburgh, 1901*)

"Hugh O'Donnell in His Pleasant Home." (*The New York World*, 17 July 1892)

"BEESWAX," THOS. W. TAYLOR.

Thomas Crawford, the leader of the workers' Advisory Committee, Homestead 1892. (Myron R. Stowell, *"Fort Frick," Or the Siege of Homestead* [Pittsburgh: Pittsburgh Printing Co., 1893])

Thomas Taylor, known as "Old Beeswax." Burgess of Homestead, 1888–89, occasional entrepreneur, and nationally prominent labor leader. (*Homestead Local News*, 3 March 1888)

John McLuckie, burgess of Homestead, 1890–91 and 1892. McLuckie, perhaps more than any other resident of Homestead, remained true to the ideals of the labor movement as it had taken shape in the 1870s in Greater Pittsburgh. (Borough of Homestead)

"Statement of Comparative Labor Costs in Competitive Mills—1891," prepared by William Martin, the chief of Andrew Carnegie's Bureau of Labor. Martin, former national secretary of the AAISW and vice-president of the AFL, formulated Carnegie's proposals in 1892 and stood against his former union brothers. (William Martin Papers)

The Battle of the Barges. (*Harper's Magazine*, 23 July 1892)

FRANK LESLIE'S
ILLUSTRATED
WEEKLY

HOMESTEAD TROUBLES.

Vol. LXXV.—No. 1922.
Copyright, 1892, by AMSELL WEEKLY CO.
All Rights Reserved.

NEW YORK, JULY 14, 1892.

[PRICE, 10 CENTS. ᴮʸ ᵀᴿᴬᴺˢᴵᵀ.
$5 a year, $1.00

THE LABOR TROUBLES AT HOMESTEAD, PENNSYLVANIA—ATTACK OF THE STRIKERS AND THEIR SYMPATHIZERS ON THE SURRENDERED
PINKERTON MEN.—DRAWN BY MISS G. A. DAVIS, FROM A SKETCH BY C. UPHAM.—[SEE PAGE 47.]

The Pinkertons and the gauntlet, 6 July 1892. This sketch, published in *Leslie's Weekly*, 14 July 1892, became the basis for the most famous iconographic image of the Lockout. Note the prominence of the women, particularly the one at the extreme left, who may well be Margaret Finch, the proprietor of the Rolling Mill House, a popular saloon in Homestead.

The Bost Building, Eighth Avenue, Homestead. During the Lockout of 1892, the workers' Advisory Committee established its headquarters on the third floor. (*Harper's Magazine*, 23 July 1892; collection of Randolph J. Harris)

State militia parading in Homestead, 1892. Note the Bost Building and the pennant—possibly an American flag—flying from the window of the headquarters of the workers' Advisory Committee. (Randolph J. Harris)

The Bost Building, November 1991. (Photograph by Randolph J. Harris)

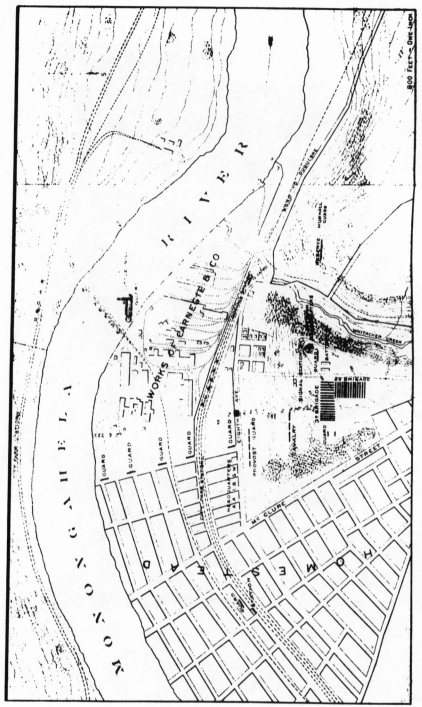

The official map of the "occupation" of Homestead by the National Guard of Pennsylvania. Note that the militia maintained a "provost guard" directly opposite the headquarters of the Advisory Committee on Eighth Avenue. (*Annual Report of the Adjutant General of Pennsylvania, 1892*)

The encampment of Company I of the Pennsylvania Militia (Col. Fred E. Windsor) in Swissvale, overlooking the Homestead Works. (Warren County Historical Society)

"Man Against Man." The steelworkers win the battle for Homestead. (*The Pittsburgh Post*, 7 July 1892)

TO ARMS! TO ARMS!

Gov. Pattison Orders the Entire National Guard to Homestead.

THERE WILL BE 8,500 MEN OUT.

Sheriff McCleary's First Actual Request For Troops.

ALL OF THE OFFICIAL ORDERS.

The Entire Army Will Likely Be in Homestead Some Time To-Morrow.

ALL ARE IN FINE CONDITION.

They Had Just Prepared for the Annual Encampmet.

WHAT ADJT. GEN. GREENLAND NOUGHT.

A LOOKOUT ABOVE THE RIVER.

SIZING UP A SUSPECT.

CHICAGO WORKMEN.

They Resolve to Give Moral, Financial and Physical Aid to the Homestead Workmen.

THE K. OF L. TO ACT.

A General Meeting to Be Held Next Wednesday Evening—Labor Unions Pass Resolutions.

RECEIVING WORD.

Gov. Pattison's Order to the Militia Spread Very Rapidly Here.

NO NOTICE TO REGIMENTS YET.

Col. Connelly Says They Will be Moving This Morning.

NATIONAL GUARD'S STRENGTH.

AT STRIKERS' HEADQUARTERS.

Governor Robert E. Pattison mobilized the Pennsylvania National Guard. The steelworkers lose. *The Pittsburgh Post,* 11 July 1892)

THE CARNEGIE STEEL COMPANY, LIMITED.

NOTICE.

THE FOLLOWING

RULES AND REGULATIONS

WILL BE IN FORCE AT THE

HOMESTEAD STEEL WORKS,

BEGINNING JULY 1st, 1892.

1. No one will be permitted to interfere with the Civil, Religious or Political opinions of the Workmen, and no political notices or posters will be allowed to be circulated or posted on the property of this Association.

2. All employes wishing to absent themselves for a turn, or longer, must first apply to and receive permission from their Foreman; and all persons working on night turn must make their application before 4 o'clock P. M. All persons violating this rule will be subject to discharge.

3. Employes are required to exercise economy in the use of all material, and to keep the machinery and works neat and clean.

4. Any employe, who through gross carelessness or malice, destroys the property of this Association, or is found stealing or carrying away the property of this Association, will be discharged.

5. Any employe, who on account of violation of the Criminal Laws of the Country is arrested, and by reason of his arrest leaves his position vacant, will be discharged and his position filled.

6. Any employe who habitually neglects or refuses to pay his debts will be subject to discharge.

7. The use of intoxicating liquor by any employe, while on duty, is absolutely forbidden, under penalty of immediate discharge.

8. All Superintendents and Foremen must pay strict attention to the rights and privileges of employes. Where a position is vacant, the employe of longest service at the Homestead Steel Works, and in the line of promotion, must fill the vacancy, without regard to his political or religious opinions; provided, however, he is fully competent to fill the higher position.

9. Excepting only where a special contract has been made, as for advice, counsel, etc., every salaried employe of this Association is expected to devote his entire service to the interests of his employer; and while no restriction is sought to be placed upon investments made by any employe, the taking of any active part in the conduct of the business in which such investment is made will not be permitted.

10. Department Superintendents and Foremen shall give hearing and prompt attention to any reasonable complaint or claim for redress, and if unable to amicably adjust the matter, shall refer the same to the General Superintendent.

11. All Department Superintendents and Foremen must see that the above Rules and Regulations are strictly complied with and rigidly enforced.

By order of the Board of Managers.

H. C. FRICK,

Chairman.

Pittsburg, Pa., July 1st, 1892.

The New Regime I: Work rules posted by Frick and John Potter, the superintendent of the Homestead Steel Works, 1 July 1892, the first full day of the lockout. (USX Archives)

THE CARNEGIE STEEL COMPANY, LIMITED.

I, ... , employed in the works of THE CARNEGIE STEEL COMPANY, LIMITED, at Munhall, Pa., prior to July 1st, 1892, as ....in the.............................mill, do hereby apply for re-instatement in the position held by me.

My age is............years,.............married, have   children.

I was not present on the grounds of The Carnegie Steel Company, Limited, in Mifflin Township on July 6th, 1892, at any time, nor did I take any part in any of the rioting or disturbances occuring in the Borough of Homestead or in Mifflin Township from July 1st, 1892, to the present time, nor do I know of my own personal knowledge of any one who did take part therein.

On July 6th, 1892, I spent the day as follows:

....

....

....

....

....

....

....

....

....

Sworn to and subscribed before me this.................day of

....1892.

....**Notary Public.**

The New Regime II: The affidavit workers were required to sign as part of their application for reemployment following the disturbances of 6 July. (USX Archives)

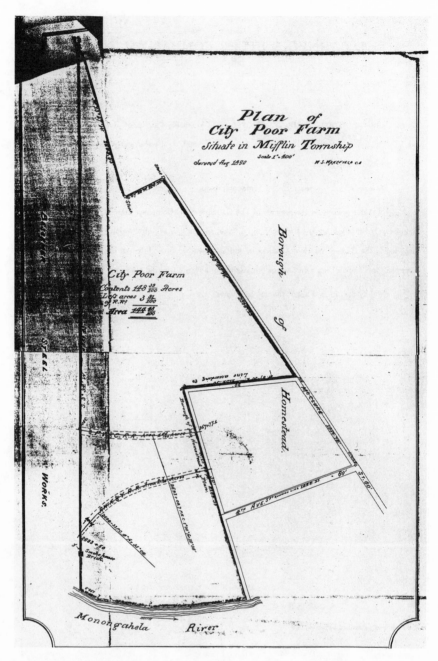

Map of the City Poor Farm and a coded telegram (on facing page) from Knox to Frick regarding the land deal, 31 July 1890. (USX Archives; the full text of the letters and telegrams is in Appendix I)

NUMBER ___ SENT BY ___ REC'D BY ___ CHECK ___

Received at _____ 188__

The Carnegie Library, Homestead. Dedicated by Carnegie in 1898, the building stands on the site used by the state militia for its campground in 1892. Carnegie bought the land in a highly suspect deal involving Philander C. Knox, Henry Clay Frick, and Christopher L. Magee. (Carnegie Library of Homestead)

The Carnegie Library, Braddock. On 30 March 1889, Carnegie came to Braddock to dedicate the first of the 2,811 public libraries that he gave to the public. (Carnegie Library, Pittsburgh)

In the wake of the Lockout of 1892, Carnegie's philanthropy often elicited satiric responses. This cartoon was published in *Harper's Weekly* in 1903. (Carnegie Library, Pittsburgh)

PART FIVE
Labor in Greater Pittsburgh During the 1880s

There is a point beyond which workmen cannot go without becoming criminals, and when they pass that point they are amenable to the law, and should be arrested, tried, convicted, and punished. . . . The safety point has been passed by the strikers at Homestead. . . . The law must be enforced at whatever cost. . . . The spirit of lawlessness shown at Homestead must be stamped out . . . (for) private rights are imperilled by mob violence."

        — *Pittsburgh Chronicle-Telegraph*, July 1889

Capitalists, merchants, and businessmen need feel proud of the conservatism that pervades the legion of labor organizations in . . . Pittsburgh

    — William Martin, national secretary,
      Amalgamated Association of Iron and Steel Workers, 1890

Chapter 14

A Tale of Two Cities: Pittsburgh and Homestead

WHILE THE PROSPECTS for labor insurgency in Pittsburgh looked grim indeed in 1882, next door in Homestead, labor was making notable strides. Workers there, spurred on by their unprecedented victory in the strike of 1882, banded together to bring into being their cherished yet ill-defined dreams for a republican community. Only six miles separated the Homestead Steel Works from the steel facilities that dominated Pittsburgh. And yet, given the radically different fortunes of labor politics in those two places in the 1880s, they might as well have been in different parts of the country.

In Pittsburgh, Thomas Armstrong had good reason to proclaim the death of labor insurgency in the wake of his calamitous defeat in the 1882 gubernatorial election. Given the humiliating blow, few labor leaders quarreled with Armstrong's categorical renunciation of independent labor politics. In their view the continued allegiance of Pennsylvania's workers to the mainstream parties indicated that it was time to concentrate on building trade unions rather than political platforms. Labor thus turned decisively away from electoral politics after 1882; the sanctuaries of the Knights of Labor and the AAISW became the hubs of trade union activity in Pittsburgh. Occasionally, labor leaders, Armstrong among them, tried to reclaim the spirit of political insurgency by renewing their efforts in the electoral arena. They met with little success, however. And despite a number of trade union victories, the overall condition of the Knights and the AAISW deteriorated badly. In fact, the two unions, which had pledged to build a grand amalgamation of all workers, found themselves at the very center of what became labor's deadly internecine brawl.[1]

The story of union relationships in Pittsburgh in the 1880s, for all its confusions and turnabouts, is an important one. Just as steelmaking had become the preeminent industry of the "second industrial revolution," so too did the metalworkers who filled the ranks of the Knights and the AAISW become the preeminent representatives of organized labor in the

205

country. Given their place in the national economy, these metalworkers set the example for all union activity at the time: their successes and their failures read like barometers of workers' strength. Workers and managers alike, therefore, looked to Pittsburgh, the very center of industrializing America, as a measure of labor solidarity on the shop floor and at the ballot box. What they saw in 1882 was a very confusing picture of two unions in disarray, each looking for a way to ensure the rights of labor, at a time when the precise nature of those rights was being disputed on all fronts.

Relations between the Knights and the AAISW in Pittsburgh had been cordial into the early 1880s. In the wake of the internal divisions that had fractured the AAISW during the Big Strike of 1882, however, leaders of that union faced declining memberships and a weakened power base. Some, like William Martin, its cautious and ambitious secretary, provoked bitter jurisdictional and policy disputes with the Knights. Under his influence, the AAISW became more and more the union of "healthy conservatism," whereas the Knights continued to pursue the ideals of labor reform and looked to a broad union of skilled and unskilled workers. The AAISW, despite some easing of membership requirements, continued to bar unskilled workers until 1889.[2]

However, in some iron and steel factories, assemblies of Knights and lodges of the AAISW did succeed in cooperating. At the Edgar Thomson Steel Works, for example, Local Assembly 1967 and Bessemer Lodge 103 supported each other despite Martin's mounting criticism of the Knights. In fact, scores of metalworkers maintained concurrent memberships in both unions. Iron Workers Assembly 1726 of the Knights was a case in point: it was "almost exclusively composed of Amalgamated men."[3]

Such instances of cooperation, however exceptional, began to rekindle the hopes of Pittsburgh labor activists in 1885. A worker known by the pseudonym Red, Jr., who lived just outside Braddock, captured some of the hopefulness of the period. His poem, "Come, Brothers, Come," echoed the familiar themes of labor republicanism and extended its promises—and demands—to women. "Come rally, noble Knights of Labor, come forth and prove your manliness" he wrote. "Come forth, ye women, . . . come help us fight that noble battle, that battle for humanity, . . . / and help to make all mankind free." In June 1885 labor leaders capitalized on such convictions: they organized another "Grand Labor Parade" that drew thousands, including 1,100 from the Edgar Thomson alone, to march through downtown Pittsburgh. And later that summer, Armstrong and other leading Knights, AAISW men, and miners organized the Trades Assembly of Western Pennsylvania. By the time 7,000 miners went on strike in the fall, however, renewed bickering between leaders of the miners' organizations and District Assembly 3 of the Knights began to eat away at whatever solidarity the Trades Assembly had been able to nurture.[4]

Conflicting impulses of solidarity and fragmentation continued to pull at Pittsburgh's labor movement in 1886, when the Great Upheaval drew hundreds of thousands of workers into the sanctuaries of the Knights of Labor all across North America. The number of local assemblies in Pittsburgh increased almost exponentially, metalworkers, who organized at least eighteen local assemblies in Pittsburgh, playing an important role. By August the membership of District Assembly 3 reached 9,000. However, the very success of the Knights in recruiting metalworkers in Pittsburgh led to further disputes with the AAISW. As a result, in late 1886 the latter overwhelmingly rejected the Knights' plan to affiliate with the order. Indeed, relations between Pittsburgh's unions had grown to acrimonious that they could not even agree to hold a Labor Day parade. The *National Labor Tribune* nonetheless proclaimed that the workers' movement in Pittsburgh had never been stronger. In terms of raw numbers this may have been true. But the movement had changed dramatically; it had lost its firm commitment to independent labor politics. Amazingly, in the 1886 election both the *Tribune* and the Trades Assembly endorsed the candidacy of "Boss" Christopher Magee.[5]

The *Tribune*'s endorsement of Magee was made in a grudging acceptance of his "ownership of the town." At the same time, however, its editor, Thomas Armstrong, helped lead a small group of activists— Homesteaders Beeswax Taylor, B. R. Culbertson, and John Miller, among them—in an effort to resuscitate the greenback-labor movement. Ultimately, however, these labor reform veterans urged fusion with the mainstream parties.[6]

The tactic of political fusion was adopted more out of necessity than out of choice, for by 1887 the labor movement in the Pittsburgh district had never been so bitterly divided. The fighting followed a byzantine trail of charge and countercharge that was cut by the leaders of the AAISW, District 3 of the Knights, and Local Assembly 300, which in effect constituted the national union of window glass workers. The official newspapers of these organizations, as well as the Trades Assembly and its paper, the *Trades Journal*, served as battleground. Virtually every week, the *Trades Journal* joined the *National Labor Tribune*, the *Commoner* (later the *Glassworker*) and the *Labor Herald* in finding new ways to discredit a putative rival.[7]

The feuding between the Knights and the AAISW was especially corrosive. The two organizations squared off at Mingo Junction, Ohio, where John McLuckie tried to play a mediating role, and at the Park brothers' Black Diamond Steel Works in Pittsburgh. In the wake of the AAISW's refusal to affiliate with the Knights, the order created its own National Trade Assembly (no. 217) of iron and steel workers. The AAISW retaliated by prohibiting its members from holding membership in the Knights and, to make its break with labor reform more complete, then joined the American Federation of Labor.[8]

The principal banner carried by the AAISW in the 1887 Labor Day parade signaled just how far the workers' movement had traveled from its postwar moorings. "Unity, Stability, Conservatism," it read, and organizers purposely cast the tone of the entire celebrations in similarly accommodating tones. One Pittsburgh daily pointed out that the parade of 1887 differed markedly from the grand parade of June 1882, when the call for the parade had frightened some Pittsburghers because it elicited memories of the Great Uprising of 1877. "There is now no necessity for a demonstration of labor organizations to show how well they can disport themselves in public. There is no expectation that they will have other than a peaceful and pleasant time." The 1887 parade coincided with the centennial of the U. S. Constitution—and an even more conservative shift in the *National Labor Tribune*'s rhetoric. The paper characterized the United States as an unparalleled "leader in progress tending to human elevation, politically, morally and physically."[9]

Such celebratory prose, no less than the well-behaved thousands who marched, marked the radical mellowing of Pittsburgh's political culture. The death of Thomas Armstrong in October 1887 allowed for some wistful declarations in the name of labor, but these eulogies were but a thin disguise for the conservative path that labor had taken. Armstrong's passing ultimately served more as a sentimental reminder than as a genuine reaffirmation of labor reform. His good friend, Beeswax Taylor, soon to be elected burgess of Homestead, joined the thousands who paid tribute to him. Others were more critical: one influential Knight in fact charged that the *Tribune* had so drastically changed by 1889 that Armstrong would "turn in his grave and weep with remorse."[10]

Armstrong would have had much to weep about in the late 1880s. Carnegie decimated the Knights at the Edgar Thomson in 1888; the defeat shattered morale in District Assembly 3 as well as in the National Trade Assembly of iron and steelworkers. Indeed, within a year the latter was dead. Moreover, the national leadership of the Knights was fighting among themselves, and the fray spilled over into the sanctuary of District 3. By 1889 the district had lost one master workman to charges of nepotism and the disclosure of secrets, and his successor described the local organization as discouraged and disheartened. A headline in a Pittsburgh daily summed up the internal fighting most succinctly: "Warring Knights." In July 1889 another paper ran the headline "The K of L is Crippled: Remarkable Falling Away of Order." By this time, District 3 had fewer than thirty local assemblies; within a year the district assembly would be close to death.[11]

Meanwhile, the AAISW was having difficulties of its own. The loss of a major strike at Singer, Nimick and Company in Pittsburgh reemphasized the thorny problem of how to maintain solidarity in the face of a resolute opponent. As the union explained: "The cause of this defeat was by some of the most prominent men of the mill becoming traitors. . . . This was a mill that . . . required the most skillful men to do the work; yet when it came to the test they became so alarmed for fear that strangers would come and do the work, they deserted." Though that strike was disheartening, union members found solace in their summertime triumph over a lockout staged by Pittsburgh metal manufacturers. William Weihe, the president of the AAISW, called it a "great and grand victory." *Iron Age* put metalworkers on notice, however, that mill owners were more determined than ever to run factories "without dictation from committees of labor associations." During the lockout, steel manufacturers, being less dependent on the skill of workers, had resisted capitulating longer than the ironmakers. The lesson of the lockout for the owners was by now a familiar one: the key to fulfilling their aspirations and running their factories as they saw fit was to substitute steel for iron production.[12]

Steelworkers understood this tactic. And in light of their successive defeats over the course of the 1880s, they also understood just how vulnerable they were. Indeed, by 1889, Homestead was the last union stronghold in the steel mills of the Pittsburgh district. And indications were that the AAISW's efforts to organize Greater Pittsburgh's newest Bessemer mill also would fail.[13]

This mill, the Allegheny Bessemer Steel Works, owned by the Park brothers and the heirs of William Clark, opened in February 1889 in Duquesne, just a few miles from Homestead. For many months, Duquesne was the scene of a violent strike. AAISW men battled with black sheep; Pinkertons and policemen were sent in to "protect" the property of the owners. Throughout their struggle, the Duquesne strikers received financial support from AAISW brothers in Homestead. To win recognition, however, they needed the assistance and support of workers who labored in the iron mills in Pittsburgh that were operated by the same owners. In asking these ironworkers to stage a sympathy strike, one Duquesne striker observed: "It won't work to say that you would not do anything for a steel worker; it's only a question of time until the puddler of today will be the steel worker of the future."

By this date, however, metalworkers in Pittsburgh were too demoralized, too disillusioned, and too intimidated to throw in their lot with the workers in Duquesne. The fate of labor solidarity in Homestead among workers and unions was quite another matter.

In an era when the fortunes—and the misfortunes—of labor activity in Pittsburgh provided the rule for the nation, Homestead was a major exception. Whereas the 1880s were a time of confusion and disarray within the union movement in Pittsburgh, they saw unmatched growth and collaboration between unions of skilled and unskilled workers in

Homestead. The AAISW itself welcomed skilled and unskilled workers into its eight Homestead lodges; by the end of the decade, almost half of the total work force belonged to these lodges. The Knights of Labor also established a formidable presence organizing scores of less skilled steelworkers, many of them immigrants, as well as machinists and coopers. Moreover, virtually every glassworker in Homestead belonged to the Knights or to the American Flint Glass Workers Union, and workers in the building trades affiliated with the United Brotherhood of Carpenters and Joiners of America. In effect, every workingman in Homestead was a union man.[14]

Looking back on this decade of union growth, John Miller, an AAISW man and veteran of the Homestead strike of 1882, proudly reflected: "Homestead in general is a thoroughly organized town. Every man that is working at whatever trade he may follow is supposed to belong to the union which governs his trade, and every stranger that comes amongst us, must have a card to show that he belongs to such an organization."[15]

Miller's remarks were published in the wake of the Homestead lockout of 1889, the most important confrontation between labor and management of its day. Remarkably, in the face of Andrew Carnegie's rough tactics, workers were able to mobilize quickly and successfully—skilled and unskilled, American-born and immigrant, men and women—to stymie the owners' determined efforts to crush unionism, once and for all. Few examples existed at the time of such resolute community solidarity. But Homestead in the 1880s was an exceptional town, to be sure. It was the last bastion of labor republicanism in Greater Pittsburgh, and its workers were able to transcend their differences in defense of their rights. At the first threat of assault, they banded together to hold the fort against the oncoming siege. And when the battle was done, they found themselves in possession not only of their jobs but of the town itself. In 1890, John McLuckie, the leader of the strike and unflinching defender of labor republicanism, was elected burgess by virtual acclamation, and union men swept a majority of seats on the town council. Given the workers' debacle taking place a mere six miles downstream, how did this happen?[16]

By virtue of its geography, Homestead occupied a unique position in Western Pennsylvania. With the railroad running through the town from east to west, the Monongahela River on one side and a precipitous hill on the other, Homestead and its steelworkers formed a self-enclosed commmunity that could be strategically sealed off from unwelcome visitors—overbearing owners or scab laborers. This is precisely what Homestead workers did in the strike of 1882 and the lockout of 1889. When threatened, therefore, the town approximated a fort in more than a metaphorical sense. However, at the same time when Homestead could, and did, close its gates to hostile intruders, it provided a ready welcome to sympathetic workers who shared its goals as a community.[17]

As in other towns in Western Pennsylvania, nativist rhetoric and feelings ran high in Homestead; but the community was able to check these impulses and accommodate a large immigrant population from Eastern Europe. Homestead in the early 1880s was still very much an Old World town of immigrants from the British Isles and of first-generation Americans, for whom labor in America promised financial security. The collective aspirations of these people conformed to a vision of labor republicanism that stretched back beyond the American Civil War to distant roots in Europe. And the principles of labor republicanism that informed the discourse of their unions urged them to cooperate with all of their co-workers. D. R. Jones, a leading Knight and president of the Miners' Association reminded union members in 1879 that they must "stand together by the beautiful principles of the Order" and ignore differences of "creed, color or race."[18]

The East European immigrants who began arriving in Homestead in 1881, for all their cultural differences, also brought with their aspirations for personal success a commitment to communal solidarity. Like their American counterparts, they came from a tradition that had known and struggled against compulsory labor. Indeed, the generation of East European immigrants who came to Homestead was the first in these countries to have been born into freedom: serfdom had been officially abolished in the Austro-Hungarian Empire only in 1848. But the freedom they were born into was qualified by lingering seigneurial privilege, and they looked to America for greater promise.[19]

Parallel aspirations between Anglo-American workers and East European immigrants existed in other working communities in Pennsylvania, of course, but most of these had trouble acknowledging such common ground. In Homestead, however, local religious and political traditions sensitized residents to the goals they might share with others and made them more receptive to the possibilities of mutual collaboration.[20]

Since the early nineteenth century the dominant religious tradition in and around Homestead had been Methodism. From the 1850s onward the preeminent Methodist family was that of William Cox; his example is not atypical of the town's citizens prior to its birth as an industrial suburb. Cox immigrated to the United States from England in 1831 and settled near Braddock, where he operated a saltworks. The family moved to Mifflin Township in the early 1840s and became successful farmers. For years, Cox served as the "class leader" of the Franklin Methodist Episcopal Church and was largely responsible for the moral integrity of the congregants. He translated his fervent Methodism into the political arena by becoming an ardent abolitionist and Republican in the prewar years. The connections Cox saw between religious and political righteousness were shared by other members of his family. His son, John F. Cox., became a leading Republican in Allegheny County, served two terms as burgess of Homestead in the 1880s, and also represented it in the state legislature as an ardent supporter of labor.[21]

Increasingly, labor needed this enthusiastic political support in Homestead, for the opening of the Homestead glassworks and the construction of the PBSW initiated extensive changes in the village that William Cox had dominated. In 1879 fewer than 300 people lived there. By June 1880 the population was 660; in November 1881, 1,500; in 1882, 3,000. During this period of rapid expansion, everything about Homestead was transformed: farming gave way to manufacturing, the unincorporated village became a borough, and merchants opened dozens of new businesses. Hundreds of industrial workers, many of them Catholic immigrants from Ireland and Eastern Europe, joined a handful of native-born Protestants, most of them farmers and small businessmen, in establishing new educational, religious, and political institutions. The first town governments were led by native-born townsmen and British and Irish immigrants, many of them skilled workers. The shared loyalties and experiences of most Homesteaders—opposing compulsory labor, fighting for the Union, voting for the Republican party, working for wages—created a community that was prepared to cooperate with and ensure the success of the unions.[22]

To speak of the unions in Homestead is to identify the two most influential labor organizations in the town, the AAISW and the Knights of Labor. Although differences in ideology and tactics had torn the two apart in Pittsburgh, in Homestead they resisted such divisiveness and adhered to the original principles upon which they had both been founded. They achieved a harmonious working relationship that allowed them to consolidate their influence separately and together.

The AAISW opened its first lodge, Homestead Lodge no. 11, in 1881; the original members were skilled workers in the rail mill who were led by John Elias Jones, a roller. A second lodge, Munhall no. 24, was founded shortly afterward, with members drawn from the converting and blooming mills. The two lodges joined together to defeat William Clark in the Homestead strike of 1882; their members emerged from the strike "tried and found faithful" and heroes among metalworkers everywhere. Shortly afterward, however, a period of economic depression led to the sale of the PBSW in 1883 and drastically reduced production there. Despite its earlier victory, the AAISW suffered too from this loss and had to close Homestead Lodge 11.[23]

In 1886, when prosperity had returned to the steel industry, Andrew Carnegie, the new owner of the mill, vowed to make it the preeminent open-hearth facility in the world. The steelworks underwent unprecedented growth during the next three years, and with the expansion in production and facilities came unprecedented expansion of the union too. In addition to defending the working rights of its members, the

AAISW's meetinghouse served as a center for sociability in the town; activities ranged from balls to funerals and included families of members in addition to the members themselves. By 1889, Munhall Lodge 24 had 250 members from the converting and blooming mills; John Kane Lodge 40 had 60 from the finishing mills of the steelworks; Armor Lodge 54 had 60 from the slabbing mill; Thomas Marlow Lodge 56 had more than 150 from the 33-inch beam mill; George Washington Lodge 99 had 50 machinists and engineers who worked throughout the plant; William T. Roberts Lodge 125 had 70 members from the mammoth 119-inch plate mill; and finally, Acme Lodge 73 had 200, many of them unskilled workers from the open-hearth department.[24]

In a review of the history of the growth of the AAISW in Homestead in the mid 1880s, two important points emerge: first, by 1889 its total membership exceeded 800; second, and perhaps more important, by this date some local lodges were admitting nonskilled labor in defiance of the national leadership. In this gesture alone, the AAISW in Homestead resembled the Knights of Labor far more than it did elsewhere in the country; the Knights, conversely, had always been willing to accept and welcome unskilled workers into their ranks.

The history of the Knights' growth in Homestead is not unlike that of the AAISW. The Knights of Labor inaugurated Homestead's first local assembly, 1785, during the Homestead steel strike of 1882. But well before then they had unofficially organized glassworkers employed at Bryce, Higbee and Company as well as workers at the PBSW. By 1887, Local Assembly 1785 represented all the unskilled laborers in the Homestead Steel Works who worked in the stocking crews as well as many of the skilled laborers in the blooming department. Some workers, like John "Yankee Jack" Thomas, a popular local poet who worked in the blooming mill, belonged to both the Knights and the AAISW; indeed, he was a leader of Local Assembly 1785 and Munhall Lodge 24, and he also served as president of the steelworkers' Beneficial Society. As a worker with dual allegiances, Thomas did not stand alone; in point of fact, in Homestead allegiance to the two unions was not really divided since it represented above all the higher allegiance to the single house of labor. And to this house the Knights were happy to welcome immigrants from all backgrounds. Indeed, "Yankee Jack" Thomas shared the leadership of Local Assembly 1785 with men as diverse as John Mikdemaro, Patrick Gilick, Joseph Smeltzer, and Thomas Clark. When, in 1889, Homestead faced the threat of a major lockout, leaders from both unions thus comfortably banded together in a huge recruitment drive to ensure solidarity and seal the town off.[25]

Through their cooperative efforts, the two unions were able to provide the workers of Homestead with an organized front and a power base from which to affect—and direct—local politics. Accordingly, it is no surprise that from the early 1880s through to the end of the decade, union men occupied a significant number of seats on the borough council. John Elias Jones, leader of the Homestead strike of 1882, served three terms on the borough council; later he led the lockout of 1889. George J. Gessner, a glassworker whose brother, Frank, led Local Assembly 1785 in the early 1880s, was a councilman from 1883 through 1887. Benjamin Culbertson, a veteran labor reformer of the 1870s, served on the council in 1882, 1888, and again in 1889. And there were many, many more. Some union men rose even higher: James Mcdonald, a retired glassworker, was elected burgess in 1885; D. R. Jones, former president of the Miners' Association, succeeded Macdonald in 1886 and was again elected in 1887; and "Old Beeswax" Taylor was elected in 1888.[26]

The successful trajectory of Homestead unionism in the 1880s thus represents the reverse of the negative labor experience that befell Pittsburgh workers during these same years. As we have seen, many factors contributed to the making of a workers' republic in Homestead. These rarely affected the community in isolation, for what made the town a sanctuary of labor reform during this decade was the unique conjunction of political and religious traditions, demographic changes, union activism, and the fortuitous presence of forceful labor leaders such as John Elias Jones. No man, however, better embodied the sum of these disparate effects than John McLuckie.

A former miner, an early member of the Knights of Labor, a GLP candidate in 1876, and later a steelworker at the Edgar Thomson Steel Works, McLuckie led the AAISW workers against Andrew Carnegie in Braddock in 1882. As a steelworker and city councilman in Bellaire, Ohio, he tried to mediate the bitter jurisdictional disputes between Knights and the AAISW that racked that town's steelworks in 1887. Soon after, he came to Homestead to work in the converting mill, joined Munhall Lodge 24, and helped lead workers in the lockout of 1889, when he also served as a police official to ensure security in the town during the disturbances. His long history of dedication to labor reform made him one of the most respected members of the community: "a simple, earnest, straightforward man, whose rugged eloquence told . . . forcibly with the brawny multitude who heard him." And that brawny multitude was a sizable one indeed, for in 1890 John McLuckie was elected burgess of Homestead with an astounding total of 811 votes; his three opponents received a combined total of 5. Two of them, William Tunstall and M. F. Rayburn, were rabid nativists.[27]

Coming on the heels of Homestead's successful stand in 1889, when skilled and unskilled workers, native-born Americans and immigrants, had joined hands in the name of one cause, McLuckie's acclamation represented no less than a decisive victory for all citizens of the republic of labor.

Chapter 15

Republican Recruits: East Europeans in Homestead

The general invitation to the oppressed of all lands to come to America . . . certainly never contemplated the introduction of so miserly low carrion as these Huns, the worst probably of the civilized world's people. . . . The republic cannot afford to have such ignorant animals within its borders

— *National Labor Tribune*, August 1882

Live Forever the United States

— Banner carried by East European workers,
Fourth of July parade,
Mt. Pleasant, Pennsylvania, 1886

Homestead in the 1880s actively sought to reconcile the various tensions that might divide its pursuit of a workers' republic. An obvious one was the result of the arrival of hundreds of unskilled workers from Eastern Europe. As we have seen, their reception, although tainted by some of the nativist bias that pervaded Western Pennsylvania, was exceptionally hospitable in Homestead. The combined influence of the unions, with their firm commitment to worker solidarity, and local religious and political traditions encouraged the general acceptance of the newest citizens as brothers in labor. The importance of this achievement cannot be overestimated, for it highlights, yet again, the distinctive values in Homestead that permitted this town to become, for a brief time, a prototype for a republic of labor.

It is true that the effects of nativist hatred were widespread in Western Pennsylvania in the 1880s and, moreover, invariably infected Homestead as well. Nativists there were led by George W. Sarver, who had been active in the labor movement at least since 1876, when he attended the Pittsburgh Labor Convention as a miners' delegate from Elizabeth,

215

Pennsylvania. In Homestead, Sarver became a steelworker and a leader of the AAISW. By 1882 he was the president of Homestead Council no. 355 of the Order of United American Mechanics, which had approximately sixty members. The mechanics, like the more popular Junior Order of United American Mechanics, appealed to native-born workers distraught about immigrant "hordes": both organizations advocated a patently xenophobic and anti-Catholic program and saw "papists" as a threat to the American common school. Sarver capitalized on this fear and was elected president of the Homestead School Board from 1890 through 1892. In the face of the political success enjoyed by Sarver and several other nativist leaders, who initiated more than three hundred members into their organizations by 1892, the triumph of interethnic solidarity in Homestead is all the more stunning.[1]

However, the full import of Homestead's willingness to accept the East Europeans can be appreciated only against the hateful standards of nativism that were the measure of the day and that formed an important part of labor's own constellation of practices and beliefs. Conspicuous among Pittsburgh's nativist leaders was none other than its leading labor reformer, Thomas Armstrong, the editor of the *National Labor Tribune*.

In August 1882, just months after East European immigrants had helped secure the AAISW's victory in Homestead at the PBSW, the *Tribune* published a virulently racist article entitled "The Filthy Huns," which purported to describe the work and personal habits of the Pittsburgh district's newest arrivals. "They have already brought filth and immorality, and will, if the importation continues, follow these in time with theft, disorder, arson, and murder. . . . No words that can be formulated can exaggerate the utter brutality of the Huns now in Pennsylvania. Their uncleanliness of person is only equaled by their beastliness as to morals and depravity of appetite." Among the most horrifying examples of such depravity was "a thoroughly authenticated account" from the Connelsville region that detailed how a party of immigrant coal workers caught a dead colt in a river and ate it, not out of need but simply because of the appetite for diseased meat common to all "Huns."[2]

In Pittsburgh, according to the *Tribune*, dozens of such people were then living at the county poorhouse, where the staff had been horrified with their general filth and diseased skin. Indeed, these immigrants were so vile that even Chinese-Americans, themselves utterly loathsome, would be shocked to observe them: "From their own accounts, they lived in a manner that would disgust any crescent-eyed leper on the Pacific coast, and if they do not breed a pestilence . . . it will not be their fault."[3]

The *Tribune*'s attack on the "Huns" was part of the mounting nativist tide that accompanied growing tensions between "American" workers and their bosses in the 1880s. The arrival of large numbers of immigrants from Eastern and Southern Europe prompted the labor press everywhere to claim that particular groups of workers and their bosses were threatening to undermine the Republic. As the *Tribune* tried to explain, however, these bestial immigrants were themselves unwitting victims of organized capital. Degraded though the East Europeans certainly were, the "heartless capitalists" who had brought them to Pennsylvania were the true culprits. "Already bands of these Hungarians roam the country unemployed and cast off by persons worse morally than themselves. . . . The money graspers who brought them to the State to supplant decent labor [are] responsible for this influx of pariahs."[4]

The answer to the problem of "The Filthy Huns," according to the *National Labor Tribune*, was to impose strict limits on immigration. "The general invitation to the oppressed of all lands to come to America . . . certainly never contemplated the introduction of so miserly [sic] low carrion as these Huns, the worst probably of the civilized world's people." There was no place for the "Huns" in America: "The republic cannot afford to have such ignorant animals within its borders."[5]

Astonishingly, this editorial, written by Armstrong, was printed right next to the *Tribune*'s register of GLP nominees for state and county office. At the top of the ticket was Armstrong himself, the party's candidate for governor. The others were equally committed leaders of the labor reform movement in Pittsburgh: two glassworkers, Isaac Cline and James Campbell, a molder, Alexander C. Rankin, and two metalworkers, James Shipman and John McLuckie. All of these men, trade unionists and Knights of Labor, had made it their career to seek the promise of amalgamation: a new American republic grounded upon cooperative social relations and equal rights for all. The *Tribune*, under Armstrong's stewardship, had been at the forefront of this effort.[6]

The noble rhetoric of amalgamation, equality, and cooperation, however, provided little more than a veneer for the widespread feelings of racism and xenophobia to which even labor's most dedicated leaders fell victim. What made an editorial like "The Filthy Huns" possible in a paper devoted to the rights of working people was the assumption that these immigrants somehow fell outside acceptable definitions of peoplehood. No doubt Thomas Armstrong was earnest in his belief that "the republic"—including his own sought-after workers' republic—"could not afford to have such ignorant animals within its borders." These same earnest feelings were expressed and approved elsewhere throughout Pittsburgh's working community. Just months later, when the nativist Junior Order of United American Mechanics marched in Pittsburgh, the parade was given full sanction by the *Tribune*.

The earnest, well-intentioned rhetoric of leaders such as Thomas Armstrong was neither without precedent nor without long-term effect. Indeed, it has long been a truism of American history that the arrival of the "new" immigrants inflamed an endemic racialism and hastened the fragmentation of the labor movement. Commentators have tended to "blame" the East European immigrants for the enormous gulf that divided American labor. Many of these immigrants came from the Austro-Hungarian Empire, and, in the words of the U.S. consul to the empire in 1884, "certain national characteristics" rendered them incapable of understanding American institutions and principles. A quarter-century later, nativist discourse found its authoritative justification when the Dillingham Immigration Commission concluded that East European immigrants not only retarded the labor movement but threatened the very fabric of American society.[7]

Thousands of these immigrants ended up working in the iron and steel mills of Pittsburgh. The Progressive scholars who first studied that city in order to understand urban America saw the East Europeans as a menace, too. Indeed, a dominant theme of the Pittsburgh Survey was that civilization itself would not survive the arrival of these people unless radical steps were taken to "Americanize" them. The immigrants "are left in ignorance of our language, our laws, our government and our history," Peter Roberts, one of the more enlightened members of the Survey's investigative team, stated in 1909. "This rich inheritance we cherish, and we believe it is more excellent than any of which the older countries of Europe can boast. . . . If the cause of civilization is to be served, . . . is it not our privilege to train these peoples of southeastern Europe in the principles of democracy?"[8]

According to Roberts, the immigrants had made the demanding job of Americanization even more troublesome by clinging to a primitive "racial consciousness" that their fraternal societies worked hard to nurture. An immigrant group "will either thrust its own concepts and ideals into the social elements around it and modify them, or it will build around itself a wall which the customs and habits of the country will find difficulty in penetrating. This is seen going on in Pittsburgh."[9]

With particular reference to immigrant steelworkers in Homestead and other steel towns in the Pittsburgh area, the investigators Margaret Byington and John Fitch in 1910 each found abundant evidence to back up Roberts's assertion. "The Slavic [fraternal] lodges," Byington reported, "are usually limited to the members of one nationality, . . . and in so far as they tend to perpetuate racial and religious feuds, miss their opportunity to amalgamate the immigrant colony." Moreover, she found that there were no labor unions in Homestead that might give "a common interest" to immigrant and native-born and thus "pave the way for mutual understanding and citizenship." Clearly, Byington's observation of the East European workers in Homestead was filtered through respectable nativist commonplaces she had brought with her to the town; for indeed, had she only read the press, she would have seem ample mention of East European membership in the AAISW in the lockout of 1892.[10]

Fitch, for his part, gave fullest expression to the proposition that a virtually irreparable gap separated East European immigrants from "Americans" in the steel towns of the Monongahela Valley: "The Slavic peasant, accustomed to subservience to authority, and taught it by all the force of tradition, is distrusted and disliked by his more independent American neighbor. Stolid and willing, living amid unsanitary surroundings, hoarding his earnings and spending only for immediate necessities, he is misunderstood and despised by the more liberal, wide-awake Anglo-Saxon, until 'Hunky' has come to be a convenient designation and a term of opprobrium as well."[11]

Passages such as these are representative of the entire corpus of the Survey's published findings, which, with their implicit condescension, continue to exert a profound influence on scholarly perceptions of East European immigrants and their interaction with "Americans." True, over the last twenty years historians have argued with increasing forcefulness that in some venues East European immigrants were eager to join unions created by native-born workers. But the overarching conclusion remains: relations were insurmountably fractious between (and among) East European immigrant groups and "Americans" in Greater Pittsburgh from the Gilded Age through the New Deal. Indeed, this is a central theme of *Out of This Furnace*, an autobiographical novel written by Thomas Bell, the son of Slovak immigrants who settled in Braddock. In our own day, this theme continues in the shared oral tradition of the Monongahela steel towns. "There was an absolute iron curtain between ethnic groups," recalls Albert Elko, a Rusyn steelworker and labor organizer who served as mayor of McKeesport in the late 1960s.[12]

Notwithstanding the nativist limitations of the American scholarship that has addressed the history of East European workers, there is nevertheless little doubt that the Pittsburgh area became bitterly divided along ethnic lines in the wake of the great immigration. As the Survey suggested, this division was only exacerbated by the fact that virtually all East European immigrants arrived as unskilled laborers; they occupied the lowest tier of jobs in the steel industry while the skilled positions belonged to "Americans." In light of this hierarchy and the nativist bias of even the most enlightened labor leaders, the alliance that East Europeans and Anglo-Americans forged in Homestead in the 1880s is all the more outstanding.

Curiously, however, scholars have ignored—or been blind to—the exceptional history of the East Europeans in Homestead. Historians have on the whole applied the general rule of xenophobia to their understanding of the community; in so doing, they have misrepresented the important facts of interethnic collaboration and solidarity and have inadvertently promoted the nativist message themselves. One labor historian has recently asserted, for instance, that the mutual support of skilled Anglo-Americans and unskilled East European immigrants stands out as an example of solidarity that "is impossible to forget." For most historians, however, it has been equally impossible to account for. Indeed, in the entire corpus of writing on Homestead, there are but few references to the nationality of the East European workers. Following the practice codified by the Pittsburgh Survey, most historians have incorrectly used the term *Slavic* in describing the East European residents.[13]

There is, however, no single "Slavic" people and no single "Slavic" language; to employ such categories uncritically is to deny the particular experiences of the diverse groups of East Europeans who immigrated to America—Ukrainians, Poles, Slovaks, to name but three. The term *Slavic* is thus best reserved for those occasions when a more specific appellation is inappropriate either because the precise ethnic origin of an individual cannot be determined or because reference is made to members of more than one ethnic group.

In Homestead prior to the lockout of 1892, most East European immigrants were, in fact, Slovaks. Even a cursory examination of their background and heritage begins to clarify the riddle of their success in Homestead. No written accounts of the 1892 lockout or of life in the town seem to have been left by the first East Europeans; but it is possible to reconstruct through church records and newspaper reports important features of the East European community in its earliest years. The picture that emerges indicates that these immigrants actively helped to forge a workers' version of a modern American republic in their adopted town.

East European immigrants to Homestead brought with them their own dreams for modest material comfort and independence that were summed up in the Slovak expression *za chlebom*. The full idiom, *ist' za chlebom*, means "to seek livelihood or employement," but literally the expression translates as "going for bread." Variations of this idiom were common to all Slavic emigrants. *Za chlebom* was essentially the slogan of the Slavic immigrants and it encapsulated the simple material desires of these new Americans: desires that were, in the end, not so different from those of Anglo-American Homesteaders who rallied together to protect their right to earn "a fair day's wages for a fair day's work" and to achieve a competence.[14]

Ironically, like their unskilled Slavic colleagues, skilled Homesteaders who were native-born or first- and second-generation German-, Irish-, or British-Americans were sometimes wont to invoke their rights in images that echoed both *za chlebom* and the Lord's Prayer. Indeed, in simple terms, what image could better sum up a worker's plea for his republican rights than the first request to the Lord, "Give us this day our daily bread." One such worker, an anonymous balladeer, conflated the plea for republican virtue with bread in the popular poem "Peter Puddler and the Mill Boy."[15] Peter Puddler, a worker skilled in ironmaking as in republican eloquence, takes under his protective care an unskilled mill boy whom he educates on the subject of workers' rights.

> The rich provide our food, you said,
> Their tyranny we should not foil,
> My little friend, our daily bread,
> We earn it dearly by our toil.
> . . . I'll strike until my latest breath,
> Against our wrongs, our rights to save,
> I'd rather see you cold in death,
> Than live to be a tyrant's slave.
> . . . Look yonder, see the banner wave—
> It is the standard of the free!
> Beneath it none shall be a slave,
> Nor will it shelter tyranny!
> We ever shall uphold our cause,
> Our rights as Sons of Liberty!
> We shall uphold our country's laws,
> And only ask equality.[15]

It is easy to see how the discourse of Peter Puddler, the proudest of all skilled craftworkers, could accommodate the strivings of new, unskilled workers who had come to America *za chlebom*. For them too, the freedom to work and earn a fair wage implied a freedom from tyranny that they had known all too well in Eastern Europe: until 1848, when serfdom was officially, although conditionally, abolished in the Austro-Hungarian Empire, their dearly earned daily bread had been bought at the cost of virtual enslavement. And it was to escape life as "a tyrant's slave" that Slavic workers, like the mill boy, would now defend the "standard of the free."

Immigrants from Eastern Europe began to arrive in Homestead just as operations were beginning in the PBSW in 1881. Among the first to work in the mill were John Jerowiski and Joseph Rosinski, who settled in Homestead with his wife, Mary, brother Simon, and sister-in-law Alice. There are no definitive records of the ethnic origin of Simon and Joseph Rosinski or Jerowiski, the first of many to die during the next decade in industrial accidents at the steelworks. The last names of these three men, as well as certain church records, clearly suggest that they were Polish. These records also indicate that the Rosinskis were a leading family in Homestead: they witnessed many marriages and regularly served as godparents to Slavic children born in the town.[16]

The Rosinskis enjoyed good relations with the Anglo-American community in Homestead. Simon, who remained a resident into the 1890s, served as the translator and trusted mediator between the English-speaking community and immigrant Slavs. In the early 1880s he left the steelworks and opened up a peanut stand. By 1883 he had achieved a modicum of economic success and owned his own house; in 1884 he built a shoe shop; later in the decade he became a grocer and then a contractor. Joseph, too, eventually left the steelworks; even after his departure, his name often appeared in the *Homestead Times*, the mouth-piece of town government. His integration into Anglo-American Home-stead was thorough and telling; indeed, the woman he married was named Mary Crowley. Moreover, records indicate that both Joseph and Simon were welcomed into the ranks of the Irish National Land League during the Homestead strike of 1882.[17]

Despite the early presence of the Rosinskis, it was Slovak immigrants who, by virtue of their sheer numbers and their organizational initiatives in work and fraternal and religious life, shaped Homestead's East Euro-pean community through the early 1890s. Pavel Olšav and Juraj Terek were the first Slovaks to settle in the town; they took up residence, proba-bly in a boarding house known as Castle Garden, in 1881 or 1882 near St. Mary Magdalene Church on a steep hill overlooking the steelworks.[18]

Like thousands of other Slovaks who came to the Pittsburgh area beginning in the early 1880s, Olšav and Terek grew up in the region of the Hapsburg Empire where a variety of economic, political, and demo-graphic forces had created rapidly growing numbers of landless agricul-tural laborers. In search of livelihood—*za chlebom*—they moved from village to village, from the countryside to the urban centers of Hungary, and finally, from Hungary to North America. Zemplín Province, the birthplace of Olšav and Terek, was the principal source of Slovak emigra-tion: between 1879 and 1901, almost 33,000 *Zemplíncania* left, a figure that represents an astounding 77 percent of the province's population. Zemplín was the home of many of the first Slovaks who came to the Pittsburgh district. Like the sixteen-year-old Olšav, Terek left his home (both came from the Žalobin area) as a young man, an experience com-mon to most Slovak immigrants.

Olšav and Terek soon were joined by two young women from the Žalobin region, who, after crossing the Atlantic, found work as domestic servants in New York City until they made enough money to continue on to Homestead. One of them, Zuzanna Tirpaková, married Olšav shortly after her arrival. The other, Anna Tereková, probably Terek's sister, mar-ried another immigrant, Ján Špan, who had previously worked in a min-ing town in Eastern Pennsylvania, and who was to play an important role in Homestead's Slovak community. Precisely how these first five Slovak Homesteaders learned of the town is not known. But the one account that traces their convergence in the United States, as well as the scattered notations of a parish priest in the 1890s, suggests that the dynamic of "chain migration" that characterized Slovak immigration to the Pittsburgh district and indeed to all of North America also brought Olšav, Terek, Tereková, Tirpaková, and Španuto Homestead.[19]

In the ten years following the arrival of Olsav and other pioneer *Zemplíncania*, the East European settlement in Homestead grew to over one thousand persons. (A handful of Galician Jews, Magyars, and Italians also lived in the town prior to the lockout of 1892.) Like Pavel and Zuzanna Olšav, most of the immigrants came from the provinces of north-central Hungary and were Roman Catholics. Some, however, were neither Slovak nor Roman Catholic but, like steelworker John Hornak, Carpatho-Rusyns who had been raised in the Byzantine Rite Catholic Church. Smaller numbers of Protestant Slovaks and Catholic Poles also settled in Homestead. Yet the Slavic settlement constituted a unified community since the overwhelming majority of its members worked and worshiped together, lived in the same neighborhood, and joined the same fraternal benefit societies.[20]

In Homestead the focal point of Slavic religious life was St. Mary Magdalene Church, organized by Irish-American Catholics in 1881. From the beginning, though, this church was not a typical "Irish" parish, for Slavic families who came to the town in the 1880s attended mass, baptized their children, and prayed for their departed in the same sanctuary and with the same priest who ministered to the Irish Catholics. Only after 1891, when the first Slovak parish in the Pittsburgh area was organized in Braddock, did Slovaks venture beyond the town to fulfill their spiritual needs.[21]

While East European steelworkers and their families worshiped with the families of many leading Irish-American steelworkers such as Hugh O'Donnell, John Rattigan, John O'Donnell, and George Fitzgerald, they looked to their own for leadership in religious life. Nearly every child born to Slavic Homesteaders, for example, had Slavic godparents, and Slavs invariably served as witnesses at Slavic weddings. Pavel and Zuzanna Olšav and Ján and Anna Španuwere the godparents and witnesses most often chosen for Slavic baptisms and weddings at St. Mary Magdalene Church and, after 1891, at St. Michael's in Braddock. Olšav and Španu along with Michael Mašley and several other Slovaks who arrived in Homestead in 1883, also provided leadership in other areas of the religious and institutional life of the East European community.[22]

Španu the owner of a butcher shop by 1890, and Mašley, a grocer, were key figures in the fraternal life of the East European Homesteaders. Together they helped organize Homestead Lodge no. 26 of the First Catholic Slovak Union, the leading fraternal benefit society of Slovak immigrants. Mašley served as the first president of the First Hungarian Slovak Sick Benefit Society of Saint Michael the Archangel, named after the patron saint chosen by the Slovak parishes of Braddock and Homestead. The Slovak laborers of Homestead chose Olšav, a steelworker, as the unofficial leader of Lodge no. 26.[23]

In the Homestead Steel Works, Olšav and virtually every other East European immigrant was employed as a laborer. This meant that the East European workers were responsible chiefly for loading and stocking the furnaces and converters and moving raw and finished materials between the mill and the yard. The friendly taverns in or near the East European settlement in the second ward provided the men with their chief recreation after a hard turn in the steelworks. The back room of one such establishment, owned by Vincent Waasilefski, occasionally served as a meeting place for East European women too, especially those who worked as domestic servants. But the handsome billiard tables in the front room were the big draw for the men; Anglo-Irish workers joined Slovak-Americans in this, the town's finest pool-hall. In fact, the editor of the *Homestead Eagle* singled out Waasilefski's for high praise as an elegant establishment and an "ornament to the town." Waasilefski's taproom was just one of the places where Slavic workers would mingle happily with their Anglo co-workers. His home was further proof of successful interethnic relations in Homestead, for his wife, Elizabeth Anderson, was of Irish origin. (Relations between Irish Catholics and Protestants apparently were not so cordial: John Sheets, a steelworker found dead on the railroad tracks one August morning in 1890, was the victim of what Pittsburgh papers characterized as warfare between the two groups.)[24]

The East European immigrants quickly adapted to the daily routines of work and leisure in Homestead. There are accounts in the foreign press about how they marked the Fourth of July, and how they sponsored Mardi Gras balls in the American fashion. In 1886 the immigrants' celebration of the Fourth of July in nearby Mt. Pleasant was so American that it even drew page-one coverage from the normally nativist *National Labor Tribune*. "The biggest jubilee over American independence ever held by representatives of a foreign dynasty" very likely attracted East European immigrants from Homestead and all over the Pittsburgh district.[25]

The highlight of the "jubilee" was a parade led by "Director General" Josef Stefanki. Leaving his headquarters, which were bedecked with the flags of his native land and the United States, he mounted a horse to lead hundreds of East European immigrants dressed in military attire, a band of "American" musicians and an immigrant drill team through the streets of Mt. Pleasant. Stefanki wore the "uniform of the [peasant] Revolution of 1848"; and the marchers, "armed with everything from a double-barrel shotgun to a broomstick," carried flags and banners. The big banner at the head of the parade recalled Peter Puddler's vision of "the standard of the free," and it proclaimed "Live Forever the United States."

Of the East European immigrants—most of them Slovaks—who marched behind that banner on 4 July 1886, many were coke workers employed by the coal magnate Henry Clay Frick. Known among them as a scandalously disreputable manager, Frick was Andrew Carnegie's partner and the chairman of the company that owned the Homestead Steel Works. In the days before the parade, however, employees in the coke region had successfully subdued Frick to end yet another of their bitter and violent disputes. The immigrants who greeted Stefanki with "tremors of admiration," then, were cheering not only "the representative of patriotic forefathers" but also an "amicable" settlement of their difficulties with Frick and the renewed opportunity to work *za chlebom*.[26]

As the celebration of the Fourth of July in Mt. Pleasant indicates, American-born workers were not the sole proprietors of republican aspirations. East European immigrants, too, made the connection between work grievances and republicanism. Drawing on their own revolutionary heritage, which, like America's, was rooted in the abolition of compulsory labor, the Slavic-Americans who marched in Mt. Pleasant declared an allegiance to the American independence that allowed them to pursue their livelihood. In Homestead the joint initiatives of American-born and Slavic immigrants demonstrated how deeply shared such an understanding of independence could be.

Six years later, on 6 July 1892, when Pavel Olšav, Peter Fares, and other East European Homesteaders ran to the front line of the town's defense, they were therefore reaffirming a solidarity that residents already took for granted. So, too, was Joseph Sotak when he jumped to the aid of Martin Murray, an Anglo-American steelworker wounded in the gunfight with the Pinkertons hired by Frick. Sotak was shot and killed. Fares was carrying a loaf of bread to his position when he was caught in the gunfire. As he lay dying, he shook the loaf at the Pinkertons. "You cannot take this from our mouths," were his last words. With these sentiments Peter Puddler would have agreed.[27]

Apparently, so would have Andrew Carnegie. In an effort to explain the bloody events of that day, Carnegie wrote to his sympathetic friend William E. Gladstone, the Liberal prime minister of Great Britain, who had always been an appreciative fan of Carnegie's philanthropy and kindhearted writings on labor relations. Carnegie confided to Gladstone that it had been an awful mistake to ask the Pinkertons to clear the way for new nonunion workers. In a telling reference to his famous comment that employers should never hire scabs, he declared: "It is a test to which workingmen should not be subjected.—It is expecting too much to expect poor men to stand by and see their work taken by others.—*Their daily bread.*"[28]

As compassionate as Carnegie purported to be, however, the fact remains that it was he who gave the order for the union to be broken at

Homestead and he who explicitly gave Frick carte blanche to carry it out. In fact, upon learning of the riverbank battle while vacationing in Britain, Carnegie's initial directive to Frick had been as follows: "Cable received. All anxiety gone since you stand firm. Never employ one of these rioters. Let grass grow over works. Must not fail now. You will win easily next trial only stand firm law and order wish I could support you in any form."[29]

Which of these Carnegies—the hard-nosed union buster utterly committed to crushing organized labor, or the compassionate employer who understood the travails of workers—are we to believe? The question addresses the contradictions that racked not only Carnegie but an entire era as well.

Chapter 16

Andrew Carnegie: Robber Baron and Philanthropist

ANDREW CARNEGIE

Bow down, ye folks whose worldly store
Is miserably slim;
In abject reverence before
This dignitary grim;
That plenipotential beard of his,
And stony British stare,
Betoken clearly that he is
A multi-millionaire.

From Scotland's heather-covered braes,
In babyhood he came,
And early fixed his childish gaze,
On lucre and on fame;
As a messenger boy he went so slow,
That none with him could vie,
And so he got an extra show
A lofty kite to fly.

So skillfully he flew his kite,
That wondrous was his luck;
He reached for all the cash in sight;
And rich investments struck;
At railroads, likewise coke and coal,
He took full many a fling,
And was cast at length for the glorious role
Of steel and iron king.

His boodle grew at rapid rate,
But bitter was his cup,
So fast did the wealth accumulate,
He couldn't count it up;
Of grief he might have died, they say,
If he hadn't struck the plan

Of giving a few odd millions away,
Which made him a happy man.

On public libraries he spent
Of shekels not a few;
A goodly slice to Pittsburgh went,
And to Allegheny, too;
But still the loss he doesn't feel,
It cannot hurt his health,
For his mills keep on with endless zeal
A-piling up the wealth.

Since he became a prince sublime,
This burg for him's too small;
New York upon his royal time
And interest has his call;
His courtiers puff him to his face,
As the stary-spangled Scot,
But he can't go back on this good old place,
Which gave him all he's got.[1]

— Arthur G. Burgoyne, 1892

Free libraries maintained by the people are cradles of democracy,
and their spread can never fail to extend and strengthen the democratic idea, the equality of the citizen, the royalty of man.

— Andrew Carnegie, 1903[2]

THERE ARE two legends of Andrew Carnegie. The first is that of the
ruthless robber baron, the second, that of the great philanthropist who
honored America with libraries and art institutions bearing his name.[3]

Most historians have tended to regard these two legends as contradictory and mutually exclusive. Indeed, virtually all interpretations of Carnegie's philanthropy have followed a similar strategy of exposition, one that
might be called the syntactic strategy of "Yes, but." Yes, Carnegie was a
robber baron, but he was also a cultural benefactor. As one critic recently
put it, "Aggressive, ruthless, and no friend of the unions, Carnegie was
nevertheless a robber baron with a difference." For all his failings and
despotism, this critic asserts, Carnegie was a genuine philanthropist;
moreover, philanthropy somehow redeemed whatever questionable activities he engaged in as a businessman.[4]

Clearly, this general view corresponds to the way in which Carnegie
himself wanted his philanthropic offerings to be interpreted—as a lasting legacy of his wealth that would erase and supersede the grimy
details of its accumulation. Carnegie persistently sought to portray himself as the righteous prototype for all men of wealth, who, he believed,

were obliged to elevate and educate the men who worked for them. William Gladstone, who often corresponded with Carnegie, took appropriately appreciative note of Carnegie's philanthropic endeavors in 1892, just months before the Homestead Lockout: "Wealth is at present like a monster threatening to swallow up the moral life of man. . . . You by precept and example have been teaching him to disgorge. I, for one, applaud . . . your gallant efforts to direct rich men into a course of action more enlightened than they usually follow."[5]

Shortly after this laudatory message, the lockout at the Homestead Steel Works left ten men dead and killed unionism in the steel industry for forty years. Yet even as Carnegie had been preparing to smash this stronghold of trade unionism, he also pursued his dreams of philanthropic beneficence for the Steel City. In the wake of the bloody confrontation at Homestead, however, thousands of Pittsburghers chose to refuse a substantial gift of money from Carnegie for the institute and library in Schenley Park that now bear his name. Carnegie, true to form, pleaded that they accept his offerings.

> It was indeed pitiable if the wage-earners for whom these [gifts] were chiefly intended should be permanently prejudiced against them by any shortcomings of the donor, however grievous, for, sadly as he may fail in his efforts to live worthily and do his duty—and no one, alas, knows as well as himself how far he falls short of his own ideal—yet his gifts to Pittsburgh must ever remain stainless and work good continuously and never evil. I hope, therefore, that . . . my fellow workmen [for I have a right to use this title] . . . see that fair play requires them to separate the donor and his many faults from libraries and music halls and art galleries, which have none. If they will only do this, I gladly risk their some day expunging the votes of censure passed upon me personally.[6]

As appealing as Carnegie's interpretation of his own philanthropy may be, there are problems with it. By what material or moral criteria did his acts of generosity cancel the shortcomings to which he himself alluded? Conversely, on what grounds should we dismiss Carnegie's philanthropy as mere hypocrisy? Each of the interpretations implicit in these questions perpetuates the notion that his philanthropy and ruthlessness were somehow contradictory or paradoxical and can therefore be explained only through a rhetorical concession—"Yes, but."

In truth, the concurrent acts of magnificent philanthropy and vicious union busting are not mutually exclusive; nor do they simply signify some form of social or psychological perversity on Carnegie's part. Both derive from the single coherent system of belief that underlay his ambitious agenda for modern America, an agenda that he repeatedly spelled out in no uncertain terms in his writings. Carnegie's initiatives in the world of business, together with his published statements on wealth, progress,

and democracy, suggest that his cultural benefactions and industrial despotism were informed by a shared logic. Simply put, it is a matter not of
"Yes, a robber baron, but a benefactor" but rather of "Yes, a robber baron
and a benefactor." The activities of these two personae must be examined
together in the context of Carnegie's larger intellectual and social agenda.
For both Carnegies were intent on achieving a single, overarching goal: in
the name of the morality of improvement and an unwavering faith in
progress, he sought nothing less than full control over the instruments of
material and cultural production in America. Indeed, his conscious strivings toward what can only be called hegemony point to the indissoluble
ties between two forms of activity typically considered separate realms of
human endeavor.[7]

Carnegie did not present himself in such light. Like other great phi-
lanthropists, he represented himself as what Thorstein Veblen called the
"keeper of the National Integrity" and "guide to literature and art,
church and state, science and education, law and morals—the standard
container of civic virtue." In this spirit, Carnegie built his libraries, muse-
ums, and trade schools and hoped they would convey to their patrons
and to the larger public that version of civic virtue which was his.[8]

The ritual initiation of Carnegie's career as a philanthropist in Braddock in 1889 provides clues to the complex nature of the man whose
name became synonymous with philanthropy; it also offers insights into
the complex nature of philanthropy—and steelmaking—in modern
America. It is telling indeed that the first instance of Carnegie's legendary philanthropy in the United States coincided with a major instance of
his legendary ruthlessness. Perhaps more telling, historians of Carnegie
have consistently overlooked or suppressed this conjunction in their
obstinate narratives of the "Yes, but" version of his life. Here I seek to
restore Carnegie's first major philanthropic endowment in America, the
Carnegie Free Library in Braddock, to the violent context of labor conflict
from which it emerged. Reduced to the simplest skeleton of a narrative:
yes, Andrew Carnegie busted the union in Braddock, and then he gave
the town a magnificent library.[9]

On 30 March 1889, Andrew Carnegie went to Braddock to dedicate
the Carnegie Free Library and, as he put it, "to hand it over" to the
mixed community of workers he employed at the Edgar Thomson Steel
Works. Over the course of his life, Carnegie would finance 2,811 public
libraries, most of them in Great Britain and the United States, but all
intended to "improve the minds" of workers. Carnegie attended many
of the dedication ceremonies. He especially enjoyed the ceremonies in
Britain, where he often received the freedom of the city, the medieval
equivalent of the key to the city, in recognition of his gift. Nothing
seemed to please him more than the pseudofeudal pageantry of these

festivities. Carnegie, the committed "republican" and lifelong Chartist who secretly coveted the friendship of kings and emperors, loved it all: riding in an open carriage through winding streets amid throngs of cheering townspeople; meeting with the mayor and other officials at the town hall; receiving the small parchment that attested to the freedom.[10]

Dedicating the new Braddock library, with its Scottish baronial design, also brought the "Laird of Skibo" extraordinary pleasure. In a telling reference to his philosophical mentor, Herbert Spencer, Carnegie inaugurated his first American library by declaring that life's "highest award . . . is the purchase of satisfactions." His purchase of the Braddock library was "a great satisfaction, one of the greatest I have ever acquired." In fact, he saw not merely the library but all of Braddock as his creation. And he was convinced that Braddock and its steelworks, a cornerstone of his industrial empire, were the majestic harbingers of the harmonious social order that Spencer had promised.[11]

It was around this conviction and principles such as those propounded in his essay on "Wealth" that Carnegie built his speech at Braddock. At the time, the first installment of the essay had not yet been published, and he borrowed freely from it for his dedication. In "Wealth" he argued that the preeminent problem of the era was indeed "the proper administration of wealth." For him, the single solution—the only true antidote for what he characterized as "the temporary unequal distribution of wealth"—was for the rich man "to consider all surplus revenues which come to him simply as trust funds which he is called upon to administer" for the benefit of "his poorer brethren." The successful businessman was a "trustee for the poor" and for the entire community; the charge of the trustee is to administer the wealth of the community "far better than it could or would have done for itself." To Carnegie the most appealing expression of this public trusteeship was the establishment of free public libraries, because the library offered to "the industrious and the ambitious" the surest means of self-advancement.[12]

Carnegie steadfastly maintained that he was a democrat in the truest sense of the word. "Fellow workmen," were the words he chose to begin his dedication of the Braddock library. "Believe me, fellow workmen," he repeated, "the interests of Capital and Labor are one." He went on to say that wealth had not merely made him a custodian of the public good but had confirmed his position as a full and equal member of the laboring community.

> Gentlemen, I am very jealous of my title to the name "fellow workman." . . . Let it always be understood that we are workers together, and although I no longer work with my hands, as I am proud to say I once did, yet when I pass through the works I object to the airs which the men . . . seem to put on as I pass along. I am just as much entitled to the proud appellation of "working-

man" as any of you, and I hope you will remember this hereafter and treat me with proper respect as one of the great guild of those who labor and perform a use in the community, and who upon that basis alone founds his claim to live in comfort.[13]

In Carnegie's view, the greatest testament to this mutuality of interest had been achieved only recently in Braddock. In 1888 he and the Edgar Thomson steelworkers had signed an agreement based on a sliding scale that pegged their wages to the market price of steel. The result, he said, was a genuine partnership between management and labor under which workers "are no longer only employees" but also "sharers with us in the profits of our business." It was out of his share of these profits that Carnegie had fulfilled his obligation as a public trustee and built the library "to express his care for the well-being of those upon whose labor he depends for success." The library was "a centre of light and learning, a never-failing spring of all good influences"; only education could ensure labor's progressive march away from serfdom and toward the universal recognition it deserved. "If you want to make labor what it should be, educate yourself in useful knowledge," he counseled. "This is the moral I would emphasize."[14]

Carnegie elaborated on this moral, and indeed the very ethic of his library: "Useful knowledge" did not embrace classical learning, what we today call the liberal arts. Rather, the "new idea of education" was to concentrate, as the new library most assuredly would, on the study of business and science alone. Success in these realms ensured the advance of civilization and also brought enormous, and just, fiscal rewards to individuals. The heroes of the era, those who owned modern-day "titles of honor" such as mechanical engineer and manager of steel mill, were those who had rescued metalmaking from puddlers by creating the remarkably efficient and profitable Bessemer steel industry.[15]

Carnegie saw the Braddock free library as something more than a means of ensuring progress. Something in the construction of the library, and indeed in all of his "charity," exceeded even his thirst for fame. The larger issue that tormented him was the solution to the outstanding ethical problem of his professional life: how to make money and simultaneously be a kind employer—and a good man.[16]

This problem had weighed heavily on Carnegie for decades. In 1868, at the age of 33, he wrote a note to himself that became his most celebrated piece of writing and which his most recent biographer has aptly characterized as a "remarkable document of self-analysis and adjuration." In it he made plans to "cast aside business forever" within two years. "The amassing of wealth is one of the worst species of idolatry. [There is] no idol more debasing than the worship of money. . . . To continue much longer overwhelmed by business cares and with most of my thoughts wholly upon the way to make more money in the shortest time, must degrade me beyond hope of permanent recovery."[17]

Carnegie, of course, did not forsake the pursuit of money within two years or limit his income to the annual maximum of $50,000, as he had planned in his private memo. Nor did he forsake the desire for "making the acquaintance of literary men" and "taking part in public matters . . . connected with eduction and improvement of the poorer classes." Indeed, at the time he dedicated America's first Carnegie library, not only could Carnegie count "literary men" such as Herbert Spencer, Matthew Arnold, and Mark Twain as friends, but he also counted profits from his steelmaking enterprises alone in excess of $3.5 million per year. A year later, in 1890, his total take-home earnings were $25 million—more than $200 million in today's dollars. While it is impossible for most of us to imagine the fabulous dimension of such sums, it is possible to appreciate the troubling contradictions that the amassing of such wealth created for a man of Carnegie's avowed convictions, for he faced a struggle between two powerful impulses: a genuine, if condescending, Christian humanitarianism and an insatiable acquisitiveness that sanctioned, as his biographers have shown, the ruthless pursuit of financial gain.[18]

Carnegie did not experience this dilemma alone, but few experienced it so intensely. Many ambitious men had to confront the moral contradictions of acquisitiveness; some concluded that the contradictions could not be ethically reconciled. Carnegie, for one, struggled toward a solution for twenty years while continuing, in the words of his cautionary note, to "push inordinately" toward the pinnacles of wealth. In the end, he believed that he had found the way to make piles of money and simultaneously avoid, as he put it, degradation.

Just as work was about to commence on the Braddock library in the midst of labor's Great Upheaval of 1886, Carnegie published two essays that discussed how to make money while remaining principled. He defended unionism and faulted employers for contributing to industrial unrest. Although he criticized workers for their role in the disturbances of 1886, he declared that the "right of workingmen to combine and form trades-unions is . . . sacred," and he also denounced the practice of hiring nonunion workers. "To expect that one dependent upon his daily wage for the necessaries of life will stand peaceably and see a new man employed in his stead is to expect much. . . . The employer of labor will find it much more to his interest, wherever possible, to allow his works to remain idle and await the result of a dispute than to employ a class of men that can be induced to take the place of other men who have stopped work." Carnegie went further: he suggested that union opposition to nonunion labor was justified and that employers need observe the first union commandment. "There is an unwritten law among the best workmen: 'Thou shalt not take thy neighbor's job.' No wise employer will lightly lose his old employees. Length of service counts for much in many ways. Calling upon strange men should be the last resort."[19]

The open-ended qualification of the last resort notwithstanding, Carnegie's 1886 essays brought him recognition as a defender of the rights of organized labor. True, his condemnation of strikebreaking by means of hiring nonunion workers incurred the wrath of his colleagues—most notably Henry Clay Frick—but Carnegie was delighted by the kudos he received from union officials.

The year 1886 also brought Carnegie tremendous satisfaction from another literary quarter: *Triumphant Democracy*, his homage to America that catalogued its industrial achievements, sold thirty thousand copies in the United States and forty thousand in Britain. The principal idea of the book was that the United States had triumphed materially because it was a democracy, the ultimate purpose of which was material progress. To make this argument, he defined democracy in narrow political terms: free access to the ballot. For Carnegie, then, Chartism's most reductive definition continued to hold; he did not recognize that inequality might arise from sources other than the denial of the suffrage. And like his fellow advocates of the morality of improvement, he saw the advance of civilization as equivalent to increases in productive capacity—and profits.[20]

Triumphant Democracy was more than Carnegie's simple defense of plutocracy or a personal effort to reconcile himself with his "republican" past. It provided the self-justification that he sought in answer to the warning that the pursuit of wealth could "degrade . . . beyond hope of permanent recovery." America itself was indeed "thunder[ing] past with the rush of the express" to still greater heights of production and consumption. But rather than check the reckless advance of runaway "progress," he took pride in the role he played therein. To be sure, the metaphor of America as an express train was not innocent, for Carnegie's own wealth was being stoked daily by the Edgar Thomson Steel Works, the world's largest producer of steel rails. Such paradoxes might have troubled a man who thought of himself as an enlightened and principled liberal. But what might seem from our vantage point a dilemma was ultimately resolved by Carnegie within the logic of his personal and political agenda.[21]

In truth, from the beginning of operations at the Edgar Thomson, Carnegie easily managed to do whatever was necessary to ensure that production quotas for the "express" would be met in his premier rail-making facility. In the late 1870s, as we have seen, he ousted the AAISW from the mill in the union's inaugural effort to organize Bessemer steelworkers. Between 1882 and 1885, he moved often, and decisively, to counter further initiatives of the AAISW and the Knights of Labor. In 1883 an innovation known as the direct process allowed Carnegie to dismiss three hundred AAISW men. He won a large wage reduction from both unions in 1883, and in 1884 he extracted yet another reduction. In August 1884 he discharged three hundred workers made redundant by the introduction of natural gas into the production process. In 1885, Carnegie finally succeeded in destroying two lodges of the AAISW and one assembly of the Knights.[22]

Tensions ran high at the Edgar Thomson throughout this period. There were many work stoppages, and Carnegie called in the police. In the midst of an 1885 shutdown in Braddock, he said he was uncertain when he would be able to reopen the mill. Labor costs were no longer competitive, and for this he held the unions responsible. Nevertheless, he professed utter confidence that harmony eventually would prevail at the Edgar Thomson and indeed wherever workers and employers struggled. "I believe that socialism is the grandest theory ever presented, and I am sure some day it will rule the world," Carnegie told the *New York Times*. "Then we will have attained the millennium."[23]

Thomas Armstrong, the editor of the *National Labor Tribune*, responded quickly to Carnegie's cloying remarks. What Carnegie was really intimating, Armstrong wrote in the *Tribune*, was that the division between workers and employers would continue until the Second Coming. Carnegie might well approve of socialism when he read Charles Fourier or contemplated the teachings of the Savior. Then there was no doubt that he "look[ed] upon all men as his brothers, and could wish that all were on a happy equality morally and materially." But when it came to the management of the affairs of this world, he operated with different priorities: "At present . . . Mr. Carnegie means business primarily and emphatically, and that business is his own."

In 1886, while Carnegie enjoyed considerable literary success, he was less happy with the course of labor relations in Braddock. In his protracted dispute with organized workers, he was forced to move from a twelve- to an eight-hour day and to hire an additional three hundred men. "The spirit of unionism is not yet dead at Braddock," the *Tribune* assured its readers. The Laird of Skibo was not pleased. Once and for all, he decided, it was time to end unionism at the Edgar Thomson. The opportunity came in December 1887 when the annual contract expired. Carnegie responded by closing the mill, discharging hundreds of men, and demanding a return to the twelve-hour day. He directly managed the lockout—as significant a labor dispute as any in the Pittsburgh of the 1880s—from start to finish. As part of his agenda, he sought substantial wage reductions, which were to be achieved through the imposition of his celebrated sliding scale.[24]

In 1886, Carnegie had argued in "An Employer's View of the Labor Question" that a sliding scale ensured the "partnership" between labor and management. He repeated this argument in his dedication speech at Braddock library. The partnership offered to the Braddock steelworkers, however, clearly favored one partner alone. The sliding scale that he proposed would change the steelworkers' piece rates by linking them to the fluctuating market price of steel; until then, their wages had been determined by an annual contract that was based on the consistently higher market price of iron. The steelworkers claimed that because Carnegie's new scale would drastically reduce the base that set the ratio between their piece rates and market prices, the scale would transfer an inequitable portion of the profits to Carnegie. He, on the other hand, argued that the Edgar Thomson owed its unprecedented productivity and fabulous success less to the efforts of workers than to the technological improvements he had set in place. He therefore justified the sliding scale, with its reduced base, on grounds that it would guarantee him a just and reasonable return on his investment. For the workers, however, Carnegie's scale demeaned the value of their work, offended their sense of natural justice and made a mockery of republican virtue.

Thus, in many ways, the views of the Edgar Thomson steelworkers reflected the very concerns that Pittsburgh metalworkers had expressed since the end of the Civil War: most striking, perhaps, were the similarities in public statements made by the Edgar Thomson workers in 1886 and by the Sons of Vulcan in the lockout of 1874–75. Though iron had been supplanted by steel and the great shop floor battles had shifted from puddling mills to giant Bessemer works, in Braddock the familiar struggles for control of the production process and the definition of republican justice still held true.

The steelworkers of Local Assembly no. 1967 of the Knights of Labor, for instance, charged that Carnegie's intent was to transform workers at the Edgar Thomson into white slaves, and that, despite his professions of republicanism, he had always opposed unions and "always treated his workers as though they were his creatures—body and soul."

Consider David Gibson, like Carnegie himself, a native of Dunfermline, Scotland. As a young man, he had occasion to hear Carnegie speak about the promise America offered new immigrants. "During his remarks," Gibson recalled, "he advised all young men to migrate to America, where a large field was before them, to better their condition. He said further that all those taking advantage of his advice would meet with his support and he would certainly find them positions." Gibson took Carnegie's advice and invitation to heart: he emigrated to America, settled in Braddock, and found work at the Edgar Thomson. During the lockout of 1888, however, Gibson, along with other union men, lost his job. When he tried to find work at the Homestead Steel Works and, later, at facilities owned by other steelmakers, Gibson discovered that Carnegie had blacklisted him.[25]

The Braddock lockout, which historians have afforded only passing notice, was a disaster not only for Gibson. In direct violation of his own commandment, "Thou shalt not take thy neighbor's job," Carnegie hired nonunion workers—and enough Pinkertons to protect them. When the mill reopened, Braddock was a town under siege. Carnegie told his former employees that if they wanted to return to work, they could sign an ironclad agreement that barred membership in the union. Although the Knights of Labor managed to withstand the lockout until May, partly because of assistance offered by members of the AAISW in Homestead, the workers ultimately capitulated. With this victory, Carnegie effectively ended unionism at the Edgar Thomson for decades. Moreover, the lockout mortally wounded District Assembly 3 of the Knights of Labor and fueled the jurisdictional battles between the Knights and the national leadership of the AAISW. The immediate result was that for advocates of a wide amalgamation of all workers, it became more difficult than ever to inject life into Pittsburgh's foundering labor movement.[26]

Carnegie celebrated his victory in Braddock by giving his repentant workers a library and calling it a monument to his partnership with them. As he was wont to repeat at subsequent library dedications: "There is not such a cradle of pure democracy upon the earth as in the Free Public Library, this republic of letters, where neither rank, office nor wealth receives the slightest consideration; where all men are equal. More than this, here in many instances the poor man, having more knowledge of books than the noble or millionaire, is the larger partner in the library."[27]

Few in the audience at Braddock, however, were fooled by such wistful invocations of their larger partnership with the noble or millionaire. To men who risked their livelihoods to defend the ideals of the American Republic, the offer of quiet reading time in the "Republic of Letters" rang more ironic than magnanimous. Even the steadfastly entrepreneurial *Homestead Local News* noted that the recipients of Carnegie's largesse recognized it was by no means unencumbered: "There seemed to be a sort of 'grin and bear it' feeling prevailing, as if the library and good advice tendered was counting for one for the people and a half dozen for Mr. Carnegie."[28]

In his dedication speech, Carnegie announced that, just weeks before, he had received a letter from Homestead asking if he also planned "to do something" for that town. "Do something for Homestead?" he retorted. "Well, we have expected for a long time, but so far in vain, that Homestead should do something for us." If Homestead would only do something for him, he would be pleased to build a library there, too. "I am only too anxious to do for them what I have done for you, . . . I hope one day I may have the privilege of erecting at Homestead such a building as you have here; but . . . our works at Homestead are not to us as our works at Edgar Thomson. Our men there are not partners." The AAISW, Carnegie continued, had strong lodges in Homestead that compelled him to pay exorbitant wages. "Of course . . . the firm may decide to give the men at Homestead the benefit of the sliding scale which you enjoy. I know that for the success of [the] Homestead works, regarded from the point of view of the capital invested, . . . the present system at Homestead must be changed."[29]

Within months, Carnegie was hard at work trying to make this change. What ensued was the lockout at Homestead in 1889. Carnegie wanted to "give" Homestead steelworkers a sliding scale as well as an ironclad contract of their own, and he hired nonunion labor and Pinkertons to ensure that his "gifts" were delivered. Homesteaders such as John McLuckie, who had led the AAISW's Braddock lodges until Carnegie destroyed them, and Councilman John Elias Jones, a leader of the local union since the Homestead strike of 1882, joined other workers in rejecting Carnegie's generosity. These steelworkers and their families wanted no part of his partnership. They believed that it would undermine their American rights. "King Carnegie," one labor paper warned the Homestead workers, "had his gun loaded" for them too.[30]

The Homestead workers needed little warning, for they had all witnessed the coercive assault on their union brothers across the river and knew full well the cost of the commanding "feudalesque" library that now adorned their sister town. "All or most of you have read the speech of Mr. Carnegie to the workmen of Braddock," one Homestead steelworker wrote in the *National Labor Tribune*. "Now the question is, Are you still willing to act as the tools for others—to sell your rights as free men and to remain slaves?"[31]

Well into the twentieth century, Braddock steelworkers would frequent the baths and athletic facilities housed in the library, but bitter feelings about the terms of Carnegie's bequests smoldered in the steeltowns of the Monongahela Valley. "I would sooner enter a building built with the dirty silver Judas received for betraying Christ than enter a Carnegie library," said a writer for the *Commoner and Glassworker.* And John Fitch, a more disinterested observer, noted in the Pittsburgh Survey that "there is a great deal of prejudice against the gift of Mr. Carnegie on account of the several labor conflicts that have occurred in the mills formerly controlled by him." Indeed, in the thirty-three years during which Carnegie bestowed libraries, 225 communities turned down his offer. Not surprisingly, this sentiment was especially strong in Pennsylvania: 20 of the 46 towns Carnegie solicited said no.[32]

Marcel Mauss, the French anthropologist who has explored the complex social, moral, and political dynamics of the seemingly simple ritual of gift giving, argues that gifts "are in theory voluntary, disinterested and spontaneous, but are in fact obligatory and interested. The form usually taken is that of the gift generously offered, but the accompany-ing behavior is formal pretense and social deception. For the transaction itself is based on obligation and economic self-interest" that reflects "nothing less than the division of labour itself." One Homestead steel-worker expressed the inherent ironies of Carnegie's gift thus: "Carnegie builds libraries for the working men, but what good are libraries to me, working practically eighteen hours a day?"[33]

As the stormy history of work relations at the Edgar Thomson demon-strates, many of the great political and moral questions then at the very center of America's divided allegiances were embedded in the gift of the library: Who would control the factories and the seats of government? Who would be best equipped to shape the cultural values of modern America? What was the meaning of democracy? What was the measure of a good life? These questions, also encoded in Carnegie's remarks directed at the workers of Homestead, surely weighed on him, too. Clearly, though, their challenge did not stand in Carnegie's way as he pushed "inordinately" beyond his own warning about the risks of ac-quisitiveness, toward the unparalleled wealth that he won. That this wealth did in fact bring with it an element of degradation surely was one reason he so insistently sought to disburse it.[34]

Yet Carnegie's philanthropy has retained its mythic aura, an aura perhaps nowhere more evident than in the celebration of the Carnegie Hall centennial in New York in 1991. The Carnegie Free Library in Braddock, which stands even today amid the industrial ruins of the Steel Valley, also continues to elicit flattering, if less grandiose, commentary. As a critic has recently observed, the Braddock library remains a lumi-nous example of Carnegie's "extraordinary philanthropy," for the "sole condition" attached to most of his library gifts was a pledge from munici-pal authorities to support them with a minimal tax assessment.[35]

In truth, Carnegie's gifts presupposed an exchange—an unequal and involuntary exchange—and the personal assessments he extracted from Braddock, Homestead, and the Monongahela steel towns that have their own Carnegie Library far exceeded the value of his gift. According to the *Commoner:* "Mr. Carnegie is a fair representative of a class of men who gain fame and fortune at the expense of the poor. The money which has gone to the erection of the structures which he presents represents so much money taken away from the men who really earned it. . . . The world is no richer by such gifts, but immeasurably poorer."[36]

In no sense, then, were Carnegie's libraries free to the people, and in 1889 the town of Homestead was in a position to defend this point of view. When Carnegie informed its residents that "they evidently need a li-brary," the workers, reading between his lines, knew that his offer was more threat than promise. Indeed, they could expect to pay a heavy fine.[37]

Chapter 17

The Homestead Lockout of 1889:
The Making of a "Workers' Republic"

> This is a contest concentrated at Homestead by Mr. Carnegie's express invitation. . . . It is a battle in the revolution of the steel industry.
>
> — *National Labor Tribune*, July 1889

ANDREW CARNEGIE's visit to Braddock on 30 March 1889 was one of many he made to the Pittsburgh area after establishing his permanent residence in New York City in the late 1860s. The trip to Braddock, as we have seen, was especially important to Carnegie because it gave him the occasion to reiterate his gospel of wealth and expound upon it. In this little-known speech he argued that wealth had not merely made him a custodian of the public good but had also confirmed his position as a full and equal member of the laboring community. "We have all our special uses to fulfill and I resent the idea that because the interest of the firm compelled me to remove to New York and attend to a special department, I am to lose my rank as a worker with you in the business."[1]

In boasting that he was a proud but quite ordinary workingman, Carnegie neglected to mention that as the working owner of the Edgar Thomson Steel Works he had cut wages, extended the working day, and destroyed workers' organizations. He based his claim to worker status on a novel interpretation of the sliding scale he had installed at the Edgar Thomson following his victory there. Like all workers, he earned his "wage" on the basis of the sliding scale; however, because his compensation was not protected by a minimum, he in fact had no guarantee of any remuneration at all: "I am a tonnage man under a sliding scale, dependent solely upon product and prices for my compensation, if any. But unfortunately for me, my sliding scale has no minimum, as yours has. I cannot tell how low it may fall."[2]

Having defended the partnership offered by the sliding scale and left his partners with their own library in Braddock, Carnegie dangled the promise of more partnership to the workers in Homestead. He then left Pittsburgh for New York and, according to his biographers, set sail for Europe. By the two most authoritative accounts, Carnegie, before packing, directed William L. Abbott, the chairman of Carnegie, Phipps, and Company, to take full charge of any untoward situation that might arise in connection with the expiration of the Homestead contract on 30 June. His most reliable biographer notes that he left the country with the knowledge "that there was apt to be trouble" at Homestead over any effort to introduce a contract modeled after the one at the Edgar Thomson. But neither Joseph Frazier Wall nor Burton J. Hendrick addresses the question of precisely what Carnegie intended to do when the Homestead contract expired. In fact, both indicate that he remained basically indifferent to the situation.[3]

In reality, Carnegie had been eager to move against organized labor in Homestead since late 1888. On 29 December he wrote to Abbott, "I had a very serious talk with Captain Jones yesterday about Homestead, which has made me more anxious than ever." He went on to say that it was imperative to reduce the work force and impose an overall wage reduction, initiatives that he discussed with Abbott on 29 March, just a day before he dedicated the free library in Braddock. During the second week of May, Carnegie was back in Pittsburgh—not vacationing in Europe—making concrete plans with Abbott, Jones, and other lieutenants to change "the present system" at Homestead. "Reduced Wages—Rumors That Mr. Carnegie's Visit Has Much to Do with a New Scale," was the headline in the *Pittsburgh Chronicle-Telegraph* on 9 May. On the basis of conversations with company officials, the paper went on, Carnegie's presence "in the city at this time is owing not a little to [the] intended revision of the [Homestead] scale" and that all questions about the company's proposal "will be decided upon before Mr. Carnegie leaves the city next week."[4]

Nine days later, on Saturday 18 May, management posted notices throughout the Homestead Steel Works and called the AAISW's mill committee, comprised of the leaders of all lodges, into the office to receive the company's proposal personally. The company informed the men that it was determined "once and for all [to] place the relations of capital and labor at these works upon a basis which may enable us to compete with others." To do this, the company would impose on 1 July a sliding scale that would reduce overall wages by approximately 25 percent and place the entire work force on a twelve-hour day. Although the proposal specifically mentioned neither the AAISW nor the Knights of Labor, Carnegie's decision with regard to the unions was quite clear. The company declared all positions in the mill vacant as of 1 June; old hands would have to reapply for work and could then, *as individuals*, sign three-year ironclad contracts.[5]

Thus neither union would be recognized as bargaining agent. "The superintendent will receive applications for employment from men at present in our service, and will select from among those whom he thinks best qualified. . . . No man will be employed who cannot bring satisfactory certificates as to his skill, sobriety and general good character." The new contract would depart from normal practice and expire in January, not June, thus ensuring that employees would have to negotiate a new contract in winter when they would be most vulnerable.

The *Chronicle-Telegraph* commented that, whereas the institution of a sliding scale was an important new provision, the most dramatic gesture was clearly the virtual dismissal of all the workers. The proposals were bound to "claim the attention of the manufacturing world and the public at large." Carnegie recognized this, and, in an effort to avoid adverse publicity, he made certain to leave town before the notices were posted. Nestled in his New York City mansion, protected by some measure of "plausible deniability," Carnegie received intelligence reports from his private detectives stationed in Homestead. Amid the "humanitarian texts and quaint heraldic devices in honor of the toiler" that lined his library walls, his personal secretary later noted, Carnegie then proceeded to plan "a strenuous campaign" for the lockout. And having mapped out these plans to his satisfaction, then—and only then—he left for Scotland.[6]

The stage was thus set for what would become the "greatest struggle" of the AAISW against "the richest manufacturing aggregation in the country." For all his posturing, Carnegie's initiative in Homestead came as no surprise, however. Since the opening of the Edgar Thomson in the mid 1870s, Carnegie had opposed unions at every opportune juncture. By the spring of 1889 he and the Homestead steelworkers were well aware that a decisive confrontation was close at hand, and that it would mark a turning point in a decades-long war fought in every mill in Greater Pittsburgh, at its polling places, and in the hearts and minds of its residents. In the course of the protracted struggle, Homesteaders had managed, against considerable odds, to defy the morality of improvement; the town had emerged as a bastion of labor republicanism. As thousands across the Pittsburgh district understood, however, a victory for Carnegie at Homestead in 1889 might end the war once and for all.[7]

The site (and the immediate spoils) of the battle in Homestead was Carnegie, Phipps, and Company's immense manufacturing complex, which covered 90 acres and required approximately 2,500 men to operate. The works included the original structures erected by the PBSW in consultation with Alexander Holley: a converting department with two five-ton Bessemer vessels in a building that measured 115 feet long and 72 feet wide; Kloman's finishing mill, 600 feet by 84 feet; and the 180-by-72-foot blooming mill. To the east of these structures loomed the giant open-hearth department, where Carnegie had installed four furnaces in a building that covered more than 43,000 square feet. Here hundreds of workers turned out massive steel ingots weighing as much as 60 tons. The steelworks also had six finishing mills; the largest was the 119-inch plate mill, housed in a 501-by-176-foot building that included a colossal array of heating furnaces, shears, rolls, hydraulic cranes, and cooling tables. Attached to the plate mill and two other finishing mills were batteries of warehouses, toolsheds, machine shops, and miles of railroad tracks that integrated operations within the works and connected it to the outside world.[8]

Like the enormous dimensions of the physical plant, Carnegie's commitment to technological innovation in the Homestead Steel Works was equally huge. The mill, as we have seen, was a fully modern Bessemer works when Carnegie purchased it in 1883. At the time, its output of steel rails did not come close to that of the Edgar Thomson; yet with an average monthly capacity of eight thousand tons, Homestead ranked among the top five plants in the country. To avoid duplication, Carnegie decided that it should concentrate on producing structural shapes, and in 1884–85 he installed a structural mill, the first of many additions. From the outset, he experimented with new techniques in an effort to overcome what he characterized in his Braddock library speech as the ignorance of the ironmaking era. Just three months after acquiring the Homestead plant, for example, management was testing a new method of producing low-carbon steel that Superintendent Charles Taylor advertised as a revolutionary assault on puddling. The company, Taylor said, was trying to do "away with that process altogether."[9]

The processes that Carnegie installed at the Homestead Steel Works following the depression of the mid 1880s did eventually play a central role in the downfall of puddling. Though the Bessemer process had mortally wounded the craft (at one Pittsburgh mill in 1882–83, for example, puddlers averaged only three days of work per week) the demand for wrought iron did not immediately disappear. Bessemer steel was cheaper to produce, to be sure, but its overall quality remained approximate; most Bessemer ingots therefore ended up as rails, and wrought iron continued to be used for high-quality speciality items. As railroad construction fell off, and as the demand for low-cost, high-quality building materials rose, however, metalmakers looked for ways to improve the Bessemer process. In the Siemens-Martin method, they found a production technique that was stunningly brilliant in its simplicity: large refractory furnaces, or hearths, could be used to achieve heat of such intensity that puddlers were no longer required in order to cook pig iron into a malleable, durable metal.[10]

As modified by Sidney Gilchrist-Thomas, open-hearth steelmaking allowed metalmakers to use low-cost, high-phosphoric ores to manufacture hitherto impossibly large quantities. In the United States this modification, called the basic process, opened up the possibility of fully exploiting the vast iron ore deposits of the Great Lakes region. It was to these that Carnegie looked when in April 1886 he decided to construct in Homestead the nation's first basic open-hearth furnaces.[11]

These furnaces, which had a combined capacity of 120 tons, required correspondingly large crews, but, as in Bessemer steelmaking, the overall skill requirements were far lower than those of puddling. Melters and their first-helpers, the workers directly in charge of maintaining proper temperatures and mixtures in the furnaces, possessed highly specialized knowledge. But the men who charged the furnaces with iron and then added all kinds of scrap to the molten bath required little familiarity with metallurgy. Even less was required of the scores of laborers who worked in the stocking crews that maintained the flow of materials. The technical expertise that went into the design of the steelworks was extraordinary, however. Hauling tons of raw materials, tapping the furnace, running the molten steel into ingot molds, and then transporting the ingots to the appropriate finishing mill to produce, for instance, a steel plate that weighed 50 tons and measured 206 inches by 9 inches by 3 inches required the careful integration of highly complex processes. Needless to say, Carnegie also installed the most advanced system of overhead cranes, ladles, and moving tables.[12]

Thus the Homestead Steel Works stood at the very pinnacle of the new technology of steelmaking. Indeed, on 10 May 1889, just a day after the *Chronicle-Telegraph* disclosed that Carnegie was in town to plan his revision of the Homestead sliding scale, a long article that hailed the plant's technical advances was published in another Pittsburgh paper, the *American Manufacturer and Iron World*. It began, however, not with a physical description of the mill but with a panegyric to the values underlying the Homestead Steel Works and the entire American steel industry. Carnegie deserved hearty congratulations because he had proven himself the most "fit." Echoing Carnegie's mentor, Herbert Spencer, the article celebrated "the mechanical habit of mind" that had propelled the steel industry to unprecedented heights.

> In most industries, as in life, in these days of severe competition and progress, the survival of the fittest is the rule. Nowhere it is more noticeable than in the iron and steel trades. The firms who are holding their own . . . are those who have supplemented their skill by taking advantage of the latest improvements, and have substituted machines in every possible instance for mere brute force, thereby increasing their output, effecting economy, and reducing to a minimum the risks of life. An admirable instance is the firm of Messers Carnegie, Phipps & Co., Pittsburgh, who have spared neither pains nor expense in the arrangement and equipment of their various plants at

Homestead. Their aim is to keep abreast, and, if possible, ahead of the times; to make a profitable business for themselves while furnishing materials of the highest character at the lowest market prices.[13]

The devaluation and dehumanization of labor implied in the phrase *brute force* and the fatuous assertion that machinery would reduce the risks of physical injury spoke eloquently of the steelmakers' ultimate purpose: to run their factories with as few workers, particularly skilled workers, as possible. In 1885 in Braddock, for example, Carnegie's mechanical improvements had displaced 57 of 69 men who worked at heating furnaces and 51 of the 63 who worked at the rolls in the rail mill. Carnegie's 119-inch plate mill commanded the admiration of all metalmakers as much for its great reduction in skilled labor as for its sheer size. In a mill that could heat 5,000 tons of ingots and roll 3,500 tons of high-quality plates each month, only 7 men were employed at the rolls and 8 in the heating department. From these places the plate mill must have seemed like a morgue.[14]

A reduction of such magnitude in the labor force, combined with the dramatic increase in outputs that had been reported by the Homestead Steel Works, was precisely what Carnegie had been aiming for. The handful of monthly production reports that survive from this period testify to these concerns. Carnegie's speech at the free library in Braddock, on the other hand, signaled his unwillingness to attribute the increased productivity at Homestead to the workers; moreover, it declared his determination to decrease labor costs. Indeed, a key point in Carnegie's remarks directed at his Homestead workers when he dedicated the Braddock library was that, through the AAISW, they had compelled him to pay such high wages that he could not compete with other manufacturers. In his view, technological enhancement accounted for the increase. No matter, for example, that with the original four-ton converters installed by the PBSC in 1881, workers had broken the world tonnage record in March 1887. For Carnegie the calculus of cutting labor costs to receive what he considered fair remuneration for his capital outlays at Homestead meant that there was virtually no connection between earnings and output: the labor market and the price of steel, not productivity, should determine wages.[15]

The company maintained that the Homestead Steel Works could not be "operated successfully under a scale of wages established to appy to iron products, nor under conditions that have radically changed and which did not contemplate the use of appliances and methods admitting of a largely increased output without a corresponding increase of labor." The sliding scale offer that the company made to the men was thus based on the price of steel blooms, billets, and slabs of sectional material, which was $27.50 per ton at the time. Under the proposal, wages were to be advanced or reduced as the average monthly selling price changed, but $25 was to be the minimum below which wages would not fall. This would amount to an overall reduction of 20–25 percent, but larger cuts were reserved for those skilled workers who, in the opinion of the company, earned exorbitantly high salaries under the old tonnage scale.

The cupola man and the vessel man in the converting department, for example, would have their wages cut by approximately 30 percent. Similar reductions applied to heaters in the blooming and the 33-inch beam mills. Laborers' wages were not to be cut at all: in the 119-inch plate mill, stocking crews would continue to earn 14 cents per hour. The wages of some skilled workers, such as those in the 23-inch mill, would rise: the company evidently understood that a proposal that seemed to elevate some wages offered good evidence of just how "reasonable" it was. The increases were not quite what they seemed, however. Since Carnegie's proposal called for the imposition of a twelve-hour day in the 23-inch mill, in three other finishing mills, and in the open-hearth departments, in reality all wages per unit of output would be reduced. Moreover, changing to a two-turn day would allow Carnegie to reduce the overall size of the work force. Added to all of these proposals—which the *National Labor Tribune* characterized as revolutionary—was the outright elimination of several skilled positions in the open-hearth departments and the blooming mill.[16]

In the eyes of devoted trade unionists such as John McLuckie and John Elias Jones, Carnegie's changes violated the underlying principles of labor reform that they had brought to Homestead. The right to a fair day's wages, the right to organize, the right to an ill-defined but equitable portion of the profits created at least in part by their labor—all of these claims were threatened by Carnegie's initiative. In the spirit of their union leaders, Homestead steelworkers unanimously resolved on 27 June 1889 that to accept Carnegie's proposal "would be giving up everything that is dear to the heart of every true workingman." Tellingly, the decision to end negotiations with the company was made over the strenuous objections of William Weihe and William Martin, respectively the national president and secretary of the AAISW. While these two officials were preaching the doctrine of "healthy conservatism," Homestead steelworkers remained committed to the more defiant unionism of the AAISW's past.[17]

To counter Carnegie the unions in Homestead embarked on campaigns to boost the official membership of the AAISW, which counted in its seven Homestead lodges approximately 800 of the 2,500 men employed at the works. They also sought to cement the ties between skilled and less skilled, many of whom were Slavic immigrants. Accordingly, skilled AAISW men in the blooming and converting mills unanimously voted in early June to go on strike if the company discharged any unskilled worker who refused to sign the new scale. McLuckie, Jones, and other steelworkers understood that a successful defense of their rights depended on tight-knit organization. The Knights of Labor also began an organizational drive and further made certain that Slavic laborers were included in the planning for a possible work stoppage. Indeed, the right to "earn bread" and the workers' sense of what constituted a fair wage drew together the entire Homestead community.[18]

Having rejected Carnegie's proposal, the steelworkers recognized that the crucial problem for them would be preventing new workers from starting operations in the mill after the company closed it down. The events in Braddock had taught that Carnegie would willingly, "commandments" notwithstanding, hire new men and protect them with Pinkertons. The steelworkers of Homestead therefore decided to move just as they had in 1882; they took possession of the town and sealed it off. Directed by the paramilitary Advisory Committee of men chosen from each AAISW lodge, armed steelworkers guarded all approaches to the town, allowing no one to enter unless proof was furnished that he was not a black sheep.[19]

Calm prevailed from 1 July, when management closed the works, until 10 July. That morning, one hundred Pinkertons arrived in Pittsburgh. Though management did not dispatch them immediately to Homestead, it did send off a train carrying thirty-one workers—blacks, Italians, and East Europeans—under the friendly escort of the county sheriff.[20]

Nearly two thousand Homesteaders awaited the train as it pulled into town, and they formed a barrier between it and the steelworks. Frightened by the crowd, most of the scabs fled into the nearby woods; then the sheriff tried to lead several of his charges into the mill. The townspeople made way for the sheriff but barred the workers who tried to follow. Three scabs and the unemployment agent who had hired and accompanied them were assaulted physically and verbally by men, young boys, and women, who formed a mile-long column. The agent had the roughest going: "Through the town, the women and boys on the streets incensed others to strike the man. . . . Before he had marched a hundred yards, his face was almost unrecognizable from the blows he had received. The running of the gauntlet through hives of savages could not have been worse." At the end of the column of people, four women pounced on him. One shouted, "What does he mean by coming here trying to take the bread out of our mouths?" To Homesteaders his meaning was clear enough. The daily press, however, interpreted their response to the intruders as "misrule."

Two days later, the sheriff returned to Homestead with 125 men he had deputized and an order barring the workers from congregating on property owned by Carnegie, Phipps, and Company. Disembarking from a railroad car, the authorities were greeted by an even larger crowd—as many as three thousand persons. This time Homesteaders would not allow the sheriff to move. "The strikers at Carnegie's steel plant have . . . full charge of the town, . . . and none dare to interfere." Homestead was "on the verge of riot."

Women and children ran from the town to the mill, joining the circle of workers who surrounded the deputies. For twenty minutes the crowd and the deputies faced each other in silence. Then "an angry murmur ran through the crowd and broke into a sullen roar." Women "urged the men to defend their homes" and "threatened what their intentions were if the deputies would attempt to go through the gates." Just as the crowd verged on assaulting the deputies, one of them broke ranks. He tore off his badge and coat, threw his revolver to the ground, and announced that he was going home. To the cheers of the crowd, the other deputies followed suit.

By late afternoon all the deputies but one had boarded return trains to Pittsburgh. "The strikers treated the officers very kindly after they saw they had won a victory, and paid some of their fares home. Many of the strikers gave them the coats off their backs in exchange for their uniforms." The lone deputy who refused to leave was physically assaulted. One of his assailants was a woman who smashed a parasol over his head.[21]

With the departure of the county sheriff and the deputies, Homestead was left in an uneasy quiet. Hugh O'Donnell, the chairman of the workers' Advisory Committee, agreed to lead the negotiations with management on the condition that it make no effort to open the mill for two days. The workers remained on guard, nonetheless, for the press continued to report that Pinkertons and more new workers were on their way. Meanwhile, a group of workers appointed by the Advisory Committee accompanied O'Donnell to Pittsburgh to meet with company officials.

The result was a complicated three-year agreement that recognized the AAISW as the representative of all workers, including the less skilled. Although the new contract guaranteed the workers reinstatement, it provided Carnegie with a good deal of satisfaction too, for the steelworkers consented to his sliding scale of reduced wages; while the base used to calculate the wages of some skilled workers remained the same, the pay of roughly sixteen hundred others was cut. Some of the skilled workers ended up with wage reductions as large as 30 percent. They were predictably irritated, but they put aside their objections when the steelworkers met to ratify the agreement. "It looks like a cold deal," one of the skilled men said, "but we're all in the same boat, and the minority must be sacrificed to the majority."

Certainly, all the steelworkers had some reason to be pleased with the agreement: it preserved the right of the skilled and less skilled to work; it maintained fair wages for many; and it left intact the power exercised by AAISW men in directing work operations on the mill floor. To celebrate, cheering women and children joined the workers on the streets of the town amid fireworks and cannon fire.

Not everyone in Homestead joined the festivities on 14 July, however. John Elko, a Slovak (or possibly Rusyn) laborer in the plate mill, for one, was on the lookout for Pinkertons or scabs that night. While the workers' representatives were putting the finishing touches on the agreement with Carnegie, Elko, accompanied by his wife and five-month-old daughter, was patrolling the bridge that connected Braddock and Homestead. He saw a train approach and, to determine who was inside, jumped onto it. He became entangled in the wheels, his leg was severed, and soon after, he died. Steelworkers carried the bloody body back to town. "The scene of his rudely amputated foot in his shoe lying on the board on which he was carried home is a horrible spectacle hundreds will never forget," observed one reporter. "Died for the Cause," read the headline in the *Pittsburgh Post*.[22]

For the East European community in town, the death of Elko provided the immediate impetus for organizing the First Hungarian Slovak Sick Benefit Society of St. Michael the Archangel. The society was the precursor of Lodge no. 26 of the First Catholic Slovak Union, which was to serve as the fraternal benefit society and semiofficial labor union of East European immigrants. For the Anglo steelworkers the death of Elko provided an occasion to acknowledge publicly the importance of his contribution and of the interethnic cooperation that it symbolized. Accordingly, the AAISW men of Homestead raised $200 for Elko's family and pledged to support them as long as they remained in town.

Elko's funeral became in fact a solemn occasion for all Homesteaders. Steelworkers and their families filled the sanctuary of St. Mary Magdalene Church, which served an overwhelmingly Irish parish, and nearly two thousand men, marching four abreast, accompanied the body to the cemetery. The Anglo steelworkers saw Elko "in the light of a patriot who falls at his post. . . . Although a Hungarian, he had imbibed American principles, and was one of the foremost in the late strike." At the mass meeting of all steelworkers called to ratify their agreement with Carnegie, Elko's East European colleagues also received accolades "for their valuable assistance"—they had guarded one of Homestead's railroad stations during the lockout. Even the *Homestead Local News*, which had become a mouthpiece for virulent nativism, was compelled to acknowledge Elko's contributions.

Compared to the triumph of the workers whom he had provoked, the gains Carnegie scored for himself in the lockout of 1889 were finally rather slim. In addition to the victory he conceded to the union, in addition to the jobs he had been forced to reinstate, he had, inadvertently, also given the town the opportunity to realize its solidarity as a defiant workers' republic, united beyond differences of skill or ethnic background in the name of labor. The Homestead workers, and the AAISW, emeged more determined and more powerful than ever. The union's committees now had a decisive say in the apportionment of work, the regulation of hours, the alteration of machinery, and personnel decisions in the event of vacancies. In short, the "mastery" of the steelworks lay squarely in the hands of union men. One year later, the town's government, too, would lie squarely in the hands of the union, with John McLuckie, a veteran AAISW man and leader in the 1889 lockout, acclaimed burgess.[23]

The truth was that Carnegie could have broken the union in 1889—if he had been willing to use lethal force. But the resolute opposition of the Homestead steelworkers, and a large number of unfilled back-orders, convinced him that a partial victory would do. After all, he could now look forward to three years of relative tranquility, and he had learned much about the tactics and determination of Homestead's community of steelworkers. From his perspective, the 1889 lockout was a successful reconnaissance. When the steel market was glutted in 1892, he could use the lessons of 1889 and employ the necessary measures: law enforcement would have to be in more formidable hands, and the executors of the rule of law would have to enter the town surreptitiously.[24]

It was, in fact, violations of the rule of law that troubled so many observers of the lockout of 1889. The effective seizure of the town, the rejection of the sheriff's authority, the cheeky denial of a private concern's right to hire whomever it pleased—all constituted an ominous assault on the social order that called forth the most unhappy associations of mass insurgency. The *Pittsburgh Press* commented: "The lessons of 1877 are too fresh in our minds not to be vividly recalled by open defiance of law and its official representatives."[25]

Another Pittsburgh paper, the *Chronicle-Telegraph*, spelled out the lessons in great detail:

> Violence has been committed at Homestead; force has been used to prevent men from going to work; and the officers of the law have been interfered with and prevented from performing their duties. We are free to admit the right of every man to sell his labor at the highest possible price, to combine with others and strike to enforce his demands, and to resort to any peaceful, lawful means to prevent others from coming in to fill the places vacated by the strikers. . . . But unlawful means must not be taken to enforce the demands of labor. There is a point beyond which workmen cannot go without becoming criminals, and when they pass that point they are amenable to the law, and should be arrested, tried, convicted and punished. . . . The safety point has been passed by the strikers at Homestead, and they are now liable to all the pains and penalties of the law.[26]

One of the many effects of the Homestead lockout of 1889 was an urgent foregrounding of the single major question that for decades had been preoccupying owners and workers across the nation: To what rights may those who work in a given industrial property lay claim? In other words, what are the rights of labor in industrial America? Whereas the lockout did not yet provide any conclusive answers, it did dramatize in an inescapable way just how high both Andrew Carnegie and the Homestead steelworkers were prepared to raise the stakes.

Prior to 1889 workers in Homestead had clung to a version of labor reform forged in the immediate postwar years; while staunchly upholding the rights of labor, however, even the most resolute reading of the republican legacy could not sustain an alternative vision of America in which empowered workers might effectively challenge the tyranny of organized capital. In 1889 the workers of Homestead proposed, on the other hand, that the meaning of republicanism itself be extended to assert the real, albeit ill-defined, rights of labor to the putatively private concern of Carnegie, Phipps, and Company—the Homestead Steel Works. And first among these rights was the right to work, a right to one's own job, a right that Carnegie himself had defended in no uncertain terms: "To expect that one dependent upon his daily wage for the necessaries of life will stand peaceably and see a new man employed in his stead is to expect much. . . . 'Thou shalt not take thy neighbor's job.' " On the heels of Homestead's audacious threat to the authority of the corporate order in 1889, Carnegie in 1892 lived not only to eat his words but also to steal the daily bread he had so sanctimoniously guaranteed.[27]

Chapter 18

The Life and Times of "Beeswax" Taylor: Exemplary Paradoxes of American Labor

T‍HE 1880s, as reflected in the distinct trajectories of the labor movement in Homestead and Pittsburgh, are best characterized by the conflicting impulses toward solidarity and dissolution that marked each town. There were only six miles between these communities, and yet how utterly separated they seemed by the differences that marked their respective fortunes in the realm of labor politics. The same decade that in Pittsburgh witnessed the breakdown of labor insurgency and the alliance of trade unions with machine politics gave rise in Homestead to the unprecedented success of an independent politics that extended labor's power from the factory floor to the town hall. However local to Pittsburgh and Homestead these apparent contradictions within the labor movement may seem to us now, at the broadest level nonetheless they epitomize the competing allegiances pulling at an entire generation of American workers who sought to define their place in the new industrial order.[1]

More often than not, the drama of this struggle was acted out not just on the public stage of municipal politics but in the very private space of individual lives and choices. Indeed, the same tensions that rode the six miles separating Homestead from Pittsburgh were capable of provoking conflicts not only among Homestead's own residents but within the hearts of a single earnest and committed individual as well. And perhaps the life of no individual Homesteader better captures the essential paradoxes of this era—paradoxes that many historians have yet fully to grasp—than that of Thomas W. Taylor.

From the time of the American Revolution, the tradition of republicanism, which Thomas Taylor would come to embrace and defend, cut two ways, leaving room for both defiance and accommodation, protecting the common good and endorsing personal aggrandizement. Few reformers in the late nineteenth century were as fervent and creative in their commitment to the defiant and critical heritage of republicanism as Taylor; and yet, even as he represented in his life and beliefs the deepest roots of radical republicanism, he never entirely gave up the pursuit of his own

self-interest. Whereas in his passionate devotion to insurgent republicanism, Taylor can be seen as embodying the dissident spirit of Homestead in
the 1880s, his parallel and persistent concern for personal security and
success epitomized the more compliant spirit of Pittsburgh.[2]

Taylor (1819–92), better known in his day as Old Beeswax, was a mill
worker and weaver, a militant abolitionist, an author of popular satires
and cheap verse, and a nationally recognized labor activist. He was one of
the most prominent, and idiosyncratic, leaders of the U.S. labor movement in the Gilded Age. A Chartist in his native England, Taylor was a
founding member of the American Federation of Labor and attended its
first convention, held in Pittsburgh in November 1881. Old Beeswax was
also a leader of the Knights of Labor, for which he wrote the foremost
workers' anthem of the era, "Storm the Fort, Ye Knights of Labor." In the
late 1880s, Taylor concluded his career in the labor movement by winning
election as burgess of the nation's preeminent labor town, Homestead.[3]

The election of Taylor as Homestead's chief municipal officer was, in
certain respects, most apposite. For throughout his adult life, he had
pleaded the case for republicanism and against acquisitiveness—the
very case that Homestead steelworkers and their families would plead in
the Lockout of 1892. And yet, for a time, Taylor had also been an avid
businessman. He was a cotton dealer during the Civil War, then a successful businessman in the lumber trade, and at the end of his life he prospered in the sale of residential real estate. In his choice to pursue these
private commercial ventures during a busy life of public commitment,
Taylor gives substance to the critical observation of Joseph P. McDonnell,
another important but largely unheralded labor leader of that era, that in
America the "capitalist enemy resides in the breast of almost everyone."[4]

In recent years a number of historians, far removed from the adventures of "Beeswax" Taylor, have appropriated McDonnell's remarks in
order to reconsider the grand problem of American labor history initially
posed by Werner Sombart in 1906, Why is there no socialism in the
United States? A series of essays, including one on McDonnell, published in the 1970s by the late Herbert G. Gutman helped resurrect this
question of American "exceptionalism" for the current generation.
Gutman, for his part, endeavored to show that, contrary to Sombart's
findings, the material success of American capitalism had not transformed the American worker into a "sober, calculating businessman
without ideals." There was an oppositional workers' culture that challenged the great industrialists and political bosses of the era. McDonnell,
a Fenian and socialist, figured prominently in this opposition.[5]

So, too, did Taylor, assiduous labor leader and occasional entrepreneur. An examination of the paradoxes embedded in his life thus sheds
light not only on Homestead and Pittsburgh in the late nineteenth century
but also on the larger problems of U.S. exceptionalism, the nineteenth-

century workers' movement, and the complicated relationship of that movement to the meaning of American republicanism.

To speak of Taylor is, indeed, to speak of republicanism: he was as great a republican as anyone of his era. Seeking recruits for the Knights of Labor, stumping on behalf of labor candidates or running for office himself, canvassing for greenback financial reforms, establishing cooperatives, writing satirical newspaper columns or rousing odes, lecturing on temperance, reading poetry—these were the efforts of a man who placed the Knights' call to "educate, agitate, organize" at the center of his life. This man lent talents to the job of building a cooperative society by combining initiatives in the interrelated realms of work, politics, economics, and culture.

Yet this man also ventured into the competitive marketplace in pursuit of his material self-interest. That Taylor was so diverted from labor's republican dream of a cooperative commonwealth testifies to the truly transformative power of the capitalist enemy at its most personal, and most effectual, level. It also testifies to the ambiguities of the republican tradition with which Taylor and many thousands of American workers so ardently identified, for into the world of business Old Beeswax carried the aspirations for individual proprietorship that also formed part of the republican legacy. In this regard, Taylor closely resembled a fellow Briton and devout republican with similarly close ties to Homestead: Andrew Carnegie. The parallels between the two, their origins and the origins of their discourse, are easily eclipsed by the more stunning dissymmetries of their respective careers. The parallels are, nevertheless, notable, for cannot it be said of Carnegie that he too was in his way as great a republican as anyone of his generation?

Whereas Carnegie's life has been told many times, history has not been particularly kind to the memory of Taylor. Yet his life, for all its quirkiness and apparent caprice, is in many ways just as exemplary of the convictions and the confusions, the dreams and frustrations, the conflicts and changes, that shaped the emergence of modern America. Just as the life of Andrew Carnegie represents far more than the tale of one ruthless robber baron, the story of Old Beeswax is that of not just one labor leader but of the dreams and dilemmas of all workers in nineteenth-century America.[6]

The narrative of Taylor's life begins in 1819 in Middleton, England, not far from Manchester, where he was born into a family of silk weavers. At the age of seven, he began work in a cotton mill, where he was often beaten by the mill's overseer. He continued laboring as a cotton worker in the Manchester area late into his teens. As he once told an audience of American workers, Old Beeswax gained his nickname from his earliest experiences in the mills. The work was so hard, he said, "that all the sweetness of [my] life was extracted, and there [was] nothing left but the wax which sticks after the honey has been taken out."[7]

Taylor's sense of humor—and of melodrama—did not obscure the fact that as a youth he began what for him became the most important work of his life: building a cooperative society. His commitment to such an alternative arose from personal experience. But it was also formed by the deep social egalitarianism that characterized the collective lives of the weavers in whose midst he was raised and by their allegiance to the most radical interpretations of Painite republicanism. Decades later, on the other side of the Atlantic, Taylor would continue to see in this tradition possibilities for a radically different kind of society.[8]

In England, Taylor embarked on his career as a labor activist in the late 1830s just as the Chartist movement was coalescing. In 1837 he "became a striker" and, like thousands of other English men and women, joined the movement for the Charter. His goal was to end the monarchy. "I was one who sought to overthrow the British government and endeavored to establish a Republican government." For his efforts Taylor narrowly escaped imprisonment, but he remained an active Chartist and went on to organize a workers' club pledged to self-help and temperance. Taylor also was active in the cooperative movement in the early 1840s. He later claimed that he assisted in founding the first cooperative store in England, four years before the Rochdale Pioneers began their work.[9]

Old Beeswax remained an active Chartist until 1842, when a series of events permanently altered his life. A devastating depression, the defeat of massive summertime uprisings, and the failure of a general strike for the Charter convinced Taylor that the time was right to change his personal life and political goals. Like thousands of other Chartists, he realized that the movement had reached a decisive juncture. Again faced with likely imprisonment, Taylor this time joined the growing number of radical emigrants and set sail for America. Some six years later, young Andrew Carnegie, the son of an active Scottish Chartist and handloom weaver, and himself an aspiring weaver, would similarly leave Great Britain behind to seek out a better and more just life in the New World.[10]

Taylor's arrival in the New World was not auspicious; finding a job, he discovered, was not a simple matter. Eventually, he found employment in a cotton mill in Rhode Island, and later he worked in mills in Massachusetts. In the early 1850s, Taylor headed west along with thousands of others searching for a better life. He lived for a short time in Indiana and then moved to Nebraska, where he joined militant abolitionists in the effort to halt the expansion of slavery. After a heroic (and possibly fictive) escape from Indians who had captured him, he returned to the East.[11]

Back in Massachusetts, Taylor became active in the antebellum labor movement, but this involvement cost him his job in the mid 1850s. The dismissal, on grounds of "inciting discontent" among co-workers, provided the impetus for a change in his working life that took him into the world of business for more than a decade.

First, Taylor tried his hand at inventing. He obtained a patent for an improved spinning frame, but a duplicitous partner ended his plans to market the device in England. Nevertheless, Taylor traveled to England in 1857, a year after his wife died, and in 1858 in Middleton he remarried in the church he had attended as a boy. Soon afterward, he returned to the United States accompanied by his new wife, a milliner by trade, and he embarked upon a career as a cotton dealer.[12]

Taylor never explained how or why he became a cotton dealer. But after thirty years of struggling as a mill operative, after the death of his first wife, the loss of his job, and the collapse of his plans for the spinning frame, he had reason to translate the philosophy of self-help into commercial terms. While in the cotton business, he accumulated money rapidly. Given his prominence in the postwar workers' movement and his stinging criticisms of self-made men and the ethic of accumulation, it seems unlikely that Taylor entered commercial life with the sole idea of becoming wealthy. However, it seems likely that his business ventures during the Civil War were not a source of pride to him—which may account for his silence on the subject—and that at some point he did business with Southern planters.[13]

After the war ended, Taylor entered the lumber business and, again, he prospered. But the Panic of 1873 wiped out all of his assets. An immediate result was that he resumed his career as a mill worker. By 1875 he was working as a weaver in Rochester, Pennsylvania, a small town about thirty miles downstream from Pittsburgh on the Ohio River. He had by this time also become active in the labor movement on a national level. In fact, by the late 1870s he was the master workman of the largest district assembly of the Knights of Labor, District Assembly 3 in Pittsburgh. He was now a widely read columnist in the labor press as well and counted among his friends the single-taxer Henry George and the editor of the *Irish World and American Industrial Liberator,* Patrick Ford.

Taylor, like other labor leaders, saw the Great Uprising of 1877 as the pivotal event of the decade and as labor's great chance to redeem the American Republic. In Pittsburgh, as we have seen, the uprising amounted to a revolt of the entire community against the Pennsylvania Railroad and all of organized capital. Taylor hoped to channel the violence and frustration of 1877 into a political movement. In the opinion of the *National Labor Tribune* in the wake of the uprising, the ballot, not the bullet, was labor's only hope of supplanting the wage system with a cooperative social and economic order.[14]

At the time of the uprising, Taylor had moved from Rochester to

Beaver, just a few miles away. He had also left his job as a weaver to become a salesman of galvanized ironware. Traveling from town to town in Clarion and other counties north of the Iron City, Taylor usually combined his sales job with informal cavasses and meetings designed to rally support for Pennsylvania's GLP. Whereas little is known about Taylor's activities immediately after the railroad disturbances, by early 1878 the *Tribune* was reporting regularly on his campaign appearances for the GLP, and later in the year it began publishing his poetry.[15]

Old Beeswax's poems are, at best, irregular in their literary merit; they are nonetheless consistent in their sharp and passionate critiques of corporate wealth. One of the more noteworthy poems on this subject is entitled "The Bankers and I Are Out." The poem highlights ideas Taylor shared with thousands in the workers' movement: First, that workers, because labor produces all value, should be society's foremost citizens. Second, that workers, who had fought and died to save the Republic in the Civil War were the true guardians of the republican legacy. Third, that accumulating wealth was both immoral and unrepublican; true republicans had no greater material aspiration than the acquisition of a competence, or a sufficiency of means for living comfortably. And fourth, that workers from all regions should unite to defeat corrupt politicians and thereby redeem the Christian Republic.[16]

Taylor constructed the poem around a conversation between John, a wage-earning worker, and his spouse, Nancy Jane, whose domestic labors are as arduous as his. John explains that he cannot understand why he and Nancy Jane work hard but never have enough money for sufficient food, clothing, and shelter. At the same time, Banker Jones, who does "no useful work, . . . rolls in wealth and style" with his extravagantly clad wife, who commands a coach and four coachmen. Worse yet, in John's view, is that Banker Jones and his wife strive to demonstrate their devotion to Christianity while fleecing hard-working laborers. Invoking the stereotype of the cheating Jew (Taylor and other labor reformers often resorted to the Shylock metaphor), John unmasks Banker Jones's hypocrisy as he explains to his wife how bankers profited in the Civil War and its aftermath.

You ought to see them go to chruch and sit in cushioned pews,
And make believe they're Christians; and yet they're naught but 'Jews."
They live six days by shaving notes and robbing honest toil,
And then they try to cheat the Lord with sanctimonious smiles.

You will remember, Nancy Jane, when first the war broke out,
The workmen left the plow and loom, and loudly they did shout—
"To arms! To arms! Your country calls—she needs strong men and means."
And soon three hundred thousand men were marching o'er the plains.
. . . .

"Yes, dear John," says Nancy Jane, as the tears ran from her eyes,
"I well remembered those dark days when we lost our darling boys."

"And widow Smith, whose husband fell at Gettysburg, you know,
Was left with six small boys and girls, to share her want and woe;
She went to Banker Jones one day and borrowed on her farm,
He charged her twelve per cent, or more, and thought he'd done no harm.

"Her farm was taken for Jones' bonds, and interest running on,
Until the farm was swallowed up and all she had was gone.
Now, John, it seems so strange to me, I've puzzled night and day
To know why bonds should go untaxed and soldiers' widows pay."[17]

John responds to Nancy Jane's question by generalizing from the experience of widow Smith and Banker Jones. Bankers such as Jones were so powerful during the Civil War that they dictated the terms under which they loaned money to the Union. The result was huge profits for the banking community that were generated through the greenback-financed purchases of government bonds and the subsequent repayment of the bonds, with interest, in "hard money." Uncle Sam tells the Money King:

"May it please your Majesty, our country sorely needs
Some gold to carry on the war—see how the nation bleeds.

"Men are cheap and if they die, we've others for their place;
But your gold's a sacred thing, so may it please your Grace
To name the terms you'll loan it on—we'll meet it if we can:
We'll make our laws to suit your wants if you will state you plan.[18]

After describing the government-financier nexus, John goes on to offer a solution to the problems faced by workers and their families.

"Now, Nancy Jane, to tell the truth, our freedom's all a sham—
We vote and fights for knaves and fools, who plunder Uncle Sam.

"They make our laws to suit the rich, and then divide the spoil,
And we, like fools, don't seem to know it's robbing honest toil;
'Tis gold that rules the Church and State, in fact it rules the world
And will until the people rise, with freedom's flag unfurled.

"And let that flag this motto bear, in letters all can read:
" 'Tis labor that produces all, let it be first to feed!"
Let drones and knaves pick up the crumbs, that's all that they deserve,
Until they do some useful work, some useful purpose serve.

"Let East, and West, and North, and South, unite with heart and hand,
And rout the thieves and party hacks who've ruined this fair land;
Or let us bow our head in shame, in sack cloth let us fix,
And own ourselves unworthy sons of sires of seventy-six."

"The Bankers and I Are Out" describes a world perverted by bankers and politicians: Mammon and corruption, rather than God and virtue, are the controlling forces. For John—and for Beeswax—only labor had the power to right the world and restore virtue to America. Uniting behind candidates committed to labor would allow workers to unfurl freedom's flag and claim it and the Republic as their own. Indeed, emblazoning a motto on the American flag that proclaimed society's ultimate dependence on labor suggested that labor was not merely a part of the Republic but actually constituted it.

When Taylor stakes a claim to the most important symbol of American republicanism in the name of American labor, he indicates the extent to which he understood that the meaning of republicanism was up for grabs. Defining it was more than a literary exercise, however, as he also understood. Its definition was the very problem that stood at the center of labor's struggle to erect an alternative social system. Though Taylor and his colleagues were never very clear about the details of such a definition, they were certain that the American Republic would have to be a republic of labor if it were to be a republic at all.[19] Taylor's suggestion that the American flag bear a motto that proclaimed labor's dominance in the social order thus represented a call to engage in practical politics and also, insofar as the suggestion amounted to an assault on the received notions of the culture's most powerful symbol, a political act in itself. Like Andrew Carnegie, a master of symbolic gestures and significant terms, Taylor grasped the importance of symbols and language as contested terrain and understood that in its effort to build a cooperative commonwealth and to overcome the real and symbolic monopolies of corporate ownership, labor had to arrogate to itself the key words and symbols of political discourse.[20]

Such appropriation meant engaging in a cultural battle of the highest order. Taylor brought a good deal of experience to that battle. As "The Bankers and I Are Out" suggests, Taylor also brought to the American labor movement of the 1870s and 1880s virtually the whole constellation of ideas that had animated the movement for the People's Charter. To be sure, the American republican tradition, independent of individuals such as Taylor, was heavily informed by many of the premises of Chartism. Preeminent among these, themselves rooted in seventeenth- and eighteenth-century English radicalism, was the conviction that the distinction between virtue and corruption, between industrious "bees" and idle "drones," marked the most basic division in society and that virtue could be assured and industriousness rewarded primarily through political means. The case for enacting the Chartist platform had been above all that poverty and oppression would end when British workers won the franchise, thereby abolishing the monopoly of lawmaking that supported those who had property but did no real work. It was a small leap indeed from such a position to one that considered the state as the corrupt protector, as Beeswax put it, of the Money King and saw the triumph of a political party of the genuine wealth producers as committing a quite justifiable regicide.[21]

In a wistful moment late in his life, Andrew Carnegie himself confessed, "My childhood's desire was to get to be a man and kill a king." Once in America, however, he had determined that things were rather different. "We have the Charter," he stated in 1853, meaning that workers had achieved their political rights and were free from the unjust tyranny of monarchs. Hence it was easy to abandon the unseemly aspirations of his youth in this New World that, for him, represented in effect "the realized Utopia of a young Scot's Chartist dreams."[22]

There were, however, no such easy decisions for Taylor. Running for the Pennsylvania Senate in 1878 to represent Beaver, Clarion, and several other counties north of Pittsburgh, he and his fellow labor-greenbackers organized a campaign rich in the themes that had informed Chartism. The *National Labor Tribune's* description of his arrival in Beaver City on his first campaign swing began, for example, with an extended metaphor that contrasted monarchical power with that of the true nobility—workers. The account described how "Greenback" Taylor, prouder than if his "sovereign" had rewarded him with a badge for fidelity and bravery, was carried not to a regal throne but to a simple chair trimmed in green. "Honest workingmen" then hoisted him on their shoulders and carried him into a parade.[23]

Taylor and most other labor-greenbackers who ran in 1878 were defeated, however. The *Tribune* charged that because voting was open, employers succeeded in pressuring workers to vote for the mainstream parties. The allegations, combined with the intense effort of the Republican and Democratic parties to discredit the GLP, imply that its opponents believed that the party represented a serious challenge. But the results of the 1878 elections persuaded Taylor and other Pennsylvania labor leaders to redirect their energies, and union building became their chief concern. Taylor nonetheless continued to organize for the GLP in and around Pittsburgh and in 1879 took his personal campaign across Pennsylvania and into New Jersey, New York, Ohio, Massachusetts, and Maine. It was also in 1879 that he began writing his "Beeswacks" column for the *Irish World*. In all of this fervent activity on behalf of the GLP, there was something of the drive and ambition of a businessman.[24]

Indeed, Taylor's column for the *Irish World* brought him a good measure of fame, and his appearances on behalf of the GLP invariably drew enthusiastic responses. "Large audiences greet him wherever he speaks"; he was noted for his "earnest truthfulness, . . . keen sarcasm and manly appeal to the workers." Despite Taylor's personal popularity, the GLP was trounced in Pennsylvania elections in 1879, 1880, and 1881. By then the mood of Old Beeswax and his associates bordered on resignation: it was clear that the GLP would not achieve a foothold in American politics. Taylor himself, in the race for director of the Allegheny County poorhouse, received a mere 817 of 11,100 votes cast.[25]

To judge from his remarks at the founding convention of the American Federation of Labor, which met in Pittsburgh just a few days prior to the 1881 elections, Taylor must have intimated that he and other labor-greenbackers were destined for another stunning defeat. Described as possessing "a wide reputation as an advocate of principles calculated to advance the best interests of the workingmen," he did not temper his survey of the electoral situation with any of the humor for which he was noted. "If workingmen did not enjoy the rights belonging to them," a newspaper paraphrased him as saying, "they had no person to blame but themselves." Taylor warned that "until workingmen joined together in cooperative societies and established mills and manufactories, there would continue to be a conflict between capital and labor."[26]

In this speech, Taylor gave vent to years of frustration. He also reaffirmed his longstanding belief that though electoral politics were important, cooperative ownership offered the ultimate answer to the problem of wage slavery. In establishing cooperative enterprises, he said later, workers could succeed in harmonizing the conflicting interests of workers and employers because they would become their own employers. This was a peculiarly American way of saying that workers should own the means of production.[27].

In supporting such views Taylor was not alone. By the early 1880s many of his fellow Knights agreed that the creation of an egalitarian social order was tied to the question of who owned the factories of America. For them, political democracy and the franchise could never ensure equal rights; the core meaning of republicanism involved more than the abolition of a titled nobility. Here, then, is where Old Beeswax and Andrew Carnegie, his fellow Chartist, parted company: Carnegie believed that the American Republic had put the People's Charter into practice. As the official newspaper of the Knights of Labor put it, however, building a democratic society in America presupposed fundamental changes in economic organization. "The remedy must be in a change of ownership."[28]

Despite its inability to effect such a change of ownership, and despite the poor fortunes of the GLP, the labor movement of the 1870s and 1880s was formidable; entrepreneurs and their managers, as well as their allies in politics, went to considerable lengths to contain it. When, in Pittsburgh in the early 1880s, businessmen stood on the threshold of victory, there were still significant pockets of resistance in the neighborhood, none so strident in its resistance as in nearby Homestead. And here, in

Homestead, Taylor at last found some success. Defeated in the larger arenas of work and politics in city, state, and nation, he came to Homestead in 1881 and helped forge a small though noteworthy victory for labor's cause.

It does not seem entirely fortuitous that Taylor ended up in Homestead or that from his home there he wrote the workers' hymn "Storm the Fort" shortly after steelworkers defeated William Clark in the strike of 1882. The song embodied the aspirations of trade unionist and Knight alike and set upon the achievement of equal rights the condition that workers use their brains by voting for independent labor candidates. For Taylor, a dedicated labor republican, the song summed up many of the themes and problems that had given purpose to a lifetime's striving.

STORM THE FORT, YE KNIGHTS OF LABOR

Toiling millions now are waking,
See them marching on,
And the tyrants now are shaking
Ere their power is gone.

Chorus:
Storm the fort, ye Knights of Labor,
God defend our cause;
Equal rights for self and neighbor;
Down with unjust laws.

'Tis labor that sustains the nation,
And 'tis just and fair
That all should help, whate'er their station,
To produce their share.

But now the drones steal all the honey,
From industry's hives;
Banks control the nation's money,
And control our lives.

In time of war the workmen rally
At their country's call;
From the hilltops and the valley
Come they one and all.

In time of peace the loom and anvil,
Reaper, plow and spade.
Join their chorus with the mandril;
Each man at his trade.

Do not load the workman's shoulder
With an unjust debt;
Do not let the rich bondholder
Live by blood and sweat.

The land and air by God was given,
And they should be free,
For our title came from heaven—
Not by man's decree.

Why should those who fought for freedom
Go in bonded chains?
Workingmen no longer need them
When they use their brains.[29]

Into the mid 1880s, Old Beeswax remained active in independent labor politics. He was elected burgess of Homestead in the spring of 1888. His one-year term was largely uneventful, and his health was often poor; in the autumn of 1888 newspapers carried false reports of his death. (When this happened again a few years later, he remarked that though he found the premature obituaries quite flattering, he "thought he would remain here a while longer, since people thought he was such a good fellow.") Despite poor health, Taylor began writing for a Pittsburgh newspaper and later in the fall set off to campaign in Indiana. He spoke on the stump every night for six consecutive weeks.

The party on whose behalf Taylor now spoke, however, was rather removed from the aspirations of the GLP; indeed, it was the party of Andrew Carnegie himself, for, following the example of many of his colleagues in labor reform, Taylor had gone to work for the Republican party. No doubt he was finally admitting that the prospects for a labor party were poor. But he had other reasons, too: he hoped to win a patronage appointment from President Benjamin Harrison. In fact, Taylor had, by this time, so closely tied his personal future to the Republican party that he now boasted of carrying on a correspondence with the infamous boss of Pennsylvania politics, Senator Matthew Quay. So certain was he of winning a government job that in 1889 he declined to run again for burgess of Homestead.[30]

The appointment did not come, however, and once again, in his disappointment, Taylor turned his efforts to the world of business, this time as a real estate agent. The focus of his activity was Wilmerding, not far from Homestead, on the north bank of the Monongahela River. By 1891 he had moved there and his business was doing so well that he and his wife were able to afford a winter vacation in Florida.[31]

Beeswax Taylor died in Wilmerding on 19 January 1892, six months before the lockout that effectively ended his republican dreams. The *Homestead Local News*, which printed his obituary under the headline, "An Eventful Life Ended," published alongside it his final poem, "Men and Monkeys." Here are the concluding verses:

And now, my friends, my story ends;
This moral fits the case:

Let working men cooperate
And free the human race.
Cooperation leads the way—
The only way to freedom—
The way to rid the earth of drones;
The world no longer needs 'em.

Shake off the chains that bind you down
And stand erect like men!
And if you stumble by the way
You'll soon get up again.
And if we all cooperate
For labor's true salvation,
The joyful sound will then resound—
A free and happy nation.[32]

Thomas Taylor himself often fell short of this parting advice to American workers. When Homestead steelworkers stood against Carnegie in 1889 and again 1892, he ended his political career as an active supporter of the party of big business, groveling for a patronage appointment by invoking the name of Matt Quay and garnering neat profits in real estate by selling residential property to workers. As Joseph McDonnell noted, virtually all Americans did indeed carry the capitalist enemy within their breasts. But what, after all, was Taylor, in poor health and lacking steady employment, to do?

The specific question of Taylor's personal choices would seem to be subsumed by McDonnell's general observations; but how are we to understand McDonnell's comment on this era of confusion? Clearly, McDonnell was not suggesting that Taylor and other American workers lacked class consciousness—whatever that term means—or, to put it another way, that they willingly endorsed the competitive wage system. Rather, McDonnell understood that the lure of acquisitiveness was powerful enough to entice even its most dedicated opponents into active complicity, particularly in a polity that offered fewer and fewer possibilities for democratic expression and in a culture that increasingly identified the pursuit of self-interest as the hallmark of moral life.

In the late nineteenth century few, if any, people made greater contributions to curbing the prospects for democracy, and to falsely identifying the ethos of acquisitive individualism with it, than Andrew Carnegie. He did this by mounting creative initiatives in the very domains where Beeswax Taylor toiled—on the factory floor, in politics, in the definition and production of culture. Whereas Taylor tried to build a cooperative society based on cooperatively owned enterprises, Carnegie created new forms of social hierarchy by transforming the technology and management of the nation's largest private industry. Whereas Taylor struggled to build a political insurgency, Carnegie supported and helped define the agenda of the Republican party. And whereas Taylor poked fun at bankers and self-made men, Carnegie offered alluring justifications for competitive ruthlessness in his countless public speeches, in his famous books, and above all in the seductive example of his own success.[33]

Throughout these endeavors, nonetheless, Carnegie thought of himself as an ordinary workman and reformer who wanted only to actualize his deepest dream of a noble, harmonious social order grounded upon Chartist principles, Christian morality, and republican politics. And he persisted in expressing his ambitions for himself and America in the very language of reform that at the time was being invoked to challenge his authority. Consider what he said in dedicating the cornerstone of his philanthropic empire, the Carnegie Library of Pittsburgh: "Every thoughtful man must at first glance be troubled at the unequal distribution of wealth, the luxuries of the few, the lack of necessaries of the many. . . . What was more natural than that the social condition of men, and especially the problem of the creation and distribution of wealth, should force themselves upon me?"[34]

The ironies of Carnegie's discourse, of course, did not go unnoticed by the many who still lacked necessaries. The title of his most famous book, *Triumphant Democracy*, provoked predictable jabs: one journalist visiting the Homestead Steel Works wrote that what he witnessed on site, far from resembling "Triumphant Democracy," "might be described under the title 'Fedualism Restored.' " Nevertheless, it is clear that Andrew Carnegie, whose life was subject to many of the same shaping forces as Beeswax Taylor's, and whose discourse bears a striking resemblance to his, was truly troubled by social conditions and apparently sincere in harboring similar dreams for betterment, even as he worked to destroy the hopes of those he employed.[35]

What Carnegie shared with Taylor, therefore, was not just Chartist origins and republican rhetoric but also a set of seemingly irreducible contradictions. Certainly, both epitomize an age of tremendous contradiction and possibility, an age marked by the simultaneous pull of powerful callings in different directions. Taylor's career, like Carnegie's, was hardly without ironies: the tireless "knight' of labor, who had spent his life fighting against feudal as well as economic privilege, in his final years became a respectable businessman and threw his support behind the party of Mark Hanna, William McKinley, and Andrew Carnegie himself.

What, then, are we to make of this odd little man who spent so much of his life in pursuit of an elusive alternative to the wage system yet flirted with its promise and ended up enmeshed in it? Perhaps Taylor was merely a sore loser in the game of capitalism, always looking for another opportunity. Perhaps he saw labor reform as the forum where his modest gifts might be consistently appreciated. Perhaps the unifying thread in his life as a worker, politician, and businessman was after all the desire for personal aggrandizement. Were his poems and newspaper columns, his campaign speeches, mere fluff, "eulogistic coverings," as one historian has characterized the utterances of radicals of the period?[36]

Doubtless, Taylor wanted to rise from the ranks; he was ambitious; he looked for success and enjoyed it when it was his. In these attributes and desires he plainly resembled Carnegie, who saw in the promise of upward mobility the greatest testimony to democracy. But then again, why should this coincidence be surprising? The republican discourse and ideals that shaped them, and that they helped shape, clearly contained within them the promise of labor reform and a cooperative commonwealth for the Gilded Age; but it also contained within it, just as surely, the promise of individual triumph in the form of self-made manhood and corporate rule. Taylor's life, for all its odd detours, may not, in the end, correspond to the ideal model of a heroic labor leader. His life of commitments, however, exemplifies in a very real way the tensions that Joseph McDonnell sadly, wisely, identified.

To his credit, Taylor learned firsthand that the untrammeled pursuit of self-interest, as conceived by the market calculus of net comparative advantage, contradicted the very prospect of success for all Americans that he so cherished. While Carnegie was blind to this contradiction, Taylor suggested that Americans seek a new kind of success, one that emphasized the common good but did not abridge individual rights. How, precisely, to do this, he did not know, but he was not the only nineteenth-century social critic who fell short in the effort.

In the end, though, Old Beeswax did capitulate; but this capitulation does not mean that he was merely a "possessive individualist" all along. To resist the enemy, capitalism, or to accommodate, to fight or to submit, to choose between personal aggrandizement and the common good, between an individualist and mutualist response to capitalism—these were questions that Taylor and countless other Americans time and again confronted in the late nineteenth century. Finally, but certainly not unequivocally, most chose accommodation. Their ultimate choice did not necessarily mean that they endorsed the competitive wage system. For many there was in fact no choice—only resignation to the very narrowing of democratic possibility that Taylor for many years had the courage to contest. To see self-interest as the sole measure by which he ordered his life is vastly to underestimate the complexity and ambiguity not only of that life but also of an entire era.

PART SIX
1892 and Beyond: Legacies of Homestead

I am of the opinion, on the whole, that the manufacturing aristocracy which is growing up under our eyes is one of the harshest
that ever existed in the world. . . . The friends of democracy
should keep their eyes anxiously fixed in this direction; for if ever
a permanent inequality of conditions and aristocracy again pene-
trates into the world, it may be predicted that this is the gate by
which they will enter.

— ALEXIS DE TOCQUEVILLE,
Democracy in America, 1840

Chapter 19

Captains of Business, Captains of Politics

There are more things in heaven and city hall, Horatio, than are dreamed of in our philosophy.

— *The Pittsburgh Post,*
September 1890

"We now know that freedom is a thing incompatible with corporate life and a blessing probably peculiar to the solitary robber." This was said by a distinguished writer referring to the individual units who have constructed the political systems under which society is organized. It applies with equal truth to the governments they have created.

— Secretary of State Philander C. Knox,
"International Unity,"
December 1909

DURING THE Great Depression of the 1870s, Andrew Carnegie had built the Edgar Thomson Steel Works in Braddock and staked his fortune on it. Unlike other steelmen, he recognized that the depression presented profitable opportunities to expand, and he possessed the requisite insight and resources to take advantage of them. While his competitors stood idly by, Carnegie found suppliers willing to sell construction materials and equipment at tremendously reduced prices; he also found workers who were eager to work for low wages. He was thus able to build the Edgar Thomson for three-quarters of what it would have cost after the depression ended.[1]

Within a year of the Homestead lockout of 1889, Carnegie recognized that he and all other American metal manufacturers were facing a new economic problem that could render many of their mills as idle as had the depression. To be sure, 1890 seemed like a stellar year for Carnegie's companies: profits were higher than the capitalization of all his plants combined, including the newly acquired Allegheny Bessemer Steel Works in Duquesne. Moreover, the demand for steel had never been greater. At the same time, however, prices had taken a precipitous dive. Carnegie needed only to survey his own rapidly expanding empire to deduce the reason: the increase in the demand for steel had simply not kept pace with the colossal expansion of productive capacity. He himself had just spent $3 million—$1 million in the Homestead mill alone—on technological improvements. The result, painfully evident to all steel-men by the spring of 1890, was a crisis of overproduction.[2]

Carnegie, true to form, rejected conventional wisdom that steelmen should "check the tendency of overproduction" in order to create "that scarcity in supply which is so essential to a rise in prices." In fact, at the very time the American Iron and Steel Association was urging its members to do just this, Carnegie was making bold arrangements to expand. Increasing the productive capacity of his mills was so critical a part of his long-term business plans that he moved swiftly and unhesitatingly when, in the midst of the overproduction crisis, he saw an opportunity to buy land next to the Homestead Steel Works.[3]

The byzantine background to Carnegie's purchase is telling, for it illumines the behind-the-scenes business practices of Carnegie, Henry Clay Frick, and their close associate, the Republican boss of Pittsburgh, Christopher L. Magee. Before reviewing the secret negotiations leading to that purchase, however, it is worth pausing to consider the long-term career and strategic significance of a fourth player in the deal, the chief corporate counsel for Carnegie, Phipps, and Company, Philander Chase Knox.

Of the many friends and associates to emerge from the business empire of Andrew Carnegie, few attained the stature and power of Philander Knox (1853–1921). As U.S. senator from Pennsylvania, attorney general in the McKinley and Theodore Roosevelt administrations, secretary of state under President William Howard Taft, and a presidential candidate himself, Knox was recognized as a key leader of conservative Republicans and an influential figure in international politics.[4]

Despite his weighty governmental responsibilities, Knox was never known for maintaining a particularly demanding schedule. In presiding over the Department of State from 1909 to 1913, for example, he would work at home until late morning, enjoy a leisurely lunch, and then play golf. During one of his afternoons on the links, a partner asked if Knox might travel to China in order to gain firsthand knowledge of the growing crisis there. "I'm just starting to learn this game [golf]," the secretary replied, "and I'm not going to let anything as unimportant as China interfere." Knox's unhurried approach to government also marked his tenure as attorney general from 1901 to 1904. At the Department of Justice he was known as Sleepy Phil. Given that his tenure coincided with the most rapid growth of trusts in American history, the appellation was well suited indeed.[5]

Whereas Knox did not publicly present himself as a man of intense energy and commitment, there was no doubt that his allegiances always stood firmly with his many friends in business. While working for Carnegie, he became chummy with the most prominent members of the American financial community. He moved in a circle of millionaires that included, in addition to the Republican kingmaker Mark Hanna, men such as George W. Perkins of the House of Morgan, A. J. Cassatt of the Pennsylvania Railroad, and James Stillman, the mastermind of the Rockefeller brothers' ever expanding interests. Prior to entering politics, Knox led the prestigious Pittsburgh law firm of Knox and Reed, earned wide recognition as the most dexterous of corporate attorneys, and served as president of the Pennsylvania Bar Association. But it was by working as chief counsel for Carnegie, Phipps, and Company and Carnegie, Brothers and Company that Knox began his ascent to the highest levels of national office.[6]

In the view of both Carnegie and his chief executive, Frick, Knox was indeed the consummate corporation lawyer. He provided more than just expert advice; he functioned as a field lieutenant who could handle unseemly details in utter confidence while simultaneously maintaining a gentlemanly public posture. In was, in fact, Knox who surreptitiously helped plan and execute the firm's legal and military strategy during the Homestead Lockout of 1892 and who secretly arranged with local authorities for the Pinkertons' riverboat landing. Moreover, it was he who, on the company's behalf, brought the charges of riot, conspiracy, and murder against the Homestead steelworkers and proudly acted as the guiding hand behind the extraordinary charges of treason brought against the workers' Advisory Committee. Of these charges, Knox declared:

> This will be the first case of treason ever tried in the State of Pennsylvania. In fact, there was never anything exactly similar. The only case coming near it was the proceedings growing out of the French Commune. This case will attract as much, if not more interest, than did the famous trial of Aaron Burr. We are bringing these proceedings to see whether the laws of Pennsylvania or the edicts of the Homestead Advisory Committee are to rule this Commonwealth. The committee took the law in their own hands, ignoring the government of the state. We think this constitutes treason.[7]

These were strong words. With the possible exception of Chief Justice Edward Paxson of the Pennsylvania Supreme Court, no one surpassed Knox in so roundly denouncing the steelworkers for subverting the rule of law. Knox soon had other legal problems to consider, however—problems that demanded his most subtle flair to defend Carnegie's probity as a corporate citizen.

In 1894, four Homestead steelworkers informed the federal government that company officials had deliberately defrauded the Navy Department by supplying it with defective armor plate. After a thorough investigation and a series of embarrassing public hearings, the government found Carnegie Steel guilty and imposed a hefty fine of $140,000. Attorney General Richard Olney also authorized an arrangement that compelled the company to pay, over and above the fine, more than $35,000 to the four informants (who of course had been summarily fired for their disloyalty).[8]

Needless to say, Carnegie and Frick hoped to avoid any further entanglements of a similar nature. Hence in 1896, when the opportunity arose to place the Department of Justice in "safer" hands, they moved quickly. Within weeks of Republican William McKinley's presidential victory over William Jennings Bryan, Frick and Carnegie requested that their man, Knox, be appointed attorney general of the United States. Carnegie wrote to McKinley that Knox "ranks with me as the best lawyer I have ever had for our interests, a veritable 'little giant.' " Frick described him as the quintessential corporation lawyer: "As counsel for the Carnegie Company, and other interests with which I have been connected, I have had abundant opportunity, from a business man's standpoint, to judge of his ability as a lawyer and his character as a man. . . . He is intensely loyal, . . . [and] has well been described to me by a Pittsburgh lawyer as a crystal thinker."[9]

When Carnegie and Frick put pen to paper in December 1896 to recommend Knox, they had reason to believe their advice would be heeded. Both were, after all, ardent Republicans: Carnegie, in fact, had contributed thousands to McKinley's campaign and had received an effusive thank-you note from Mark Hanna, his campaign manager and the national chairman of the Republican party. Moreover, McKinley and Knox had been friends for nearly twenty years. As it turned out, McKinley did nominate Knox to be his attorney general, but not until 1901. And from that point on, Knox remained in the public eye, succeeding Matt Quay in the U.S. Senate in 1904, returning to the executive branch in 1909 when President Taft named him secretary of state, and later serving again in the Senate.[10]

It was during his term as secretary of state that Knox achieved his greatest prominence, afternoon golf matches and leisurely lunches notwithstanding. He streamlined the organization of the state department by making it function, not surprisingly, more like a corporation: he introduced the system of departmental specialists responsible for separate regions of the world. Although criticized for his lack of experience and expertise in foreign affairs, he was viewed by many Washington insiders as the dominant force in the notoriously weak Taft administration; some believed that it was Knox who chose the entire cabinet for Taft and to a large degree directed his administration.[11]

In the realm of foreign affairs proper, Knox became known as the principal architect of Taft's Dollar Diplomacy. Politely stated, this policy held that American investment in the nonindustrialized world could prevent disorder and simultaneously turn neat profits for domestic corporations. In principle, Knox maintained that American capital should replace the big stick approach to world affairs made famous by Teddy Roosevelt. In practice, however, Knox often resorted to force and what he called the moral value of U.S. naval power in a wide range of overseas initiatives aimed at securing American political and financial domination.[12]

It was, for instance, Knox who between 1908 and 1911 negotiated clandestine schemes with the Honduran government, J. P. Morgan (at the time head of U.S. Steel), and Samuel "Sam the Banana Man" Zemurray (who later was to become the flamboyant president of the United Fruit Company) that effectively brought Honduras under American control. And in Nicaragua in 1912, it was Knox who, by sending in 2,700 U.S. troops to uphold a friendly government he had personally installed, set in motion not only twenty years of American armed occupation but the forty-five-year dictatorship of Anastasio Somoza and the Sandinista revolution that toppled him. The Central American Court of Justice, created in 1907 with the blessing of the U.S. government, condemned Knox's intervention as contrary to international law, but the United States ignored the decision. Knox defiantly explained American policy thus: "We are in the eyes of the world . . . held responsible for the order of Central America."

Ironically, the ruling of the Central American Court of Justice was issued from a building in Cartago, Costa Rica, that had been constructed with $150,000 donated by Knox's crony and former employer, Andrew Carnegie, who by then had left the world of commerce to campaign for world peace. As the historian Walter LaFeber suggests, Carnegie's gift to the Central American Court of Justice may well have represented one of his "few bad investments." It is unlikely, however, that he was surprised when his former legal advisor, who had so passionately upheld the rule of law in condemning the workers of Homestead, had so little use for the law when it proved inconvenient to his purposes; for Knox, along with Frick and other officials of Carnegie, Phipps, and Company, had, on at least the one notable occasion alluded to above, themselves conspired to circumvent the law.[13]

On that occasion the scheming did not involve heads of state, American naval power, or jumbo banana plantations in Central America. It did, however, directly involve Republican politics and one very valuable piece of domestic real estate: to be precise, 144.48 acres situated in Mifflin Township between the borough of Homestead and the site of the Homestead Steel Works (located, more precisely, in Munhall). Called the City Farm, the land rose from a large, flat plain that abutted the Monongahela River up to one of Homestead's schoolhouses, which stood atop a steep hill. There were two main structures on the land: the City Poor House, where as many as 300 paupers might live at any one time, and the Home for the Insane, which had a capacity of 150 patients. The residents of each building who were physically and emotionally able to work were required to help farm the surrounding land.[14]

The City Poor House, built in 1851, was by 1890 hardly considered out of date. Nevertheless, the Pittsburgh city councils, at the direction of the Republican boss, Christopher L. Magee, decided that it was time to sell the property, buy new land, and construct a new poorhouse. Accordingly, the Select and Common councils enacted an ordinace on 11 July 1890 that authorized the sale of the City Poor Farm and instructed R. C. Elliott, the chief of the Department of Charities, to advertise for bids.[15]

The story of how this land came to be sold by the city of Pittsburgh and then bought by Carnegie is replete with juicy conspiratorial details. It also provides a case study of how businessmen such as Carnegie and Frick and machine politicians such as Magee—with the aid of well-connected Republican attorneys—effected their much cited but little-studied alliance. Moreover, for modern readers looking back on the vigorous efforts of the Homestead workers to carve out an alternative model of workplace and governmental organization, the story is, above all, a poignant one; for it reveals the extent to which these men were unwittingly and inescapably tangled in the web of big business, machine politics, and ultimately Dollar Diplomacy woven by Magee, Knox, Carnegie, Frick.

When Carnegie, Phipps, and Company and the city of Pittsburgh consummated the deal for the 144.48 acres, the city's Democratic newspaper, the *Post*, joined a handful of concerned citizens in charging that there had been an "outrageous swindle." But no one could prove that any party to the transaction had broken the law or in any way acted improperly. A series of letters, cables, and telegrams sent by Carnegie, Knox, and Frick (only recently uncovered in the archives of the USX Corporation) provides the kind of evidence that the outspoken critics of the "job" would have savored: incontrovertible proof that Carnegie, Phipps, and Company, Christopher Magee, and a real estate broker by the name of Milton I. Baird had conspired to defraud the city of Pittsburgh, and that Magee had breached the public trust. The documents also suggest that officials for Carnegie, Phipps, and Company, most probably at the direction of Knox, perjured themselves in court.[16]

Carnegie himself set the deal in motion on 22 March when he sent two letters to Knox outlining his position on acquiring the land next to the Homestead Steel Works. He said that he was willing to pay $3,000 per acre—roughly $433,000—for the parcel and that for three years the city could retain, rent free, the use of the land and buildings. Should Knox succeed in obtaining the land for less than $3,000 per acre, he would split the "savings" with the firm and win an additional $50,000 bonus from Carnegie. Three days later both Carnegie and Frick wrote to Knox authorizing for him an additional $25,000 for "all expenses in connection with the purchase."[17]

Given that the final form of the transaction did indeed allow the city of Pittsburgh to retain the land, rent free for three years, it is probable that Carnegie discussed matters with Magee as early as March. However, Carnegie's files offer no conclusive evidence of any direct communication between himself or his subordinates and Magee prior to the opening of bids on 27 July. On that day, Carnegie, Phipps, and Company offered $2,805 per acre for the land; Joshua Rhodes, owner of the Pennsylvania Tube Works, bid $2,715; and Milton I. Baird, of Black and Baird, bid $2,903. As Baird's bid was the highest, it was immediately accepted. City officials then opened envelopes containing offers of sale to the city of land for a new poor farm. One was from Baird himself and another from H. S. A. Stewart, a prominent Pittsburgh realtor and businessman. Mayor Henry I. Gourley responded cautiously, to say the least, to the bids for the poor farm and to the offers for new land. "In view of the ridiculously low bids for the farm and the wonderfully high prices asked for land twenty-five miles from the city [the site for a new farm], I do not think this offer should be accepted." While Gourley's legal authority to quash the sale was problematic, he did succeed in temporarily delaying the deal.[18]

Gourley had good reason to be suspicious: the principals in the sale had close connections with one another. Carnegie was Magee's good friend, and Frick was his business partner, facts that were widely acknowledged at the time but that historians have managed to overlook. H. S. A. Stewart, a former city councillor and chairman of the city's finance committee, was also Magee's partner: he was a director of Magee's Citizens' Traction Company and in fact served as chief collaborator in virtually all of his commercial endeavors. Rhodes, too, had ties with these businesses: he was on the board of the Citizens' Traction Company and, at the time of Magee's death, was described as having enjoyed "very close" social and business relations with him for many years. Baird directed a large real estate firm and, as indicated by certain communications exchanged by Knox and Frick, enjoyed a privileged relationship with those two men as well as with Magee.[19]

In point of fact, what appeared to be three bids on land from separate interests amounted to a planned effort on behalf of at least three collaborators: on 1 August, scarcely a week after the bids on the old poor farm had been opened and assessed, Milton Baird agreed to sell his rights to the property to Andrew Carnegie for a cool $75,000. Even taking into account Baird's profit, Carnegie could hardly complain of his success in acquiring this choice piece of land; real estate brokers and city councilmen at the time placed its actual value in excess of $1,000,000.[20]

Whereas historians have ignored many of the important details of this negotiation, on a general level the concerns of Mayor Gourley have been acknowledged as legitimate. Indeed, since the early twentieth century when Lincoln Steffens published his caustic indictment of political bossism, *The Shame of the Cities*, it has been clear that Magee, in personally directing Pittsburgh's finances, took a less than selfless interest in the awarding of municipal contracts.

As far as the intrepid Steffens understood matters, however, Magee pursued his own pecuniary ambitions in a perfectly legal manner: he was not corrupt, he simply "owned" the city and always took care to operate within the law. This general characterization of Magee's tenure has been repeated down to the present day. The historian Joel Tarr, in the most recently published discussion of the Pittsburgh ring, writes, for example, that the consolidation of power effected by Magee and his colleague William Flinn did indeed allow them to channel municipal "contracts and patronage to their own companies and those of their followers." The question of legality does not enter into his discussion. If anything, Tarr suggests that the ring actually aided municipal development: the malodorous details of municipal corruption, not to mention the much larger problem of identifying the winners and losers in the political tourney organized by Magee and Flinn, are subsumed under the respectable goals of "better control" over "administrative policies and the city-building process."[21]

Magee and Flinn did indeed put their shoulders to the wheel of city building: Magee was perfectly happy to acknowledge publicly that he favored industrial development of the City Poor Farm site.[22] And, as the story of the transaction suggests, the ring did indeed succeed in streamlining certain administrative practices and exerting superior control over city hall. The transaction also demonstrates, however, that beneath such neat abstractions, culled from the disciplines of urban history and public policy studies, there lay certain untoward particulars of city building inevitably associated with a most fundamental question of history—the question "of who rides whom and how?" With regard to the City Poor Farm, at least, this question points well beyond the boundaries of local history.[23]

The most revealing evidence of the smoothly interlocking vectors of power and interest that coordinated the City Poor Farm transaction was generated just a few days after the bids were opened, between 31 July and 2 August. Unbeknown to the general public, Knox, Frick, Carnegie, Magee, and Baird were all engaged in their own private bidding game for control of the site. Whereas the documents detailing this game yield a somewhat confused picture of the stakes, two things are certain: that Magee, Carnegie's company, and Baird engaged in extralegal collusion; and that in this collusion, Philander Chase Knox negotiated for Frick and Carnegie.

To judge from the cable Carnegie sent Frick on the morning of 31 July, all had not gone according to plan. In notifying Frick that the flat part of the City Poor Farm tract was essential at any price, Carnegie also advised that the company should arrange for a prompt settlement with an un-named "interloper" in the deal. Just who this was the documents generated by Carnegie and his associates do not disclose. But the secret communications issued in the wake of Carnegie's urgent telegram to Frick establish beyond doubt that some third party had his own eyes on the land. Moreover, they establish that Christopher Magee was kind enough to "fix" for his friends Carnegie and Frick whatever concerns this third party had raised in their eyes and that Philander Knox was a full and knowing accomplice in effecting this arrangement.[24]

It is, in fact, a telegram that Knox sent to Frick about ten hours after Carnegie cabled on 31 July that is most revealing. It demonstrates that the company's officers fully understood that their activities were of questionable propriety and that they would prove incriminating should they be disclosed: the telegram was consequently drafted in a special code that a disloyal office boy or messenger could not penetrate. Of course, the business practice of communicating in code was by no means limited to the City Poor Farm deal. Typically the communications between Carnegie and his associates were written in a peculiar, and often colorful, language that required a lengthy codebook for translation. In the code used for everyday transactions, for example, *stone* stood for "puddlers," *slop* stood for "heaters," and *storm* stood for "rollers." Though the one codebook pertaining to these details of day-to-day steelmaking has survived, other codes designed for more specialized, or secretive, transactions have not been so easily cracked.[25] As a result, no handy key is available to decipher fully the cables and telegrams exchanged by company officials in late July and early August 1890. As luck would have it, however, the clerk who received these messages penciled in the names of important actors and a sum of money that figured in the City Poor Farm deal. The full text of Knox's telegram to Frick on 31 July reads:

> Angel [Magee] sent success [Baird] to me demanded dot band fifty [$150,000] con down now to give or take half success represents the people we thought

am on whole combination are trying to work it from both side am satisfied attempt will be made Monday or Tuesday to Pittsburgh must act   Eagle [Knox][26]

Roughly translated, the telegram establishes that Christopher Magee sent Milton I. Baird to Philander Knox with a demand for $150,000 to set the deal right for Carnegie, Phipps, and Company. We also know that Baird represented a certain interested party who was somehow working two ends of the transaction and was on the verge of undercutting Carnegie. Whether Baird demanded the $150,000 on behalf of Magee, of the third party, or possibly of both is unclear; whatever the case, Frick was doubtless alarmed that his "Angel" had apparently skewed the plan and that the entire deal might fall through. The next day, 1 August, brought Frick another telegram from Knox. This time the news was considerably more encouraging: "Everything fixed Suspend judgment on Angel [Magee] until you get all facts." And evidently everything was "fixed," for later that same day Baird willingly signed over the property rights to Carnegie, Phipps, and Company.[27]

While Knox, Magee, and Baird were negotiating and Carnegie was sending off cables from Europe, the public in Pittsburgh was being treated to a exercise in political charades and self-righteous indignation by Mayor Gourley. Shortly after questioning the transaction, he backed off, repeated his reservations, and then adopted a stance that can be generously described as equivocal. The mayor, in any event, seemed to be out of the official picture: the ordinance authorizing the sale and purchase of poor farm lands gave full power to the head of the Department of Charities, Elliott, and the city councils—both, not surprisingly, in Magee's full control. Given Gourley's public waffling on the bidding, it seems likely that Magee, Frick, Carnegie, Knox, and Baird were not the only men maneuvering behind the scenes to close the deals in an opportune manner. What, if anything, was at stake for Gourley is not certain; but when he finally announced on 4 August that he had decided, after all, to endorse the sale of the land to Baird and, moreover, that he now approved the purchase of the property owned by Stewart, Magee's partner, for a new poor farm, it signaled to everyone that the transaction was unassailable.[28]

Some untoward complications had in fact arisen at a certain point: as Knox indicated in a telegram to Frick on 2 August, messy kinks in the transaction had required Frick's presence—evidently at the negotiating table with Magee—to ensure that there be no further slipups. Carnegie, for his part, was kept informed of developments. Moreover, the telegram he sent Frick on 2 August suggests he had some inside information of his own that he had not previously disclosed even to company officials: the unnamed broker who had entered into the negotiations posed no problem if he was acting on behalf of certain insiders. Go ahead with the deal, Carnegie counseled. Frick followed the advice and later that day won assurances that there would be no further complications. Carnegie cabled back his reply: "Glad hearty congratulations price high but firm Will never regret." After receiving the telegram, Frick left town for a seaside vacation with the chief engineer of the city of Pittsburgh.[29]

Two days later, the Pittsburgh city councils formally approved the sale of the City Poor Farm to Baird and the purchase of the Stewart property for a new farm. The deal was consummated, the *Post* reported, "with an alacrity surprising to some people." The vote in the Select and Common councils was overwhelming. Indeed, so large was the majority that it utterly confirms Lincoln Steffens's characterization of Magee as the owner of councils. For the purchase of the Stewart land, the vote was 30 to 1 in the Select Council and 35 to 5 in the Common Council. The voting followed a similar pattern on Baird's bid for the City Farm: 31 to 1 in the Select Council and 34 to 1 in the Common Council.[30]

In the wake of the vote, the *Post* and other papers carried reports that suggested improprieties and collusion—reports that were vehemently denied by William L. Abbott, chairman of Carnegie, Phipps, and Company. "There have been stories afloat that our firm offered the amount it did with the understanding that there would be no higher bids. All such statements are false." Abbott even denied that the firm was particularly keen on purchasing the poor farm, Carnegie's forceful and specific orders to the contrary notwithstanding. In truth, Abbott said, the company had sufficient land for any contemplated expansion over the course of the next several years.[31]

The *Post*, responding in a blistering editorial entitled "Plundering the People," charged that "vast private fortunes" were being amassed through deals such as the City Poor Farm transaction.

> Those who know how the city of Pittsburgh is regularly milked by the professional politicians who acquire their living and their fortunes through its necessities, real or imagined, will not readily discard the idea that there was a job, and a big one, in the poor farm sale and purchase. There has been so much jobbery, there is now so much, and probably will continue for many years to be so much, in connection with the affairs of this city, that few transactions indeed will bear admission of the light of day into their vitals.[32]

The *Post* had hit upon an important truth: if indeed the light of day had found its way into the boardroom of Carnegie, Phipps, and Company to expose the secret communications of Frick, Carnegie, and Knox, no doubt the "jobbery" would have been exposed. As it happened, one Pittsburgh city councilman did publicly charge that Baird had acted as a figurehead in the deal. He had heard reports that Baird was acting on behalf of Christopher Magee, H. S. A. Stewart, or William Flinn's construction company (Booth and Flinn). "I cannot say anything [more specific] about that, but I know that one of those gentlemen is interested to some extent." Baird, for his part, endeavored to maintain the public charade: three weeks after signing the contract with Carnegie, Phipps, and Company, he was still solemnly avowing his intention to develop the poor farm tract as residential property.[33]

In early September public doubts about the propriety of the deal were given legal status when a certain Charles L. Straub sued the city of Pittsburgh, Mayor Gourley, Elliott, Baird, and Carnegie, Phipps, and Company over the irregular nature of this business transaction. Attempting to void the poor farm sales, Straub charged that the enabling ordinance authorizing Elliott to advertise the land was illegal and, more important, that those who bid on the property had reached an illegal understanding. The bids were submitted only for the appearance of competing with Baird, and Baird himself had bid "only in the interest of Carnegie, Phipps & Co."[34]

Needless to say, Carnegie, Phipps, and Company denied all allegations of fraud and collusion. Responding to Straub's suit, the company—in direct contradiction of the telegrams sent by Frick, Carnegie, and Knox—declared that none of its officers, agents, or employes had any understanding or agreement with Rhodes, Baird, or their agents. And in a brief that was doubtless prepared by Knox himself, the company specifically stated that it had no "knowledge that Baird would be the bidder." Had the contents of Knox's telegram of 31 July been available to the court, a charge of perjury in all likelihood would have followed.[35]

Knox, for his part, was kept rather busy by the lawsuit: in an astoundingly brazen display of conflict of interest, he represented not only Carnegie, Phipps, and Company but also the city of Pittsburgh. Unbelievably, Knox was joined by Baird's lawyer, D. T. Watson, in presenting the city's defense. Knox won the case for both his clients; the two judges who presided, one of whom was to prove particularly friendly to company officials and hostile to union leaders during the Homestead Lockout of 1892, held that there had been no collusion and that the ordinance authorizing the sale of the farm had been properly drawn. The *Post* was outraged; in an editorial entitled "The City Poor Farm Job," the paper called the whole deal an outrageous swindle. It paraphrased Hamlet: " 'There are more things in heaven and city hall, Horatio, than are dreamed of in our philosophy.' "[36]

Still odder developments ensued when, on Straub's appeal, the case reached the Pennsylvania Supreme Court. Knox represented his accomplice, Baird, and again was victorious. Baird, for his part, received $125,000 from Knox's employers, $50,000 as reimbursement of his deposit and $75,000 for having sold the property to them. And on 12 November the sale became official; Mayor Gourley signed over the deed to the company for the sum of $370,906. The total cost of the land, exclusive of the commission and fee paid to Knox, thus came to about $496,000. Even with legal costs, however, Carnegie had made an extraordinary bargain: he had acquired the land for about half of its market value.[37]

Aside from the thrill of closing such a profitable deal, Carnegie had good reason for pursuing the City Poor Farm property so energetically. On 20 November 1890, scarcely a week after officially signing the agreement with the city of Pittsburgh, he won a $4 million contract from the Navy Department to supply 5,909 tons of battleship armor. The Homestead Steel Works already possessed a fully functioning armor plate mill, which was soon to provide material to fit the battleships *Maine* and *Texas* and the cruisers *Raleigh* and *Cincinnati*. But the military contracts on which Carnegie now set his sights and the new military-industrial ambitions that now fueled his imagination demanded a major expansion of the mill that only the poor farm property could make possible. Indeed, it was on this sleepy piece of land that the Homestead Steel Works would eventually become a vast corporate behemoth embodying not only the incredible fortune of Andrew Carnegie but also the intimate, powerful relationship between industrial technology and military might that would shape the contours of modern American history.[38]

In capitalizing on the extraordinary military demand for steel that wartime would sooner or later provide, Carnegie thus demonstrated not only his much touted business sense but also a political foresight that he could boast of, even if it squarely contradicted his firmest public avowals of pacifism. "It is one of the chief glories of the Republic that she spends her money for better ends and has nothing worthy to rank as a ship of war," Carnegie had proudly written in *Triumphant Democracy*, published in 1886. In the copy he sent to the secretary of the navy at the time, he had taken care to underline this sentence and, as a personal postscript, added: "Compliments to my friend the Sec'y of the Navy who I am sorry to see trying to rob his Country of one of its chief glories." Three short years later, however, Carnegie was whistling a rather different tune: "There may be millions for us in armor," he wrote to his partner, W. L. Abbott. Whereas, out of pacifist principles he had at one time censured the manufacture of guns, he now managed to justify battleship armor as a purely defensive product.[39]

Comfortable with this righteous accommodation, Carnegie now went on to pursue the millions that "defensive" armor offered. Like his delegates in the City Poor Farm deal, he did not hesitate to exploit less than righteous means to win U.S. government contracts extralegally for his armor mill at Homestead. Among his inside contacts in the U.S. government he counted some of the highest officials, including one of Philander Knox's predecessors at Foggy Bottom, Secretary of State James G. Blaine, who virtually delivered to him enormous foreign naval contracts.

It was with the help of men such as Blaine, Knox, Magee, and Frick, powerful politicians and crafty financiers who operated in the grand arenas of national and international government—as well as in the backrooms of Pittsburgh's businesses and city hall—that Carnegie was able to construct his immense industrial fiefdom. In so doing he created the foundation for the world's first billion-dollar corporation, U.S. Steel. And it is only against this larger picture that the significance of the convoluted transfer of 145 acres of poor farm property outside Pittsburgh becomes apparent. This deal, which appears on the surface—and indeed appeared at the time to all but Carnegie and his most intimate colleagues—to be just one more local case of unscrupulous real estate development, implied a vast network of influence and power that extended well beyond the Monongahela Valley, reverberating through state, national and ultimately global channels. The City Poor Farm deal not only tied Pittsburgh interests to the steelworks and steelworkers of Homestead but also tied Homstead and its residents to an emerging order of American economic and military dominance in a world that few, at the time, were privileged to foresee.

Over and above the personal glory reflected by Carnegie's entrepreneurial successes, his holdings came to embody the triumph of corporate management and values that had occurred over the course of his working life. This triumph, to say the least, was not without larger consequences. As Paul Kennedy observes: "Of all the changes which were taking place in the global power balances during the late nineteenth and early twentieth centuries, there can be no doubt that the most decisive one for the future was the growth of the United States. With the Civil War over, the United States was able to exploit . . . many advantages . . .—rich agricultural land, vast raw materials, and the marvelously convenient evolution of technology . . . to develop such resources . . . [and] transform itself at a stunning pace." In Kennedy's eyes, Carnegie Steel stands as the outstanding example of the industrial "gigantism" that signaled America's emergence as a world power.[40]

As we have seen, this gigantism was built cumulatively upon the globally imperceptible negotiations of men such as Carnegie and his partners. Just as the Pittsburgh poor farm deal ultimately signals, beyond its immediate deceits, the questionable relation between corrupt business practices, local politics, and the expansion of American military-industrial authority, the career of a properly dull individual such as Philander C. Knox is emblematic of the rise of American corporate power. With the unwavering support of Carnegie, Knox was able to move gracefully from the boardrooms of Pittsburgh businesses to the chambers of the U.S. Senate and the Department of Justice, to the intimacy of the White House, and finally, to the Central American Court of Justice. The influence of Philander Knox, whose political ascent begins propitiously with a shady real estate deal on behalf of Carnegie in Homestead in 1890, thus ends just as tellingly with the shady rise of Anastasio Somoza in Managua in 1936. What the trajectory of his success connotes above all is the unholy alliance between American corporate interests and imperial ambition that would mark the entire twentieth century.

Given that the historical ironies behind these careers and deals are still so difficult to reconstruct today, is it any wonder that honorable journalists such as Lincoln Steffens, not to mention upright workers such as John McLuckie, John Miller, and many of their colleagues, did not fathom the implications for world histroy of the jobs they performed? Fighting to redeem the American Republic and to secure the rights of all workers to an honest livelihood, how could they possibly have known that their efforts would, in the end, subsidize the profitable overseas ventures of the very men and values they opposed?

When, in 1883, the powerful ironmaster and politician Abram S. Hewitt dedicated the Brooklyn Bridge, built with Andrew Carnegie's steel, he proudly pronounced it a fitting monument to the moral qualities of the time. Some fifteen years later, the battleship *Maine,* also built with Carnegie's steel (and later sabotaged in Havana harbor), would be quickly appropriated as the new moral monument to America's unself-conscious commitment to progress, justice, and democracy. However, just as the Brooklyn Bridge did indeed stand as a moral measure of the times, in ways Abram Hewitt could not imagine, the battleship *Maine,* the end product of years of corporate scheming and political adventurism, likewise embodied the broader morality of the era. And when we now "remember the *Maine,*" without knowing it we not only recall the deaths of innocent American shipmen but also acknowledge, indirectly, the efforts of the dauntless workers at Homestead who rolled its armor: their resistance to and their defeat by the captains of business, the captains of politics.

Chapter 20

1892: The Stakes for Labor

As THE 1890s began, groups of Americans, as diverse as they were spread out, recognized that they were being squeezed out of the civic life of the Republic. For many workers, urban and agrarian alike, the new decade signaled what they hoped would be one last grand opportunity to rechart the course of the Republic and create a cooperative social order. But whereas some strove boldly to assert their claim to political and economic entitlement, others resigned themselves to what seemed to be the inevitable, undemocratic forces of mass production, modernization, and progress.

All across the South and into the Western plains, agrarian insurgency was cresting: hundreds of thousands of farmers, black and white, struggling to escape debt and poverty and to secure some measure of autonomy, had joined the Farmers Alliance and were preparing to enter electoral politics. (Their efforts, though valiant, would prove ultimately desperate and fruitless.) For native Americans all across the continent, the 1890s marked the effective end of any hope for independence. At the very beginning of the decade, the Census Bureau officially declared the Western frontier closed and, as if in awful recognition of this fact, the army completed its suppression of the Plains Indians in December 1890 at Wounded Knee, South Dakota. Meanwhile, in the industrial North and Midwest, the labor movement, though badly wounded in the aftermath of the Great Upheaval of 1886, still commanded an impressive army: two hundred thousand workers belonged to the American Federation of Labor (AFL), and one hundred thousand loyal Knights of Labor clung tenaciously to their memberships. But even before the debacles at Homestead, Pullman, and Coeur d'Alene, many working Americans, defeated in spirit, had already withdrawn from the fray and taken reluctant shelter in a conservative compromise with former adversaries.[1]

For a select handful of Americans, however, the 1890s pointed unequivocally toward an era of unsurpassed prosperity and triumph. Capitalizing on the profits from their burgeoning industries, members of a new elite enjoyed a life of extraordinary privilege and opulence in virtually every major city in America. And for no one were the nineties more "Gay" than the great steelmasters. It was in 1890 that the United States outstripped Great Britain in the manufacture of iron and steel; in that year, Abram S. Hewitt, a steelmaster and Democratic kingmaker, received the Bessemer Gold Medal in recognition of this achievement. With his shrewd eye cast toward the twentieth century, he predicted that the new methods of steel production he helped pioneer had cleared the way for nothing less than a "higher civilization."[2]

Hewitt, of course, was not alone in prophesying a grand future for the Republic. But with the Western frontier officially closed, swelling ranks of Americans who, like Hewitt, believed in their country's Manifest Destiny, were forced to look beyond the continental United States to fulfill their imperial aspirations. "Whether they will or no, Americans must now begin to look outward," wrote Captain Alfred T. Mahan in *The Influence of Sea Power upon History, 1660–1783.* "The growing production of the country demands it. An increasing volume of public sentiment demands it." Mahan's influential book, published in 1890, not only called for an offensive military strategy to fulfill the demands of American production and popular opinion but also stressed the need for a large merchant marine and navy—based, of course, on a powerful steel industry.[3]

The publication of Mahan's book and the blossoming of America's expansionist dreams, the closing of the frontier and the rise of the populist insurgency, the defeat of Britain in iron and steel production and the ascent of the great American steelmasters, the surge and precipitous decline of worker militancy—the conjunction of these events and trends was not fortuitous. Each grew out of the mighty political and economic forces that had been unleashed by the Civil War and had stoked America's industrial takeoff in the succeeding decades. And while the implications for world history of these weighty developments made the early 1890s a watershed, other, smaller but related initiatives also heralded the beginning of the new decade and its ethos.

It was, after all, in November 1890 that Andrew Carnegie concluded his agreement with the city of Pittsburgh to purchase the poor farm, on which he would expand the Homestead Steel Works, and also won a $4 million contract from the U.S. Navy for armor plate produced at the plant. This contract for the plate that would eventually fit the *Maine* and other battleships represented an early triumph of what the historian Walter LaFeber has called America's "first military-industrial complex." It also represented a personal victory for Mahan and Carnegie, who had joined forces to construct the great imperial navy Mahan had envisioned.[4]

Less than two years after Carnegie signed these prized compacts with

Pittsburgh and the federal government, he moved to consolidate his vast holdings, thereby giving concrete expression to the gigantism of the U.S. steel industry. In creating the Carnegie Steel Company, the canny Scot married Carnegie, Phipps, and Company, which had operated the Homestead Steel Works, and Carnegie, Brothers, and Company, which had overseen the Edgar Thomson Works in Braddock. Capitalized at a whopping $25 million, the company owned, in addition to these two giant mills, a mammoth Bessemer facility in Duquesne, a vast array of iron and bridge works in Greater Pittsburgh, and mining and coking concerns elsewhere in Pennsylvania. With a capacity equal to more than half that of all the steel mills in Great Britain, the Carnegie Steel Company, which employed thirteen thousand men, was the world's largest steelmaker.[5]

The birthdate of Carnegie Steel was 1 July 1892, perhaps as momentous a day as any in the history of American business. Andrew Carnegie and Henry Clay Frick had ample reason to be proud of their new company. It was, as its enormous physical assets and work force indicated, a true behemoth. No less impressive were the combined profits and production figures for Carnegie, Phipps, and Company and Carnegie, Brothers, and Company on the eve of consolidation: $4.3 million and 797,286 tons of steel ingots, respectively. The 110-acre Homestead plant alone boasted sixteen open-hearth furnaces with an annual capacity of two-hundred and fifty thousand tons of steel ingots, two ten-ton Bessemer converters capable of producing almost as much, and a wide variety of rolling and finishing mills that turned out armor plate, bridge steel, and structural beams and girders. Carnegie's new company, eight years before its controlling partner left the steel business in a $40 million blaze of profits, came close to meeting the challenges that Frederick Overman had put to American metalmakers in 1854.[6]

Since entering the steel business in the 1870s, Carnegie, as we have seen, pursued a relentless course of technological innovation, union-busting, and managerial reform, all in an effort to reduce costs and emerge from the great contest of world steelmaking as its undisputed king. On 1 July 1892, he could rightfully claim this title as his own; he might proudly affirm that "the Carnegie spirit," to borrow the historian David Brody's apt characterization, did indeed rule the American steel industry.[7]

And yet, as Carnegie plainly realized, all was not well within the realm. The Homestead Steel Works, which he acquired in 1883, had been a persistent souce of business problems and therefore of personal discomfort as well: despite his best efforts to oust them, the AAISW and the Knights of Labor not only had managed to thwart him but had in fact flourished, enjoying more power in Homestead than in any other mill. Indeed, one reason why Carnegie had approved the plan for corporate reorganization—a plan pushed by Henry Clay Frick—was to ensure utmost strength in what both men hoped would be the final showdown with organized labor in Homestead.[8]

Throughout the 1880s, as his Homestead records attest, Carnegie had kept a particularly watchful eye on the twin barometers of cost-efficient production, union strength and labor costs. A letter to the Homestead superintendent, William L. Abbott, in which Carnegie recounts "a long and serious talk . . . about Homestead" with W. R. Jones, his expert on personnel matters, spells out Carnegie's concerns. The talk made him "more anxious than ever" about affairs at the plant; his advice to Abbott was therefore to trim the work force by 10 percent "so that each man getting more wages would be required to do more work."[9]

Abbott and Carnegie, of course, had tried to achieve this goal and others, notably a nonunion mill, in the Homestead lockout of 1889. And though Carnegie had been pleased with some of the cost-cutting effects of the lockout, he was deeply disturbed by having made an agreement with the AAISW in the first place. He wrote to Abbott shortly after the lockout that the wage reductions in three of the Homestead departments represented an important success: "So much is clear gain." However, not only did the AAISW remain a power in the mill, but the agreement with it had been made under duress and had set what Carnegie feared was a dangerous precedent. "The great objection to the compromise is of course that it was made under intimidation—our men in other works now know that we will 'confer' with law breakers. . . . I don't like this feature at all." Not long afterward he received the alarming news that an old corporate nemesis, Park Brothers, was enjoying a 51-cent-per-ton cost advantage over Homestead in the production of steel plates. This report only served to reinforce Carneige's own publicly declared intentions "that the present system at Homestead must be changed."[10]

Appropriately enough, the efforts of Carnegie to change the system made page-one news across the country on 1 July 1892, the very day that Carnegie Steel itself came into being. "Carnegie's Gates Shut against Union Labor" was the *New York Herald's* headline. Abbott, who was regarded as a coward by Frick since the disastrous "compromise" of 1889, and who had previously left the Homestead superintendency, formally resigned from the company on that day. His replacement at Homestead, John A. Potter, demonstrated his own uncompromising spirit early that morning when, outside the entrance to the mill, he kicked and badly injured a locked-out worker who refused to obey a command to leave his post outside the gate. Meanwhile, in Pittsburgh, F. T. F. Lovejoy, the new secretary of Carnegie Steel, served public notice of his superiors' long-standing intent: "No trade union will ever be recognized at the Homestead Steel Works hereafter. This has been positively decided upon, and there is no reason that there should be any secrecy about the matter any longer." An observation in the *Pittsburgh Commercial-Gazette* seemed ominously on the mark: 1 July 1892, the paper reported, marked "the opening of a campaign that will be memorable in the industrial history of the country."[11]

Though Potter's kick constituted the first overtly violent act in a dispute that would become famous for its violence, Carnegie himself had initiated the most recent round of assaults against metalworkers much earlier. In a move that dramatized the technological changes he had championed for decades, he closed down and ordered dismantled all thirty-eight puddling furnaces at his Twenty-Ninth Street Mill in late April; two hundred puddlers were summarily fired, and there were reports that those at Carnegie's Thirty-Third Street Mill would also be dismissed. Startling though it was, Carnegie's initiative constituted only the latest in a series of corporate decisions that had shifted production away from puddled iron and toward steel: as early as January 1890 the press carried reports from Carnegie's mills "that the end of puddling is not distant."[12]

The fact was that in 1892 puddlers in all Pittsburgh mills were facing the end, and Carnegie and his fellow steelmasters recognized that the long-awaited opportunity to deliver a knockout punch to the AAISW was also close at hand. In February, Jones and Laughlin closed thirty-five puddling furnaces and dismissed their puddlers; in May the *American Manufacturer*, the industry's mouthpiece, reported that the cost advantage of steel had reached a point that indicated puddled iron would finally be a thing of the past; and in June, in the midst of the annual negotiations for the puddlers' sliding scale, the president of one large iron company warned all puddlers that, given the cost-effectiveness of steel, they would be unwise "to take any stand that will result in the stoppage of the puddling furnaces." A Pittsburgh ironmaster, Henry Oliver, commented, "Steel is selling in the open market at prices [for] which . . . it is utterly impossible to make and sell iron unless at a loss."[13]

Under pressure from the disintegrating market for iron and the technological innovation that had precipitated it, many puddlers buckled at the pointed threats of their employers and, along with hundreds of other skilled ironworkers, helped steer the AAISW in a cautious direction. The the new technology of steel, moreover, had succeeded in isolating puddlers and ironworkers from their brother steelworkers. The union, which counted 24,068 members in 1891, was in fact so dominated by ironworkers, and particularly by puddlers, that when it met in convention that year, delegates from steel mills openly complained that few of their colleagues could understand them or their concerns. When, in 1889, the Duquesne steelworkers had issued a plea for a sympathy strike on the part of the iron puddlers, it fell on deaf ears. "It's only a question of time," the steelworkers predicted, "until the puddler of today will be the steel worker of the future." By 1891 these words rang truer than ever. As if to compound the divisions that already existed between the iron-and steelworkers in the AAISW, many iron finishers had begun to believe that they could no longer count on the union, and in the early 1890s some of them moved to secede.[14]

On the eve of the Homestead Lockout of 1892, then, the national organization of the AAISW was plagued by internal dissension and external assault and had no effective strategy to counter either. True, its membership was larger than ever, but only 25 percent of those eligible carried union cards. The union was further weakened by some of its own practices, in particular, its reluctance, as a matter of national policy, to admit unskilled workers. After 1890 they could be admitted at the discretion of local lodges, as they were at Homestead, but the national union had in general remained an organization of the skilled. "There is no doubt that the Amalgamated Association is seriously menaced on all sides with the approaching dangers of disintegration," one prominent Pittsburgh labor leader said. "I should not be surprised to see the Amalgamated Association reorganize under another name and begin under vastly different rules and regulations. The trouble has always been that the association has extended protection to the few at the expense of the so-called unskilled laborer."[15]

The "trouble" with the AAISW was even deeper than this labor leader acknowledged. The *Pittsburgh Post* reported just weeks before the Homestead Lockout that the union's "internecine strife and contention" had forced President William Weihe and several others from office. One, James H. Nutt, had left to assume an important position with the Mahoning and Shenango Valley Iron Association, where, one labor paper observed, he would be "engaged in the congenial occupation of aiding the robber barons . . . in their efforts to reduce the wages of labor." In crossing the floor, Nutt was joined by a former AAISW president, John Jarrett. These defections, coupled with recent defeats at the Black Diamond Steel Works and the Solar Iron Works, prompted another Pittsburgh labor leader to suggest that the general sense among his colleagues was that the AAISW had "simply not been 'in it' for the last ten or twelve years."[16]

These comments came from a trade unionist whose allegiance to the labor movement extended back to the mid-1870s, when many organizers of the AAISW had tried to direct it toward a goal more clearly enunciated by the Knights of Labor: building an amalgamation of all workers, skilled and unskilled, in a grand effort to transform the wage system and redeem the American Republic. In the early 1880s, however, the leadership of the AAISW had publicly declared its allegiance to "conservatism," and by decade's end it had routed the Knights' national assembly of iron- and steelworkers in a series of bitter disputes.[17]

In these endeavors the point man for the AAISW had been its secretary, William Martin, a former steel roller, who edited the union's pages in the *National Labor Tribune*, helped direct the Western Pennsylvania Trades Assembly, and served as a vice president of the AFL. Looking back on his decade of accomplishments in Pittsburgh, Martin, a practical man, said with pride: "Capitalists, merchants, and businessmen need feel proud of the conservatism that pervades the legion of labor organizations in this city. . . . Pittsburgh is looked upon as being the hot-bed of unionism, but the many years of practical experience of those in the labor movement has reduced the percentage of labor troubles to a minimum."[18]

Throughout the 1880s it had been Martin, arguably the most knowledgeable and ambitious man in the AAISW, who had held it together, even as he began to see that the real political power for which he thirsted lay outside the union's lodges. While encouraging conservative tactics, he tried to map out his own accommodation by seeking the directorship of the new federal Bureau of Labor. He met with no success, but his power and influence nonetheless grew: he knew the leaders of every local union lodge and the officers of every iron and steel company in the region, and he was familiar with the most particular, plant-specific concerns of each side. It was Martin who helped formulate workers grievances and shaped their demands; it was he who compiled wage proposals and the accompanying job descriptions that were submitted to employers as a basis for negotiating the yearly scale; and it was he who often smoothed the way for settlements.[19]

In June 1890, Martin inexplicably left the AAISW and resigned from the AFL. "A trades union to be successful must be run on business principles," he stated in parting, in the *Tribune*. Like his brother in trade unionism "Beeswax" Taylor, Martin went after the main chance and entered the real estate business in September 1890. By July 1891 he was finally appointed head of a bureau of labor—not by the government, but by a more appreciative employer, Andrew Carnegie. As one Pittsburgh paper observed, three of the AAISW's most powerful men now worked for the owners of iron and steel mills and were being handsomely rewarded for their services: "The acquisition of Jarrett, Martin, and Nutt by the manufacturers at this time has the appearance of a prearranged plan to wipe out the most potent forces of the Amalgamated Association with cash."[20]

Whatever the appearance, one thing was clear about the hiring of William Martin: it was a heavy blow for the union, for it meant that Carnegie had obtained the expertise of the most skilled wage worker in the American steel industry. Indeed, it was William Martin, erstwhile AAISW man and leader of the AFL, who drafted the wage scales first presented to the Homestead steelworkers in January 1892, which incited them to protest in June and July.[21]

The scales that Martin prepared for Carnegie were built on the compromise wage scales that effectively ended the Homestead lockout of 1889. The 1889 scale, which was to terminate on 30 June 1892, had effected wholesale reductions for skilled workers in three of the largest departments. Martin, acting on directions from Carnegie, then under intense pressure to cut costs because of the overproduction crisis in the U.S. steel industry, began a comprehensive survey of Pittsburgh metalmakers in early 1892 in order to ascertain comparative wage rates in the region's mills. To judge from letters he exchanged with the ironmaster David B. Oliver in 1893 and from the specificity of detail included in Martin's wage studies, Pittsburgh manufacturers were only too happy to oblige any request Martin made for information that might prove useful to his cause. Their cooperation lends credence to the charge that there was some kind of "prearranged plan to wipe out" the AAISW by way of defeating its Homestead lodges, the last bastion of unionism in the Bessemer steel industry.[22]

In researching area wage scales, Martin found that at Homestead's two open-hearth departments, the company was operating at a comparative disadvantage, paying skilled workers (whose wages were determined by the sliding scale) an average of almost 50 percent more than their counterparts in ten other mills. Moreover, Carnegie was also paying higher wages in the 32-inch slabbing mill and the mammoth 119-inch plate mill. To make matters worse, Martin calculated that the wages Carnegie paid to skilled day laborers (masons, blacksmiths, boiler makers, machinists, and engineers, among others) throughout the Homestead works exceeded those of men who did the equivalent work in Carnegie's nonunion mills in Braddock and Duquesne. While some skilled workers at Homestead—rollers in the 23-inch mill, for example—were in fact paid less than their counterparts in competing establishments, company officials clearly felt that the AAISW had put a "tax" on labor at Homestead and "therefore the Amalgamated had to go." And, as if to bolster this conclusion, Martin's wage analysis confirmed Carnegie's own long-held belief, restated in urgent cables to Frick in June 1892, that in Homestead "it is not only the wages paid, but the number of men required by Amalgamated rules, which makes our labor rates so much higher" and forced the company to employ "far too many men."[23]

The negotiations for the new scale began early in January, even as Martin was conducting his research. Two features stand out. First, the negotiations were confusing. Whereas on the surface, the main issue of debate was the wage rates, Carnegie officials and union representatives spent much of their time pondering how the company and the workers should divide the material benefits generated by technological change. Both issues were addressed—or, in the case of the firm's representatives, often consciously ignored—in the complicated, substantive questions that were brought up during the negotiating sessions. The questions before the union and the company were in fact so abstruse that the congressmen who investigated the lockout and examined scores of witnesses did not always understand them.[24]

A second notable feature is the forthright democratic principles that governed the representation and participation of the AAISW men of Homestead. All but one of the negotiators for the union were Homestead steelworkers, usually members of the mill committee that represented the men in a given department, and all of these middle-level leaders were directly responsible to their co-workers. There was some overlap between mill committee members and officers of the eight Homestead lodges of the union; it was in fact in the lodge sanctuaries that the steelworkers first broached the subject of the contract in 1892. As the union president, William Weihe, testified before congressional investigators, the procedure began when individual workers came to their lodge with a complaint or suggestion about the contract. All the lodge members then discussed the workers' presentations and voted them up or down; the office of the national union entered the picture only much later. Weihe himself, for example, did not participate in the negotiations until late spring, and then only as a union representative; neither he nor other national officers set union policy regarding the Homestead negotiations.[25]

William T. Roberts, a leading member of the workers' Advisory Committee, was a heater's helper in the 32-inch slabbing mill; he was also the chief union negotiator and one of the key, though largely unheralded, figures in the Homestead Lockout. Roberts judiciously mediated between workers and the company as well as between the union's local and national forums. In his testimony to congressional investigators, he took pains to emphasise how frequently he consulted with his colleagues. And yet, for all the local concentration of his activity, Roberts became one of the most influential figures in the national union. He represented his lodge, no. 54 "Armor," at the national convention, sat on a number of its important committees, and even challenged M. M. Garland for the union presidency in 1892. Despite his considerable popularity, however, Roberts was roundly defeated when the overwhelming majority of members outside Homestead chose to support the "conservative" trade unionism of men such as Garland and Martin.[26]

In Homestead, however, Roberts's style of leadership was the rule, and his personal commitment to union democracy at the local level was highly valued by his colleagues: in tribute, the union lodge of the 119-inch plate mill was named after him. For men such as Roberts and his co-workers, democracy in the union hall and at the workplace possessed very different meanings from those ascribed to it by most trade unionists of today. Democracy was not simply a matter of a union member exercising the privilege of denouncing or supporting a leader

or a contract proposal, or even organizing to overthrow a coterie of
unresponsive officials who had little knowledge of the day-to-day concerns of their constituents. Before it shaped the union's interactions
with the company, democracy for these men defined relations within
the collective itself. Democracy as practiced by Homestead trade unionists was participatory in fact and not just in theory, and it built from the
shop floor up.[27]

As practiced in the late 1880s and early 1890s, the basic organizational unit of the AAISW at Homestead was the lodge, which elected its
own president and officers and also appointed a mill committee to enforce union rules inside a given department of the steelworks. The union
maintained a joint committee of the entire works, which usually convened to consider contractual matters with the firm, and each lodge sent
several representatives to the executive board, a combined legislature,
tribunal, and executive charged with "administering" the entire steelworks. The board, which was expanded during the disputes of 1889 and
1892 and renamed the Advisory Committee, enacted basic policy and
also appointed its own president. But the president—Hugh O'Donnell,
when the 1892 lockout began—did not have great power; he served
mainly as the executive of the Advisory Committee and was answerable
to it. In fact, when he presumed to act without the committee's authorization, he could be, as O'Donnell eventually was, replaced. Over and
above the Advisory Committee stood the mass meeting, convened only
during extraordinary times, and often open to all workers, not just
AAISW men.[28]

Andrew Carnegie and his associates did not publicly comment on the
issue of union democracy; nevertheless, they were deeply troubled by its
effects in the workplace. So troubled, in fact, that beyond the issue of
wages or any issues related to it, it was unionism itself that was the
primary target of Carnegie's concern. The following passage by James H.
Bridge, Carnegie's secretary, shows just how irksome the company
found the mill committees, particularly after the settlement of the 1889
lockout:

> Every department and sub-department had its workmens' "committee,"
> with a "chairman" and full corps of officers, who, fearing that their authority
> might decay through disuse, were ever on the alert to exercise it. During the
> ensuing three years hardly a day passed that a "committee" did not come
> forward with some demand or grievance. If a man with a desirable job died
> or left the works, his position could not be filled without the consent and
> approval of an Amalgamated committee. Usually this committee had a man
> in waiting for it; and the firm dared not give it to anyone else. The method of
> apportioning work, of regulating the turns, of altering the machinery, in
> short, every detail of working the great plant, was subject to the interference
> of some busybody representing the Amalgamated Association.[29]

Bridge's vexed view of the work relations at Homestead was not isolated. On 3 July 1892, F. T. F. Lovejoy, a high-ranking executive in Carnegie Steel, identified the powerful presence of the AAISW on the shop floor as the chief impetus for moving against the union.

> Our principal reason for repudiating the Amalgamated Association at Homestead is the annoyance it puts on us by the mill committee. At all hours we were worried by this committee. We had no power to discharge a man. When we did discharge one, the committee held a so-called investigation, and invariably found that we were wrong. There were several cases of this nature that were positively outrageous. If we didn't take them back, we were told there would be a strike. . . . But [now] we have decided to run our Homestead mill ourselves.

A day later, Lovejoy added the following statement, approved by Frick: "While the Amalgamated dealt at Homestead, they seemed to run our mill. We are going to do that ourselves hereafter." In short, public records notwithstanding, the labor difficulties that precipitated the Homestead Lockout had less to do with quantifiable matters such as wages and wage scales than with the politics of the workers' claim to a franchise within the mill—that is, the legitimacy, authority, and power of the union.[30]

John A. Fitch, who in 1907–08 interviewed company officials as well as forty-five steelworkers active in the Homestead lodges at the time of the lockout, also concluded that its chief cause was unionism—a particular kind of unionism for which even Fitch, sympathetic to labor's cause as he was, had little use. "A prominent official of the Carnegie Steel Company told me that before the strike of 1892, when the union was firmly entrenched at Homestead, the men ran the mill and the foreman had little authority. . . . There were innumerable vexations." This official voiced familiar complaints regarding the union's forcing the retention of "incompetent men" and demanding the right to approve technical innovations. Many of Fitch's union informants seemed only too willing to corroborate these complaints: "The evidence gathered from the steel workers and from manufacturers in Pittsburgh seems to indicate that repeatedly, when a lodge of the Association was strongly entrenched, a sufficient number of its members misused and abused their power to discredit, to a certain extent, the whole organization. . . . The arbitrary and arrogant spirit of some of the men in the local lodges was, it is generally admitted, more in evidence at Homestead than in any other important plant."[31]

According to Fitch, the mill committees at Homestead often sought out the superintendent "to secure the adjustment of grievances which were largely imaginary" and which committeemen themselves knew to be "unworthy of consideration." Fitch used the recollections of one particular committee member to illustrate forcefully the "arbitrary and arrogant spirit" of the AAISW men. On one occasion when this man met with Superintendent Potter, the latter charged that the committeeman clearly recognized just how groundless many of his grievances were. Fitch recounts the crucial interview that formed the basis for many of his generalizations thus: "A member of the mill committee at Homestead in 1892 said to me, 'I was in the office with the committee one day, with a grievance, and Superintendent Potter said to me, "John, there have been a good many times since you've been on the committee, that you have come into this office with a grievance, when you were ashamed to state your case [because the grievance was unfounded]." I didn't tell him so, but, by George, he was right.' "[32]

Interesting though this incident may be, it did not happen quite the way that Fitch presented it. In Fitch's own transcription of the interview with the committeeman, Potter's remarks came at a negotiating session just before the lockout began, and not at a meeting in his office to discuss a grievance. Moreover, those remarks are both briefer and less personal than the version in the book. Though these appear to be minor, they nonetheless illustrate that the author did in fact alter his own records in the process of writing *The Steel Workers*. Were the changes confined to the words attributed to Potter and the specific circumstances in which they were spoken, we might simply conclude that Fitch was trying to construct a more appealing narrative. But he augmented his notes in a third and much more damaging manner.[33]

In *The Steel Workers*, Fitch reconstructed the encounter with Potter in such a way as to suggest, quite clearly, that the committeeman acknowledged the legitimacy of Potter's reproach when he offered it at a grievance meeting sometime prior to the lockout. The committeeman says, "I didn't tell him so, but, by George, he was right." In Fitch's transcription of the interview however, there is no such quotation but only Fitch's own gloss on the event: "He [the committeeman] would not admit this to Potter, but stated to me that it was true." The crucial questions raised by Fitch's doctoring of his own notes are these: Did the committeeman recognize at the time of his meeting with Potter that the latter was right? Or did that recognition come to him only with the benefit of fifteen years' hindsight and in the encouraging presence of an aspiring academic who harbored his own ideas about proper trade union behavior— and who, incidentally, pointed to William Martin's criticism of the "unpremeditated and arbitrary" inclinations of "the rank and file" as the hallmark of wise, "conservative," trade union practice?[34]

A second encounter between Potter and the mill committeeman that the latter recounted to Fitch raises even more serious questions— questions relating to the integrity of the committeeman as well as to Fitch's larger claim that the general feeling among all 145 of his steelworker informants was that the Homestead men did in fact exceed the limits of acceptable union practice. Though it is impossible to know with utter certainty his identity, we do know that the committeeman, whom Fitch called Nubia-5, identified himself as a highly skilled "screw-down" in the 119-inch plate mill, chairman of its mill committee, and a member of the plantwide Advisory Committee. He also told Fitch that, as a result of his participation in the lockout, he was indicted for conspiracy, treason, riot, and murder, and that at one point soon after the lockout began, Potter approached him with the offer of a high-paying, five-year contract if he would forsake the union and return to work. Fitch's notes about this incident warrant extended quotation:

> He put the superintendent off by saying that he wanted to go on a vacation. He was then offered money for his vacation expenses. This he also refused and went on his vacation at his own expense. After he came back from his vacation, Potter again approached him with his five-year proposition. He told Potter "to go to a warmer climate." This was Friday, that night a friend came to him and told him that unless he had $20,000 to put up for bail [he] had better get out of town. He left that night on a freight train for Philadelphia. He had a letter which he showed me, stating that he was one of the Homestead strikers, requesting railroad men to extend him courtesies. With this he was able to travel anywhere he wanted to go. . . . He went to Chester, Pa., near Philadelphia, and worked there until March [1893]. By that time the trouble had blown over. . . . He came back to the Pittsburgh district and got a job in the mill where he now is. He received information that he could have gotten back in Homestead, but he preferred to go elsewhere.[35]

There are several peculiar features about the recollections of Nubia-5. First, it is known that of the three screw-downs in the 119-inch plate mill (H. Lank, F. Pifer, and William McQuade), none was indicted for conspiracy, treason, riot, or murder. It is also known that at a mass meeting of all Homestead workers on 30 June, it was unanimously and most forcefully decided that no worker should leave town except under extraordinary circumstances; defections had been a problem in the labor disputes of 1882 and 1889, and all workers understood that absolute solidarity had to be maintained if there were to be any hope of defeating Carnegie in 1892. Even after the first indictments were handed down on 18 July, those workers who were charged with criminal offenses did not physically abandon Homestead, and it is inconceivable that the colleagues of Nubia-5 would have considered his desire for a vacation as sufficient reason to leave town. The letter that Nubia-5 showed Fitch must therefore have been the product of his own pen; the members of the Advisory Committee, all of whom were in fact indicted on a variety of charges, would hardly have authorized such a note. Finally, we know that neither Lank, Pifer, nor McQuade served on the Advisory Committee; their names are absent from the list of its members provided by Burgoyne as well as by all other contemporary accounts of the lockout.[36]

Simply put, in his interview with Fitch, Nubia-5 did not tell the truth about his activities during the lockout: he was not a member of the Advisory Committee, he was not charged with any criminal offense, and he did not leave Homestead to vacation in the summer of 1892. It is true, however, that he was a member of the mill committee for the 119-inch mill, and that he left town in July—not quietly for a vacation but, fearfully, on a late-night, eastbound train.

Given the profiles of the three screw-downs in the 119-inch plate mill, we can be virtually certain that Nubia-5 was William McQuade, for only he was prominent enough to be publicly recognized as a leader. And though not a member of the Advisory Committee, McQuade, screw-down and mill committeeman, did negotiate with Superintendent Potter and was one of the seven steelworkers to testify before the congressional committees that investigated the lockout.[37]

McQuade's testimony before Congress, interestingly enough, differed quite significantly from the information he would give Fitch some fifteen years later. Where Nubia-5 was critical of the mill committee and even went as far as to tell Fitch that union leaders (David Lynch, in particular) sold out to the company, McQuade was, like all workers who testified, highly critical of the company. And where Nubia-5 conceded that Superintendent Potter's criticism about mill committee grievances was accurate, McQuade publicly embarrassed Potter by repeating classified company information that Potter had inadvertently divulged.[38]

On other matters too, McQuade's testimony challenged the version of events offered by company officials, who, in their defense before the congressional committee, had claimed that improved machinery, and not a more demanding work routine, had raised outputs in the 119-inch mill and that it was therefore the company, and not the workers, who should receive a larger portion of the profits. McQuade took the stand feistily to demonstrate, on the contrary, how the overworked steelmen, held to a schedule that was, quite literally, nauseating, had been directly and painfully responsible for increased productivity. In an eight-hour turn the men stopped only once, just for a few minutes, during which time they tried desperately to grab a bite to eat—invariably with oil-covered hands. "We work these eight hours consecutively right straight through. We stop only the time it takes to oil the engine. . . . I have worked in that mill and labored there when I was throwing up, sick, and I could not leave my post."

How are we to account for the discrepancies in substance and affect between McQuade's public utterances of 1892 and his private conversation with Fitch fifteen years later? Even taking into account Fitch's own embellishments, it is clear that in 1907 McQuade, like so many others, had not only changed mills as a result of his experience at Homestead but had also had a change of heart about the role he had played there. In interviews with others who had participated in the lockout, Fitch un-covered this same general but not surprising tendency among many to discount their past deeds and accomplishments. Moreover, he found among them a profound feeling of resignation and defeat. Fitch captured this mood most poignantly in the transcription of an interview he con-ducted with Ch-1, that is, Carnegie Homestead informant number 1, a heater's helper in U.S. Steel's Homestead plant in 1907, who had worked in the Homestead rail mill at the time of the lockout. "In all of the [U.S. Steel] corporation mills, the men are kept down just as much as possible, but for oppression there is no mill like the one where this man is now employed. He used to be a correspondent for the *National Labor Tribune,* but he cannot do that anymore. He wishes he were free to speak and tell things he knows, publicly. He would like to be free to declare the truth over his own signature, but he has to make a living and a policy of silence is his only reasonable one now."[39]

And yet, even in his role as the hardened Nubia-5, McQuade still clung to some of the proud memories that bound him to the past. He told Fitch that he was instrumental in opening up the Homestead lodges of the AAISW to unskilled workers, and, he happily claimed, "most of the laborers came into the union." Nor, for all his hardness, could McQuade entirely reconcile himself to the political realities of the pres-ent: "If the socialists would change their name, they would bring a great many more laboring men into their ranks. Most of the mill men [now] are Republicans, and this man is a Republican," Fitch wrote, "but he sees no hope through that party."[40]

Hardened resignation and proud memories aside, still we are faced with the odd and patently fictive tale that Nubia-5 created. Perhaps McQuade saw in his interview with Fitch the occasion to introduce a little vicarious adventure into his beleagurered life. Such whimsical in-dulgence, however, does not adequately explain what drove the man to rewrite his own history—one in which he might well have taken pride—to invent a vacation, the offer and proud refusal of a company bribe, and an escape from Homestead in order to avoid imprisonment on charges that in reality were never brought.

The key may lie in a seemingly insignificant detail. Nubia 5 "told Potter 'to go to a warmer climate.' This was Friday, that night a friend came to him and told him that unless he had $20,000 to put up for bail, [he] had better get out of town." The syntax of these sentences is ambigu-ous: was it on Friday that McQuade told Potter to go to hell, or was it on Friday that a friend warned him that he was about to be indicted, or did he refuse Potter's offer and entertain his friend's warning on the same day? It does not matter. What is noteworthy, however, is that McQuade remembered Friday as the key day.

And here, at least, his memory did not fail him. For it was on Thursday 14 July 1892, late in the afternoon, that William McQuade took the witness stand before a committee of the U.S. House of Representatives and proudly, defiantly, indicted the Carnegie Steel Company and Superintendent John Potter himself. And it was on Monday 18 July that the first round of indictments, bearing the full weight of law, were served on the steelworkers of Homestead. In the interim, most likely on Friday, the day after his testimony, McQuade may well have been approached by Potter, perhaps with the offer of a job, perhaps with the threat of a permanent place on the company's blacklist, perhaps with both, in appropriate sequence. And perhaps a friend did warn him on Friday 15 July that he would be charged. In any event, McQuade remembered, it was on Friday that he abandoned Homestead on a train bound for Philadelphia. Is it any wonder then that, fifteen years later, settled again in Western Pennsylvania and working in a mill in McKeesport, this former union man may have invented a story that allowed him to live and work with some measure of lost dignity?[41]

In leaving Homestead furtively on 15 July 1892, what McQuade had given up—not without some remorse, it would seem—were the collective aspirations for enfranchisement that the workers of Homestead had struggled for, won, and defended with their lives. Recognizing the impending loss of that enfranchisement, many, like McQuade, chose to bolt and restart their lives and careers elsewhere by making accommodations with the very system they had resisted. But there were others, however dismayed by the crushing blow of 1892, who maintained their belief that democracy and unionism as practiced in Homestead were inextricably bound.

Given that the essential issue in the Homestead Lockout of 1892 was unionism and all that it represented, the negotiations that began in January of that year assumed a curious character from the outset. In a sense, the negotiations were little more than a charade: the company officials who sat opposite William T. Roberts of the AAISW—Henry Clay Frick, Superintendent John Potter, Secretary F. T. F. Lovejoy, and William Martin—all understood that their ultimate purpose, as per Andrew Carnegie's directives, was to force a conflict that would result in a nonunion mill. For this reason the key proposals put forward by the firm's representatives were intended to be unacceptable and confusing: unacceptable because a settlement was not part of their agenda, and confusing because they realized that confusion over the contract proposals would obscure their real goal and, it was hoped, cut into the public support enjoyed by the union. Despite the deliberate obliqueness, the negotiations nevertheless did bring to the fore many of the great problems in the iron and steel industry that had troubled workers and employers alike since the lockout by ironmasters in 1874–75.[42]

The negotiations began in January when company officials summoned Roberts and other members of the mill committees to the offices of the Homestead Steel Works. Superintendent Potter opened this first session by politely asking the men to formulate their proposals and then to return for substantive discussions as soon as possible. But, he added, the company would be able to entertain the proposals of the committees of only four of the ten departments of the plant: the two open-hearth furnaces, the 119-inch mill, and the 32-inch slabbing mill, where the armor plate ordered by the navy was being produced. Potter asked the indulgence of the union on the matter of formulating wage scales for six other departments, explaining that because the company was contemplating "mechanical changes" there, it would be impossible to draw up a scale at the present time. The union representatives agreed to Potter's request though, as they were to learn in the ensuing months, it masked an important company objective.[43]

At this first meeting, Potter made a point of assuring Roberts and the other AAISW representatives that the company did not want a conflict. "It was not the policy of the Carnegie firm . . . to leave the way open for a strike"—this is how Burgoyne summarized Potter's stated position. Should there be any significant differences, Potter said, they could be settled by friendly arbitration. For this reason it was important to begin early consideration of the scales; this would allow sufficient time for an "amicable adjustment" of any disputed points before the contract expired on 30 June.

Roberts and the other mill representatives thanked Potter for his consideration and left to consult with their respective lodges. Soon afterward they forwarded to Potter proposals that called for small advances in the tonnage rates for some workers, advances intended largely for the purposes of bargaining, which essentially extended the terms of the 1889 contract. After an interval of several weeks, Potter sent word that Roberts and his colleagues should come to the downtown Pittsburgh headquarters of Carnegie, Phipps, and Company, there to meet with Potter himself, Martin, and several other officials of the firm.

Roberts and his colleagues made the short trip to Pittsburgh one day in early February to discuss their submissions. When Potter, to the amazement of Roberts and the other AAISW men, angrily rejected the union scales and distributed Martin's company proposals, it was evident that both the tone and the substance of the negotiations had drastically changed and that the company had abandoned its public commitment of settling all differences with the union. In the first place, Martin's proposals for the four departments reduced the minimum of the scale from $25 to $22 per ton of steel billets measuring 4 feet by 4 feet, the market item to which the wages of all tonnage men were pegged; the scales also reduced the base embedded in them—the ratio that fixed the relationship between output and tonnage rates at what the men considered a fair level.[44]

Publicly, the company maintained that a reduction in the minimum was not only fair but also necessary because of the depressed market for steel. In 1889, when the Homestead steelworkers reached their compromise with William Abbott, the market price for steel billets had been $27 per ton. From then until 31 March 1891, the price of billets fluctuated, never falling below $27 and occasionally rising as high as $36. Under the agreement, wages were recalculated at quarterly intervals, and through March 1891 they had risen in accord with market prices. But by 1892 billets could be bought for as little as $23 a ton; because of the current minimum, however, Carnegie was still paying his employees wage rates that corresponded to a market price of $25 a ton.[45]

In seeking a reduction in the base, the firm argued that improved machinery in its mills had increased production while decreasing the work load, and therefore it was only just to make an appropriate adjustment in the wage rates. "We had put in new improvements in some departments which increased the output and reduced the work, and we thought we were entitled to some of the benefits," Superintendent Potter said later. Specifically, the company's initial proposal envisioned a reduction in the tonnage rates for about 280 workers in the two open-hearth departments, the 119-inch plate mill, and the 32-inch slabbing mill. With the proposed cut in the minimum, which would immediately affect 45 workers, the company claimed, its offer meant that only 325 out of 3,800 employees at Homestead would have to accept lower salaries in what were, for everyone in the steel industry, very hard times indeed.

At the February meeting at Carnegie headquarters, Potter and his associates refused to discuss any of these matters with the union representatives. "They asked me if I would present their proposition to our people and I told them that I would do it, providing they would give me a reason why they had demanded such a reduction in the scale[s] submitted by us," Roberts told congressional investigators. "They did not seem disposed to talk the matter over and said they had not given it that much thought." Roberts pressed Potter for an explanation of the reductions; Potter responded that the firm had simply concluded that heaters, for example, were making too much money. In any event, said Potter, there was no point in continuing the discussion because Roberts and the others did not have the power to sign an agreement; the full membership of the various lodges might demand changes, or the national convention of the AAISW might reject the settlement.[46]

It was at this point that Roberts understood the real intent of the company, for Potter knew full well, as Roberts reminded him, that the mill committees were fully authorized to act on behalf of the lodges, that the lodges invariably signed agreements approved by the mill committees, and that AAISW procedures held that the national union should not interfere with local settlements. Clearly, Potter was now stalling rather than moving toward the "amicable adjustment" he had invoked in January. Roberts nonetheless tried to persuade Potter to proceed. "I then said," Roberts later recalled, "that if we went on talking the scale over and an agreement was arrived at that would be satisfactory to the firm and the men, they need not be a particle afraid of the [national] convention making any alterations in that scale or anybody else making alterations in it." Potter, Martin, and the other Carnegie officials answered that Roberts's assurance was not satisfactory, and there ended the negotiating session.

The union negotiators held firm for several weeks. Sometime in March, Roberts, who was well aware of the preparations the firm had been making for a lockout, considered it prudent to ask his lodge to confer upon him the singular "privilege," as he put it, of securing "the best arrangements possible." This concession, though it contradicted traditional democratic practice, seemed most sensible: the company had completed work on a fence to enclose the steelworks; a foreman had told Roberts that he would not be paid after July, and, of course, Potter's behavior had been undeniably suspicious.

Roberts, like other union members, knew that Carnegie had secured the $4 million contract from the navy and was under pressure to meet its production schedule. But it seemed that unless negotiations resumed quickly, there would be a work stoppage, and the men did not want that to happen. Roberts rehearsed these points at a union meeting, and reluctantly the men authorized him "to make any amicable agreement that could be made." He then notified Potter that the discussions could begin again. The chairmen of the three other mill committees then negotiating with the firm secured the same kind of authority, and their discussions with the company likewise resumed.[47]

Though the complete chronology of the ensuing negotiating sessions is not known, William Martin's own notations on various scale proposals indicate that on 6 April company officials met with the mill committee from Open Hearth Department no. 2 and that on 15 April they met with Roberts to discuss the scale for the 32-inch mill. But before these meetings commenced in Pittsburgh, Carnegie had already decided to bury permanently the AAISW—and the Knights of Labor—in Homestead: it was on 4 April that he drafted the notice to his employees announcing that the steelworks "will be necessarily Non-Union after the expiration of the present agreement" on 30 June. On this notice, Carnegie appended a personal note to Frick: to ensure that the company fulfill its contractual obligations to the navy, Potter should "roll a large lot of [armor] plates ahead" so that they might be finished in Braddock or Duquesne.[48]

Frick, more troubled than Carnegie about the political consequences of assuming the role of the aggressor, "pigeon-holed" the notice, according to his biographer, and proceeded along the course he had already charted: namely, to offer the union unacceptable terms and then present them to the public as eminently reasonable. Predictably, nothing close to an agreement was achieved in the April meetings with the mill committees. Carnegie, who left for England late in the month, formally approved Frick's tactics on 4 May in a communication from Coworth Park, Sunningdale.[49]

While Carnegie vacationed abroad, Frick was preparing for what was now the inevitable confrontation with organized labor at Homestead. It was important, of course, for the company to maintain the fiction of bargaining in good faith, yet Frick did not want to convene another meeting too soon. Accordingly, he waited until 30 May to move. On that day he traveled to Homestead early in the morning to confer with Potter and, in two letters, formally instructed the superintendent to meet immediately with the joint committee of the union and present it with an ultimatum stating that it must accept the proposal by 24 June.[50]

In these memoranda, Frick was careful to instruct Potter to inform the committee that the firm did "not care whether a man belongs to a union or not. . . . He may belong to as many unions or organizations as he chooses." But unless the joint committee accepted the company's offer by the deadline, the company would negotiate only with individuals. In making this point, Frick echoed the message Carnegie had delivered to the workers of Homestead from the steps of the Braddock library in 1889. "We think," Frick said, "our employees at [the] Homestead Steel Works would fare much better working under the system in vogue at [the] Edgar Thomson."

Shortly after Frick left Homestead, Potter called Roberts and the other mill committeemen to an urgent meeting in the plant office. There Potter delivered the ultimatum. With the exception of one additional demand, it amounted to little more than a restatement of the position the firm had first enunciated in February: the minimum on the scale would be reduced from $25 to $22, and tonnage rates in the two open-hearth departments, the plate mill, and the slabbing mill would be reduced by 15–18 percent for most workers and by as much as 35 percent for some. The added section proposed that the agreement stay in effect for at least eighteen months, thereby terminating on 31 December 1893 instead of on the traditional date of 30 June. Having restated the company's position, Potter threatened to cut off negotiations if Roberts did not accept this proposal on behalf of all the AAISW workers: "Unless this scale is accepted by the 24th of June, we intend to deal with our men individually."[51]

Roberts studied the proposal for a few moments and then turned to face Potter, pointedly reminding him that the company had now gone back on its promise to negotiate. "Do you think this is fair? Do you think this is giving us a chance to talk the matter over? You people, when I was here last, told me if I would come back with power to make a scale, then you were willing to enter negotiations and try to arrange the thing in an amicable manner." For his part, Potter had little to say, other than: "I cannot help it. It is Mr. Frick's ultimatum." With these words the negotiations ended. Roberts and his co-workers returned to their positions in the steelworks—there seemed to be nothing else to do. One Pittsburgh paper warned: "Developments now indicate that Homestead will be the scene of a great conflict between capital and labor. . . . When the strike comes, and it seems imminent, it will be the most bitter this section has ever seen."[52]

On the eve of the lockout of 1874–75, nearly two decades before the Carnegie company issued its ultimatum to the Homestead steelworkers, a puddler named David Harris, responding to the demands of Pittsburgh ironmasters, had declared, "The puddlers do not look through the same spectacles as you." Though puddling furnaces had given way to the Bessemer converter and the open hearth, the Sons of Vulcan had been replaced by the AAISW and ironmasters had become steelmasters, the city's greatest factory owner and his employees still did not see eye to eye. Each part of the final proposal put forward by Carnegie and his associates violated the very tenets of trade union practice in the American metals industry that had found such forceful expression in the lockout of 1874–75 and in the movement for amalgamation that it spawned. Moreover, contrary to the repeated and insistent avowals of Frick, Potter, and other company officials, virtually all of Homestead's 3,800 employees, not just 325, were destined to feel the impact of the firm's plan for a new "system" in the mill.[53]

The proposal to change the expiration date of the contract from June to December, for one thing, was seen by the AAISW men of Homestead as a direct and potentially lethal assault against the union itself. Frick, of course, claimed that this adjustment would cause the workers no hardship, for in the event of future disputes over the contract, it would be preferable for both the workers and the company to endure a stoppage in the winter, when business was slow, rather than during the brisk business months of June and July.[54]

Union members interpreted the impact of such a change rather differently, however. As wintertime living expenses are higher than those in the summer, moving the contract negotiations could only serve to weaken the ability of union members to hold out during a lockout or strike. Furthermore, years of experience in the steel industry had taught that, because unemployment is also higher in winter, the firm could anticipate a relatively easy time in filling whatever vacancies might occur during a dispute. As William Roberts noted, "I can state a reason why we object to ending the scale in the winter time, and that is that the burnt child dreads the fire. We know from past experience, . . . that when winter time comes around and our contract ends in the winter, . . . [employers] take that opportunity at that time of the year to starve us into submission." For this reason, just as Frick had anticipated, the union men found any change in the contract date to be unacceptable.

The two other components of the company's ultimatum, the reductions in the tonnage rates and in the minimum, represented an assault less on unionism than on its principle of fairness. As Frick and Potter interpreted the question, fairness demanded rate reductions because new production processes had increased output while lowering the need for physical labor. And, although the base of the scale would be reduced, they argued, take-home pay was bound to increase: the greater productivity of workers would more than compensate for lowered tonnage rates, and workers would thus earn more money, not less. In addition, it was only "fair" to eliminate certain inequities in the wage scales—a goal that could be achieved, of course, only through a reduction in the tonnage rates.[55]

The volatile connection between productivity and tonnage rates crystallized in discussions regarding the 119-inch plate mill. Both Frick and Potter asserted that it was the new machinery that had increased outputs by 50 percent while reducing labor by an equivalent amount. In other words, Frick claimed, one man there could do the work that formerly required four.[56]

In truth, the company had installed no improvements in the 119-inch mill since its construction in 1888. Moreover, as William McQuade and his co-workers told congressional investigators, increased productivity in that mill arose from the imposition by management of a rigorous three-turn, eight-hour work shift (previously there had been two shifts of twelve hours) and from the construction of an altogether new plant facility, the 32-inch slabbing mill. George Rylands, a steelworker, explained that the manufacture of a single armor plate typically required twelve or fifteen ingots from the open-hearth furnace. In Homestead, however, the massive slabbing mill had served to speed up the process dramatically. Only one or two giant ingots were required from the open-hearth department before the slabbing mill, in a prefinishing maneuver, would turn out a plate as thick as 10 inches for final processing in the plate mill. Workers in the plate mill did indeed benefit from its greater productivity, but there were fewer of them: remarkably, only seven at the rolls and eight in the heating department. Moreover, because the slabs came to the plate mill hot, they required continuous and much more careful working than in any other mill in the country. In short, increased productivity in the plate mill was the result, first, of the efficiency of the workers there and, second, of mechanical innovations in the slabbing mill.

In their testimony to the House committee that investigated the lockout, both Frick and Potter obliquely acknowledged that it was the new slabbing mill (as well as improvements in the open-hearth department), and not improvements in the plate mill, that accounted for the larger output of armor plates. But Frick steadfastly maintained that the new slabbing mill had made work easier in the plate mill and that, therefore, tonnage rates should be reduced there. In fact, he claimed that the firm had lost money in 1891–92 on every single steel bloom, billet, and slab that it had sold; tellingly, he said nothing about plates.[57]

Congressional investigators were understandably befuddled by the array of products, not to mention the details of production processes and wage scales, that were discussed. Not for nothing did the Homestead workers publicly declare that "arranging scales of wages to govern iron and steel workers" was sufficiently complex to "render liable erroneous views to be drawn by those not familiar with the trade." But the congressmen who questioned Frick were more than confused; they were deferential. They did not, for example, press him and other officials on questions about the tonnage reductions. One congressman did ask Frick if the alleged losses on billets, blooms, and slabs were related to wages, but he allowed him to ignore the question. Twice Frick was asked to relate wages to costs, but the committee deferred to his claim: "The principal reason for not answering, . . . is that we have competitors in business and it would hardly be fair to us that they should know what our cost is as we do not know what it costs them."

Frick had apparently forgotten that, through the stellar efforts of William Martin, he had in fact obtained precisely such information from his competitors. He also neglected to state that corporate profits for 1891 ($4.3 million) were gratifying, to say the least, and that he had every indication that 1892 would be no less profitable. (In fact, profits would fall off slightly, to $4 million—a remarkable sum, nonetheless, in light of the losses attendant on the Homestead Lockout.) Such profits represented more than 16 percent of the initial capitalization of Carnegie Steel; Fitch later observed that "these figures do not cry for wage retrenchment."[58]

It was around the discussion of the tonnage question that Fitch noted how difficult, if not impossible, it was to say precisely what constituted a fair wage. "That is a matter upon which doctors disagree." Here he unwittingly hit upon what was perhaps the most crucial point of the issue. For Frick, as for every other iron- or steelmaster in the nation, labor constituted a factor of production the value of which is determined by the imperatives of the competitive marketplace. For the Homestead men, as for thousands of other metalworkers, labor was, however, something else. For them labor still possessed an intrinsic and customary value that ought not to be affected by the vagaries of the market—which is why the Homestead steelworkers, like the puddlers before them, insisted on maintaining the minimum. And, like the puddlers, they believed that they too had the right to a fair wage, no matter how ill defined this standard might be. Indeed, this point was emphasized by William Weihe in his speech to thousands of Homestead steelworkers just days after Frick and Potter issued the ultimatum about the scale. "The foremost principle of the Amalgamated Association is 'a fair day's wages for a fair day's work.' We do not want to ask anything unreasonable, we only want what justly belongs to us."[59]

Precisely how to fix this reasonable standard of fairness was never directly addressed by the Homestead men. They did, however, make it clear that they did not hold technological innovation in the workplace to be the categorical source of unfairness. Weihe himself told congressional investigators: "If there are improvements that do away with certain jobs, they make no objection. They believe in the American idea that the genius of the country should not be retarded." In contrast to the evidence of workers' resistance to innovation about which the iron- and steelmasters of Pittsburgh had complained for two decades, at Homestead there is no evidence of anything remotely resembling Luddism. In 1889 and again in 1892, the workers understood and accepted the need for innovation.[60]

Perhaps the most ominous feature of the company's proposal for the AAISW workers was, public pronouncements to the contrary, the plain intent of Frick and Potter unilaterally to enforce rate reductions in *all* the departments in the Homestead Steel Works. In his congressional testimony, William T. Roberts read a crucial portion of the contract that was affixed to each of the various mill scales put forward by the company. The language is quite clear: "This scale to be subject to revision in the event of the introduction of new methods and appliances."[61]

Frick reaffirmed the meaning of this key item when he told congressional investigators that the scales for the entire steelworks would be subject to revision once improvements, then underway or merely contemplated, were installed. Superintendent Potter, according to William McQuade, personally confirmed the plan; he told McQuade that all but the very least skilled laborers would eventually be paid on the basis of the reduced tonnage rates. As there were fewer than 400 such men in the plant, more than 3,400 workers would ultimately be affected.[62]

From the moment Potter handed Roberts the ultimatum, he and the other leaders of the union recognized that they were at a severe disadvantage in the public debate over the contested issues. From the start, Frick had taken the upper hand: by limiting the negotiations to scales that would reduce the tonnage rates for only 280 men and the minimum for an additional 45, he succeeded in minimizing the apparent impact of the company's proposal. "An attempt is made to lead the public into the belief that the number of men affected by the reduction are few," the workers pointed out. But the truth was that, while each of the three components of the ultimatum (the reductions in the tonnage rate, the cut in the minimum, and the change in the termination date) "do not affect the whole of the Homestead workmen, few of the 3,800 employees of that place escape without being affected by one or more of its provisions. What does not affect the one, does affect the other, and it might be said that instead of the company's proposing altering the condition of employment of 325, the change is general, and the whole are involved."[63]

A handful of astute reporters discerned the company's strategy, but most commentators did not and were therefore at a loss to explain the determined solidarity of more than 700 AAISW men, not to mention 2,500 other workers, who were supposedly unaffected by the proposals. Among the dailies in Pittsburgh, only the *Post* recognized the true dimensions of Frick's plan: "Ultimatum Given by Firm. It Demands Heavy Reduction for All Tonnage Workers."[64]

As the proposals put forth by Frick and Potter clearly indicate, Carnegie's call for a "new system" at Homestead, first enunciated in his dedication of the free library in Braddock, was clearly understood by his field lieutenants. The AAISW men also understood the company's plans. "The people employed in Homestead thought that it was simply a proposition made by the firm that they knew we would not accept," one of their leaders told the Senate investigators. "They did it with the intention of forcing this trouble." Significantly, this leader spoke of "the people employed in Homestead," and not merely of the members of the union, for unlike so many outside observers, he knew very well why his nonunion colleagues also regarded the company's proposal as unacceptable: previous agreements had contained a clause stating that the wages of nonunion workers could not be cut so long as the contract remained in force. The firm's plan to pay most workers on a reduced tonnage basis and its self-awarded carte blanche for future reductions would render moot whatever protection the AAISW might afford unorganized labor.[65]

In a dramatic expression of unity following the announcement of Frick's ultimatum, thousands of Homestead steelworkers met on 5 June at the Opera House on Fifth Avenue. The meeting, which convened on the eve of the AAISW's annual convention in Pittsburgh, captured the attention of all iron- and steelworkers, who, the *National Labor Tribune* observed, saw the dispute that loomed at Homestead as the "key" to the union's future. Even this newspaper, now a staunch advocate of conservative trade unionism, described the ultimatum of Carnegie, Phipps, and Company as radical, a characterization echoed by the typically cautious William Weihe in his keynote address at the mass meeting. The national convention followed his lead a few days later when it voted to support the position of the Homestead lodges and formally endorsed the scales drawn up by them.[66]

Into the last week of June, there were few developments in Homestead or in the headquarters of Carnegie, Phipps, and Company. But throughout Greater Pittsburgh everyone was talking about the impending struggle. The *Pittsburgh Post*, the organ of the Democratic party, was only too happy to lend its voice to the agitation: a series of articles argued that the inevitable conflict at Homestead would be prosecuted by Carnegie Steel on behalf of all iron and steel manufacturers in a great effort to destroy "the most powerful independent labor organization in the world." Carnegie, an ardent Republican whose business had profited handsomely by virtue of the McKinley Tariff, would stand to gain the most. But, said the paper, there were undeniable indications that his company was now preparing for what one AAISW man called "the long-expected fight for the life of the organization." Inevitably, the conflict would involve the destruction of property, the loss of life, and the mobilization of the state militia, according to the *Post*.[67]

In mid June, the newspaper's reporting may have struck some readers as nothing short of fantastic. But the subsequent "course of events gave it a strong coloring of probability." Indeed, as Frick's deadline of 24 June approached, Roberts and the other union leaders, mindful of the monumental effects a loss at Homestead would unleash, decided to offer Frick a series of concessions. Uncertain how these might be received, union members and their unorganized co-workers moved to consolidate the ranks of all Carnegie employees in Homestead.[68]

By this time, Frick, with the capable assistance of Philander C. Knox, had preparations well in hand for the mustering of three hundred agents from the Pinkerton National Detective Agency. Nevertheless, Frick played out the charade of negotiating to the end: along with Potter and several other company officials, he met with Weihe, Roberts, and other AAISW men in the firm's downtown offices at 10:00 A.M. on 23 June.

At this meeting, Frick and Potter reiterated the company's position on the minimum, the expiration date for the contract, and the reduction in the base for tonnage work. Roberts and his co-workers realized that the company "was somewhat determined in maintaining their position," as Weihe later put it, and therefore they asked for an adjournment to formulate what they hoped would be an acceptable compromise. When they returned, Roberts told Frick that the men were willing to reduce the minimum from $25 to $24, accept tonnage reductions of up to 15 percent, and sign an agreement that lasted as long as five years in order to assuage the company's fears about future labor difficulties.

Frick categorically refused to yield on the question of the tonnage rates and the termination of the contract; he did, however, make a token gesture of conciliation by agreeing to a $23 minimum instead of the $22 of his ultimatum. He plainly recognized, however, that it was the termination date that was the vital point for the men: on this they would not budge. "Gentlemen," Frick exclaimed to Roberts and his colleagues, "this ends all conferences between you and this firm." The union negotiators collected their notes, left the Carnegie offices, and went back to Homestead. Frick had succeeded in maneuvering the AAISW into a confrontation.

Frick calmly allowed the deadline of 24 June to pass without comment; he shored up his own defenses for the coming battle and ordered completion of the work on "Fort Frick," as the fortification of the Homestead Steel Works was to become known. The works and the mill offices were encased in a three-mile-long fence that was topped with barbed wire and perforated at strategic intervals "as if for the convenience of sharpshooters." Twelve-foot-high platforms, equipped with searchlights, were constructed near the mill buildings, and water cannon were positioned at each entrance to the plant. According to some newspapers, Frick even installed pressurized pipes to spray boiling water on any unwanted intruders. "There was," Burgoyne noted, "a cold and sanguinary determination about these provisions which boded ill for the workmen. . . . One of King John's barons could not equip his feudal castle with more elaborate offensiveness than this nineteenth-century ironmaster displayed in fortifying his mill, with the apparent intention of making war—actual war with arms upon the men of Homestead."[69]

On 25 June, a Saturday, Frick and Potter posted notices throughout the town and the mill that the company no longer would deal with the AAISW and that the contracts with individual workers would expire in January. To install the new system would require force: it was on this day, too, that Frick formally requested the Pinkerton Agency to dispatch three hundred guards to Homestead on 5 July, and that Philander Knox met with Sheriff William McCleary to work out the details of the Pinkertons' arrival.[70]

By now the logic of the events that led up to the battle of the barges was firmly in place. On 28 June the company installed two powerful water pumps on rail flatcars in preparation for the expected difficulties and then formally initiated the lockout by closing the 119-inch plate mill and one of the open-hearth departments. "This was the beginning of the lockout, for a lockout it was, and not a strike, as has been very generally represented." Later that day, laborers in the steelworks, very likely affiliated with the Knights of Labor, decided to walk out in support of the AAISW lodges. The night of 28 June brought more angry solidarity: hundreds of steelworkers hung effigies of Frick, Potter, and William McBroom, a former steelworker who had signed on as chief company policeman in the late 1880s.[71]

The following day, 29 June, Frick and Potter closed the rest of the mill, and virtually every steelworker in Homestead attended another mass meeting in the Opera House, this time to ratify Roberts's report on the final negotiating session and initiate more formal preparations for the lockout. Roberts pointed out that the firm had broken its contract with the men by laying off the full work force a day before the expiration date of 30 June. "We filled our contract," Roberts said. "Now the firm has laid the entire mill off one day ahead of time. Has it lived up to its contract?" More than three thousand steelworkers shouted, "No" and then, without dissent, endorsed Roberts's refusal to accept Frick's ultimatum. "When, after two hours, the meeting adjourned, there remained not the least doubt as to the unity of feeling among all classes of workers in the town."[72]

It was immediately after this meeting that the workers' Advisory Committee effectively assumed control in Homestead. According to the *Pittsburgh Commercial-Gazette*, a newspaper that spoke for the business community, the committee was composed of the "most intelligent and conservative members" of the AAISW, who counseled moderation and "deprecate[d] violence in every shape and form." The committee, acting with Burgess John McLuckie, moved immediately to close all saloons in the town and establish regular police patrols manned by the most dedicated union men. It also established a picket system, just as it had in 1889, to guard against the introduction of outside workers and Pinkertons. The government of the town "had now passed absolutely into the hands of the advisory committee of the Amalgamated lodges, and the committee was determined to use its arbitrary authority for the preservation of order and decency and the protection of life and property as well as the exclusion from Homestead of non-union men."[73]

This authority found its most forceful expression on 30 June, when, following another mass meeting, the Advisory Committee began what the press termed active "military preparations." Officials of the company declared that the final battle with Homestead unionism was close at hand, and, not surprisingly, the men concluded that the firm would soon attempt to introduce Pinkertons and new workers. To meet them, a small flotilla of river skiffs began to patrol the Monongahela, and the workers, who had been divided into an elaborate system of brigades and divisions, guarded all approaches to the town. The key positions were commanded by veterans of the Homestead strike of 1882 and the lockout of 1889.[74]

Although some of the men were armed, Hugh O'Donnel declared that there would be no violence: the steelworkers, he said, intend only to "very gently, but very firmly, push [the scabs] away from here." The Advisory Committee made every effort to ensure that the integrity of the mill and town would be maintained through peaceful means, although it was not averse to issuing threats. When members noticed that two furnaces in Open Hearth Department no. 2 had been fired up by supervisory personnel, for example, they sent a letter to the assistant superintendent advising that such actions might provoke some of the men. "If the gas is not shut off, we cannot be held responsible for any act that may be committed." The company's watchmen, apparently acting on their own, allowed members of the committee to enter the mill and extinguish the furnace fires, but later the committee relit them to prevent the loss of the materials already in the furnaces. Indeed, the mill seemed so well "protected" by the union men that the firm's own defenses seemed unnecessary. One paper commented, "The men are better deputies than stone wall and cannon."[75]

By Sunday 3 July it seemed certain that Pinkertons were on the way. Even the names of the barges that would eventually carry them to the company wharf—the *Iron Mountain* and the *Monongahela*—were common knowledge. The *New York Herald* carried a story that correctly identified the date and approximate time of the eventual attack: the two barges were to "be towed up to the river gate [of the steelworks] on Tuesday night." The paper also reported that the mobilization of the state militia was also a virtual certainty: "Troops to Crush the Strikers," was the page-one headline. "It Is Believed the Firm Are Trying to Hasten a Conflict with the Men So They Can Appeal for State Bayonets to Protect the New Employees."[76]

On this last peaceful Sunday in Homestead, steelworkers flocked to church and heard a number of sermons on the crisis. The Reverend John Bullion of St. Mary Magdalene Church told his parishioners, predictably enough, to obey the law: "To keep peace should be your first endeavor." The Reverend J. J. McIlyar of the First Methodist Episcopal Church was more supportive of the steelworkers—and more critical of their employers. Preaching on "The Master and the Men," McIlyar, who would win considerable fame for his eulogy of a worker killed on 6 July, warned that "a suppressed volcano exists among American workmen, and some day there will be an uprising that will become history. The question is often asked, what would Homestead be without the mills? Why not ask, where would Andrew Carnegie be without the millions he has made from his mills? . . . What would Mr. Carnegie be without his men? Capitalists should remember that men do not sell their self-respect when they sell their labor."[77]

Homesteaders had occasion to pause for more reflection on the following day, the Fourth of July, which was marked by only a handful of picnics and a small fireworks display in the evening. As one paper observed, the locked-out men "celebrated" by increasing the number of guards from 350 to 1,000. In the view of some reporters, the town was now distinguished by the remarkable level of "organized anarchy" the AAISW men had imposed upon it. In truth, all remained peaceful, and the men were subdued. McLuckie, with characteristic humor, explained: "We can't celebrate the Fourth until we know whether or not the Declaration of Independence is still in force in this country. . . . You see, H. C. Frick wasn't consulted when that document was drawn, and he may think it necessary to revoke its provisions."[78]

Later that evening, Frick set in motion the chain of events that would, in the eyes of McLuckie and his fellow steelwokers, "revoke" their claims to citizenship and to any stake at all in the Homestead Steel Works. Citing the Advisory Committee's threatening letter about operations at Open Hearth Department no. 2, Frick formally requested Sheriff McCleary to intervene. "To protect our property from violence, damage and destruction, and to protect us in its free use and enjoyment," he wrote, the sheriff was now obliged to disperse the union men from the vicinity of the mill. Early on the morning of 5 July, McCleary honored Frick's request. The locked-out steelworkers, he commanded, were to "abstain from assembling or congregating" at the works "and from interfering with the workmen, business, or operation of said works, and in all respects to observe the peace and to return to their respective homes or places of residence, as the right of the workmen to work and the owners to operate their works will be fully protected, and in case of failure to observe these instructions all persons offending will be dealt with according to law."[79]

The battle for Homestead had thus become a battle over conflicting property rights. The firm, which over the weekend had officially become the Carnegie Steel Company, claimed that it enjoyed the right to manage the mill to suit itself and to hire whomever it pleased; the steelworkers claimed that they had earned the right to employment in the mill and to defend the integrity of the institution—the AAISW—that, as William Roberts testified before the Senate investigating committee, had made their jobs and homes secure.[80]

It is hardly surprising that the steelworkers categorically refused to recognize the authority of McCleary when he arrived in town on the morning of 5 July to post his notices and secure the steelworks on behalf of Carnegie Steel. The Advisory Committee extended a "cordial" greeting to him and to the eleven deputies who accompanied him, allowed him to inspect the steelworks (he pronounced them in good order), and then volunteered to be deputized for guard duty themselves. At union headquarters in the Bost Building, Hugh O'Donnell assured McCleary that the steelworkers would "perform their duty as sworn officers, even though it cost them their lives." The sheriff claimed that he saw no reason for additional protection of the steelworks, but that since Frick had requested it, he was obligated to provide it. Therefore it was "out of the question" that the steelworkers themselves be deputized, for "they were the men whom the Carnegie company complained of." Members

of the Advisory Committee responded that neither McCleary nor anyone else would be allowed to bring nonunion workers into the plant.[81]

The committeemen adjourned for a brief canvass and then informed
McCleary that the Advisory Committee had disbanded and was no
longer responsible for public order—or, for that matter, for anything.
One by one they deposited their badges on the table in front of the
sheriff; O'Donnell then collected the badges and all of the committee's
records, threw them into the fireplace, struck a match, and announced:
"Sheriff McCleary, the last meeting of the Advisory Committee has just
concluded. The Advisory Committee from now on will not be responsible for any disorder or lawless act perpetrated either in Homestead or
Mifflin Township. Do you understand? Our responsibility ceases from
this very moment. . . . We are not at the head of the men any longer in
this lockout. We are not responsible for what may hereafter develop." In
answer to this ominous abdication from power, McCleary offered a polite bow. "Good day, then, gentlemen. I shall send my deputies this
afternoon."[82]

When these deputies arrived, they too were assured that the property
of the Carnegie Steel Company was perfectly safe. Pointing to the mammoth mill, a steelworker said to one of them: "Do you see those steel
works? Do they look as though they needed guarding? Has that board
fence been broken down? You yourself can best judge from the manner in
which you have been received, even at this trying hour, whether the
peace has been broken." With this, the steelworkers and their families,
led by O'Donnell and McLuckie, escorted all of McCleary's men out of
town.[83]

It was now 6:00 P.M. on 5 July. As McCleary's men left town, another
crew of law enforcers was speeding toward Homestead to protect the
property of Andrew Carnegie and his associates. As for Carnegie himself, he was sleeping comfortably at Haddo House in Aberdeen; it had
been a good day. He had dedicated the library he had given to Aberdeen, and in return he had received the freedom of the city. On the
following day, he would be fishing at Loch Rannoch.[84]

Chapter 21

Silenced Minorites

FOR ALL that we think we know about the people and events that contributed to the Homestead Lockout of 1892, it remains both remarkable and curious just how much information has been overlooked. Archival difficulties aside, when we look back on the lockout and its subsequent historiography with one hundred years' hindsight, we are struck by the numbers of people, indeed groups of people, who seem to have been judiciously written out of the story. As important as it is to write these people back in, it is equally important to ask why they were omitted in the first place.

It is clear, in the case of powerful men such as Philander Knox and Christopher Magee, that the roles they played in the events of July 1892 were conveniently suppressed, perhaps at their own instigation. In the case of other key actors, who boldly took a stand in public, the existing literature on Homestead has neglected or dismissed the roles they played. Indeed, the literature has allowed whole communities of people to recede into the background—so far into the background that they have become invisible to most historians. I refer, on the one hand, to the East European workers, and on the other, to the women of Homestead, native- and foreign-born.

In 1892 the ethnic composition of Homestead was diverse, encompassing large numbers of East European workers as well as British, Irish, and native-born Americans. This much is known. And we have of course always known, even without the help of archival material, that there were women there.[1] And yet women and East Europeans appear for the most part as bits of local color in the margins of scholarly accounts. This, despite compelling evidence of the active and influential role they played in the politics and events that mark the town's history. Their voices, which were once very loud and strong, have been silenced not merely by the political and economic forces that overwhelmed Homestead in 1892 but by a historical tradition that continues to perpetuate a

315

particular narrative of good guys and bad guys in which both sides are indistinguishably Anglo-American and male.

Contemporary accounts of the 1892 lockout report, for example, that between eight hundred and one thousand East Europeans were employed in the steelworks; and yet even the most recently published commentary on the lockout, one that accompanied a highly successful public exhibition in Pittsburgh, explains that "at the time of the 1892 Strike, the Homestead Works employed a handful of workers from Eastern Europe." The author thus ignores one of the most intriguing facts about the town: that despite its reputation as a highly exclusive and conservative craft union, the AAISW nonetheless entertained the interethnic solidarity of its predominantly native-born, British, and Irish workers on the one hand and the East Europeans on the other.[2]

The tradition of excluding East Europeans has been so powerful that even writers emerging from that community were not immune to its effects. In his well-known novel *Out of This Furnace*, Thomas Bell, himself the son of Slovak immigrants who had settled in Braddock, chronicles the lives of three generations of Slovak-American steelworkers and their families. Bell portrays the first generation, the immigrants, as represented by George Kracha, as utterly cut off from the larger world of work and politics, which so many Homesteaders helped shape. For Bell, Slovak-Americans attain political maturity only in the 1930s, when Kracha's grandson begins work as a union organizer. The message is that it took decades for these Eastern European immigrants to become active participants in communal life. What Bell, like less sympathetic writers, overlooked was that the Krachas' real-life counterparts, men and women, had been actively involved in the labor struggle from the outset.[3]

In point of fact, few of the Slovaks living in Homestead in 1892 were as dislocated and apolitical as the fictional George Kracha. In response to the events of 6 July, Bell has him sputter indifferently and walk away: "If it's the mill, let the Irish take care of it. I want no trouble." On the contrary, the East European immigrants occupied center stage for the battle of the barges. Moreover, their participation in the defense of Homestead, hardly a fluke, was the logical expression of a decade of the immigrants' collective life—one that from its beginnings in 1881 had been appreciated and valued by many Anglo-American steelworkers.[4]

The participation of East European immigrants in the larger life of Homestead found its first forceful expression, as we have seen, in the strike of 1882, when Anglo-American steelworkers welcomed East Europeans into the ranks of the Irish National Land League in a battle for their shared "American" rights. Interethnic cooperation was advanced as Local Assembly 1785 of the Knights of Labor, organized during that strike, opened its doors to common mill laborers, many of them East European immigrants. By 1887 this assembly spoke for all the unskilled members of the steelworks' stocking crews; it also represented skilled workers in the blooming mill, some of whom maintained membership also in the AAISW. In the Homestead lockout of 1889, members of both unions made common cause and took care to include immigrant laborers in a united effort to check Andrew Carnegie. Their participation in the 1889 lockout was, in fact, utterly crucial and intergral to the success of the steelworkers. As the *New York Herald* noted, "the strikers are, to no small degree, of foreign extraction." Indeed, the town's overwhelming support of the family of John Elko, the Slovak laborer who was fatally injured while on patrol, was typical of the community's reliance upon and pride in its immigrant workers. Even the *Homestead Local News*, edited by M. P. Schooley, a virulent racist and nativist, was compelled to acknowledge Elko's contributions.[5]

The acknowledgment did not come easy, however. In offering it, Schooley managed to distinguish Elko from the genuine "strikers" and "men" of Homestead—who, as only genuine men were entitled to do, had fought for their American rights. Elko "proved to be one of the most active and useful men in the aid of the strikers. . . . He understood several languages and rendered valuable service in interpreting to other Hungarians . . . who came out for the rights for which the men were contending. It is said that he displayed great bravery and untiring zeal." Elko's funeral, concluded Schooley in a characteristically patronizing tone, led the people of Braddock to note "the great respect that the Homestead people showed to their Hungarians": one thousand of Elko's colleagues, marching four abreast to dirges played by a band of steel-workers, accompanied his body to the cemetery.

Clearly, Schooley wanted people such as Elko to disappear. This is the message encoded in his prose—and in the frustrating holes in his newspaper's coverage of Homestead's immigrant communities. But whereas the wishful disappearance of East Europeans from Schooley's narrative can be traced back to his avowed and conscious nativism, to what may we attribute their effective disappearance from the received historical discourse? Has "historical wisdom" simply taken its cue, wittingly or unwittingly, from men such as Schooley? Or have twentieth-century ethnic tensions in the labor movement, particularly among steel-workers, skewed our perspective on Homestead in the late 1800s?[6]

Schooley, responding to the increased visibility of East Europeans in the work force, afforded generous coverage to nativist organizations; his opinion of East Europeans in no sense departed from the norms of his era. Nor, for that matter, did Schooley's views on women and their proper place. Just as his begrudging reports on East European workers encode a discourse of disgust common at the time, his accounts of women's roles in local conflicts encode a discourse of disdain that reflected the general societal discomfort with "unfeminine" behavior.[7]

Schooley's coverage of women from the early 1880s through the 1892 lockout reflects the sensibilities he shared with his projected readers: petit bourgeois shopkeepers and small merchants; craftsmen who had pulled themselves up by their own bootstraps or were trying to; Progressive euchre players and devotees of "junior socials" and polite evening strolls; Methodist teetotalers. Staunch union men who had "succeeded" were also among Schooley's favored readers; together with their social and financial betters, many of them agreed that women should be confined to the domestic sphere. For them the "Our Ladies" column in the *Local News*, which commenced in May 1892, was appropriate fare: it contained the typical array of recipes and household hints and, in the issue distributed on the eve of the Pinkerton assault, asserted that "every woman adores love letters." For most of Schooley's readers the interests of women belonged properly to the world of romantic love; the world of work was too rough for the weaker sex. It was in fact so rough that it threatened to invade "the sacred precincts of the domestic circle" and tear "assunder affects that were almost divine."[8]

Schooley offered this assessment in his introduction to a series of fictional letters exchanged by a betrothed couple during the Homestead strike of 1882. The "letters," published in 1885, recount the story of Frank and Mamie from their courtship in Keokuk, Iowa, through Frank's search for respectable employment, which lands him in the Homestead Steel Works, to Mamie's disenchantment with Frank because of his participation in the 1882 strike.

"Why did you go into the mill to work?" Mamie askes. "A clerkship would be preferable I think. . . . O, I cannot bear to think of you working amid the smoke and dirt of a large steel works." Later, after Frank has declared his allegiance to the strikers, Mamie replies: "It is not possible, surely, that you will become identified with any of their *revolutionary* and *communistic* proceedings. Frank, I have always entertained the hope that you were above mingling with the ordinary affairs of everyday life. O, Frank, my ideal, are there not better things in store for us?"

Apparently there were not, for Frank refused to forsake the union: "I am sure that if you were here and knew how dear to me were the principles that actuate working men to a struggle for a fair division of the proceeds resulting from their daily labor, you would readily understand how I could willingly 'become identified with their revolutionary and communistic proceedings.' " To this Mamie responded: "Really, the character of a striker, which you have assumed, fills me with terror. A skull and cross bones engraved on the back of your letter could not have caused greater misgivings than the burning sentences contained in it. . . . Are you so filled with that despicable spirit of communism . . . that you must breath it forth to me?" Shortly after Frank received this letter, the romance ended. Frank declared, however, that he was confident of finding a Homestead "lady" who would appreciate his support of labor organizations. In truth, a real-life Frank could very likely have found such a lady locally.

Over the course of the 1880s, wives and female friends of AAISW members invariably supported the union. Homestead women raised money for their husbands when the American Flint Glass Workers Union went on strike, and many women worked in the Homestead Co-operative Boot and Shoe Manufacturing Company, a venture organized by the Knights of Labor. By the time of the lockout of 1889, the behavior of Homestead women was very far removed from Schooley's vision of domesticated, genteel womanhood: as we have seen, women were eager participants in the effort to enforce communal sanctions against outside workers.[9]

Just how eager may be inferred from the warning to women issued by the Reverend John Bullion, the priest at St. Mary Magdalene Church: "As for the women, they must keep off the street. During the disturbance the other day, I saw them collected in knots at all corners, many of them holding their babies, and all of them inciting the workmen to acts of violence. Women are not very formidable antagonists in a fight, . . . let the women stay indoors." According to the daily press, however, the women were formidable indeed: ignoring Father Bullion's appeal, they rushed deputies and assaulted them with clubs, pieces of iron, and scalding water. Moreover, "a band of about two hundred women" organized to spell their husbands on an all-night watch. "The Women Stood on Guard," proclaimed the page-one headline in the *New York World*. "Carnegie's Men Slept While Their Wives and Sweethearts Watched."[10]

In a telling move reporters for the daily press used the same language to characterize the women participants in the 1889 lockout as they had for the East European immigrants: uncivilized, riotous, savage. The *Pittsburgh Press*, feeding rampant nativist fears, described the strikers guarding the railroad station as fierce "Hungarians, who look savagely at all strangers." The women, another reporter wrote, were "wild with excitement" as they "savagely" moved to assault scabs and sheriff's deputies. In general, the press saw the behavior of Homesteaders as troublesome examples of "disorder" and "misrule."[11]

The coverage of the Homestead Lockout of 1892 was informed by these same themes. Unruliness, savagery, hysteria—this was how the press interpreted the initiatives of the residents who rushed to the riverbank on 6 July to defend their town against the Pinkerton "invaders." Time and again, reporters took care to distinguish between the Anglo-Americans who led the Advisory Committee and tried to maintain some semblance of order, and the unruly mob of immigrants and women who perpetrated the most vicious attacks of the day.

The fact is that by June 1892, the East European steelworkers of

Homestead were well organized, well governed, and utterly loyal partners of their Anglo-American colleagues. Many of the immigrants belonged to the Knights of Labor, and, though it has been universally
overlooked, the workers' Advisory Committee that directed Homestead's preparation for the lockout was a joint venture of the AAISW and
the Knights. In accord with the broad mandates of the Knights and the
local lodges of the AAISW, the committee took care to ensure that all
members of the community were involved in the planning.[12]

Accordingly, on 19 June, at the steelworkers' first public demonstration of solidarity, a certain B. Maverick, identified only as a leader of
the "Pittsburgh Slavonic Order," followed Burgess John McLuckie onto
the speakers' platform to rally East European workers and assure them
that their cause and the AAISW were one. The press did not record a
single word of Maverick's ten-minute address—delivered in several
languages—but it did report that he translated McLuckie's speech on
what was by then a familiar theme to all Homestead steelworkers: "The
constitution of this country guarantees all men the right to live, but in
order to live we must keep up a continuous struggle." The message
spoke to the great concern of Anglo-American labor reformers—securing a competence—and to the ethos of *za chlebom* that had brought
hundreds of East Europeans to Homestead.[13]

A few days later, East European immigrants took the first formal steps
to organize themselves as a lodge of the AAISW. On 22 June, "Slavs"
pledged "a solemn oath of fealty of obligation to the Amalgamated Association" and "effected a temporary organization, which will soon be made
permanent by the forming of a large lodge of laborers of that nationality."
Mike Sutton, a leader of Slovak workers whose name had obviously been
Anglicized, met with all the day workers and mechanics, some of them
from Eastern Europe, to shore up plans for the anticipated lockout. And
on 26 June, amid charges that Maverick was a company spy (charges that
ultimately proved groundless), the "Slav"steelworkers of Homestead officially "banded themselves together in a labor organization of that nationality which is to be a lodge of the Amalgamated Association."[14]

It is true that the national office of the AAISW made no move to
endorse these initiatives. Nonetheless, the daily press reported repeated
avowals of solidarity on the part of these self-proclaimed AAISW men.
"There are nearly 1000 Slavs employed in the mill; most of them as
laborers. Their loyalty to the AA rivals that of the English-speaking
men." By 3 July, East European workers had organized the "permanent"
lodge about which the press had written. It was "under the command of
an intelligent man of their nationality who is a fluent speaker of English.
This man has gotten his fellows into good discipline." However, this
lodge was "to be kept in reserve and not given post duty" because the
immigrants were so "excitable."[15]

That East European immigrants created their own lodge of the AAISW violates received wisdom regarding the immigrants as well as the union. In Homestead, at least, the union was not the prototype for an "aristocracy of labor," and when Peter Fares and Joseph Sotak died defending the rights of organized workers on 6 July, the whole town marked their devotion to a shared cause. Sotak's funeral on 8 July fascinated the press: the "typical Hungarians—stoical, morose, and silent" who attended the services in the Methodist Episcopal Church "chanted a weird dirge" and "set their teeth together more fiercely" when the officiating minister denounced the Pinkertons. Hundreds of Homesteaders, East Europeans and Anglo-Americans alike, accompanied his body to the cemetery. Fares, too, was honored by the town: "Fully 800 members of the Amalgamated Association from the lodge in which Fares was a member, and the other lodges in the city, attended his funeral."[16]

Within the context of such examples of the shared enterprise of native-born and East European and English-speaking immigrant steelworkers, the comments of one sociologist who has studied Homestead would be laughable, were they not representative of nearly a century of scholarship. "Steelworkers understood the minute details of repression, intensified work, and great physical danger, within their historical experience of conflict with steel companies. They did not express any coherent understanding of the impact of the immigration upon wages, labor organization, and repression. In fact, the same means workers developed to fight against employers blocked any welcome to immigrant workers." "Hostility towards immigrants was embedded" in the world of the "Amercian" members of the AAISW; while totally ignoring the hundreds of East European immigrants who labored in Homestead, this writer asserts that they "neither understood nor much cared for" the world of their "Anglo" co-workers.[17]

East European and Anglo-American Homesteaders certainly did come from and live in separate worlds. But these worlds could, and often did, converge at the point of production. When Superintendent John Potter dismissed three-hundred common laborers, many of them East European immigrants, on 11 March 1892—dismissals that historians have themselves dismissed—he advanced the cause of worker solidarity. For even the most poorly paid immigrant worker was bound to recognize, following dismissal, that no job in the Homestead Steel Works was safe so long as its managers' power was unchecked. It is therefore hardly surprising that Pavel Olšav, František Fagula, and their Anglo-American colleagues understood the importance of solidarity and that they publicly testified to it at virtually every mass meeting during the 1892 lockout. Indeed, even the nativist *National Labor Tribune* took note of interethnic cooperation at Homestead: "The Huns have not forgotten that Kossuth was their countryman, that they came to America for freedom, and that the Carnegie Company is doing more against American freedom than did the biggest victory of British troops in the War of Independence."[18]

Just as scholars have ignored the organized participation of East-European immigrants in the Homestead Lockout, so, too, have the initiatives of women been overlooked. This, in the face of overwhelming evidence that they were quick to defend the town when the Pinkertons landed, and that they worked side by side with the men. In fact, the most famous iconographic image we have of the lockout prominently features women; arms raised, mouths open, fists clenched, they stand in the front lines of the crowd as the surrendering Pinkertons are marched into town from the steelworks. The journalists covering the lockout were uniformly transfixed by this image, and by what they described as the "warlike," "frenzied," and "boldly aggressive" quality of Homestead's "fiendish," "frantic" women. As the daily press saw it, the running of the gauntlet was a demonic, savage, barbarian act, "a carnival of revenge," as Burgoyne termed it, that was led by scores of "fierce Amazons" and ugly, "shrill-voiced shrews and harridans" who had been "converted for the nonce into veritable furies." Seizing the very symbol of feminine delicacy, the parasol, some women pounced on the Pinkertons, while others ripped off the agents' clothes and beat them with clubs and sticks. "Kill them all," the women shouted. "We are the people!" In the process of "releasing their pent up rage," they committed "the most shocking and dastardly deeds" and abused the Pinkertons "in every way imaginable." Clearly, though, it was less the deeds that shocked observers than the gender of the dastards; equivalent acts of rage by the aggrieved men, however deplorable, still found some form of explanation in the press. But when it came to the women, "mere words [could not] describe the scene."[19]

In the view of most reporters, the march into town from the steelworks was the most brutal part of the Pinkertons' day, and the daily press regaled the public with screaming headlines and sensational narratives. Perhaps the most representative of the headlines was the *Pittsburgh Post's:* "The Pinkerton Detectives Marched from the Barges Defeated. Workmen Allowed Them Life, but Heaped All Sorts of Indignities on the Prisoners. Compelled to Run a Gauntlet. . . ." The *New York World* seemed to sum up the conventional readings of the day's events with the headline, "Women and Boys Join in the Horrible Work." And although it described the violence of only one particular woman, the *Wheeling Daily Intelligencer's* commentary on Homestead women in general typified the reports in most papers: "The women were the most violent and savage after the surrender, and it was due largely to their acts and to their goading of the men that the leaders were unable to restrain the mob. Tales in numbers are told of the scenes along the line of the gauntlet. The

Madame Dufarge [*sic*] of the movement was a woman who stood near headquarters and outdid all the men."[20]

Several scenes on Eighth Avenue were singled out by the press to underscore the notoriously violent acts of the women. For some reason the assaults on the Pinkertons had come to a lull early along the route into town. Then a woman in a blue calico dress attacked one of them: immediately, another woman threw a handful of dust in his eyes. "My God, I'm blinded," he moaned. "Serves you right, you dirty cur," the woman responded, and this time hurled a handful of jagged stones into his face. The Pinkerton, six feet tall and weighing two hundred pounds, fell down, only to be dragged to "safety" by the guards of the Advisory Committee.[21]

As the press described the scene, the crowd was emboldened to new levels of violence by these two women. Having been identified as the killer of one of the dead workers, one Pinkerton was beaten to the ground with the heavy blows of a bull whip. When, prostrate, he shouted, "Mercy, mercy," another woman rushed to the spot with a large pole and started smashing the agent's head. Other women, newly arrived on Eighth Avenue, hurled stones at the agents and chased them down the street. "One fat, red-headed woman in a calico dress was especially violent and abusive. She cursed as roundly as any man could and, holding her hands high in the air, shrieked loudly for vengeance on these men who had shot down the people of Homestead in cold blood. Twice the procession halted as the guards tried to tear this woman away, but she would not be repulsed, . . . throwing stones with an accurate aim." And yet another woman prevented a worker from bringing water to a wounded agent. When she knocked the water to the ground, the crowd responded with shouts of "Good."[22]

Shocked by the role of the Homestead women in the crowd, journalists were also scandalized by the virulence of the anti-Pinkerton attacks led by "foreign-born" or "Hungarian" immigrants, both male and female. According to one account, based on the testimony of John Martin, a Homestead railroad ticket agent, it was the "Hungarian" women who were the most violent. They seemed "worse than the men," Martin was quoted as saying. "They gathered around and tore the clothes from the backs of the [agents]. . . . Women and girls . . . with sticks and clubs beat the poor wretches. One woman had a stocking filled with iron, and with it she struck one of the Pinkerton men over the head." One journalist wrote: "It was plain to everybody that the mad, blood-thirsting multitude was not composed of the Homestead men who had, at the risk of their lives, fought a battle on the riverfront early in the day, but consisted for the most part of rough, unthinking Hungarians and foreigners."[23]

Interstingly enough, in another account based on Martin's observations, published in the *New York Sun,* the relationship between "Hungarians" and American workers was presented somewhat differently; here the ticket agent made a point of explaining how all workers—not just the East European immigrants and their female relatives—were actively engaged in assaulting the Pinkertons. Similarly, the *Pittsburgh Post* recounted the story of one agent who, upon seeing the crowd on Eighth Avenue, told the assembled townspeople that he was an upright American who belonged to a leading nativist organization, the Junior Order of United American Mechanics. "Fellow citizens, American brothers, hear me just a moment. I came here because I did not have the least idea in the world where I was coming. I was told that I would only be compelled to meet foreigners, and I did not know that I was to fight Americans. I do not want to be abused by you. I am a member of the Junior Order . . . , and I want your protection. I promise you I will not be in a scrape of the like again." The Homesteaders cheered him and let him pass without striking him. Clearly, not all active members of the crowd were furies and "foreigners."[24]

Throughout the day, Margaret Finch, the feisty proprietor of the Rolling Mill House, a steelworkers' saloon on Fourth Avenue, led the women. She was, by all accounts, one tough customer—very popular with the mill hands, a scourge on the polite world of Mr. Schooley and the Reverend Bullion. Her behavior intrigued the daily press:

> The leader of the women, a white-haired old beldam who has seen forty strikes in her long life, strode to the front, and brandishing the hand-billy which she always keeps about her house for just such emergencies, shrieked aloud: "The dirty black sheep, the dirty black sheep. Let me get at them. Let me get at them." This was Mrs. Finch, the leader of the Amazons wherever this dark Dahomey land of labor goes to war. High and shrill and strong for all her years as the voice of the lustiest fisherwoman who marched on Versailles, it rose in the night air and a hundred voices answered it. "Good for you Mother Finch. Damn the black sheep. We'll send them home on stretchers."[25]

With less detail, the narrative of the Pinkerton's ordeal and humiliation has been reproduced in virtually all subsequent accounts, both popular and scholarly. "One of the blackest scenes in American labor history," is how one scholar sums it up. The Pinkertons, wrote Wall, "had to run a gauntlet of screaming, cursing lunatics. The women of Homestead were worse than the men." "Worse than the men" is the common refrain that echoes from the contemporary press reports through more recent interpretations; and yet, by all accounts, the actions of the women in no way exceeded those of the men. Together they fought, as equals, to defend their town, and together they raged at their aggressors.[26]

Like other commentators, Wall fails to address the importance of that moment when the women physically intervened to protect the integrity of Homestead's republic of labor. Nor does he address the powerful fascination that the assault on the Pinkertons provoked in all who witnessed it; in fact, his uncritical repetition of the frenzied descriptions of the crowd, with the addition of lurid (often fictional) details, merely suggests that he shares in this fascination.[27]

What, then, does it mean that, as in the now famous etching, the women of Homestead were at the forefront of the assault on 6 July? What does it mean that no journalist there—male or female, pro- or antilabor, serious or casual—could forget that haunting image? And what does it mean that alongside these women were hundreds of East European immigrants who also enlisted to protect the town from the Pinkertons? Who similarly horrified reporters covering the assault? And who have been likewise silenced by historical tradition?

Men—and women—have been at once unable to forget and unable to talk about the women of Homestead because what they did seemed so "savage," so "demonic," in fact, so threatening. Threatening not just to the sense of order represented by Pinkertons, but to the very order of a society that might imagine the empowerment of workers in a mill, even as it deplored their tactics, but could not tolerate or even conceptualize the empowerment of willful women in a man's world.

The tradition of denial is so powerful that one of the most outraged accounts of what Homestead women did in 1892 came from the pen of an otherwise emancipated woman journalist. Mary Temple Bayard, the scion of one of Pittsburgh's most established families and a regular columnist for the *Pittsburgh Dispatch*, was, for all her emancipation and independence, as firmly entrenched as any man in the system of values that confined women's place to the home: "Woman as originally planned was a delicate creation, intended to hold within herself all capabilities of good cheer, tenderness, and grace; but the women at Homestead who felt called upon to get out and fight like men for what they felt was theirs . . . have become sadly perverted from the primal idea. That is not what heaven meant womankind to be."[28]

Bayard, who enjoyed the "painful privilege" of visiting several residences in the days immediately following the battle, found that the women of Homestead were not only unfeminine but also shockingly poor. In a passage enunciating many of the themes of social reform that Margaret Byington would explore (in a similarly condescending manner) in the Pittsburgh Survey, Bayard observed: "That people could live in such squalor, I had always before then doubted. There is nothing more true than that one-half of the world does not know how the other half lives. We, of the other half, are too prone to draw our silked [sic] robes about us and keep as much distance between us and the other half as possible, and in a measure forget, or for this very reason fail to realize, that these people are as human as ourselves."[29]

Touched as she may have been by the surprising "humanity" of the women, Bayard described them as helpless, pitiable "victims" unable to fulfill their God-appointed task, motherhood, and moving inexorably toward prostitution. "I pity those women from the depths of my heart. They are the victims. . . . I could not but wonder what [would become of the] kind of women I found in some of the worst homes . . . and I could not even imagine. From my heart I wished I could rescue them."

The rescue Bayard envisioned—"heaven's plan," she called it—was to "found beautiful homes where all unprotected women could tarry together. . . . There they would sing, paint, do fine needlework, and teach girl children to be what the Lord intended them to be—delicate, pure, high-minded, and womanly beings, and we should have the salvation of the future race assured." In cases where women were fortunate enough to find "protection," that is, a husband, "the gift of motherhood" would be certain to "set them apart from the harsh dealings of life" and "take the load off from both back and heart for sake of future generations."

The Homestead women's assertion of their power and rights, of their place and stake in the workers' republic, signaled, however, that they had refused to be domesticated, interiorized, or harnessed for the purpose of lovely embroidery. Rather, they chose to break the conventions of female behavior by going into the streets, asserting themselves in word and even deed in what the historian Mary Ryan has called the "public sphere."[30]

This unleashing of physical female energy so flouted accepted middle-class norms of feminine behavior that observers could only dismiss the self-assertion of Homestead's women as a barbaric mutation that was described as hysterical, that is, pathologically female. Members of the House committee that investigated the lockout were so shocked by the evidence of the women's forceful performance that they could only conclude: "We are loth to believe that any of these women were native Americans." In fact, not only were there native-born Americans in the crowd of angry women, but there were solidly middle-class matrons, "well-bred and well-dressed," standing on their front steps, cheering the crowd on.[31]

Nevertheless, these wishful assumptions reinforce the two sets of exclusionary values that inform most accounts of the Homestead community. And it is no surprise that in 1892, as in 1889, observers consistently invoked the same epithets when dismissing either the East European immigrants or the spirited women with their respective gestures of self-empowerment: "savage," "barbarian," "degraded."

Clearly, the politically sophisticated, courageous behavior of the depraved "Huns" was viewed by polite, civilized Americans as profoundly threatening. While there was room in the social imagination of most middle-class Amercians for a scenario in which white Anglo-American workers might rise to power (after all, Carnegie, their antagonist, came from the same stock, and look where he stood!) the entitlement of ignorant peasants who had come to the center of the industrialized world from the backward villages of the Hapsburg Empire was utterly unthinkable. So unthinkable was it, in fact, that when they presumed to seize some measure of entitlement on their own terms, John R. Commons and other social reformers he gathered to study Pittsburgh spearheaded an attempt to "Americanize" these people properly and speedily.[32]

As the behavior of women and East European immigrants was judged aberrant by the mainstream press, so, too, was the response of the most defiant Homesteaders judged unacceptable. One hundred thirty-two indictments on charges of riot, conspiracy, murder, and treason were brought against the steelworkers who had contested Carnegie and the rule of law that upheld his power. Every effort was made to disenfranchise the men who had challenged the authority of corporate America. As the post-1892 careers of the leading steelworkers testify, that effort was overwhelmingly successful.[33]

In the end, it would seem that the extravagant metaphor of an appalled journalist provides an apt summation to the story of Homestead: a "carnival of revenge." Though Burgoyne did not employ this phrase self-consciously, his narrative most assuredly captures the underlying logic of the carnival as it has been explored by the influential Russian literary critic Mikhail Bakhtin: "The carnivalesque crowd . . . in the streets is not merely a crowd. It is the people as a whole, but organized *in their own way*, the way of the people. It is outside of and contrary to all existing forms of the coercive socioeconomic and political organization."[34]

As described by Emmanuel Le Roy Ladurie and other historians who have built on Bakhtin, the carnival dictates the temporary suspension of all hierarchies and the symbolic inversion of power relations—the world turned topsy-turvy. In Homestead this was a world in which the orders of submission and domination, immigrant and "host," weaker sex and stronger sex, were reversed. A world, that is, in which workers may challenge the rule of law and the principle of private property; East Europeans may challenge nativist prejudice; and women who refuse to be cloistered away take to the streets, "like men," and shout, "We are the people!"[35]

Like the historic carnival whose ritual recurrence served as a kind of salutory purge to the community as well as a symbolic redress of political grievance, the Homestead Lockout of 1892, with its frenzy of riotous activity, unleashed years of pent-up energy and authorized bold role reversals and challenges to authority. When women joined East European and "native-American" men to turn the world of the steelmasters and political bosses upside down, the power they assumed was so threatening that ultimately it could not go unchecked: on 10 July, Governor

Robert E. Pattison at last heeded the calls of Henry Clay Frick, Sheriff William H. McCleary and "Boss" Christopher L. Magee and ordered 8,500 troops to seize control of the town, thereby setting the world back "right side up."[36]

And while working to set the world right side up, the mainstream voices of people such as M. P. Scholley and Mary Temple Bayard, representing the dominant values of industrial America, also sought to set the record "right" by silencing some of its more troublesome and unconventional actors and relegating them to the margins of history. It is time that we recognize just how incomplete that record is and just how pervasive its influence has been; it is also time that we openly challenge the unfortunate cultural presuppositions it has sustained.

Chapter 22

Winners and Losers

In late January 1893, John Miller, a former steelworker in the Homestead blooming mill, wrote to William Martin at Andrew Carnegie's Bureau of Labor asking for help in regaining the job he had lost as a result of the "troubles" of 1892. A leader of the AAISW's Munhall Lodge no. 24 since its inception in 1881, Miller had helped direct workers in the strike of 1882, had inspired them with his ode "The Homestead Strike," and had gone on to play an active role in independent labor politics through the mid 1880s. In 1889 and again in 1892, Miller was one of the veteran activists who defended Homestead against the offensives launched by Carnegie Steel.[1]

In the 1892 lockout, Miller stood by his fellow workers and remained loyal to the AAISW right through the bitter end. As a result of his participation, he was charged with conspiracy and treason, and he and his son, a laborer in the steelworks, were blacklisted; Miller could find no other job in the steel industry. By January 1893 he had to acknowledge his painful defeat. Swallowing principles and pride, he addressed a plea to Martin, his former union brother, who to his mind had surely committed the greater act of treason.

> Dear Sir,
>
> You may think it strange perhaps that I pen you a few lines, but I deem it my duty as we have always been good friends. You know all about the trouble we had at Homestead. Well through this trouble, I lost my position . . . and I am at a loss to know why I am put out this way. I was always on friendly relations with the firm and I think I have been the cause of settling many disputes which may have brought on trouble. Now I think my record is good, as far as I can learn, as a workman. I always tried to do the best I knew how between employer and employee. Now William, what I want you to do is to see Mr. Frick and see if he could not do something for me. I want them if possible to try and withdraw the case that is pending against me. Not that I am afraid of any serious result in the matter at all, but it will save me a great

deal of time and expense which I can ill afford at the present time. I have
started a little business trying to make a living for myself and family. But I
find it is a very uphill job. If my boy could get his work back, it would not be
so hard on us, but as it is we are both idle. The boy was making $1.68 a day
before the trouble occurred, and if they don't feel like giving me my work
back, I would like very well if they could give the boy employment. Now
William, do not let this pass your notice but rather do all you possibly can for
me and I will ever remain your friend and brother. . . .

—John Miller.

Miller's letter underscores the pathos and reluctance of thousands of
steelworkers who were forced to come begging in the aftermath of 1892. It
would be wrong, however, simply to equate the desperate gestures of
committed union men, reduced to pathetic indignity, with the scheming
accommodations of others. The ambitious personal strivings of men such
as Martin in no way matched the distressing compromises of men such as
Miller. This much, at least, even Martin must have recognized, for after
leaving Carnegie Steel in 1893, he was never able to bring himself to
comment publicly on the fruits of his labors for Andrew Carnegie. Approached by a reporter on the day after the Pinkerton assault, Martin,
seen chatting with a prominent member of the AAISW, could only mutter,
"I have nothing to say." As far as we know, he had nothing to say to Miller,
either: there is no extant record of a reply to Miller's appeal.[2]

While John Miller had to grovel, some of his colleagues managed to
emerge with some dignity from the events of 1892. John McLuckie, we
recall, became a miner in northern Mexico. Hugh O'Donnell, who served
as the first chairman of the Advisory Committee, left town to manage the
"Edwards Family," a small orchestra comprised of another blacklisted steelworker from Homestead, "Professor" John Edwards, and his five gifted
children. According to the *Homestead Local News*, O'Donnell traveled in
advance of the orchestra and made bookings for them through 1893; later
he moved to Chicago and worked for a weekly newspaper there.[3]

The careers of other prominent members of the Advisory Committee—William T. Roberts, Hugh Ross, Jack Clifford, and David Lynch—
followed similarly humble paths. Roberts worked as a professional
speechmaker, first as a Democrat and then as a Republican, and then
disappeared from public view. Lynch, who served on the borough
council at the time of the lockout, went into the liquor business. And
Clifford and Ross, who had distinguished themselves by directing the
initial counterattack on the Pinkertons, became, respectively, a book
salesman and a permanent member of the unemployed. What became
of Pavel Olšav, František Fagula, and other leading East European steelworkers is simply not known.

Thomas Crawford, the only identifiable leader of the AAISW who
was living in Homestead at the end of the century, was able to make a

decent living as a roller, first at a mill in Uniontown, Pennsylvania, and later in a Pittsburgh steelworks that had not blacklisted him. Interviewed in 1899 by the social reformer Charles B. Spahr, Crawford, then 36, complained of premature old age due to the long hours and brutal working conditions at the nonunion mill in which he worked. It was Crawford, and not O'Donnell, Spahr correctly noted, who maintained "the real direction of affairs" during the 1892 lockout. "He had been born in England and felt somewhat keenly his want of schooling, though it is doubtful if schooling would have developed his executive ability more than the postgraduate course he had been compelled to take."[4]

Crawford, unlike so many of his former co-workers, did not hesitate to voice his support for unionism even in the depths of the nonunion era. Nor, for that matter, was he afraid to mock Carnegie and the vaunted embodiment of his philanthropy, the town's free library that Carnegie himself had dedicated only a year before. "I have always hoped to educate myself. But, after my day's work, I haven't been able to do much studying. . . . After working twelve hours, how can a man go to a library?"[5]

Crawford had been head of the Advisory Committee from mid July 1892 onward. In one of many confrontations during the lockout, he and several of his colleagues on the committee were arrested by Sheriff William McCleary's deputies on 30 September while chatting on a street corner. The deputies escorted Crawford to a temporary holding cell in a tent manned by the state militia and informed him that he had been charged with treason against the Commonwealth of Pennsylvania. He was to learn that it had been Philander C. Knox, chief counsel for Carnegie Steel, who had drawn up the charge and submitted it to Edward H. Paxson, the chief justice of the Pennsylvania Supreme Court for his personal, and quite enthusiastic, approval.[6]

Crawford, needless to say, was astounded by the charge of treason, the circumstances of his arrest, and the news that all members of the Advisory Committee faced the same indictment. Handcuffed and taken to the Homestead train station for the ride to the county jail in Pittsburgh, Crawford was cheered by a boisterous crowd that had assembled to protest his departure. "They can persecute us," he shouted, "but they can't make us work. The truth was, however, that by this time, Carnegie Steel had found hundreds of eager new men only too willing to work; in the view of company officials, Crawford's defiant words were mere rhetoric, and rhetoric alone. Still, into the autumn, the steelworkers were able to maintain a credible defense. A few days after his arrest, Crawford was back in charge of the Advisory Committee; he succeeded in coming up with the requisite bail, set at a hefty $10,000 by Justice Paxson, when Homestead friends came to his aid. Similarly, Lynch and others who had been arrested for treason were released on bail through the good offices of friends and neighbors.

The man who served as Lynch's bondsman, Vincent Waasilefski, had also provided bail for Crawford earlier that summer when he had been incarcerated on other charges stemming from his participation in the lockout. Waasilefski, a native of Poland, was one of Homestead's most successful East European immigrants: his saloon and billiard room were known as the town's finest and served as a meeting place for East European steelworkers and their native-born and British immigrant colleagues. In providing bail for Crawford, Lynch, and others, Waasilefski, whose own son had been locked out by Carnegie Steel, thus reaffirmed a long-held symbolic bond between the East European and Anglo-American communities of Homestead.[7]

Waasilefski's generosity underscores the extraordinary solidarity and communal strength exhibited by the steelworkers and their friends during the summer of 1892. Going into the lockout, the labor community of Homestead was stronger than it had ever been. The AAISW, which had counted more than one thousand members in its eight Homestead lodges in 1891, claimed to have enlisted more than three thousand by the second week of July 1892. John McLuckie, longtime leader of the AAISW and the Knights of Labor, had been reelected burgess of the town in the spring of that year. And steelworkers, for the first time in the town's history, held an outright majority on the town council; they also served as chairmen of its most important committees. Moreover, beyond personal friendships, the institutional ties that linked skilled and unskilled workers and Anglo-Americans and East Europeans were tighter than ever: in mid 1892, East European workers had prepared for the impending confrontation with Carnegie Steel by forming their own lodge of the AAISW.[8]

To be sure, the goals of labor republicanism were never so well served in Homestead as in 1892. And yet these same goals were dismantled with a speed no less extraordinary than the solidarity displayed by the town's steelworkers, families, and friends. Even as the workers celebrated their victory over the Pinkertons on 6 July—a celebration cut short by the funerals of their fallen colleagues—they recognized that the town's resistance, no matter how well organized, would ultimately prove no match for Carnegie Steel, should it succeed in persuading Governor Robert E. Pattison to mobilize the state militia. As one report pointed out, "The men know that the company, if it wants to, can win the strike." Hugh O'Donnell himself acknowledged that the men would be obliged to yield if Carnegie Steel, with the protection afforded by the Pennsylvania militia, decided to hire new men. As early as 7 July, therefore, he and other leaders of the Advisory Committee tried to assure Pattison, as well as the public at large, that law and order had been restored. "There is no occasion for the State sending any troops here," said one member of the committee. "We are not destroying the property of the company—merely protecting our rights."[9]

Sheriff McCleary and his "bondsman," Christopher L. Magee, took a decidedly different view of the recent events. McCleary, acting on orders from Magee, contrived once again to raise a posse for the ostensible purpose of reasserting the county's authority in Homestead and returning control of the steelworks to Carnegie Steel. The plan, unveiled at a meeting over which Magee presided on the evening of 7 July, was to deputize twenty prominent Pittsburghers and an equal number of Homesteaders to replace the workers then guarding the mill. The members of the Advisory Committee who attended this meeting—John McLuckie, David Lynch, and William Roberts among them—had no use for Magee's proposal. In their view, his intent was quite clear: if they agreed to relinquish control to the deputies, the company could easily introduce new workers. If, on the other hand, the committee declined to go along, that was likely to pecipitate a rapid mobilization of the state militia—which also would allow for the introduction of scabs. Magee, for his part, was betting heavily on the latter option and, therefore, later that night ordered McCleary to consult with militia officers about preparations for mobilization. This meeting "excited considerable interest" in Homestead: military intervention, everyone knew, would play directly into the hands of Henry Clay Frick.[10]

Disgusted with Magee and his henchman, John F. Cox, a prominent Republican and former Homestead burgess who had helped arrange the meeting with the "boss," the Advisory Committee decided "to pay no more attention to Pittsburgh politicians" and sent representatives directly to Governor Pattison. Before they left early on 8 July, McLuckie wired the governor, emphasizing that all was peaceful in Homsetead and asking that he take no action, at least until he met with the town's emissaries. Unknown to McLuckie and the other steelworkers, however, Pattison had already dispatched his representatives to Homestead to assess the situation secretly. Their report of "disagreeable encounters with the pickets and workmens' committees," as the governor would later phrase it, only confirmed the latest newspaper stories, all quite alarming, that had come to his desk. "The strikers are the masters in every sense. They feel their power; they order men about with more impunity than a Chicago policeman."[11]

As O'Donnell and other Homestead representatives made their way to Harrisburg, the workers convened yet another mass meeting to consider their next move. William Weihe and William Brennen, representing the conservative politics and tactics espoused by the national leadership of the AAISW, urged the members to surrender the works and allow McCleary, on behalf of the company, to assume possession of them. The men, predictably, would have none of this plan: when McCleary arrived later in the afternoon to report that his latest efforts to raise a posse had been futile, he was surrounded by a large crowd and personally threatened by Edward "Rioter" Burke, a heater in the 119-inch plate mill. The sheriff, having demonstrated to his own satisfaction that matters were indeed out of hand, immediately returned to Pittsburgh to confer with Magee.[12]

Meanwhile, in Harrisburg, O'Donnell tried desperately to convince Pattison that order had been restored and that the property of Carnegie Steel was secure. In fact, he said proudly, company watchmen were back on the grounds. (He neglected to mention that they were serving at the pleasure of the Advisory Committee, which had allowed them to enter the steelworks.) Pattison indicated that he had received rather different reports from his agents and, though he was not prepared to act immediately, he was now inclined to dispatch troops to Homestead. Pattison adjourned the meeting shortly after midnight. It was now 9 July. On the following day, Sunday, after receiving another formal request from McCleary for "a large military force," Pattison ordered Major General George R. Snowden, commander of the National Guard of Pennsylvania, to arm 8,500 troops and lead them to Homestead. Their job was "to maintain the peace" and to "protect all persons in their rights under the constitution and laws of the state."[13]

News of Pattison's decision quickly reached Homestead on 11 July, and it demoralized many residents. "The men can think of nothing but the fact that the fight is lost and that they will have to surrender without striking a blow," one reporter wrote. But the men were angry as well: angry that Pattison had sent spies into town and, of course, that he had decided to support the company. "I cannot believe it," said O'Donnell, "I cannot believe it." Other leaders of the Advisory Committee were demonstrably less shocked. McLuckie, for one, recognized that the battle was effectively lost when McCleary had met with the state militia officers on the evening of 7 July. His sardonic remarks to the press regarding the mobilization of the militia therefore had the unmiskable ring of a rehearsed speech: "We will welcome them. It would be folly to attempt to oppose them, even if any people from Homestead desired it. We will receive the militia in a fraternal spirit, and accord to them that respect due to the representatives of the grandeur and dignity of the great state of Pennsylvania."[14]

McLuckie's little speech gently masked Homestead's contempt for the duly constituted authorities of the Commonwealth of Pennsylvania, even as he and his colleagues were preparing to "welcome" them. What, after all, could Homestead do but welcome the National Guard? O'Donnell, never one for rhetorical bluff, said as much: "We can't fight the state of Pennsylvania, and even if we could, we cannot fight the United States government."[15]

It was precisely this kind of resignation, publicly expressed, that would cost O'Donnell the chair of the Advisory Committee a few weeks later. At this point, however, he was still very much a part of what the press was calling the Homestead "insurrection" and "great labor rebellion." Indeed, the daily press was nothing less than aghast at what it had witnessed in the town since 6 July.

> Among themselves these men are orderly. [But] towards strangers or visitors they are savages. They justify their conduct by saying the fight against them is a desperate one, that it is a fight for their homes and their wives and their children, as well as for their lives. The laws of the whole state are set at naught and the liberties of citizens are restricted. . . . The strikers, who practically compose the town, do not realize the amazing nature of their doings [and] seem to think that they are an orderly, law-abiding lot of American citizens simply exercising their right to defend themselves against their enemies. . . . The law is defied, . . . the Constitution is violated . . . daily, . . . yet the state has made no move to put down the rebellion.[16]

By the time these words had been printed, the state was moving, quite expeditiously, to restore constitutional rule in Homestead. In the view of McLuckie, the borough's chief municipal officer, and of his colleagues on the Advisory Committee, the introduction of troops meant that the lives of all residents were potentially at risk: any attempt to resist might result in more bloodshed. Resisting the militia, McLuckie recognized, would also irrevocably cast the steelworkers in the role of insurrectionists. In an effort to restore its own rule and thereby minimize the chance of an armed confrontation with the militia, the Advisory Committee therefore formally reconstituted itself and then convened a mass meeting. Five thousand people attended on the morning of Monday 11 July and were told by McLuckie:

> "We want every man, woman, and child in this town to welcome the militia with open arms, because just as true as I stand here, their arrival is the best thing that could possibly have occurred to our people. . . . This man Pattison is acting wisely and judiciously. He understands our cause, and our position. He is a just man and will not cater to monopoly, and will not permit the troops of our state, the servants of the people, the defenders of the dignity of the Commonwealth, which is as dear to us as it is to any human being that ever breathed, to outrage a community of people situated as we are.[17]

In this speech, McLuckie flexed what little political muscle was left him in the hope that Governor Pattison would not allow the militia to ease the way for Carnegie Steel to employ new workers. Misreading his words, some modern interpreters have too hastily condemned him and fellow Homesteaders for selling out. However, the counsel McLuckie offered was not, as the political scientist Linda Schneider suggests, born of any kind of "identification" that he, or his colleagues, had forged with "legitimate authority." McLuckie, one must not forget, had led virtually every political and trade union campaign in Western Pennsylvania against such authority since the 1870s. Nor, for that matter, was the advice born of his, or the steelworkers', belief in the neutrality of the state, as Schneider also indicates. McLuckie and thousands of other employees of the company had more than a decade's worth of experience that taught that such neutrality was chimerical, to say the least: the police and sheriff had on numerous occasions intervened, gladly, on behalf of Carnegie and his fellow steelmasters, and Homestead steelworkers, in 1882 and again in 1889, had answered these interventions with strident resistance.[18]

The truth is that by 11 July, McLuckie—and Homestead—simply had no choice. Most townspeople understood that to engage in armed resistance against 8,500 armed militiamen, as a handful of steelworkers suggested, was tantamount to suicide. Following the "riots" of 1877, Pennsylvania had modernized its militia to preclude future mass public uprisings, and by 1892 it was regarded as one of the nation's finest. (Indeed, it was the bloody intervention of the militia in 1877, conducted on behalf of the Pennsylvania Railroad, that had incited Pittsburgh workers, McLuckie included, to launch one of their most forceful political challenges against "legitimate" government.) Schneider concludes, wishfully, that Homestead offered "insurrectionary potential" on the grand, perhaps national, scale; with unthinking condescension she asserts, however, that this potential was undermined by the steelworkers' unwillingness to resist once the state intervened—an unwillingness that "led directly to their defeat."[19]

The fact was, however, that resistance did not end when the militia arrived; the steelworkers and their families were merely provoked by Pattison's announcement of the mobilization. James Boyce, one of the leaders of the AAISW, expressed the prevailing opinion: "Instead of ending the fight at Homestead, the militia will just end the first chapter of it." So infuriated were the residents that the Advisory Committee was forced to swear in one hundred special deputies to preserve order. The East European steelworkers, many of whose relatives had confronted Frick's Pinkertons in the Connellsville coke region, were especially incensed. In addressing his East European colleagues, František Fagula therefore echoed McLuckie's call to refrain from violence shortly after the burgess finished his speech at the mass meeting of 11 July.[20]

As that meeting concluded, one member of the Advisory Committee was asked what, in truth, the arrival of the troops would mean. His answer summed up the view of thousands: "What does it mean? It means just this—that the entire National Guard of the State of Pennsylvania had been called out to enable the Carnegie company to employ scab labor. That's what it means."

It was with full possession of this knowledge that the town went ahead with its elaborate plans to welcome the National Guard and to demonstrate its allegiance to the rule of law. McLuckie was to lead a procession comprised of more than 3,500 steelworkers and various town officials, all marching behind the banners of the AAISW and Knights of Labor, to greet General Snowden officially at the railroad station and, in a solemn ceremony, present him with the freedom of the city. Then the soldiers would disembark and march into Homestead to the tune of the "Star Spangled Banner" and other patriotic music. The soldiers were to be greeted by the applause of thousands. Perhaps this demonstration of friendly respect would win the goodwill—or sympathy?—of the visiting guardsmen.[21]

While McLuckie and his colleagues were completing their plans to welcome the troops, General Snowden was making elaborate preparations of his own. He decided to take the town by surprise and succeeded in keeping secret the location of all 8,500 militiamen until the very moment of their arrival at 9:00 A.M. on 12 July—not, as expected, at the Homestead station but at the Munhall station, near the steelworks. Within minutes ninety-five rail cars had deposited more than 4,000 heavily armed troops near the front gate of the mill; Snowden ordered several companies to secure the entrance and then dispatched an entire regiment to make camp on the commanding heights of the hill overlooking the steelworks and the town. Fittingly, the hill lay on the City Poor Farm property that Carnegie had recently acquired; Snowden made his headquarters in the little Carnegie School House at the top of the hill. As Carnegie had indicated when the deal was signed, the firm would always make good use of this land.[22]

For the Homestead steelworkers the arrival of the state militia signaled the beginnning of the end; the mood of the entire town turned to sour defeat. "The Strikers Much Chagrined," read the headline of one New York paper. "As soon as the soldiers came in, there was a complete surrender of the town," reported another newspaper. O'Donnell, for a second time, stated publicly that to all intents, the cause was now lost because new workers would be able to enter the mill. And, indeed, by 9:20 A.M., only twenty minutes after their arrival, the militia had displaced the steelworker pickets who had been guarding the mill. By 10:00 A.M. company officials were fully established in the mill office. "It was a complete acquiescence to the power of the state, and as gracefully as they could, the strikers philosophically accepted the inevitable." Burgess McLuckie had no choice but to cancel the welcoming parade—"The Parade That Never Was," in the words of the *New York Herald*.[23]

Later in the morning a delegation of Homesteaders, after considerable difficulty, succeeded in obtaining an audience with General Snowden, then conferring with Sheriff McCleary in the Carnegie School House. "Captain" O. C. Coon, a former state militiaman with close ties

to the steelworkers, led the delegation representing the town government and the AAISW. The purpose of the visit, he told Snowden, was to
assure him that the union and indeed all residents intended to cooperate
fully in the maintenance of law and order. "I need no assistance; I shall
preserve order myself," replied Snowden. Coon then stated that the
townspeople themselves had done just that. Pointing to the mill, Snowden shot back, "Yes, I have heard of that." Both Coon and O'Donnell,
who was representing the Advisory Committee, protested. "Ask the
sheriff," Coon said, turning toward McCleary. McCleary, visibly agitated, declared: "You turned back my deputies. You didn't allow my
deputies to take charge of the works."[24]

It was at this point that Snowden brought the meeting to a swift
conclusion, saying that he was obliged to decline the offer of assistance
from the union and the town because he recognized the authority of
neither. "Gentlemen, I thank you for your offer, but I only recognize you
as citizens. I am here by order of the governor to cooperate with the
sheriff in the maintenance of order and the protection of the Carnegie
Steel Company in the possession of its property. I wish you good morning." Coon said nothing; O'Donnell could only mutter: "Well, I believe
we have nothing further to say."

As Coon and O'Donnell left Snowden's headquarters, they saw the
Little Bill, one of the tugs that Frick had rented for the Pinkertons' landing, steaming toward the company wharf below the mill; this time, in
the service of General Snowden, it proudly flew the flag of the Commonwealth of Pennsylvania. O'Donnell had told Snowden that Homestead
had always recognized the legal authority of the state; it was only the
"illegal" authority of the Pinkertons that it had rejected. Watching the
Little Bill return to the site of the Pinkerton landing, he sadly understood
that, when it came to the issue of trade unionism and property rights,
these distinctions did not exist.

Over the course of the next three days, the National Guard of Pennsylvania went to extraordinary lengths to ensure that Carnegie Steel
could move forward with its plans to reopen the steelworks. Hundreds
of troops patrolled the mill yard and the river and rail approaches to it,
and sentries manned the entire perimeter of the works, which had been
enclosed by Frick's fence. Immediately after the company secured the
mill on 12 July, supervisory personnel installed makeshift quarters for
the new workers they planned to welcome. And the very next day the
first scabs began to arrive. Union men persuaded these workers to leave,
but by 15 July the company had succeeded in smuggling fifty new men
into the mill—enough to light several of the furnaces.[25]

Although it would be weeks before steel was produced, the response
of the locked-out men to the sight of smoke rising from the steelworks
was understandably furious. Hundreds of townspeople advanced to-

ward the front gate; they stopped only when the militiamen stationed there drew their bayonets and took aim with their rifles. The East European community was particularly enraged: an irate crowd tried to storm the mill by tearing down part of the fence. Only after militiamen had stabbed six did the East Europeans retreat.[26]

These abortive assaults on the mill provoked the first of the AAISW's many efforts to explain the violent turn that Homestead's resistance often took. Boyce, who had predicted earlier that the mobilization of the militia would only harden resistance, related the angry outburst to the steelworkers' claim to unspecified "rights" in the Homestead Steel Works. "The people outside do not understand this Homestead position. Most of us, expecting continuous employment here, have put our savings into homes, which will be lost if we are to be driven away from this town. The Carnegie mills were built up by us, the great profits of the concern were made by us. Our labor was expended for Scotch castles, and library advertising. We do not say that Carnegie, Phipps, and Company does not own the mill property, but we do say that we have some rights in it ourselves." It was for this reason, Boyce suggested, that his co-workers had decided to prevent new men from going to work for Carnegie Steel and "stealing" the jobs of the Homestead steelworkers.

Boyce's assertion underscored what was perceived by many contemporary observers as the core issue of the lockout: the respective rights of workers and employers. Even before he had sought to justify the defiant stand, the daily press, universally shocked by the values embedded in his formulation, recognized that the conflict called into question fundamental principles of industrial society, particularly the inviolate nature of the individual's right to private property. As the *Pittsburgh Post* explained, "the Homestead mills belong to the Carnegie Company, and their right to put into those mills non-union workers if they should see proper to do so is undeniable. With such a movement, no one has any right . . . to interfere; and when such interference takes places, it is unjustifiable and lawless. . . . [The workers' efforts to] stop the owners of the mills from doing with their property just as they please is wrong, altogether wrong, and without excuse or justification."[27]

Out-of-town papers such as the *Chicago Times*, the *Cleveland Plain Dealer*, and the *New York Herald* joined a chorus of Pittsburgh dailies that saw in Homestead the specter of 1877 and, with it, profoundly disturbing threats to the very fabric of American society. The *Herald*, which, like many newspapers, was only too eager to criticize Carnegie, stressed the admirable qualities of the workers:

The most remarkable feature of the situation is the character of the men. . . . They are not desperadoes or anarchists. They are not reckless aliens. They do not belong to the criminal classes. They are honest, intelligent and mostly

American citizens and voters. They are sober, industrious workmen, and many of them property holders, owning homes bought by their savings. They have carefully abstained from injuring the property where they were recently employed. They even offered to Sheriff McCleary men from their own ranks to serve as deputy sheriffs to guard the works from which they have been locked out.[28]

For all its empathy for the workers, however, the *Herald* was obliged to point out that even "the most ardent sympathizer of these men must see that their present attitude is beyond the pale of the law and in defiance of the authority of the Commonwealth" because the workers had denied Carnegie and his partners "free access to their works" and the right to "operate them unmolested." As Ezra B. Taylor, a congressman from Ohio who served on the House investigating committee, put it, in Homestead "there seems to be some queer ideas of the rights of property."

The idea that the Homestead steelworkers, by virtue of their having worked in the mill, had "some rights" in it, certainly seemed queer indeed to the vast majority of Americans. In the immediate aftermath of 6 July, Boyce and his fellows found themselves with few friends willing to defend the workers' claim to rights in the mill. Among the few were: Senator John A. Palmer, Democrat, of Illinios; an unidentified (though prominent) Republican lawyer from Youngstown, Ohio; and two relatively obscure journalists, one who wrote for the *Independent* and the other for *Twentieth Century* magazine.[29]

In a speech that shocked even the most committed liberals of the day, Senator Palmer told his esteemed colleagues on 7 July that Homestead had proved that the cherished tenets of American individualism were woefully outmoded. "Within my lifetime, I have seen marvelous changes. There was a time when individualism was the universal rule and men lived almost alone because they could support themselves; but matters have changed." The most significant of these changes was the emergence of two distinct groups of Americans: workers and employers. Because of the vast power that employers—organized capital, Palmer called them— had accumulated, it was now necessary for the state to protect the rights of employees. The affirmation of the worker's right to freedom of contract afforded him insufficient protection: "You cannot do it by asserting . . . that every man has a right to the control of his own property in his own way; if he does not like to go to work for the Carnegies, he may go to work for somebody else."[30]

In arguing that the state must take an active role to ensure the welfare of its working citizens, Palmer acknowledged that, in some cases, individual rights would have to be abridged. The protection of Carnegie's right to employ whomsoever he pleased, for example, could only abrogate the rights of labor, and of society in general. Palmer, echoing Alexis de Tocqueville's warning about the dangers of a "manufacturing aristocracy," warned: "If some solution is not found, this army of employees will be controlled by the employers, and there will be established an aristocracy more terrible than exists in any free country, and this nobility of wealth will become our governors."[31]

Palmer did not offer a solution to the vexing problem of balancing individual and group rights. But in his view this much was clear: the state now had an obligation to limit the freedom of the employer to dispose of his property as he saw fit when that property was invested, as the Homestead Steel Works most assuredly were, with the "public interest." The steelworkers in Homestead had a "moral right" to employment in the mill, and the mill itself should be seen as a "public" institution whose owners "must hereafter be regarded as holding their property subject to the correlative rights of those without whose services [such] property would be utterly worthless."

Palmer was vilified for privileging the workers' rights to employment. The *Pittsburgh Commercial Gazette* asked: "What is this but socialism, pure and simple? If this does not strike at individual liberty and the right of property in the most direct and dangerous manner, then no socialist ever assailed those rights." Other publications labeled Palmer as something "worse than a Populist"; to claim a right to employment did nothing less than undermine the foundation of American society—what one Southern paper called the "good old rule" that allowed the property owner to "do whatever he pleases with his own." The *Nation,* too, joined the criticism of Palmer's defense of the workers' occupation of the steelworks: Palmer, who denied that the men had in fact trespassed, maintained that they were within their rights to use force to answer force, for it was clearly the only way that they could protect their rights. In the view of the *Nation,* however, if indeed these rights did exist, they were of such "recent birth" that any claim based upon them was virtually worthless.[32]

In truth, the rights claimed by Boyce and other steelworkers and defended by Senator Palmer were hardly new. They were of long and respectable heritage, as the Youngstown lawyer who defended the steelworkers was quick to point out: it was English common law that justified the privileging of public over private rights. Common law, he wrote in the *Youngstown Evening Vindicator,* holds that "private right shall be subject and subservient to the public good." Moreover, private property rights in particular are always subservient to the public good. "The stickler for property right would vehemently assert that he had the right to buy with his own money any lawful commodity on the market, and as much as he saw fit of it. Yet the common law very easily made it a crime to create a corner in the necessaries of life. And the law protects the weak against the strong."[33]

In arguing this position, one that has been retrieved by E. P. Thompson and other historians of the moral economy, the lawyer drew upon a well-defined juridical tradition. As the legal historian Harry Scheiber argues, American legal doctrine "has strongly suggested that some kinds of property should not be held exclusively in private hands, but should be open to the public or at least subject to what Roman law called the *jus publicum*, that is, the public right." This doctrine, Scheiber writes, found what was perhaps its clearest nineteenth-century expression in an 1851 case, *Commonwealth v. Alger*, adjudicated by Justice Lemuel Shaw of the Supreme Court of Massachusetts. Shaw ruled that all private property is subject to some restraint to protect the general good; moreover, all such property is in fact held on condition that it not be used to harm the "the public rights and interests of the community."[34]

Justice Shaw's understanding of property rights, as Scheiber explains, has never constituted the dominant view in American jurisprudence. It does, however, reflect a central tension in the law between a tradition that seeks to protect public rights and one that privileges entrepreneurial interests. For much of the nineteenth century and most of the twentieth, the latter tradition had prevailed. Viewed from the dominant libertarian perspective of today, Shaw's ruling in *Commonwealth v. Alger*, no less than the solitary voices of Senator Palmer and the Youngstown lawyer, no doubt seem misguided and the efforts of the Homestead steelworkers to enforce the *jus publicum* dangerously romantic.

Yet, from the days of the Puritan Saints onward, successive generations of Americans have challenged the supremacy of individual property rights, and the ethos of self-interest and material gain that serves as its justification, to assert an alternative politics. In the Gilded Age, as we have seen, hundreds of thousands of urban and agricultural laborers succeeded, for a time, in carrying this assertion into the center of a great national debate on the future of the country. At the heart of their effort lay the problem of how to reconcile individual and communal rights, which bedeviled them and many of their heirs in the twentieth-century labor movement from the rousing campaigns of the socialist Eugene Victor Debs to the frontal assault on private property rights manifest in the sit-down strikes of the depression of the 1930s and through the civil rights movement of the 1960s. In the steel industry the problem has had even more immediate significance: in the 1970s and 1980s, a bold affirmation of public rights helped guide the efforts of community activists in Pittsburgh and Youngstown who sought to forestall the massive plant closings ordered by the United States Steel Corporation.[35]

Seen in this light, James Boyce's declaration that the Homestead steelworkers had a claim to rights in the mill owned by Carnegie Steel represents a peculiar combination of traditional and more modern efforts to grapple with the perplexing problem of safeguarding community interests in a polity that treasures individual liberty. Boyce, we recall, charged that many steelworkers would lose their homes if they lost their jobs, and he held that the Homestead steelworkers owned their jobs. In so doing he gave expression to some of the most powerful ideas that had animated the post–Civil War labor movement in Greater Pittsburgh through the early 1880s and, in Homestead, had found fertile ground. For Boyce, after all, was claiming that he and his co-workers had a right to a competence, a sufficiency of the means to live comfortably, and a right to the means to ensure that such a life was indeed possible, that is, a right to a job.[36]

In affirming the workers' claims to a competence and to a job, Boyce, speaking for his fellow steelworkers, did more than invoke the republican legacy that they had brought to and defended in Homestead; he extended it in a new direction. He based these claims on an explicit assertion that the workers had rights not only to a competence and a job but to property that was in fact owned by their employer. Boyce did not deny that Carnegie Steel owned the Homestead Steel Works, but he did assert that, if the rights of the workers were to be protected, title to the mill could no longer mean that its owners possessed absolute control over it.

In the days immediately following publication of Boyce's remarks, tensions between the militia and the residents grew, and the town attracted even more attention from the outside world. Frick instructed Potter to notify all former employees that they could have their old jobs back if they applied, as individuals, prior to 21 July and if they could demonstrate that they had taken no part in "any of the rioting or disturbances" in Homestead after 30 June. The locked-out steelworkers met this stipulation with silence.[37]

There were, however, reports that some men had threatened Frick's life. The AAISW leadership plainly realized that "no one act could injure the cause of the locked-out men as much as an attack on Mr. Frick." Yet Homestead remained defiant, and General Snowden became convinced that only an extension of his control beyond the mill and into the town would quell the "communism" of the townspeople who, he said, "believe the works are theirs." He therefore moved to place the town under what was in effect martial law. On Sunday 17 July, Snowden conducted a formal drill of all 8,500 militimen that was witnessed by as many as 20,000 spectators. Responding to this forceful display of state power, the *New York Sun*'s page-one headline that day was: "Strikers Losing Ground."

As the chain of events that began on that day were to indicate—events that were to a large extent orchestrated by Christopher L. Magee—the *Sun*'s headline was on target. Early in the morning, John L. Milholland, chairman of the Republican party's national committee on industrial affairs, arrived with an associate in Homestead to confer with Hugh O'Donnell. Milholland, on Magee's instructions, had come from New York to ask O'Donnell if he could make one additional overture that might lead to a settlement. Magee's interest in ending the dispute was twofold: first, he was a close friend of Carnegie and Frick as well as being the latter's business partner; and second, as a national power in the Republican party, he was concerned that the lockout would hurt President Benjamin Harrison's chances in the November elections. Magee, who had effectively secured Harrison's nomination in 1888, was above all interested in muzzling McLuckie, who had consistently attacked the GOP, particularly for its stand on the tariff. He hoped to enlist O'Donnell in the endeavor.[38]

O'Donnell, ultimately much to the chagrin of his colleagues, agreed to take Milholland up on the suggestion that he help silence McLuckie in return for whatever assistance the national GOP could render in persuading Frick and Carnegie to reopen negotiations. Accordingly, O'Donnell, without authorization from the Advisory Committee, left Homestead with Milholland on what the press called a secret mission. Convinced that Carnegie Steel was certain to win, he had unilaterally decided to seek a settlement on virtually any terms that might allow the union lodges at Homestead to survive. Magee, well attuned to the thinking of each of the AAISW leaders, clearly recognized that O'Donnell, who had publicly predicted the defeat of the union, could be used to undermine members' morale further. Once O'Donnell's effort to end the lockout became public knowledge, Magee hoped, it would signal that the union was hopelessly crippled.[39]

Milholland and O'Donnell's secret mission took them to the New York office of Whitelaw Reid, the editor and publisher of the *New York Tribune*, who had just been chosen as President Harrison's running mate. Following Reid's suggestion, O'Donnell dictated a letter, antedated from Homestead, that asked Reid to intercede on behalf of the workers. The AAISW, whose spirit was now "conciliatory in the extreme," O'Donnell wrote, was now willing to concede anything. Through the good offices of Secretary of State John Foster, who was acting on instructions from President Harrison, Reid promptly cabled Carnegie through the American consul in London that O'Donnell had assured him that the workers were prepared to "waive every other thing in dispute, and submit to whatever you think it right to require" if Carnegie would only reopen negotiations and recognize the union. Carnegie, receiving the message after several days, initially considered O'Donnell's offer, but he ultimately chose to reject it out of hand: after all, he himself had drawn the line at Homestead over the very issue of union recognition. O'Donnell's plea, Carnegie wired Frick, was "useful showing distress of Amalgamated Association."[40]

As Magee had anticipated and Carnegie had understood, O'Donnell's compromise—which became highly publicized within days—signaled a weakening of Homestead's resistance. The AAISW lodges were heartened by the sympathy strikes initiated at Carnegie's operation in Pittsburgh, Duquesne, and Beaver Falls, but all of these endeavors ultimately proved fruitless. O'Donnell, who had been replaced by Thomas Crawford as interim chairman of the Advisory Committee, never regained the confidence of the steelworkers after his return from New York. He publicly quarreled with McLuckie over the tariff issue, and he further alienated fellow workers by proudly announcing that he had received a $200-per-week acting contract (possibly in a New York drama about Homestead). While in New York, he boasted, he had lived high off the hog: "I dined at the Holland, lunched at the Fifth Avenue, and smoked cigars at the Hoffman."[41]

On Monday 18 July several murder and riot charges prepared by the company lawyer, Philander C. Knox, were served; more were to follow. McLuckie was one of the first members of the Advisory Committee to be arrested. "The law has put its label on the late secession of the free and independent borough of Homestead," said the *New York Herald* "and the words of its label spell 'murder.' " From the county jail, McLuckie made it known that he would counter Frick and Knox with charges of his own: "We propose to give Mr. Frick a dose of his own medicine, and informations against the officials of the company are now being prepared." McLuckie's audacity was cooled by the trial judge who set bail at $10,000 and found that anyone in the town who had made no effort to suppress the "riot" of 6 July was guilty of any crimes that had been committed. The ruling, one paper noted, had "fallen on the late seceded borough with even more depressing weight" than General Snowden's announcement that the troops would remain for an indefinite period.[42]

McLuckie, unlike O'Donnell, continued to enjoy the full support of the town, and his friends quickly provided bail. When he returned to Homestead, thousands cheered him and staged an impromptu parade. McLuckie and other members of the borough council and the Advisory Committee were hoisted onto carriages, and a steelworkers' band, marching behind the American flag, played "Hail to the Chief." General Snowden quickly dispatched an armed guard to end the proceedings. C. K. Bryce, the owner of Bryce, Higbee, and Company's glassworks, who for years had enjoyed good relations with workers, publicly challenged the militia. The parade was entirely peaceful, said Bryce, who had been acting burgess in McLuckie's absence. The militiamen replied that they had specific orders to disperse the crowd; civil authority in Homestead had now passed to General Snowden.[43]

Over the course of the week, county authorities arrested more steelworkers, including O'Donnell, who warned from his jail cell that confinement would kill him because his once rugged constitution had been shattered by recent "exposures" about him in the press. Meanwhile the company stepped up the pace of its initiatives: it evicted more than twenty steelworkers who rented company-owned homes.

Governor Pattison arrived on 21 July, the deadline for union men to reapply at the works, to supervise the annual review of the National Guard, which, he announced, would remain in the town as long as necessary to "settle this fight." While in town, Pattison, who was quartered in Superintendent Potter's house, conferred with company officials and national leaders of the AAISW; he also toured Homestead's Shantytown, the site of some of its worst tenements. Immediately afterward, William McBroom, chief of Carnegie Steel's private police force, evicted another fifty families. Prior to his departure, Pattison announced that General Snowden would no longer be permitted to halt peaceful gatherings. The directive may have pleased some residents, but it had no practical effect, for there were to be no more mass celebrations of worker solidarity in Homestead that summer. Indeed, by 22 July nonunion black and white workers were engaged in a race war inside the Homestead Steel Works.[44]

The employment of black workers by Carnegie Steel effectively marked a new era in the labor practices of the steel industry. In their effort to defeat the Sons of Vulcan in the lockout of 1874–75, owners had hired black puddlers from Richmond, Virginia. But it was not until July 1892, in Homestead, that large numbers of black workers began to enter the steel mills of the industrial North. And the violence that greeted them there was the beginning of a pattern that would endure across the country for decades. Superintendent Potter, in an immediate attempt to lessen tensions among the new workers, promised to build separate housing facilities for the "coloreds."[45]

Racial unrest simmered throughout the summer and fall and finally exploded in a massive antiblack riot on 13 November that saw twothousand whites, many of them East European immigrants, attack the fifty black families who by then were living in Shantytown. "Let's lynch the nigger black sheep. Let's hang 'em," they cried. Although gunfire was exchanged and several people were badly wounded, there were no fatalities. Two days later, however, Mack Schudy, a Hungarian Jew who worked in the mill, shot and instantly killed Pat Coyne, an Irish coworker. Though racism and ethnic tension had always been a part of Homestead, through July 1892 the workers had effectively contained the more virulent expressions of these ugly forces. Thus, in addition to permanently altering the career trajectories of thousands of individual workers, the Homestead Lockout modified the overall quality of race and ethnic relations in—and beyond—the town.

The legacy of the lockout is by no means without its redeeming aspects, however. On 22 July, the very day that black and white scabs squared off within the Homestead Steel Works, the workers' Advisory Committee issued "An Address to the Public" intended to clarify its public position on the great issues of the dispute. Although it embraced many of the key concepts embedded in Boyce's earlier statement on the respective rights of the workers and owners of the Homestead Steel Works, it authorship remains uncertain. O'Donnell, for one, was most certainly not involved, for he had been in New York and then in the Allegheny County jail in the days immediately before publication; more-over, its politics were far too bold for his liking. And though McLuckie's political vision closely corresponded to that of the address, the prose is clearly not his. If it was the product of a single pen, most likely it belonged to William Roberts or, possibly, to the sympathetic though unidentified lawyer in Youngstown. It was once a testimony to the leg-acy of labor republicanism and a departure from it. [46]

The most evident characteristic of our time and country is the phenomenon of industrial centralization, which is putting the control of each of our great national industries into the hands of one or a few men and giving these men an enormous and despotic power over the lives and the fortunes of their employees and subordinates—the great mass of the people; a power which eviscerates our national constitution and our common law and directly an-tagonizes the spirit of universal history in its world-wide struggle after law-ful liberty–a power which, though expressed in terms of current speech as "The right of employers to manage their business to suit themselves," is causing to mean [*sic*] in effect nothing less than a right to manage the country to suit themselves.

The employees in the mill of Messrs. Carnegie, Phipps & Co., at Home-stead, Pa., have built there a town with its homes, its schools and its churches; have for many years been faithful co-workers with the company in the business of the mill; have invested thousands of dollars of their savings in said mill in the expectation of spending their lives in Homestead and of working in the mill during the period of their efficiency.

. . .Therefore, the committee desires to express to the public as its firm belief that both the public and the employees aforesaid have equitable rights and interests in the said mill which cannot be modified or diverted without due process of law; that the employees have the right to continuous employ-ment in the said mill during efficiency and good behavior without regard to religious, political or economic opinions or associations; that it is against pub-lic policy and subversive of the fundamental principles of American liberty that a whole community of workers should be denied employment or suffer any other social detriment on account of membership in a church, a political party or a trade union; that it is our duty as American citizens to resist by every legal and ordinary means the unconstitutional, anarchic and revolutionary policy of the Carnegie Company, which seems to evince a contempt of public and private interests and a disdain of the public conscience. . . .

The committee wish it known that we will prosecute the said public and private interests in the courts of law and equity, and that we demand of

Congress and the State Legislature distinct assertion of the principle that the public has an interest in such concerns as that at Homestead. . . .

Finally, we desire to state emphatically that as defenders of and petitioners for law and order, we pledge ourselves to refrain from violence and lawlessness, and that we rest our cause, which is the people's cause—the cause of American liberty—against anarchy on the one hand and despotism on the other, with the courts, the legislatures and the public conscience.

In the legislatures the cause of the Homestead steelworkers achieved some measure of success. In 1893 the Pennsylvania legislature passed an "anti-Pinkerton" law, which prohibited civil authorities from deputizing nonresidents of the state; within a year, twelve other states had enacted similar measures. But the effectiveness of this legislation in circumscribing the activities of the Pinkerton National Detective Agency was limited; companies were still free to hire private guards in labor disputes. Carnegie Steel, for one, found other means to protect its interests. As early as September 1892 it succeeded in persuading Sheriff McCleary to deputize its own policemen so that scabs could be protected on the streets of Homestead.[47]

In the courts the steelworkers found that their cause met considerable hostility. Though no jury would convict any of them for murder, riot, or conspiracy (only Jack Clifford, Hugh O'Donnell, and Sylvester Critchlow were ever tried on these charges) the judiciary proved unsympathetic; trial judges uniformly spoke out against the workers, and their charges to juries were unabashedly hostile. One of the most sensational cases arising from the lockout involved Hugh Dempsey, the master workman of District Assembly no. 3 of the Knights of Labor. An active supporter of the AAISW at Homestead, he was found guilty of conspiring to poison nonunion workers in the mill. The prosecution's star witness at one point recanted his story, avowing that employees of Carnegie Steel had suborned perjured testimony from him. But Dempsey's conviction stood, and he served seven year in prison.[48]

Many of the Homestead workers, unable to raise sufficient funds for bail, were incarcerated for extended periods, and a number of those who had helped lead the sympathy strike at Duquesne also received prison sentences. But all prosecutions ceased when, following O'Donnell's acquittal in February 1893, Philander Knox, who had played a key role in the prosecution, engineered an agreement with what remained of the Advisory Committee: the workers dropped the murder charges McLuckie and Hugh Ross had brought against Frick and other company officials in return for an equivalent action from Knox and the district attorney.

The most astonishing of all the cases involving the steelworkers was instigated by Knox, who, acting on a suggestion offered by General

Snowden and in close consultation with Chief Justice Edward Paxson of the Pennsylvania Supreme Court, prepared charges of treason against thirty-three members of the Advisory Committee. Knox submitted his briefs to the Supreme Court for its private consideration sometime in July; he based them on Pennsylvania's Crimes Act of 1860, which held that any citizen of the state who levied "war" against it or aided its "enemies" was guilty of treason and could be sentenced to twelve years in prison. This statute, never before invoked, had been aimed at those who might have been inclined to aid the Confederacy. In the hands of Knox and Paxson—himself a close friend as of Christopher L. Magee— the law found a novel interpretation indeed.[49]

Sitting in Pittsburgh for the fall term of the Supreme Court, Paxson, after conferring with Knox, decided that the Homestead workers, by virtue of their usurpation of civil authority prior to the arrival of the state militia, their denial of the rights of new workers to find employment in the mill, and their abrogation of Carnegie Steel's property rights, had levied "war, insurrection, and rebellion against the Commonwealth of Pennsylvania." In resisting the Pinkertons they had engaged in "unlawful violence." Indeed, "the moment they attempted to control the works, they placed themselves outside the pale of the law."[50]

Paxson, in an unusual move, brought the treason charges himself, delivering a lengthy indictment from the bench of the Allegheny County Court of Oyer and Terminer that chronicled the "treasonous" actions of the Advisory Committee. Whereas the workers, in their address to the public, had charged Carnegie Steel with pursuing an "unconstitutional, anarchic and revolutionary policy," Paxson declared that it was the committee that had moved to undermine the Republic: "When a large number of men arm and organize themselves by divisions and companies, appoint officers, and engage in common purpose to defy the law, to resist its officers, and to deprive any portion of their fellow citizens of the rights to which they are entitled under the Constitution and the laws, it is levying war against the state, and the offense is treason."

Although Paxson's reasoning won approval from the steel industry's trade journals, some daily newspapers, and the *Nation*, it inspired heated criticism from legal scholars. The *American Law Review* maintained categorically that no reasonable person could comprehend how the actions of the Advisory Committee could be construed as having constituted treason. The labor press, of course, was shocked: "Never before in America has law been so abominably misused. Never, heretofore, has civil authority permitted itself to be employed as a tool to a corporation so palpably." Recognizing the specious character of the indictments, state authorities ultimately decided to forgo prosecution.[51]

Nonetheless, the treason charges discouraged the steelworkers, deepened the financial woes of the Advisory Committee, and indicated to them, and to all Americans, that the state, in partnership with its largest corporate citizens, would go to considerable lengths to ensure the rights and privileges most valued by those citizens. Paxson's declaration that the assertion of workers' rights in Homestead was equivalent to insurrection against the Republic, no less than the workers' address, which set forth and defended those rights, underscored the degree to which the events of 6 July were not determined by simple economics. As even Justice Paxson understood, the logic behind the unruly "carnival of revenge" was undeniably and profoundly political; the residents, he argued, had not acted as "a mere mob" but were plainly guided by a shared consciousness of purpose.[52]

Seen in this light, Homestead illustrates the link in American history—one all too often overlooked—between industrial violence and political protest, for the events of July 1892 presupposed two visions, diametrically opposed, of what the Republic should be. Considered on the level of politics alone, Homestead thus encapsulates a decades-long struggle over what the historian Charles Tilly has called "established places in the structure of power."[53]

As we have seen, however, neither this struggle nor the conflicting visions that informed it was confined to the realm of politics proper. The battle for Homestead dramatized the great cultural entanglements of the era no less than the great questions of politics and labor. Thus it was not entirely fortuitous that Andrew Carnegie began his summer holiday of 1892 by donating a library to Aberdeen and ended it by giving one to Ayr, the latter dedicated in a solemn speech delivered just two days after Justice Paxson's treason warrants were issued in Pittsburgh.[54]

In this speech, Carnegie publicly acknowledged, albeit obliquely, that he had failed to fulfill the promise he had made to himself when, in 1868, as a young man of 33, he vowed to give up his relentless quest for financial success for fear that it would permanently "degrade" him. "I feel more strongly bound than ever to devote the remaining years of my life less to aims ending in self and more to the service of others." That Carnegie understood the events of July 1892 as a result of the dogged pursuit of "aims ending in self" seems unlikely. And whereas he doubtless regretted the course those events had taken, in the end his tender feelings counted for little in the view of the countless commentators, on both sides of the Atlantic, who vilified him.[55]

Like Carnegie, however, even the most vicious of his critics in the daily press and the mainstream political parties failed to identify the malignant ethos of "aims ending in self" as a determining factor in the Homestead Lockout. Carnegie, for his part, continued to preach the "Gospel of Wealth" as the only credible alternative to unbridled individualism: he told the people of Ayr that he was now pledged to use his "surplus wealth and spare time in the manner most likely to produce the greatest good to the masses of people. From these masses comes the wealth which is entrusted to the owner only as administrator."

These words, summing up as they did Carnegie's answer to the inequities of industrial society, elicited a skeptical response from Homestead. Burgoyne wrote that "at the very moment when Mr. Carnegie was speaking [at Ayr], the wealth-givers in his own employ were being hunted down as traitors . . . [and] locked up in jail." The *St. Louis Post-Dispatch* put it this way: "Ten thousand 'Carnegie Public Libraries' would not compensate the country for the direct and indirect evils resulting from the Homestead Lockout."[56]

Little did the editorial writers for the *Post-Dispatch* know—little did Americans know—that just two months before Carnegie Steel locked out its Homestead employees, Carnegie himself had finalized plans for the Carnegie Library of Homestead. In so doing he signaled his intention to fulfill the pledge announced in his dedication of the Braddock library: to change "the present system at Homestead." In a gesture fitting to his tainted philanthropy, he came to Homestead in late April 1892 accompanied by "a Pullman-car-full of his guests," during the preparations he and Frick were making for the lockout, to choose a site for his Homestead benefaction. "Mr. Carnegie selected a rising ground on the poor-farm purchase as the site for a library and music hall building at Homestead similar to the one he erected in Braddock." Thus the Carnegie Library of Homestead, which he would dedicate in 1898, was to be built on the land that Knox, Frick, and Magee had conspired to convey to him; it would rise on the very grounds occupied by the state militia in the summer of 1892.[57]

Though Carnegie did not busy himself worrying about the larger sources of the Homestead conflict, the Advisory Committee in its address to the public clearly indicated that it had. It had been the ostensible right of private individuals to pursue unchecked "aims ending in self" that had led directly to "the phenomenon of industrial centralization" and its attendant concentration of "enormous and despotic power" in the hands of a few Americans. To counter this power it was necessary to assert over and against it the public right.[58]

In affirming this right the Advisory Committee confronted—though clearly it did not resolve—the perplexing dilemma that has stood at the heart of American political culture since colonial times: how to square the pursuit of individual liberty with the protection of the common good. In the era immediately preceding that of Carnegie and the Homestead steelworkers, it had seemed to many Americans that the nation afforded such vast opportunities for advancement to all its citizens that the dilemma did not, in fact, exist. Abraham Lincoln, perhaps more clearly than anyone, embodied this myth of universal self-advancement, and no less a critic than Alexis de Tocqueville maintained that the pursuit of "self interest rightly understood" would, somehow, enable Americans to maintain the proper balance between private and public right.[59]

De Tocqueville, nonetheless, for all his apparent enthusiasm about the American Republic, harbored profound reservations about the future, not only for it but for all democracies, where "personal interest" was bound to become "the principal if not the sole spring of men's actions." The reason was that no one could foretell precisely how "self interest rightly understood" would in fact be understood. De Tocqueville himself feared that secular democracy, unchecked by religious sanctions, would give full vent to the darkest expressions of selfishness. He warned: "It remains to be seen how each man will understand his personal interest. If the members of the community, as they become more equal, become more ignorant and coarse, it is difficult to foresee to what pitch of stupid excesses their selfishness may lead them; and no one can foretell into what disgrace and wretchedness they would plunge themselves lest they should have to sacrifice something of their own well-being to the prosperity of their fellow creatures."[60]

Had he been alive in 1892, de Tocqueville, his longings for the ancien régime notwithstanding, would have acknowledged that his worst fears not only about self-interest but also about a new aristocracy—one based not on inherited wealth but on manufacturing—had indeed been realized. "I am of the opinion . . . that the manufacturing aristocracy which is growing up under our eyes is one of the harshest that ever existed in the world. . . . The friends of democracy should keep their eyes anxiously fixed in this direction; for if ever a permanent inequality of conditions and aristocracy again permeates into the world, it may be predicted that this is the gate by which they will enter."[61]

It is unlikely that the steelworkers of Homestead knew the works of de Tocqueville. A familiarity with *Democracy in America*, however, was not required in order to see that by 1892 glaring inequalities defined the social and political landscape of America and that a forceful aristocracy of "manufactures," as de Tocqueville termed it, had come into being.

This new and seemingly permanent inequality had no place in a republic: this was the central meaning of the Advisory Committee's address, which summed up the hopes and fears of America's nineteenth-century labor movement. In large measure, that movement had been defined by native-born and British and German immigrant workers. But in Homestead, the "new" immigrants, those from Eastern Europe, stood enthusiastically within the republican fold. To say this is not to overlook or undervalue the differences between, say, a Pavel Olšav and a William Roberts. It is merely to recognize that the new immigrants, as Herbert Gutman suggested, "hadn't come to America to be proletarianized." In the 1880s workers such as Olšav and Roberts, workers from very different backgrounds, workers not just in Homestead but all across the country, asked, in Gutman's paraphrase: "What in hell is going on in America? What kind of country is this becoming?" In the eyes of the Homestead Advisory Committee, at least, some form of governmental intervention was necessary to set America back on course, to protect the rights of the public against the zealous assertion of private interest.[62]

Seen in this light, assertions that Homestead's republicanism of 1892 "failed to challenge any of the basic economic institutions of capitalism" or that, because of the deep allegiance that home-owning workers held to the right of private ownership, this republicanism "was less radical" than that of the 1870s, seem off target. To be sure, some workers maintained over the course of the lockout that their cause was rooted in the defense of home. But, as Roberts explained to the Senate investigating committee, in the eyes of the Homestead steelworkers, defense of home was closely tied to resistance against unjust wage reductions, loss of job, and ultimately the company's effort to eliminate the guarantor of a decent dwelling place, salary, and position in the mill, that is, the union. "To be denied the privilege of belonging to an organization that had done so much for them, . . . and . . . to be forced into accepting a reduction that they didn't think was right or just at that time, and then to be confronted with a gang of loafers and cut-throats from all over the country, coming there, as they thought, to take their jobs, why, they naturally wanted to go down and defend their homes and their property and their lives, with force, if necessary."[63]

The formal politics of Roberts's gloss on the events of 6 July found expression in the Advisory Committee's address. Rather than signaling a retreat from the insurgent republicanism of the 1870s, the address embraced it and moved toward an accommodation with an emergent American socialism. This is not to suggest any kind of linear development between the labor republicanism of workers in the Gilded Age, in Homestead or elsewhere, and the vision of Eugene Debs and his supporters (though in Homestead Debs would enjoy considerable support after the turn of the century). Rather, it is to suggest that, in the wake of the lockout of 1892, Homestead workers realized that in order to check and challenge the pressing assault of organized capital, they needed a more aggressive program than the one labor republicanism had bequeathed them. They had, perhaps, finally acknowledged the worst fears of Thomas Armstrong, the tireless editor of the *National Labor Tribune*, who, as early as 1875 had declared: "We find our boasted republicanism of no avail to save us from the oppression of capital. . . . [But] we, as a people, have great faith in republicanism. . . . We will keep on . . . trusting until we find our mistake."[64]

The Homestead workers made no "mistake," however, in clinging to what may, with the benefit of twentieth-century hindsight, be called a residual set of political beliefs and practices. In legitimizing and thus helping to secure a measure of political and workplace autonomy that few workers elsewhere in America enjoyed, republicanism had served the steelworkers of Homestead quite well for more than a decade. During this period they had tried to work within the framework of existing property rights, a framework that was, at this time, simply beyond challenge on the national level.

By 1892 the possibilities for republican justice within this framework seemed exhausted: while the steelworkers continued to see themselves as citizens entitled to a just wage and a decent home, their employers saw them as mere factors of production. In truth, the idea of laborer as citizen versus that of laborer as factor of production amounted to a contradiction that could never be resolved within the competitive wage system. This is the very insight that informed the Advisory Committee's call for state intervention to protect the rights of Homestead workers and of the public in general.[65]

The contemporary opponents of the steelworkers were quick to recognize the menace behind their bold stand. The address of the Advisory Committee smacked of "socialism," said *Iron Age*, the journal of metal manufacturers; its sister publication, the *American Manufacturer*, of like mind, applauded Frick for helping to stamp out the "sentiment of socialism . . . in the ranks of the steelworkers." Predictably, the *Pittsburgh Commercial Gazette*, which spoke for the business community, called the committee's statement "a monstrous doctrine." The *New York Herald*'s reaction to the workers' demands squarely met the limits of late nineteenth-century liberalism head on: the lockout represented much "more than a struggle between an employer and an employee. It has become a conflict between the citizens of Homestead and public authority." In such cases "there can be but one course and one result—the enforcement of the law and the restoration of order."[66]

As publicly threatening as the Advisory Committee's address may have seemed when it first appeared in the press on 23 July, it was another incident that pushed the calls for law and order to fever pitch. For it was on that day, in Carnegie Steel's downtown headquarters, that the anarchist Alexander Berkman, referred to by one paper as a "Russian Hebrew Nihilist," shot and stabbed Henry Clay Frick. Though seriously wounded, Frick helped J. G. A. Leishman, vice president of Carnegie Steel, wrestle Berkman to the floor, then allowed a doctor to remove one bullet from his neck and another from his back without the aid of an anaesthetic. Frick then cabled Carnegie, urging him to remain in Scotland and telling him, "I am still in shape to fight the battle out." He then sat down to finish his day's work, "specifying the final terms of an essential loan which he had been negotiating," his biographer tells us. Finally, before leaving for home in an ambulance, he dictated the following message to the press: "This incident will not change the attitude of the Carnegie Company toward the Amalgamated Association. I do not think I shall die, but whether I do or not, the Company will pursue the same policy and it will win."[67]

Even if Frick had not drawn a connection between the assassination attempt and the AAISW, the union was bound to suffer in the arena of public opinion. The Advisory Committee moved quickly to deflect criticism and passed a resolution that condemned Berkman's action. Nevertheless, the press and the public in general followed Frick's lead in associating the assault with the treasonous cause of the Homestead steelworkers. "The conquered secession of the free and independent borough of Homestead has produced its J. Wilkes Booth. His name is Alexander Berkman. He hails from St. Petersburg via New York." McLuckie, unlike his colleagues on the Advisory Committee, was typically frank in his public reaction to the assassination attempt. In Youngstown to raise money for the locked-out men, McLuckie said: "When I got off the train here this afternoon, I heard that Frick had been shot, but I can't say that I am very sorry. This man Frick sent a lot of thugs and cut-throats into the peaceful village of Homestead, over which I have the honor to preside as burgess, and they murdered my friends and fellow citizens."[68]

"Honest" John was not the only person who shed no tears for Frick. On learning of the attempt on Frick's life, a young state militiamen stationed in Homestead, W. L. Iams, shouted his approval. At the command of General Snowden, Iams was placed in the stockade and then hung by the thumbs. He refused to apologize and, after thirty minutes, passed out. Snowden then ordered that Iams be dishonorably discharged and drummed out of the encampment: "His crime is that of treason. His conduct was aiding, abetting, and giving comfort to our enemy."[69]

Whereas the Iams incident did not have an appreciable effect on the course of the lockout, Berkman's foolish attempt to kill Frick led directly to the demise of the steelworkers' resistance. Again it was O'Donnell who played the central role. In jail on charges of murder when Frick was shot, O'Donnell had grown concerned that his previous trip to New York would be associated with Berkman's assassination attempt. In fact, the *Washington Post* published a story that linked the two men, a story that O'Donnell vehemently denied and for which he threatened to sue. "I shall find out the authors of these stories and punish them." But in private he proceeded in an altogether different direction. He had just been released from jail a few days after the assassination attempt. Understandably frightened, he secretly moved to end the dispute by offering Carnegie Steel what amounted to an unconditional surrender. O'Donnell then arranged to have his plan made public, feigned mild displeasure over the disclosure, and solemnly announced: "This attempted assassination of Mr. Frick, you know, has created a bad impression all over the country, and for the sake of the men, I would recommend an almost unconditional surrender."*70

O'Donnell, without the knowledge of his colleagues on the Advisory Committee, had authorized two newspapermen to confer with Sheriff McCleary and Superintendent Potter about terms for surrender. He had told the reporters, F. D. Madiera of the *New York Recorder* and J. Hampton Moore of the *Philadelphia Public Ledger,* to inform Potter that the steelworkers were willing to return to work on the company's terms; they simply wanted their jobs back. Potter was pleased to hear the news, but he informed Madiera and Moore that roughly 160 men, the most prominent union members, would never be rehired by Carnegie Steel. When word got out that O'Donnell had offered to surrender, the Advisory Committee immediately convened, declined O'Donnell's invitation to hear a "report" on the meeting of Potter, Madiera, and Moore, officially censured O'Donnell, and then, after an acrimonious debate, replaced him, permanently this time, by electing Thomas Crawford as chairman.

All of Homestead was astounded by what O'Donnell had done, and he himself was shaken to the point of physical collapse at his own cravenness. When he emerged from the committee's meeting he nervously denied that he had offered to surrender; he had only been "joking." O'Donnell assured the press that he had not been replaced as chairman and that he planned to leave town "for a seaside resort" only because of "exhaustion." But the truth was that he had been unceremoniously removed for his "joke."

The *New York Sun* summed up the effects of O'Donnell's private initiative to end the lockout this way: "Through the efforts to two newspapermen to bring about the settlement of the strike, the weakness of the men, the discordance of the Advisory Committee, the strength of the company, and above all Hugh O'Donnell's fall from power, have come out in a light that was unexpected and sudden." The *New York Herald,* which often invoked the metaphor of Southern secession in its attempts to explain the Homestead "treason," wrote, under the banner headline, "Leader Hugh No Longer," that O'Donnell's mistake signaled the beginning of "the reconstruction period in the borough of Homestead." O'Donnell himself told the *Herald* that the cause was lost. Pathetically, two years later, in a letter to Professor Edward Bemis of the University of Chicago, he maintained that he could not fathom why he had been "misunderstood and maligned by an unthinking crowd—a modern Ishmael doomed to wander in the desert of ingratitude."71

In the wake of O'Donnell's downfall, and with railroad cars and river tugs arriving each day with new workers, the Advisory Committee was racked by increasing tensions and problems. By 12 August, Superintendent Potter claimed that the Homestead Steel Works were officially back in business and that seventeen hundred men were now working there.

McLuckie, Roberts, and other leaders set out on numerous speaking tours in an effort to raise funds, but when the AFL declined to call a boycott of Carnegie products, the men knew they would never last the winter. By the first week of September, Olšav could no longer claim that his fellow East European immigrants were holding the line. And Crawford acknowledged that the Advisory Committee no longer had any influence whatsoever over "the Huns and the Slavs." Clearly, the interethnic solidarity had by this time all but vanished. By 13 October the situation was well enough in control, in the view of General Snowden, for him to order an end to the "occupation" of Homestead. It had lasted ninety-five days.[72]

McLuckie spent a good part of the ninety-five days in Youngstown, chiefly to avoid incarceration. He resigned as burgess of Homestead on 7 November, amid reports of mass union defections. Ten days later, "the first big break" occurred as 300 of the locked-out men applied for work and were rehired. Soon after, Crawford, still publicly denying that resistance had collapsed, was making plans to leave town. On Sunday 20 November the steelworkers convened what would be their last mass meeting. Only 192 attended; Crawford, one of the most steadfast of the union men, was not among them: he had resigned as chairman of the Advisory Committee to take a new position in Uniontown. By a vote of 101 to 91, his former colleagues decided to go back to work on the company's terms. The Homestead Lockout was over.[73]

In the wake of the AAISW's calamitous defeat in 1892, labor in Homestead veered away from the insurgency that had guided it through the 1880s, and moved toward an overt accommodation with business. In this regard the fate of Reid Kennedy was not atypical. He worked as a screw-down in the 32-inch slabbing mill at the time of the lockout; a member of the Advisory Committee, he was indicted for riot, conspiracy, and treason. In the late 1890s, Kennedy was elected burgess, but by then spoke for the dominant values of the "new" Homestead. Indeed, it was he who, on behalf of the town, personally accepted what he characterized as Carnegie's splendid gift of a library in 1898. Kennedy called the building "a temple of education and knowledge," a monument to the "pleasant relations of Homestead workers to their employers," and an "example that capital was engaged in dividing with their workmen the fruits of their labor."[74]

Too often workers such as Kennedy have been blamed for a putatively cowardly turn to conservatism at the end of the nineteenth century. As the adventure of the labor movement in Homestead illustrates, however, the retreat to a more conservative trade unionism reflects less a growing enthusiasm for the emergent corporate order than what the historian James Holt wisely called "a resigned acknowledgement that in a land where . . . the big corporations ruled supreme in industry, accommodation was more appropriate than confrontation." In this sense, the situation in Homestead must be read as the exemplary, rather than exceptional, episode in modern American labor history.[75]

The defeat of Homestead's stillborn republic of labor, for all it might teach us of the limits of labor republicanism in industrial America, did not represent a weakness of purpose or even organization on the part of its citizens. As Holt argues, the lockout showed all Americans "that a great corporation could refuse to negotiate with a strong trade union, use the most oppressive strike-breaking tactics available, and ignore the flood of adverse publicity which resulted." Ultimately, Homestead points to the immeasurable power of men such as Frick and Carnegie, who, with the full support of their allies in government—Magee, to name but one—could crush a united and determined community.[76]

By the end of the lockout, employers found themselves where they wanted to be, in the saddle, not only in Homestead but all across the country. They had won the right "to manage their business to suit themselves," which, as the Advisory Committee had feared, quickly came to mean managing "the country to suit themselves." The spirit of many workers, like that of John Miller, was broken; it was said that Homestead became a place where, "if you want to talk, . . . you must talk to yourself."[77]

And workers were well warned to keep their more serious thoughts to themselves. By the mid 1890s, Carnegie Steel was operating a sophisticated internal espionage system that monitored the work and leisure habits of its employees. A letter from J. R. Mack, head of the company's Bureau of Information, to an operative, Scott McCollough, more than hints at the labor practices of the post-1892 managerial regime. "Dear Sir, We are advised, and on pretty good authority, that there is a move on foot to organize the Structural and Shop men in all the Bridge Works in this district. Please keep your eyes and ears open, and the minute you get into anything of this kind, advise us at once. Be especially particular to give the names of any one connected with this movement." Company spies notwithstanding, a small core of committed workers remained defiant beyond their defeat. McLuckie, for one, no longer living in Homestead, returned there in 1894 to help Elmer Bales, a fellow member of the Advisory committee from 1892, rally the town's Populists. It was to be "Honest" John's last visit to Homestead.[78]

Though it was McLuckie who, in carrying to Homestead the cooperative vision shared by the AAISW and the Knights of Labor in the 1870s, embodied the insurgent spirit of the town through the lockout of 1892, other individuals, quite different from him typified the spirit of accommodation with which many, Kennedy included, would make their peace. By 1892, David R. Jones, the ex-checkweighman and former burgess of

Homestead who had helped organize the Monongahela miners for the Knights of Labor, was living in a two-story mansion in Homestead and enjoying the fruits of a respectable law practice. His eyes fixed on finical opportunity, Jones held property valued at close to $11,000.[79]

Needless to say, scores of other individuals who resided in Homestead and Pittsburgh and had once campaigned along with McLuckie and Jones for the cause of labor reform also reconciled themselves with the industrial order. Robert Layton, who, as national secretary and treasurer of the Knights of Labor, had privately declared his allegiance to socialism in the early 1880s, was by 1892 working on behalf of corporate America. In the presidential election of 1888, he campaigned for the successful Republican candidate, Benjamin Harrison, along with "Beeswax" Taylor and Christopher Magee. For his efforts, Layton was rewarded with a well-paid patronage appointment; he became Harrison's immigration inspector for Greater Pittsburgh and in that capacity inspected the Homestead Steel Works in August 1892 to ensure that no aliens were working there in violation of the federal anticontract labor law. To his pleasure, he was able to report that Carnegie Steel was in strict compliance with all immigration statutes. Moreover, he publicly announced that the company was doing all it could "to ensure the health and comfort" of the men hired to replace the locked-out steelworkers. Ten years later, Layton rode at the front of Pittsburgh's Labor Day Parade. Next to him sat William Brennen, the former ironworker and attorney for the AAISW, who had become chairman of the county Democratic party.[80]

The activities of men such as Kennedy, David R. Jones, Layton, and Brennen have largely faded from public memory. So, too, have the dealings of Taylor, whose life encapsulates the contradictory paths of these and so many other nineteenth-century labor activists. In light of the events of 1892, the curious lives of these individuals oblige us to reframe old questions and rethink just what it means to straddle the line between resistance to and accommodation with the emerging order of corporate America.

To consider the puzzling logic of resistance and accommodation is to step beyond the tired question of class and begin to confront the ways all spheres of life reinforce relations of domination and subordination by making them seem natural. It is to step beyond questions of cooptation versus willing consent, strategic versus ideological shortcomings, or state coercion versus false (or even "divided") consciousness. It is, rather, to begin to consider, as the historian Joyce Appleby suggests, "the complex way that human beings initiate actions, comply with conventions, and dissent from norms." It is to begin to consider, as we have here for the workers of Homestead, the sources of personal and collective empowerment that individuals and collectivities draw on when they dare to challenge received structures of power and authority. And it is to begin to consider the sources of deference to that power and authority.[81]

For workers trying to bring into balance individual and public rights—no less than for us, trying to make sense of this balancing act— the battle for Homestead posed all the big questions but in the end provided no sure answers. Even for Andrew Carnegie, the man who stood as the country's most forceful and convincing proponent of the wage system, Homestead left some questions unresolved. In response to Frick's cables informing him that the lockout ended with a victory for the company, Carnegie had responded: "Life worth living again! . . . Europe has rung with Homestead, Homestead, until we are all sick of the name, but it is all over now." Try as he might, however, Carnegie would never be able to part with Homestead. Indeed, when he returned to the United States from his extended European holiday of 1892, he immediately set off for the town. There, in the first of many disingenuous efforts to make rhetorical peace with its residents, he told a gathering of his employees that there had been "no genuine victory for either side" in the recent lockout, "only the defeat of both." Employers and employees, he said, were like "twin brothers."[82]

When Carnegie traveled to Homestead in 1898 to dedicate his library, he told Kennedy and his fellow townspeople that the day marked an occasion to which he had "long looked forward." Never had there been so long a lapse between a promise he had made and its fulfillment. The reason was that the "Homestead Works were probably the most difficult we ever had anything to do with"; the workers "were not such men as we have been blessed with at our other works, and such as we now rejoice in having here." So dreadful a place was pre-1892 Homestead and its steelworks, he sighed, that "many good man were sent from our other works, only to return, giving as their reasons that it was no place for their wives and children, nor even for themselves."[83]

Although the lockout had paved the way for better conditions in the town and the mill, Carnegie was forced to acknowledge that the event was "deplorable" for him. It was "the one great pain . . . which startled us when far away, and which even yet has not lost its power to sadden our lives." Giving the library to Homestead allowed him at long last to devote sacredly the very first returns he had earned in the town to an appropriate cause. "As it was by the labor of my hands I first earned my living," he concluded, "my title to the name of workingman must pass unchallenged in any part of this world. Take, therefore, this building as the gift of one workingman to other workingmen. . . . Under our social and political system, labor is noble." Carnegie, ever the master of appropriating key ideas and imparting to them his own unique meanings (and nonmeanings), had for years worked to thwart the political vision that lay behind workers' affirmations that "labor is noble." In Homestead and elsewhere he had stood against the efforts of workers to achieve the material embodiment of that nobility, a competence. And yet he vowed that a competence was all he ever wanted. All citizens should seek "a competency for the reasonable and necessary wants of life for yourself and those dependent upon you, without which . . . no man can be independent, scarcely honest." Having achieved his competence, workingman Carnegie explained, he then devoted his time to considering the problem of wealth and how to distribute it.[84]

Carnegie offered these comments to the curators of Pittsburgh's politics, culture, and commerce. Well beyond the achievement of mere competences of their own, these men no doubt stood in awe of the simple Scotsman whose steel companies would earn a handy $5 million in profits in 1895, $21 million in 1899, and go on to double that figure just one year later.[85]

Although Carnegie repeatedly denied that there had been a winner in the Homestead Lockout, the American public, not to mention Carnegie's own personal secretary, took a rather different view. It was common knowledge that the monumental profits earned by Carnegie Steel in the 1890s grew directly from the defeat of unionism at Homestead. "It is believed by the Carnegie officials, and with some show of reason," James H. Bridge wrote, "that this magnificent record was to a great extent made possible by the company's victory at Homestead." Without the encumbrance of the union, Carnegie was able to slash wages, impose twelve-hour workdays, eliminate five hundred jobs, and suitably assuage his republican conscience with the endowment of a library.

When, near the end of his life, Carnegie looked back on the events of July 1892, he sadly concluded that they had been unnecessary. Given his own ambition and the demands it placed on him—which included running the Homestead Works to suit himself—given, indeed, the ambitious demands of personal advancement that he helped legitimize for so many Americans, there was, however, little of the incidental about the Homestead Lockout.[86]

Just a few years before Carnegie penned his famous note about the pitfalls of self-advancement, another committed republican author, Herman Melville, had cautioned Americans that their inextricably linked personal ambition and mindless fascination with the powers of technology posed dire threats to the Republic: "Like negroes, these powers own man sullenly; mindful of their higher master; while serving, plot revenge. The world is apoplectic with high-living of ambition; and apoplexy has its fall. Seeking to conquer a larger liberty, man but extends the empire of necessity."[87]

This book has explored some of the necessary implications of the ethos of ambition and uncritical technological advancement and the way in which, in no small way, Andrew Carnegie and his associates endeavored to portray this "high-living of ambition" as the equivalent of liberty itself. Although Carnegie loved books and enjoyed chatting with literary figures, he appears never to have encountered Melville or any of his works. Even if he had, it is doubtful that he, the ostensible winner of 1892, could have heeded Melville's warnings. That we may be similarly heedless points to a still greater loss than that suffered by the residents of Homestead one hundred years ago and, potentially, to a still greater national tragedy than the Homestead Lockout of 1892.[88]

Appendices
Abbreviations
Notes
Bibliography
Index

Appendix A

What Is Steel?

Henry Bessemer's invention of a process to manufacture iron "without fuel" raised many metallurgical problems. It also raised semantic and commercial ones. Bessemer's method of inexpensively producing a malleable yet strong metal without the labor of puddlers called into question definitions of iron and steel that had held for centuries. Indeed, the development of Bessemer steelmaking sparked a controversy in the ranks of American and British metalmakers about the very meaning of iron and steel.[1]

The controversy arose mainly because the manufacturers who used the Bessemer process, which its inventor initially said would yield malleable iron, decided, for marketing purposes, to call their product steel. Alexander Holley, who invented the modern Bessemer steel mill, was among the leading advocates of the name *steel* for the product. On the other side of the controversy were some of the leading chemists and metallurgists in the international metalmaking community, who wanted to maintain the traditional definitions of iron and steel that were based not only on the characteristics of the metals, but also on the methods of production.[2]

Holley, among others, urged the AIME and other professional engineering organizations to adopt a definition of steel that would embrace all compounds of iron that had been cast and were malleable. According to Holley, the classification *wrought iron* would include any malleable metal that was not cast but made from a "pasty mass." Thus the product of the Bessemer converter would be steel. Holley hoped that by virtue of this name, the metal would acquire a heightened value over its chief competitor, the wrought iron that puddlers made from a pasty mass.

Prior to the development of the Bessemer process, the definitions of iron and steel held that steel was a product situated about halfway between cast iron and wrought iron. Steel, though, possessed few if any of the disadvantages of cast or wrought iron, and most if not all of their advantages.

The production of cast and wrought iron, and of steel, began by smelting iron ore in a blast furnace. The resulting product was known either as cast iron or pig iron, depending on its use. Cast iron was essentially a finished product. Metal from a blast furnace designated as cast iron was poured into molds of various shapes and then sold. Because cast iron contained a relatively high amount of carbon (2.5–4.5 percent), it was very hard and very brittle and could therefore be

365

shaped only by pouring it into a mold. And because cast iron could not bear much stress, it could be used only for those products subject to minimal compression and torsion.

During the seventeenth and eighteenth centuries in Western Europe, the demand rose for products that were larger and capable of withstanding greater stress; these therefore could be made only from a material more malleable, elastic, and ductile than cast iron. The material that fitted these needs was called wrought iron, and it was refined from the product of the blast furnace known as pig iron. Pig iron thus was an intermediate product that required further working to be transformed into malleable iron.

Beginning in the 1780s, the overwhelming portion of wrought iron was made by puddling and rolling. Puddling consisted substantially of heating and stirring pig iron in a furnace to bring its carbon content to below 0.1 percent, and usually to within a range of 0.01–0.08 percent. Such metal was malleable and ductile, whereas cast iron, with its higher carbon content, was hard and brittle. Steel, which possessed anywhere from about 0.07 to about 2 percent carbon, was both hard and malleable as well as ductile.[3]

While the carbon content of steel gave it distinctive qualities, the microscopic arrangement of its chemical constituents was in reality the primary characteristic that distinguished it from both cast and wrought iron. However, the manufacture of steel did not depend on a precise knowledge of the molecular composition of metals; for centuries, metalmakers produced steel in ignorance of its inner structure. The peculiarities of the inner structure were rooted in the proportions of carbon, phosphorus, silicon sulphur, and other components of the metal, by the intensity and duration of its exposure to heat during processing, and by the relative length and abruptness of the methods used to cool it after it had been refined to possess the desired amount of carbon.[4]

Thus it was carbon content that set the perimeters of what differentiated steel from both cast and wrought iron. By the mid 1800s most metallurgists maintained that steel was any refined metal that was at once malleable and strong and had a carbon content between that of cast iron and wrought iron. Its definition therefore was arbitrary. As one prominent metallurgist put it, "It cannot even be said where steel begins or ends."[5]

It is possible, however, to gain an understanding of what constituted steel, both for commercial purposes and within the broad realm of public discourse, by surveying the most important methods of production as they were carried out prior to the introduction of the Bessemer process.

Through the late 1800s steel could be made by one of three methods. First, it could be extracted directly from iron ore; second, it could be refined from pig iron; third, it could be made from wrought iron. In each case the goal was to produce a metal that had less carbon than cast iron but more than wrought iron. For a variety of reasons, this goal was difficult to reach by direct extraction from the ore or by refining pig iron. Steelmaking by means of adding carbon to wrought iron therefore was the method of choice, even though wrought iron achieved its distinctive qualities by means of reducing the carbon content of pig iron.[6]

The manufacture of steel, then, usually began only after the manufacture of wrought iron. Prior to 1856, when Bessemer developed the process that bears his name, most steel was made either by cementation or by the crucible method.

The cementation process, which yielded a product called blister steel, had its origins in antiquity. The modern practice, outlined in 1722 by the great French metallurgist René-Antoine Ferchault de Réaumur, consisted of packing wrought iron bars together with charcoal dust—called cement—into long boxes lined with firebrick. The boxes were covered and subjected to intense heat. Though the iron bars did not melt, they became hot enough to interact with the cement and to absorb some carbon from it. Making blister steel sometimes took as long as twelve days: it took about two days to heat the furnace to the temperatures required, and it took as many as ten days for the iron bars to absorb adequate amounts of carbon. Moreover, because the wrought iron bars did not melt and because they absorbed carbon from the outside, the carbon content of blister steel ranged from a high level on the surface to a low level in the core. In fact, the core of some grades of blister steel remained wrought iron.[7]

The heterogeneity of blister steel led steelmakers to look for a process than would yield a more even product. One such method was to break blister steel into pieces, pile them into a "faggot," heat it to a welding temperature, and then hammer it into a bar of steel that, because of the additional processing, had a more even distribution of carbon. Steel made in this way was called shear steel. If a higher-quality metal of greater homogeneity was required, the bars of shear steel could be "sheared" or broken again, reheated, and then rehammered. In Britain in the 1800s, twice-hammered shear steel was the best. In Germany shear steel was broken, heated, and hammered so many times that some bars consisted of 320 separate layers of steel. "This kind of work took time."[8]

Though shear steel attained a greater degree of homogeneity than blister steel, it still remained an inadequate material for intricately shaped products that required a uniform quality of metal throughout. The problem of heterogeneity was initially addressed by Benjamin Huntsman, a British watch- and clock-maker, who found a way of producing steel of a more uniform quality. His innovation, the crucible process, was the one significant advance in steelmaking of the Industrial Revolution. The manufacture of crucible steel, though, was even more labor- and capital-intensive than the cementation method, for crucible steel had to be made from blister steel.[9]

Huntsman's innovation, in effect a recovery of a method practiced in ancient India, consisted of melting blister steel bars and then casting the molten metal. The blister bars were broken into small pieces and packed into firebrick-lined crucibles, or pots, which then were placed in a furnace. As the heating progressed, workers added a special flux to the crucibles to draw off chemical impurities. Then the steel would be "teemed" into ingot molds.[10]

Refining steel by the crucible process yielded a metal that was superior to all others. Yet crucible steelmaking was very expensive and difficult to execute, particularly in the United States, where clay suitable for use in the crucibles was hard to find; therefore the importance of crucible steel as a commercial product paled in comparison to that of wrought iron. However, the crucible technique foreshadowed steelmaking in the era of mass production, for it made possible the manufacture of extremely large pieces of metal even though each crucible usually held no more than sixty pounds: the contents of several crucibles could be poured into a single huge mold.[11]

The manufacture of such products demanded the coordination of hundreds of tasks, many of which required highly skilled labor. Moreover, great skill was also required in the finishing processes that followed. Unlike wrought iron, though, cast steel was not rolled. Because it was less malleable, workers used large hammers to shape it. Often the ingots had to be reheated and then rehammered to achieve the desired shape, and maintaining the proper heat was always a vexing problem. As a contemporary treatise put it, "to hit the exact heat required . . . is a matter of extreme delicacy, . . . [and] no amount of attention is superfluous."[12]

The production of cast steel, then, required even more—much more— expertise than the manufacture of its "raw material," wrought iron: quality cast steel depended, first, on the production of quality wrought iron and, second, on the production of quality blister steel. Cast steel therefore was not only difficult to make but also very expensive. It was, though, a superior metal—and one with which the product of the Bessemer converter could not compete for items demanding the traditional attributes of steel.[13]

Appendix B

The Homestead Census of 1880

James MacDonald, Sr., a retired glassworker, served as federal census enumerator for Homestead in 1880. His findings suggest that the demographics of Homestead, like its politics, were dominated by workers in 1880. Of 592 residents, 144, all but 1 of them men, earned their livelihood by doing manual labor, and over half of these pursued occupations that required considerable skill. The glassworkers who labored at Bryce, Higbee, and Company constituted the largest category of wage earners, and the 140 wives, mothers, and children who performed domestic work comprised the largest category of laborers.[1]

Homestead's census figures for 1880 also reveal that native-born Americans (499) far outnumbered immigrants (93). The numerical dominance of native-born and also of Pennsylvania-born Homesteaders—84 percent and 79 percent, respectively—suggests that the town was thoroughly American in 1880.

This conclusion, however, runs counter to a more detailed analysis, for almost 40 percent of the native-born had foreign-born parents. Together with the immigrant residents, those who were first-generation Americans comprised a majority (54 percent) of the population. First-generation Americans and immigrants also predominated in the ranks of the town's wage-earners: 58 percent of all workers were born abroad or had at least one foreign-born parent. Indeed, immigrants and first-generation Americans constituted a majority in each subcategory of the work force: skilled laborer, unskilled laborer, skilled glassworker, and glassworker.[2]

Thus the federal census of 1880 shows that Homestead was, to a large degree, an Old World town. Among the immigrants from Europe, those who left the British Isles held a substantial numerical dominance, constituting 61 percent of the foreign-born.

OVERVIEW:

Total population: 592
   Male: 303
   Female: 289

Total married: 213 (36%)
   Male: 109 (51%)
   Female: 104 (49%)
Total infants and school-aged children: 240 (41%)

Native-born: 499 (84%)
  Male: 255
  Female: 244
  Born in Pennsylvania: 465 (79%)

Immigrants: 93 (16%)
  Male: 48
  Female: 45

Residents with at least one non-native parent: 228 (39%)

Total, first-generation American and immigrant: 321 (54%)
  Male: 169
  Female: 152

Total, both parents native: 271 (46%)
  Male: 134
  Female: 137

White: 586 (99%)
Black: 6 (1%)

Head of Household:
  Male: 103
  Female: 4

  Native: 69 (64%)
  Immigrant: 39 (36%)

  With at least one non-native parent: 22
  Total, first-generation American and immigrant: 61 (56%)

Total dwellings: 97

NATIVE & NON-NATIVE RESIDENTS, BY AGE & GENDER

Age	Total	Male	Female	Native	Non-native
0–21	320	155	165	312	8
22–50	231	126	105	164	67
51–80	40	22	18	22	18
TOTAL		303	288	499	93

Note: The age of one female is not listed in the census.

IMMIGRANTS' PLACE OF BIRTH:

  Ireland: 21
  Germany: 32
  England: 25
  Scotland: 1

Wales: 10
France: 3
Switz.: 1

  Total: 93

OCCUPATIONS:

Iron molder: 2
Skilled glassworker: 14
Glassworker: 37 (includes one female)
  Total glassworkers: 51
Laborer: 33
Skilled laborer (includes caulker,
carpenter, blacksmith, etc.): 58

Total, laborer and skilled laborer: 144
  Native: 107
  Immigrant: 37
    Irish: 11
    German: 12
    English: 7
    Welsh: 5
    French: 2
  Total, first-generation
      American and immigrant: 84 (58%)

Total, skilled workers: (includes skilled laborers,
iron moulders and skilled glassworkers): 74
  Native: 54
  Immigrant: 20
  Total, first-generation
      American and immigrant: 38 (51%)

Total, unskilled: 70
  Native: 53
  Immigrant: 17
  Total, first-generation American and immigrant: 46 (66%)

Glassworkers: 51
  Native: 46
  Immigrant: 5
  Total, first-generation American and immigrant: 33 (65%)

Skilled glassworkers: 114
  Native: 10
  Immigrant: 4
  Total, first-generation American and immigrant: 10 (71%)

Housekeeper: 140 (all female)
School: 114
Infant; non-school: 126
Servant: 14 (all female)
Merchant: 16
Farmer: 3
Manufacturer: 2
Minister: 1
Clerk: 4
Dressmaker: 1 (female)
Physician: 1
Teacher: 1
Barber: 2 (includes apprentice; both black)
Indentured servant: 1 (male)
Retired: 3
Attorney: 1
Saloon keeper: 2
Hotelier: 1
Salesman: 1

Appendix C

Homestead Steelworkers, 1880–1882

Materials about the first Homestead steelworkers that would yield quantifiably satisfying information are unfortunately not available, for two reasons. First, because operations at the PBSW did not commence until 1881, virtually no steelworkers who settled in Homestead appear in the 1880 population schedules of the federal census. Second, none of the extensive employee records maintained by Andrew Carnegie has survived: the repositories of Carnegie's archives maintained by the USX Corporation, the Library of Congress, and the New York Public Library contain materials with but scant mention of workers' names and jobs. Similarly, the papers of Charles Schwab, who managed the Homestead Steel Works beginning in the late 1880s and subsequently directed Carnegie Steel, contain no employee records. (Schwab's papers are at the Hagley Museum in Wilmington, Del.) Henry Clay Frick, himself a careful record keeper, may have maintained employee files from pre-1892 Homestead, but the Helen Clay Frick Foundation, which oversees his papers, has repeatedly denied access to them.

In an effort to compensate for these difficulties, I conducted an informal census of my own. Based principally on the weekly and monthly newspapers published in Homestead, the daily press of Pittsburgh, the *National Labor Tribune*, various church records, and the *Proceedings* of the AAISW, my census surveys approximately one-third of those men engaged in the production of steel in Homestead from 1880 through the spring of 1882, when the mill employed approximately five hundred laborers. Details about workers whose names appear even in multiple sources were hard to come by. And because the sources heavily favored union members, even less can be said regarding hundreds of their less skilled co-workers. What follows, then, is a necessarily incomplete overview.

TOTAL COUNTED: 166

LEADERS (13)

Barkly, George	James, John P.
Blanford, Edward	Jones, John Elias
Fitzgerald, George	Lysett, Martin

373

McFarland, P.
Miller, John
O'Donnell, John J.
Olšav, Pavel

Rattigan, John
Redpath, Alexander
Thomas, John

Leaders who belonged to Homestead Lodge 11 (Rail Mill), AAISW (6)

Barkly, George
Blanford, Edward
James, John P.

Jones, John Elias
Lysett, Martin
Thomas, John

Leaders who belonged to Munhall Lodge 24 (Converting and Blooming Mills), AAISW (4)

Fitzgerald, George
Miller, John

Rattigan, John
Redpath, Alexander

Members of the AAISW (48)

Barkly, Charles
Barkly, George (roller)
Blanford, Edward
Boniface, George
Bulmer, Robert
Casey, William
Critchlow, Albert
Cush, Thomas (hooker)
Cush, William
Davis, Morgan (heater)
Evans, Thomas
Fitzgerald, George
Gamble, Harry (heater)
Gardner, Thomas
Glorey, George N.
Griffiths, Charles
Harrigan, M. J.
Havican, John G.
James, John P.
Jones, Isaac (roller)
Jones, John Elias (roller)
Korbler, Andrew
Lewis, John
Lloyd, Evan (catcher)

Lysett, Martin
Maddock, Thomas
Maloney, George
Maloney, James
Maloney,Thomas
McFarland, P.
Miller, John
Montague, James
Murphy, Matthew
Murray, Martin
O'Donnell, John J.
Parry, William
Price, William
Quinn, Patrick
Rattigan, John
Redpath, Alexander
Reynolds, Milton
Stevick, Adam
Sullivan, J. J.
Sweeney, Michael
Thomas, John
Williams, Albert
Williams, Thomas R. (heater)
Williams, William

Members of Lodge 11 (18)

Barkly, George
Blanford, Edward
Davis, Morgan
Griffiths, Charles

James, John P.
Jones, Isaac
Jones, John Elias
Korbler, Andrew

Lloyd, Evan
Lysett, Martin
Maddock, Thomas
Maloney, James
Murphy, Matthew

Parry, William
Price, William
Sweeney, Michael
Thomas, John
Williams, William

Members of Lodge 24 (7)

Boniface, George
Fitzgerald, George
Havican, John G.
Miller, John

Quinn, Patrick
Rattigan, John
Redpath, Alexander

Members of the Michael Davitt Branch of the Irish National Land League (all members of the AAISW) (6)

Havican, John G.
Jones, John Elias
McFarland, P.

O'Donnell, John J.
Rattigan, John
Redpath, Alexander

Strikers, 1882 (all AAISW members) (32)

Barkly, Charles
Barkly, George
Blanford, Edward
Boniface, George
Casey, William
Cush, William
Evans, Thomas
Fitzgerald, George
Gardner, Thomas
Griffiths, Charles
Harrigan, M. J.
Jones, Isaac (roller)
Jones, John Elias
Korbler, Andrew
Lewis, John
Lloyd, Evan (catcher)

Lysett, Martin
Maddock, Thomas
Maloney, James
McFarland, P.
Miller, John
Murphy, Matthew
O'Donnell, John J.
Parry, William
Price, William
Rattigan, John
Reynolds, Milton
Stevick, Adam
Sullivan, J. J.
Sweeney, Michael
Thomas, John
Williams, William

Strike leaders (10)

Barkly, George
Blanford, Edward
Fitzgerald, George
Jones, John Elias
Lysett, Martin

McFarland, P.
Miller, John
O'Donnell, John J.
Rattigan, John
Thomas, John

Those who worked during the strike (24)

Brush, Harvey (foreman)
Chidlow, Thomas (policeman)

Clark, F. L. (chemist)
Clark, William (manager)

Davis
Dickson, Robert P. (laborer)
Dickson, William Brown (laborer)
Floyd, William (foreman)
Fowley, John
Gamble, Harry (heater)
Grayther, Thomas
Haven, Kirt
Healy, Henry (carpenter)
Hooker

Kelly, James S.
Kelly, William E.
Killcrere, William (machinist)
Knauff, Joseph
Knauff, Richard
Marsden, Isaac
McCaffery, John (policeman)
McCarty, Jerry
McKay, Angus
Orr, R. J. (policeman)

Identified as supervisors accountable strictly to management (30)

Bealis, Max (clerk)
Beaty, Thomas W. (clerk)
Brown, Bobby
Brush, Harvey (manager)
Burkenbush, Charles (supervisor)
Burns, Frank X. (clerk)
Cabbot, J. W.
Chidlow, Thomas (policeman)
Clark, F. L. (chemist/assistant general
    manager)
Clark, William (general manager)
Dixon (clerk)
Donovan, Tim (railroad track man-
    ager)
Fleegar, J. B. (clerk)
Hanlon, Michael (policeman)
Humbert, George J. (clerk/
    weighmaster)

Irwin, Larry (inspector)
Mackey, David (clerk)
McDonald, Robert (clerk)
McCaffery, John (policeman)
Morrison, Al (supervisor)
Naughton, Harry (clerk)
Naughton, J. Ambrose (clerk)
Nichols, David (paymaster)
Northcraft, John (supervisor)
Orr, R. J. (policeman)
Reif, Adam (clerk)
Reynolds, (clerk)
Taylor, Charles S. (chemist)
Van Gordon, Grant (clerk)
Williams, David (plant supervisor/
    general manager)

Appendix D

Homestead Glassworkers, 1879–1882

Total, 1880–82: 89[1]
Glassworkers: 71
Skilled glassworkers: 18

Skilled Glassworkers, 1880

Baldwin, Daniel (mold maker)
Bossert, Charles (presser)
Bossert, Valentine (presser)
Bower, Peter (presser)
Engle, Jacob (finisher)
Farquhar, William (mold maker)
Hoffman, Eugene (mold maker)
Jones, John (presser)
Jones, John B. (presser)
McDonald, J. J., Jr., (finisher)
Miller, Jacob (teaser)
Stemler, Peter (presser)
Stoche, Gilbert (mold maker)
Taylor, William (presser)

Less Skilled Glassworkers, 1880

Barnes, William
Blockinger, Michael
Bossert, Val., Jr.
Briggs, Nettie
Cashdollar, James
Cole, Aaron
Cole, Aaron W.
Cole, Kenneth
Crouse, John L.
Doyle, Francis
Duke, Thomas J.
Getsinger, John
Getsinger, William
Grein, Conrad
Grein, Frederick
Jenkins, Thomas
Kaull, Henry
Kaull, Jacob
King, James
Lloyd, David
Maser, John
McCaslin, Robert
Metz, Frederick
Metz, John
Metz, Phillip
Nestler, Andrew
Nestler, John
Rogers, David
Rogers, Owen
Roy, Christ
Roy, Frank
Roy, John
Stemler, Charles
Switzer, William
Weaver, William
Woods, George
Woods, Robert

Skilled glassworkers, 1880–1882

Baldwin, Daniel
Bossert, Charles
Bossert, John
Bossert, Valentine
Bower, Peter
Engle, Jacob
Farquhar, William
Hand, Henry
Hill, Joseph

Hoffman, Eugene
Jones, John B.
Jones, John, Jr.
McDonald, James J.
Miller, Jacob
Stemler, Peter
Stoche, Gilbert
Taylor, William
Thomas, W. L.

Glassworkers, 1880–1882

Armer, William
Armour, Clark
Barnes, William
Beatty
Bitner, John
Blockinger, Michael
Bosler, George
Bossert, Val., Jr.
Briggs, Nettie
Carr, Robert
Cashdollar, James
Cole, Aaron
Cole, Aaron W.
Cole, Kenneth
Conner, William J.
Crouse, John L.
Dell, Grant
Doyle, Francis
Duke, Otis
Duke, Thomas J.
Gessner, George J.
Getsinger, John
Getsinger, William
Gilhooley
Grein, Conrad
Grein, Frederick
Grein, John
Humphrey, M.
Jenkins, Thomas
Jones, Louis
Kaull, Henry
Kaull, Jacob
Kerr, Robert
Kerr, William
Kessler, William

King, James
Klein, C.
Kritzenberger
Kuhn
Lloyd, David
Lloyd, Thomas
Maser, John
McCaslin, Robert
Messer
Metz, Frederick
Metz, John
Metz, Phillip
Miller, Adolph
Mosier, John
Nestler, Andrew
Nestler, John
Nutt, Jim
Rogers, Ben
Rogers, David
Rogers, Owen
Roy, Christ
Roy, Frank
Roy, John
Stemler, Charles
Sweitzer, Louis
Sweitzer, William
Wand, John
Weaver, William
Weigand,
White, Oliver
Wilkinson, Herb
Wilkinson, James
Wilkinson, Ozro
Williams, John T.
Woods, George
Woods, Robert

Appendix E

Founding Members of General Griffin Post 207, Grand Army of the Republic

The following men organized the Homestead lodge of the GAR, the organization of Union veterans.[1] The members' names are followed by their birthplace, job, and political affiliation (if known).

Boniface, Alexander (Pennsylvania, laborer)
Bryson, John (Ireland, skilled laborer, Republican)
Cole, Joseph (Pennsylvania, skilled laborer)
Hays, James D. (Pennsylvania, skilled laborer)
Hoover, J. M. (Pennsylvania, skilled laborer, Greenback-Labor and Democrat)
Horne, Christian (Germany, laborer)
Izenour, Arthur (Pennsylvania, skilled laborer)
Jones, J. B., Sr. (Wales, skilled glassworker, Republican)
MacDonald, J. J., Jr. (Pennsylvania, skilled glassworker, Republican)
McClure, M. L. (Pennsylvania, skilled laborer, Republican)
McCrea, W. E. (West Virginia, minister)
McLaughlin, W. W. (Pennsylvania, skilled laborer, Democrat)
Murphy, Richard (Ireland, laborer)
Rogers, Benjamin (Wales, laborer)
Spellman, John (Ireland, skilled laborer)
Stemler, Peter (Germany, skilled glassworker)
Stewart, William L. (Pennsylvania, skilled laborer)
Thomas, B. T. (Ohio, minister)
Weaver, William (Pennsylvania, glassworker)
Will, C. C. (Wisconsin, merchant and jeweler, Republican)
Woods, James W. (Pennsylvania, skilled laborer)

Appendix F

Incorporators of Homestead

The following thirty-seven persons petitioned Allegheny County in 1880 to incorporate Homestead as a borough.[1] The petitioners' names are followed, when known, by their sex, birthplace, job, and political affiliation. Members of the GAR are so designated.

Ackard, A. C. (male, Pennsylvania, skilled laborer, Democrat)
Baldwin, F. E. (male, Virginia, skilled laborer, Republican)
Barton, Abram M. (male, Pennsylvania, physican, Democrat)
Brown, Henry (male, Pennsylvania, Democrat)
Bryson, John (male, Ireland, skilled laborer, Republican, GAR)
Bullock, Mary E. (female, Pennsylvania, domestic worker)
Bullock, William S. (male, Pennsylvania, merchant, Republican)
Cox, William (male, England, retired farmer, Republican)
Hays, J. D. (male, Pennsylvania, skilled laborer, Republican, GAR)
Izenour, Elizabeth (female, England, domestic worker)
Kunkle, J. A. (male)
Lloyd, Thomas (male, Wales, laborer)
Lowry, John (male, skilled laborer)
Lynn, William (male)
MacDonald, James, Jr. (male, Pennsylvania, skilled glassworker, Republican, GAR)
MacDonald, James, Sr. (male, Pennsylvania, retired skilled glassworker, Republican)
Marshall, Elizabeth (female, Pennsylvania, domestic worker)
Martin, Robert (male)
McKenzie, J. W. (male, Virginia, skilled laborer)
McLaughlin, W. W. (male, Pennsylvania, skilled laborer, Democrat, GAR)
McVay, M. T. (male, Pennsylvania, merchant, Democrat)
Ramsay, Mary (female)
Ried, P. W. (male)
Smart, J. W. (male, Pennsylvania, skilled laborer)
Spellman, John R. (male, Ireland, skilled laborer, GAR)
Stenger, Benj. J. (male, Pennsylvania, merchant)
Stenger, Mary A. (female, Pennsylvania, domestic worker)

380

Stewart, Ed. S. (male, New Jersey, salesman, Democrat)
Stewart, Joseph S. (male, New Jersey, manufacturer, Republican)
Thomas, W. L. (male, Wales, skilled laborer)
Thompson, Mrs. M. H. (female, Pennsylvania, domestic worker)
West, Alexander (male, Pennsylvania, skilled laborer)
West, Edward (male, Pennsylvania, skilled laborer, Democrat)
West, L. H. (male, Pennsylvania, merchant)
Wilkinson, Samuel (male, Ireland, laborer)
Will, Charles C. (male, Wisconsin, merchant and jeweler, Republican, GAR)
Williams, John A. (male, Maryland, skilled laborer)

Appendix G

Homestead Councilmen, 1880–1881[1]

1880

Ackard, A. C. (Pennsylvania, skilled laborer, Democrat)
Atwood, E. J. (England, merchant)
Bryson, John (Ireland, skilled laborer, Republican, GAR)
Fairfield, J. G. (England, skilled laborer, Republican)
Lloyd, Thomas (Wales, glassworker and laborer)
Lowry, John (Ireland, skilled laborer)
Will, Charles C. (Wisconsin, merchant and jeweler, Republican, GAR)

1881

Ackard, A. C. (Pennsylvania, skilled laborer, Democrat)
Atwood, E. J. (England, merchant)
Bullock, William S. (Pennsylvania, merchant, Republican)
Fairfield, J. G. (England, skilled laborer, Republican)
McLaughlin, W. W. (Pennsylvania, skilled laborer, Democrat, GAR)
Smart, J. W. (Pennsylvania, skilled laborer)
Stewart, Jos., Sr., (New Jersey, manufacturer, Republican)

Appendix H

Selected Officeholders, Homestead, 1880–1892[1]

1880

Burgess: C. C. Will (merchant, Republican, Civil War veteran)

Councilmen
  A. C. Ackard (engineer, Democrat)
  J. G. Fairfield (engineer)
  John Lowry (saddler)
  John Bryson (carpenter, Republican, Civil War veteran)
  E. J. Atwood (merchant)
  Thomas Lloyd (glassworker)

Solicitor: John F. Cox

1881

Burgess: W. S. Bullock (merchant)

Councilmen
  W. W. McLaughlin (engineer/steelworker, Democrat, Civil War veteran)
  A. C. Ackard (engineer/steelworker)
  J. G. Fairfield (engineer)
  Joseph Stewart, Sr. (manufacturer)
  John Bryson (carpenter)
  J. W. Smart (skilled worker, Republican)

1882

Burgess: August Hirth (merchant)

Councilmen
  B. R. Culbertson (skilled worker, Greenback-Labor)
  John Bryson (carpenter)
  W. S. Bullock
  Joseph Stewart
  Jacob Trautman (merchant)
  M. L. McClure (builder)

1883

Burgess: John F. Cox (lawyer, Republican)

Councilmen
  John Bryson (carpenter)
  George Gessner (Knights of Labor, glassworker)
  R. D. Bryce (glass manufacturer)
  Fred Schuchman (merchant)
  F. E. Baldwin (skilled worker, Republican)
  Joseph Stewart, Sr.

1884

Burgess: John F. Cox

Councilmen
  John Bryson
  Geoorge Gessner (Knights of Labor—defeats T. B. Bridges, leader of Junior
    Order of American Mechanics)
  Joseph Stewart
  August Hirth
  D. R. McClure (builder)
  Robert O. Young (bricklayer, Junior Order of United American Mechanics)

1885

Burgess: James MacDonald (retired glassworker)

Councilmen
  John Bryson
  George Gessner
  Joseph Stewart, Sr.
  August Hirth
  Robert O. Young
  D. R. McClure

1886

Burgess: D. R. Jones (lawyer/union leader)

Councilmen
  William Tunstall (carpenter, Junior Order of United American Mechanics)
  Robert O. Young
  William Evans (coal miner/blacksmith)
  D. R. McLure
  Geoorge Gessner
  August Hirth

1887

Burgess: D. R. Jones

Councilmen
  John Elias Jones (steelworker)

William Tunstall
George Gessner
William Russell (steelworker)
D. R. McLure
William Evans

1888

Burgess: Thomas W. Taylor (labor leader)

Councilmen
John Elias Jones (steelworker)
Robert McWhinney (Junior Order of United American Mechanics)
B. R. Culbertson
Jacob Bauer (mason)
R. M. Eliott (building contractor)
William Evans
O. Swisher (carpenter, Junior Order of United American Mechanics)
James M. Hoover (painter, Greenback-Labor)
A. C. Ackard (engineer)

1889

Burgess: L. L. Davis (lawyer, Junior Order of United American Mechanics)

Councilmen
John Elias Jones (steelworker)
Robert McWhinney (Junior Order of United American Mechanics)
William Tunstall (Junior Order of United American Mechanics)
B. R. Culbertson (Greenback-Labor)
James Hoover
A. C. Ackard (engineer)
Louis Rott (clerk and bank cashier)
John Osborne (physician)
Jacob Bauer (mason)

1890

Burgess: John McLuckie (steelworker/labor leader)

Councilmen
Robert McWhinney
James M. Hoover
Fred Schuchman (defeats J. M. Colgan, Junior Order of United American Mechanics)
Oren Swisher (Junior Order of United American Mechanics)
John C. Schultz (machinist)
B. R. Culbertson
A. C. Ackard
William Tunstall
Jacob Bauer

1891

Burgess: M. M. Wilson (liveryman—defeats R. M. Elliott, contractor, McLuckie does not run)

Councilmen
  William Tunstall
  J. M. Hoover
  Fred Schuchman
  C. K. Bryce (glass manufacturer)
  J. J. Rattigan (steelworker)
  Oren Swisher
  John K. Lowry (saddler)
  Louis Rott
  A. C. Ackard (real estate and insurance salesman)

1892

Burgess: John McLuckie (steelworker/labor leader)

Councilmen
  Fred Schuchman (merchant)
  C. K. Bryce (glass manufacturer)
  David Lynch (steelworker and leader of AAISW in Homestead)
  William Tunstall (carpenter, Junior Order of United American Mechanics)
  J. J. Rattigan (steelworker and AAISW leader)
  John Dierken (steelworker)
  T. H. Williamson (steelworker/roller)
  John K. Lowry (saddler)
  William Lloyd (steelworker—defeats O. Swisher, Junior Order of United American Mechanics)

Appendix I

The City Poor Farm: Selected Documents

ANDREW CARNEGIE TO PHILANDER C. KNOX, 22 MARCH 1890

Carnegie, Phipps & Co., Limited
Pittsburgh, March 22nd, 1890
P. C. Knox, Esq.

Dear Sir:
  Will agree to pay $3,000 per acre for City Farm.
  . . . City to retain free of rent the buildings and ground around, necessary to their use until new buildings are obtained, not exceeding 3 years, when City to have right to remove buildings.
  Yours very truly,
  AC[1]

CARNEGIE TO KNOX, 22 MARCH 1890

Carnegie, Phipps & Co., Limited
Pittsburgh, March 22nd, 1890
P. C. Knox, Esq.

My Dear Sir:
  In event of purchase being made of City Farm for us, at price given you in letter of this date, we will, on obtaining a satisfactory deed for same, pay you the sum of Fifty thousand dollars Commission, and any saving to us under $3,000 per acre, we will divide with you.
  Yours very truly,
  AC

CARNEGIE TO KNOX, 25 MARCH 1890

Carnegie, Phipps & Co., Limited
Pittsburgh, March 22nd, 1890
P. C. Knox, Esq.

Dear Sir:

Referring to two letters of the 22nd inst., regarding purchase of City Farm, we beg to say that if deed is received for said property, at cost not to exceed amounts named in said letters, we will pay you Twenty five thousand dollars additional Commission, which amount is to be in full for all expenses in connection with the purchase of said property; this amount to be in addition to Fifty thousand dollars named in one of said letters.

Yours very truly,
AC

H. M. CURRY AND HENRY CLAY FRICK TO KNOX, 25 MARCH 1890

March 25th, 1890
P. C. Knox, Esq.

Dear Sir:

Referring to two letters of the 22nd inst., regarding purchase of City Farm, we beg to say that if deed is received for said property, at cost not to exceed amounts named in said letters, we will pay you Twenty five thousand dollars additional Commission, which amount is to be in full for all expenses in connection with the purchase of said property; this amount to be in addition to Fifty thousand dollars named in one of said letters.

Yours very truly,
Carnegie, Phipps & Co., Limited
H. M. Curry, Vice Chairman
H. C. Frick, Manager

CARNEGIE TO FRICK, 31 JULY 1890 (WESTERN UNION CABLE)

To Frick
Pgh. (Repeated to Mr. Frick July 31/90 10 A.M.) answer can wait advise prompt settlement farm interloper flat part essential any price

Knox to Frick, 31 July 1890 (Western Union telegram)

Received: 8:28 p.[m.]
Dated: Allegheny, Pa.
To: H. C. Frick
Angel [Magee] sent success [Baird] to me demanded dot band fifty [$150,000] con down now to give or take half success represents the people we thought am on whole combination are trying to work it from both side am satisfied attempt will be made Monday or Tuesday to Pittsburgh must act
Eagle [Knox]

Knox to Frick, 1 August 1890 (Western Union telegram)

Dated: Pittsburgh, Pa.
To: H. C. Frick
Everything fixed Suspend judgment on Angel [Magee] until you get all facts. . . .
Eagle [Knox]

Knox to Frick, 2 August 1890 (Western Union telegram)

Dated: Allegheny, Pa.
To: H. C. Frick
Final meeting Monday afternoon in view of what has happened best to be prepared for emergencies and be in shape to act instantly under any new complications. Rome [Curry] agrees with me you should be here acknowledge receipt
Eagle [Knox]

Carnegie to Frick, 2 August 1890 (Western Union cable)

To: Frick
Pgh America (Repeated to Mr. Frick 9:30 a.m. Aug 2/90)
If Broker acted for insiders need not be afraid lauder [George Lauder, Jr.] myself vote half million limit fees included. . . .

Carnegie to Frick, 2 August 1890 (Western Union cable)

To Frick Pgh (Repeated to Mr. Frick 3:35 p.m. Aug 2/90)
Glad hearty Congratulations price high but firm Will never regret.

Appendix J

Selected Leaders of the Homestead Steelworkers, 1892

Arthur Burgoyne's account of the Homestead Lockout identifies most of the steelworkers who were charged with murder, treason, riot, and conspiracy. Whereas he reports that a total of 167 indictments were issued, my calculations yield a smaller figure: 133.[1] Of these, 19 were for murder, 33 were for treason, and 81 were for either riot or conspiracy. Bernard Hogg concludes that a total of 185 indictments were handed down.[2]

Among the questions suggested by this overview: Why were no East European workers charged in connection with the events of 6 July? And what was the precise role played in those events by Samuel Burkett, a teamster and the only identifiable African-American to have participated in the lockout?

OVERVIEW

Abbott, William J. Leader of AAISW Basic Lodge no. 72 in 1892.

Akers, Joseph. Charged with riot/conspiracy.

Allen, Peter. Owner of a three-story frame house, valued at $2,375, at 421 Fifth Avenue. Charged with murder, riot/conspiracy.

Antiss, Oliver P. Leader of Acme Lodge no. 73. Charged with riot/conspiracy.

Antiss, Thomas. Charged with riot/conspiracy.

Atwood, Charles. Charged with riot/conspiracy.

Bail, Elmer E. Owner of a house, valued at $1,990, at 436 Fourth Avenue. A union mainstay since 1882. Charged with treason and riot/conspiracy.

Baird, William. Owner of a home, valued at $860, at 227 Ninth Avenue. Charged with treason and riot/conspiracy.

Bakely, William. Chared with riot/conspiracy.

Bakewell, James. Leader of Thomas Marlow Lodge no. 56 in 1892.

Baldwin, Mark E. Charged with riot/conspiracy.

Bandura, Jan. Laborer in 119-inch and 32-inch mills. Arrested during the lockout for harrassing nonunion workers. Slovak-American.

Barry, Mike. Leader of mechanical workers' union (probably organized by Knights of Labor) in 1892.

Barzowiscz, John. Laborer. Translator for East European workers.

Bayard, William. Charged with riot/conspiracy.

Bayne, Harry. Charged with treason and riot/conspiracy. Elected secretary of the Advisory Committee in early September 1892.

Baynes, Thomas M. Owner of a home valued at $2,500. Charged with riot/conspiracy.

Benke, Ed. Charged with riot/conspiracy.

Bickerton, Harry. Charged with riot/conspiracy.

Boyce, James G. Union spokesman. Active in the battle of 6 July.

Boyle, John. Charged with riot/conspiracy.

Bridge, Jack. Charged with riot/conspiracy.

Brown, Harry. Leader of the mechanical workers.

Brown, T. W. Machinist. Charged with treason. Led mass meeting of locked-out men in early August 1892.

Burke, Edward. Heater in 119-inch mill. Known as "Rioter" Burke. Charged with treason, riot/conspiracy, and unlawful assemblage.

Burkett, Samuel. Teamster. Charged with murder and riot/conspiracy. African-American.

Byers, Isaac. Union leader during the 1880s. Charged with treason and riot/conspiracy.

Champeno, George W. Second ladleman, Open Hearth no. 2. Leader of Basic Lodge no. 72 in 1892; former president of Munhall Lodge no. 24. Union leader during the 1880s. Good friend of John McLuckie. Charged with treason and riot/conspiracy.

Clifford, Jack. Shear helper, 119-inch mill. Along with Hugh Ross, led the attack on the Pinkertons. Charged with murder, treason, and riot/conspiracy.

Clifford, Thomas. Leader of Acme Lodge no. 73 in 1892.

Close, James. Charger and drawer in Open Hearth Department. Charged with murder and riot/conspiracy.

Colflesh, Oscar. Tableman, 119-inch mill. Owner of a house, valued at $2,000, at 416 Third Avenue and of rental property, valued at $1,200, on McClure Street. Leader of AAISW at least since 1889. Testified before the House investigating committee.

Colgan, J. Miller. Worked in Bessemer mill. Owner of a house, valued at $1,300, on Ninth Avenue. Leader of Munhall Lodge no. 24 during the 1880s. Charged with treason and riot/conspiracy.

Combs, William M. Melter's second helper, Open Hearth no. 2. Charged with treason and riot/conspiracy.

Conneghy, William. Charged with riot/conspiracy.

Connelly, Thomas. Charged with riot/conspiracy.

Conroy, S. S. Possible member of the Advisory Committee. With W. T. Roberts and David Lynch, traveled to New York to raise money for locked-out men in early August 1892.

Coon, Oliver C. Owner of a billiard room. Ex-member of the Pennsylvania National Guard. Tried to negotiate with General Snowden on behalf of the town. Charged with riot/conspiracy.

Corcoran, John. Charged with riot/conspiracy.

Coyle, John. Owner of a house, valued at $1,700, on Twelfth Avenue. Delegate to the national convention of the AAISW in 1891. Charged with treason.

Crawford, Thomas J. Roller. Owner of a house, valued at $1,250, at 608 Ammon

Street. Leader of AAISW in Homestead since 1884. Led Advisory Committee through most of the lockout. Charged with treason and riot/conspiracy.

Critchlow, Isaac. Part of a very large family of steelworkers that included his brother Sylvester. Charged with treason and riot/conspiracy.

Critchlow, Sylvester. Roller. His father, Albert, was a leader in the Homestead strike of 1882. Charged with murder and riot/conspiracy.

Cudia, Anthony. Reportedly wounded on 6 July 1892.

Cummings, Michael. One of the principal leaders of the Advisory Committee. Charged with treason and riot/conspiracy.

Cush, Dennis M. A leader of the Advisory Committee. His brother Thomas was a hooker and an active union member during the Homestead strike of 1882. Charged with treason.

Daeska, Charles. Reportedly wounded on 6 July 1892.

Daily, John. Charged with riot/conspiracy.

Dalton, Robert. Charged with riot/conspiracy.

Diebold, George. Charged with murder.

Dierken, John. Owner of a house, valued at $2,275, on Sixth Avenue. Member of borough council in 1892. One of the wealthiest steelworkers in Homestead. Charged with riot/conspiracy.

Durham, Richard. Melter, Open Hearth no. 2. Reportedly wounded on 6 July 1892.

Durkes, John. Charged with treason.

Fagan, Patrick J. Ladleman, Open Hearth no. 1. Owner of a house, valued at $1,175, on Eighth Avenue. Leader of Acme Lodge no. 73. Charged with treason and riot/conspiracy.

Fagula, František. Leader of East European steelworkers. Slovak-American.

Fares, Peter. Pitman, second helper, Open Hearth no. 2. Killed on 6 July 1892. Slovak-American.

Flaherty, Anthony. Charged with murder and riot/conspiracy.

Flanagan, James. Charged with murder and riot/conspiracy.

Foy, Matthew H. Owner of a house, valued at $1,000, on Plum Alley. Helped lead assault against the Pinkertons.

Foy, William. Several family members, including Matthew, worked in the mill. Wounded by Pinkertons. Charged with murder.

Francis, David S. Leader of John Kane Lodge no. 40 in 1892.

Gaches, W. S. Shear helper, 119-inch mill. Prominent Republican in Homestead. Charged with treason and riot/conspiracy.

Gunston, Fred. Charged with riot/conspiracy.

Hadfield, George. Mechanic. One of the many leaders of non-AAISW workers who supported the union. Probably a member of the Advisory Committee.

Hall, James H. Charged with riot/conspiracy.

Hannon, D. H. Charged with riot/conspiracy.

Harris, Matthew. Owner of a house valued at $1,000. Charged with riot/conspiracy.

Harris, Nathan. Charged with treason.

Haws, Charles. Delegate to the national convention of the AAISW in 1892.

Hayes, Patrick. Charged with riot/conspiracy.

Hotchkiss, Richard. Sole member of the Advisory Committee not to be charged with treason. Replaced Thomas Crawford as head of the committee near the end of the lockout.

Hughes, Harry N. Wounded on 6 July 1892.

Hulse, John. Worked in Homestead at least since 1884, when he was a hammerman in the blooming mill. Leader in the lockout of 1889. Worked in the cogging mill at the time of the 1892 lockout. Owner of a house, valued at $2,200, on Fourth Avenue. One of the premier leaders of the Advisory Committee. Correspondent for the *National Labor Tribune*. Had ties to the Homestead Co-operative Boot and Shoe Factory. Probably a member of the Knights of Labor.

Inchico, David. Charged with riot/conspiracy.

Jones, Evan. Charged with riot/conspiracy.

Jones, James. Hurt in the violence against black scabs in November 1892.

Kane, John. Hooker, 119-inch mill. Wounded on 6 July 1892.

Kennedy, Reid. Screw-down, 32-inch slabbing mill. Owner of a house, valued at $1,050, on Second Avenue. Charged with treason and riot/conspiracy. Became burgess of Homestead in late 1890s.

Lamb, G. T. Leader of non-AAISW machinists.

Lewis, Lewis. Charged with riot/conspiracy.

Lloyd, William. Owner of a house, valued at $3,000, on Fifteenth Avenue. Served on the borough council in 1892.

Loyo, Joseph. Reportedly wounded on 6 July 1892.

Lynch, David. Served on borough council in 1892 after defeating fellow steelworker John Miller. One of the leaders of the Advisory Committee. Charged with treason and riot/conspiracy.

McAllister, Peter. Charged with riot/conspiracy.

McConegly, William L. Worked in the 32-inch slabbing mill. Active in Homestead politics. Close friend of Hugh O'Donnell. Charged with treason and riot/conspiracy.

McFadden, Peter. Hurt in the riot against black steelworkers in November 1892.

McLuckie, John. Burgess in 1892. Leader of the Advisory Committee as well. Charged with murder, treason, and riot/conspiracy.

McQuade, William. Screw-down, 119-inch plate mill. Testified before House committee.

McVay, Edward. Charged with murder and riot/conspiracy.

Markowisky, Jules. Reportedly wounded on 6 July 1892.

Martz, Charles. Charged with murder.

Maverick, B. Leader of and translator for East European steelworkers. Slovak-American.

Miller, John. Owner of a house, valued at $1,600, on Eleventh Avenue. Stalwart member of AAISW in Homestead since 1881. Active in Greenback-Labor politics.

Morris, John E. Craneman, Open Hearth no. 1. Owner of house, valued at $960, on Ninth Avenue. Killed on 6 July 1892.

Murphy, Owen. Owner of a house valued at $2,100. Charged with riot/conspiracy.

Murray, John. Owner of a house valued at $1,300. Charged with treason and riot/conspiracy.

Murray, Martin. Heater. Leader of the Homestead strike of 1882. Wounded on 6 July 1892. Charged with treason.

Nau, Peter. Charged with riot/conspiracy.

Naughton, Mike. Charged with riot/conspiracy.

O'Donnell, Hugh. Heater, 119-inch mill. Owner of a house, valued at $2,700, on Fifth Avenue. President of Acme Lodge no. 73 in 1889. In 1890, became leader of new lodge, no. 125, named in honor of W. T. Roberts. Charged with murder, treason, and riot/conspiracy.

Oeffner, William. Charged with riot/conspiracy.

Olšav, Pavel. Preemmient leader of East European immigrants. Slovak-American.

Osmunger, Joseph. Reportedly wounded on 6 July 1892.

Palatka, Antonio. Reportedly wounded on 6 July 1892.

Parry, Thomas L. Roller. Owner of a house, valued at $1,100, on Eighth Avenue. Led several meetings during the lockout. Became a successful businessman afterward.

Prichard, ———. Hurt in the violence against black steelworkers in November 1892.

Prion, John Alonzo. Charged with riot/conspiracy.

Rattigan, John. Roller. Also co-proprietor of a real estate agency. Owned property valued at $6,600 in 1892. Without question the wealthiest of the Homestead steelworkers. Served on borough council in 1892. Had been leader of the Irish National Land League in 1882. Returned to work on company terms in September 1892, prompting councilmen Lynch, Lloyd, Dierken, and John K. Lowry to leave a meeting of the borough council.

Redshaw, James. Convicted of disorderly conduct for verbally assaulting non-union workers during lockout.

Reed, James G. Delegate to AAISW convention in 1892 from W. T. Roberts Lodge.

Richards, Edward. Leader of workers in 1889 lockout. Led mass meetings during 1892 lockout.

Roberts, William T. Heater's first helper, 32-inch slabbing mill. Along with Thomas Crawford, the real force behind the Advisory Committee. Chief union negotiator in 1892. Charged with treason and riot/conspiracy.

Rogers, Samuel. Arrested for drunkenness.

Ross, Hugh. One of the premier leaders of the Advisory Committee. Directed the assault against the Pinkertons on 6 July 1892. Charged with murder, treason, and riot/conspiracy.

Rusiski, Henry. Reportedly wounded on 6 July 1892.

Rutter, George. Wounded on 6 July and died on 17 July 1892.

Rylands, George. Heater, 119-inch mill. Charged with treason and riot/conspiracy.

Sanderson, ———. Charged with murder.

Sarver, George. Worked in Bessemer mill. Leader of nativist forces in Homestead. President of school board. Owner of a house, valued at $975, on Fifth Avenue. Charged with treason and riot/conspiracy.

Scott, Richard. Former Chicago policeman wounded in the Haymarket "riot" of 1886. Charged with aggravated riot.

Searight, Oliver S. Screwman, 32-inch slabbing mill. Charged with treason and riot/conspiracy.

Shannon, David H. One of the leaders of the Advisory Committee. Charged with treason and riot/conspiracy.

Sharpe, Newton. Charged with riot/conspiracy.

Shoemaker, Oden. Charged with riot/conspiracy.

Sotak, Joseph. Leader of the East European immigrant steelworkers. Killed 6 July 1892. Slovak-American.

Sotak, Mike. Brother of Joseph. Leader of East European steelworkers.

Soulier, Andrew. Melter's third helper, Open Hearth no. 2. Along with William Foy, spearheaded the attack against the Pinkertons.

Stinner, Jacob. Charged with murder.

Sullivan, John. Charged with riot/conspiracy.

Sutton, Mike. Leader of East European steelworkers. Served as interpreter at a meeting of mechanics and day laborers, 23 June 1892. Slovak-American.

Sweeney, Ed. Served as special constable for the borough during the lockout.

Taylor, ———. Charged with riot/conspiracy.

Thomas, Benjamin. Charged with riot/conspiracy.

Thompson, M. H. Owner of property valued at $1,450. Charged with treason.

Trautman, H. Charged with riot/conspiracy.

Tuchigo, David. Charged with riot/conspiracy.

Verbullion (Vabelunas), Frank. Translator for and leader of East European steelworkers. Slovak-American.

Wain, Silas. Killed on 6 July 1892.

Ward, James. Charged with riot/conspiracy.

Watts, William. Leader of William T. Roberts Lodge no. 125 in 1892.

Weber, John F. Leader of Acme Lodge no. 73 in 1892.

Weldon, Thomas. Laborer, possibly a hooker, in 1892. Shot and killed on 6 July 1892. Member of John Kane Lodge no. 40.

Williams, W. Edward. Charged with riot/conspiracy.

Williams, W. H. Charged with riot/conspiracy.

Williamson, T. H. Roller. Elected to the borough council in 1892.

Wolley, George. Charged with riot/conspiracy.

MEMBERS OF THE ADVISORY COMMITTEE, 1892 (34)

Bail, Elmer E.	Cummings, Michael	Murray, John
Baird, William	Cush, Dennis M.	Murray, Martin
Bayne, Harry	Durkes, John	O'Donnell, Hugh C.
Brown, T. W.	Fagan, Patrick J.	Roberts, William T.
Byers, Isaac	Gaches, W. S.	Ross, Hugh
Champeno, George W.	Harris, Nathan	Rylands, George
Clifford, Jack	Hotchkiss, Richard	Sarver, George
Colgan, J. Miller	Kennedy, Reid	Searight, Oliver S.
Combs, William M.	Lynch, David	Shannon, David H.
Coyle, John	McConegly, William L.	Thompson, M. H.
Crawford, Thomas J.	McLuckie, John	
Critchlow, Isaac	Miller, John	

CHARGED WITH MURDER (19)

Allen, Peter
Burke, Edward
Burkett, Samuel
Clifford, Jack
Close, James
Crawford, Thomas J.
Critchlow, Sylvester
Diebold, George
Flaherty, Anthony
Flanagan, James
Foy, Matthew H.
Foy, William
McLuckie, John
McVay, Edward
Martz, Charles
O'Donnell, Hugh C.
Ross, Hugh
Sanderson,
Stinner, Jacob

CHARGED WITH TREASON (33)

Bail, Elmer E.
Baird, William
Bayne, Harry
Brown, T. W.
Byers, Isaac
Champeno, George W.
Clifford, Jack
Colgan, J. Miller
Combs, William M.
Coyle, John
Crawford, Thomas J.
Critchlow, Isaac
Cummings, Michael
Cush, Dennis M.
Durkes, John
Fagan, Patrick
Gaches, W. S.
Harris, Nathan
Kennedy, Reid
Lynch, David
McConegly, William L.
McLuckie, John
Miller, John
Murray, John
Murray, Martin
O'Donnell, Hugh C.
Roberts, William T.
Ross, Hugh
Rylands, George
Sarver, George W.
Searight, Oliver S.
Shannon, David H.
Thompson, M. H.

CHARGED WITH RIOT AND/OR CONSPIRACY (81)

Akers, Joseph
Allen, Peter
Antiss, Oliver P.
Antiss, Thomas
Atwood, Charles
Bail, Elmer E.
Baird, William
Bakely, William
Baldwin, Mark E.
Bayard, William
Bayne, Harry
Baynes, Thomas M.
Benke, Ed
Bickerton, Harry
Boyle, John
Bridge, Jack
Burke, Edward
Burkett, Samuel
Byers, Isaac
Champeno, George W.
Clifford, Jack
Close, James
Colflesh, Oscar
Colgan, J. Miller
Combs, William M.
Conneghy, William
Connelly, Thomas
Coon, Oliver C.
Corcoran, John
Crawford, Thomas J.
Critchlow, Isaac
Critchlow, Sylvester
Cummings, Michael
Daily, John
Dalton, Robert
Dierken, John
Fagan, Patrick J.
Flaherty, Anthony
Flanagan, James
Foy, Matthew H.
Gaches, W. S.
Gunston, Fred
Hall, James H.
Hannon, D. H.
Harris, Matthew
Hayes, Patrick
Inchico, David
Jones, Evan
Kennedy, Reid
Lewis, Lewis
Lynch, David
McAllister, Peter
McConegly, William L.
McLuckie, John
McVay, Edward
Miller, John
Murphy, Owen
Murray, John
Nau, Peter
Naughton, Mike
O'Donnell, Hugh C.
Oeffner, William
Prion, John Alonzo
Roberts, William T.
Ross, Hugh
Rylands, George
Sarver, George
Scott, Richard
Searight, Oliver S.

Shannon, David H.
Sharpe, Newton
Shoemaker, Oden
Sullivan, John

Taylor,
Thomas, Benjamin
Trautman, H.
Tuchigo, David

Ward, James
Williams, W. Edward
Williams, W. H.
Wolley, George

PROPERTY-OWNING UNION LEADERS, 1892 (25)

Allen, Peter
Bail, Elmer E.
Baird, William
Baynes, Thomas M.
Boyle, John
Colflesh, Oscar
Colgan, J. Miller
Coyle, John
Crawford, Thomas J.

Dierken, John
Fagan, Patrick J.
Foy, Matthew H.
Harris, Matthew
Hulse, John
Kennedy, Reid
Lloyd, William
Miller, John
Morris, John E.

Murray, John
O'Donnell, Hugh C.
Parry, Thomas L.
Rattigan, John
Rylands, George
Sarver, George
Thompson, M. H.

PROPERTY-OWNING MEMBERS OF THE ADVISORY COMMITTEE, 1892 (13)

Bail, Elmer E.
Baird, William
Colgan, J. Miller
Coyle, John
Crawford, Thomas J.

Fagan, Patrick J.
Kennedy, Reid
Miller, John
Murray, John
O'Donnell, Hugh C.

Rylands, George
Sarver, George
Thompson, M. H.

Appendix K

Selected Members of the East European Community in Homestead, 1892

Most of Homestead's East European immigrants lived in the borough's second ward during the period covered by this study. The ward was bounded by the Monongahela River, Ann Street, City Farm Lane, and Thirteenth Avenue.[1]

LEADERS (18)

Fagula, František. Slovak. Steelworker. Attended St. Michael's Church, Braddock. Married, with children. Lived in Munhall. Arrived in 1883. Later, moved to McKeesport, and then returned to Homestead/Munhall prior to the lockout of 1892. Served as translator during the dispute. The godfather of many Slovak children.

Fares, Peter. Slovak. Steelworker (pitman, second helper). Attended St. Michael's Church, Braddock. Born in Šariš Province, Hungary. Killed, at age 28, on 6 July 1892.

Leskanic, Michal. Slovak. Attended St. Michael's, Braddock, and St. Mary Magdalene Church, Homestead. In 1892, age 30. Married, with children. Organizer of St. Michael's Church, Homestead.

Luteran, Juraj. Slovak. Steelworker. In 1892, age 26. Organizer of St. Michael's Church, Homestead.

Mašley, Michal. Slovak. Grocer. Attended St. Michael's Church, Braddock. Married, with children. Age 33 in 1892. Arrived in Homestead in 1883. One of the founding members of St. Michael's Church, Homestead.

Maverick, B. Slovak. Steelworker. Translator in lockout of 1892. One of the leaders of the First Catholic Slovak Union, Lodge no. 26.

Olšav, Pavel. Slovak, born in Zemplín Province, Hungary. Steelworker. Attended St. Michael's Church, Braddock. Lived in Munhall Hollow in the 1880s; later moved to the second ward, Homestead. Premier leader of the East European steelworkers.

Rosinski, Simon. Probably Polish. Arrived in Homestead with his brother Joseph in the early 1880s. Worked as a steelworker, then became a grocer. Attended St. Francis Church, Homestead. Married, with children.

Sanitrik, Jozef. Attended St. Michael's Church, Braddock, and St. Mary Magdalene, Homestead. Age 25 in 1892. Helped organize St. Michael's Church, Homestead.

398

Sotak, Joseph (Jan). Slovak. Steelworker. Killed on 6 July 1892.

Sotak, Mike (Michal). Slovak. Steelworker. Attended St. Michael's Church, Braddock. Helped organize St. Michael's, Homestead.

Špahn, Ján. Slovak. Butcher. Age 29 in 1892. Organizer of St. Michael's, Homestead. Close friend of Pavel Olšav and his family.

Stefancin, Imro. Slovak. Attended St. Michael's, Braddock, and St. Francis Church, Homestead. Married, with children, in 1892. Arrived in Homestead in 1881. Cousin of Peter Farris. Organizer of St. Michael's Church, Homestead.

Sutton, Mike. Steelworker. Translator during the lockout of 1892.

Tomas, Stefan. Organizing member of St. Michael's Church, Homestead.

Ulicny, John. Steelworker. Organizer of St. Michael's, Homestead.

Verbullion, Frank. Steelworker. Translator during the lockout of 1892.

Waasilefski, Vincent. Polish. Hotelier and saloon owner. Attended St. Mary Magdalene Church, Homestead. His pool hall served as a center of sociability for many steelworkers, Anglo-American and East European alike. His son Vincent was a steelworker.

PROPERTY OWNERS (28)

Brozenski, Martin. Laborer, Open Hearth no. 1. Owned a house, valued at $800, on Second Avenue.

Brozinski, John. Laborer, 119-inch and 32-inch mills. Owned a house at 612 Ammon Street and a lot on Third Avenue, the combined value of which was $1,345.

Frankaritch, J. Laborer, 32-inch mill. Owned a house, valued at $700, on Second Avenue.

Frankiewicz, John. Steelworker. Owned a house, valued at $700, on Second Avenue.

Ihnath, Juraj. Owned a house, valued at $825, on Plummer Place.

Kochanik, George. Steelworker. Owned a lot, valued at $400, on Third Avenue.

Kraintzki, George. Steelworker. Owned a house, valued at $1,100, at 470 Third Avenue.

Macko, Andrej. Steelworker. Owned a house, valued at $725, on Fourth Avenue. Arrived in Homestead in 1883, age 17.

Noraski, Mary. Polish. Owner of a house, valued at $220, on Plummer Place.

Petrasavich, Anthony. Laborer, Open Hearth no. 2. Owned a house, valued at $1,075, at 323 Seventeenth Avenue. Arrived in Homestead in 1883. Continued to attend St. Mary Magdalene Church even after St. Francis Church was organized.

Povilanski, Christian. Steelworker. Owner of a house, valued at $1,010, at 542 Second Avenue.

Prosiski, John. Owned a house, valued at $775, on Second Avenue.

Radyshivski, Enoch. Steelworker. Owned a house, located in the third ward, that was valued at $550.

Rosinski, Joseph. Owned property valued at $700 in the third ward. Arrived in Homestead in 1881, when he began working in the mill. Later, opened a restaurant in Pittsburgh.

Rosinski, Simon. Grocer and contractor; formerly a steelworker. Owned a number of parcels in Homestead, the combined value of which was $1,600, in 1892.
Shalkoski, Joseph. Steelworker. Owned a house, valued at $900, on Third Avenue.
Shalkoski, Paul. Steelworker. Owned a house, valued at $900, on Third Avenue.
Stivick, G. W. Steelworker. Owned a house, valued at $999, in the third ward.
Topanczer, Alexander. Steelworker. Owned a house, valued at $1,100, on Third Avenue.
Ulicny, John. Steelworker. Owned a house, valued at $800, on Plummer Place.
Vargoncek, Michal. Steelworker. Owned property valued at $2,300 in 1892.
Vebolunas, Joseph. Steelworker. Owned property on Plummer Place valued at $650.
Vebolurzas, Joseph. Steelworker. Owned a house, on Third Avenue, valued at $650.
Verick, John. Steelworker. Owned a house, valued at $580, on Second Avenue.
Warga, Michael. Steelworker. Owned a house, valued at $650, at 467 Third Avenue.
Waasilefski, Vincent. Owned property valued at $7,425, which made him the wealthiest member of the East European community.
Wicestas, A. Steelworker. Owned property on Plummer Place valued at $850.
Wiskinkiwis, John. Steelworker. Owned two houses, with a combined value of $3,150, on Fourth Avenue.

MEMBERS OF THE FIRST CATHOLIC SLOVAK UNION, LODGE NO. 26 (119)

Azmondă, Ján	Fenár, Ján	Kerestyi, Ján
Balint, Andrej	Fred, Michal	Kohut, Ján
Bandura, Ján	Furda, Ján	Koritko, Jan
Bardar, Jozef	Furdoš, Ján	Koritko, Juraj
Beništak, Michal	Gajdoš, Ján	Korpol, Andrej
Berecin, Jan	Geči, Ján	Koško, Juraj
Berecin, Michal	Goč, Michal	Kostisak, Juraj
Berecin, Michal (son)	Goga, Ján	Kostisak, Juraj (son)
Biereš, Jan	Greč, Juraj	Kusnir, Andrej
Billi, Jan	Hirko, Jan	Kusnir, Pavel
Breris, Micko	Hondáš, Juraj	Ladok, Jan
Bukovsky, Stefan	Hornák Andrej	Lakatoš, Andrej
Cacko, Andrej	Hornák, Jozef	Leškanič, Michal
Calfa, Andrej	Horny, Jan	Leškanits, Andrej
Ceplicky, Frank	Hotončik, Ján	Lukáč, Michal
Cigas, Andrej	Hricz, Miko	Luteran, Juraj
Demko, Michal	Hudak, Jan	Macko, Andrej
Drabant, Andrej	Ignacz, Michal	Majersky, Peter
Dudáš, Andrej	Ihath, Ján	Majoros, Stephan
Dundala, Ján	Ihnath, Juraj	Maruščak, Michal
Dziak, Michael	Ježko, Jozef	Masley, Michal
Elko, Jakub	Juhàsz, Ján	Mikula, Jan
Estok, Juraj	Kapriva, Jozef	Mražik, Andrej

Mražik, Michal
Mucha, Valent
Novák, Ján
Novák, Miklóš
Novák, Stefan
Olšav, Pavel
Paulik, Andrej
Paulik, Ján
Perža, Jan
Petka, Karol
Petrik, Jozef
Priputer, Leško
Priškar, Juraj
Ragan, Andrej
Ragan, Andrej (son)
Ragan, Juraj
Ragan, Michael

Rebak, Jozef
Rečicar, Ján
Roskoš, Ján
Sanitrik, Jozef
Scelecky, Andrej
Schwarz, Andrej
Serdy, Andrej
Silady, Andrej
Simej, Andrej
Slebodnik, Matej
Sokira, Pavel
Sotak, Jan
Sotak, Michal
Spahn, Jan
Stefancin, Imro
Stolar, Jan
Szerdy, Michael

Takáč, Jozef
Terek, Jan
Top, Jozef
Uhorčak, Juraj
Valovsky, Jan
Varga, Ján
Varga, Juraj
Vargovits, Ján
Vasko, Jan
Vessik, Jan
Vinter, Jozef
Vyrostko, Jan
Zibaj Sabol, Jan
Zïdó, Jozef
Zïdó, Juraj
Zipay, Michal

Overview: Identifiable Males (333)

Ander, Jan
Azmonda, Jan
Balint, Andrej
Ballock, Michal
Ballok, John
Bandura, Jan
Bardar, Jozef
Barlow, John
Barzowiscz, John
Basak, G.
Beatty, Michael
Benistak, Michal
Berecin, Jan
Berecin, Michal
Berecin, Michal (son)
Beresok, Joe
Betco, Mike
Bidock, Peter
Bieres, Jan
Bieres, Mike
Bille, Mike
Billi, Jan
Billick, Joe
Bonijou, Steve
Breris, Micko
Brozenski, Martin
Brozinski, H.
Brozinski, John

Bukoski, John
Bukosku, Steve
Bukovsky, Stefan
Bushka, John
Buskoski, Stephen
Cabouch, J.
Cacko, Andrej
Cacko, Michal
Calfa, Andrej
Ceplicky, Frank
Chortas, L.
Choushda, Pete
Cigas, Andrej
Cintala, Andrej
Coscoe, G.
Costellnick, Stephan
Csopko, Michal
Cudia, Anthony
Daeska, Charles
Dakosh, Joseph L.
Damyel, J.
Daryel, M.
Demko, Michal
Ditromazo, Grose
Dorosko, John
Drabant, Andrej
Dubranski, John
Dudas, Andrej

Dudas, Mike
Dukosh, George
Dukosh, Joe
Dukoste, Frank
Dundala, Jan
Dyerko, A.
Dyerko, M.
Dziak, Michael
Elko, Jakub
Elko, Mike
Emanuel, Fred
Estok, Juraj
Fagula, František
Farbarak, M.
Farbarik, John
Fares, Peter
Fargosh, Steve
Fenar, Jan
Finco, Mike
Fordorkok, Joseph
Forish, John
Frankaritch, J.
Frankiewicz, John
Fred, Michal
Furda, Jan
Furdos, Jan
Gajdos, Jan
Gargo, John

Geboyske, William
Geci, Jan
Gladish, Andy
Goc, Michal
Goga, Jan
Grec, Juraj
Halibuta, John
Hirko, Jan
Hodeck, John
Hollar, John
Hondas, Juraj
Hornack, Anthony
Hornak, Andrej
Hornak, Jozef
Hornuck, Andrew
Horny, Jan
Hotalhan, John
Hotoncik, Jan
Houyack, Andy
Houyack, Mike
Hricz, Miko
Hudak, Jan
Hudock, John
Hudock, Paul
Humenick, Andrew
Hunchar, Mike
Hurra, John
Hurra, Mike
Ignacz, Michal
Ihath, Jan
Ihnath, Juraj
Jaklofsky, Joseph
Jemburski, Andrew
Jezko, Jozef
Juhasz, Jan
Kakash, Michal
Kanda, Michal
Kapriva, Jozef
Karch, Imero
Karch, Pavel
Keish, Joe
Kerestyi, Jan
Kochanik, George
Kohut, Jan
Kohute, Mike
Kohutz, Nick
Konute, John
Konute, Nick

Kooacs, J.
Kopco, Jozef
Koritko, Jan
Koritko, Juraj
Koropo, A.
Korotz, George
Korpol, Andrej
Kosko, Juraj
Kosock, M.
Kossun, Andy
Kostisak, Juraj
Kostisak, Juraj (son)
Kovosh, John
Kowacz, John
Kraintzki, George
Kundash, Joseph
Kusnir, Andrej
Kusnir, Jan
Kusnir, Pavel
Kustre, John
Kuzak, Michael
Ladok, Jan
Ladowsky, Otto
Lakatos, Andrej
Lapiansky, Stefan
Laskody, Juraj
Latofski, Joseph
Latowski, Andrew
Latroske, Andrew
Lepras, Francis
Lescsak, Peter
Leskanic, Michal
Leskanits, Andrej
Lesko, Priputan
Loyo, Joseph
Lukac, Michal
Luteran, Juraj
Macko, Andrej
Majernick, Jan
Majersky, Peter
Majoros, Stephan
Marko, John
Markowisky, Jules
Marto, John
Maruscak, Michal
Masley, Michal
Mata, Jozef
Matisco, John

Maures, N.
Maverick, B.
Mikula, Jan
Mikula, Paul
Mislinkiewicz, John
Mozek, Joseph
Mrazik, Andrej
Mrazik, Michal
Mucha, Valent
Myroshe, Mike
Noraski, Mary
Noroski, Anthony
Noroski, Anton W.
Noroski, Francis
Noroski, John
Novak, Jan
Novak, Miklos
Novak, Stefan
Olšav, Pavel
Osmunger, Joseph
Otzski, Herman
Palatka, Antonio
Palko, Jozef
Palszo, J.
Parlotski, Andy
Parlotski, Joe
Paulik, Andrej
Paulik, Jan
Pedo, J.
Perch, George
Perza, Jan
Petka, Karol
Petras, Jozef
Petras, Michal
Petrasavich, Anthony
Petrik, Jozef
Pido, Peter
Plapopen, M.
Porish, George
Poskar, George
Poskar, John
Povilanski, Christian
Presaski, Joseph
Priputer, Lesko
Priskar, Juraj
Prosiski, John
Prososkey, John
Pundick, Jan

Radyshivski, Enoch
Ragan, Andrej
Ragan, Andrej (son)
Ragan, Juraj
Ragan, Michael
Rebak, Jozef
Recicar, Jan
Recto, Andy
Rosinski, Joseph
Rosinski, Simon
Roskos, Jan
Rusiski, Henry
Sabo, F.
Sabo, M.
Sabol, Andrej
Sanitrik, Jozef
Sato, John
Scelecky, Andrej
Scerbak, Jan
Schwarz, Andrej
Scinick, Andrew
Sedlyak, Stefan
Seenic, George
Senatric, George
Serdy, Andrej
Shalkoski, Joseph
Shalkoski, Paul
Shatlack, Joseph
Shatlack, Martin
Shatlack, Paul
Silady, Andrej
Simej, Andrej
Sindric, Thomas
Sirdy, Andy
Slebodnik, Matej

Sokira, Pavel
Solvitz, A.
Sotak, Jan
Sotak, Michal
Soxkua, P.
Spahn, Jan
Stafuro, Jozef
Stefancin, Imro
Stevick, G. W.
Stevick, G. W. (son)
Stolar, Jan
Stopko, Andy
Sunco, John
Sutton, Mike
Szerdy, Michael
Takac, Jozef
Teckcz, Joseph
Terek, Jan
Timko, John
Tomas, Stefan
Tomko, Andy
Top, Jozef
Topanczer, Alexander
Topko, Joe
Topsrezer, Ed.
Torgosge, James
Treko, George
Tusack, Michael
Uargo, Mike
Uhorcak, Juraj
Ulicny, John
Uskat, George
Vabaloon, Charles
Valovsky, Jan
Vamist, George

Varga, Jan
Varga, Juraj
Vargoncek, Michal
Vargovits, Jan
Vasko, Jan
Vebolunas, Joseph
Vebolurzas, Joseph
Verbullion, Frank
Veretski, John
Verick, John
Vessik, Jan
Vinter, Jozef
Vislie, John
Vitro, Mike
Volenski, J.
Vyrostko, Jan
Wacha, Jozef
Walkic, Aaron
Warga, Michael
Waruscak, Michal
Waasilefski, Paul
Waasilefski, Vincent
Waasilefski, Vincent P.
Wessak, John
Wicestas, A.
Wiskinkiwis, John
Yapanitzki, Mike
Zamborski, Andrej
Zamroskie, Julius
Zerco, J.
Zesko, Jozef
Zibaj, Jan
Zido, Jozef
Zido, Juraj
Zipay, Michal

Appendix L

Selected Disputes in Greater Pittsburgh, Metalmaking Industries, 1867–1892

The following table is an overview of the major industrial disputes discussed in the text. The table is by no means exhaustive; in virtually every year, there were important confrontations in the mills of Pittsburgh.

DATE	SITE	OWNER	TYPE	OUTCOME
1866–67	All puddling mills in Pittsburgh	All owners of puddling mills	Lockout	Puddlers win; iron-masters recognize Sons of Vulcan
1867	Iron foundries in Pittsburgh	Virtually all foundry owners	Strike	International Mold-ers Union is decimated
1874–75	All puddling mills in Pittsburgh	All owners of puddling mills	Lockout	Puddlers win; campaign for "amalgam-ation" begins
1876	Edgar Thomson Steel Works (Braddock)	Andrew Carnegie	Strike	Carnegie wins; lodge of the AAISW ousted from the mill
1878	Black Diamond Steel Works (Pittsburgh)	James Park, Jr.	Strike	Compromise
1878–79	Solar Iron Works (Pittsburgh)	William Clark	Strike	Compromise
1879	Hussey's Crucible Steel Mill (Pittsburgh)	Hussey, Howe, & Co.	Strike	Compromise
1880	Crescent Steel Works (Pittsburgh)	Reuben Miller, Jr.	Strike	Compromise
1882	Edgar Thomson Steel Works	Andrew Carnegie	Strike	Victory for Carnegie; AAISW lodges collapse
1882	Pittsburgh Bes-semer Steel Works[a] (Homestead)	Pittsburgh Bes-semer Steel Co. (Clark, Miller, Hussey, Park, and others)	Strike	Victory for the AAISW and the Knights of Labor

404

DATE	SITE	OWNER	TYPE	OUTCOME
1882	Virtually all iron works in Pittsburgh	Virtually all ironmasters	Strike	AAISW defeated in the "Big Strike"
1884–85	Edgar Thomson Steel Works	Carnegie	Shut down, ostensibly for repairs and improvements	Victory for Carnegie; workers accept reduction and 12-hour shifts; AAISW lodges disband
1887–88	Edgar Thomson Steel Works	Carnegie	Lockout	Knights of Labor ousted from the mill; District Assembly 3 decimated
1889	Homestead Steel Works	Carnegie	Lockout	AAISW and Knights of Labor forestall Carnegie; compromise on wages
1892	Homestead Steel Works	Carnegie	Lockout	AAISW and Knights ousted from mill; sympathy strikes fail

a. Carnegie, Phipps, and Company purchased the Pittsburgh Bessemer Steel Works in 1883 and operated it under that name until 1886, when the name was changed to the Homestead Steel Works. Along with Andrew Carnegie's other major holdings in the steel industry, Carnegie, Phipps, and Company was consolidated with Carnegie Brothers and Company on 1 July 1892 to form the Carnegie Steel Company.

Abbreviations

ACLC	Andrew Carnegie Papers, Library of Congress
AIME Transactions	*Transactions of the American Institute of Mining Engineers*
AISI Bulletin	*Bulletin of the American Iron and Steel Institute*
AM	*American Manufacturer and Iron World*
ASME Transactions	*Transactions of the American Society of Mechanical Engineers*
BT	*Braddock Tribune*
CDN	*Chicago Daily News*
CT	*Chicago Tribune*
EMJ	*Engineering and Mining Journal*
FCSU	First Catholic Slovak Union
HLN	*Homestead Local News*
HM	*Homestead Mirror*
HT	*Homestead Times*
IA	*Iron Age*
ILWCH	*International Labor and Working Class History*
IW	*Irish World and American Industrial Liberator*
JAH	*Journal of American History*
JEH	*Journal of Economic History*
JIH	*Journal of Interdisciplinary History*
JSH	*Journal of Social History*
JSP	*John Swinton's Paper*
JUL	*Journal of United Labor*
LH	*Labor History*
NLT	*National Labor Tribune*
NYH	*New York Herald*
NYS	*(New York) Sun*
NYT	*New York Times*
NYTR	*(New York) Tribune*
NYW	*(New York) World*
OVB	*Ohio Valley Budget*
PBIS	Pennsylvania Bureau of Industrial Statistics
PC	*Pittsburgh Commercial*
PCG	*Pittsburgh Commercial-Gazette*
PCT	*Pittsburgh Chronicle-Telegraph*

PD	*Pittsburgh Dispatch*
PEC	*Pittsburgh Evening Chronicle*
PET	*Pittsburgh Evening Telegraph*
PG	*Pittsburgh Gazette*
PL	*Pittsburgh Leader*
PP	*Pittsburgh Post*
PPG	*Pittsburgh Post-Gazette*
PSM	*Popular Science Monthly*
PT	*Pittsburgh Times*
RHR	*Radical History Review*
TC	*Technology and Culture*
TJ	*(Pittsburgh) Trades Journal*
WDI	*Wheeling (W. Va.) Daily Intelligencer*
YEV	*Youngstown (Ohio) Evening Vindicator*
YWT	*Youngstown (Ohio) Weekly Telegram*

Notes

INTRODUCTION

1. This account is drawn from: Hewitt, "Brooklyn Bridge," *Selected Writings*, 295–311; Alan Trachtenberg, *Brooklyn Bridge*, 8–9, 93–113, 117–25; McCullough, *Great Bridge*, 372–96, 415–16, 535–36; Wall, *Carnegie*, 291, 654; Lears, *No Place of Grace*, 8–9.

CHAPTER 1. *Homestead and the American Republic*

1. Contemporary accounts of the lockout are Burgoyne, *Homestead Strike*; Stowell, *Fort Frick*. In addition to daily press accounts, other relevant primary sources are: U.S. Congress, House of Representatives, Committee on the Judiciary, *Report 2447: Investigation of Homestead Troubles*, hereafter cited as U.S. House, *Report 2447*; U.S. Congress, Senate, Committee on Labor and Education, *Report 1280: Investigation in Relation to the Employment for Private Purposes of Armed Bodies of Men*, hereafter cited as U.S. Senate, *Report 1280*; Bemis, "Homestead Strike." The quotation is from Roger Butterfield, forward to Wolff, *Lockout*, ix.

2. Accounts of the battle on 6 July contain numerous discrepancies regarding the number and the identities of the casualties. In an earlier essay, "*Za Chlebom*," 143, I wrote that three Pinkertons and nine workers were killed. Further examination of the sources has led me to conclude that, in fact, seven workers were killed: Peter Fares, Silas Wain, John E. Morris, Joseph Sotak, Thomas Weldon, George Rutter, and Henry Striegel. (Striegel was not employed at the Homestead Steel Works; he was a teamster for a small company.) The Pinkerton agents who died were Thomas J. Connors, Edward A. R. Speer, and J. W. Kline. These findings are drawn from the standard accounts of the lockout and the July 1892 issues of the following newspapers: CDN, CT, HLN, NLT, NYH, NYS, NYT, NYTR, NYW, PCG, PD, PP, PT, WDI, YEV. See, in particular: *CT*, 7 and 9 Jul. 1892; *NYS*, 7 and 8 Jul. 1892; *NYH*, 7, 8, and 9 Jul. 1892; *NYW*, 6, 7, 8, 9, 11, and 17 Jul. 1892; *WDI*, 7 and 8 Jul. 1892; *NYTR*, 8 and 9 Jul. 1892; *PCG*, 7 Jul. 1892; *PP*, 7 Jul. 1892. Also see Burgoyne, *Homestead Strike*, 61, 65–66, 67, 73, 92–93, 102; Stowell, *Fort Frick*, 83–85, 86, 89, 96.

3. This paragraph and the succeeding one are based on the accounts cited in 1, above, and: *PP,* 21–23, 26, and 28 June, and 4 Jul. 1892; *NYTR,* 7 Jul. 1892; *NYW,* 7 and 8 Jul. 1892; *NYS,* 7 and 8 Jul., and 7 Aug. 1892; *NYH,* 8 Jul. 1892; *PCG,* 6 June, 7 and 9 Jul. 1892; Pennsylvania, *Annual Report of the Adjutant General, 1892,* 34–125; E. Y. Breck, ed., *Pittsburgh Legal Journal* 23 (Aug. 1892–Aug. 1893): 106–10; David, "Upheaval at Homestead"; Brody, *Steelworkers in America,* 51–56; Carnegie, *Autobiography,* 219–30.

4. Following Burgoyne, *Homestead Strike,* 194, virtually all the secondary accounts state that a total of 167 charges were brought against the steelworkers. My calculations, based on a wide range of primary sources as well as on Burgoyne's reporting, yield a smaller figure: 133 indictments—81 for riot or conspiracy, 33 for treason, and 19 for murder. A total of 93 workers were charged. See app. J for additional details.

5. The texts of "Father Was Killed" and several other songs about the lockout are in P. Foner, *American Labor Songs,* 242–45. For other songs see: *HLN,* 3 Jul. 1892; Swetnam, "Labor-Management Relations," 325; "Songs of a Strike," *Pittsburgh Press,* 5 Feb. 1967, clipping in "Homestead Folder," Western Pennsylvania Historical Society, Pittsburgh.

6. Fitch, *Steel Workers;* Byington, *Homestead;* Gutman, review of Wolff, *Lockout.* There is one valuable unpublished account: Hogg, "Homestead Strike of 1892." The University of Pittsburgh Press has reprinted the studies by Fitch and Byington.

7. Among recent works that consider the 1892 lockout: Miner, *Homestead,* chap. 1; Montgomery, *House of Labor,* 36–40; Wall, *Carnegie,* chap. 16; Schneider, "Republicanism Reinterpreted"; Schneider, "Citizen Striker," 47–66; Cohen, "Steelworkers Rethink." The quotation is from p. 155.

8. Gutman, review of *Lockout,* 274. The best of the many essays on the lockout is David, "Upheaval at Homestead." Narratives may also be found in: Brecher, *Strike;* Lens, *Labor Wars;* Yellen, *American Labor Struggles.*

9. On the sweeping changes that marked Pittsburgh's history in the late nineteenth century, see Couvares, *Remaking of Pittsburgh.*

10. On the proposition that technology is not value-free but, rather, shaped by the people who develop, control, and bring it into the production process, see: Mumford, *Technics and Civilization;* Marcuse, "Social Implications"; Noble, *America by Design,* esp. xvii–xxvi; Lazonick, "Production Relations."

11. Montgomery, *Beyond Equality,* 30–31, 249–60; Roediger, "Steward"; Hofstadter, *American Political Tradition,* 118–74; E. Foner, *Reconstruction,* 124–75; E. Foner; *Nothing but Freedom,* 39–73; S. Walker, "Abolish the Wage System."

12. "The Grand Problem," *NLT,* 23 Dec. 1876. Also see "Capital and Machinery," *NLT,* 27 Jan. 1877. On the celebratory effusions occasioned by the Centennial Exposition, see Kasson, *Civilizing the Machine,* 156–64.

13. Among the many studies that document this war: Forbath, "Ambiguities"; Fink, *Workingmen's Democracy;* Goodwyn, *Populist Moment;* Gutman, *Work, Culture, and Society;* Holt, "Trade Unionism"; Oestreicher, *Solidarity and Fragmentation;* Ross, *Workers on the Edge;* Levine, *Labor's True Woman;* Montgomery, "Labor and the Republic"; Salvatore, *Debs;* Hahn, "Common Right and Commonwealth." Also see Kealey and Palmer, *Dreaming.*

14. This overview of republicanism is drawn from Wilentz, *Chants Demo-*

cratic, 14; Wood, *Creation of the American Republic*, 48–74; E. Foner, *Paine*, chap. 3; Pocock, "Machiavelli"; Pocock, "Virtue and Commerce"; Kramnick, "Republican Revisionism Revisited"; Kramnick, "Great National Discussion." The quotation is from p. 4.

15. Some of the works that document the centrality of republicanism in the discourse of those opposed to competitive capitalism: Rock, *Artisans;* Faler, *Mechanics and Manufacturers;* Dublin, *Women at Work;* John Alexander, "Fort Wilson Incident"; Young, "Hewes"; Wilentz, "Against Exceptionalism"; E. Foner, *Politics and Ideology.* Salvatore, "Class and Citizenship," suggests that it was racism, not republicanism, that provided white Americans with a common basis for developing their collective identity.

16. McCloskey, *American Conservatism*, 1–22, 168–74.

17. Armstrong, "Labor Reform," *NLT,* 22 May 1874. Also see E. Foner, *Reconstruction*, 477–78.

18. *NLT,* 13 Mar. and 19 June 1875, and 8 Jan. 1876; Krause, *"Za Chlebom,"* 148–49; J. A. H. Murray, ed., *The Oxford English Dictionary* (Oxford: Clarendon Press, 1933), 2:718–19; Dawley, *Class and Community,* 151.

19. Locke, *Second Treatise,* 18–30; Macpherson, *Democratic Theory, 55,* 231–32. The distinction between property for use and property for accumulation has been overlooked by most Western political theorists since the time of Locke. Marx, however, did make the distinction. It is therefore doubtful that he would see in the idea of competence an unwavering commitment to the sanctity of private property, a commitment to which many Marxists have attributed the absence of "class consciousness" in the United States.

20. McCloskey, *American Conservatism,* 1–22. This was a battle that included a fight over the possession of meaning as well as over the formal instruments of power. On this issue see Bender, "Wholes and Parts." For a celebratory view of the conjunctures of republicanism and capitalism, see Berthoff, "Peasants and Artisans."

21. *NLT,* 23 Sept. 1882, as quoted in Stromquist, "Working Class Organization," 38.

CHAPTER 2. *6 July 1892*

1. David, "Upheaval at Homestead," 133. The quotation is from the *New Nation*, the publication of Edward Bellamy's Nationalist movement, as cited by David, 134.

2. Fitch, *Steel Workers,* pts. 2, 3. Not long after steelworkers finally did succeed in organizing a new union in 1937, they pointed to the conspicuous memory of Homestead. Homestead Local 1397 of the Steel Workers Organizing Committee dedicated a monument to the slain workers thus: "In memory of the Iron and Steel Workers who were killed in Homestead, Pa., on July 6, 1892, while striking against the Carnegie Steel Company in defense of their American rights" (David P. Demarest, Jr., Afterword, to Burgoyne, *Homestead Strike,* 301). The monument, built in 1941, still stands in Homestead near the site of the former steelworks.

3. U.S. House, *Report 2447*, ix. Among the publications that covered the

events of 6 July 1892 that were consulted for this study: *AISA Bulletin, AM, BT, CDN, CT, Elizabeth Herald, Harper's Weekly, HLN, IA, Leslie's Weekly, NLT, NYH, NYS, NYT, NYTR, NYW, North American Review, Pittsburgh Catholic, PCT, PCG, PD, PP, Pittsburgh Press, PT, WDI, YEV, YWT.*

4. Fitch, *Steel Workers*, 130; Hogg, "Homestead Strike," 91; Wall, *Carnegie*, 559. Hogg, "Pinkertonism," his only published piece that touches on the lock-out, remarked that in assaulting the Pinkertons, Homesteaders were "transformed into a blood-thirsty mob" whose behavior departed altogether from civilized norms (179).

5. Wall, *Carnegie*, 557; Fitch, *Steel Workers*, 122, David, "Upheaval at Homestead," 148. Also of interest is the decade-old observation of a sociologist, Linda Schneider: "There has been no scholarly work produced about Homestead which adequately unifies a narrative of events with discussion of the economic and ideological underpinnings of the strike. Instead several popular labor histories have regaled readers with the dramatic tale of the Homestead battle" ("Citizen Striker," 29).

6. This account has been compiled from the sources cited in n. 3 above; U.S. House, *Report 2447*; U.S. Senate, *Report 1280*; and the most reliable of the secondary accounts—Burgoyne, *Homestead Strike*; David, "Upheaval at Homestead"; and above all, Hogg, "Homestead Strike." In the notes that follow, more specific references are provided where they seem warranted, and particularly when details depart from received wisdom about the events.

7. Burgoyne, *Homestead Strike*, 51–53; *PCG*, 6 and 7 Jul. 1892; *NLT*, 9 Jul. and 26 Nov. 1892; U.S. House Report 2447, vii, 38; *PP, NYW*, and *NYS*, 7 Jul. 1892; Bridge, *Inside History*, 212. See also Harvey, *Frick*, 116–17.

8. This paragraph and the succeeding two are based principally on: *PP, NYH*, and *WDI*, 7 Jul. 1892; *CT*, 6 and 7 Jul. 1892; *PCG*, 6 Jul. 1892; *NLT*, 9 Jul. 1892; Hogg, "Homestead Strike," 82–83; Burgoyne, *Homestead Strike*, 52–56; Harvey, *Frick*, 118; U.S. House, *Report 2447*, vii, 129. Some of the details regarding the Pinkertons' uniforms are drawn from Wolff, *Lockout*, 104.

9. An armed riverboat assault on Homestead hardly came as a surprise to the steelworkers and their families. For days journalists had reported the persistent rumors of company plans to launch just such an assault. Indeed, on 5 July the son of William Rogers, captain of the *Little Bill*, actually told a reporter that Pinkertons would be dispatched to Homestead on barges.

10. This paragraph and the succeeding one are based on: *NYH* and *PCG*, 7 Jul. 1892; *NYS*, 11 Jul. 1892; *CT*, 6 and 7 Jul. 1892; *PP* and *NYW*, 8 Jul. 1892; *WDI*, 7 and 8 Jul. 1892; U.S. House, *Report 2447*, 5, 14; Bemis, "Homestead Strike," 381–82; Burgoyne, *Homestead Strike*, 60–61. Information about O'Donnell and the other steelworkers who participated in the events of 6 July 1892 has been gleaned from a wide range of additional sources. See app. J for details.

11. On Mrs. Finch, see: *NYH*, 7 Jul. 1892; *CT*, 6 Jul. 1892; *HLN*, 14 Apr. and 28 Sept. 1888, 27 Apr. 1889, 22 Feb., 26 Apr. 1890, and 27 Feb. 1892.

12. Burgoyne, *Homestead Strike*, 54–58; U.S. Senate, *Report 1280*, 240, 268; U.S. House, *Report 2447*, 90, 117, 133; *PCG*, 6 Jul. 1892; *NYS, NYW, PP*, and *WDI*, 7 Jul. 1892; Hogg, "Homestead Strike," 83.

13. Burgoyne, *Homestead Strike*, 56, 58; *NYS, NYTR, NYW, PD, PP*, and *WDI*, 7 Jul. 1892; U.S. House, *Report 2447*, 133.

14. *CT* and *CDN*, 6 Jul. 1892; *NYH, NYT, PP,* and *WDI,* 7 Jul. 1892; Hogg, "Homestead Strike," 83; Burgoyne, *Homestead Strike,* 56. The contemporary press invariably referred to immigrants from Eastern Europe as Hungarians or Huns; in point of fact, there were few, if any, ethnic Hungarians, or Magyars, among the East European immigrants who settled in Homestead prior to the lockout of 1892. See chaps. 17 and 21 below for details.

15. This paragraph and the following three are based on: Burgoyne, *Homestead Strike,* 58, 59; *PCG, NYH, NYS,* and *NYW,* 7 Jul. 1892; U.S. House, *Report 2447,* 8, 133; Stowell, *Fort Frick,* 45–46.

16. On Martin Murray see: *HT,* 5 Aug. 1882 and 21 Apr. 1883; *NLT,* 26 Apr. 1890; Burgoyne, *Homestead Strike,* 197; AAISW, *Proceedings,* 1891, 3245. On Joseph Sotak see FCSU, Membership List; *CT,* 9 Jul. 1892; Burgoyne, *Homestead Strike,* 92; *NYTR* and *NYW,* 8 and 9 Jul. 1892; *NYS,* 7 Jul. 1892; *NYH,* 9 Jul. 1892.

17. *NYH* and *PCG,* 7 Jul. 1892; U.S. House, *Report 2447,* 90–91; Burgoyne, *Homestead Strike,* 60.

18. *CDN, CT, NYW, NYH, NYTR, NYS, PCG,* and *PP,* 7 Jul. 1892; U.S. House, *Report 2447,* 115–21, 133–37, 179 (which includes the testimony of the reporter for the *HLN*); *NLT,* 26 Nov. 1892; *PD,* 19 and 20 Nov. 1892; Hogg, "Homestead Strike," 85; Burgoyne, *Homestead Strike,* 59. The *NYW* offered contradictory reports regarding the first shot, while the *NYH,* the *CDN,* and the *CT* reported that it came from the Pinkertons. Hogg's informant named the man who allegedly fired first, but Hogg chose not to identify him. Hogg's comments on the question merit quotation: "Probably the best judgment is that at the time all witnesses were interested, directly or indirectly, and since murder was to be charged by both sides, testimony must have been given with an eye toward future developments."

19. This paragraph and the succeeding two are based on: *YEV,* 6 Jul. 1892; *CT, CDN, NYH, NYS, NYTR, NYW, PCG, PD, PP,* and *WDI,* 7 Jul. 1892; *NYH, NYW,* and *WDI,* 8 Jul. 1892; *NYS,* 17 Jul. 1892; *NYTR* 17 and 18 Jul. 1892; *CT, WDI, NYW,* and *NYH,* 18 Jul. 1892; Burgoyne, *Homestead Strike,* 59, 61, 67, 92–93; U.S. House, *Report 2447,* 90–91; Stowell, *Fort Frick,* 42, 254.

20. I have been unable to corroborate the identities of many of the East European workers listed by the daily press as having been wounded on 6 July. Hogg, "Homestead Strike," 84, incorrectly concludes that no one was killed in the initial confrontation and, moreover, that Foy later died of his wounds.

21. Burgoyne, *Homestead Strike,* 61; *NYW* and *WDI,* 7 Jul. 1892; U.S. House, *Report 2447,* 117–21, 129–30; Hogg, "Homestead Strike," 85.

22. Burgoyne, *Homestead Strike,* 61, 65; Hogg, "Homestead Strike," 86; Schooley and Schooley, *Homestead Directory, 1890,* 176; *NYW* and *WDI,* 7 Jul. 1892. Atkinson was one of two participants interviewed by Hogg in the early 1940s.

23. Burgoyne, *Homestead Strike,* 60–61, 282–93; *NYW,* 7 Jul. 1892; AAISW, *Proceedings,* 1890, 3064; U.S. House, *Report 2447,* 5. On Clifford see also *PD,* 4 Sept. 1892. O'Donnell's leadership is discussed in greater detail in chap. 27, below.

24. Burgoyne, *Homestead Strike,* 62; U.S. House, *Report 2447,* 98; *NLT,* 4 Dec. 1890; *NYW,* 7 Jul. 1892.

25. *NYW,* 7 Jul. 1892; Burgoyne, *Homestead Strike,* 61, 62. The GAR was the organization of Union Veterans of the Civil War.

26. The details in this paragraph and the succeeding one are drawn from: *HLN,* 27 Dec. 1890; *CT, PP,* and *NYS,* 7 Jul. 1892; *NYH* and *WDI,* 7 and 8 Jul. 1892; *NYW,* 7, 8, and 17 Jul. 1892; *WDI,* 8 Jul. 1892; Stowell, *Fort Frick,* 51, 81–86, 89, 254; Burgoyne, *Homestead Strike,* 65–66, 67, 93.

27. *CT, PD, PP, NYS,* and *NYH,* 7 Jul. 1892; *NYW,* 6–8 and 11 Jul. 1892; *PP, NYH,* and *WDI,* 8 Jul. 1892; Burgoyne, *Homestead Strike,* 65–66, 93; Stowell, *Fort Frick,* 48, 86.

28. *PP, NYH, NYS,* and *YEV,* 7 Jul. 1892; *WDI,* 8 Jul. 1892; *NYH,* 9 Jul. 1892; *NYW,* 8 and 9 Jul. 1892; Burgoyne, *Homestead Strike,* 67, 102.

29. *PP, NYS,* and *NYH,* 7 and 8 Jul. 1892; *CT,* 7 Jul. 1892; *NYW* and *WDI,* 8 Jul. 1892; Burgoyne, *Homestead Strike,* 93; St. Michael's Roman Catholic Church, Register of Death, 1891–1952, 3–4; FCSU, Membership List; St. Michael Church, Munhall, *75th Anniversary* (Pittsburgh: n.p., 1972), 1; St. Mary Magdalene Church, Register of Marriage, vol. 1 (1881–1908), 59; Kushner, *Slováci Katolíci,* 56; U.S. House, *Report 2447,* 12; Stowell, *Fort Frick,* 86.

30. Hogg, "Homestead Strike," 84, 88; U.S. House, *Report 2447,* 135, 137.

31. *PP,* 7 Jul. 1892; Burgoyne, *Homestead Strike,* 67, 68; Hogg, "Homestead Strike," 87.

32. This paragraph and the following one are based principally on Burgoyne, *Homestead Strike,* 62, 67–70, 73; *NYH* and *PCG,* 7 Jul. 1892.

33. This paragraph and the following two are based on: *PP* and *NYH,* 7 Jul. 1892; Burgoyne, *Homestead Strike,* 62–63; *PCT,* 6 Jul. 1892, as quoted by Hogg, "Homestead Strike," 88.

34. This paragraph and the succeeding one are based on: *PCG, PD, PP, PT, NYH, NYHR, NYS, NYW, WDI,* and *YEV,* 6 Jul. 1892; U.S. House, *Report 2447,* viii, 36–37, 56–66, 66–68; Burgoyne, *Homestead Strike,* 48–49; Bridge, *Inside History,* 212; Harvey, *Frick,* 112–13.

35. Hogg, "Homestead Strike," 79; *NYH* and *NYW,* 6 Jul. 1892; *WDI,* 7 Jul. 1892.

36. This paragraph and the following one are based on: *PP,* 6 Jul. 1892; Frick to Robert A. Pinkerton, 25 June 1892, as quoted in Harvey, *Frick,* 114–15; U.S. House, *Report 2447,* vi, xi, 32, 60–64; Hogg, "Homestead Strike," 81; Harvey, *Frick,* 117–18.

37. This paragraph and the following one are based on: Hogg, "Homestead Strike," 81–82; *HLN,* 2 May 1891; U.S. House, *Report 2447,* xi; Burgoyne, *Homestead Strike,* 50; *NYTR,* 17 and 18 Jul. 1892; *NYH, NYW, WDI,* and *CT,* 18 Jul. 1892; *NYS,* 17 Jul. 1892.

38. On the business and personal relations of Frick and Magee—described as "close personal friends" and "connected . . . in many . . . enterprises"—see *PT* and *PCG,* 9 Mar. 1901. These newspapers also contain an encomium from Carnegie on the occasion of Magee's death. Relationships involving Frick, Carnegie, Knox, and the Magee are explored in chap. 25, below.

39. This paragraph and the preceding one are based on: Burgoyne, *Homestead Strike,* 86, and the daily papers that most carefully followed the activities of Magee and McCleary: *PP, NYH,* and *NYW,* 7, 8, and 9 Jul. 1892. The quotation from the *NYW* appeared on 9 July. (Also of interest is Stowell, *Fort Frick,* 68.) The classic study of Magee as the consummate urban boss is Steffens, *Shame of the Cities,* 147–89.

40. Burgoyne, *Homestead Strike*, 96; Montgomery, *House of Labor*, 37. Burgoyne's widely accepted treatment of the simple relationships among the key actors—more significantly, his silence with regard to the more complex relationships among them—has long been incorporated into the received wisdom about the Homestead Lockout. But his book—originally titled *Homestead, A Complete History of the Struggle of July, 1892, between the Carnegie Steel Company, Limited, and the Amalgamated Association of Iron and Steel Workers* and written in 1893 at the behest of organized labor—is plainly not as complete as he might have made it. It would seem that Burgoyne, for all the splendid, juicy details he revealed, chose to obscure the elaborate network of political intrigue that governed the events. His reasons lie well beyond the scope of this account; that he did and that his incomplete history has not been challenged do, however, render suspect an entire historical tradition of writing on Homestead that has reverently drawn upon Burgoyne's "gospel." Hogg, writing a half-century ago, offered the barbed observation—one that still contains more than a kernel of truth—that most accounts of the Homestead Lockout seemed to be plagiarisms of Burgoyne's work (see Hogg, "Homestead Strike," 88; Hogg, "Pinkertonism," 179).

The question at hand goes beyond the relationship of a gifted journalist and the persons about whom he wrote, interesting as those relationships may have been. We now know, for example, that prior to the lockout, Burgoyne worked for the newspaper owned by Magee, the *Pittsburgh Times* (by 1892 he was writing for the *Pittsburgh Leader*), and that Burgoyne counted Philander C. Knox among many influential friends who stood, as one newspaper put it, "in the highest places of Pittsburgh's commercial and professional life."

On Burgoyne see: Pittsburgh Writers' Club, *Book of Writers*, 22; *Pittsburgh Bulletin*, 1 Apr. 1911; David P. Demarest, Jr., Afterword to Burgoyne, *Homestead Strike*, 315–16, which provides an accessible biographical sketch but does not take note of Burgoyne's having worked for Magee.

41. This paragraph and the succeeding one are based principally on *PP, CT,* and *NYH,* 7 Jul. 1892, the latter two of which contain the texts of the communications exchanged on 6 July by McCleary and Pattison. (Also see U.S. House, *Report 2447,* 57–60.) Burgoyne, *Homestead Strike,* 62, asserts that it was McCleary himself who concluded that state intervention was necessary.

42. *PP, CT,* and *WDI,* 7 Jul. 1892; Burgoyne, *Homestead Strike,* 62; *PL,* 9 Mar. 1901; *NYW,* 10 Feb. and 3 Mar., 1890; and *PCG,* 6 Nov. 1890. In his own ward, the fourteenth, a rock-solid Republican stronghold where the party's candidates usually won by a margin of four to one, Magee brought back an overwhelming majority for Pattison.

43. *HLN,* 8 Nov. 1890. Homestead's returns in the gubernatorial election of 1890 have been all too easily overlooked by many historians largely because the town acquired a reputation as a Republican stronghold prior to the 1892 lockout. Cf. Montgomery, *House of Labor,* 39.

44. *PP,* 7 Jul. 1892; Burgoyne, *Homestead Strike,* 50, 71.

45. *NYH, WDI,* and *PP,* 7 Jul. 1892; Burgoyne, *Homestead Strike,* 70–72.

46. *PP, WDI,* and *NYH,* 7 Jul. 1892.

47. *PP* and *NYH,* 7 Jul. 1892

48. *PCG, PP,* and *WDI,* 7 Jul. 1892; Burgoyne, *Homestead Strike,* 79–80.

49. This paragraph and the two succeeding ones are based principally on the reports in *PP* and *NYH,* 7 Jul. 1892.

50. Pattison was incorrect about the predominance of homeowners in Homestead. See below, chap. 27.

51. *PP* and *NYH,* 7 Jul. 1892; Hogg, "Homestead Strike," 89; Burgoyne, *Homestead Strike,* 94–95. In the end, only thirty-two men reported for duty; McCleary relieved them by declaring it futile to go to Homestead with so few.

52. Burgoyne, *Homestead Strike,* 76, 78–79; *WDI, PP,* and *NYH,* 7 Jul. 1892.

53. *PCG, PP,* and *WDI,* 7 Jul. 1892; Burgoyne, *Homestead Strike,* 79–80.

54. This paragraph and the succeeding one are based on: *PP, PCG, NYW, WDI,* and *NYH,* 7 Jul. 1892; Burgoyne, *Homestead Strike,* 81; U.S. House, *Report 2447,* 92; Hogg, "Homestead Strike," 90

55. The quotation is from Burgoyne, *Homestead Strike,* 81. Hogg, "Homestead Strike," 90, is among the many commentators who overlooks the surrender plan envisioned by the steelworkers.

56. *CT* and *PP,* 7 Jul. 1892; *NYW,* 7 and 8 Jul. 1892; *PD,* 4 Sept. 1892; U.S. House, *Report 2447,* 92; Burgoyne, *Homestead Strike,* 82. In his testimony before the House investigating committee, O'Donnell made no mention of the plan to arrest the Pinkertons and charge them with murder.

57. *PP,* 7 Jul. 1892; *CT, NYW,* and *NYH,* 9 Jul. 1892; *PD,* 10 Jul. 1892; Burgoyne, *Homestead Strike,* 83.

58. Burgoyne, *Homestead Strike,* 83–84; *PCG, NYW, NYTR,* and *CT,* 7 Jul. 1892.

59. *PP,* 7 Jul. 1892

60. Burgoyne, *Homestead Strike,* 84–85.

61. *PP,* 7 Jul. 1892; Stowell, *Fort Frick,* 66; Burgoyne, *Homestead Strike,* 87.

62. *PP,* 7 Jul. 1892; *PCG,* 9 Jul. 1892; Stowell, *Fort Frick,* 64.

63. *NYH* and *PP,* 7 Jul. 1892.

64. *NYW, NYS,* and *NYH,* 7 Jul. 1892.

65. *NYW, NYS,* and *PP,* 7 Jul. 1892.

66. This paragraph and the succeeding two are based on *PP, NYS,* and *NYW,* 9 Jul. 1892; Burgoyne, *Homestead Strike,* 85, 86.

67. Burgoyne, *Homestead Strike,* 85–86; *PP, NYW,* and *NYS,* 7 Jul. 1892. Cf. Wall, *Carnegie,* 559, who asserts that three Pinkertons were killed on the march to the Opera House. At the time of the lockout, there were reports that one or more of the agents had committed suicide during the battle. However, none of these reports was ever confirmed.

68. This paragraph and the succeeding one are based on: *PP, NYW,* and NYS, 7 Jul. 1892; A. J. Blochinger, "The Homestead Strike" (1892), as quoted in the *Homestead Messenger,* 1 Jul. 1976.; Burgoyne, *Homestead Strike,* 86.

69. According to the *WDI,* for example, McLuckie was the actual leader of the Advisory Committee, and David Lynch and Hugh O'Donnell served as "his two assistants" (*WDI,* 8 Jul. 1892). The membership of the Homestead Borough Council is discussed below, in chaps. 20, 27.

70. This paragraph and the next one are based on: *CT, PP, NYH,* and *NYW,* 7 Jul. 1892; Stowell, *Fort Frick,* 68; Burgoyne, *Homestead Strike,* 86.

71. This paragraph and the next one are based on: *NYS, WDI,* and *NYH,* 8 Jul. 1892.

72. *PP,* 7 Jul. 1892.

73. Steffens, *Shame of the Cities,* 150, 158; *PP,* 7 Jul. 1892; Stowell, *Fort Frick,* 99; *NYW,* 8 Jul. 1892. With regard to the Pinkertons' departure, the *PP* observed: "The arrangements . . . had been accomplished so stealthily, that no one could ascertain in what manner they were to be disposed of. The local [railroad] officials were utterly ignorant of the matter, and concluded that negotiations must have been carried on with the president of the Road."

74. *PP,* 7 Jul. 1892. On Brennen see: Weber, *Don't Call Me Boss,* 11–14. Like Lawrence, the mighty Democratic boss of twentieth-century Pittsburgh who was Brennen's most famous political protégé, Brennen possessed, as Weber observes, an "unusual ability to deal successfully with affluent, protestant, Republicans while at the same time acting as a spokesman for organized labor." The key word here is *acting,* for in no way was Brennen a genuine spokesman for organized workers in Homestead; he blatantly ignored their instructions regarding the Pinkertons. He, together with other national leaders of the AAISW, had already made his peace with men such as Frick, Knox, Carnegie, and Magee.

75. *PP,* 7 Jul. 1892; Burgoyne, *Homestead Strike,* 87.

76. This paragraph and the next one are based on: *NYW,* 6 Jul. 1892; *NYH,* 10 Jul. 1892; Wall, *Carnegie,* 546, 815; William Isherwood to Carnegie, 7 Jul. 1892, ACLC, vol. 17.

77. In his *Autobiography,* Carnegie claimed that he did not learn of the events of 6 July until two days later (223).

78. *WDI,* 9 Jul. 1892; Wall, *Carnegie,* 560; *NYH,* 10 Jul. 1892.

79. *HT,* 20 Nov. 1883; Carnegie to Frick, 4 Apr. 1892, as quoted in Bridge, *Inside History,* 204–05; Carnegie to Frick, 4 May 1892, as quoted in Harvey, *Frick,* 165–66; Carnegie to Frick, 10 June 1892, as quoted in Bridge, *Inside History,* 205.

80. Carnegie to Frick, 7 Jul. 1892, as quoted in Harvey, *Frick,* 166; Carnegie, *Autobiography,* 219. Also relevant in Hogg, "Homestead Strike," 59–60.

81. On the Braddock lockout of 1888, see below, chap. 22.

82. Carnegie, *Autobiography,* 223.

CHAPTER 3. *The "Mechanical Habit of Mind"*

1. This paragraph and the next one are based on Overman, *Metallurgy,* 484–85.

2. Wall, *Carnegie,* 792. On puddling see: Camp and Francis, *Making Steel,* 214–22; James O. Edwards, "Theory versus Practice," *Vulcan Record,* 1873, 5–7; J. Davis, *Iron Puddler,* 98–99, 110–12; Durfee, "Development of American Industries, II"; Aston and Storey, *Wrought Iron,* 4–6, 11–13; Courtheaux, "Le Puddleur"; Joynson, *Iron and Steel Maker,* 89–91; Keeler and Fenn, "Taking of Pittsburgh," 233, 236–38; Morton and Mutton, "Cort's Puddling Process"; Roberts, "Puddling Process."

3. J. Davis, *Iron Puddler,* 91.

4. Durfee, "Development of American Industries, II"; Hunt, "American Rolling Mills"; Morgan, "Landmarks"; Kindl, "Rolling Mill Industry."

5. Couvares, "Work Leisure, and Reform," 13–25; Bennett, "Iron Workers," 10–14.

6. Smith, *Wealth of Nations, An Inquiry into the Nature and Causes of the,* 7–10. On the transformation of the English textile trades in the industrial revolution, see Thompson, *English Working Class.* On Lowell see Dalzell, *Enterprising Elite;* Kasson, *Civilizing the Machine;* 55–106.

7. Babbage, *Machinery and Manufactures,* 169–76; Braverman, *Labor and Monopoly Capital;* 76–81; Berg, *Machinery Question,* 182–84.

8. Tawney, *Religion and the Rise of Capitalism:* Polanyi, *Great Transformation;* Weber, *Economy and Society,* 1:63–74, 2:635–40; R. Williams, *Country and City,* 64; R. Williams, *Marxism and Literature,* 60–67. On the emergence of a moral code peculiar to capitalism, see R. Williams, *Culture and Society;* R. Williams, *Long Revolution;* Macpherson, *Possessive Individualism.* Also of interest is Greenberg, "Social Change in the Early Nineteenth Century," 393–714.

9. Mumford, *Technics and Civilization,* 45–55; Blake, "Mumford"; Berg, *Machinery Question,* chap. 3; Winch, *Adam Smith's Politics,* chap. 4.; Heilbroner, *The Worldly Philosophers,* 16–72.

10. Babbage, *Machinery and Manufactures,* 2, 119, 211–16; Braverman, *Labor and Monopoly Capital,* 80. Also see Noble, *America by Design,* 259–60. Babbage understood that his "principle" was contested by workers; in a certain sense, this understanding informs *Machinery and Manufactures* in its entirety, but see esp. 228–30, 296–305, 334–36. Both Braverman and, to a lesser extent, Noble imply that the Babbage principle was a substantive achievement rather than a working hypothesis that informed managerial efforts to restructure and reorganize the production process.

11. Overman, *Manufacture of Iron,* 484–85.

12. Noble, *America by Design,* chaps. 1–3; Mumford, *Technics and Civilization,* 53.

13. Bessemer, *Autobiography,* 156–61; *Times* (London), 12 and 14 Aug., 1856; Hendrick, *Carnegie,* 1:155.

14. Bessemer, *Autobiography,* 159, 162–63, 165ff.; Birch, *Economic History,* 323; Carr and Taplin, *British Steel,* 20–21; Hendrick, *Carnegie,* 1:159–60; Fisher, *Epic of Steel,* 116–17; Wertime, *Age of Steel,* 287; McHugh, *Holley,* 287.

15. Bessemer, *Autobiography,* 160; Camp and Francis, *Making Steel,* 277–79, 320–23; H. Campbell, *Iron and Steel,* 217.

16. See, for example, Durfee, "Development of American Industries, VIII," 15–28, 39–40, 743–49; Durfee, "Chemical Laboratory"; Knight, "First Century," 216–17; Hunt, "Original Bessemer Steel Plant," 61–70. Also see McHugh, *Holley,* 174–89; Fisher, *Epic of Steel,* 116–21; Casson, *Romance of Steel,* passim; Hendrick, *Carnegie,* 150–77.

17. Bessemer, *Autobiography,* 161.

18. Gilfillan, *Sociology of Invention;* Temin, *Iron and Steel,* 126; Phillips, "Pneumatic Process"; Wertime, *Age of Steel,* 285; Swank, *Iron in All Ages,* 397–99; Boucher, *Kelly,* 47–51; Weeks, "Bessemer Process"; Fisher, *Epic of Steel,* 120–21; McHugh, *Holley,* 112–35.

19. J. Williams, "Danks Furnace"; Durfee, "Development of American Industries II," 327–31; Percival Roberts, "Puddling Process"; *AISA Bulletin,* 6 Feb. and 13 Nov. 1867; U.S. Senate, *Report on the Conditions of Employment in the Iron and Steel Industry, Vol. III,* 33–36. Also see Bennett, "Iron Workers," 21–25.

20. The definition of steel is discussed in app. A.

21. Bessemer, *Autobiography*, 135; Bessemer to James Kitson, president of the British Iron and Steel Association, 10 Sept. 1890, reprinted in Boucher, *Kelly*, 67–76; Birch, *Economic History*, 320–21; Carr and Taplin, *British Steel*, 19.

22. Bessemer, *Autobiography*, 138; Bessemer to Kitson in Boucher, *Kelly*, 67–76; Hendrick, *Carnegie*, 1:152; Carr and Taplin, *British Steel*, 21; Landes, *Unbound Prometheus*, 255. Shear steel was produced by the following steps: smelting iron ore in a blast furnace; puddling pig iron into wrought iron; rolling wrought iron into merchant bar; converting iron into blister steel by "cooking" it in large vaults (known as the cementation process); resmelting in crucibles and then recasting it into small ingots; rolling the ingots; compressing many layers of ingots into shear steel bars; and finally, shaping the bars into a finished product. See app. A for additional details.

23. Bessemer, *Autobiography*, 138; Bessemer to Kitson in Boucher, *Kelly* 67–76. Mumford, *Technics and Civilization*, 89–91, discusses earlier ties between metal-making and the military.

24. The quotation is from Bessemer, *Autobiography*, 142. The description of the invention and practice of Bessemer steelmaking in this and in succeeding paragraphs is drawn principally from ibid., 156–61; Holley, "Adaptation"; Holley, "Recent Improvements"; Hunt, "Original Bessemer Steel Plant"; Weeks, "Bessemer Process," Hall, "Manufacture of Bessemer Steel," 121–28; Tchernoff, "Manufacture of Bessemer Steel"; U.S. Senate, *Report on the Conditions of Employment in the Iron and Steel Industry in the United States, Vol. I: Wages and Hours of Labor*, 52–55; Slade, "Bessemer Steel," in Hewitt, "The Production of Iron and Steel," 2:63–84; Frederick A. P. Barnard, "Machinery and Processes of the Industrial Arts, and Apparatus of the Exact Sciences,"in U.S. Senate, *Reports on the Paris Exposition*, 3:284–89; Camp and Francis, *Making Steel*, 262ff.; Hendrick, *Carnegie*, 1:150–60.

25. Bessemer, *Autobiography*, 142–44. Compared to most descriptions of the Bessemer converter in action, the inventor's own account of the initial blow is not melodramatic in the least. The converter was a favorite (and fetishized) subject for graphic artists, lay journalists, scientists, and novelists well into the twentieth century.

26. Bessemer, *Autobiography*, 143–44, 170; Boucher, *Kelly*, 29.

27. Wertime, *Age of Steel*, 287–90; Birch, *Economic History*, 326–27; Carr and Taplin, *British Steel*, 22–23; McHugh, *Holley*, 142–67; Temin, *Iron and Steel*, 125–26; Camp and Francis, *Making Steel*, 27, 262–63, 280, 284–85; Hall, "Manufacture of Bessemer Steel," 122–23.

28. This paragraph and the following one are drawn from: Birch, *Economic History*, 325; Landes, *Unbound Prometheus*, 256; Wall, *Carnegie*, 263–65; Hendrick, *Carnegie*, 1:160–63; Wertime, *Age of Steel*, 292–93; Carr and Taplin, *British Steel*, 22–23; Camp and Francis, *Making Steel*, 278. The enhancement that allowed the Bessemer process to use phosphoric ores was developed by Sidney Gilchrist-Thomas and Percy Carlyle Gilchrist. Called the basic process, its principal application in the United States was in the manufacture of open-hearth steel.

29. Despite its production problems, the Bessemer process became a commercial success for Henry Bessemer not long after he began operations in his mill in Sheffield. The principal reason was that irregularities in the quality of Bessemer steel did not detract from its usefulness for items that did not require exactness

of chemical specification. Chief among these were rails. In the United States, too, the commercial success of the product arose in part from the demand for steel rails. See Temin, *Iron and Steel*, 130–32.

CHAPTER 4. *Captains of Steel*

1. This overview of American metalmakers is based principally on the *Transactions* of the AIME and the ASME. The *Proceedings* of the Engineers Society of Western Pennsylvania also have been helpful. Among the relevant secondary works: Layton, *Revolt of the Engineers;* Layton, "American Ideologies"; Layton, "Science, Business, and the American Engineer," 51–72; Layton, "Veblen and the Engineers"; Calvert, *Mechanical Engineer;* Noble, *America by Design*, 1–49; Sinclair, *Centennial History;* Rae, "Engineer as Business Man"; Redlich, *American Business Leaders*, vol. 1, passim; Urwick, "Management's Debt." Horowitz, "Industrialization," chaps. 8–10, also is helpful; as is Hutton, *American Society of Mechanical Engineers*.

2. Holley, "Intermediate Power," 167; Bledstein, *Culture of Professionalism*, 80–92, 104–05.

3. "The Age of Steel," *AISA Bulletin*, 23 Nov. 1867. The article was first published in *Engineering*, a British journal that served the same constituency. Also see *AISA Bulletin*, 30 Nov. 1867, which includes a glowing account of Bessemer steel based on the exhibits of the Paris Exposition of 1867.

4. Bledstein, *Culture of Professionalism*, 87–88, 90, 92, 104–05. Also see Lears, *No Place of Grace*, 17–19.

5. "Rules," *AIME Transactions* 4 (1875–76): 21; Layton, *Revolt of the Engineers*, 29–35, 50; Calvert, *Mechanical Engineer*, 210–13.

6. Holley, "Mechanical Engineering," 5; "Proceedings of the Hartford Meeting," *ASME Transactions* 2 (1881): 3–4; Thurston, "Mechanical Engineer"; Thurston, "Inaugural Address," 6; ASME, *Mechanical Engineers in America Born Prior to 1861*, 297–98; Layton, "American Ideologies," 693–95; Durand, *Thurston*, 95–114; Noble, *America by Design*, 36–37; Horowitz, "Industrialization," 232; Layton, *Revolt of the Engineers*, 35–37; Sinclair, *Centennial History*, 24–30; Calvert, *Mechanical Engineer*, 45ff., 97–104, 210–13, 225–27; Hutton, *American Society of Mechanical Engineers*, 26.

7. Holley, "Inadequate Union," 201.

8. Richardson, "Traveling by Telegraph," 21–22. Also of interest is Garland, "Homestead," and the accompanying illustrations by Orson Lowell. On the technological sublime see Klingender, *Art and the Industrial Revolution*, 83–103; Kasson, *Civilizing the Machine*, 166–71.

9. Durfee, "Development of American Industries, VIII," 30; Kazin, *On Native Grounds*, 18.

10. Kitson, "Iron and Steel Industries," 625; *AIME Transactions* 19 (1890–91): xxxi–xlii; Burn, *Economic History*, 11. Also see Kitson, Preface to British Iron and Steel Institute, *Institute in America*, v–xi.

11. Hewitt, "Iron and Labor"; Kitson, "Iron and Steel Industries," 625; I. Bell, "American Iron Trade," 2–3; Nevins, Introduction to Hewitt, "Iron and Labor," *Selected Writings*, 113; Swank, *Iron in All Ages*, 519–24. The British Insti-

tute's decision to honor Hewitt arose partly from his unwavering support of lower tariffs on metal products. See Hewitt, "American Worker under High Tariffs," *Selected Writings,* 227–48, esp. 246; Nevins, *Hewitt,* 419–29, 573. Hewitt understood that the award of the medal to him rather than to Carnegie, who was a staunch protectionist, could be construed as "compensation for services rendered," as Hewitt himself put it.

12. The standard biography of Hewitt is Nevins, *Hewitt.* More critical sketches may be found in Alan Trachtenberg, *Brooklyn Bridge,* 7–8, 101–09, 118–24; McCullough, *Great Bridge,* 373–80, 399–92, 415–16.

In calling Hewitt an entrepreneur, I have followed the definition codified by Cole, "Tribute to Gay," and embellished by Pollard, *Genesis of Modern Management,* 1–3: one who unites all the means of production to create goods by determining the objectives of the business enterprise; by developing and maintaining the business organization and building "efficient" relations with workers; by securing adequate financial resources; by acquiring "efficient" technology and updating it with the best innovations; by developing new markets and products; and by nurturing good relations with the government and the public. Though this definition is helpful, neither Cole nor his colleagues in entrepreneurial history assess the role of the entrepreneur in creating and re-creating social hierarchy.

13. Hewitt's report is in U.S. Senate, *Reports on the Paris Exposition,* 2:1–183. Some of the points in this and in succeeding paragraphs are drawn from Appendix H of the *Reports,* "Evidence Given by Abram S. Hewitt before the Trades Union Commission in London, in 1867," 150–70, as well as United Kingdom, Parliament, *Second Report of the Commissioners Appointed to Inquire into the Organization and Rules of Trades Unions and Other Associations,* Parliamentary Sessional Papers, 1867, vol. 32, c3893, testimony of Abram S. Hewitt, 1–13, microfilm, Perkins Library, Duke University.

14. This paragraph and the succeeding two are based on Hewitt, "Statistics and Geography," as quoted in Nevins, *Hewitt,* 95; Hewitt, "Production of Iron and Steel," in U.S. Senate, *Reports on the Paris Exposition,* 2:39, 55; Hewitt, "Evidence," in U.S. Senate, *Reports on the Paris Exposition, app. H, pp.* 157, 160–61. For examples of Hewitt's explicit antipathy toward labor and labor organizations, see P. Foner, *Labor Movement,* 2:125–26; Nevins, *Hewitt,* 510, 516.

15. By 1890, Hewitt was publicly avowing his "support" of trade unions—but only if they acted according to principles that in no way threatened the domain of capital. See Hewitt, "Iron and Labor," *Selected Writings,* 125–26; Hewitt, "Bessemer," *Selected Writings,* 139.

16. Testimony of Hewitt, United Kingdom, Parliamentary Sessional Papers, 1867, vol. 32, c3893, pp. 6, 8; Hewitt, "Production of Iron and Steel," in U.S. Senate, *Reports on the Paris Exposition,* 2:54, 62. Scobey, "Boycotting the Politics Factory," 285, correctly point out that Hewitt possessed "a liberal's animus against class-conscious politics," but his characterization of Hewitt as "a liberal defender of trade unionism" is inaccurate.

17. *Vulcan Record,* Jan. 1868, 14.

18. Hewitt to W. F. Durfee, 13 Feb. 1891, as quoted in Durfee, "Development of American Industries, VIII," 746; Hewitt, "Production of Iron and Steel," in U.S. Senate, *Reports on the Paris Exposition,* 2:31; Nevins, *Hewitt,* 125–33; Temin, *Iron and Steel,* 110, 126, 139; Redlich, *American Business Leaders,* 2:93–94. Hewitt's

reservations about Bessemer steel proved costly to him, since the American metals industry relied heavily on it through the 1880s. However, Hewitt's assessment was generally on target when in 1867 he concluded that it was "not safe to use Bessemer metal in any case involving the security of life or limb, unless, in the process of manufacture, it has been subjected to such tests as will certainly show all its defects." While the quality did improve, even after the turn of the century Bessemer metal was liable to give way "in a treacherous manner under shock." (See H. Campbell, *Iron and Steel*, 529; Temin, *Iron and Steel*, 145–52.) Open-hearth metal, which was stronger, ultimately became the dominant product of the American metals industry.

19. Like other ironmasters, Hewitt was deeply interested in mechanizing puddling. Mechanical puddling "could be introduced with great advantage to both masters and men." He noted, though, that English puddlers had "declined" to use mechanical puddling devices. J. Williams, "Danks Furnace," noted a similar response by puddlers in Pittsburgh. The sketch of the open-hearth process in this and in succeeding paragraphs is based on: Hewitt, "Iron and Steel Production," 32–35; Nevins, *Hewitt*, 236–46; Camp and Francis, *Making Steel*, 288–91; Wellman, "Open-Hearth Manufacture"; Seaver, "Manufacture of Open-Hearth Steel," 133–54; Durfee, "Development of American Industries, VIII," 741–43; Carr and Taplin, *British Steel*, 30–35; Temin, *Iron and Steel*, 138–39; Fisher, *Epic of Steel*, 125–26; Birch, *Economic History*, 371–78; Wertime, *Age of Steel*, 290–92; McHugh, *Holley*, 274–93; Swank, *Iron in All Ages*, 418–25; Landes, *Unbound Prometheus*, 256–57; Hogan, *Economic History*, 1:221–23.

20. Temin, *Iron and Steel*, 110, 131, 141–42; Nevins, *Hewitt*, 235, 244–45, 250; Wellman, "Open-Hearth Manufacture," 79–82; Redlich, *American Business Leaders*, 98–99. Temin notes that Hewitt "was always among the first to try new techniques and introduce new products" and therefore was "often, in fact, too early to make a commercial success of these experiments."

21. On the 1886 mayoralty election in New York, see Scobey, "Boycotting the Politics Factory." As chairman of Sameul Tilden's presidential campaign, Hewitt played a peripheral role in the negotiations that culminated in the Compromise of 1877. See Hewitt, "Disputed Election, 1876–77," *Selected Writings*, 155–94; Woodward, *Reunion and Reaction*, 5, 153–56.

22. Hewitt, "Mutual Relations," *Selected Writings*, 277–91; U.S. House, Select Committee, *Causes of the General Depression*, esp. 181–208, 464–76, 476–91, 506–15; Nevins, *Hewitt*, 264–66, 292–98, 306–19, 432–40.

23. Hewitt, "Mutual Relations," *Selected Writings*, 277, 286–89, 290.

24. Ibid., 286, 288. Also see Kirkland, *Dream and Thought*, 12.

25. Hewitt, "Mutual Relations," *Selected Writings*, 288–89; Hewitt, "Production of Iron and Steel," in U.S. Senate, *Reports on the Paris Exposition*, 53; Ware, *Labor Movement*, 362; P. Foner, *Labor Movement*, 2:125–28; Perlman, "Upheaval and Reorganisation," 2:450–54; Scobey, "Boycotting the Politics Factory."

26. Hewitt, eulogy of Alexander Lyman Holley, in AIME, *Holley Memorial*, 24; Hewitt, "Bessemer," *Selected Writings*, 138–39; *NYT*, 1 and 2 Oct. 1890; Noble, "Present Tense Technology," 1.

27. Howe, "Bessemer Process," 1120–67, esp. 1120, 1135–38. The principles of increasing outputs outlined by Howe also applied to open-hearth mills. Howe claimed that the ever increasing pace of production caused no ill effects to the

steelworkers: "You will find no signs of unwholesome exhaustion in our Bessemer works." Where the eight-hour day still prevailed in 1890, Howe's observation may have had some truth to it. But twelve-hour shifts became the rule after the Homestead Lockout of 1892. For a harrowing account of the effects of overwork in the post-Homestead era, see Fitch, "Old Age at Forty."

28. *NYT*, 30 Sept.–3 Oct. 1890; Nevins, Introduction to Hewitt, "Bessemer," *Selected Writings*, 137; Howe, "Bessemer Process," 1120, 1148–50, 1166ff. In calling Holley an engineer-entrepreneur, I have followed: Redlich, *American Business Leaders*, 1:96, 101; Rae, "Engineer as Business Man," 95, 97–98; Calvert, *Mechanical Engineer*, 225–26. As Calvert has suggested, Holley was not the only nineteenth-century engineer who saw his job as embracing that of the entrepreneur. Among engineers and businessmen, though, Holley's "name was frequently mentioned as representing the ideal, . . . and Holley himself was one of the earliest to formulate the engineer-entrepreneur as an ideal." Among the best examples of his thinking on the subject are: Holley, "Mechanical Engineering"; Holley, "Inadequate Union." For a formal definition of the engineer-entrepreneur, see Rae, "Engineer-Entrepreneur"; note, however, that in formulating his definition, Rae overlooks workplace relations.

29. McHugh, *Holley*, 46, 350, 369–70, 372; *NYT*, 30 Sept. and 3 Oct. 1890.

30. See, among others: "Pittsburgh Testimonial," in AIME, *Holley Memorial*, 162–65; Bayles, "Tribute to Holley," 34–48. For a twentieth-century example of the reverence afforded Holley, see McHugh, *Holley*, passim. Brief and more dispassionate assessments of his technical achievements are: Temin, *Iron and Steel*, 132–40; Wall, *Carnegie*, 312–21; Camp and Francis, *Making Steel*, 264ff. The clearest statement of the ties between Holley and management "science" is Urwick, "Management's Debt," esp. 9. On Holley's importance in the ASME, see Sinclair, *Centennial History*, 32, 38–39.

31. Holley, "Inadequate Union," esp. 201, 207. Also see Calvert, *Mechanical Engineer*, 225–26.

32. Holley, "Intermediate Power"; Holley, "Inadequate Union"; Holley, "Mechanical Engineering"; Kent, "Relation of Engineering to Economics"; Thurston, "Inaugural Address"; Lears, *No Place of Grace*, 4–26.

33. Holley, "Inadequate Union," esp. 193, 198.

34. The quotations are from Holley, *Ordnance and Armor*, 396, as quoted in McHugh, *Holley*, 171. The details in this paragraph and the succeeding ones are based on: Bayles, "Tribute to Holley," 39–44; Hunt, "Bessemer Manufacture," 201, 213–15; Hunt, "Original Bessemer Plant at Troy," 173–74; Hogan, *Economic History*, 1:31–38; McHugh, *Holley*, 190–205; Swank, *Iron in All Ages*, 409–10; Durfee, "Development of American Industries, IX; Temin, *Iron and Steel*, 133–36; Fritz, *Autobiography*, 160–61.

35. Fritz, *Autobiography*, 160–61. Some of the other members of the group were Fritz's brother, George, Robert W. Hunt, and Eckley B. Coxe, who went on to become a Pennsylvania state senator and the president of ASME. Hunt, who was the first professional chemist employed in an American steelworks, W. R. Jones, and the Fritz brothers were all employed for a time by the Cambria Works in Johnstown.

36. The quotations are from Holley, "Wrought Iron and Steel." In discussing the Edgar Thomson, I have drawn from the same writing that informs my discus-

sion of Holley's career in general, and from: Holley, Blueprints; *NLT,* 11 Sept. 1875; *AISA Bulletin,* 10 Sept. 1875; *IA,* 5 Aug. 1875; *PC,* 16 Sept. 1875; Carnegie, Brothers, and Co., *Edgar Thomson Steel Works;* Wall, *Carnegie,* 311–21; Camp and Francis, *Making Steel,* 264ff.; Chandler, *Visible Hand,* 259–66. Chandler's discussion of the Edgar Thomson is very helpful—as far as it goes. Building on his consideration of the goals of postwar industrialists, Chandler argues that steelmasters wanted to increase the volume and speed of production while decreasing capital outlays for the inputs of labor, capital, and materials. The semitechnical term for increasing the output and the rate of flow of materials is *throughput.* As Chandler suggests, Holley sought to increase throughput. The question of labor relations does not enter into Chandler's equation, however.

37. Chandler defines mass production as that which yielded high throughput by means of technological and organizational innovation that replaced manual labor and consolidated successive processes into a single establishment. See Chandler, *Visible Hand,* 241.

38. Holley, "Inadequate Union," 119–201, 204, 206, 207.

39. John Fritz also was a talented engineer as well as an opponent of labor unions. Many of his innovations were in the rolling sector of the metals industry and were incorporated in the design of the Edgar Thomson. On Fritz see, in addition to his *Autobiography:* Fackenthal, "Fritz"; McHugh, *Holley,* 233–43. The production records of the Edgar Thomson are in USX Corporation, Miscellaneous Historical Records, 1853–1907, USX Archives.

40. Jones, "Manufacture of Bessemer Steel, also published in *AM,* 20 May 1881; Holley, "Inadequate Union"; Holley, "Memo Concerning American Bessemer Works to Lord Stafford," 2 June 1881, Holley Letterbooks, vol. 7; Thurston, "Mechanical Engineer."

41. Towne, "Engineer as Economist"; Noble, *America by Design,* 267. Noble offers a concise definition of scientific management by identifying its five successive yet overlapping stages: (1) the accumulation by management of information about machines and workers; (2) the systemization of this information into "laws"; (3) the "scientific" determination of optimal work standards for machines and laborers; (4) eliciting from the machines and the workers this optimal standard by reorganizing the work process; and (5) gaining the cooperation of workers by making them feel "content." Noble dates the start of the movement for scientific management at 1890, but American steelmasters were active in all five stages of the technique as early as the 1860s.

42. Towne, "Engineer as Economist," 428–49.

43. The historian most attentive to the pathbreaking role of American metalmasters in the origin of modern production and management techniques is Chandler: "Modern factory management was first fully worked out in the metal-making and metal-working industries" (*Visible Hand,* 258). The men credited by Chandler with helping to create "the economies of speed" in the steel industry—Holley, Jones, and Fritz—were well aware that modernization was in reality a move not only to increase production and integrate disparate processes but also to wrest control of the work process away from workers. For further evidence that mechanical engineers began to focus on managerial problems well before Towne's speech, see Nelson, *Managers and Workers,* 49; Litterer, "Systematic Management: Design"; Litterer, "Systematic Management: Search"; Jenks, "Early Phases."

44. Holley, "Pressing Needs"; Temin, *Iron and Steel*, 135–36; Bayles, "Tribute to Holley," 42–43; AIME, *Holley Memorial*, 69–70.

45. Hogan, *Economic History*, 1:37; Fritz, *Autobiography*, 155–57; Temin, *Iron and Steel*, 135.

46. Hunt, "Bessemer Manufacture," 214–15; Hunt, "Original Bessemer Plant"; Bayles, "Tribute to Holley," 38; Hogan, *Economic History*, 1:37; Temin, *Iron and Steel*, 136.

47. Holley, "Bessemer Machinery," 10, as quoted in Hogan, *Economic History*, 1:36–37, emphasis in the original; Hunt, "Bessemer Manufacture," 215; Camp and Francis, *Making Steel*, 264, 273–75; Bayles, "Tribute to Holley," 40; Temin, *Iron and Steel*, 136.

48. This paragraph and the succeeding two are drawn from: U.S. Department of Labor, Bureau of Labor Statistics, *Wages and Hours of Labor in the Iron and Steel Industry, 1907 to 1915*, 475–81; U.S. Senate, *Report on the Conditions of Employment in the Iron and Steel Industry in the United States, Vol. 1: Wages and Hours of Labor*, 52–66; Hogan, *Economic History*, 1:20–21; Swank, "Iron and Steel Production," 124–25; Bennett, "Iron Workers," 27–29.

49. Hunt, "Bessemer Manufacture," 215. The labor policies of the Cambria Works were pathbreaking, to say the least, according to Bennett, "Iron Workers." The superintendents of the largest Bessemer mills, including the one in Homestead, were trained at Cambria. See W. Jones, "Manufacture of Bessemer Steel," 32–33. Holley, too, endorsed a policy of hiring men with little skill because he found that they—in the words of his biographer—had "fewer preconceived notions and prejudices." See McHugh, *Holley*, 221.

50. *AISA Bulletin*, 10 Sept. 1875; *NLT*, 11 Sept. 1875; W. Jones, "Comments on Report," 366–67; Raymond, "William R. Jones"; Wall, *Carnegie*, 311–16. Jones summarized his management philosophy in a letter to one of the owners of the Edgar Thomson. For the full text of the letter, see Bridge, *Inside History*, 81–82; McHugh, *Holley*, 257. The Mr. Metcalf in Jones's remarks was a prominent Pittsburgh steelmaker.

51. Holley, "Intermediate Power," 168.

CHAPTER 5. *The Civilization of the Nineteenth Century*

1. There is a vast literature that considers the issues but alluded to here. Above all, see: Montgomery, *Beyond Equality*; E. Foner, *Reconstruction*; E. Foner, *Nothing but Freedom*. Also relevant is Bernstein, *Draft Riots*.

2. Lincoln, as quoted in Hofstadter, *American Political Tradition*, 133–34.

3. *NYT*, 22 Feb. 1869, as quoted in Montgomery, *Beyond Equality*, 25–26.

4. Montgomery, *Beyond Equality*, 30; Montgomery, "Labor and the Republic"; Rodgers, *Work Ethic*, 30–34; L. Fink, *Workingmen's Democracy*, 6–7.

5. Forbath, "Ambiguities," 774–75, 801–12; E. Foner, *Paine*, 123–24; Montgomery, *Beyond Equality*, 30–31, 249–60, 448–52; Pocock, "Machiavelli"; E. Morgan, "Slavery and Freedom," esp. 7–9; G. Nash, "Popular Political Thinking"; Wilentz, "Artisan Republican Festivals."

6. Ware, *Labor Movement*, 74; Montgomery, "Labor and the Republic," 204–05; Montgomery, *Beyond Equality*, 140–41; Andrews, "Nationalisation," 2:92–93,

151–52; McNeill, "Problem of Today," esp. 459, 462, 456, 468. For an alternative interpretation of the Knights, see Grob, *Workers and Utopia*, esp. 39–42. On McNeill also see Gutman, *Work, Culture, and Society*, 99–101.

7. This sketch of Armstrong is drawn principally from *NLT*, 26 Aug. 1882 and 7 Dec. 1889. Also see Richards, "Armstrong"; Couvares, "Work, Leisure, and Reform," 48–49; Montgomery, *Beyond Equality*, 176–78.

8. The editorials upon which this paragraph is based appeared in the *NLT* from late 1873 through 1877. See, in particular: "Labor Reform," 22 May 1874; "The Coming Struggle," 22 May 1875; "The Coming Struggle," 28 Aug. 1875; "What Shall We Do?" 9 Sept. 1875; "Still in Slavery," 18 Nov. 1876; "The Grand Problem," 23 Dec. 1876; "If," 27 Jan. 1877. Also see Couvares, "Work, Leisure, and Reform," 50; Oestreicher, "Working-Class Formation," 124. The *NLT* occasionally has been referred to as conservative (see, for example, Gutman, *Work, Culture, and Society*, 104). However, the paper's conservatism was an acquired characteristic and, as the career of Armstrong himself illustrates, only grudgingly acquired.

9. "Certificate of Non-Liability to be Given by the Board of Enrollment," 19 Jul. 1864, Miscellaneous Historical Records, Box 39, Carnegie Papers, USX Archives; Bridge, *Inside History*, 101; Wall, *Carnegie*, 189–90, 222–23, 319, and chap. 7, passim.

10. Harvey, *Frick*, 16, 29–66, 69; Wall, *Carnegie*, 479. Frick continues to be the object of uncritical scholarship. See, for example, Warren, "Business Career."

11. *AM*, 18 Feb. 1881, 10 and 17 Oct. 1884.

12. *HT*, 17 Sept. 1881; *NLT*, 22 June 1889; William B. Dickson, "Account of 1882 Strike," and Robert P. Dickson, "Addendum to Account of 1882 Strike," both in Dickson Papers; Eggert, *Steelmasters*, xvi, 3–4, 17–18; Wall, *Carnegie*, 484–85, 530–32; Stevens, "Men Who Run the Mills," manuscript; Charles M. Schwab Letterbook, Miscellaneous Historical Records, box 3, Carnegie Papers, USX Archives. For an unabashedly celebratory account of Schwab's career, see Hessen, *Schwab*.

13. This sketch of McLuckie is based primarily on *NLT*, 28 Oct. 1876, 1 Apr., 8 and 15 Jul., and 18 Nov. 1882, 12 May 1887, and 11 Dec. 1892; Garlock, *Guide to Local Assemblies*, 407; *PCT*, 12 Jul. 1889; *HLN*, 2 Jan. 1886, 8 Feb., 1 Mar., and 22 Nov. 1890, 23 Jan. and 12 Mar. 1892; *HT*, 13 Jan. 1883; U.S. House, *Report 2447*, 98–106; *YEV*, 23 and 27 Sept. 1892; *WDI*, 1. Oct. 1892; *PP*, 4 Oct. 1892; *PD*, 22 Sept., 1 and 6 Oct., and 8 Nov. 1892; Burgoyne, *Homestead Strike*, 180ff., 194–97, 202, 209; Carnegie, *Autobiography*, 226–30.

14. *WDI*, 20 Jul. 1892.

15. Information on J. E. Jones and Crawford has been gathered from a wide variety of sources, including: M. P. Schooley and J. R. Schooley, *Homestead Directory, 1892*, 8–9; Spahr, *America's Working People*, 154–56; *HLN*, 29 Jan., 2 and 20 Feb., and 20 Dec. 1884, 24 Jan., 19 and 26 Dec. 1885, 2 Jan. and 17 Feb. 1886, 19 Feb. 1887, 25 Mar. 1888, 9 Mar. 1889, 22 Feb. 1890, 21 Feb. 1891, and 20 Feb. 1892; *HT*, 25 Feb. and 10 Jun. 1882, 13 and 20 Jan. and 24 Feb. 1883; AAISW, *Proceedings*, 1881, 771; AAISW, *Proceedings*, 1889, 2851–53, and "Membership Abstract"; *Homestead Eagle*, 10 Mar. 1888; Burgoyne, *Homestead Strike*, 38; *NYTR*, 17 and 18 Jul. 1892; *WDI*, 18, 19, and 28 Jul., 3, 4, and 8 Aug. 1892; *NYH*, 18 Jul. 1892; *CT*, 18 Jul. 1892; *NYS*, 17 Jul. 1892; *NYW*, 18 and 28 Jul. 1892;

PP, 2 and 3 Aug., 3 Sept., and 21 Nov. 1892; *PD,* 2, 3, 4, and 7 Aug., 3 and 4 Sept., and 1 Oct. 1892.

16. *PP,* 3 and 5 Sept. 1892; *PD,* 3, 4, 5, 8, and 9 Sept. 1892; *WDI,* 5 Sept. 1892; Stowell, *Fort Frick,* 250; *HT,* 20 Aug. 1881, 11 Mar. and 2 Apr. 1882; Kushner, *Slováci Katolíci,* 49, 56; St. Mary Magdalene Church, *One Hundredth Anniversary,* 1; FCSU, Membership list, 322; Krause, *"Za Chlebom,"* passim. Also see June Alexander, "Staying Together," 59–61; Stolarik, "Immigration and Urbanization," chap. 1.

17. This sketch of D. R. Jones is drawn primarily from: H. C. Cooper, *Twentieth-Century Bench and Bar,* 2:954; Burgoyne, *Homestead Strike,* 219–20; Chris Evans, *United Mine Workers,* 89–90; Roy, *Coal Miners,* 184–85; McBride, "Coal Miners," 252–53; *AM,* 4 Mar. 1881; *HT,* 2 Dec. 1882; *HLN,* 17 and 31 Jan. 1885, 13 Feb. 1886, 19 Feb. 1887, 2 June and 11 Nov. 1888; *IW,* 11 Oct. 1879; *NLT,* 16 Aug. 1879, 1, 15, 22, and 29 Jan., 12, 19, and 26 Feb., 26 Mar., 29 Oct., and 5 Nov. 1881, 10 Jun., 15 Jul., and 28 Oct. 1882, 6 Jan. and 6 Oct. 1883, 2 Feb. 1886, and 19 Feb. 1887.

18. Armstrong to Powderly, 1 Jan. 1880, reel no. 2, Powderly Papers, emphasis in the original. Also see D. R. Jones to Uriah Stephens, 13 Oct. 1879, and Jones to Powderly, 16 Oct. 1879, reel no. 1 Powderly Papers.

19. Northwestern Historical Association, *Allegheny County,* 1:444–45; Layton to Powderly 18, 23, and 25 May, and 21 June 1882, reel no. 3, Layton to Powderly, 14 June 1882, reel no. 4, and Powderly to Layton, 8 Jun. 1882, reel no. 45, all in the Powderly Papers; Gompers, *Autobiography,* 68; *PCT,* 12 Jul. 1889.

20. *JUL,* 15 Nov. 1880, and Layton to John Samuel, 25 Jan. 1882, as quoted in Horner, "Producers' Co-operatives," 220–21; *JUL,* 15 Jan. 1882.

21. *NLT,* 26 Apr. 1890, and 31 Oct. 1891; *PCT,* 12 July 1889; Northwestern Historical Association, *Allegheny County,* 2:445; Powderly, *Autobiography,* 294, 298.

22. *NLT,* 27 May 1882, and 10 Sept. 1888; *HLN,* 3 Mar., 15 Sept., 27 Oct., and 22 Dec. 1888. Among the most revealing of the contemporary accounts of Quay are the articles by William Shaw Bowen in the *NYW,* 10 Feb. and 3 Mar., 1890; Blackenburg, "Forty Years in the Wilderness"; Blackenburg, "Ills of Pennsylvania"; Pennypacker, "Quay of Pennsylvania." Recent scholarship includes Blair, "Quay"; Kehl, *Quay.*

CHAPTER 6. *Labor Reform and Machine Politics*

1. Keeler and Fenn, "Taking of Pittsburgh" and accompanying illustrations (quotation from 238); Lorant, *Pittsburgh,* 467; Korson, *Coal Dust,* 5. Birmingham, today's South Side, became a part of Pittsburgh in 1872. Allegheny, now known as the North Side, was incorporated by the city in 1906.

2. Keeler and Fenn, "Taking of Pittsburgh," 238, 262; Montgomery, *Beyond Equality,* 5–6; Couvares, "Work, Leisure, and Reform," 1–3, 9, 10; Andrews, "Civil War," 129–76.

3. This paragraph and the following one are based on: Keeler and Fenn, "Taking of Pittsburgh," 238; G. Davis, "Greater Pittsburgh's Commercial Development," 323, 326; V. Clark, *History of Manufactures,* 2:88–89; Couvares, "Work,

Leisure, and Reform," 11; Hunter, "Influence of the Market," 246–54; Thurston, *Pittsburgh's Progress*, 45; Andrews, "Civil War," 160; Wall, *Carnegie*, 323–24; Temin, *Iron and Steel*, 159; Lesley, *Iron Manufacturer's Guide*, 247–51.

4. Warner, *Allegheny County*, 233–36, 254–58; Keeler and Fenn, "Taking of Pittsburgh," 262; Kitson, "Iron and Steel Industries of America," 630–31; Thurston, "Pittsburgh and Allegheny," in PBIS, *Annual Report*, vol. 4 (1875–76), 104–05, 128–30; Glazier, *Peculiarities of American Cities*, 338–39; Andrews, "Civil War," 147.

5. The sketch of the coal industry is based primarily on Thurston, "Pittsburgh and Allegheny," 131–38, 148–50; Thurston, *Pittsburgh's Progress*, 117–35. Also see Montgomery, *Beyond Equality*, 10–11.

6. Thurston, "Pittsburgh and Allegheny," in PBIS, *Annual Report*, vol. 4 (1875–76), 128; Thurston, *Pittsburgh's Progress*, 103; Couvares, "Work Leisure, and Reform," 10; Andrews, "Civil War," 148.

7. Kitson, "Iron and Steel Industries," 630–31; Keeler and Fenn, "Taking of Pittsburgh," 262; Livesay, *Carnegie*, 20; Thurston, *Pittsburgh's Progress*, 26–30; Thurston, "Pittsburgh and Allegheny," in PBIS, *Annual Report*, vol. 4 (1875–76), 109–13; Hunter, "Influence of the Market," 245; "Manufactures—Rolling Mills," PBIS, *Annual Report*, vol. 4 (1875–76), 586–635; Andrews, "Civil War," 129, 147.

8. Bridge, *Inside History*, 73; Thurston, "Pittsburgh and Allegheny," in PBIS, *Annual Report*, vol. 4 (1875–76), 132; American Iron and Steel Institute, *Bulletin*, 10 Sept. 1875; Keeler and Fenn, "Taking of Pittsburgh," 262–63. Fenn's accompanying illustrations of a blast furnace at work are reprinted in Lorant, *Pittsburgh*, 161. Unlike many illustrations of metalmaking operations that were published by popular magazines in the late 1800s, Fenn's do not convey a sense of terror and human powerlessness before machinery.

9. Linaberger, "Rolling Mill Riots of 1850"; "Labor Troubles in Pennsylvania," in PBIS, *Annual Report*, vol. 10 (1881–82), 273–75; Robinson, *Amalgamated Association*, 10–12; Jarrett, "Iron Workers," 269–72. Also see Swetnam, "Labor-Management Relations, 322–24.

10. "The Pittsburgh Scale of Prices," *Vulcan Record* (1873), 34–37; "Views of Mr. Miles F. Humphries," in U.S. House, Select Committee, *Causes of the General Depression*, 506–07; Jarrett, "Iron Workers," 272–74, 300–302, 306; Foster, "The Amalgamated Association of Iron and Steel Workers," in PBIS, *Annual Report*, vol. 15 (1887), G2, G15–16; "Labor Troubles in Pennsylvania," 281–84; Robinson, *Amalgamated Association*, 10–14, 87–88; Bridge, *Inside History*, 184–85; Fitch, *Steel Workers*, 78–79.

11. Grossman, *Sylvis*, 173–180; Andrews, "Nationalisation," 48–56; P. Foner, *History of Labor*, 1:417–20.

12. Sylvis, in an 1867 article, as quoted by Andrews, "Nationalisation," 48–56; Grossman, *Sylvis*, 200–04, 189–219; Grossman, "Co-operative Foundries." Also see "Labor Troubles in Pennsylvania," in PBIS, *Annual Report*, vol. 10 (1881–82), 281.

13. McBride, "Coal Miners," 244; Wieck, *American Miners' Association*, 156; Amsden and Brier, "Coal Miners on Strike," 137–70, esp. 156–58; Trachtenberg, *History of Legislation*, chaps. 2, 4, 5.

14. Ehmann and Smith, "Flint Glass Workers," and J. Campbell, "Window

Glass Blowers' Association," in PBIS, *Annual Report,* vol. 16 (1889), F1–37. Also see O'Connor, "Cinderheads and Iron Lungs."

15. McNeill, *Labor Movement,* 606; Montgomery, *Beyond Equality,* 389–92, 464.

16. Commons et al., *Documentary History* 9:141–68; Montgomery, *Beyond Equality,* 177–80.

17. Bennett, "Iron Workers," 311; C. Wright, "Amalgamated Association," 410; *Vulcan Record* (1868), 14; *Vulcan Record* (1873), 34, 36; *NLT,* 15 Oct. 1887.

18. *PC,* 12 Sept. 1867; Kerr, "Mayors of Pittsburgh," 133–41; Montgomery, *Beyond Equality,* 391.

19. *PT,* 9 Mar. 1901, *PCG,* 9 Mar. 1901, *PL,* 10 and 12 Mar. 1901, *PP,* 9 Mar. 1901, and *PD,* 9 and 11 Mar. 1901, all in Flinn Scrapbooks, reel 4, vols. 14–19, Nov. 1900–Apr. 1901; Thrasher, "Magee-Flinn Political Machine," 2–5; Tarr, "Infrastructure and City-Building," 232.

Even before the war was over, Magee had begun to make his influence felt: by 1869 he held an important position in the city treasurer's office; by 1870 he had succeeded in reorganizing the fire department, thereby securing for himself an important political base.

20. Kleppner, "Government, Parties, and Voters," 152.

21. *PC,* 11, 16, 18, 25, 27, 28, and 29 Dec. 1865, and 3 Jan. 1866; *PP,* 11, 12, 18, 19, 22, 24, 25, and 30 Dec. 1865, 3 and 6 Jan. 1866, and 30 Nov. 1867; *PG,* 16 Dec. 1865, as quoted in Kerr, "Mayors of Pittsburgh," 136; Couvares, "Work, Leisure, and Reform," 48–49, 86; Kerr, "Mayors of Pittsburgh," 133–38, 138–41.

22. This paragraph and the following one are based on: Montgomery, *Beyond Equality,* 390–91; Couvares, "Work, Leisure, and Reform," 48; Couvares, *Remaking of Pittsburgh,* 28–29, 62–68; Oestreicher, "Working-Class Formation," 128; French, "Whirlwind," 99–100; *PC,* 30 Oct., 7, 18, 19 Nov., and 11 Dec., 1867; *PP,* 16, 18, 19, 28, and 30 Nov., 2, 3, 11, and 17 Dec. 1867; Kerr, "Mayors of Pittsburgh," 144–55.

23. *PC,* 11, 12, and 30 Sept., 9, 10, 11, and 14 Oct. 1867; *NLT,* 9 Jul. 1881, as quoted in Montgomery, *Beyond Equality,* 391; *NLT,* 7 Dec. 1889.

24. *PG,* 27 and 31 Jul., 17 Aug., 15 and 16 Sept. 1868, 24 Oct., and 4 Dec. 1871; *PC,* 11 Jul., 19 Sept., and 13 Oct. 1868; Metcalf et al., "In Memoriam: James Park, Jr."; Kerr, "Mayors of Pittsburgh," 146, 148, 156–60; Couvares, "Work, Leisure, and Reform," 48; Montgomery, *Beyond Equality,* 463.

25. *PC,* 19 and 26 Sept., 3, 10, and 17 Oct., 1868; *PG,* 29 and 30 Sept., and 8 Oct. 1868; Kerr, "Mayors of Pittsburgh," 146, 149, 155.

26. *PG,* 19 and 28 Sept., 13, 14, 15, and 17 Oct. 1868; Kerr, "Mayors of Pittsburgh," 156.

27. Kerr, "Mayors of Pittsburgh," 179; Montgomery, *"Beyond Equality,* 208, 211.

28. On the farmers' revolt, see Goodwyn, *Democratic Promise.*

29. Andrews, "Nationalisation," 151–52; Bennett, "Iron Workers," 220–27.

30. Keeler and Fenn, "Taking of Pittsburgh," 262, 273–74.

CHAPTER 7. *Custom Confronts Capital*

1. Foner, *History of Labor,* vol. 1, chaps. 22–24; Stromquist, "Working Class Organization," 7–10; Wall, *Carnegie,* 317; "The Scale Agitation," *NLT,* 28 Nov.

1874; Temin, *Iron and Steel*, 274, 284; "Views of Mr. Joseph Bishop," in U.S. House, Select Committee, *Causes of the Depression*, 491. The quotation is from *AISI Bulletin*, 6 Feb. 1875.

2. *NLT*, 28 Nov. 1874, and 8 Jan. 1876.

3. Overman, *Metallurgy*, 484–85.

4. For an alternative interpretation of the origins of the AAISW, see Trusilo, "Ironworkers' Case."

5. *AISA Bulletin*, 12 Nov. 1874; *NLT*, 28 Nov. 1874; *Vulcan Record* (1875), 12–14, 30–37; Jarrett, "Iron Workers," 302–03; "Labor Troubles in Pennsylvania," in PBIS, *Annual Report*, vol. 10 (1881–82), 311–13. On customary notions of labor and workplace justice, see Hobsbawm, *Labouring Men*, 344–70.

6. This paragraph and the following three are based on *PG*, 16, 23, and 24 Nov., and 12 Dec. 1874; *PET*, 16 and 23 Nov., 7 and 17 Dec. 1874; *NLT*, 7, 14, 21, and 28 Nov. 1874; Wright, "Amalgamated Association," 407–08; Jarrett, "Iron Workers," 302; Hogan, *Economic History*, 1:86–87; Foster, "Amalgamated Association," G16; "Labor Troubles in Pennsylvania," in PBIS, *Annual Report*, vol. 10 (1881–82), 311; *Vulcan Record* (1875), 30–37; *Vulcan Record* (1873), 36–37; Doeringer, "Piece Rate Wage Structures" 265; Robinson, *Amalgamated Association*, 14, 87; *Amalgamated Journal*, 27 Aug. 1942, 9–10.

7. *NLT*, 7 and 28 Nov. 1874; *AISA Bulletin*, 12 Nov. 1874; *PG*, 16, 23, and 24 Nov. 1874; *PET*, 16 and 23 Nov., and 7 Dec. 1874; Wright, "Analgamated Association," 408; Jarrett, "Iron Workers," 302. The market for pig iron and rails also fell off dramatically in 1874. In 1872 pig sold for $48.88 a ton; in 1873, $42.75; and in 1874, $30.25. The downward trend continued until 1879. Rail prices followed a similar pattern. See Swank, *Iron in All Ages*, 514.; Novack and Perlman, "Structure of Wages," 338.

8. This paragraph and the following two are based on *AISA Bulletin*, 26 Nov. 1874; *NLT*, 7 and 28 Nov. 1874; Wright, "Amalgamated Association," 408.

9. This paragraph and the next one are based on the *Vulcan Record* (1875), 31–32, 34–35; *NLT*, 28 Nov. 1874; Jarrett, "Iron Workers," 303.

10. This paragraph and the succeeding two are based principally on *NLT*, 28 Nov. 1874; *Vulcan Record* (1875), 13–14, 30–33. Also see *PG*, 16, 23 and 24 Nov. 1874; *PET*, 16 and 23 Nov., and 7 Dec. 1874.

11. Boiling iron was a process that closely resembled puddling, and many puddlers often referred to themselves as boilers.

12. *Vulcan Record* (1870), 4; Robinson, *Amalgamated Association*, 105–07; Schneider, "Workers' Consciousness," 220–21; Couvares, "Work Leisure, and Reform," 18; Montgomery, "Workers' Control," 15–18.

13. Even after the turn of the century, officials of the AAISW expressed similar views. The scale, they said, was based on the idea that the workers should get a "fair" share. Neither these officials nor their predecessors in the AAISW or the Sons of Vulcan ever offered a precise definition of *fair*. As Robinson, *Amalgamated Association*, 145–46, comments, "just what [was] meant by 'fair' is uncertain. . . . The scale [was] not developed in accord with scientific principles. The scale was not made; it grew." (Doeringer, "Wage Structures," 265, offers a markedly different interpretation of how the puddlers regarded the scale; however, it is based on a questionable reading of Jarrett's explanation.) During the 1874–75 lockout, David Harris, a puddler, tried to determine what

the base of the scale should be in terms of an ill-defined "reserve fund" that amounted to what puddlers might manage to save after buying nine "principal commodities."

14. *Vulcan Record* (1873), 34–35; Robinson, *Amalgamated Association*, 146; Jarrett, "Iron Workers," 301–02; Temin, *Iron and Steel*, 284; Novack and Perlman, "Structure of Wages," 342; Wright, "Amalgamated Association," 405–07.

15. *Vulcan Record* (1873), 35; Schneider, "Workers' Consciousness," 220; Novack and Perlman, "Structure of Wages," 342. Also see U.S. Department of Labor, Bureau of Labor Statistics, *History of Wages in the United States from Colonial Times to 1928*, 241–50. In order to appreciate the position of the puddlers, one must consider the ground they occupied, and fought to hold, as standing somewhere between a "precapitalist" or "traditional" order and mature industrial capitalism. The risk, otherwise, is a facile dismissal of the puddlers' desire for "harmony" with capital as the crass aspiration of "petty bourgeois," would-be capitalists. Puddlers do not fit into such neat categories. On the one hand, they did produce goods for profit, not for use, and the production and distribution of such goods was regulated partly by the market. On the other hand, their labor was not a commodity; at any rate, they did not regard it as such.

The puddlers might be said to belong to what Macpherson characterizes as a "simple market society" (*Possessive Individualism*, 49–61). One of the attributes of such a society, he argues, is that no one gains at the expense of another—"no one converts more of the powers of others to his use than they convert of his." This formulation goes a long way toward explicating the ethic of the puddlers. Even their employment of helpers conforms to Macpherson's description of how jobs are allocated and rewards determined in customary society: by groups and on the basis of performance, as judged by an empowered group. For a discussion of puddlers and other metalworkers that sees expressions of the desire for harmony as tantamount, if not wholly equivalent, to an "acceptance of the basic terms of the capitalist system," see Freifeld, "Roots of Division," 413–20.

16. *NLT*, 28 Nov. 1874; *PG*, 23 Nov. 1874. See also *NLT*, 17 Apr. 1875.

17. *NLT*, 28 Nov. 1874.

18. *NLT*, 28 Nov. 1874; Robinson, *Amalgamated Association*, 139; Schneider, "Workers' Consciousness," 220–21.

19. *NLT*, 28 Nov. 1874; *PG*, 23 Nov. 1874.

20. *NLT*, 28 Nov. 1874; "Views of Mr. Joseph Bishop," in U.S. House, Select Committee, *Causes of the Depression*, 479.

21. *AISA Bulletin*, 10 Dec. 1874, 6 Feb., 12 Mar., and 2 Apr. 1875; *NLT*, 28 Nov. and 12 Dec. 1874, 2 and 30 Jan., 27 Feb., 13 Mar., and 3 Apr. 1875; *Vulcan Record* (1875), 33; "Labor Troubles in Pennsylvania," in PBIS, *Annual Report*, vol. 10 (1881–82), 312; Freifeld, "Roots of Division," 399.

22. *PG*, 16 Nov. and 7 Dec. 1874, 2, 5, and 12 Mar., 5 and 15 Apr. 1875; *PET*, 16, 23, and 30 Nov., 3 and 7 Dec. 1874, 16 Jan., 11, 13, 15, 16, 17, 20, 24, and 25 Feb., 29 and 30 Mar. 1875; *PP*, 13 Mar., 5 and 8 Apr. 1875; *Vulcan Record* (1875), 12–14, 30–37; "Labor Troubles in Pennsylvania," in PBIS, *Annual Report*, vol. 10 (1881–82), 311–13.

23. *NLT*, 2 and 30 Jan. 1875; *Vulcan Record* (1875), 33. *Black sheep* was a term of disapprobation applied by puddlers to those workers, regardless of union membership, who failed to honor a union directive against working.

In some cities the finishers had their own organizations. The two principal unions were the Associated Brotherhood of Iron and Steel Heaters, Rollers, and Roughers of the United States and the Iron and Steel Roll Hands Union. Neither was as strong as the Sons of Vulcan, partly because the two finishers' unions were often involved in jurisdictional disputes. The Associated Brotherhood did not allow heaters' helpers to join, for example, and was comprised only of rollers and the most highly skilled laborers who worked under them. The Roll Hands, on the other hand, did accept helpers and also tried to keep rollers from joining the Associated Brotherhood. Though cooperation between the finishers' unions was tenuous, the two organizations occasionally did engage in unified actions. The relations between the puddlers and the finishers, though, were normally bitter: each group sought to protect its interests, often at the expense of the other. See Wright, "Amalgamated Association," 411–14; Jarrett, "Iron Workers," 277–81; Robinson, *Amalgamated Association*, 14–16; Fitch, *Steel Workers*, 81–85; Bennett, "Iron Workers," 40–58.

24. *NLT*, 2 and 30 Jan. 1875. Also see Martin, *Minute Book of Iron and Steel Roll Hands*, 3 June 1874, Martin Papers.

25. *PET*, 2 Mar. 1875; *PG*, 2 Mar. 1875; *NLT*, 6 Mar. 1875; Stromquist, "Working Class Organization," 28–29; Bennett, "Iron Workers," 58–59.

26. *NLT*, 1873–74, particularly 11 Apr., and 2, 9, and 16 May 1874; Campbell, "Window Glass Blowers," in PBIS, *Annual Report*, vol. 16 (1889), F30; Stromquist, "Working Class Organization," 29.

27. *NLT*, 13 Mar. 1875, as quoted in Stromquist, "Working Class Organization," 29; *NLT*, 19 June 1875. Also see the follwoing editorials in the *NLT*: "Labor Reform," 22 May 1874; "The Coming Struggle," 22 May 1875; "The Coming Struggle," 28 Aug. 1875; "What Shall We Do?" 9 Sept. 1875; "Still in Slavery," 18 Nov. 1876; "The Grand Problem," 23 Dec. 1876; "If," 27 Jan. 1877.

28. *AISA Bulletin*, 12 Mar. 1875; *NLT*, 13 Mar. 1875; *Vulcan Record* (1875), 32–33; "Labor Troubles in Pennsylvania," in PBIS, *Annual Report*, vol. 10 (1881–82), 312.

29. Some of the complex patterns of race and labor relations in the Reconstruction Era are explored in Bernstein, *Draft Riots*, passim.

30. *PG*, 5 Mar. 1875; *PET*, 3, 4, 5, 6, 9, 10, 11, 13, 30, and 31 Mar., and 9 Apr. 1875; *PC*, 3 and 5 Mar. 1875; *PP*, 5 Apr. 1875; *Vulcan Record* (1875), 33; "Labor Troubles in Pennsylvania," in PBIS, *Annual Report*, vol. 10 (1881–82), 312; *AISA Bulletin*, 12 Mar. 1875.

31. *AISA Bulletin*, 12 Mar. 1875; *Vulcan Record* (1870), 10; *Vulcan Record* (1873), 10; Robinson, *Amalgamated Association*, 46–47; Freifeld, "Roots of Division," 514–27, which differs from the interpretation offered here. The decision of the AAISW ultimately to admit blacks grew directly out of the union's experience at James Park's Black Diamond Steel Works: in an effort to break a strike, Park once again hired black ironworkers from Richmond, Virginia. (See Rachleff, *Black Labor*, 101–02.)

32. Commons et al., *Documentary History*, 9:158–59. Also see Montgomery, *Beyond Equality*, 179–80.

33. *NLT*, 13 Mar. 1875; Richards, "Armstrong," 9–13; Grossman, *Sylvis*, 229–32; Montgomery, *Beyond Equality*, 227–28.

34. *NLT*, 20 Mar. 1875, as quoted in Freifeld, "Roots of Division," 517.

35. *NLT,* 12 Sept. 1874.

36. *NLT,* 17 Apr. 1875; *Vulcan Record* (1875), 30.

37. *PET,* 7, 11, 12, and 13 Apr.; *PC,* 15 Apr.; *PG,* 15 Apr. 1875; *PP,* 13 Mar. and 8 Apr. 1875; "Labor Troubles in Pennsylvania," in PBIS, *Annual Report,* vol. 10 (1881–82), 312–13; *NLT,* 3 and 17 Apr. 1875; *AISA Bulletin,* 2, 9, and 23 Apr. 1875; *Vulcan Record* (1875), 32–34; *Vulcan Record* (1874), 16; *AM,* 28 Jul. 1882; Freifeld, "Roots of Division," 397.

38. *NLT,* 17 Apr. 1875; *Vulcan Record* (1874), 16; *Vulcan Record* (1875), 30.

39. *Vulcan Record* (1875), 16–17; *NLT,* 17 Apr. and 22 May 1875.

40. *Vulcan Record* (1877), 39–41.

CHAPTER 8. *The Knights of Labor*

1. *Vulcan Record* (1874), 17; *Vulcan Record* (1875), 32; *NLT,* 28 Nov. 1874, and 8 Jan. 1876.

2. *NLT,* 19 June 1875. On the antipathy between helpers and skilled iron-workers, see Bennett, "Iron Workers," 53–58.

3. The quotations in this and the following paragraph are from an editorial entitled, "Amalgamation," *NLT,* 8 Jan. 1876.

4. McBride, "Coal Miners," 251; Ware, *Labor Movement,* 31; P. Foner, *Labor Movement,* 1:505; Roy, *Coal Miners,* 183–84; Garlock, *Guide to Local Assemblies,* 406–417, 435; Couvares, *Remaking of Pittsburgh,* 27–28.

5. Ware, *Labor Movement,* 31–32; Garlock, *Guide to Local Assemblies,* 406–17. Ware also noted that the Pittsburgh Knights were influenced by "socialist thought." While the miners achieved notable successes in Western Pennsylvania, the mid 1870s were not banner years for miners elsewhere in the United States. The "long strike" against the railroad and mine magnate Frank Gowen resulted in the destruction of the organization of anthracite miners in Eastern Pennsylvania. And the arrest and conspiracy trial of John Siney and Xingo Parks, who were organizing bituminous miners closer to Pittsburgh in Clearfield County, decimated the National Miners' Association. The conviction and imprisonment of Parks under Pennsylvania's anticonspiracy statute underscored the tenuous claim of miners, and indeed of all workers, to the right to organize. See Ware, *Labor Movement,* 33–35, 45; McBride, "Coal Miners," 251; Kuritz, "Labor Controls," 49–57. Also see Roy, *Coal Miners,* chaps. 14, 15; Chris Evans, *United Mine Workers,* 1:73–81.

6. *NLT,* 31 Nov. 1874, 20 Mar. and 31 Jul. 1875, and 8 Jan. 1876; Perlman, "Upheaval and Reorganisation," 201–02, 235–36. The best discussion of Kellogg and "Kelloggism" remains Destler, *American Radicalism,* 50–77. Also see Sharkey, *Money, Class, and Party,* 183–99.

7. *NLT,* 8, 15, and 29 Jan., 5 and 12 Feb., 11, 18, and 25 Mar. 1876; Bennett, "Iron Workers," 277–79; Korson, *Coal Dust,* 402–04.

8. *NLT,* 22 and 29 Apr. 1876. Also see Bennett, "Iron Workers," 279–82; Perlman, "Upheaval and Reorganisation," 235–39.

9. *NLT,* 11 Mar., 22 and 29 Apr. 1876. Some of the Pittsburgh labor leaders who attended the convention: Isaac Cline, Andrew Burtt, David Harris, "Beeswax" Taylor, Homer D. McGaw, A. C. Rankin, and Thomas Grundy.

10. This paragraph and succeeding ones are based on: *NLT*, 3 Oct. 1874, 10 June, 26 Aug., 9, 16, and 30 Sept., 21 and 28 Oct., 18 and 25 Nov. 1876; *HLN*, 1 Mar. 1890; Ricker, *Greenback-Labor*, 31; French, "Whirlwind," 103–04; Unger, *Greenback Era*, 100–10.

11. There is no satisfying account of the Greenback party and its various incarnations. Kleppner, "Greenback and Prohibition Parties," 1549–66, provides the best available overview. Also see P. Foner, *History of Labor*, 1:475–79. On the origins of the Greenback party, see Andrews, "Nationalisation," 167–71.

12. "The Grand Problem," *NLT*, 23 Dec. 1876.

13. The editorials upon which this paragraph is based appeared in the *NLT* from late 1873 through 1877. See, in particular: "Labor Reform," 22 May 1874; "The Coming Struggle," 22 May 1875; "The Coming Struggle," 28 Aug. 1875; "What Shall We Do?" 9 Sept. 1875; "Still in Slavery," 18 Nov. 1876; "The Grand Problem," 23 Dec. 1876; "If," 27 Jan. 1877.

14. "The Coming Struggle," *NLT*, 22 May 1875. Also see "The Coming Struggle," *NLT*, 28 Aug. 1875.

15. *NLT*, 7 Oct. 1876, as quoted in French, "Whirlwind," 108. On the 1877 uprising see: McCabe, *Great Riots*; Dacus, *Great Strikes*; P. Foner, *Great Uprising*; Bruce, *1877*; Debouzy, "Workers' Self-Organization," 61–77; Montgomery, "Strikes," 95. The significance of the event is recaptured in *1877: The Grand Army of Starvation*, a film produced and directed by Steven Brier of the American Social History Project, Graduate Center, City University of New York.

16. Among the secondary sources I have used in this sketch of the uprising in Pittsburgh: Mann, *Our Police*, 97–116; P. Foner, *Great Uprising*, chap. 3; Bruce, *1877*, chaps. 7–9; Debouzy, "Grève et violence"; Caye, "Roundhouse Riot"; Couvares, *Remaking of Pittsburgh*, 5–8; Kuritz, "Pennsylvania State Government and Labor Controls," chap. 3.

17. The quotation is from Bruce, *1877*, 149.

18. *PCG*, 25 Jul. 1877; *PET*, 23 Jul. 1877; *NYTR*, as quoted in *AISA Bulletin*, 11 Jul. 1877; Pennsylvania General Assembly, *Report on the Railroad Riots*, 37–38; Ware, *Labor Movement*, 49.

19. Pennsylvania General Assembly, *Report on the Railroad Riots*, 18, 45; Tiers to "Sallie," 23 Jul. 1877, manuscript; Couvares, "Work, Leisure, and Reform," 42.

20. *PCG*, 20–25 Jul. 1877; *PET*, 21–27 Jul. 1877; *Pennsylvania Legislative Record*, 1876, 301, as quoted in Alexander Trachtenberg, *Coal Miners in Pennsylvania*, 78–79; Pennsylvania General Assembly, *Report on the Railroad Riots*, 18.

21. *NLT*, 28 Jul. 1877; Tiers to "Sallie," 23 Jul. 1877, manuscript; *PCG* and *PET*, 24 and 25 Jul. 1877; P. Foner, *Great Uprising*, 67; Jones Diary, pt. 1 (1875–1901), 24 Jul. 1877; Debouzy, "Grève et violence," 52–60; Couvares, "Work, Leisure, and Reform," 44; Caye, "Roundhouse Riot," 55; Bruce, *1877*, 181–82.

22. *NLT*, 28 Jul. 1877; *PET*, 23 Jul. 1877; Couvares, "Work, Leisure, and Reform," 42, 44–46; Bruce, *1877*, 168–79; Bennett, "Iron Workers," 105–06.

23. *NLT*, 21 and 28 Jul. 1877; Kuritz, "Pennsylvania State Government and Labor Controls," 85–93. Also see Couvares, *Remaking of Pittsburgh*, 30.

24. Introduction to "The Laborers' Strike," in "Clippings on 1877 Riot in Pittsburgh," Morris Scrapbook; *NLT*, 21 and 28 Jul. 1877; Mann, *Our Police*, 108; Moore, *Injustice*, chap. 1.

25. *NLT*, 28 Jul., 4, 11, and 18 Aug. 1877; Moore, *Injustice*, 15–31.

26. On the state's responsibilities to settle disputes in a fair manner and to ensure peace and security, see Moore, *Injustice*, 20–26.

27. *NLT*, 28 Jul. 1877. The *NLT*'s critique of the wage system represented a refusal to accept "the rules of the game." Such a refusal captures the essence of what E. P. Thompson has called the moral economy. On this point see Reddy, "Textile Trade," 86.

28. "The Laborers' Strike." The complete text is in "Clippings on 1877 Riot in Pittsburgh," Morris Scrapbook.

29. Campbell, "Window Glass Blowers," F30–F31, and Ehmann and Smith, "Flint Glass Workers," in PBIS, *Annual Report*, vol. 16 (1889), F7–F8; *NLT*, 28 Jul. 1877; Stromquist, "Working Class Organization," 8; French, "Whirlwind," 107–08. Campbell later became president of Local Assembly 300 of the Knights of Labor, the union that in 1880 amalgamated all crafts in the window glass industry. Campbell also became a leader of the Trades Assembly of Western Pennsylvania in the 1880s.

30. *NLT*, 28 Jul., 4, 11, and 18 Aug. 1877.

31. *NLT*, 8 Aug. 1877; "A Lost Grave Found," *National Glass Budget*, 31 Aug. 1912. Some socialists affiliated with the Workingmen's party of the United States also engaged in organizational activities in the wake of the July disturbances in Pittsburgh. See: *NLT*, 11 Aug. 1877; French, "Whirlwind," 109–111; Bennett, "Iron Workers," 283–85. In Allegheny City, several of the most influential socialist leaders joined the Greenback-Labor party.

32. *NLT*, 11 and 18 Aug., 8 and 15 Sept. 1877; French, "Whirlwind," 109.

33. Goodwyn, *Democratic Promise*, 17; Goodwyn, *Populist Moment*, 14, 101, 177; Montgomery, "On Goodwyn's Populists," 166–73.

34. *NLT*, 26 Aug. 1876, 2 Mar. 1878, 21 Jul. and 15 Nov. 1879; Ricker, *Greenback-Labor*, 33; Kleppner, "Greenback and Prohibition Parties," 1560–61; P. Foner, *History of Labor*, 1:482–83. "The Greenbackers' theories of finance were auxiliary to the labor question, and necessarily secondary," the *NLT* observed. It also noted, however, that because workers in Pittsburgh understood that financial issues affected them, the workers' party adopted "the Greenback addition to the name of a political organization which, otherwise, would have been the National Labor Party."

35. *NLT*, 15 Sept. 1877, 1 Apr. and 15 Jul. 1882; *HLN*, 1 Mar. 1890; McNeill, *Labor Movement*, 405; Bennett, "Iron Workers," 283–93.

36. *NLT*, 15 Sept. 1877, 1 Mar. 1879, 5 and 26 Nov. 1881, 2 Sept. 1882, 10 Feb., 7 Apr., 4 and 11 Aug. 1883, 27 Aug. 1884, 23 Oct. 1886, 14 June 1890; *JUL*, 15 Aug. and 15 Oct. 1880, 15 May and 15 June 1882, and Apr. 1884; *HLN*, 16 May 1885, 9 Jan. 1886; *HT*, 15 Oct. 1881, 25 Feb. and 30 Dec. 1882; 27 Jan., 10 and 24 Feb. 1883; 6 Feb. 1884; Ehmann and Smith "Flint Glass Workers," in PBIS, *Annual Report*, vol. 16 (1889), F1, F9; French, "Whirlwind," 113–14; Ricker, *Greenback-Labor*, 33–34; "A Lost Grave Found," *National Glass Budget*, 31 Aug. 1912; Allegheny County, Election Docket, vol. 3 (1885–91); Burgoyne, *All Sorts* 163.

37. *NLT*, 15 Sept. 1877. Some of the subsequent platforms of the party can be found in *NLT*, 19 Jan. 1878, 27 Aug. 1881, 3 June, 29 Jul., 2 Sept., 14 and 28 Oct. 1882.

38. Cf. L. Fink, *Workingmen's Democracy*, chap. 2.

39. *NLT,* 15 Sept. 1877; French, "Whirlwind," 115; P. Foner, *History of Labor,* 1:480; Ricker, *Greenback-Labor,* 34–35. On the rivalry between the Pittsburgh and Philadelphia Knights, see Ware, *Labor Movement,* 35–44; Perlman, "Upheaval and Reorganisation," 332–35; P. Foner, *History of Labor,* 1:506.

40. *NLT,* 22 Sept. 1877; Frank P. Dewees to Terrence V. Powderly, 27 Sept., 16 and 25 Oct. 1877, Powderly Papers; Ricker, *Greenback-Labor,* 35–37. On Emerson's commitment to monetary reform as the exclusive remedy for the problems facing wage earners, see French, "Whirlwind," 111–12. Perlman, "Upheaval and Reorganisation," 243, incorrectly reports that the state Greenback convention also nominated John Davis for auditor general, and P. Foner, *History of Labor,* 1:408, echoes the error. The resulting impression of a complete fusion between the Pennsylvania Greenback party and the labor parties of Philadelphia and Pittsburgh is wrong.

41. Dewees to Powderly, 27 Sept. and 16 and 25 Oct. 1877, Powderly Papers; Ricker, *Greenback-Labor,* 37.

42. *NLT,* 10, 17, and 24 Nov. 1877; Ricker, *Greenback-Labor,* 39; French, "Whirlwind," 117–18; Bennett, "Iron Workers," 284–85; Perlman, "Upheaval and Reorganisation," 243; Garlock, *Guide to Local Assemblies,* 406–17.

43. *NLT,* 10 Nov. 1877.

44. *NLT,* 12 Jan., 2 Feb., 2 Mar., and 11 May 1878; Dewees to Powderly, 25 Oct. 1878, Powderly Papers; Perlman, "Upheaval and Reorganisation," 244, 247; P. Foner, *History of Labor,* 1:482–83, 485; Kleppner, "Greenback and Prohibition Parties," 1562, 1599–1601. While the "National Party," as it was often called, was dominated by currency reformers, labor activists in Pittsburgh understood that affiliating with a new party that had some chance of challenging the Republicans and Democrats on a national scale would lend credibility to political insurgencies on the county and state level. Thus Thomas Armstrong was one of the signatories of the "call" for the Toledo convention. Among the other nationally known activists who signed were Wendell Phillips, Richard Trevellick, Ignatius Donnelly, James B. Weaver, and Patrick Ford.

45. *NLT,* 19 Jan., 9, 16, and 23 Feb., 2 Mar., 11 and 18 May 1878; Dewees to Powderly, Oct. 25, 1878, Powderly Papers; Bennett, "Iron Workers," 285; P. Foner, *History of Labor,* 1:484, 485; Kehl, *Quay,* 45; Richards, "Armstrong," 18–19. Mason, as it turned out, was working for the Pennsylvania Railroad at the time of his nomination.

46. This paragraph and the succeeding one are based on: *NLT,* 15 June, 21 Sept., 15 Oct., 9, 16, and 23 Nov. 1878; Kleppner, "Greenback and Prohibition Parties," 1561–62; Perlman, "Upheaval and Reorganisation," 247; Ricker, *Greenback-Labor,* 64–69. The *NLT* charged that the Greenback-Labor vote in Allegheny County would have reached about twelve thousand had it not been for the threats of employers to fire workers who supported the party.

47. *NLT,* 9 Nov. 1878.

CHAPTER 9. *Mill Owners and Machine Politicians*

1. Bruce, *1877,* 311; P. Foner, *Great Uprising,* 212; Kuritz, "State Government and Labor Controls," 105–08, 214–19; Pennsylvania General Assembly, *Report on*

the Railroad Riots, 2, 37, 798–99; Couvares, *Remaking of Pittsburgh*, 62–63. Also see Holmes, "National Guard of Pennsylvania."

2. Kuritz, "State Government and Labor Controls," 106, 107, 110–11; Kolko, *Railroads and Regulation*, 12.

3. *NLT*, 28 Jul. 1877; Max Weber, as quoted in Genovese, *Roll, Jordan, Roll*, 25. As Genovese suggests, those in power "must confront the problem of coercion in such a way as to minimize the necessity for its use, and . . . must disguise the extent to which state power does not so much rest on force as represent its actuality." See 25–49. Also see Moore, *Injustice*, 82–83.

4. This paragraph and the succeeding one are based on: *NLT*, 17 and 24 Feb., 10 March, 1877, and 7 Dec. 1889; Kerr, "Mayors of Pittsburgh," 185–88; Montgomery, *Beyond Equality*, 211; Couvares, *Remaking of Pittsburgh*, 62, 66; Walsh, "Fanatic Heart," 197.

5. *PD*, 9 Mar. 1901; *PP*, 9 Mar. 1901; Kehl, *Quay*, 35–36, 40–41; Zink, *City Bosses*, 234; Thrasher, "Magee-Flinn Political Machine," 3–4; Seilhamer, *Republican Party*, 2:310–13.

6. *PET*, 7 Feb. 1874, 1, 2, and 26 Feb., 1 and 22 Mar. 1875; *PC*, 1 and 2 Feb. 1875; *PG*, 9, 10, and 18 Feb. 1874; *PP*, 28 Jan. 1900; *PD*, 26 Jan. 1900; *PP*, 9 Mar. 1901; Seilhamer, *Republican Party*, 2:60–62; Kerr, "Mayors of Pittsburgh," 168–77, 188; Kehl, *Quay*, 45; Zink, *City Bosses*, 234; Tarr, "Infrastructure and City Building," 232.

7. This overview of the political machine headed by Magee is drawn from: *PT*, 9 Mar. 1901, *PCG*, 9 Mar. 1901, *PL*, 10 and 12 Mar. 1901, *PP*, 9 Mar. 1901, *PD*, 9 and 11 Mar. 1901, all in Flinn Scrapbooks, reel 4, vols. 14–19, Nov. 1900–Apr. 1901; Seilhamer, *Republican Party*, 2:60–62; Steffens, *Shame of the Cities*, 147–89; Fleming, *Pittsburgh*, 4:298–300; Stevens, "Hearth of the Nation," 193–96, 201, 204; Couvares, *Remaking of Pittsburgh*, 62–65; Zink, *City Bosses*, 230–56; Kehl, *Quay*, 76–78; Thrasher, "Magee-Flinn Political Machine"; Baldwin, *Pittsburgh*, 352. The quotation, a paraphrase of Magee's words, is from Steffens, *Shame of the Cities*, 152.

8. Steffens, *Shame of the Cities*, 155, 165.

9. Ibid., 156–57. The quotation is from 153. Also see Couvares, *Remaking of Pittsburgh*, 67. Between 1884 and 1912, Flinn was a frequent delegate to the Republican National Convention. He also served on the party's national executive committee. He was elected to the state house of representatives in 1877 and to the state senate in 1890. Magee served two terms in the state senate.

10. Twain and Warner, *Gilded Age*; Tarr, "Infrastructure and City Building," 232–33. On the political "professionals" of the Gilded Age, see Keller's influential study, *Affairs of State*, 238–83. Keller sees the triumph of the professional politician committed to advancing the cause of his organization as a supercession of the ideological politics of Reconstruction. Though the concerns of politicians did indeed shift as the nation entered the Gilded Age, in no way were such concerns nonideological. This is one of the most important points of the novel by Twain and Warner, not to mention the scholarship of C. Vann Woodward. Also see Alan Trachtenberg, *Incorporation of America*, 171–72, who offers the following apposite remarks: "The [machine] boss represented the visible integration of politics and economics, . . . [but] he functioned to keep the transactions between public officials and private interests behind closed doors."

11. Steffens, *Shame of the Cities*, 150, 158.

12. Ibid., 167. That the Pennsylvania Railroad and other business enterprises shared with Magee and Flinn a desire for the maintenance of public order, as well as a desire for profits, does not mean that the railroad and the business community in general entered into a conspiracy with the ring. A shared consciousness of purpose is not equivalent to a conspiracy. See Noble, *America by Design*, xxv, following William Appelman Williams.

13. Couvares, *Remaking of Pittsburgh*, 64–65. On the centrality of the fire department in the work and leisure lives of Pittsburghers, see C. Dawson, *Our Fireman*. Magee was on the Board of Fire Commissioners from 1877 to 1886. He then served as president of the board. Flinn served on the board in 1877 and 1878.

14. *NLT*, 27 Jan. 1877 (as quoted in Couvares, *Remaking of Pittsburgh*, 64), and 15 Jan., 19 Feb., and 29 Jul. 1876.

15. "The Coming Struggle," *NLT*, 28 Aug. 1875. Also see "Labor Reform," *NLT*, 22 May 1874, and "The Coming Struggle," *NLT*, 22 May, 1875.

16. "The Grand Problem," *NLT*, 23 Dec. 1876. Also see "Capital and Machinery," *NLT*, 27 Jan. 1877. On the Centennial Exposition, see Kasson, *Civilizing the Machine*, 156–64.

17. *NLT*, 23 Dec. 1876 and 27 Jan. 1877. See Walzer, *Exodus and Revolution*, for a discussion of the use of the Exodus metaphor in the discourse of insurgent political movements.

18. My account of the dispute at the Edgar Thomson is based on Joseph Bishop, "President's Report," in AAISW, *Proceedings*, 1877, 43–44; *NLT*, 9 Dec. 1876; Carnegie to W. P. Shinn, 28 Aug. 1876, Letterbooks, vol. 4, ACLC.

19. *Braddock's Fields* and *Braddock* were used interchangably. By the mid 1880s, though, the former appelation fell into disuse.

20. The steelmasters' dependence on the cooperative efforts of their employees is explored in Nuwer, "From Batch to Flow."

21. Bridge, *Inside History*, 94–99; Temin, *Iron and Steel*, 172; Hendrick, *Carnegie*, 1:214–15; Carnegie to W. P. Shinn, 10 Apr. 1876, Letterbooks, vol. 4, ACLC; *AISA Bulletin*, 26 Aug. 1875; Wall, *Carnegie*, 316, 359; Holley, "Wrought Iron and Steel," 341. Jones's salary, which he accepted "with a whoop of joy," was equal to that of the president of the United States.

22. Overman, *Manufacture of Iron*, 484–85; Wall, *Carnegie*, 337–38; Brody, *Steelworkers*, 2.

23. W. R. Jones, "Manufacture of Bessemer Steel," 130–31; W. R. Jones, "Comments on Report," 366–67. Elbaum and Wilkinson, "Industrial Relations and Uneven Development," argue that "there is no evidence that [American] unions in the iron and steel industry resisted the introduction of new methods" (296). True, William Weihe, a president of the AAISW, once said that the union "never objects to improvements"; however, this was often contradicted by the initiatives of union members.

24. W. R. Jones, "Comments on Report," 366–67; Price, "Labour Process and Labour History." Also of interest are Zeitlin, "Social Theory"; Elbaum et al., "Labour Process," 227–30. I have borrowed the phrase, *contested terrain*, from R. Edwards, *Contested Terrain*.

25. *NLT*, 28 Nov. 1874; *IA*, as quoted in Freifeld, "Roots of Division," 476;

Bennett, "Iron Workers," 75–78, and esp. 197–212; AAISW, "A Brief History of the Amalgamated Association of Iron and Steel Workers of the United States," 16, Martin Papers.

26. Freifeld, "Roots of Division," 475–76; Robinson, *Amalgamated Association,* 19–21. Freifeld contradicts her own evidence in asserting (471) that the struggle for control was interrupted by the depression of 1873–79 and the resulting (though by Freifeld undocumented) feeling of workers that they were "grateful to have any job at all."

27. Jarrett, "Iron Workers," 286–88, 307; *Amalgamated Journal,* 27 Aug. 1942, 2–3, 11; Robinson, *Amalgamated Association,* 19, 21; Swetnam, "Labor-Management Relations," 326.

28. *NLT,* 12 and 19 Jan., 14 Dec. 1878; 11 Jan., 2, 8, 15, and 22 Feb., 1, 8, 15, 22, and 29 Mar., 26 Jul. 1879, 13 Nov. 1880; AAISW, *Proceedings,* 1881, 560, 564; *AM,* 10 Oct. 1884; Metcalf et al., "In Memoriam: James Park, Jr."; Bridge, *Inside History,* 151; Fleming, *Pittsburgh,* 1:69–70; Thurston, *Pittsburgh's Progress,* 81–86; Redlich, *American Business Leaders,* 1:93, 105, 118; Warner Co., *Allegheny County,* 1:254–58.

29. This paragraph and the succeeding one are based on *NLT,* 14 Dec. 1878, 11 Jan., 2, 8, 15, and 22 Feb., 1, 8, 15, 22, and 29 Mar. 1879.

30. *NLT,* 1 Jan. and 18 Feb. 1882.

31. Jarrett, "Iron Workers," 309.

32. *NLT,* 28 Oct. 1876; Garlock, *Guide to Local Assemblies,* 407. McLuckie lived in Turtle Creek in 1876; he belonged to Local Assembly 191 (or possibly 206) of the Knights of Labor.

CHAPTER 10. *Miners Amalgamate*

1. Keeler and Fenn, "Taking of Pittsburgh," 262. Pittsburgh has been compared to hell more frequently than any other city in the United States. See Holt, "Trade Unionism," 21.

2. *AM,* 16 June 1882; Wall, *Carnegie,* 307–08; Couvares, "Work, Leisure, and Reform," 1–5, 151–54; Muller, "Metropolis and Region," 199–205; Ingham, "Steel City Aristocrats," 278–80. On the growth of Pittsburgh also see Tarr, *Transportation Innovation;* Hays, "Pittsburgh as a Social Order."

3. *Warner Co., Allegheny County,* 121–27; *Everts Co., Allegheny County,* Fleming, *Pittsburgh,* 3:731–51; Shand, "Sociological Aspects of an Industrial Community," 33–34.

4. "Homestead," photocopy of a handbill announcing the sale of lots in Homestead (Pittsburgh: n.p., 1871), in author's possession; Hopkins Co., *Atlas of Pittsburgh, Allegheny, and Adjoining Boroughs* 96–97. The sketch of Homestead and the other settlements of Mifflin Township in this and succeeding paragraphs is drawn from: Warner Co., *Allegheny County,* 71–77, 279–80, 294–95, 297–98, 400–01, 653, 702–03; Everts Co., *Allegheny County,* 114–15, 136, 150, 179, 189, and illustrations; Smeltzer, *Homestead Methodism,* 9–18, 106–09, 113–14; Northwestern Historical Association, *Allegheny County,* 1:264–66, 497–98, 2:126–27, 135–36, 141–42, 516–17; *HT,* 14 Jan. 1882; Schooley and Schooley, *Directory of Homestead, 1892,* 31–32, and *1890,* 5; Hopkins Co., *Atlas of the County of Allegheny,* 36; Ste-

vens, untitled manuscript; 10; Stitt, "My Beloved Farm," manuscript; Fleming, *Pittsburgh*, 3:772–79.

5. Everts Co., *Allegheny County*, pls. 19–25, *Homestead Daily Messenger*, 1 Jul. 1976.

6. PBIS, *Annual Report*, vol. 4 (1875–76), 132–33, 236–57.

7. "Labor Troubles in Pennsylvania," in PBIS, *Annual Report*, vol. 10 (1881–82), 366–67; *NLT*, 11 Aug. 1877, 2 Feb. and 30 Nov. 1878.

8. *NLT*, 29 Oct. 1881; McBride, "Coal Miners," 252–53; "Labor Troubles in Pennsylvania," in PBIS, *Annual Report*, vol. 10 (1881–82), 372–76; Chris Evans, *United Mine Workers*, 89–90; Roy, *Coal Miners*, 184–85; Korson, *Coal Dust*, chap. 8. The organizational drive of the miners may be followed also in the *NLT*, 29 Mar.– 20 Dec. 1879.

9. My sketch of Jones's career through 1879 is based on the sources cited in the preceding note and: *HLN*, 10 Nov. 1888; Jones to Uriah S. Stephens, 13 Oct. 1879, and Jones to Powderly, 16 Oct. 1879, both in the Powderly Papers; Cooper Co., *Twentieth-Century Bench and Bar*, 2:954; Cushing, *Allegheny County*, 388.

10. This paragraph and the succeeding one are based on: McBride, "Coal Miners," 252; Roy, *Coal Miners*, 185; *NLT*, 29 Oct. 1881 and 11 Feb. 1882; Armstrong to Powderly, 1 Jan. 1880, Jones to Powderly, 16 Oct. 1879, and Jones to Uriah Stephens, 13 Oct. 1879, all in the Powderly Papers. Roy observed that in his job as chief officer of the Miners' Association, Jones "was as much of an autocrat as the Czar of Russia." Criticism of him came not only from national figures such as Roy, Armstrong, Evans, and McBride, but also from John Bonner, the leader of the Knights in Mifflin Township, See, for example, *NLT*, 20 Nov. 1880.

11. *NLT*, 9 and 16 July 1881; *JUL*, 15 July 1881. On Jones's aversion to mixing politics and union-building efforts, see *NLT*, 2 Oct. 1880. On his arrest and subsequent trial, see *NLT*, 27 Nov. 1880, 15 Jan., 12 and 19 Feb., 26 Mar., and 29 Oct. 1881.

12. The quotations in this and the succeeding two paragraphs are drawn from a letter by Jones, "Seasonable Advice—Words of Warning," that appeared in the *NLT*, 16 Aug. 1879.

13. Ibid. On at least one occasion, Jones himself was unable to ignore differences of race with regard to black Americans. See, for example, *NLT*, 29 Jul. 1882.

14. *NLT*, 16 Aug. 1879.

15. The quotation is from Hegel, *Philosophy of Right*, 13.

CHAPTER 11. *Assaults on Labor*

1. This paragraph and the succeeding one are based on contemporary press accounts and: H. May, *Protestant Churches*, 91–107; Boyer, *Urban Masses*, 123–31; Lears, *No Place of Grace*, 28–29; Kuritz, "State Government and Labor Controls," 105–12; David, "Upheaval at Homestead," 152–57, 161–65; Hogg, "Homestead Strike," chap. 11.

2. The quotation is from *NYS*, 7 Jul. 1892.

3. *PCG*, 25 Jul. 1877; *Independent*, 26 Jul. and 2 Aug. 1877, as quoted in May, *Protestant Churches*, 92–93.

4. Pennsylvania General Assembly, *Report on the Railroad Riots*, 37–38.

5. Robinson, *Amalgamated Association*, 19–21; Jarrett, "Iron Workers," 307.

6. This paragraph and the following one are based on: *NLT*, 27 Nov. 1880, 15 Jan., 12 and 19 Feb., 29 Oct., and 29 Nov. 1881, 7 Jan., 4, 11, 18, and 25 Feb., 4 Mar., 15 Apr. 1882, and 28 Apr. 1883; vol. 10 (1881–82), 172; 1882; AAISW, *Proceedings*, 1882, 807, 917; *AM*, 3 Apr. 1881, 10 and 24 Mar. 1882; *HLN*, 19 Feb. 1887 and 10 Nov. 1888; *PP*, 9 Mar. 1882; *PT*, 9 Mar. 1882; *PEC*, 9 Mar. 1882; Allegheny County, Election Docket, vol. 3 (1885–91); Cooper Co., *Twentieth-Century Bench and Bar*, 2:954; Warner Co., *Allegheny County*, pt. 2, 219–20, 388; Lorant, *Pittsburgh*, 233.

7. *NLT*, 11 Feb. 1882; Kuritz, "State Government and Labor Controls," 50–59. The relationship of the rule of law and the labor movement in the late nineteenth century is explored in Forbath, "American Labor Movement," 1111–1236.

8. This paragraph and the following one are based on: *NLT*, 27 Nov. 1880, 15 Jan., 12 and 19 Feb., and 29 Oct. 1881; Kuritz, "State Government and Labor Controls," 59, 151–52.

9. *NLT*, 19 Feb., 9 Apr., and 29 Oct. 1881, 11 Feb. and 26 Oct. 1882, and 6 Jan. 1883; Mellon, *Mellon*, 541–63, esp. 541, 549–50, 561; Kuritz, "State Government and Labor Controls," 151–52.

10. *NLT*, 19 Feb. 1881 and 13 Jan. 1883.

11. *NLT*, 13 Jan. 1883 and 22 May 1874.

12. *NLT*, 19 Feb. and 29 Oct. 1881; Kuritz, "State Government and Labor Controls," 152, 157, 159–61; Cooper Co., *Twentieth-Century Bench and Bar*, 2:954; Lorant, *Pittsburgh*, 196, 264. Possibly the judge was also mindful of a current in public sentiment that found expression in the reluctance of many jurors to return guilty verdicts in such cases because they too feared the growth of corporate power. Indeed, soon conspiracy convictions were obtained with enough difficulty to convince employers that the injunction was a better means to protect their profits and their property—which Pennsylvania courts had come to equate.

13. *JUL*, Jan. 1883; *NLT*, 20 Jan. 1882; Kuritz, "State Government and Labor Controls," 153. Also see Genovese, *Roll, Jordan, Roll*, 25–49.

14. *JUL*, 15 June 1880 and 15 Feb. 1881; *NLT*, 2 Sept. 1880, 22 Jul. and 2 Sept. 1882, and 10 Jul. 1886; Kuritz, "State Government and Labor Controls," 153–54.

15. *NLT*, 29 Oct. 1881, 4, 11, 18, and 25 Feb., 26 Mar., 15 Apr., and 28 Oct. 1882, 6 and 13 Jan., 21 and 28 Apr. 1883; *AM*, 4 Mar. 1881; AAISW, *Proceedings*, 1882, 797, 806–07, 808–10. Jones appealed his conviction to the Pennsylvania Supreme Court, but it refused to review the case. The Waverly case against the *NLT* was dismissed in 1883.

16. *NLT*, 25 Feb. 1882

17. On the concept of turning the world upside down, see Christopher Hill, *World Turned Upside Down*.

18. *PP*, 15, 16, and 21 Mar. 1882. In making some of the points in this paragraph, I have drawn on Reddy, "Textile Trade," 62–89; LaCapra, *Rethinking Intellectual History*, 291–324.

19. *NLT*, 8 and 15 Jan., 12 and 19 Feb. 1881.

20. U.S. Bureau of the Census, *1880 Census*, Homestead; *HT*, 23 Jul., 3 and 24 Sept. 1881, 9 and 16 Sept. 1882, and 11 Oct. 1883. The success of the town's first

newspaper, the _Homestead Herald_ was short-lived; fire destroyed its office in the fall of 1881. Soon afterward the editor, Fred H. Penny, became ill and the paper went out of business. Unfortunately, there are no extant copies either of it or of its sister publication, the _Braddock Herald_. The _HT_ was published initially by E. W. Eisenbise, the publisher of the _Braddock Times_. By late 1883, Penny had regained his health and purchased the _HT_, but Schooley continued as editor.

21. _OVB_, 28 Apr., 5 and 19 May, 1888; Scoville, _Revolution in Glassmaking_, 3; _HT_, 31 Dec. 1881, 4 Nov. and 5 Aug. 1882, 2 and 27 Jan., 24 Feb., 4 and 18 Aug. 1883; _HN_, 2 Apr. 1884; Innes, _Pittsburgh Glass_, 57; Parsons, _History and Commerce of Pittsburgh_, 106.

22. _HT_, 6 Aug. 1881, 19 Jul. 1884, 12 Sept. and 21 Nov. 1885; Parsons, _History and Commerce of Pittsburgh_, 106; Joseph Weeks, "Report on the Manufacture of Glass in the United States," _Tenth Census_ (1880), 2:1074, 1076; Scoville, _Revolution in Glassmaking_, 64–66, 78–79, 149ff., 323–38; U.S. Commissioner of Labor, _Regulation and Restriction of Output_, 653, 657–61; P. Davis, _Glass Industry_, 82–84 and chaps. 8–11; Thurston, _Pittsburgh's Progress_, 110; _HLN_, 19 Jul. and 20 Dec. 1884, and 19 Dec. 1885; _American Glass Worker_, 9 Nov. 1885, as quoted in _HLN_, 21 Nov. 1885.

23. Scoville, _Revolution in Glassmaking_, 18–19, 62, 64–66, 78–79, 149ff., 323–38; Warner Co., _Allegheny County_, pt. 2, p. 603; Fleming, _Pittsburgh_, 4:288; Weeks, "Manufacture of Glass," 1085, 1124; P. Davis, _Glass Industry_, 153–55, 275; Thurston, _Pittsburgh's Progress_, 107. As editor of their two leading trade journals, Weeks also served as spokesman for iron- and steelmasters; in this capacity he hailed each "improvement" that reduced skill requirements in metalmaking. Weeks was editor of _AM_ until 1876, then became editor of _IA_, and returned to _AM_ in 1886. Under Weeks's stewardship, _AM_ paid careful attention to the glass industry.

24. U.S. Bureau of the _Census, 1880 Census_, Homestead; Byington, _Homestead_, 5; Weeks, "Manufacture of Glass," 1057, 1079–82; Scoville, _Revolution in Glassmaking_, 14, 17–18; Larner, "Glass House Boys," 359; Keeler and Fenn, "Taking of Pittsburgh," 263; Davis, _Glass Industry_, 46–50.

25. Scoville, _Revolution in Glassmaking_, 18–19, 332–34; Larner, "Glass House Boys," 359–60; U.S. Bureau of the Census, _1880 Census_, Homestead; P. Davis, _Glass Industry_, 84–85.

26. Weeks, "Report on the Manufacture of Glass in the United States," _Tenth Census_ (1880), 2:1045, 1085; Couvares, _Remaking of Pittsburgh_, 16–18; P. Davis, _Glass Industry_, 156; Scoville, _Revolution in Glassmaking_, 32–33.

27. Lazonick, "Production Relations"; Price, "Labour Process and Labour History."

28. U.S. Bureau of the Census, _1880 Census_, Homestead; Couvares, _Remaking of Pittsburgh_, 17–18; Weeks, "Manufacture of Glass," 1045. Of the 51 glassworkers enumerated in 1880 census of Homestead, 14 were skilled. Of the 89 glassworkers I was able to identify as employees of Bryce, Higbee, and Company from 1879 through 1882, 17 (roughly 19 percent) were skilled. See app. D.

29. U.S. Commissioner of Labor, _Regulation and Restriction of Output_, 653, 657–58; P. Davis, _Glass Industry_, 155–56, 227; Garlock and Builder, "Data Bank," 234; _HM_, May 1882; _JUL_, June, Jul., and Sept. 1882; _NLT_, 27 Jan., 10 Feb., and 24 Mar. 1883; _HT_, 6 Aug. and 22 Oct. 1881, and 22 Apr. 1882; _HLN_, 16 May 1885;

National Glass Budget, 31 Aug. 1912. Some Homestead workers in the early 1880s belonged to assemblies of the Knights that were headquartered elsewhere. John A. Williams, a caulker, for example, belonged to a South Side assembly. Though not officially designated as a "mixed" assembly, Local Assembly 1785 included laborers from several different trades. See *PET,* 17 June 1882.

30. *National Glass Budget,* 31 Aug. 1912; *HM,* Oct. 1881–Aug. 1882; *NLT,* 15 Jul. 1882, 21 Jan. and 21 Apr. 1883; *JUL,* June 1882; *HT,* 30 Jul., 24 Sept., 8 and 15 Oct., and 5 Nov. 1881; U.S. Bureau of the Census, *1880 Census,* Homestead; *AM,* 3 June 1887. Gessner and Schooley were close friends.

31. *NLT,* 15, 22, and 29 Jul. 1882; *HT,* 20 Oct. 1881, 7 Oct., 4, 11, and 18 Nov., 2 and 16 Dec. 1882, and 13 Jan. 1883; *National Glass Budget,* 31 Aug. 1912; U.S. Bureau of the Census, *1880 Census,* Homestead; *HM,* Apr., June, Jul., and Aug. 1882.

32. *HT,* 29 Oct. and 31 Dec. 1881, 8 and 13 May, 18 Nov., 2, 16, and 23 Dec. 1882, 16 Jan. and 4 Aug. 1883, and 29 Jan. 1884; U.S. Bureau of the Census, *1880 Census,* Homestead; Northwestern Historical Association, *Allegheny County,* 2:119; *HM,* Nov. 1881 and Jan. 1882. Charles Stemler, Charles Bossert, John B. Jones, Jr., John B. Jones, Sr., and James J. McDonald were among those glassworkers active in Homestead politics in the early 1880s.

33. *HT,* 5 Aug. 1882 and 4 Aug. 1883; Scoville, *Revolution in Glassmaking,* 38. On volunteer fire companies, see Couvares, *Remaking of Pittsburgh,* 45–49.

34. Temin, *Iron and Steel,* 180–81, claims that Holley had nothing whatever to do with the design of the PBSW.

35. On the importance of examining relationships between and among different groups of employers and workers in efforts to understand struggles for shop floor control, see Elbaum et al., "Labour Process." Note, however, that the authors regard social and political phenomena as secondary factors in apprehending the nature of work relations.

36. Wall, *Carnegie,* 330–32; Hendrick, *Carnegie,* 1:210–13; Temin, *Iron and Steel,* 175; Holley to Julian Kennedy, 20 Oct. 1879 and 12 May 1881, and Holley to a Mr. Sandberg, 12 May 1881, all in Holley Letterbooks, 1877–1882; Holley's untitled reports to the Bessemer Steel Co., Ltd., 1880–81, box 4, Miscellaneous Historical Records, USX Archives; McHugh, *Holley,* 294–95, 300–05, 347–48.

37. *HT,* 20 Oct. 1883; Bridge, *Inside History,* 85–87, 150–51; Wall, *Carnegie,* 474–75.

38. My sketch of the owners of the PBSW is drawn from: *EMJ* 28 (July–Dec. 1879), 301; *AM,* 18 Feb. 1881, 19 Oct. 1883, and 10 Oct. 1884; *HT,* 20 Oct. 1883; *HLN,* 2 Jan. 1886; *NLT,* 12 and 19 Jan., 14 Dec. 1878; 11 Jan., 2, 8, 15, and 22 Feb., 1, 8, 15, 22, and 29 Mar., and 26 July 1879; Park and Hemphill, "Kloman Eulogy," 250–54; Metcalf et al., "In Memoriam: James Park, Jr.," 239–40; Fleming, *Pittsburgh,* 4:69–71; Warner Co., *Allegheny County,* pt. 2, 254–58; Holley to Andrew Kloman, 10 Dec. 1877, Holley to Mackintosh-Hemphill Company, 10 Dec. 1878, Holley to Julian Kennedy, 20 Nov. 1879, 11 and 12 May 1881, Holley to J. L. Bill, 5 Jan. 1878, and Holley to Carnegie, 30 Jan. 1880, all in Holley Letterbooks, 1877–82; R. W. Hunt, untitled eulogy of Holley, in AIME, *Holley Memorial,* 31; Kloman, "Improved Friction Clutch"; Bayles, "Tribute to Holley," 42; Stevens, "Men Who Run the Mills," manuscript; Bridge, *Inside History,* 54–61, 85–87, 150–52; Bennett, "Iron Workers," 93–94; Hogg, "Homestead Strike," 14–15; Jarrett, "Iron

Workers," 286–88, 307; V. Clark, *History of Manufactures,* 234; Temin, *Iron and Steel,* 127–30, 180–82; Wall, *Carnegie,* 474–75; Hendrick, *Carnegie,* 1:301; Carnegie, *Autobiography,* 225; Redlich, *American Business Leaders,* 1:92–93, 88, 104–05, 109, 111, 116, 118; McHugh, *Holley,* 301–05, 347–48.

39. Bridge, *Inside History,* 86–87; Temin, *Iron and Steel,* 180, 181, 274–75; Wall, *Carnegie,* 274; V. Clark, *History of Manufactures,* 2:159–61.

40. Carnegie, *Autobiography,* 194–200; Wall, *Carnegie,* 338–340, 475; Hogg, "Homestead Strike," 12; Park and Hemphill, "Kloman Eulogy," 252; Bridge, *Inside Story,* 66–69, 86; Hendrick, *Carnegie,* 1:218–19, 301.

41. *AM,* 2 Feb. and 8 Apr. 1881; Wall, *Carnegie,* 340, 475–76; Carnegie, *Autobiography,* 195–97; Bennett, "Iron Workers," 94; Mackintosh-Hemphill Co., *Experience for Sale,* 12.

42. AIME, *Holley Memorial,* 31; Crooker, "American Blooming Mill," 336; Hunt, "American Rolling Mills," 54; Bridge, *Inside History,* 85–87; Holley to Julian Kennedy, 20 Nov. 1879 and 12 May 1881, Holley Letterbooks; Bayles, "Tribute to Holley," 42–43; Temin, *Iron and Steel,* 136, 181–82, 213; McHugh, *Holley,* 301.

43. Carnegie, *Autobiography,* 195–97, 225; Wall, *Carnegie,* 338, 474–75; *EMJ* 28 (July–Dec. 1879): 301; *AM,* 18 Feb. 1881 and 10 Oct. 1884; Redlich, *American Business Leaders,* 1:92, 104–05, 116, 118; Park and Hemphill, "Kloman Eulogy," 250–54; Metcalf et al., "In Memoriam: James Park, Jr.," 239–40; *HT,* 20 Oct. 1883; Bridge, *Inside History,* 85–87, 150–52; Clark, *History of Manufactures,* 2:234; Temin, *Iron and Steel,* 180, 213; Hendrick, *Carnegie,* 1:301; Fitch, *Steel Workers,* 109. The PBSC was incorporated with a capitalization of $250,000 on 21 October 1879. The Park brothers, William Singer, and Hussey, Wells, and Company each owned five shares, which were valued at $10,000 each; Miller and Clark each owned four; and Kloman owned two.

44. Holley to Julian Kennedy, 20 Nov. 1879, Holley to J. L. Bill, 5 Jan. 1878, and Holley to a Mr. Sandberg, 12 May 1881, all in the Holley Letterbooks; Holley to Daniel Morrell, 21 Oct. 1876, Holley to John Slade, 29 Aug. 1877, Holley to Rossiter Raymond, 17 April 1879, as quoted in McHugh, *Holley,* 301, 305, and 332 respectively. Holley advised Kennedy that he was certain the PBSC could "build a good steel works without infringing any of your patents."

45. AIME, *Holley Memorial,* 31. Holley also had a hand in designing the most important part of the blooming mill at the PBSW, a conclusion based on the following sources: AIME, *Holley Memorial,* 31; Mackintosh-Hemphill Co., *Rolling Mills,* 38–39; Mackintosh-Hemphill Co., *Experience for Sale,* 12, 25; Mackintosh-Hemphill Co., *1803–1924,* 16; Hunt, "American Rolling Mills," 54; Hunt, "Bessemer Manufacture," 206–11, 213; McHugh, *Holley,* 227; Crooker, "American Blooming Mill," 333, 334, 336; Holley to Kloman, 10 Dec. 1877, and Holley to Mackintosh-Hemphill Company, 10 Dec. 1878, both in Holley Letterbooks.

46. Holley to Julian Kennedy, 11 and 20 Nov. 1879, and 12 May 1881, Holley to Andrew Carnegie, 30 Jan. 1880, Holley to Andrew Kloman, 10 Dec. 1877, all in the Holley Letterbooks; and Holley to Daniel Morrell, 21 Oct. 1876, as quoted in McHugh, Holley, 301; "Pittsburgh Testimonial," in AIME, *Holley Memorial,* 31, 162; McHugh, *Holley,* 301, 332, 339–40, 348–49. Holley's letterbooks from 1878 through 1881 contain numerous letters written to Park Brothers, Inc. and to James Park, Jr., who hosted a testimonial for Holley in Pittsburgh in 1879. Carnegie was noticeably absent from the gathering. See Holly to Sandberg, 12 May

1881, as well as a number of other letters quoted in McHugh, *Holley,* chaps. 21–25, for additional evidence of Holley's increasing hostility toward the pool.

47. Bridge, *Inside History,* 152; Hendrick, *Carnegie,* 1:301; Wall, *Carnegie,* 475. For an alternative interpretation of Hunt's remarks, see Temin, *Iron and Steel,* 180–81.

48. *NLT,* 5 Feb. 1881; *AM,* 4 Feb. 1881; Holley to Mackintosh-Hemphill Company, 10 Dec. 1878, Holley Letterbooks; Mackintosh-Hemphill Co., *1803–1924,* 16; Mackintosh-Hemphill Co., *Experience for Sale,* 12, 25; Mackintosh-Hemphill Company, *Rolling Mills,* 38–39; Crooker, "American Blooming Mill," 336; Bridge, *Inside History,* 151; W. R. Jones, "Manufacture of Bessemer Steel," 129; Bridge, *Inside History,* 97; Wall, *Carnegie,* 475–76.

49. Wall, *Carnegie,* 275.

50. *HT,* 19 Nov., 3 and 24 Dec. 1881; *NLT,* 16 Dec. 1881, and 7 Jan. 1882; *AM,* 18 Feb. 1881 and 10 Oct. 1884.

51. *NLT,* 18 Feb. 1882; *HM,* Jan. 1882; *HT,* 30 Jul., 6 Aug., 3 Sept., 19 Nov., 10 and 31 Dec. 1881, 1 Apr. 1882, and 5 May 1883; *AM,* 20 May 1881; W. R. Jones, "Manufacture of Bessemer Steel," 133.

52. *HT,* 23 Jul., 13 and 27 Aug., 17 Sept., and 17 Dec. 1881; *HLN,* 17 Jul. 1886; *NLT,* 8 Dec. 1877, 2 Jul. 1881, 7 Jan. 1882, and 6 Jan. 1883; Freifeld, "Roots of Division," 460–61.

53. Mauss, *The Gift;* Freifeld, "Roots of Division," 461. Freifeld's assessment of the gift-giving problem conforms to a main argument of her study: that there was no political revolution in nineteenth-century America, as there should have been, because workers failed to develop class consciousness.

54. My account of Clark's life is based primarily on *AM,* 18 Feb. 1881, 10 and 17 Oct. 1884.

55. *PEC,* 28 Feb. 1882; Bridge, *Inside History,* 153; *PP,* 6 Mar. 1882.

56. This sketch of the first Homestead steelworkers is drawn from a variety of sources, but chiefly from the weekly "Steel Sparks" column in the *HT* and the reports of the AAISW in the *NLT.* Also see app. C.

57. Fitch, research notes, card 1, CH-29 (Carnegie-Homestead, interview no. 29); Schooley and Schooley, *Homestead Directory, 1890,* 82, *Homestead Directory, 1891,* p. 89, and *Homestead Directory, 1892,* pp. 9, 112; AAISW, *Proceedings,* 1881, 771; AAISW, *Proceedings,* 1890, 2965, 2970–71; *HLN,* 7 Nov. and 19 Dec. 1885, and 19 Feb. 1887; *HT,* 24 June and 26 Aug. 1882; *NLT,* 10 June 1882.

58. *NLT,* 3 Sept. and 29 Oct. 1881, 4 Mar. and 8 Apr. 1882; Bennett, "Iron Workers," 93–95, 309–10; Northwestern Historical Association, *Allegheny County,* 2:117; *HLN,* 12 Feb. 1884.

59. *HT,* 17 Sept. 1881; Eggert, *Steelmasters,* xvi, 3, 17; William B. Dickson, "Account of 1882 Strike," and Robert P. Dickson, "Addendum to Account of 1882 Strike," both in Dickson Papers.

60. *HT,* 30 Jul., 6, 13, and 27 Aug. 1881, 26 Aug., 14 and 28 Oct. 1882, 17 Mar. 1883, and 1 Mar. 1884; *IW,* 29 Jul. 1882; St. Mary Magdalene Church, Register of Baptism vol. 1 (1881–1890), 1, 8; Allegheny County, Board of Assessment, Real Property and Assessment Books: Homestead and Mifflin Township, 1883.

Carpatho-Rusyns, an East-European people who speak several dialects formally classified as Ukrainian, began arriving in the United States from the Kingdom of Hungary in the early 1880s. Also known as Ruthenians, Rusnaks,

Carpatho-Russians, or Carpatho-Ukrainians, their name derives from their homeland—the Carpathian Mountains—and their ancient origins as Eastern Slavs. (The appellation, *Rus'*, applied to all such people in the Middle Ages.) Today, the original homeland of the Carpatho-Rusyns is located in the Western Ukraine and in northeastern Slovakia. See Magocsi, "Carpatho-Rusyns," 200–10.

61. This paragraph and the following one are based on: *NLT*, 2 and 9 Jul. 1881 and 7 Jan. 1882; PBIS, *Annual Report*, vol. 10 (1881–82), 170; AAISW, *Proceedings*, 1881, 723, 729, 735, 741–742; AAISW, *Proceedings*, 1882, 806; *PP*, 6 Mar. 1882.

62. *HT*, 23 Jul. and 27 Aug. 1881; *NLT*, 17 Sept. 1881. On Jones, Blanford, and Homestead Lodge 11, see: AAISW, *Proceedings*, 1881, 729, 741, 747, 771, 786, 1039; AAISW, *Proceedings*, 1882, 786, 795, 1031; *NLT*, 10 June, 29 Jul., and 19 Aug. 1882, and 20 Jan. 1883; *HT*, 20 Jan. and 10 Feb. 1883; *HLN*, 19 Feb. 1887. On Fitzgerald and Lodge 24, see: AAISW, *Proceedings*, 1882, 795; AAISW, *Proceedings*, 1881, 77, 742; *NLT*, 7 Jan., 6 May, and 10 June 1882; *PP*, 3 Mar. 1882.

63. PBIS, *Annual Report*, vol. 10 (1881–82), 171; *HT*, 31 Dec. 1881; *HM*, Jan. 1882; AAISW, *Proceedings*, 1882, 806.

64. *NLT*, 7 Jan. 1882; PBIS, *Annual Report*, vol. 10 (1881–82), 171; AAISW, *Proceedings*, 1882, 806, 918–19; *PP*, 2, 6, 15, 16, and 21 Mar. 1882; *PT*, 3, 6, and 9 Mar. 1882; *AM*, 10 and 24 Mar. 1882; *IA*, 9 and 23 Mar. 1882; Bridge, *Inside History*, 154.

CHAPTER 12. *The Homestead Strike of 1882*

1. *NLT*, 6 May, 1882.

2. My account of the Homestead strike of 1882 is based on reports from labor and trade journals, the daily and weekly press of Pittsburgh and Homestead, union and government records, and personal memoirs. Among the most helpful: *NLT*, 9 Jul. 1881 and 7 Jan., 4, 11, and 18 Feb., 18 Mar., and 6 May 1882; PBIS, *Annual Report*, vol. 10 (1881–82), 171–75; AAISW, *Proceedings*, 1882, 806, 19; W. Dickson, "Account of 1882 Strike," and R. Dickson, "Addendum"; *IW*, 29 Jul. 1882; *HM*, Jan., Feb., and Mar. 1882; *HT*, 31 Dec. 1881 and 4 Feb. 1882; *PP*, 2, 4, 6, 9, 11, 13–16, and 21 Mar. 1882; *PT*, 3, 6, 9, and 15 Mar. 1882; *AM*, 10 and 24 Mar., and 25 Aug. 1882; *PEC*, 28 Feb. and 2 Mar. 1882; *PET*, 2, 3, 4, 6, and 14 Mar. 1882; *PCG*, 28 Feb., 4 and 6 Mar. 1882; *IA*, 9 and 23 Mar. 1882.

3. *NLT*, 7 Jan., 4 and 11 Feb. 1881; *PCG*, 4 Mar. 1882; *IA*, 23 Mar. 1882.

4. The Homestead strike of 1882 receives brief consideration in: Fitch, *Steel Workers*, 109; Holt, "Trade Unionism," 12; Freifeld, "Roots of Division," 482; Stromquist, "Working Class Organization," 33; Temin, *Iron and Steel*, 180–81. Also see Krause, " *'Za Chlebom,'* "151.

5. *PP*, 9, 11, and 13 Mar. 1882; *PT*, 9 Mar. 1882; *PEC*, 9 Mar. 1882; *AM*, 10 Mar. 1882.

6. *PT*, 3 Mar. 1882; *PEC*, 2 Mar. 1882; *PP*, 2 Mar. 1882.

7. *HM*, Feb. 1882.

8. *PET*, 3 and 14 Mar. 1882, emphasis in the original; *PP*, 6 Mar. 1882.

9. *NLT*, 3 Sept. 1881 and 8 Apr. 1882; *HT*, 17 and 24 June 1882, and 21 Apr. 1883; *PT*, 15 Mar. 1882; *IW*, 29 Jul., 5 and 12 Aug. 1882. On the Irish National

Land League in Pittsburgh, see Walsh, "Fanatic Heart," 187–204. For a treatment that is more sensitive to the league's critique of American capitalism, see E. Foner, *Politics and Ideology*, 150–200.

10. *PP*, 6 Mar. 1882; *IW*, 29 Jul. 1882; *HT*, 13 Aug. 1881, 6 May and 9 Sept. 1882. Prior to the opening of Ellis Island, Castle Garden was the port of entry for most European immigrants.

11. Garlock and Builder, "Data Bank," 234; *HM*, May 1882; *JUL*, June 1882 and Jul. 1883; *HT*, 22 April 1882; *NLT*, 24 Mar. 1883 and 29 Jan. 1887.

12. This argument runs counter to the accounts of Stromquist, "Working Class organization," 33, and Freifeld, "Roots of Division," 482–83, who maintain that it was the threat of a citywide strike that alone made possible the workers' victory at Homestead.

13. On the functional autonomy of industrial artisans, including those cited in the text, see Soffer, "Trade Union Development"; Montgomery, *Workers' Control*, 11–15.

14. Robinson, *Amalgamated Association*, 18–21; Holt, "Trade Unionism," 10–12; Freifeld, "Roots of Division," 477–80. In 1879 the AAISW began a campaign that saw membership triple to sixteen thousand within three years. During this period, the union established lodges in seven of the nation's eleven Bessemer plants.

15. *PP*, 6 Mar. 1882; *PEC*, 28 Feb. 1882. "To gain their point, the men at Homestead had one time struck when the ingots were in the furnace and the firm was compelled to grant an increase in wages or suffer a great loss," William Singer, an owner, explained. "This is the cause of the present lockout." Although Singer called the dispute a lockout, workers and virtually all contemporary observers called it a strike. And in truth it was a strike, for the workers withheld their labor rather than sign Clark's ironclad contract.

16. *PEC*, 28 Feb. 1882; *PT*, 6 Mar. 1882; *PP*, 6 Mar. 1882. On Johnstown as a company town, see Bennett, "Iron Workers," chap. 5.

17. *NLT*, 6 May 1882; PBIS, *Annual Report*, vol. 10 (1881–82), 171; AAISW, *Proceedings*, 1882, 919, 806; *AM*, 10 Mar. 1882

18. This paragraph and the following one are based on: *IA*, 23 Mar. 1882; *PP*, 17 and 18 Mar. 1882; *AM*, 24 Mar. 1882; R. Dickson, "Addendum," and W. Dickson, "Account of 1882 Strike." Also see Eggert, *Steelmasters*, 17–18.

19. Robert Dickson recalled that between the time of Gardner's hearing and his trial in March, William Dickson was threatened many times. Following the strike he continued to carry a revolver to work. He was later discharged for this but then was rehired as a foreman of converting mill laborers.

20. This paragraph and the subsequent one are based on: *NLT*, 11 and 18 Feb. 1882; AAISW, *Proceedings*, 1882, 806; *HM*, Feb. 1882; *PET*, 3 Mar. 1882; *PT*, 3 Mar. 1882; *PP*, 6 Mar. 1882; *HT*, 4 Feb. 1882; W. R. Jones, "Manufacture of Bessemer Steel," 133.

21. *AM*, 24 Mar. 1882, which offers a somewhat different version of the assault from Dickson's own; *PP*, 15 and 18 Mar. 1882; *PT*, 3, 4, and 6 Mar. 1882; *PET*, 14 Mar. 1882.

22. *HT*, 21 Jan. 1882; PBIS, *Annual Report*, vol. 10 (1881–82), 170 and 172; *NLT*, 4 June 1881, 4, 11, and 18 Feb., 4 Mar., and 7 Oct. 1882; AAISW, *Proceedings*, 1882, 807, 917; Bennett, "Iron Workers," 309–10. The conspiracy charges

prompted the *NLT* to caution the strikers about the appropriate manner to dissuade others from going to work: "Any person engaged in a strike has the right, under the law, to state his case to any other person whom he supposes is going to work. This must be done, however, as individuals, and not in twos or threes, and off of the company's premises." Gusky, known for his charitable work, received many accolades from the AAISW.

23. PBIS, *Annual Report*, vol. 10 (1881–82), 170; *NLT*, 18 Feb. 1882; *HT*, 18 Feb. 1882; *PCG*, 28 Feb. 1882; *PEC*, 28 Feb. 1882.

24. This paragraph is drawn from a reading of the daily and weekly newspapers published in Homestead and Pittsburgh during the strike and from Berman, "Democracy," 12–17. On union self-government see also Robinson, *Amalgamated Association*, chap. 2.

25. *PCG*, 28 Feb. 1882; *NLT*, 4 Mar. 1882; *HT*, 18 Feb. 1882; *PEC*, 28 Feb. 1882.

26. PBIS, *Annual Report*, vol. 10 (1881–82), 172; *PP*, 2 Mar. 1882; *PCG*, 2 Mar. 1882; *PEC*, 2 Mar. 1882; *PET*, 2 Mar. 1882; *PT*, 3 Mar. 1882; *AM*, 25 Aug. 1882. Later in 1882 the PBSC was in fact sued by at least one disgruntled customer that charged that the rails it had purchased from the company were virtually worthless.

27. *PT*, 11 Mar. 1882; *NLT*, 11 Mar. 1882.

28. PBIS, *Annual Report*, vol. 10 (1881–82), 172; *PT*, 3 Mar. 1882; *PP*, 2 and 3 Mar. 1882; *PEC*, 2 Mar. 1882; PET, 2 Mar. 1882. Bullock also requested assistance from the Pittsburgh police. The request was denied, although authorities later dispatched six policemen to the City Poor Farm, which adjoined the steelworks.

29. PBIS, *Annual Report*, vol. 10 (1881–82), 172–73; *PP*, 3 Mar. 1882; *PT*, 3 Mar. 1882.

30. *PET*, 2 Mar. 1882; *PP*, 3 Mar. 1882; *PT*, 3 Mar. 1882; PBIS, *Annual Report*, vol. 10 (1881–82), 172.

31. PBIS, *Annual Report*, vol. 10 (1881–82), 173; *PP*, 3 Mar. 1882; *PCG*, 3 Mar. 1882; *PEC*, 3 Mar. 1882; *AM*, 10 Mar. 1882.

32. *PET*, 3 Mar. 1882; *PT*, 3 and 4 Mar 1882; *PEC*, 3 Mar. 1882; PBIS, *Annual Report*, vol. 10 (1881–82), 173.

33. *PP*, 4 Mar. 1882; *PCG*, 4 Mar. 1882; *PT*, 4 Mar. 1882; *PEC*, 3 and 4 Mar. 1882.

34. PBIS, *Annual Report*, vol. 10 (1881–82), 173; *PET*, 4 Mar. 1882; *PCG*, 4 Mar. 1882; *PT*, 4 Mar. 1882.

35. *PP*, 4 and 6 Mar. 1882; *PCG*, 6 Mar. 1882; *IA*, 9 Mar. 1882; *NLT*, 4 Mar. 1882; *PT*, 6 Mar. 1882; *AM*, 10 Mar. 1882. The mills owned in part or in whole by the operators of the PBSC were: Singer, Nimick, and Company; Hussey, Howe, and Company; the Solar Iron Works; the Superior Mill; the Black Diamond Steel Works; the Crescent Steel Works.

36. *PP* and *PCG*, 6 Mar. 1882.

37. *PT*, 10 Mar. 1882; *AM*, 10 Mar. 1882; *PP*, 9, 11, and 13 Mar. 1882; *PT*, 9 Mar. 1882; *PEC*, 9 Mar. 1882; *PET*, 6 Mar. 1882.

38. *PT*, 11 and 14 Mar. 1882; *NLT*, 11 Mar. 1882; *PP*, 13 and 14 Mar. 1882.

39. This paragraph and the subsequent one are based on *PP*, 13 and 14 Mar. 1882.

40. Ibid.; *PT*, 14 Mar. 1882; *PCG*, 14 Mar. 1882; *PEC*, 15 Mar. 1882. While the strikers asserted that they had been duped by Clark, it is entirely possible that Jarrett was party to a sellout. He was absent from Pittsburgh on 13 March,

claiming that there was an illness in his family in Sharon. When he returned, he said he had been ill.

41. This paragraph and the following two are based on: *PP,* 15 Mar. 1882; PBIS, *Annual Report,* vol. 10 (1881–82), 173–74; *PET,* 14 and 15 Mar. 1882; *PEC,* 14 Mar. 1882; *PT,* 15 Mar. 1882; *PP,* 15, 16, and 21 Mar. 1882; Bridge, *Inside History,* 157.

42. *AM,* 24 Mar. 1882; *PP,* 16 Mar. 1882; PBIS, *Annual Report,* vol. 10 (1881–82), 173–74; AAISW, *Proceedings,* 1882, 807; *NLT,* 18 Mar. 1882. That the Homestead men pressed for an agreement that granted them authority to sign a contract suggests that they were not pleased with Jarrett's leadership. Other union men shared this opinion, and Jarrett eventually stepped down.

43. AAISW, *Proceedings,* 1882, 806–07; *HT,* 25 Mar. 1882; *PT,* 20 Mar. 1882; *IA,* 23 Mar. 1882; *AM,* 25 Aug. 1882.

44. *NLT,* 6 May and 24 June 1882; *IW,* 1 Jul. 1882; *PP,* 17 and 19 June 1882; *PET,* 17 June 1882; *PCG,* 19 June 1882; *HT,* 10 and 17 June, and 1 Jul. 1882.

CHAPTER 13. *Defeat in the City and the State*

1. My account of 17 June 1882 is drawn principally from *NLT,* 29 Apr., 6, 20, and 27 May, 10 and 24 June 1882; *IW,* 1 Jul. 1882; *PP,* 17 and 19 June 1882; *PET,* 17 June 1882; *PT,* 17 and 19 June 1882; *PEC,* 16 and 17 June 1882; *PCG,* 19 June 1882. Also see Stromquist, "Working Class Organization," 17–24. Schnapper, *American Labor,* 172, reproduces a contemporary illustration of the parade.

2. The *NLT* placed the number of onlookers at three hundred thousand persons, but the daily press reported more conservative figures. Even the steadfastly entrepreneurial *PCG,* however, estimated that a minimum of thirty thousand workers marched in the parade.

3. The figures on the number of Homesteaders in the parade are drawn from *HT,* 10 and 17 June, and 1 Jul. 1882; *PET,* 17 June 1882; *PCG,* 19 June 1882; *PP,* 19 June 1882; PBIS, *Annual Report,* vol. 11 (1882–83), 24a.

4. *NLT,* 7 Jan., 11 and 18 Feb., 4 Mar., 6 May, 10 June, and 7 Aug. 1882; *PP,* 19 June 1882; *PET,* 17 June 1882; *HLN,* 3 Jan. 1890; AAISW, *Proceedings,* 1882, 788.

5. *PET,* 17 June 1882; *PCG,* 19 June 1882; *NLT,* 1 and 22 Apr. 1882; Knights of Labor, *District Assembly 9, Proceedings,* 3 and 4 Jan., 4 Apr., 5 and 6 Jul. 1882, Powderly Papers, reel 65; *JUL,* 18 May 1882; *Workingman,* 29 Aug. 1882.

6. Armstrong to Powderly, 15 and 21 May, 9 and 26 June 1882, Robert D. Layton to Powderly, 23 May and 14 June 1882, and Powderly to Armstrong, 17 and 24 May 1882, all in the Powderly Papers; *PD,* 21 Aug. 1882; *NLT,* 6 and 13 June, 17 Sept., 5 and 12 Nov. 1881, 4 and 25 Mar., 1, 8, 15, 22, and 29 Apr., 6, 13, 20, and 27 May, 3, 17, and 24 June 1882; *Workingman,* 29 Aug. 1882; Stromquist, "Working Class Organization," 19; Couvares, *Remaking of Pittsburgh,* 68–69; Bennett, "Iron Workers," 289–92.

7. *PET,* 19 Nov. 1881; *HT,* 5 Nov. 1881; *NLT,* 5 and 26 Feb., 16 Apr., 21 May, 18 and 25 June, 6 Aug., 29 Oct., 5 and 12 Nov. 1881.

8. *NLT,* 17 June 1882; *JUL,* Jul. 1882.

9. *PP,* 28 and 30 Aug. 1882; *PD,* 29 Aug. 1882; *NLT,* 4 and 25 Mar., 1, 8, 15, 22, and 29 Apr.; *IW,* 24 June 1882; *PD,* 23 and 29 Aug. 1882; Bennett, "Iron Workers," 290–91; Walsh, "Fanatic Heart," 198; S. Walker, "Powderly," 242–43.

10. Unsigned letter from an official in the Land League's New York office to Powderly, 21 May 1882, Powderly to Armstrong, 17 and 24 May 1882, Powderly to Frank Heath, 11 and 24 May 1882, Armstrong to Powderly, 22 May 1882 (emphasis in original), all in the Powderly Papers; *NLT*, 3 June 1882, which reprints in full the critical editorial (also republished in the *PP*) cited by Armstrong in his letter to Powderly; S. Walker, "Powderly," 250–54; Richards, "Armstrong," 20.

11. R. D. Layton to Powderly, 23 and 25 May and 14 June 1882, Charles Litchman to Powderly, 5 June 1882, Powderly to Armstrong, 17 and 24 May, 20 June 1882, Powderly to Frank Heath, 24 May and 2 June 1882, Powderly to A. C. Rankin, 7 June 1883, and Armstrong to Powderly 9 and 26 June 1882, all in the Powderly Papers; Stromquist, "Working Class Organization," 22; S. Walker, "Powderly," 254; Falzone, *Powderly*, 55. Powderly's public opposition to labor politics became quite strident by 1883, when he told the Knights' general assembly that "a labor party . . . is not in accord with the genius of American institutions."

12. *Vulcan Record* (1875), 16; AAISW, *Proceedings* 1877, 39–41; AAISW, *Proceedings*, 1878, 122; AAISW, *Proceedings*, 1881, 583–84; *NLT*, "The Coming Struggle," 27 May 1882; Stromquist, "Working Class Organization," 30–32.

13. *NLT*, "Amalgamated Association Policy," 18 June 1881; *IW*, 30 Sept. 1882; Stromquist, "Working Class Organization," 33–34.

14. *NLT*, 27 May and 17 June 1882; *AM*, 25 May, 2 and 9 June 1882; *IW*, 24 June 1882.

15. *NLT*, 15 Apr. and 27 May 1882; *IW*, 17 June and 7 Oct. 1882; AAISW, *Proceedings*, 1882, 815; *AM*, 26 May, 2 and 23 June, and 28 Jul. 1882; Jarrett, "Iron Workers," 293–94, 307; Bennett, "Iron Workers," 117. With few (and very brief) exceptions—notably Stromquist, "Working Class Organization," 35–38, and Fitch, *Steel Workers*, 108–110—the "Big Strike" of 1882 has received little attention from historians. In addition to the *NLT*, the *IW* and the *AM*, which provide good weekly coverage, the best contemporary account is "Labor Troubles in Pennsylvania," in PBIS, *Annual Report*, vol. 10 (1881–82), 174–92.

16. *NLT*, 27 May and 1 Jul. 1882; Bennett, "Iron Workers," 118.

17. *NLT*, 3 and 24 June 1882; *IW*, 1 Jul. 1882; *PP*, 19 June 1882; *PET*, 17 June 1882; *PEC*, 17 June 1882; *PCG*, 19 June 1882.

18. *NLT*, 24 June 1882. There also was considerable cooperation between local assemblies of Knights and lodges of the AAISW during the Big Strike. In fact, some ironworkers maintained memberships in both organizations.

19. In interpreting the grand parade, I have profited from Darnton's reading of a procession in eighteenth-century Montpellier; see Darnton, *Great Cat Massacre*, 107–43.

20. *PCG*, 19 June 1882; *PP*, 19 June 1882; *PT*, 19 June 1882; *PEC*, 17 June 1882; *NLT*, 24 June 1882.

21. *PD*, 4 Jul. 1882; *AM*, 9 and 23 June, 11, 18, and 25 Aug., 8, 15, and 22 Sept. 1882; *IW*, 17 and 24 June, 8 and 22 Jul., 5, 12, and 26 Aug., 9 and 30 Sept., 7 and 28 Oct., and 18 Nov. 1882; *JUL*, Feb. 1883; AAISW, *Proceedings*, 1882, 814–17, 967; AAISW, *Proceedings*, 1884, 1084–87, 1112; Jarrett, "Iron Workers," 293–94; "Labor Troubles in Pennsylvania," in PBIS, *Annual Report*, vol. 10 (1881–82), 174–192; Robinson, *Amalgamated Association*, 21; Stromquist, "Working Class Organization," 36–37; Fitch, *Steel Workers*, 110.

22. *NLT,* 1 Apr. and 28 Oct. 1882 and 6 Jan. 1883; *JUL,* Apr. 1883; *HT,* 2 Dec. 1882; *HLN,* 19 Feb. 1887; A. C. Rankin to Powderly, 26 June 1882, Powderly Papers, reel 4; Stromquist, "Working Class Organization," 23–24, 38; Friefeld, "Roots of Division," 469, 483–88, 534. District Assembly 3 suffered from petty battles among some of its leaders even before the grand parade. The problem became much more troublesome by the end of the decade.

23. *NLT,* 24 June, 8, 15, 22, and 29 Jul., 5 and 19 Aug., 2, 23, and 30 Sept., 11 and 18 Nov. 1882; Allegheny County, Election Docket, vol. 2 (1877–85); R. D. Layton to Powderly, 6 and 21 June 1882, and Rankin to Powderly, 26 June 1882 both in Powderly Papers, reel 3; Bennett, "Iron Workers," 289–91, which discusses the disaffection of Irish workers in Pittsburgh from the GLP; Couvares, *Remaking of Pittsburgh,* 68.

24. *PP,* 14 Nov. 1882; *NLT,* 18 and 25 Nov. 1882; Couvares, *Remaking of Pittsburgh,* 68; Allegheny County, Election Docket, vol. 2 (1877–85). Armstrong also failed to carry Mifflin Township, even with its heavy concentration of miners, and he also lost in the steel towns of Braddock and McKeesport.

25. *PD,* 5 and 9 Nov. 1882; *PP,* 7 and 8 Nov. 1882; *NLT,* 18 Nov. 1882; *HT,* 11 Nov. 1882; Stromquist, "Working Class Organization," 24, 38.

26. *NLT,* 22 May 1874; Holt, "Trade Unionism," 35.

27. *NLT,* 24 June 1882.

CHAPTER 14. *A Tale of Two Cities*

1. *NLT,* 18 Nov. 1882, 3 May, and 27 Sept. 1884, 29 Aug. 1885, 17 and 24 Jul., 28 Aug., 11 and 25 Sept., and 16 Oct. 1886; Allegheny County, Election Dockets, vol. 2 (1877–85), and vol. 3 (1885–91).

2. *NLT,* 23 Sept. 1882, as quoted in Stromquist, "Working Class Organization," 38; AAISW, *Constitution, By-Laws, and Rules of Order,* 1876, 16; AAISW, *Constitution, By-Laws, and Rules of Order,* 1878, 7; Fitch, *Steel Workers,* 97–98, 257–58; Brody, *Steelworkers,* 125–26; Robinson, *Amalgamated Association,* 49–50. By the late 1880s, Martin was urging the AAISW to admit unskilled workers. His criticism of the Knights, as well as his career ambitions, may be traced through the AAISW's page in the *NLT* that he edited. See, among other issues: 7 and 14 Jul. 1883, 8 Mar. 1884, 27 Feb. and 10 Apr. 1886, 24 Mar. 1888, 13 Apr., 11 May, and 29 June 1889, 3 Feb., 28 June, and 27 Sept. 1890, and 19 Mar. 1892. Mavrinac, "Labor Organization," 3–47, offers an uncritical overview of Martin's career.

3. *NLT,* 4 Mar. 1882, 10 and 31 Mar., 14 and 28 Apr., 5 May, 7 and 14 Jul., and 2 Sept. 1883; Robinson, *Amalgamated Association,* 21; Hogan, *Economic History,* 1:227; Wright, "Amalgamated Association, 1892–1901," 40; Holt, "Trade Unionism," 10, 12–13.

4. *JSP,* 9 and 23 Aug., 20 Sept., and 1 Nov. 1885; *Alarm,* 21 Feb. 1885, as quoted in P. Foner, *American Labor Songs,* 150; Fitch, research notes, CD-6; *NLT,* 3 Jul., 1, 15, 22, and 29 Aug. 1885; *AM,* 22 May and 5 June 1885.

5. Garlock, "Data Bank," 234–39; Holt, "Trade Unionism," 13; *JSP,* 25 Apr., 8 Aug., 19 Sept., 14 and 28 Nov., 5 and 12 Dec. 1886; *NLT,* 13 Mar., 11 and 25 Sept., 30 Oct., 6 and 27 Nov., 4 and 18 Dec. 1886; AAISW, *Proceedings,* 1886, 1806–07, 1822–23; AAISW, *Proceedings,* 1888, 1959–62; *AM,* 4 and 11 June 1886;

Trades Assembly Political Committee, "Report of Auditing Committee," n.p., n.d., Martin Papers.

6. Couvares, *Remaking of Pittsburgh*, 72; Allegheny County, Election Docket, vol. 2 (1877–85), and vol. 3 (1885–91); *NLT*, 3 May and 27 Sept. 1884; 17 Jul., 28 Aug., 11 and 25 Sept., and 16 Oct. 1886; *HLN*, 14 May, 6 Sept., and 8 Nov., 1884.

7. *NLT*, 2 Oct. 1886, 1 and 15 Oct. 1887, 6 Apr. 1889, 29 Mar. 1890, and 18 Jul. 1891; *TJ*, 5 and 19 May, 30 June, 7 and 28 Jul., 1 and 27 Sept. 1888; AAISW, *Proceedings*, 1887, 2360–63, 2389–92; Knights of Labor, Local Assembly 300, *National Convention*, 1889, 62–63. For some details in this and succeeding paragraphs, I have also drawn on Couvares, *Remaking of Pittsburgh*, 70–75.

8. *NLT*, 26 Feb., 5 and 12 Mar., 23 and 30 Jul., 6 and 20 Aug., 17 Sept., 1, 8, 15, 22, and 29 Oct., 26 Nov. 1887, 18 and 25 Feb., 5 Mar, 12 May, and 13 Dec. 1887, and 21 Apr. 1888; *Commoner*, 10 Sept. and 3 Dec. 1887, 1 Jan., 18 Feb., 17 Mar., and 9 June 1888; AAISW, *Proceedings*, 1887, 1769, 1936–45, 2360–2363; AAISW, *Proceedings*, 1888, 2026–30, 2336.

9. *NLT*, 23 Jul., 13, 20, and 27 Aug., 3, 10, and 17 Sept. 1887.

10. *NLT*, 8 and 15 Oct., 7 Dec. 1887, 5 May 1888, 6 Apr., 8 and 15 Oct. 1889, 13 June and 11 Jul. 1891; *Commoner*, 2 Oct. 1887; AAISW, *Proceedings*, 1887, 2389–92. Also see Richards, "Armstrong," 26–27.

11. *PCT*, 5 and 20 May 1889; *NLT*, 28 Jan. and 6 Oct. 1888, 5 and 26 Jan. 1889, 1 Mar. 1890; *PD*, 26 Feb. 1890; *Commoner*, 26 Jan. 1888, 19 Jan., 16 Mar., 20 Apr., 4 May, 6 and 13 Jul., 1889; *OVB*, 23 Feb. and 19 May. 1888; *PP*, 31 Jul. 1889; *TJ*, 21 Jul., 1888; and Knights of Labor, District Assembly 3, *Proceedings, First Quarterly Meeting, January 1889*, pp. 7, 13, 23, *Proceedings, Second Quarterly Meeting, April 1889*, pp. 4–5, and *Proceedings, First Quarterly Meeting, January 1890*, 6–7, 14.

12. AAISW, *Proceedings*, 1889, 2633–38, 2643–44; *AM*, 19 June 1885, 15 June, 6 and 20 Jul. 1888; Couvares, *Remaking of Pittsburgh*, 85–86.

13. This paragraph and the succeeding one are based on: *Duquesne Times*, 7 and 14 Mar., 4, 18, and 25 Apr., 1889; *Commoner*, 27 Apr. 1889; *NLT*, 30 Mar., 18 and 25 May, 8, 15, 22, and 29 June, and 20 Jul., 1889; *HLN*, 4 May 1889; *OVB*, 23 Feb. 1889; *PCT*, 5, 9, 13, 15, 16, 20, 23, 24, and 27 May 1889; AAISW, *Proceedings*, 1889, 2612–13.

14. *HLN*, 28 Mar. and 20 June 1891; *NLT*, 29 Jan. 1887 and 30 May 1890; *OVB*, 5 and 19 May 1888; AAISW, *Proceedings*, 1889, 2851–53, 2601; AAISW, *Proceedings*, 1890, "Membership Abstract," and 2966–70. Also see Marcus, "Homestead," esp. 4. A second glass factory, the Windsor Glass Works, opened in 1886.

15. *HLN*, 1 Nov. 1890.

16. The data on Homestead town officials have been gathered from a variety of sources, including: Schooley and Schooley, *Homestead Directory, 1890, Homestead Directory, 1891*, and *Homestead Directory, 1892*; *HLN*, 29 Jan., 2 and 20 Feb. 1884, 24 Jan. and 26 Dec. 1885, 2 Jan. and 17 Feb. 1886, 19 Feb. 1887, 25 Mar. 1888, 9 Mar. 1889, 22 Feb. 1890, 21 Feb. 1891, and 20 Feb. 1892; *HT*, Feb. 1882, 13 and 20 Jan., and 24 Feb. 1883; AAISW, *Proceedings*, 1889, 2851–53; *Homestead Eagle*, 10 Mar. 1888.

17. Hopkins Co., *Atlas of the Vicinity of Pittsburgh, 1886*, pl. 17; Hopkins Co., *Atlas of the County of Allegheny*, 36.

18. *NLT*, 16 Aug. 1879.

19. U.S. Bureau of the Census, *1880 Census*, 391–485, which is discussed in

greater detail in app. B; FCSU, Membership List, 320–34; Higham, *Strangers in the Land*, chap. 3; S. Alexander, "Immigrant Church," chap. 1; Stolarik, "Immigration and Urbanization," chap. 1; Blum, *End of the Old Order*, pt. 3.

20. On the conjuncture of the aspirations of East Europeans and American "republicans," see Berthoff, "Peasants and Artisans." Note, however, that in these shared aspirations, Berthoff sees an "ideological consensus" on the virtues of private enterprise and acquisitiveness. Such a view overlooks the findings of Montgomery and Gutman, among others. On the repudiation of acquisitiveness by East European immigrants, see Bodnar, "Immigration and Modernization," 336–37; also see Bodnar, *The Transplanted*, 45–56.

21. Smeltzer, *Homestead Methodism*, chap. 5 and pp. 83–87, 106–09, 114, 131–32, 153; Cameron, "Church Divides," 2:22–39; U.S. Bureau of the Census, *1880 Census*, Homestead; Northwestern Historical Association, *Allegheny County*, 1:497–98, 2:296, 516–17; *HT*, 30 Jul., 13 Aug., 24 Sept., 15 and 29 Oct. 1881, 7 Oct., 2, 9, and 30 Dec. 1882, 27 Jan., 24 Feb., 25 Aug., and 11 Oct. 1883, 21 May and 8 Nov. 1884; *HLN*, 26 Apr. and 12 June 1884, 10 Mar., 18 Apr., and 30 May 1885; Warner Co., *Allegheny County*, pt. 1, pp. 195, 201–02, 300, pt. 2, pp. 279–80, 293–94, 297–98, 663; Burgoyne, *All Sorts*, 104–05; Cooper Co., *Twentieth-Century Bench and Bar*, 2:944. Within Homestead's Presbyterian congregations, too, religious commitments had a secular analogue in Republican politics. For example, Abdiel McClure, a Presbyterian leader, was elected recorder of Allegheny County from 1863 through 1866, a period when Radicals dominated the county Republican party. During the Civil War, many Presbyterian as well as Methodist Homesteaders gave substantive expression to this Radicalism by enlisting in the Union army.

22. U.S. Bureau of the Census, *1880 Census*, Homestead; *HT*, 23 Jul., 20 Aug., 17 Sept., 1 Oct., 5, 12, and 19 Nov. 1881, 14 Jan. and 21 Oct. 1882; *HLN*, 11 Oct. 1884 and 14 Feb., 18 Apr., 23 and 30 May, and 9 Nov. 1885; *HT*, 30 Jul. and 5 Nov. 1881, 23 Sept. and 28 Oct. 1882, and 17 Mar. 1883; *Homestead Directory, 1891*, pp. 7, 13–15; *Homestead Directory, 1892*, pp. 5–11; Smeltzer, *Homestead Methodism*, 65–67, 114, 153; Warner Co., *Allegheny County*, pt. 2, pp. 76–77, 603, 704, 706; St. Mary Magdalene Church, *One Hundredth Anniversary: St. Mary Magdalene Church* (Homestead: St. Mary Magdalene Church, 1980), 3; Northwestern Historical Association, *Allegheny County*, 1:510; Hopkins Co., *Atlas of Allegheny County, 1876*, 36. Also see apps. E through H.

23. AAISW, *Proceedings, 1881*, 729, 741, 742, 747, 771; AAISW, *Proceedings, 1882*, 795; AAISW, *Proceedings, 1885*, 1538–39; *HT*, 24 June 1882; *NLT*, 10 June 1882, 3 Feb. and 21 Apr. 1883; *HLN*, 7 Nov. 1885; *PCG*, 19 June 1882; Temin, *Iron and Steel*, 181–82; Bridge, *Inside History*, 159–60; Wall, *Carnegie*, 475–76.

24. *HLN*, 21 Mar., 25 Apr., 8 and 22 Aug. 1885; *AM*, 1 Jan., 5 and 26 Mar., 23 Apr., 11 June, and 10 Sept. 1886, 18 Nov. 1887, 29 June 1888, 10, 17, and 31 May 1889; *NLT*, 27 Jan., 24 Mar., 14 Apr., and 8 Sept. 1883, 26 Apr. 1884, 3 Apr. 1886, 29 Mar. 1890, and 16 May 1891; *HT*, 31 Mar. and 5 May 1883; AAISW, *Proceedings, 1890*, 2966–77; AAISW, *Proceedings, 1888*, 2311–14; Bridge, *Inside History*, 161–64; Brier, "Technological Change"; Marcus, "Struggle Continues," 4–5. Information on the composition of the AAISW lodges in Homestead is drawn from: AAISW, *Proceedings, 1885*, 1538–39; AAISW, *Proceedings, 1887*, 2404; AAISW, *Proceedings, 1889*, 2601, 2851–53, and "Membership Abstract"; AAISW, *Proceedings, 1890*,

2966–73, 3218, and "Membership Abstract"; *NLT*, 2 Feb. and 12 Jul. 1884, 23 Jan., 17 Jul., and 11 Sept. 1886, 15 Oct. 1887, 7 Jan. 1888, 20 and 27 Apr., 15 and 21 June, and 6 Jul. 1889, 22 Mar., 12 Apr., and 30 May 1890, and 16 May 1891; *AM*, 29 Mar. 1888, 12 Apr. and 21 June 1889; *Commoner*, 25 May 1889; *PP*, 15 Jul. 1889.

25. *NLT*, 24 Mar. 1883, 29 Jan. 1887, 3, 13, 20, and 27 Apr., 15 June, and 20 Jul. 1889; *Commoner*, 27 Apr. and 6 Jul. 1889; Garlock, "Data Bank," 234; *HM*, May 1882; *JUL*, June 1882; *HT*, 6 Aug. and 22 Oct. 1881, 31 Mar., 21 Apr., and 5 May 1883.

26. Information on town officers has been gathered from a wide variety of sources, including: Schooley and Schooley, *Homestead Directory, 1890, Homestead Directory, 1891*, and *Homestead Directory, 1892*; *HLN*, 29 Jan., 2 and 20 Feb. 1884, 24 Jan. and 26 Dec. 1885, 2 Jan. and 17 Feb. 1886, 19 Feb. 1887, 25 Mar. 1888, 9 Mar. 1889, 22 Feb. 1890, 21 Feb. 1891, and 20 Feb. 1892; *HT*, 25 Feb. 1882, 13 and 20 Jan., and 24 Feb. 1883; AAISW, *Proceedings*, 1889, 2851–53, and "Membership Abstract"; *Homestead Eagle*, 10 Mar. 1888. Also see appendix H.

27. AAISW, *Proceedings*, 1882, 788; *NLT*, 28 Oct. 1876, 1 Apr., 8 and 15 Jul., 18 Nov. 1882, 12 May 1887; Garlock, *Guide to Local Assemblies*, 407; *PCT*, 12 Jul. 1889; *HLN*, 2 Jan. 1886, 8 Feb. and 1 Mar. 1890, 23 Jan. and 12 Mar. 1892; *HT*, 13 Jan. 1883; U.S. House, *Report 2447*, 98; Burgoyne, *Homestead Strike*, 24.

CHAPTER 15. *East Europeans in Homestead*

1. *NLT*, 22 Apr. 1876; Burgoyne, *Homestead Strike*, 38, 192–97; *PCT*, 12 June and 18 Jul. 1889; AAISW, *Proceedings*, 1890, 2965; Schooley and Schooley, *Homestead Directory, 1890*, 9, *Homestead Directory, 1891*, p. 16, and *Homestead Directory, 1892*, 10, 14, 164; *HLN*, 19 Jan., 6 Feb and 4 Oct. 1884, 9 May 1885, 2 Nov. 1889, 12 and 19 Sept. 1891, 23 Jan. and 12 Mar. 1892; *HT*, 18 Nov. 1882 and 1 Jan. 1883; Higham, *Strangers in the Land*, 58–60. Also see below, app. H.

2. The quotations in this paragraph and the succeeding three are drawn from *NLT*, 26 Aug. 1882.

3. The description of the immigrants at the poorhouse was reprinted from a previously published report in the *PD*.

4. Higham, *Strangers in the Land*, chap. 3, esp. 45–63. Higham observes that "the immigrants seemed both symbols and agents of the widening gulf between capital and labor. The hatred of them was a hatred of corporations for trying (as one Pennsylvania newspaper put it) 'to degrade native labor by the introduction of a class who, in following the customs of their ancestors, live more like brutes than human beings.' "

5. In 1882, Congress did enact a restrictive immigration law; however, it was not until the 1891 act that immigration policies became sufficiently restrictive to begin to satisfy nativist zealots.

6. This paragraph and the succeeding one are based on *NLT*, 18 Mar. and 10 June 1882, and 30 June 1883; Higham, *Strangers in the Land*, 57.

7. U.S. House, *Labor in Europe*, 48th Cong., 2d sess. (Washington, D.C.: GPO, 1884), 2:1212–87, esp. 1219; Stolarik, "From Field to Factory," esp. 96–97; Ehrlich, "Immigrant Strikebreaking." Most instructive of the Dillingham Commission's 42 published volumes are U.S. Immigration Commission, *Reports on Immigrants in Industries, Iron and Steel Manufacturing*, vols. 8, 9.

8. Peter Roberts, "New Pittsburghers," 552. For a more appreciative view of Roberts's scholarship, see Stolarik, "From Field to Factory," 97. The Pittsburgh Survey was published in *Charities and the Commons* beginning in January 1909, and then in a six-volume series that included Fitch, *Steel Workers;* Byington, *Homestead.* Also of interest are two companion studies: Balch, *Our Slavic Fellow Citizens;* Commons, *Races and Immigrants.* Commons worked on the Survey. The outstanding commentary on the Survey is McClymer, "Pittsburgh Survey" (see 174–81 for a discussion of nativism and the Survey's portrait of East European immigrants). Also see: Samuel P. Hays, "Homestead Revisited," xvii–xxxiv, in Byington, *Homestead;* Hill and Cohen, "Fitch and the Pittsburgh Survey," 17–32; Cohen, "Industrial Conflict and Democracy"; Chambers, *Kellogg and the Survey.*

9. Peter Roberts, "New Pittsburghers," 549.

10. Byington, *Homestead,* 164.

11. Fitch, *Steel Workers,* 164.

12. This paragraph and the succeeding one are based principally on: Bodnar, *The Transplanted,* chap. 3; Bodnar *Immigration and Industrialization,* esp. 41; Brody, "Labor"; Brody, *Steelworkers in America,* chap. 5; Couvares, *Remaking of Pittsburgh,* 87–92; Greene, *Slavic Community,* passim; L. Fink, *Workingmen's Democracy,* chap. 7; Serene, "Immigrant Steelworkers," passim; Graziosi, "Common Laborers"; Holt, "Trade Unionism," esp. 17–18; Stolarik, "From Field to Factory," 96–99; Leonard, "Ethnic Cleavage"; T. Bell, *Out of This Furnace,* esp. pt. 1; Albert Elko, interview with the author, 20 June 1983. Elko's father, a steelworker who immigrated from the Austo-Hungarian Empire, was a leader of the Rusyn community in McKeesport at the turn of the century.

13. Graziosi, "Common Laborers," 536. Faires, "Immigrants and Industry," 14, 29, while criticizing historians for collapsing members of diverse nationality groups into the category of "Slavic," follows received historical practice herself in merely alluding to interethnic cooperation during the Homestead Lockout of 1892 and in failing to identify the nationalities and ethnic origins of the East European workers. In this regard she has large company—virtually every author who has written about the 1892 lockout. The most offensive is Wolff, *Lockout,* esp. 124, 127–30, where East European immigrants are described as "impetuous," "semi-hysterical," "the most blood-thirsty of all," and incapable of reason because they did not understand English. Cohen, "Steelworkers Rethink," is the most striking recent example of scholarship written in a vein that, while totally ignoring East European workers, nonetheless charges that they "neither understood nor much cared for" the world inhabited by "American" Homesteaders.

14. The Slovak expression *ist' za chlebom* connotes "independence." *Na svojom chlebe,* for example, means "to be on one's own"; *byt' na vlastnom chlebe* means "to be on one's own" or "to be one's own boss." A translation of *za chlebom* that pins its meaning on "looking for money" is decidedly limited. Unfortunately, this mistranslation has influenced most of the literature on East European immigrants. See, for example, Greene, *Slavic Community,* 28, 221. For a more thoughtful discussion of *za chlebom,* see S. Alexander, "Immigrant Church," chap. 1.

15. *NLT,* 17 Apr. 1875. This poem also is discussed above, chap. 10.

16. This paragraph and the next one are based on: *HT,* 13 and 27 Aug. 1881, 26 Aug., 14 and 28 Oct. 1882, and 17 Mar. 1883; *HLN,* 1 Mar. 1884; *IW,* 29 Jul. 1882; St. Mary Magdalene Church, Register of Baptism, vol. 1 (1881–90), 1, 7, 8,

33, 90; Allegheny County, Board of Assessment, Real Property and Assessment Books: Homestead and Mifflin Township, 1883; St. Francis Church, Register of Baptism, Marriage, and Death, 13; Schooley and Schooley, *Homestead Directory, 1890*, p. 129, and *Homestead Directory, 1891*, p. 132.

17. St. Anthony's Church, *Souvenir Booklet of the Golden Jubilee of St. Anthony's Church, Homestead, Pennsylvania* (Pittsburgh: Pittsburgher Publications, 1949), 11. The Polish community in Homestead remained small until after the lockout of 1892, and the Polish Catholic parish, St. Anthony's, was not organized until 1899. U.S. Immigration Commission, *Reports on Immigrants in Industries, Iron and Steel Manufacturing*, vols. 8, 9, pt. 2, pp. 236–37, states that "Hungarians" came to Homestead to work in the mill in 1882, but I have been unable to confirm this. As *Hungarian* remained a term of disapprobation for virtually all East European immigrants well into this century, it seems likely that the commission was referring not to ethnic Magyars but instead to Slovak and/or Carpatho-Rusyn immigrants from "Hungary."

18. This paragraph and the following one are based on: *HT*, 20 Aug. 1881, 11 Mar. and 2 Apr. 1882; Kushner, *Slováci Katolíci*, 54–61, esp. 49, 56; St. Mary Magdalene Church, *One Hundredth Anniversary* (Pittsburgh: n.p., 1980), 1; FCSU, Membership List, 322; June Alexander, "Staying Together," S. Alexander, "Immigrant Church," chap. 1, esp. 31–32; Bodnar, *The Transplanted*, 12; Stolarik, "Immigration and Urbanization," chap. 1; Stolarik, "Slovaks," 927–28. Also see Serene, "Immigrant Steelworkers," chap. 2.

19. Kushner, *Slováci Katolíci*, 49, 56, 101; St. Michael's Roman Catholic Church, Register of Death, 1891–1952, 3–4, 28, 29; *PP*, 2 Jan. 1891; Alexander, "Staying Together," 47–49, 60–61. John Bullion, the priest who ministered to most East European Homesteaders in the 1880s, made no reference to the country or province of birth of his East European parishioners when entering their names in parish registers. However, those of St. Michael's, the "Slovak" parish organized in 1891 in Braddock, contain some entries that note the place of birth of its Homestead parishioners. One, a steelworker whose name is recorded in the Register of Death, was born in the same village as Olšav and Terek, and another, in a nearby town in Zemplín Province. Usually, though, the priest at St. Michael's in Braddock noted only that his parishioners were from "Hungary." The chain of Slovak migration to Homestead may have been initiated by Joseph Wolf, who operated a tavern and boardinghouse in Braddock near the Edgar Thompson. A Jew born in Slovakia, he recruited laborers for Andrew Carnegie; into the 1890s his establishments served as the principal meeting place in Braddock for Slovak steelworkers. As the initial group of Slovak immigrants in Braddock were from Šariš Province, however, it is possible that the first Slovaks who arrived in Homestead learned of the town through the efforts of Jan Lesniansky, a Zemplín Slovak who arranged for his countrymen still in Europe to obtain jobs in Allegheny City. Lesniansky was a native of Falkusovce, a southern Zemplín village not far from Žalobin.

20. Kushner, *Slováci Katolíci*, 57; Joseph Hornak, interview with the author, 11 June 1983. Hornak's father arrived in Homestead in 1888. It is difficult to estimate the number of Carpatho-Rusyns in Homestead prior to the 1892 lockout because Carpatho-Rusyn and Slovak last names are virtually indistinguishable and the former did not have a Byzantine Rite, or "Greek Catholic," church in the

town until 1896. Furthermore, there are no available parish records that would allow comparisons between my census of East European Homesteaders, compiled from a variety of sources dating from 1880 to 1892, and those who later affiliated with the Byzantine Rite Church at the Cathedral of St. John the Baptist in Homestead or with any of the Byzantine Rite churches in adjacent towns. Homestead later became a center of Carpatho-Rusyn immigrant life, as both the Greek Catholic Union, a fraternal benefit society comprised mostly of Carpatho-Rusyns, and the *Amerikansky Russky Viestnik*, the society's official organ, established headquarters there. The definitive work on Carpatho-Rusyns is Magocsi, *Shaping of a National Identity*, an exhaustive study that focuses on the Carpatho-Rusyn intelligentsia.

21. These conclusions are drawn primarily from the diocesan histories and parish registers of St. Michael's Church, Braddock, and St. Mary Magdalene and St. Francis, Homestead. (St. Francis was established in 1890 by Roman Catholics of German origin. Most of the St. Mary Magdalene parishioners whose last names indicate Polish origin affiliated with St. Francis at the time.) While some Slovaks from Braddock traveled to St. Wenceslaus Church—a Czech congregation in Allegheny City—to get married, records of that parish indicate no such practice on the part of Homestead Slovaks. (See St. Wenceslaus Roman Catholic Church, Records, 1871–96.) On the close relations of Carpatho-Rusyn and Slovak immigrants, see Rev. A. Kazincy to Bishop R. F. Canevin, 3 Mar. 1914, Miscellaneous Letters, archives of the Roman Catholic Diocese of Pittsburgh, as well as: Morawska, "East European Immigrant Communities," 84; Warzeski, *Byzantine Rite Rusins*, chap. 7, esp. p. 101; Procko, "Ruthenian Church," 140.

22. Kushner, *Slováci Katolíci*, 56–57; St. Michael Church, Munhall, *75th Anniversary* (Pittsburgh: n.p., 1972), 1; and FCSU, Membership List. This paragraph is also based on an examination of the parish records at St. Mary's and St. Michael's Church, Braddock. St. Michael's Church in Munhall—which adjoined Homestead and actually was the site of the Homestead Steel Works—was organized by Homestead Slovaks only in 1897.

23. Schooley and Schooley, *Directory of Homestead, 1890*, pp. 130 and 172, and *Directory of Homestead, 1892*, pp. 114 and 148; *BT*, 17 Sept. 1892; Burgoyne, *Homestead Strike*, 192; Stowell, *Fort Frick*, 250; Kushner, *Slováci Katolíci*, 57; FCSU, Membership List, 320, 322; Allegheny County, Board of Assessment, Real Property and Assessment Books: Homestead, 1890. Interestingly, Olšav's leadership of and contributions to the Slovak community of Homestead have been dropped from Kushner's official history of Pittsburgh Slovaks. Kushner also incorrectly reports that Pavel and Zuzanna Olšav permanently left town shortly after their arrival, an error he repeats in his discussion of other Slovak immigrants who settled in Homestead. While the Olšavs may have moved upriver to McKeesport for a short period, by 1890 they were residents of Homestead and had accumulated enough savings to pay a minimal tax on it. Later the family moved to Munhall Hollow, which became another large Slovak neighborhood. On the FCSU and other Slovak fraternal organizations, see Stolarik, "Immigration and Urbanization," chap. 3; S. Alexander, "Immigrant Church," chap. 4.

24. Schooley and Schooley, *Homestead Directory, 1892*, p. 182; *HT*, 1 Apr. and 18 Nov. 1882, 4 and 14 Feb. 1884, 21 Mar. 1885, 26 Apr. 1890, and 2 May 1891; St. Mary's Church, Register of Baptism, vol. 1: 1881–90, 59; *Homestead Eagle*, 12 and

19 May, 1888; *HLN,* 16 and 23 Aug., 1890; and Evelyn Patterson, interview with the author, 11 Oct. 1981. Mrs. Patterson is a descendant of one of the steelworkers involved in the 1892 lockout. The best sources on the occupations of the East European steelworkers in Homestead are: U.S. House, *Report 2447,* 5–18; Allegheny County, Board of Assessment, Real Property and Assessment Books: Homestead and Mifflin Township, 1883–1892.

25. This paragraph and the following one are based on: *Národnie noviny,* 4 Feb. 1890; *Mount Pleasant Journal,* reprinted in *NLT,* 10 Jul. 1886. Stolarik has found that Slovak immigrants often celebrated the Fourth of July and that the festivities typically were held in honor of a Slovak national hero. On the commingling of Old and New World traditions in East European communities in the U.S., see Bodnar, "Immigration and Modernization," 333–60.

26. *NLT,* 6 Feb., 3 and 10 Jul. 1886, and miscellaneous clippings in Max Schamberg Papers, collection of Jane Berkey, Pittsburgh. Schamberg, the Austro-Hungarian consul in Pittsburgh during the 1880s, helped settle a number of the violent disputes involving Frick and the East European workers he employed.

27. Krause, " 'Za Chlebom,' " 160.

28. Gladstone to Carnegie, 19 May 1892, vol. 16, Gladstone to Carnegie, 19 Sept. 1892, vol. 17, and Carnegie to Gladstone, 24 Sept. 1892, vol. 17, emphasis in the original, all in ACLC; Carnegie, "Employer's View," *Forum* 1 (Apr. 1886): 114–25, and Carnegie, "Results of the Labor Struggle," *Forum* 1 (Aug. 1886): 538–51, both reprinted in Carnegie, *Gospel of Wealth.*

29. Bridge, *Inside History,* 204–06; Wall, *Carnegie,* 541–46; Harvey, *Frick,* 165–67; Carnegie to Frick, 7 Jul. 1892, as quoted in Harvey, *Frick,* 166.

CHAPTER 16. *Andrew Carnegie*

1. Burgoyne, *All Sorts,* 5. Burgoyne was one of Pittsburgh's leading journalists in the late nineteenth century. He published this poem just weeks before the Homestead Lockout of 1892; his book on that event was published in 1893.

2. *NYT,* 8 Jan. 1903

3. Characteristic of the first genre is Josephson, *Robber Barons;* representative of the many Carnegie hagiographies is Hendrick, *Carnegie.* Barry Paris, "The Canny Scot," *PPG,* 25 Nov. 1985, is a discerning piece of daily journalism that identifies some of the contradictions in Carnegie's life.

4. Pepper, "Department Store."

5. Gladstone to Carnegie, 19 May 1892, ACLC, vol. 16.

6. Carnegie to C. W. Scotell, 17 Dec. 1892 (published in *NYT,* 18 Dec. 1892), ACLC, vol. 17. Despite the opposition in 1892, the city of Pittsburgh soon afterward accepted the gifts.

7. On the material basis of culture, see R. Williams, *Marxism and Literature,* 11–20; on hegemony see ibid., 108–14. Munslow, "Carnegie," endeavors to address a number of relevant issues. Also see Crockatt, "Response to Munslow," as well as Munslow's rejoinder.

8. Veblen, as quoted in Josephson, *Robber Barons,* 316–17; Carnegie, *Dedication;* W. F. Stevens, "Carnegie Library, Homestead," in Byington, *Homestead,* 255–70.

9. The following works probe some of the questions related to Carnegie's library gifts: Mickelson, "Public Library"; Ditzion, *Democratic Culture*, 149–64; Farrah, "Carnegie," 8–28; Rosenberg, "Wages versus the Library."

10. Carnegie, *Dedication*, 1; Carnegie to an unnamed correspondent, 18 Oct. 1884, ACLC, vol. 8; *NLT*, 6 Apr. 1889; *IA*, 4 Apr. 1889; Pepper, "Department Store"; Wall, *Carnegie*, 82–85, 97, 815–20, 828; McCloskey, *American Conservatism*, 137–38. On Carnegie's notorious delight in receiving the freedom of the city, see William W. Delaney's popular song about the Homestead Lockout of 1892, "Father Was Killed by the Pinkerton Men," cited above, chap. 1.

11. *AM*, 9 Sept. 1882; Carnegie, *Dedication*, 1; Wall, *Carnegie*, 384–86, 689; Hendrick, *Carnegie*, 1:240–41; Pepper, "Department Store"; Kidney, *Landmark Architecture*, 286. "I know of no pleasure in life," Carnegie once remarked, "which for me is comparable to creating a library which is not mine when created, but belongs to the people" (Mickelson, "Public Library," 128).

In 1882, Herbert Spencer visited Braddock as Carnegie's guest; however, the former did not concur that the seeds of utopia were to be found there: "Six months' residence here would justify suicide."

Skibo is the medieval castle and manorial estate over which Carnegie presided. It is located in Sutherland in the Scottish Highlands. Carnegie purchased Skibo in 1897.

12. "Wealth" appeared in *North American Review* 148 (June 1889): 653–64, and was continued as "The Best Fields for Philanthropy" in ibid., 149 (Dec. 1889): 682–98. The essay was reprinted in Carnegie, *Gospel of Wealth*. For discussions of the essay, see Wall, *Carnegie*, 806–15; McCloskey, *American Conservatism*, 162–65. The quotations in the text are drawn from these works. See also Lubove, "Pitttsburgh and the Uses of Social Welfare History," 311–14; Fine, *Laissez Faire*, 113–17.

13. Carnegie, *Dedication*, 1, 5, 17–18; *HLN*, 6 Apr. 1889.

14. Carnegie, *Dedication*, 1, 3, 5, 7–8, 15, 21–22, 30–31; *AM*, 2 and 11 May 1888; *Commoner*, 5 and 12 May, 2 and 9 June, 1 and 13 Sept. 1888; *NLT*, 14 and 28 Apr., 5 May, 6 Oct., and 3 Nov. 1888; *IA*, 5 and 12 Apr., 10 May, and 23 June 1888.

15. Carnegie, *Dedication*, 21–22.

16. Wall, *Carnegie*, 522. Carnegie enjoyed the tremendous publicity won by his philanthropic ventures. Poultney Bigelow, an informed contemporary, was probably correct when he suggested that "never before in the history of plutocratic America had one man purchased by mere money so much social advertising and flattery." (Wall, *Carnegie*, 822.)

17. Photoduplication, ACLC, vol. 3. Carnegie's note is reprinted in Wall, *Carnegie*, 224–25; and McCloskey, *American Conservatism*, 144.

18. Bridge, *Inside History*, 294–95; Paris, "The Canny Scot," *PPG*, 25 Nov. 1985. For some of the points in this paragraph and the succeeding one, I have drawn on McCloskey, *American Conservatism*, chap. 6, esp. pp. 145–47.

19. Carnegie, "Employer's View"; Carnegie, "Results of the Labor Struggle." For discussions of Carnegie's 1886 essays, see: Wall, *Carnegie*, 523–27; Bridge, *Inside History*, 186–88; McCloskey, *American Conservatism*, 147–49. The quotations in the text are drawn from these sources.

20. This paragraph and the next one are drawn from Carnegie, *Triumphant Democracy*, passim; Wall, *Carnegie*, 442–47, 526; McCloskey, *American Conservatism*, 153–58.

21. Carnegie, *Triumphant Democracy*, 1.

22. *NLT,* 9 Dec. 1876; 1 and 29 Apr., 24 June, and 8 Jul. 1882, 21 Jan., 10 and 31 Mar., 14 and 28 Apr., 31 Mar., 5 May, 14 Jul., 2 Sept., and 22 Dec. 1883, 2 Sept., 6, 13, 20, and 27 Dec. 1884; 10 Jan., 7 and 14 Feb., 28 Mar., and 3 Apr. 1885; *AM,* 21 Dec. 1883, 26 Dec. 1884, 6 Feb., 20 Mar., and 20 Nov. 1885; Fitch, *Steel Workers,* 11, 112–14, and the comments of two unidentified steelworkers, CH-1 and CD-6, in his research notes; AAISW, *Proceedings,* 1877, 43–44; AAISW, *Proceedings,* 1882, 796; *JSP,* 22 Feb. 1885; *IA,* 5 and 26 Feb. 1885; Holt, "Trade Unionism," 12–13; Bridge, *Inside History,* 185; Garlock and Builder, "Data Bank," 234–39; *Commoner,* 23 Oct. 1887 and 28 Jan. 1888.

23. The quotations in this and in the succeeding paragraph are drawn from *NLT,* 10 Jan. 1885.

24. My account of the Braddock lockout is based on: *AM,* 27 Jan., 17 Feb., 30 Mar., 6, 13, 20, and 27 Apr., 2 and 11 May 1888; *Commoner,* 21 Jan., 11 and 18 Feb., 3, 10, 17, and 31 Mar., 7, 14, 21, and 28 Apr., 5 and 12 May, 2 and 9 June, 1 and 13 Sept. 1888, 1 Jan., 2 Mar., and 25 May 1889; *OVB,* 5 May 1888; R. D. Layton to Powderly, 3 Apr. 1888, Powderly Papers, reel 25, microfilm at Davis Library, University of North Carolina-Chapel Hill; Knights of Labor, District Assembly 3, *Minutes of the 2nd Quarterly Meeting, April 1888* (Pittsburgh: Snowden & Harrison, 1888), Powderly Papers, reel 65, microfilm at Hillman Library, University of Pittsburgh, pp. 9–10, 14, 16, 25, and 43–44; *HLN,* 10 Mar. 1888; *TJ,* 5 May, 23 and 30 June, 28 Jul., and 8 Sept. 1888; *NLT,* 9 and 16 Jan., 24 Apr. 1886, 14 and 28 Apr., 5 May, 6 Oct. and 3 Nov. 1888; *IA,* 5 and 12 Apr., 10 and 23 May, and 23 June 1888; *NYW,* 3 Jul. 1892; Carnegie, *Dedication,* passim; Fitch, research notes, CD-6; Fitch, *Steel Workers,* 114.

25. *NLT,* 3 Nov. 1888.

26. Hendrick, *Carnegie,* 1:372–76, gives a radically different account of the lockout, asserting that it demonstrated Carnegie's commitment to the principles enunciated in his 1886 essays. Wall, *Carnegie,* 527–28, while acknowledging that Carnegie did not quite live up to his stated principles, overlooks the use of nonunion labor and the hiring of Pinkertons.

27. Carnegie offered these remarks at the dedication of the Carnegie Library in Pittsburgh; he repeated them in a speech at Leicester, England, 8 May 1905. See *PCG,* 5 and 6 Nov. 1895; Ditzion, *Democratic Culture,* 154.

28. *HLN,* 6 Apr. 1889.

29. Carnegie, *Dedication,* 12–13, 15.

30. This paragraph and the succeeding one are based on: *NLT,* 3, 13, 20, and 27 Apr., 15 June, and 20 Jul. 1889; *Commoner,* 27 Apr. 1889; *PP,* 11, 12, and 16 Jul. 1889; *PT,* 16 Jul. 1889; *PCT,* 11 and 12 Jul. 1889; *Pittsburgh Press,* 12, 13, and 14 Jul. 1889.

31. On the "simple Richardson Romanesque design" of the Carnegie Free Library in Braddock, see Kidney, *Landmark Architecture,* 286. Photographs of several other Carnegie libraries are reprinted in Dickson, *Library in America,* 48–52.

32. Fitch, *Steel Workers,* 203; Paris, "The Canny Scot," *PPG,* 25 Nov. 1985. Whereas the precise circumstances surrounding the various rejections await further consideration, it is the general fact of these negative responses to Carnegie's generosity that is of interest here.

33. Mauss, *The Gift*, 1; Fitch, research notes, Nubia-1. The comments of the Homestead steelworker quoted in the text were confirmed in other interviews conducted by Fitch. A steelworker ("CH-1") who had labored in the Edgar Thomson and in the Homestead Works prior to the 1892 lockout told Fitch that he never used the library, nor did other mill men. "As a rule, they do not care for it, but they couldn't use it even if they wanted to, for they work too long hours to permit the use of any such thing as a library." On the operations of the Homestead library in the early twentieth century, see Miner, "Deserted Parthenon."

34. This interpretation is suggested by McCloskey, *American Conservatism*, 163.

35. *NYT*, 5 and 6 May 1991; Pepper, "Department Store." Pepper mistakenly notes that Carnegie promised libraries to Homestead and Duquesne in his Braddock speech. A similar misreading can be found in Kidney, *Landmark Architecture*, 284, and many other secondary accounts. Also of interest is a recent observation of Robert Gangewere, the editor of *Carnegie Magazine:* Carnegie "organized the giving of libraries so that they became a major cultural influence. The free library was a very important matter in what he saw as generating a new citizenry" (Gangewere, quoted by Salem Alaton, "Steel Town Fights to Spruce Up Carnegie Legacy," *Toronto Globe and Mail*, 8 May 1989).

36. *Commoner*, as quoted in *NYW*, 3 Jul. 1892.

37. Carnegie, *Dedication*, 13.

CHAPTER 17. *The Homestead Lockout of 1889*

1. Wall, *Carnegie*, 221; Kidney, *Landmark Architecture*, 286; Carnegie, *Dedication*, 17–18.

2. Carnegie, *Dedication*, 18; *AM*, 2 and 11 May 1888; *Commoner*, 5 and 12 May, 2 and 9 June 1888; *OVB*, 5 May 1888; *NLT*, 14 and 28 Apr., 5 May, 6 Oct., and 3 Nov. 1888; *IA*, 5 and 12 Apr., 10 May, and 23 June 1888; Fitch, *Steel Workers*, 115–18.

3. Carnegie, *Dedication*, 31; Wall, *Carnegie*, 528–29; Hendrick, *Carnegie*, 1:376; AAISW, *Proceedings*, 1888, 2311–14. Also see Livesay, *Carnegie*, 138, which follows the accounts of Wall and Hendrick.

4. Carnegie to Abbott, 29 Dec. 1888 and 20 Mar. 1889, ACLC, vol. 10; Carnegie, *Dedication*, 13; *PCT*, 9, 18, and 20 May 1889.

5. This paragraph and the following one are based on: *PCT*, 18 May 1889, 11, 12, 15, and 18 Jul. 1889; *PCG*, 12 and 13 Jul. 1889; *IA*, 23 May 1889; *AM*, 24 May and 21 June 1889; *Commoner*, 6 Jul. 1889; *NLT*, 25 May and 15 June 1889; AAISW, *Proceedings*, 1890, 2962–64; Hogg, "Homestead Srike," 32–33; Fitch, *Steel Workers*, 119–120.

6. *PCT*, 18 May 1889; Bridge, *Inside History*, 200.

7. *PCT*, 20 and 21 June, and 2 Jul. 1889; *Pittsburgh Press*, 29 June and 13 Jul. 1889; *PP*, 4 Jul. 1889; *NYTR*, 11 Jul. 1889; *NYH*, 13 Jul. 1889.

8. My description of the Homestead Steel Works as it stood in 1889 is drawn from: *AM*, 19 Oct. 1883, 1 Aug. 1884, 23 Apr., 11 June, 10 Sept., and 31 Dec. 1886, 1 Apr., 18 and 25 Nov. 1887, 29 June 1888, 10, 17, and 31 May 1889, and 9 May 1890; AAISW, *Proceedings*, 1890, 2966–77; AAISW, *Proceedings*, 1888, 2311–14; *Commoner*, 25 May 1889; *PP*, 15 Jul. 1889; *Pittsburgh Press*, 29 June and 16 Jul.

1889; *PCG,* 11 Jul. 1889; *NLT,* 23 Apr. 1892; Bridge, *Inside History,* 161–64; Thurston, *Allegheny County's Hundred Years,* 176–77; Parsons, *History and Commerce of Pittsburgh,* 73; United States Steel Corp., *Homestead Works,* 35; Mackintosh-Hemphill Co., *Experience for Sale,* 12, 16; Curtis, "Apparatus," 347–51; Warner Co., *Allegheny County,* pt. 2, p. 77. Also see Brier, "Technological Change."

9. *HT,* 29 Jul. 1882, 26 May, 23 June, 20 and 27 Oct. 1883; Carnegie, *Dedication,* 22; *JSP,* 2 Dec. 1883.

10. The literature on the open hearth process is nearly as vast (and as hagiographic) as that pertaining to Bessemer steelmaking. Virtually all the references cited in chap. 2 on the Bessemer method also include discussions of the open hearth. In this and in succeeding paragraphs, I have relied principally on: Landes, *Unbound Prometheus,* 256–60; "The Basic Open-Hearth Process," *AM,* 31 Jul. 1885; U.S. House, *Report 2447,* 11–13; James Riley, "On Recent Improvements in the Method of the Manufacture of Open-Hearth Steel," *AM,* 14 Nov. 1884; Durfee, "Development of American Industries, VIII," 741–73; Wellman, "Open-Hearth Manufacture"; "Homestead as Seen by One of Its Workmen," *McClure's Magazine* 3 (Jul. 1894): 163–69; Bennett, "Iron Workers," 37; Fitch, *Steel Workers,* 42–44; Hogan, *Economic History,* 1:221–24; Reitell, *Machinery and Its Benefits,* 21–33; Seaver, "Manufacture of Open-Hearth Steel," 133–54.

11. Wall, *Carnegie,* 320–21; Bridge, *Inside History,* 163–64; Brier, "Technological Change," 10; *AM,* 23 Apr., 11 June, and 10 Sept. 1886.

12. *AM,* 23 Apr., 23 Jul., and 10 Sept. 1886, 29 June 1888, and 24 May 1889.

13. *AM,* 10 May 1889. Weeks, the former editor of *Iron Age,* also served as secretary to various incarnations of the iron and steel manufacturers' associations of Western Pennsylvania. During strikes and lockouts at Homestead, as well as at other plants throughout the region, he functioned as management's public voice.

14. *AM,* 10 and 31 May, and 22 Nov. 1889; U.S. House, *Report 2447,* 5–8; *NLT,* 6 Feb. and 20 Mar. 1885; Brody, *Steelworkers in America,* 51; Brier, "Technological Change," 9.

15. This paragraph and the next one are based on: Pittsburgh Bessemer Steel Co., Limited, "Comparative Statement of Cost," 6 Mar. 1884, "Statement of the Net Earnings of the Pittsburgh Bessemer Steel Co., Limited," 31 May 1884, and H. P. Smith to Carnegie, 24 Nov. 1883 and 19 Jan. 1886, all in box 37, USX Archives; Carnegie, *Dedication,* 13; *AM,* 21 June 1889; *IA,* 27 June 1889; *PCT,* 15 Jul. 1889; *Journal of the Iron and Steel Institute* (1887), 423; Bridge, *Inside History,* 161; Brody, *Steelworkers in America,* 40–43.

16. *IA,* 23 May and 27 June 1889; *AM,* 24 May and 21 June 1889; *NLT,* 15 June and 13 Jul. 1889; *IA,* 23 May and 27 June 1889; and *PCT,* 18 May and 15 Jul. 1889. The twelve-hour provision is not mentioned in any of the secondary accounts of the 1889 lockout.

17. *NLT,* 25 May, 15 June, and 1 Jul. 1889; *WDI,* 1 Jul. 1889; *IA,* 23 May and 27 June 1889; *AM,* 24 May and 21 June 1889; *PCT,* 15, 18, 20, and 23 May, 20 and 21 June, and 15 Jul. 1889; *PP,* 15 Jul. 1889; AAISW, *Proceedings,* 1890, 2962.

18. *NLT,* 28 Apr. 1888, 3, 13, 20, and 27 Apr., 15 June, and 20 Jul. 1889; *Commoner,* 28 Apr. 1888, 27 Apr. and 6 Jul. 1889; *PP,* 1, 3, 14, and 15 Jul. 1889; *PT,* 1 Jul. 1889; *IA,* 2 Apr. 1888. My estimate of AAISW membership is also based on AAISW, *Proceedings,* 1890, 2966–77, and "Membership Abstract." There is little

information about the activities of specific assemblies of the Knights of Labor during the lockout. However, the Knights' National Trade District no. 217 supported the AAISW in the 1889 lockout. Even William Martin, the conservative leader of the latter union, was obliged to thank the Knights for "valuable, timely pointers."

19. *Commoner,* 28 Apr. 1888 and 6 Jul. 1889; *PP,* 1, 3, 14, and 15 Jul. 1889; *PT,* 1 Jul. 1889; *IA,* 2 Apr. 1888; *NLT,* 28 Apr. 1888; Robinson, *Amalgamated Association,* 43.

20. The details in this and succeeding paragraphs are drawn principally from: *WDI,* 1, 10, 11, 12, 13, and 15 Jul. 1889; AAISW, *Proceedings,* 1890, 2962–64; *AM,* 24 May, 21 June, 12 and 19 Jul. 1892; *CDN,* 12 Jul. 1889; *Commoner,* 6 Jul. 1889; *HLN,* 13 May, 8 June, 13 and 20 Jul. 1892; *IA,* 23 May; *PP,* 1, 3, 11, 12, 14, 15, and 16 Jul. 1889; *PCT,* 10, 11, 12, 15, and 18 Jul. 1889; *PCG,* 12 and 13 Jul. 1889; *Pittsburgh Press,* 12–14 Jul. 1889; *PT,* 1, 12, and 13 Jul. 1889; *NLT,* 15 June, 13 and 20 Jul. 1892; *NYTR,* 13 Jul. 1889; *NYW,* 14 Jul. 1889; *NYH,* 13 Jul. 1889; *CDN,* 12 and 13 Jul. 1889; *CT,* 15 Jul. 1889; Stowell, *Fort Frick,* 23.

21. One reason why the deputies left their posts was that some were workers. One, a glassworker who belonged to the Knights, exchanged his uniform with a locked-out engineer, W. W. McLaughlin, who was on the Homestead school board.

22. This paragraph and the following two are based on: Kushner, *Slováci Katolíci,* 57; *HLN,* 20 Jul. 1889; *NYH,* 13 Jul. 1889; *Pittsburgh Press,* 14 Jul. 1889; *PP* and *PT,* 16 Jul. 1889; *Pittsburgh Press,* 15 Jul. 1889; FCSU, Membership List; St. Mary Magdelene Church, *Register of Baptism, 1881–90,* 76; *BT,* 17 Sept. 1892; Albert Elko, interview with the author, 20 June 1983. Elko is a familiar name in the Rusyn communities of the Monongahela Valley, and members of at least one Elko family have played an important role in political and religious life for the last ninety years. Albert Elko, a former steelworker, was elected mayor of Mc-Keesport in 1967. His father, also a steelworker, was a founder of the Rusyn parish in the town. There is no hard evidence, however, linking the family of Albert Elko to John Elko.

23. Bridge, *Inside History,* 201–02.

24. Hogg, "Homestead Strike," 39; Wall, *Carnegie,* 540.

25. *Pittsburgh Press,* 13 Jul. 1889.

26. *PCT,* 13 Jul. 1889.

27. Carnegie, "Results of the Labor Struggle," as quoted in Wall, *Carnegie,* 525.

CHAPTER 18. *The Life of "Beeswax" Taylor*

1. On the relationship of labor and urban politics, see Shefter, "Trade Unions," 197–276.

2. On the contradictions embedded in the republican tradition, see, among others, Wilentz, *Chants Democratic;* Wilentz, "Artisan Republican Festivals"; Forbath, "Ambiguities"; E. Foner, *Paine;* E. Foner, *Free Soil.*

3. The text of "Storm the Fort" appeared under Taylor's by-line in *NLT,* 27 May 1882.

4. McDonnell, as quoted in Salvatore, "Response to Wilentz," 26. McDonnell's observations resonate with Faustian overtones. See J. W. von Goethe, *Faust*, trans. Walter Kaufmann (New York: Anchor Books, 1963), 145: "Two souls, alas, are dwelling in my breast, And one is striving to forsake its brother."

5. Sombart, *Why Is There No Socialism?* 106; Gutman, *Power and Culture*, 93–116.

Gutman's early essays, published in his *Work, Culture, and Society*, were roundly criticized for overestimating the power of labor radicals such as McDonnell and for arguing that there were real possibilities in Gilded Age America for building an alternative to industrial capitalism. Much of this criticism came from historians who see American workers as having failed in this endeavor and who charged that Gutman ignored their failure and any effort to explain it. Gutman never fully responded to this criticism or to the charge of romanticism that lay behind it; however, he did suggest that historians reach beyond reductivist readings of U.S. labor history to see the ambiguities and contradictions that have shaped it. Instead of focusing, as he himself often had done, on the "irregular outbursts of collective, democratic protest," Gutman asked historians to begin to examine the "central tension" that "exists within all modern dependent groups between individualist (utilitarian) and collective (mutualist) ways of dealing with and sometimes overcoming historically specific patterns of dependence and inequality." One way to explore this tension and to rekindle the popular and scholarly historical imagination, he wrote, is to examine the life of a single individual. See Gutman, *Power and Culture*, 335, 404, 407, 408, 412.

The most forceful of the earlier reviews of Gutman's work is Genovese and Fox-Genovese, "Political Crisis of Social History." Also see Montgomery, "Gutman's Nineteenth-Century America." A recent critical overview is Hahn, "Gutman's History." Berlin, "Herbert G. Gutman and the American Working Class," in Gutman, *Power and Culture*, 3–69, provides a key to the scholarly debates generated by Gutman's work.

For alternative interpretations of McDonnell's remarks, see Salvatore, "Response to Wilentz," 26; Diggins, "Comrades and Citizens," 625. Salvatore argues that McDonnell correctly located the failure of American socialism in the failure of American workers to achieve class consciousness; Diggins takes a rather different tack—that McDonnell stands in the "vital center" of American politics because his thinking anticipates the Progressive agenda. Wilentz, "Against Exceptionalism," 14; Wilentz, Reply to Criticism," 49–50, in offering a more nuanced reading of McDonnell, essentially restates Gutman's interpretation.

6. The only published accounts that touch on Beeswax Taylor are Krause, "Old Beeswax"; Krause, *"Za Chlebom,"* 146, 151, 164.

7. *HLN*, 3 Mar. 1888 and 23 Jan. 1892; *NLT*, 15 Jul. 1882 and 30 Jan. 1892.

8. Thompson, *English Working Class*, 155–57, 294–95; Sykes, "Early Chartism," 165–66.

9. *NLT*, 22 Apr. 1876; *HT*, 8 Nov. 1883; *HLN*, 23 Jan. 1892; and Epstein, *Lion of Freedom*, chap. 3.

10. Boston, *British Chartists in America*, 18, 21–22, 35, 80; *HLN*, 23 Jan. 1892; Epstein, *Lion of Freedom*, 212, 215, 294–302, 310. On Carnegie's origins see Wall, *Carnegie*, chap. 3; Carnegie, *Autobiography*, chap. 1. Carnegie's uncle, Tom Morri-

son, Jr., like his father, was an active Chartist. Morrison was arrested in 1842 for his activities on behalf of the People's Charter.

11. This paragraph and the succeeding four are based on: *HLN*, 3 Mar. 1888 and 23 Jan. 1892; *NLT*, 22 Apr. 1876.

12. *HLN*, 7 May 1884. There is virtually no available information about either of Taylor's wives.

13. Two examples of Taylor's critique of the self-made man are in *IW*, 25 Jan. and 15 Feb. 1879. For his views on profiteering during the Civil War and on accumulating wealth in general, see his poems, "The Bankers and I Are Out," *NLT*, 22 June 1878, discussed below, and "Men and Monkeys," *HLN*, 23 Jan. 1892. It is conceivable that Taylor did not trade with Southern planters during the war: he might have done business with Northern abolitionists who established themselves in 1862–63 on the Carolina Sea Islands and in Louisiana.

14. *NLT*, 28 Jul., 4, 11, and 18 Aug. 1877.

15. *NLT*, 27 Apr., 22 June, and 5 Oct. 1878.

16. *NLT*, 22 June 1878.

17. Additional examples of Taylor's use of the Shylock metaphor are in *IW*, 4 Jan. and 19 Apr. 1879; and *NLT*, 4 Sept. 1880. Though the metaphor is disturbing, there is little that was metaphoric about the profiteering of the Eastern financial community during and immediately after the Civil War. One source of Taylor's anti-Semitism is in Chartist discourse. See, for example, the reference to the "Jewocracy" in *Northern Star*, 4 Aug. 1838, as quoted in G. S. Jones, "Language of Chartism," 14. It also should be noted that implicit in "The Bankers and I Are Out" are some contradictory views of women's place in society. On the one hand, Nancy Jane and John are partners: he works for wages and she works at home in a joint effort to maintain the household economy. However, John's description of the activities of the wife of Banker Jones suggests that John might prefer an arrangement that would allow Nancy Jane to devote more time to "womanly" activities and less to manual labor. See Levine, *Labor's True Woman*, for an extended consideration of women and women's rights in the Gilded Age labor movement.

18. The decision to repay wartime obligations with currency backed by specie, as opposed to greenbacks, meant in effect that though the war had been fought with dollars worth fifty cents each, the debt would be paid in dollars worth one hundred cents each. See Goodwyn, *Populist Moment*, 11.

19. This is a very different problem from those raised by Salvatore's critique of historians, who, he charges, have mistakenly portrayed republicanism as an interpretive framework for understanding nineteenth-century America. See Salvatore, "Class and Citizenship."

20. On the multivalency of political discourse, see Pocock, *Politics, Language, and Time*, 17–25.

21. Epstein, "Rethinking the Categories of Working Class History," 195–208; G. Jones, *Languages of Class*, 90–178; G. Jones, "Language of Chartism," 13–18, 34–35, 44–45.

22. Wall, *Carnegie*, 2, 109.

23. *NLT*, 5 Oct. 1878; Ricker, *Greenback-Labor*, 61. By contrast, when Carnegie had succeeded in consolidating his manly aspirations as a "worker," he busily recuperated for his own aggrandizement the nostalgic trappings (and titles) of a feudal monarchy.

24. *NLT,* 9, 16, and 30 Nov. 1878, 4 Jan., 26 Apr., 10 May, 14 and 21 June, 12 and 19 Jul., 13 and 27 Sept., 25 Oct., 1, 8, and 15 Nov. 1879; *IW,* 2 and 30 Aug., 13 and 27 Sept. 1879; Ricker, *Greenback-Labor,* 51–63, 79, 125.

25. *IW,* 13, 20, and 27 Sept. 1879, and 28 Apr. 1888; *NLT,* 12 Jul., 1, 15, and 22 Nov. 1879, 4 and 11 Sept., 2 and 23 Oct., 20 Nov. 1880, 5 and 26 Feb., 16 Apr., 21 May, 18 and 25 June, 6 Aug., 29 Oct., 5 and 12 Nov. 1881; *PET,* 19 Nov. 1881; *HT,* 5 Nov. 1881; Ricker, *Greenback-Labor,* 83, 93, 100; Berthoff, *British Immigrants,* 102–03.

26. James, "First Convention of the AFL," 214–15.

27. *HT,* 4 Feb. 1882; Horner, "Producers' Co-operatives," chap. 5. Taylor noted that cooperation provided the surest way of ending the "false relations" that underlay the wage system and robbed labor of the wealth it produced. "After forty years of experience" in the labor movement, he was "forced to the conclusion that the only sure way out of the antagonism now existing between labor and capital is co-operation."

28. Wall, *Carnegie,* 80–109; *JUL,* 15 Nov. 1880.

29. For other versions of "Storm the Fort," see P. Foner, *American Labor Songs,* 154; Dawley, *Class and Community,* 3, 193.

30. *NLT,* 10 Sept. 1888; *HLN,* 16 Apr. 1887, 3 Mar., 15 Sept., 27 Oct., and 22 Dec. 1888, 12 Jan. and 8 June 1889, and 30 Jan. 1892.

31. *HLN,* 13 Dec. 1890 and 21 Nov. 1891.

32. *HLN,* 23 Jan. 1892.

33. McCloskey, *American Conservatism,* 1–22, 145–49.

34. *PCG,* 6 Nov. 1895.

35. Spahr, *America's Working People,* 148.

36. Diggins, "Comrades and Citizens," 629.

CHAPTER 19. *Captains of Business, Captains of Politics*

1. Wall, *Carnegie,* 318–19; Bridge, *Inside History,* 75–78; Hogg, "Homestead Strike," 14; Livesay, *Carnegie,* 95–98.

2. Hogg, "Homestead Strike," 19–20, 39–47; Bridge, *Inside History,* 294–95. See also U.S. House, *Report 2447,* 25.

3. Carnegie to Knox, 22 (two letters) and 25 Mar. 1890, H. M. Curry and H. C. Frick to Knox, 25 Mar. 1890, and Carnegie to Frick, 31 Jul. 1890, all in Real Estate Document Files, Carnegie-Illinois, Plant: Homestead, box 13, USX Archives. The quotation is from James M. Swank's 1890 report for the American Iron and Steel Association, as cited in Hogg, "Homestead Strike," 40.

4. Mowry, *Era of Theodore Roosevelt,* 227. Two readily accessible sketches of Knox are: Wright, "Philander Chase Knox,"; H. Wright "Knox, Philander Chase," 5:478–80. Knox launched a short-lived campaign for the 1908 Republican nomination.

5. Dobson, *America's Ascent,* 204; LeFeber, *American Age,* 242; Wall, *Carnegie,* 645; Kolko, *Triumph of Conservatism,* 67–68; Hofstadter, *American Political Tradition,* 293–295. Knox prosecuted the Northern Securities case for the justice department—a case that won wide publicity for Roosevelt as a trustbuster but changed virtually nothing about the concentration of economic power held by

James J. Hill, J. P. Morgan, or their chief competitor in the Northwest, E. H. Harriman.

Knox evidently mastered the game of golf within a few years. A Mr. Burke, who eulogized Knox shortly after he died in 1921, told the Allegheny County Bar Association that "he drove a gold ball with the precision of an accomplished devotee of the royal and ancient game." Burke went on to say that principle was Knox's constant guide, "and the banner of expediency under which the opportunist finds a refuge was always a subject of his contempt" (H. Wright, "Philander Chase Knox," 9:309–10).

6. H. Wright, "Philander Chase Knox," 9:305; Josephson, *Politicos,* 645–46; Josephson, *Robber Barons,* 398–400, 449; Munro, *Dollar Diplomacy,* 160; Hofstadter, *American Political Tradition,* 287; Harvey, *Frick,* 290–91; Burgoyne, *Homestead Strike,* 47.

7. *PD,* 3 and 11 Oct. 1892; *WDI,* 4 and 11 Oct. 1892; U.S. House, *Report 2447,* 36–37, 60–64, 130; U.S. Senate, *Report 1280,* 165, 240; Hogg, "Homestead Strike," 81; Wolff, *Lockout,* 211; Burgoyne, *Homestead Strike,* 46–47, 201; Stowell, *Fort Frick,* 257–59, 264; Harvey, *Frick,* 116–18, 291. Knox's quotation is from *PD,* 1 Oct. 1892.

8. Josephson, *Robber Barons,* 391–92; Hessen, *Steel Titan,* 45–58, 307–10; Wall, *Carnegie,* 650–52.

9. Carnegie to McKinley, 17 Dec. 1896, ACLC, vol. 40, as quoted in Wall, *Carnegie,* 645; Frick to McKinley, 16 Dec. 1896, as quoted in Harvey, *Frick,* 290–91.

10. Wall, *Carnegie,* 466–68, 644–45; Harvey, *Frick,* 290–92. Harvey and Wall give conflicting accounts of why Knox did not become attorney general in 1896. Harvey writes that the offer was made but that Knox declined for financial reasons. Wall, on the other hand, states that McKinley did not offer Knox the job until 1901. H. Wright, "Knox, Philander Chase," 5:479, says that Knox was offered the job in 1899 but turned it down because he was "deeply engrossed" in Carnegie's business operations—very likely the impending creation of U.S. Steel.

11. Wall, *Carnegie,* 982–83; Munro, *Dollar Diplomacy,* 160–61; LaFeber, *American Age,* 242; H. Wright, "Philander Chase Knox," 9:320–26; Dobson, *America's Ascent,* 204.

12. My sketch of Knox as secretary of state is based primarily on: Dobson, *America's Ascent,* 204–05, 208–17; LaFeber, *American Age,* 222, 240–49; LaFeber, *Inevitable Revolutions,* 38, 42–49; Munro, *Dollar Diplomacy,* 160–268; Link, *Wilson,* 94, 96. Also see Langley, *United States and the Caribbean,* 49–62; H. Wright, "Philander Chase Knox," 9:327–49.

13. On Carnegie's contributions to the Central American Court of Justice, see LaFeber, *Inevitable Revolutions,* 41; Wall, *Carnegie,* 910–11.

14. Warner Co., *Allegheny County,* pt. 1, pp. 702–03; Hopkins Co., *Atlas of the Vicinity of Pittsburgh and Allegheny* pl. 17.

15. *PD,* 12 Jul. 1890; *PP,* 3 Sept. 1890; Plan of City Poor Farm and Deed for City Poor Farm, Real Estate Document Files, Carnegie-Illinois Steel Company, Plant: Homestead, box 13, USX Archives.

16. In reconstructing the City Farm transaction, I have relied on the *PP* and the *PD,* from July through November 1890. See, in particular: *PP,* 4, 8, and 30 Aug., 3, 6, 12, 13, 19, and 22 Sept., 1 Oct., 4 Nov. 1890, *PD,* 12, 29, and 31 Jul., 2,

4, and 5 Aug., and 11 Sept. 1890. Also see *HLN,* 23 and 30 Aug. 1890. Relevant letters, cables, and telegrams, as well as deeds, indentures, attestations, and articles of agreement, are located in Real Estate Document Files, Carnegie-Illinois, Plant: Homestead, box 13, and in Document File no. 5840, Carnegie Steel Co., Ltd., Abstract of Title, Homestead Steel Works, pts. 1, 2, both in the USX Archives. A number of these documents are reproduced in app. I.

17. Carnegie to Knox, 22 (two letters) and 25 Mar. 1890, and Curry and Frick to Knox, 25 Mar. 1890, Carnegie Papers, USX Archives. The text of the letter that Knox received from Frick and Curry, who was vice chairman of Carnegie, Phipps, and Company, is exactly the same as Carnegie's letter to Knox.

18. *PP,* 28 and 31 Jul., and 1 Aug. 1890; *PD,* 29 Jul. 1890; *HLN,* 2 Aug. 1890.

19. *PP,* 30 Aug. 1882 and 18 Nov. 1890; *PT,* 9 Mar. 1901; *PD,* 29 Jul. 1890; *PCG,* 9 Mar. 1901; Warner Co., *Allegheny County,* pt. 2, pp. 562–63; *Directory of Pittsburgh and Allegheny Cities,* 997; Knox to Frick, 31 Jul. and 1 Aug. 1890, USX Archives. Rhoads later became chairman of the board of the giant National Tube Works in McKeesport.

20. *PP,* 4 and 8 Aug 1890; *PD,* 29 and 31 Jul., 2, 4, and 5 Aug. 1890.

21. Steffens, *Shame of the Cities,* 155, 165; Tarr, "Infrastructure and City-Building," 232.

22. *PD,* 29 Jul. 1890.

23. Genovese and Fox-Genovese, *Fruits of Merchant Capital,* 212.

24. Carnegie to Frick, 31 Jul. 1890, Knox to Frick, 31 Jul. 1890, and Knox to Frick, 1 Aug. 1890, all in Carnegie Papers, USX Archives.

25. The codebook is located in Carnegie Papers, box 31, USX Archives.

26. Knox to Frick, 31 Jul. 1890.

27. Knox to Frick, 1 Aug. 1890, Carnegie Papers, USX Archives; Milton I. Baird and William L. Abbott et al., "Articles of Agreement," 1 Aug. 1890, and Deed for City Poor Farm, both in the Real Estate Document Files, Carnegie-Illinois Steel Company, USX Archives.

28. *PP,* 29, 30, and 31 Jul., 1, 2, and 4 Aug. 1890; *PD,* 29 and 31 Jul., and 2 Aug. 1890; *HLN,* 2 Aug. 1890. Gourley's equivocations reflect his contradictory position within the ring. As it turned out, his tentative criticism of the poor farm bidding added to Magee's growing displeasure with him: in 1893, Magee saw to it that Gourley, who had served the ring as president of the Select Council from 1879 through 1890, was not renominated for mayor. Flinn, however, tried to secure Gourley's nomination for controller. He failed, but Gourley was nominated nonetheless—by Democrats and independents. Despite a bitter personal campaign against him by Magee, Gourley was elected controller. From this position he investigated several prominent members of the ring on grounds of financial misconduct; they were subsequently prosecuted and convicted. Magee then decided to engineer Gourley's renomination for controller, this time, of course, as a Republican. Though his power was no match for Magee, Gourley thus proved a skillful political operative. Clearly he was a force to be reckoned with: his public criticisms of the poor farm deal may well have been intended as threats to expose the affair; his eventual support may be read as an indication that he, too, had profited from the transaction, possibly as the unnamed "farm interloper" alluded to by Carnegie in his telegram to Frick on 31 July. On Gourley see Kerr, "Mayors of Pittsburgh," 197–202.

29. Knox to Frick, 2 Aug. 1890, Carnegie to Frick, 2 Aug. 1890, 9:30 A.M., and Carnegie to Frick, 2 Aug. 1890, 3:35 P.M., all in Carnegie Papers, USX Archives; and *PP* and *PD*, 2 and 3 Aug. 1890.

30. *PP* and *PD*, 5 Aug. 1890.

31. *PP,* 4 Aug. 1890. Also see *PD*, 4 Aug. 1890. Interestingly enough, the ubiquitous hands of Andrew W. Mellon, the good friend of both Frick and Carnegie, may have figured in the City Poor Farm deal. He was quoted by the *PD* as saying that the bid offered by Baird was in fact too high and that Baird had asked him to buy into the property.

32. *PP,* 8 Aug. 1890.

33. *PP,* 13 Aug. 1890; *HLN,* 23 and 30 Aug. 1890.

34. *PP,* 3 and 6 Sept. 1890. Straub also sought to block the purchase of the Stewart property. Unfortunately, little is known about Straub himself or his position in Pittsburgh politics.

35. *PP,* 12 Sept. 1890. The company's brief continued: Carnegie, Phipps, and Company's "relation to the sale was that after the bid of Baird had been accepted by the city and the property awarded to him as the highest bidder, Baird, for a valuable consideration by deed duly executed and acknowledged, assigned the contract to this defendant [Carnegie, Phipps, and Company] and granted and sold to them all his interest therein, and in the assignment directed the city to deliver to this defendant the deed for the farm. . . . The city was [then] informed of the transfer and agreed to it, and a deed was prepared."

36. *PP,* 22 Sept. 1890; *WDI, PD, NYW,* and *PP,* 4 Aug. 1892; *NLT,* 6 Aug. 1892; Wolff, *Lockout,* 210. Judges Ewing and White heard the Straub case. In 1892, Ewing refused even to hear testimony on bail applications for a number of the workers charged in connection with the disturbances of 6 July. The reason he gave at the bail hearing was that it was utterly impossible to construe the actions of the workers as an exercise in self-defense. When the workers charged Frick and his colleagues with crimes, however, Ewing prepared the bail orders in advance.

The *Post*'s allusion to Hamlet is to act 2, scene 1: "There are more things in heaven and earth, Horatio, / Than are dreamt of in your philosophy."

37. *PP,* 12, 13, and 22 Sept., and 4 Nov. 1890, and *PD,* 11 Sept. 1890, as quoted in *PP,* 12 Sept. 1890; Baird, Abbott et al., "Articles of Agreement," Carnegie Papers, USX Archives; and Carnegie, Phipps, and Company and City of Pittsburgh, "Articles of Agreement," 12 Nov. 1890, Real Estate Document Files, Carnegie-Illinois Steel Company, USX Archives. The poor farm deal was framed by two acts of philanthropy initiated by the principals of Carnegie, Phipps, and Company. On 6 February 1890 Carnegie offered $1,000,000 to the city of Pittsburgh for the construction of a huge public library. On 17 November 1891, Henry Phipps offered $100,000 to for the conservatory in Schenley Park that bears his name.

38. *CT,* 23 Jul. 1892.

39. Carnegie to W. C. Whitney, February 1886, W. C. Whitney Papers, vol. 31, Library of Congress, and Carnegie to Abbott, spring 1889, ACLC, vol. 240, both as quoted in Wall, *Carnegie,* 646. This paragraph and the succeeding one also draw on ibid., 646–49.

40. P. Kennedy, *Great Powers,* 242–43. The story of Homestead is preeminently about the social truths putatively subsumed by Kennedy's colossal abstractions.

CHAPTER 20. *The Stakes for Labor*

1. Goodwyn, *Democratic Promise,* passim; Laurie, *Artisans into Workers,* chaps. 5, 6; Holt, "Trade Unionism"; L. Fink, *Workingmen's Democracy,* chap. 8. For pointing out the conjunction of some of the events cited in this and succeeding paragraphs, I am indebted to the splendid overviews by Brody, "Rural America," esp. 588; Brody, Public World," 634–37.

2. Hewitt, Holley eulogy, in AIME, *Holley Memorial,* 24; *NYT,* 1 and 2 Oct. 1890.

3. Mahan, as quoted in LaFeber, *New Empire,* 89.

4. LaFeber, *American Age,* 177; *CT,* 23 Jul. 1892.

5. U.S. House, *Report 2447,* 2; Kennedy, *Great Powers,* 242–43; Wall, *Carnegie,* 535–36; Hogg, "Homestead Strike," 19–20; Bridge, *Inside History,* 254–56.

6. Handbill announcing the formation of Carnegie Steel Company, Limited, Carnegie Papers, box 31, USX Archives; Bridge, *Inside History,* 295, 297; *NLT,* 23 Apr. 1892; *NYW,* 3 Jul. 1892; Parsons, *History and Commerce of Pittsburgh,* 73–74; Hogg, "Homestead Strike," 43; Overman, *Metallurgy,* 484–85. By 1892 the capacity of the Homestead Steel Works was four times greater than that of the giant Krupps concern in Germany.

7. Brody, *Steelworkers in America,* 2.

8. Bridge, *Inside History,* 254; Wall, *Carnegie,* 534.

9. Carnegie to Abbott, 29 Dec. 1888, ACLC, vol. 10. Also relevant is Carnegie's correspondence bearing on the Homestead Steel Works in PBSC File, Carnegie Papers, box 37, USX Archives.

10. Carnegie to Abbott, 7 Aug. 1889, ACLC, vol. 10 (also reproduced in Wall, *Carnegie,* 530); Abbott to Carnegie, 2 Sept. 1889, PBSC File, USX Archives; Carnegie, *Dedication,* 12, 13, 15.

11. Wall, *Carnegie,* 567, 660–61; *NYH, PP,* and *PCG,* 1 and 2 Jul. 1892; *CT* and *NYW,* 2 Jul. 1892; *NYS,* 2 and 3 Jul. 1892. After Potter kicked the unidentified worker, he ran back inside the steelworks, closing the gate behind him. The workers vowed to prosecute Potter but never did.

12. *PCT,* 22 Jan. 1890 and 22 Apr. 1892, as quoted in Hogg, "Homestead Strike," 46, 44.

13. Hogg, "Homestead Strike," 44–46.

14. Holt, "Trade Unionism," 10, 11, 14, 26; William Martin to Charles G. Foster, 13 Jan. 1892, in Martin Papers; *NLT,* 29 June 1889, 13 Jan. and 11 Apr. 1892.

15. *PP,* 14 June 1892; AAISW, *Proceedings,* 1890, 3031; Fitch, *Steel Workers,* 257–58; Montgomery, *House of Labor,* 35; Holt, "Trade Unionism," 14.

16. *PP,* 7 and 13–15 June 1892, and *National Glass Budget,* 11 and 18 June 1892, clippings in Martin Papers. On the defections of Martin, Nutt, and Jarrett and the weakening of the AAISW, see also *AM,* 10 June 1892.

17. This paragraph and the succeeding two are based on: *NLT,* 23 Sept. 1882, as quoted in Stromquist, "Working Class Organization," 38; *NLT,* 14 Jul. 1883, 8 Mar. 1884, 27 Feb. and 10 Apr. 1886, 24 Mar. 1888, 16 Mar., 13 Apr., 11 May, and 29 June 1889, 3 Feb., 28 June, 27 Sept., and 4 Oct. 1890.

18. The full text is in *NLT,* 19 Apr. 1890.

19. Martin lost his bid to direct the federal labor bureau to Caroll F. Wright.

20. *NLT,* 19 Apr., 28 June, 27 Sept., and 4 Oct 1890; *AM,* 10 June, 1892; *PP,* 7 June 1892; U.S. Senate, *Report 1280,* 151–53; *Pittsburgh Press,* 26 June 1890, and *Steubenville (Ohio) Star,* 4 Jul. 1891, both as quoted by Mavrinac, "Labor Organization," 95, 96; Martin to Foster, 13 Jan. 1892, Martin Papers.

21. *PCG,* 6 June 1892. Martin's work for Carnegie's Bureau of Labor and, in particular, on the Homestead wage scales, may be traced in the Martin Papers. See, among others: "Open Hearth, Average Daily Wages, 1891–92"; "32-inch Mill, Homestead, Average Daily Wages, 1891–92"; "Plate Mills, 1891–92"; "Carnegie Associations, Comparative Statement of Wages Paid for Day Labor"; "Statement of Comparative Labor Costs in Competitive Mills, 1891"; "Sliding Scale proposed by the Carnegie Steel Company, Limited, 1892"; "Wage Scale, 32-inch Mill, Homestead Steel Works," 15 Apr. 1892; "Scale—No. 2 Open Hearth Plant, Homestead Steel Works," 6 Apr. 1892; "List of Prices Paid at the Edgar Thomson Steel Works." Montgomery, *House of Labor,* 13, overlooks Martin's betrayal of the labor movement in his laudatory presentation.

22. Martin, untitled history of the Homestead scale, 1, "Open Hearth, Average Daily Wages, 1891–92," and "Statement of Comparative Labor Costs in Competitive Mills, 1891" all in Martin Papers; Hogg, "Homestead Strike," 39–42; Oliver to Martin, 10 and 23 Feb. 1893, both in Martin Papers. In his letter of 10 February, Oliver, a ranking official in the Oliver Iron and Steel Company, one of the city's largest, asked Martin to provide him with the current wage schedule for the converting and blooming departments at Homestead. Oliver, who at the time was preparing to negotiate with his employees, already had comparable information from other mills in Pittsburgh; it was his intent, he said, to "equalize" his wages with those paid by competitive concerns. Martin took Oliver's request to the Carnegie board of managers, and it was summarily rejected. Following this action, Oliver told Martin: "When you were preparing the Homestead prices (in 1892) and called on me for information, I cheerfully threw open *all* [emphasis in the original] our prices to you and laid open everything you wanted that we had. . . . I think the action of your Board, all the circumstances of the case considered, is hardly defensible." This was, of course, not the only instance of a Carnegie concern entering into a secret agreement with competitors and then pulling out when the agreement no longer proved useful to Carnegie.

23. Martin, "Open Hearth, Average Daily Wages, 1891–92," "32-inch Mill, Homestead, Average Daily Wages, 1891–92," "Plate Mills, 1891–92," and "Carnegie Associations, Comparative Statement of Wages Paid for Day Labor," all in Martin Papers; U.S. House, *Report 2447,* 112, 126–27; Martin, "Statement of Comparative Labor Costs in Competitive Mills, 1891," Martin Papers; Carnegie to Frick, 10 and 28 June 1892, as quoted in Bridge, *Inside History,* 205, 206. The remarks of the unnamed Carnegie official are quoted in Hogg, "Homestead Strike," 242.

24. Paul Berman, "Negotiations between Labor and Capital," 1, manuscript, 1976, photoduplicate in author's possession. Berman, now a writer for the *Village Voice,* explored intricacies of the negotiations while preparing a film script about the Homestead Lockout. His commentary is invaluable, and I am indebted to him for many of the observations in this and succeeding paragraphs.

25. Berman, "Negotiations," 1, 8, manuscript in author's possession;

AAISW, *Proceedings*, 1889, 2601, 2851–53, and "Membership Abstract"; AAISW, *Proceedings*, 1890, 2966–73, 3218, and "Membership Abstract"; AAISW, *Proceedings*, 1891, 3399ff., and "Membership Abstract;" U.S. Senate, *Report 1280*, 193.

26. *WDI*, 27 June 1892; *PCT*, 25 June 1892; AAISW, *Proceedings*, 1892, 3733, 3742, 3831, 4169; U.S. House, *Report 2447*, 9, 106–08, 114; Berman, "Negotiations," 23, manuscript in author's possession; Bemis, "Homestead Strike," 373.

27. This paragraph and the succeeding one are drawn from: AAISW, *Proceedings*, 1890, 3218, and "Membership Abstract"; AAISW, *Proceedings*, 1892, 3958; *NLT*, 22 Mar. 1890 and 16 May 1891; Schooley and Schooley, *Homestead Directory, 1891*, 20; Paul Berman, "Democracy in the Union and in the Mill," 3–4, 12–14, manuscript, 1976. This manuscript, like others Berman and the historian Steve Brier wrote as part of their research for a Homestead film script, has been extraordinary helpful.

28. Some of O'Donnell's difficulties with the Advisory Committee may be traced in the following: *NYW*, 27 and 28 Jul. 1892; *NYS*, *YEV*, and *PP*, 27 Jul. 1892; *NYH*, *NYW*, and *WDI*, 28 Jul. 1892; *WDI*, *NYW*, and *PD*, 1 Aug. 1892. The executive board typically met every Sunday afternoon.

29. Bridge, *Inside History*, 201–02. On the control of the shop floor exercised by skilled workers, see Soffer, "Trade Union Development"; Montgomery, "Workers' Control," 485–509.

30. *PT*, 4 and 5 Jul. 1892, reprinted in *NLT*, 9 Jul. 1892. Interestingly enough, Lovejoy's remarks were issued with an assurance that the company planned no initiatives for a week or so. "Our officials at Homestead have started on vacations," Lovejoy said. Two days later, on the very day Frick had chosen, the Pinkertons arrived, accompanied by the superintendent of the Homestead Steel Works, John A. Potter, and several of his associates.

31. Cohen, "Steelworkers Rethink," 157; Fitch, *Steel Workers*, 102–04, 123.

32. Fitch, *Steel Workers*, 103.

33. Fitch, research notes, Nubia-5, 1907, cards 1–13. Potter's remarks are on card 10. Only the following phrase attributed by the committeeman to Potter is a direct quotation: "There have been many times when you have come into the office with a grievance and have been ashamed to state your case." Fitch's notes are in the possession of his grandson, Charles Hill, who was kind enough to make photoduplicates of them available to me.

34. Fitch, *Steel Workers*, 103, 123; Fitch, research Notes, Nubia-5, cards 2–3, 9–10; Cohen, "Steelworkers Rethink," 157–58. Of the nondeferential attitude possessed by Homestead members of the AAISW, Fitch wrote: "It was undoubtedly due to this spirit that the officials of the Carnegie Company were not in an overconciliatory mood at the beginning, and that when the men would not accept their terms they demanded a dissolution of the union." Indeed, throughout *Steel Workers*, Fitch sprinkled criticism of the steel industry's post-Homestead managerial regime with comments that are, at the very least, equally censorious of the union. See, in particular, chaps. 9, 10, passim. Fitch was a 27-year-old graduate student in economics at the University of Wisconsin when he conducted the research for *Steel Workers*. For an insightful discussion of ambiguities in the book, see McClymer, "Pittsburgh Survey," esp. 178–80.

35. Fitch, research notes, Nubia-5, cards 2–3, 10–11. Nubia was a pseudonym Fitch gave to the large mill in McKeesport, doubtless the National Tube

Works, where his committeeman informant was working in 1907. The number 5 indicates that the informant was the fifth steelworker interviewed there.

Like Fitch himself, Cohen, "Steelworkers Rethink," also engages in the creative revision of Fitch's field notes, including the selection cited in the text above. See, for example, 162, 164, 165, where Nubia-5, to whom Cohen gives the pseudonym, Chandler, is made to speak in the first person, thus giving the impression that Fitch quoted him directly in his notes. In truth, the comments of Nubia-5/ Chandler on Potter's handsome offer, as well as on other matters, were paraphrased by Fitch and recounted by him in the third person. Cohen also incorrectly states that Nubia 5 was chairman of the 32-inch mill committee in Homestead.

36. U.S. House, *Report 2447*, 5, which lists the screw-downs in the 119-inch mill; *PP*, 1 Jul. 1892; *WDI, NYH, CT, NYS*, and *NYW*, 19 Jul. 1892; Burgoyne, *Homestead Strike*, 38, 141.

37. The fact that Fitch has Potter refer to the committeeman as John in no ways disqualifies McQuade as the man who was Nubia 5; Fitch often invented names for his informants. Furthermore, neither H. Lank nor F. Pifer, the other screw-downs in the 119-inch mill, are mentioned in any of the press accounts bearing on the lockout. McQuade's testimony may be found in U.S. House, *Report 2447*, 187–89. The other workers who gave evidence to the House committee, or to its counterpart in the Senate, were: John McLuckie, William T. Roberts, David Lynch, George F. Rylands, Hugh O'Donnell, and Oscar Colflesh. Rylands, O'Donnell, and Colflesh worked in the 119-inch plate mill along with McQuade; Colflesh, like McQuade, was on the mill committee and participated in negotiations with the company, but he did not serve on the Advisory Committee.

38. This paragraph and the succeeding one are based on Fitch, research notes, Nubia-5, card 11; U.S. House, *Report 2447*, 28–31, 124–26, 188–89.

39. Fitch, research notes, CH-1, 1907, card 7. See also CH-13, cards 1, 2, and CH-14, card 1.

40. Fitch, research notes, Nubia-5, cards 8–9.

41. Fitch, research notes, Nubia-5, card 2; U.S. House, *Report 2447*, 124; *WDI, NYH, CT, NYS*, and *NYW*, 19 Jul. 1892; Burgoyne, *Homestead Strike*, 141. The comments of Berman are germane: "The self-deprecation of the workers that Fitch interviewed should be taken with a grain of salt. It was some . . . years after the strike that he spoke to them, and they had in that time been badly oppressed and suffered many defeats. It was natural for them to look back and find fault in the union's behavior and to judge the past by the standards of the present. In fact, though, what they were looking back on could be interpreted as a different epoch rather than as a series of union abuses. Their defeat was so great, however, that they could not envision this" ("Negotiations," 7, manuscript in author's possession).

42. Berman, "Negotiations," 10, manuscript in author's possession. On Martin's participation, see U.S. House, *Report 2447*, 106.

43. This paragraph and the succeeding two are based on: Bemis, "Homestead Strike," 373; U.S. House, *Report 2447*, 106; U.S. Senate, *Report 1280*, 205; Burgoyne, *Homestead Strike*, 17, 19, 20; *HLN*, 2 Jul. 1892; *PP*, 4 June, 1892.

44. *PP*, 4 June, 1892; *AM*, 17 June and 1 Jul. 1892; Martin, untitled history of scale, 1, Martin Papers; *NYH*, 21 Jul. 1892; Burgoyne, *Homestead Strike*, 20; Fitch, *Steel Workers*, 123; Hogg, *Homestead Strike*, 50, 53.

45. This paragraph and the following one are based on: Martin, untitled history of scale, 1, Martin Papers; *AM*, 1 Jul. 1892; Bemis, "Homestead Srike," 376; U.S. House, *Report 2447*, 18–19, 127.

46. This paragraph and the next one are based principally on U.S. House, *Report 2447*, 106–07. On the many inconsistencies in the company proposals, see Fitch, *Steel Workers*, 128.

47. U.S. House, *Report 2447*, 107–08; A. C. Buell to a Mr. Cramp, 8 Jan. 1892, Papers of Secretary of the Navy Benjamin F. Tracy, Library of Congress, as quoted by Wall, *Carnegie*, 550–51. No account of the lockout, primary or secondary, identifies precisely when the fence enclosing the steelworks was completed. It is known, however, that construction began in early January. See AAISW, *Proceedings*, 1892, 3958.

48. This paragraph and the following one are based on: "Wage Scale, 32-inch Mill, Homestead Steel Works," 15 Apr. 1892, and "Scale—No. 2 Open Hearth Plant, Homestead Steel Works," 6 Apr. 1892, both in Martin Papers; Fitch, *Steel Workers*, 124; Wall, *Carnegie*, 541, 544–45; Harvey, *Frick*, 164–65; Bridge, *Inside History*, 203; Carnegie to Frick, 4 Apr. 1892, as cited by Bridge, *Inside History*, 204–05.

49. Carnegie to Frick, 4 May 1892, as quoted in Harvey, *Frick*, 165–66. Wall points out that sometime in April, Frick traveled to New York to confer with Carnegie prior to his departure for Europe. No written records exist; however, it apparently was at these meetings that Carnegie and Frick reached a clear-cut decision to oust the AAISW and the Knights.

50. This paragraph and the next one are based on Frick to Potter, 30 May 1892, as cited in U.S. House, *Report 2447*, 23; *PP*, 4 June 1892.

51. *AM*, 17 June, 1 and 8 Jul. 1892; *PP*, 4 June 1892; *NLT*, 11 June 1892; U.S. House, *Report 2447*, 22–25, 108, 181; U.S. Senate, *Report 1280*, 193–94; Carnegie Steel Company, Limited, "Agreement Entered into by and between the Limited Partnership Association of the Carnegie Steel Company, Limited, and the Workmen Employed by It at the Homestead Steel Works, Munhall," n.d. (c. 6 Jul. 1892), USX Archives; Fitch, *Steel Workers*, 123; Bemis, "Homestead Strike," 376.

52. U.S. Senate, *Report 1280*, 206, as quoted in Bemis, "Homestead Strike," 374; U.S. House, *Report 2447*, 108; *PP*, 4 June 1892.

53. Harris, as quoted in *NLT*, 28 Nov. 1874.

54. This paragraph and the following one are based on: U.S. House, *Report 2447*, 27, 73, 110–11; Wall *Carnegie*, 555; Berman, "Negotiations," 19–20, manuscript in author's possession; Bemis, "Homestead Strike," 379; *NLT*, 16 Jul. 1892; *AM*, 1 Jul. 1892; *AISA Bulletin*, 13 Jul. 1892.

55. U.S. House, *Report 2447*, 29, 107–09, 124–26, 163; Berman, "Negotiations," 17, manuscript in author's possession.

56. This paragraph and the next one are based on U.S. House, *Report 2447*, 29, 87, 126, 170, 183, 187, 189; Bemis, "Homestead Strike," 377; *AM*, 10 May 1889, which published a floor plan and full description of the plate mill.

57. This paragraph and succeeding the one are based on U.S. House, *Report 2447*, 29–30, 126, 163; *NLT*, 16 Jul. 1892.

58. Bridge, *Inside History*, 295; Fitch, *Steel Workers*, 127.

59. Fitch, *Steel Workers*, 127–28; Robinson, *Amalgamated Association*, 145–46; *NLT*, 11 June and 16 Jul. 1892; *PCG*, 6 June 1892. The steelworkers well knew that

Carnegie was never averse to underselling his competitors in an effort to capture a larger share of the market, and therefore that a minimum was necessary to guard against his clever manipulation of the market: "It is the experience of the iron and steel workers that some prevention is necessary to protect themselves from being reduced to an extremely low rate of pay by the acceptance by manufacturers of sales below current rates; as the workingmen do not sell the product, there must be a point where reduction in wages by reason of low-figured sales shall cease."

60. U.S. Senate, *Report 1280*, 195; Bemis, "Homestead Strike," 375, 378; *NLT*, 16 Jul. 1892; Hogg, "Homestead Strike," 55. See also Wall, *Carnegie*, 553. Frick's insistence that the scales simply could not be negotiated was most troubling to the men, for the AAISW had always agreed to a downward revision in tonnage rates when new machinery increased productivity. The Homestead workers recognized that "if increase of output without increase of labor to the workmen is brought about by improvement, there is every opportunity offered by the workmen to arrive through conference at an equitable rate; but when the employer refuses to engage with the employees on the matter, all hope of a just settlement is lost."

61. This paragraph and the following one are based on U.S. House, *Report 2447*, 20, 106, 111, 188; Carnegie Steel Company, "Agreement between Carnegie Steel and the Workmen," *Carnegie Papers*, USX Archives; *PP*, 4 June 1892.

62. Among the workers affected by the new contracts were men in six departments whose wage scales the company had previously requested not to negotiate on the grounds that mechanical changes were imminent. In accepting the company's disingenuous request, however, the union inadvertently left the workers in these departments vulnerable to the unilateral imposition of an unfair wage scale. The six departments in question were the Bessemer converting mill, the blooming mill, and the 23-inch, 33-inch, 40-inch, and 35-inch rolling mills.

63. *NLT*, 16 Jul. 1892; U.S. House, *Report 2447*, 186.

64. This paragraph and the succeeding one are based on *PP*, 4 June 1892; Hogg, "Homestead Strike," 55, 56. "The point that seems to have been overlooked by most contemporary observers," Hogg observes, "was that the old scales were to continue in the other departments only until such time as new machinery and other improvements could be introduced; then new scales would be drawn up for those mills also. . . . The Amalgamated men at Homestead exhibited a solidarity of ranks that astonished those who did not understand the true situation." The proposed reduction in the minimum seemed to be aimed at all the workers: "There is no evidence that it was limited to the four mills only." Hogg's criticism of the contemporary views of the company proposals applies with equal force to most secondary accounts as well.

The eight lodges of the AAISW had a combined membership of 1,038 in 1891, a figure that rose dramatically in the spring of 1892 (AAISW, *Proceedings*, 1891, "Membership Abstract"). Most commentators have placed the membership of the lodges at a much lower figure.

65. The AAISW leader, as quoted in Brody, *Steelworkers*, 55, and *PP*, 18 June 1892, which carried the following crucial information about those workers employed in the plant—among them, machinists, carpenters, engineers, and day laborers—who did not belong to the AAISW: "They are not required to belong

to the Amalgamated Association, and receive but little benefit from it, except that it is always included in the contracts between the employers and the association that the wages of such men shall not be cut while the contract remains in force."

66. *NLT,* 11 June 1892; *PP* 6, 7, and 8 June 1892; *PCG,* 6 June 1892; AAISW, *Proceedings,* 1892, 4080–84; Burgoyne, *Homestead Strike,* 23, 31.

67. *PP,* 7, 8, and 18 June, 1892; Burgoyne, *Homestead Strike,* 27–28. The protection afforded by the McKinley Tariff to steel manufactures—and particularly to McKinley's friend Andrew Carnegie—generated considerable discussion over the course of the lockout. The Democratic party opposed the tariff, and Grover Cleveland championed its repeal in his presidential campaign against Benjamin Harrison in 1892. In what remains the most thoughtful consideration of Homestead and the tariff, Hogg, "Homestead Strike," 143–72, concludes, however, that the lockout had little impact on Cleveland's triumph over the the protectionist Harrison. John McLuckie, in his testimony to the House investigating committee (U.S. House, *Report 2447,* 99–101), pointed out that the McKinley Tariff, which protected many steel products from foreign competition, excluded 4×4 billets. As the price of these was the very figure upon which the Homestead sliding scale was based, one result of the tariff—not in the least fortuitous, McLuckie said—was to ensure lower prices for the billets and therefore lower wages.

68. This paragraph and the succeeding three are based on: *HLN,* 2 Jul. 1892; *PD,* 24 June 1892; *PP,* 19, 21, and 22 June 1892; U.S. House, *Report 2447,* 27; Frick to William Weihe, 22 June 1892, as cited in U.S. House, *Report 2447,* 26–27; U.S. Senate, *Report 1280,* 193–94; Burgoyne, *Homestead Strike,* 12, 31–32, 36; Stowell, *Fort Frick,* 26; Wall, *Carnegie,* 494; *NYW,* 3 Jul. 1892. In a gesture symbolic of workers' solidarity to oppose the ultimatum, it is significant that on 22 June, the very day that Frick agreed to a final negotiating session, the eight hundred East European steelworkers of Homestead took a "solemn oath of fealty of obligation to the Amalgamated Association."

69. Burgoyne, *Homestead Strike,* 20–22; *PD,* 24 June 1892; *WDI,* 29 June 1892; U.S. House, *Report 2447,* 34; *NYH,* 1 Jul. 1892; *PP,* 28 and 30 June 1892; Hogg, "Homestead Strike," 60–61. Of interest is the following poem, "The Fort That Frick Built," first published in the *HLN,* 2 Jul. 1892: " 'Twixt Homestead and Munhall, / If you'll believe my word at all, / Where once a steel works noisy roar, / A thousand blessings did out pour, / There stands today with great pretense, / Enclosed within a white-washed fence, / A wondrous change of great import, / The mill's transformed into a fort."

70. Burgoyne, *Homestead Strike,* 32–34, 46–47; *PD,* 26 June 1892; *PP,* 25 June 1892; Stowell, *Fort Frick,* 28.

71. Burgoyne, *Homestead Strike,* 34–35; *PCG,* 29 June 1892; *PP,* 28 June 1892; *WDI,* 29 and 30 June 1892. Burgoyne's definition of a lockout, as opposed to a strike, warrants quotation: "A lockout originates with the employing individual or corporation, and consists in the refusal to let the employees work until they have come to terms with the employer." A strike, on the other hand "occurs when dissatisfied workingmen cease work of their own accord and refuse to return until the cause of dissatisfaction is removed." At Homestead, Frick "took the initiative," and therefore "the trouble . . . was distinctly a lockout."

72. Burgoyne, *Homestead Strike,* 35–37; *NYS,* 1 Jul. 1892; U.S. House, *Report 2447,* 28.

73. Burgoyne, *Homestead Strike,* 37–39; Bemis, "Homestead Strike," 381; *PP,* 30 June 1892; *PCG, NYW,* and *NYS,* 1 Jul. 1892; *NYW,* 2 Jul. 1892. The members of the Advisory Committee are listed in app. J. Bemis states that the Knights of Labor had representatives on the committee.

74. *NYW,* 1, 2, and 4 Jul. 1892; *NYH,* 1 and 4 Jul. 1892; *PCG,* 1 Jul. 1892; *NYS,* 1 and 4 Jul. 1892; *CT,* 1 Jul. 1892; *PP,* 30 June, 1 and 4 Jul. 1892; *YEV,* 5 Jul. 1892; *WDI,* 1 Jul. 1892.

75. *PCG,* 1 and 2 Jul. 1892; *NYW,* 2 Jul. 1892; *NYS,* 2 and 3 Jul. 1892; *CT,* 2 Jul. 1892; *PP,* 1, 2, and 6 Jul. 1892; *PP,* 2 Jul. 1892; *NYH,* 2 and 4 Jul. 1892.

76. *NYH,* 4 Jul. 1892. See also *NYW,* 4 Jul. 1892.

77. *PCG, NYW,* and *NYH,* 4 Jul. 1892; *PCG, PP, WDI,* and *NYH,* 8 Jul. 1892; *NYW,* 17 Jul. 1892. To judge from the coverage afforded McIlyar by the Homestead press over the course of the 1880s, his relationship to the steelworkers, and to the cause of labor republicanism he seemed to champion in 1892, was not particularly close. However, his public pronouncements during the lockout do suggest that his understanding of American society was anchored in a tradition far more critical of mainstream politics than that provided by the early advocates of the "social gospel."

78. Burgoyne, *Homestead Strike,* 48; *PCG, NYS,* and *NYH,* 5 Jul. 1892.

79. *NYW,* 4 and 6 Jul. 1892; *PP,* 6 Jul. 1892; *WDI,* 6 Jul. 1892; *NYH,* 5 Jul. 1892; *NYS,* 6 Jul. 1892.

80. U.S. Senate, *Report 1280,* 210–11, as quoted in Bemis, "Homestead Strike," 382.

81. *PP* and *NYS,* 6 Jul. 1892; Burgoyne, *Homestead Strike,* 48–49.

82. *PP, NYS,* and *NYH,* 6 Jul. 1892.

83. *PP, PCG, NYS, NYH,* and *NYW,* 6 Jul. 1892.

84. *NYW,* 6 Jul. 1892; *NYH,* 10 Jul. 1892; Wall, *Carnegie,* 546, 815; William Isherwood to Carnegie, 7 Jul. 1892, ACLC, vol. 17.

CHAPTER 21. *Silenced Minorities*

1. Of a total population of 592, there were 289 female residents of Homestead in 1880. In 1890 the total population was 7,911, of whom 3,541 were female. See app. B, and U.S. Bureau of the Census, *Eleventh Census* (1890), *Population,* pt. 1, 50:446. On working women in Greater Pittsburgh, see Kleinberg, *Shadow of the Mills.*

2. Gutman, review of *Lockout,* 275, first raised this question in 1966. On the number of East Europeans working at the Homestead Steel Works in July 1892, see, among others: *NYW,* 2 Jul. 1892; *PP, NYS,* and *NYH,* 4 Jul. 1892. The quotation is from Miner, *Homestead,* 17–18, a catalogue published in 1989 with an exhibition on Homestead at the Historical Society of Western Pennsylvania. Miner's account of the 1892 lockout is on pp. 7–9.

3. T. Bell, *Out of This Furnace,* esp. chap. 9, which focuses on the Homestead Lockout of 1892. On Bell see Berko, "Thomas Bell." "I as a young boy did not know anything about the history of my people," Berko quotes Bell as saying. "I

made up my mind to write a history of the Braddock Slovaks in order to tell the world that the Slovaks with their blood and lives helped build America." Bell's novel accomplishes this task to a large degree; however, his apparent allegiance to the familiar teleology, which sees immigrants engaged in a progressive march toward full participation in American life, skewed his vision with regard to the first generation of Slovak immigrants.

4. T. Bell, *Out of This Furnace*, 41.

5. *IW*, 29 Jul., 5 and 12 Aug. 1882; *NLT*, 24 Mar. 1883, 29 Jan. 1887, 28 Apr. 1888, 3, 13, 20, and 27 Apr., 15 June, and 20 Jul. 1889; *Commoner*, 28 Apr. 1888, 27 Apr. and 6 Jul. 1889; Garlock and Builder, "Data Bank," 234; *HM*, May 1882; *JUL*, June 1882; *PP*, 1, 3, 14, and 15 Jul. 1889; *NYH*, 13 Jul. 1889. Schooley's comments are in *HLN*, 20 Jul. 1889. On Elko see also *PP* and *PT*, 16 Jul. 1889; *Pittsburgh Press*, 14 and 15 Jul. 1889.

6. Brody, *Labor in Crisis*, explores ethnic tensions in the steel industry at a crucial period. For a recent overview of the role played by ethnicity in the U.S. labor movement, see Asher and Stephenson, "American Capitalism, Labor Organization, and the Racial/Ethnic Factor," 3–27. Albert Elko, a Rusyn steelworker and labor organizer who recently served as mayor of McKeesport, confirms a major theme explored by Asher and Stephenson: "There was an absolute iron curtain between ethnic groups" (interview with the author, 20 June 1983). Indeed, for Elko, whose father emigrated from the Austro-Hungarian Empire about the same time as did John Elko, the thought of interethnic solidarity in any era stretches credibility to its very limits.

7. Woman's "proper" sphere in the nineteenth century is explored by Welter, "Cult of True Womanhood"; Smith-Rosenberg, "Female World"; Kish-Sklar, *Beecher*.

8. *HLN*, 21 May and 2 Jul. 1892. The quotation is from 2 May 1885; the "Frank and Mamie" letters were published in consecutive issues from this date through 11 Jul. 1885. The coverage afforded women by the *HLN* was consistent throughout the period covered by this study, but see, in particular: a "romance" entitled "By the Waves," 13 Mar. 1886; "Fashion Notes," 20 Mar. 1886; "A Woman's Age," 27 Mar. 1886.

9. *HT*, 4, 11, and 18 Aug., 8 Sept. 1883, 26 Mar. 1884, 14 Feb. and 7 Nov. 1885; *HLN*, 18 Feb. 1888.

10. *PP*, 15 Jul. 1889; *WDI*, 13 Jul. 1889; Stowell, *Fort Frick*, 23; *NYW*, 14 Jul. 1889. Three years later, on 6 July 1892, the *NYW* noted that in the 1889 lockout women "were more violent than the men and took an active part in every demonstration." Among the accounts of the 1889 lockout that overlook the participation of women: Hogg, "Homestead Strike," 32–38; Fitch, *Steel Workers*, 119–22; Wall, *Carnegie*, 528–30; Bridge, *Inside History*, 199–201.

11. The quotations in the text, from the *Pittsburgh Press*, 14 Jul. 1889, and *WDI*, 13 Jul. 1889, are representative of the coverage afforded women and East Europeans by other daily papers that covered the 1889 lockout. See, among others: *PCT*, 12 Jul. 1889; *PP*, 1, 3, 11, 12, 14, 15, and 16 Jul. 1889; *PCG* and *PT*, 12 and 13 Jul. 1889; *NYTR* and *NYH*, 13 Jul. 1889.

12. On the participation of the Knights of Labor and the AAISW in the workers' Advisory Committee, see Bemis, "Homestead Strike," 381.

13. *PP*, 19 and 25 June 1892; *NYW*, 3 Jul. 1892; Burgoyne, *Homestead Strike*, 23–

25. Though McLuckie had spent his career trying to broaden the appeal of the labor movement, he was, like other veterans of labor reform, hardly immune to racism: in his speech of 19 June, he said that the question facing the steelworkers of Homestead was whether or not they would "live like white men" in the future.

14. *PP*, 22, 23, and 27 June 1892; Burgoyne, *Homestead Strike*, 32–34; *PD*, 26 June 1892.

15. *PP*, 28 June 1892; *PP*, and *NYW*, 2 Jul. 1892; *PP*, *NYS*, and *NYH*, 4 Jul. 1892. On 4 July the *PCG* reported that the Advisory Committee had asked the "Slavic" papers of several Eastern cities to request their readers to rebuff the efforts of Carnegie Steel to recruit new workers.

16. Stowell, *Fort Frick*, 86, 96; *CT*, 9 Jul. 1892; *PP*, *NYW*, *NYH*, and *WDI*, 8 Jul. 1892; Burgoyne, *Homestead Strike*, 93.

17. Cohen, "Steelworkers Rethink," 174, 177.

18. *HLN*, 12 Mar. 1892; *BT*, 30 Jul. 1892; *PCG*, 4 and 5 Jul. 1892; *PP*, 27 June and 4 Jul. 1892; *NYS*, 4, 16, and 17 Jul. 1892; *NYH*, 4 Jul. 1892; *NYW*, 2 and 18 Jul. 1892; *NLT*, 12 Nov. 1892; *WDI*, 18 and 19 Jul. 1892; Stowell, *Fort Frick*, 188–89, 280; Krause, *"Za Chlebom,"* 160. The quotation is from *NLT*, 24 Sept. 1892. On the leading East European steelworkers, see app. K.

19. *Leslie's Weekly*, 14 Jul. 1892; Burgoyne, *Homestead Strike*, 83–85; Stowell, *Fort Frick*, 51, 71–72; and U.S. House, *Report 2447*, ix, 93. This paragraph is also based on *BT*, *CDN*, *CT*, *HLN*, *IA*, *NYH*, *NYS*, *NYT*, *NYTR*, *NYW*, *PCG*, *PD*, *PP*, *PT*, *WDI*, and *YEV*, July 1892. See in particular: *PCG*, 5 Jul.; *NYH*, 7 Jul.; *CT*, 6 Jul.; *PP*, 7 and 8 Jul.; *NYT*, 7 Jul.; *WDI*, 7 and 8 Jul.; *NYW*, 7 Jul.; *NYS*, 7 Jul. According to the *PCG*, 9 July, the women were "boldly aggressive"; Stowell simply wrote that they were worse than the men (64).

Greenwald, "Women and Class," notes the involvement of Homestead women in the events of 6 July. See also Younger, "Paintings and Graphic Images,"224–36.

20. *PP*, *NYW*, and *WDI*, 7 Jul. 1892.

21. *NYS*, 7 Jul. 1892.

22. *PP*, *NYS*, and *NYW*, 7 Jul. 1892.

23. Stowell, *Fort Frick*, 71–72; *PP* and *NYS*, 7 Jul. 1892.

24. *NYS*, *PP*, *WDI*, and *NYH*, 7 Jul. 1892.

25. *NYH*, 7 Jul. 1892; *CT*, 6 Jul. 1892; *HLN*, 14 Apr. and 28 Sept. 1888, 27 Apr. 1889, 22 Feb. and 26 Apr. 1890, and 27 Feb. 1892.

26. Hogg, "Homestead Strike," 91; Wall, *Carnegie*, 557–59. *NYH* 7 Jul. 1892, and *CT*, 6 Jul. 1892 give the fullest account of the involvement of Homestead women in the defense of the town prior to the march to the Opera House.

Wall repeats the tired assertion that "the details of that bloody 6 July on the Monongahela have been told so often that they need no elaboration here," but he too goes on to erase and embellish parts of the historical record. While condemning the women for their bad behavior, he ignores their participation in the defense of the town, and he indicates that the Pinkertons who were killed in the gun battle with workers were in fact victims of the women who attacked them as they ran the gauntlet.

27. Of the secondary accounts, Wolff, *Lockout*, esp. 124, 127–30, is probably the most offensive with regard to East Europeans: he describes them as "impetu-

ous," "semi-hysterical," "the most blood-thirsty of all," and incapable of reason because, he maintains, they did not understand English.

28. On Bayard's family see: *Pittsburgh Bulletin*, 14 Mar. 1914; *Pittsburgh Press*, 4 Dec. 1930. The quotations in this and in succeeding paragraphs are from Bayard's column "Homestead's Women," *PD*, 10 Jul. 1892. For her consideration of properly feminine, "dainty" women, see: "Fair Woman's World," *PD*, 25 Sept. 1892; "Shopping in Paris," *PD*, 2 Oct. 1892; "Fair Woman's Realm," *PD*, 30 Oct. 1892.

29. In the early 1980s a Homestead worker I interviewed remarked that Byington, *Homestead*, was profoundly patronizing. "All she wrote about was the disgusting bathroom habits of us Slovaks." The grandfather of this worker, who did not want to be identified, participated in the 1892 lockout.

30. Ryan, *Women in Public*, 130–71.

31. *NYH*, 7 Jul. 1892; U.S. House, *Report 2224*, ix.

32. See, in addition to the volumes of the Pittsburgh Survey cited above, Commons, *Races and Immigrants*. For a critical overview of the Survey, as well as related literature, see McClymer, "Pittsburgh Survey."

33. *WDI*, 5 Sept., 1, 3, and 12 Oct, and 24 Nov. 1892; *PP*, 2 Sept., 1 and 4 Oct. 1892; *PD*, 3 and 22 Sept., 1 and 12 Oct., and 8 Nov. 1892; *YEV*, 23 and 24 Sept., 3 and 13 Oct. 1892; *NLT*, 26 Nov. and 15 Dec. 1892; Stowell, *Fort Frick*, 256, 259; Spahr, *America's Working People*, 148–58; Burgoyne, *Homestead Strike*, 296–97; Carnegie, *Autobiography*, 226–28; and the comments of an unidentified steelworker, CH-29, in Fitch, research notes, 1907.

34. Burgoyne, *Homestead Strike*, 83; Bakhtin, *Rabelais*, 255, emphasis in the original. Wolff, *Lockout*, 115, also employs the carnival metaphor.

35. Ladurie, *Carnival*, esp. 289–304; Jelavich, "Theater in Fin-de-Siècle Munich," 225–26; LaCapra, *Rethinking Intellectual History*, 294–306; Burke, *Popular Culture*, 178–204. The quotation attributed to the women of Homestead is from *NYW*, 7 Jul. 1892.

36. *WDI, CT*, and *NYH*, 11 Jul. 1892; Stowell, *Fort Frick*, 113–14; *WDI, CT*, and *NYS*, 13 Jul. 1892.

CHAPTER 22. *Winners and Losers*

1. This paragraph and the succeeding one are based on: Miller to Martin, 20 Jan. 1893, and Martin to Charles Foster, 13 Jan. 1892, both in Martin Papers; *NLT*, 3 Feb., 7 and 14 Jul. 1883, 8 Mar 1884, 27 Feb., 10 Apr., and 17 Jul. 1886, 11 May and 29 June 1889, 27 Sept. and 4 Oct. 1890, and 19 Mar. 1892; *HLN*, 21 Feb. 1885; AAISW, *Proceedings*, 1882, 787, 1039; AAISW, *Proceedings*, 1889, 2601; Burgoyne, *Homestead Strike*, 196–97.

2. *PCG*, 7 Jul. 1892; Mavrinac, "Labor Organization," 98.

3. This paragraph and the succeeding one are based on: Burgoyne, *Homestead Strike*, 183, 297; Carnegie, *Autobiography*, 227–28; *HLN*, 13 Mar. 1893, as quoted in Berman, "O'Donnell," 47.

4. My sketch of Crawford is based principally on: Spahr, *America's Working People*, 154–56; Burgoyne, *Homestead Strike*, 166, 195, 196, 197, 214, 226–27; Stowell, *Fort Frick*, 188–89, 244, 249–50; *NYTR*, 17 and 18 Jul. 1892; *WDI, NYH*,

NYW, and *CT,* 18 Jul. 1892; *NYS,* 17 Jul. 1892; *WDI* and *NYW,* 1 Aug. 1892; *PP* and *PD,* 2 and 3 Aug. 1892; *NLT,* 3 Sept. and 8 Oct. 1892; *PD,* 4 Sept. 1892; *PP,* 21 Nov. 1892.

5. It seems likely that Crawford was also interviewed by Fitch as part of his research for *Steel Workers.* Much of the information provided by the informant labeled CH-29 in Fitch's field notes conforms to the known details of Crawford's life.

6. This paragraph and the succeeding two are based on: *WDI,* 1. Oct. 1892; Stowell, *Fort Frick,* 256, 259; *PD,* 4 Sept., 1 and 3 Oct. 1892; *PP,* 4 Oct. 1892; *NLT,* 3 Sept. and 8 Oct. 1892; Burgoyne, *Homestead Strike,* 197; Spahr, *America's Working People,* 156; Hogg, "Homestead Strike," 127–28, 131; *Pittsburgh Legal Journal* 13 (26 Oct. 1892), 106–10.

7. On Waasilefski see, among others: Schooley and Schooley, *Homestead Directory, 1892,* 182; *HT,* 1 Apr. and 18 Nov. 1882, 4 and 14 Feb. 1884, 21 Mar. 1885, 26 Apr. 1890, and 2 May 1891; *Homestead Eagle,* 12 and 19 May, 1888; Evelyn Patterson, interview with the author, 11 Oct. 1981.

8. AAISW, *Proceedings,* 1891, "Membership Abstract"; *WDI,* 13 Jul. 1892; *NYH,* 12 Jul. 1892; *PP,* 21–23 and 26–28 June, 2, 4, and 8 Jul. 1892; Krause, "*Za Chlebom,*" 160. When East European and Anglo-American workers were accidentally killed in an open-hearth accident in late 1889, the Homestead lodges of the AAISW combined to honor and bury them together.

9. *NYW* and *NYS,* 8 Jul. 1892; *CT,* 9 Jul. 1892; *NYH,* 10 Jul. 1892; Burgoyne, *Homestead Strike,* 96.

10. Burgoyne, *Homestead Strike,* 86, 95–96, 103; *WDI,* 8 Jul. 1892; *NYW,* 9 Jul. 1892.

11. *WDI,* 8 Jul. 1892; *NYS* and *WDI,* 9 Jul. 1892; *CT,* 9 and 12 Jul. 1892; Burgoyne, *Homestead Strike,* 96–97; Stowell, *Fort Frick,* 104.

12. Burgoyne, *Homestead Strike,* 103; *NYW* and *NYS,* 9 Jul. 1892; *WDI,* 8 and 9 Jul. 1892; *NYH,* 9 and 12 Jul. 1892; *CT,* 10 Jul. 1892; Stowell, *Fort Frick,* 95.

13. Burgoyne, *Homestead Strike,* 97; *WDI,* 9 and 11 Jul. 1892; *CT,* 9, 11, and 12 Jul. 1892; Stowell, *Fort Frick,* 104, 113–14; Pennsylvania, *Annual Report of the Adjutant General, 1892,* 46, 71; Hogg, "Homestead Strike," 99; *NYH,* 10 and 11 Jul. 1892.

14. *NYW, NYH, WDI, CT,* and *NYS,* 11 Jul. 1892. The governor's agents who came to Homestead for a reconnaissance mission had posed as newspaper reporters. This was the chief reason for the Advisory Committee's subsequent decision to monitor carefully the activities of the press.

15. *WDI,* 12 Jul. 1892; *NYH,* 11 Jul. 1892; Berkman, *Prison Memoirs,* 25–26, as cited in Berman, "O'Donnell," 35. Berkman, the man who tried to assassinate Frick, attended the meeting of 11 July in Homestead and heard O'Donnell implore the crowd to welcome the state militia. According to Berman, even O'Donnell was not so naive as to believe that the state militiamen were friends: "Since the guard was going to occupy the town anyway, why not try to fraternize with it?"

16. *NYS,* 10 and 11 Jul. 1892; *CDN,* 11 Jul. 1892.

16. *WDI, CT,* and *NYS,* 12 Jul. 1892.

18. This paragraph and the succeeding three are based on: Burgoyne, *Homestead Strike,* 111–12; Schneider, "Citizen Striker," 64–65; *NYS, NYW, NYH,* and *WDI,* 12 Jul. 1892.

19. For Schneider the workers' decision effectively to throw in the towel was grounded in the republican tradition, which, she affirms, nurtured in them a naively fallacious belief in the inherent justice of the American state, allowed them to recognize "only some aspects of their oppression," and therefore circumscribed "the bounds of class conflict."

20. The English-language press invariably had difficulty with Slovak and other East European names, and daily newspapers spelled Fagula's name in a number of inventive ways, among them Figaro, Fugala, and Figuld. Similarly, Pavel Olšav, another Slovak leader, was often referred to as Paul Oldshue, a name familiar to residents of Mifflin Township because an Anglo-American family of that name lived there. Slovak-language sources and parish records, examined in conjunction with the English-language press, confirm, however, that it was indeed František Fagula who spoke at the meeting of 11 July and who, together with Olšav, served as an important Slovak leader throughout the lockout of 1892.

21. This paragraph and the following one are based on: Pennsylvania, *Annual Report of the Adjutant General, 1892*, 72–73; *WDI*, 13 Jul. 1892; *NYH*, 12 Jul. 1892; Burgoyne, *Homestead Strike*, 112–13, 116–19, 121; Hogg, "Homestead Strike," 100; Carnegie to Frick, 2 Aug. 1890, 3:35 P.M., Carnegie Papers, USX Archives.

22. Marsh, "Captain Fred," provides an overview of the state militia's summer-long encampment at Homestead.

23. *WDI, CT, NYS*, and *NYH*, 13 Jul. 1892.

24. This paragraph and the succeeding two are based on: *WDI, NYH*, and *CT*, 13 Jul. 1892; *NYW*, 14 Jul. 1892; Schooley and Schooley, *Homestead Directory* (1891), 48; Burgoyne, *Homestead Strike*, 120–22, 124; Stowell, *Fort Frick*, 130; Pennsylvania, *Annual Report of the Adjutant General, 1892*, 75.

25. *NYW*, 14 Jul. 1892; *NYS*, 15 Jul. 1892; Burgoyne, *Homestead Strike*, 133–34; David, "Upheaval at Homestead," 150; Stowell, *Fort Frick*, 137.

26. This paragraph and the following one are based on: *NYS, NYH*, and *WDI*, 16 Jul. 1892.

27. *PP*, 7 Jul. 1892, as quoted in Hogg, "Homestead Strike," 179.

28. This paragraph and the succeeding one are based on: *PCG, NYTR*, and *WDI*, 7 Jul. 1892; *NYH*, 11 Jul. 1892; *WDI*, 14 Jul. 1892; Hogg, "Homestead Strike," 178–81.

29. *YEV*, 11 Jul. 1892; Hogg, "Homestead Strike," 184–86.

30. This paragraph and the following two are based principally on: *Congressional Record*, 52d Cong., 1st sess., Senate, vol. 33, pt. 6, pp. 5824–25, and pt. 7, pp. 7013–14, as quoted in Hogg, "Homestead Strike," 184–85; David, "Upheaval at Homestead," 162; Burgoyne, *Homestead Strike*, 99; *NYH*, 8 Jul. 1892.

31. de Tocqueville, *Democracy in America*, 450–54.

32. *PCG*, 12 Jul. 1892, and *Richmond Times*, 10 Jul. 1892, both as quoted in Hogg, "Homestead Strike," 185; *Nation*, as quoted in David, "Upheaval at Homestead," 164; David, "Upheaval at Homestead," 162, 163.

33. *YEV*, 11 Jul. 1892.

34. Thompson, "Moral Economy"; Scheiber, "Public Rights," esp. 222–24. Also of interest is Rose, "Comedy of the Commons."

35. See, among others: Boyer and Nissenbaum, *Salem Possessed*; E. Foner, *Paine*, esp. chap. 5; Dublin, "Women, Work, and Protest"; Wilentz, "Against

Exceptionalism"; L. Fink, *Workingman's Democracy;* Goodwyn, *Democratic Promise;* Salvatore, *Debs,* pts. 1, 2; Fine, *Sit-Down.* In an important series of articles, Staughton Lynd has carefully explored the steel mill closings in Pittsburgh and Youngstown in the 1970s and 1980s: "Communal Rights"; "Resisting Plant Shutdowns"; "Community Right"; "View from Steel Country"; "Not-For-Profit Economy."

36. The labor qualification to ownership, which derives chiefly from Locke, *Second Treatise of Government* (1690), and the idea that labor is the source of all wealth, explicated by Smith in *The Wealth of Nations* (1776), were fundamental tenets of nineteenth-century labor republicanism.

37. This paragraph and the succeeding one are based on: Carnegie Steel Company Limited, "Application for Reinstatement," July 1892, box 31, Carnegie Papers, USX Archives; *NYW,* 14, 16, and 18 Jul. 1892; *NYS,* 15 Jul. 1892; *NYTR,* 17 and 18 Jul. 1892; *WDI,* 18 and 19 Jul. 1892; *NYH,* 18 Jul. 1892; *CT,* 18 Jul. 1892; *NYS,* 17 Jul. 1892; Burgoyne, *Homestead Strike,* 135; Hogg, "Homestead Strike," 102–03; Montgomery, *House of Labor,* 38; Stowell, *Fort Frick,* 188–89.

38. My account of O'Donnell's activities in this and succeeding paragraphs is drawn from: *WDI,* 18 and 19 Jul. 1892; *NYS,* 17 Jul. 1892; *CT, NYH,* and *NYW,* 18 and 24 Jul. 1892; *NYTR,* 17 and 18 Jul. 1892; Burgoyne, *Homestead Strike,* 179–83; Stowell, *Fort Frick,* 188–89; Berman, "O'Donnell" 18–20; Bemis, "Homestead Strike," 383–86; Wall, *Carnegie,* 563–65; Harvey, *Frick,* 148–50.

39. David, "Upheaval at Homestead," 166, following Bemis, "Homestead Strike," 384, incorrectly states that O'Donnell acted with the unanimous support of the Advisory Committee. This was O'Donnell's own interpretation, which he told to a very sympathetic Bemis.

40. O'Donnell to Reid, 16 Jul. 1892 (in reality, c. 19 Jul. 1892), as reproduced in Bemis, "Homestead Strike," 384–85; Reid to Carnegie, 20 Jul. 1892, in Whitelaw Reid Papers, box 146, Library of Congress, as quoted in Wall, *Carnegie,* 567 and in Harvey, *Frick,* 149; Carnegie to Frick, 28 and 29 Jul. 1892, as quoted in Harvey, *Frick,* 152.

41. *NYW,* 14, 18, 21, and 24 Jul. 1892; *NYTR,* 17 and 18 Jul. 1892; *NYS,* 15 Jul. 1892; *WDI,* 18, 19, and 23 Jul. 1892; *NYS,* 17 Jul. 1892; Stowell, *Fort Frick,* 188–89; *NYH,* 21 and 23 Jul. 1892; *CT,* 18 Jul. 1892; *BT,* 23 Jul. 1892; *PP,* 21 Jul. 1892, as quoted in Berman, "O'Donnell," 21.

42. *PCT,* 18 Jul. 1892; *WDI,* 19, 20, 21, and 22 Jul. 1892; *NYH* 19 and 21 Jul. 1892; *CT* and *NYS,* 19 Jul. 1892; *NYW,* 19 and 20 Jul. 1892.

43. *WDI* and *NYH,* 21 Jul. 1892; *NYS,* 19 and 21 Jul. 1892; Pennsylvania, *Annual Report of the Adjutant General, 1892,* 76, 100; Hogg, "Homestead Strike," 114.

44. *NYS,* 22 and 23 Jul. 1892; *CT, NYW, WDI,* and *NYH,* 22 Jul. 1892; *CDN,* 22 Jul. 1892; *CT, NYW, NYH, NYS,* and *WDI,* 23 Jul. 1892; *PCT,* 20 and 21 Jul. 1892, as cited in Hogg, "Homestead Strike," 111.

45. This paragraph and the succeeding one are based on: *WDI,* 14 and 16 Nov. 1892; *NLT,* 19 Nov. 1892; *PD* and *PP,* 14 Nov. 1892; *YEV,* 16 Nov. 1892.

46. *WDI* and *NYH,* 23 Jul. 1892; *CDN,* 22 Jul. 1892; *NLT,* 30 Jul. 1892; Berman, "O'Donnell," 22. The full text of the Advisory Committee's address may be found in *NLT,* 30 Jul. 1892; *PP,* 23 Jul. 1892.

47. Burgoyne, *Homestead Strike,* 238–40; Hogg, "Homestead Strike," 188–91; David, "Upheaval at Homestead," 165. See also Hogg, "Pinkertonism."

48. The overview, in this and succeeding paragraphs, of the criminal charges brought against the steelworkers is based on: *NLT,* 30 Jul., 6 Aug., 10 Sept., 1 and 8 Oct., and 26 Nov. 1892; *PD,* 22 Sept. 1892; *YEV,* 23 Sept. 1892; *WDI* and *PD,* 1 Oct. 1892; *PD* and *YEV,* 3 Oct. 1892; *PD* and *WDI,* 4 Oct. 1892; *PD,* 5 Oct. 1892; *WDI,* 11 and 12 Oct. 1892; David, "Upheaval at Homestead," 168–70; Hogg, "Homestead Strike," 115, 125–31, 139–42; Stowell, *Fort Frick,* 256, 264; Burgoyne, *Homestead Strike,* 107, 189–207, 241–79, 280–95.

49. On the relationship of Paxson and Magee, see Burgoyne, *Homestead Strike,* 196.

50. The full text of Paxson's charge is in *Pittsburgh Legal Journal* 13 (26 Oct. 1892): 106–10. It was widely reprinted by the contemporary press. The House investigating committee came to the same conclusion: that the Advisory Committee and "their aiders and abettors," in trying to fend off Pinkertons, were "violators of private right and of the public peace." See U.S. House, *Report 2447,* xii.

51. *American Law Review,* as quoted by David, "Upheaval at Homestead," 169; *NLT,* 8 Oct. 1892.

52. Burgoyne, *Homestead Strike,* 83; *Pittsburgh Legal Journal* 13 (26 Oct. 1892): 110; Montgomery, *House of Labor,* 39.

53. I am indebted to Melvyn Dubofsky for bringing these points to my attention. "American political history may seem placid in comparison to that of other nations because violent labor conflicts have been traditionally defined as nonpolitical modes of mass action, while labor history has appeared so bloody because phenomena perceived elsewhere as political protest have been regarded in the United States as nonpolitical. If, however, we follow Tilly's definition of collective violence as political action by men (and women) 'seeking to seize, hold, or realign the levers of power,' then, American workers have continually engaged in collective violence as part of their economic and *political* struggles." See Dubofsky, "Homestead Strike," 1; Tilly, "Collective Violence in European Perspective."

54. On the dedication of the Carnegie Library in Ayr, Scotland, see Burgoyne, *Homestead Strike,* 207–08.

55. Carnegie's note of December 1868, in which he warns of the dangers of amassing wealth, is reprinted in: Wall, *Carnegie,* 224–25; McCloskey, *American Conservatism,* 144. See Wall, *Carnegie,* 570–76, for a sampling of the criticism directed at Carnegie in the wake of the Homestead Lockout; on the public response in general, see Hogg, "Homestead Strike," 173–93. For Carnegie's retrospective account of the lockout, see his *Autobiography,* 219–30.

56. *St. Louis Post-Dispatch,* as quoted in Bridge, *Inside History,* 233–34.

57. Carnegie, *Dedication,* 12–13, 15. On the Homestead library, see: Carnegie, "Dedication of Homestead Library," unpaginated typescript, 5 Nov. 1898, box 39, Carnegie Papers, USX Archives; Miner, "Deserted Parthenon."

58. *NLT,* 30 Jul. 1892.

59. Hoftstadter, *American Political Tradition,* 118–74; de Tocqueville, *Democracy in America,* 136, 178–79, 258–59, 414–18.

60. De Tocqueville, *Democracy in America,* 417–18.

61. Ibid., 454.

62. The quotations are from Merrill, "Interview with Gutman," 334.

63. Schneider, "Republicanism Reinterpreted," 211; Schneider, "Citizen Striker," esp. 59–60. Also relevant is Schneider's unpublished essay "American

Iron and Steel Workers Reinterpret Republicanism." Roberts's testimony may be found in U.S. Senate, *Report 1280*, 210–11. They are reprinted in Bemis, "Homestead Strike," 382; and (with a significant ellipses) Schneider, "Citizen Striker," 59.

Neither Roberts nor James Boyce, who also stated that the workers' resistance grew partly out of a desire to defend their homes, was a homeowner. As Schneider herself notes, the AFL, the AAISW, and the Advisory Committee estimated that roughly 8–10 percent of the Homestead steelworkers owned their own homes. On the basis of my own review of Allegheny County, Board of Assessment Real Property and Assessment Books: Homestead and Mifflin Township, 1883–1892, this figure may be somewhat low, at least among the more prominent members of the AAISW. Of the 146 union men I was able to identify as having played a role in the lockout, 25 (17 percent) were homeowners; 13 (38 percent) of the 34 identifiable members of the Advisory Committee were homeowners. Of the 333 East European immigrants identified as steelworkers or as having close ties to them, only 28 (8 percent) were property owners. See apps. J and K for additional details.

64. Armstrong, "Coming Struggle," *NLT*, 22 May 1875. On Debs's support in Homestead, see Fitch, research notes, CH-11, 1908; M. Nash, "Conflict and Accommodation," 139–45.

65. On the paradox of the laborer as citizen as opposed to factor of production, see Montgomery, *Beyond Equality*, 252.

66. *IA*, 28 Jul. 1892; *PCG*, 27 Jul. 1892, as quoted in Hogg, "Homestead Strike," 183; *AM*, 22 Jul. 1892, as quoted in Hogg, "Pinkertonism," 189; *NYH*, 11 Jul. 1892.

67. *NYW* and *NYH*, 24 Jul. 1892; *WDI*, 25 Jul. 1892. Virtually all secondary accounts of the Homestead Lockout retell the story of Berkman's assault on Frick. Harvey, *Frick*, 136–45, is perhaps the most complete; the quotations in the text are from pp. 139, 140. Also see Burgoyne, *Homestead Strike*, 146–52. Several attempts have been made to situate Berkman's assault and his politics in general within the American political tradition, but many questions, well beyond the scope of this study, remain. See Berkman's autobiographical account, *Prison Memoirs*; Christoph, "Berkman"; Nowlin, "Berkman"; Ward, "Berkman."

68. *CT*, 24 Jul. 1892; *YEV*, 25 Jul. 1892; Burgoyne, *Homestead Strike*, 151; Stowell, *Fort Frick*, 215–16.

69. *WDI*, *NYH*, *NYW*, and *CT* 25 Jul. 1892; *PD*, 24 Jul. 1892, as reprinted in *WDI*, 26 Jul. 1892; Burgoyne, *Homestead Strike*, 152–54; Stowell, *Fort Frick*, 220–21.

70. *PP*, 26 Jul. 1892, as quoted in Berman, "O'Donnell," 22. O'Donnell's statement appeared in *NYS*, 27 Jul. 1892. My account of his maneuvering in the wake of Berkman's assassination attempt is based on: *PP*, *WDI*, *NYH*, *CT*, *NYW*, *NYS*, and *YEV*, 27 Jul. 1892; *WDI*, *NYW*, and *NYH*, 28 Jul. 1892; Stowell, *Fort Frick*, 249–50; *WDI* and *PD*, 12 Aug. 1892.

71. Bemis, "Homestead Strike," 387.

72. *WDI*, 13 Aug. 1892; *PD*, 8 and 9 Sept. 1892; Marsh, "Captain Fred," 310.

73. *PD* and *PP* 4 Oct. 1892; *PD*, 5 and 6 Oct., and 8 Nov., 1892; *YEV*, 12, 13, and 17 Oct. 1892; *WDI*, 16 Nov. 1892; *PP*, *WDI*, and *PD*, 18 Nov. 1892; *WDI*, *PD*, and *YEV*, 21 Nov. 1892; *PP*, 21 Nov. 1892; Burgoyne, *Homestead Strike*, 209–40, which differs in some details from my account of the denouement of the lockout.

74. U.S. House, *Report 2447*, 9; Stevens, "The Men Who Run the Mills,"

manuscript; "Reid Kennedy's Speech," Library Files, Carnegie Library, Homestead, as quoted in Miner, "Deserted Parthenon," 112; Rosenberg, "Wages versus the Library," 3; Burgoyne, *Homestead Strike*, 195, 196, 197.

75. Holt, "Trade Unionism," 35. Also see Merrill, "Interview with Gutman," 333.

76. Holt, "Trade Unionism," 15.

77. Byington, *Homestead*, 175; Fitch, *Steel Workers*, chaps. 16, 18, esp. pp. 216, 232, 235. Also see Garland, "Homestead." Gutman's comments are of interest: "The really critical year, I think, was 1892. If you locate events that tell us something about essential changes that shaped and reshaped the consciousness of working-class leaders and radicals, of trade unionists, on a time continuum, then 1892 was a big year. The Homestead lockout, the Buffalo switchmen's strike, the Tennessee coal strikes, the New Orleans general strike, the Idaho mining strikes in Coeur d'Alene. The use of state power in the early 1890s against these workers was staggering! In the late 1880s and early 1890s there was a growing awareness among workers that the state had become more and more inaccessible to them and especially to their political and economic needs and demands" (Merrill, "Interview with Gutman," 333).

78. Mack to McCollough, 1 Feb. 1896, Bureau of Information, Letters to Operatives, 1896–1907, box 3, Carnegie Papers, USX Archives; Burgoyne, *Homestead Strike*, 297; Marcus, "Change and Continuity," 69–70; Marcus, with Moore and Bullard, "Populist Party," 275–76.

79. *NLT*, 19 Apr. 1890; Allegheny County, Board of Assessment, Real Property and Assessment Books: Homestead, 1892, ward 1.

80. *WDI* and *PD*, 10 Aug. 1892; Northwestern Historical Association, *Allegheny County*, 444–45; *PD*, 2 Sept. 1902.

81. Appleby, "One Good Turn," 1331; Moore, *Injustice*; Merrill, "Interview with Gutman," 335; R. Williams, *Marxism and Literature*, 108–14; Lears, "Cultural Hegemony." Cf. Montgomery, *House of Labor*, 2, which takes as its starting point the questionable notion that, during the period under consideration, American workers held a "shared presumption that individualism was appropriate only for the prosperous and wellborn." Peter Wood's cautionary remarks regarding patterns of slave resistance and rebellion are most germane. To separate slave reactions into docility on the one hand, and resistance on the other, he suggests, "is to underestimate the complex nature of the contradictions each Negro felt in the face of new provocations and new penalties. It is more realistic to think in terms of a spectrum of response, ranging from complete submission to total resistance, along which any given individual could be located at a given time" (Wood, *Black Majority*, 285).

82. Carnegie to Frick, late November 1892, as quoted in Harvey, *Frick*, 172; Wall, *Carnegie*, 570, 576–77, which cites the *Times* (London), 31 Jan. 1893, as the source of Carnegie's Homestead speech.

83 The quotations in this and in the next paragraph are from Carnegie, "Dedication of Homestead Library," box 39, Carnegie Papers, USX Archives.

84. *PCG*, 5 and 6 Nov., 1895.

85. This paragraph and the succeeding one are based on: *PCG*, 5 and 6 Nov., 1895; Bridge, *Inside History*, 295–96. Carnegie made these remarks at the dedication of the Carnegie Library of Pittsburgh.

86. Carnegie, *Autobiography,* 223.

87. Epigraph to the "The Bell Tower," Herman Melville, *Billy Budd, Sailor, and Other Stories* (New York: Penguin Books, 1986), 140.

88. Most popular writing about Carnegie and American steelmaking remains largely uncritical. See, for example, McCullough, "Case for Pittsburgh," 66; Warren, "Frick," 13.

APPENDIX A. *What Is Steel?*

1. The details in this and succeeding paragraphs are drawn principaly from: Holley, "What Is Steel"; Prime, "What Steel Is"; AIME, Proceedings of the Philadelphia Meeting, October 1876, *AIME Transactions* 5 (1876–77): 19–20; Wedding, "Nomenclature of Iron"; Metcalf, "Commercial Nomenclature and Scientific Definitions"; Howe, "Nomenclature of Iron."

2. Bessemer, *Autobiography,* 156–57; Prime, "Steel," 337. Most of the papers cited in n. 1 were presented to the AIME and then discussed by its members. The discussions include a number of acknowledgments by Bessemer manufacturers that they wanted to adopt the name *steel* for business reasons. In the initial issues of the *AISA Bulletin,* advertisements appeared for licenses to produce metal by the Bessemer process; they called the product wrought iron, homogeneous iron, or steel. See, for example, *AISA Bulletin,* 3 Mar. and 21 Aug. 1867.

3. Camp and Francis, *Making Steel,* 256; Wertime, *Age of Steel,* 13; Landes, *Unbound Prometheus,* 251.

4. Hall, "Manufacture of Bessemer Steel," 121–24. Also see Wertime, *Age of Steel,* 1–43, 207–17, 274–84.

5. Louis Emmanuel Gruner, *The Manufacture of Steel,* trans. Lenox Smith (New York: Van Nostrand, 1872), 8–9, as quoted in Prime, "What Steel Is," 330. A comprehensive treatise published in the 1920s by U.S. Steel noted, "An adequate definition of steel is lacking." (See Camp and Francis, *Making Steel,* 254.)

6. Wertime, *Age of Steel,* 191, 275; Camp and Francis, *Making Steel,* 274.

7. Durfee, "Manufacture of Steel, VIII," 732–33; Wertime, *Age of Steel,* 208–10; Camp and Francis, *Making Steel,* 245–46; McHugh, *Holley,* 84; Landes, *Unbound Prometheus,* 252; Overman, *Manufacture of Iron,* 474.

8. Ashton, *Iron and Steel,* 55; Camp and Francis, *Making Steel,* 246; Overman, *Manufacture of Iron,* 246; Landes, *Unbound Prometheus,* 252.

9. Camp and Francis, *Making Steel,* 246–47; Durfee, "Manufacture of Steel, VIII," 734; Landes, *Unbound Prometheus,* 253–54.

10. Overman, *Manufacture of Iron,* 475–77; Durfee, "Manufacture of Steel, VIII," 735–36, 738–39; Camp and Francis, *Making Steel,* 246–47; Wertime, *Age of Steel,* 191–207.

11. Frederick A. P. Barnard, Machinery and Processes of the Industrial Arts and Apparatus of the Exact Sciences," in U.S. Senate, *Reports on the Paris Exposition,* 3:283–84; Hewitt, "Production of Iron and Steel," in ibid., 2:6–8; Temin, *Iron and Steel,* 19–20; Ashton, *Iron and Steel,* 56; Camp and Francis, *Making Steel,* 247.

12. Overman, *Manufacture of Iron,* 477–78; Camp and Francis, *Making Steel,* 253, 452; Durfee, "Manufacture of Steel, VIII," 38–39.

13. Barnard, "Machinery and Processes," in U.S. Senate, *Reports on the Paris Exposition,* 3:284; McHugh, *Holley,* 85; Landes, *Unbound Prometheus,* 254. Another method of making steel was to puddle it—an extremely difficult process that American steelmasters largely ignored.

APPENDIX B. *The Homestead Census of 1880*

1. My demographic profile of Homestead in 1880 is based on U.S. Bureau of the Census, *1880 Census,* population schedules for Homestead, 461–66.

2. In 1880 in Allegheny County 88,666 out of 355,869 residents, or about 25 percent of the total population, were immigrants. See U.S. Bureau of the Census, *1890 Census, Population Compendium,* 446.

APPENDIX D. *Homestead Glassworkers, 1879–1882*

1. This appendix is based on U.S. Bureau of the Census, *1880 Census,* Homestead, and the newspapers published there from 1880 through 1882.

APPENDIX E. *Founding Members of General Griffin Post 207, Grand Army of the Republic*

1. Principal sources are: *HLN,* 30 May 1885; Hopkins Co., *Atlas of the County of Allegheny,* 1876, 36; *HT,* 30 July and Oct. 29 1881, 18 Mar., 28 Oct., and 9 Dec. 1882, 7 Apr. and 10 Nov. 1883; Warner Co., *Allegheny County,* pt. 2, pp. 663, 716.

APPENDIX F. *Incorporators of Homestead*

1. Principal sources are: Schooley and Schooley, *Homestead Directory,* 1892, 5–7; U.S. Bureau of the Census, *1880 Census,* Homestead; *HLN,* 30 May 1885. The information regarding affiliation with political parties is drawn from Homestead newspapers. The fourteen petitioners (38 percent of the total) who had at least one non-native parent are: Bryson, Cox, Hays, Izenour, Lloyd, Lowry, MacDonald, Marshall, Spellman, Thomas, Edward West, Wilkinson, Will, and Williams.

APPENDIX G. *Homestead Councilmen, 1880–1881*

1. Principal sources are: Schooley and Schooley, *Homestead Directory, 1892,* 8; U.S. Bureau of the Census, *1880 Census,* Homestead; Northwestern Historical Association, *Allegheny County,* 1:510; Warner Co., *Allegheny County,* pt. 2, pp. 603, 704; *HLN,* 11 Oct. 1884 and 14 Feb., 18 Apr., 23 and 30 May 1885; *HT,* 30 July and 5 Nov. 1881, 28 Oct. and 23 Sept. 1882, and 17 Mar. 1883.

APPENDIX H. *Selected Office Holders, Homestead, 1880–1892*

1. Information on town officers comes from a variety of sources: city directories, county histories, newspapers in Pittsburgh and Homestead, and union records.

APPENDIX I. *The City Poor Farm: Selected Documents*

1. The documents reproduced in this appendix are located in Real Estate Document Files, Carnegie-Illinois, Plant: Homestead, box 13, and Document File no. 5840, Carnegie Steel Co., Ltd., Abstract of Title, Homestead Steel Works, Parts 1 and 2, both in the USX Archives.

APPENDIX J. *Selected Leaders of the Homestead Steelworkers, 1892*

1. This appendix is based principally on newspapers published in Homestead and Pittsburgh, the *National Labor Tribune*, various church records, and the *Proceedings* of the AAISW. In addition, this informal census draws upon Allegheny County Board of Assessment, Real Property and Assessment Books for Homestead from 1883 to 1892, and Burgoyne, *Homestead Strike*.

2. Burgoyne, *Homestead Strike*, 194; Hogg, "Homestead Strike," 131.

APPENDIX K. *Selected Members of the East European Community in Homestead, 1892*

1. Principal sources are the parish records of Homestead and Braddock churches, the *Homestead Local News*, the membership list of Homestead's lodge in the First Catholic Slovak Union, and Allegheny County Board of Assessment, Real Property and Assessment Books for Homestead from 1883 to 1892. In most cases, I have followed the spellings provided in the sources—sources largely created by persons unfamiliar with East European languages.

Bibliography

PRIMARY SOURCES

MANUSCRIPTS AND MANUSCRIPT COLLECTIONS

Carnegie, Andrew. Papers. Library of Congress, Washington, D.C.
———. Papers. USX Corporation, Annandale Archives, Boyers, Pa.
Carnegie Steel Company. Real Estate Document Files. USX Corporation, Annandale Archives, Boyers, Pa.
Dickson, William Brown. Papers. Pennsylvania State University Library, University Park.
First Catholic Slovak Union, Lodge 26, Homestead, Pa. Membership List. Immigration History Research Center, University of Minnesota, Minneapolis.
Fitch, John A. Research notes and field interviews for *The Steel Workers*, 1907–08. Photoduplicates in possession of the author.
Flinn, William. Scrapbooks. Microfilm. Reel 4, vols. 14–19. Archives of Industrial Society, University of Pittsburgh Libraries.
Hayes, John William. Papers. Catholic University of America, Washington, D.C. Microfilm in University of Pittsburgh Libraries.
Holley, Alexander L. Blueprints for the Edgar Thomson Steel Works. Smithsonian Library, Washington, D.C.
———. Letterbooks, 1877–1882. Microfilm. Division of Mechanical and Civil Engineering, National Museum of American History, Washington, D.C.
———. Papers. Division of Mechanical and Civil Engineering, National Museum of American History, Washington, D.C.
Holy Trinity Church, Duquesne, Pa. Miscellaneous Papers. Roman Catholic Diocesan Archives, Pittsburgh.
Jones, Benjamin Franklin. Diary. In "Historical Miscellanea," Jones and Laughlin Corporation. Archives of Industrial Society, University of Pittsburgh Libraries.
Kacinzy, Rev. A. Papers. Roman Catholic Diocesan Archives, Pittsburgh.
Mackintosh-Hemphill Company. Records. Archives of Industrial Society, University of Pittsburgh Libraries.
Martin, William. Papers. Archives of Industrial Society, University of Pittsburgh Libraries.
Morris, J. M. Scrapbook. Clippings on the 1877 "Riot" in Pittsburgh. Archives of Industrial Society, University of Pittsburgh Libraries.
Powderly, Terrence V. Papers. Catholic University of America, Washington, D.C.

Microfilm in University of Pittsburgh Libraries and Davis Library, University of North Carolina at Chapel Hill.

Roman Catholic Diocese of Pittsburgh. Annual Census of Parishes in Pittsburgh and Allegheny County, 1877–1970. Microfilm. Archives of Industrial Society, University of Pittsburgh Libraries.

———. Miscellaneous Letters on "Greek Catholics." Roman Catholic Diocesan Archives, Pittsburgh.

St. Anne's Roman Catholic Church, Homestead, Pa. Miscellaneous Papers. Archives of Industrial Society, University of Pittsburgh Libraries.

St. Anthony's Roman Catholic Church, Homestead, Pa. Miscellaneous Papers. Roman Catholic Diocesan Archives, Pittsburgh.

St. Francis Church, Homestead, Pa. Register of Baptism, Marriage, and Death, 1891– . St. Mary Magdalene Church, Homestead, Pa.

St. John the Baptist Ukrainian Catholic Church, Pittsburgh. Registers of Baptism, Marriage, and Death. St. John the Baptist Ukrainian Catholic Church, Pittsburgh.

St. Mary Magdalene Church, Homestead, Pa. Register of Baptism. Vols. 1–2 (1881–1904). St. Mary Magdalene Church, Homestead, Pa.

———. Register of Marriage. Vol. 1 (1881–1908). St. Mary Magdalene Church, Homestead, Pa.

St. Michael's Roman Catholic Church, Braddock, Pa. Baptismal Register. Vol. 1 (1891–1905). St. Michael's Roman Catholic Church, Braddock, Pa.

———. Death Register, 1891–1952. St. Michael's Roman Catholic Church, Braddock, Pa.

———. Marriage Register. Vol. 1 (1891–1905). St. Michael's Roman Catholic Church, Braddock, Pa.

St. Wenceslaus Roman Catholic Church, Pittsburgh. Miscellaneous Records. Archives of Industrial Society, University of Pittsburgh Libraries.

Schamberg, Max. Papers. Personal collection of Jane Berkey, Pittsburgh.

Stevens, W. F. "Homestead as Is." Typewritten manuscript, 1941. Carnegie Library, Homestead, Pa.

———. "The Men Who Run the Mills." Typewritten manuscript, n.d. Carnegie Library, Homestead, Pa.

———. Homestead. Untitled typewritten manuscript, n.d. Carnegie Library, Homestead, Pa.

Stitt, Hallie V. "My Beloved Farm." Manuscript, n.d. Carnegie Library, Homestead, Pa.

Tiers, C. P. Letter to "Sallie," 23 July 1877. Photoduplicate in possession of the author.

Wider, Rev. Raymond. Papers. Roman Catholic Diocesan Archives, Pittsburgh.

PUBLIC DOCUMENTS

Allegheny County, Pa., Election Docket. Vols. 2–4, 1877–97. Allegheny County Courthouse. Pittsburgh.

Allegheny County, Pa., Board of Assessment and Revision of Taxes. Real Property and Assessment Books: Homestead and Mifflin, 1833–1892. Allegheny County Courthouse. Pittsburgh. Microfilm. Archives of Industrial Society. University of Pittsburgh Libraries.

Pennsylvania. *Annual Report of the Adjutant General of Pennsylvania, 1892*. Harrisburg: Edwin K. Meyers, State Printer, 1893.

Pennsylvania Bureau of Industrial Statistics. *Annual Report*. Vol. 1 (1872–73); vol. 3 (1874–75); vol. 4 (1875–76); vol. 5 (1876–77); vol. 9 (1880–81); vol. 10 (1881–82); vol. 11 (1882–83); vol. 15 (1887); vol. 17 (1889); vol. 20 (1892).

Pennsylvania General Assembly. *Report of the Committee Appointed to Investigate the Railroad Riots in July, 1877*. Harrisburg, Pa. Lane S. Hart, State Printer, 1878.

U.K. Parliament. *Second Report to the Commissioners Appointed to Inquire into the Organization and Rules of Trade Unions and Other Associations*. Parliamentary Sessional Papers, 1867, 32, c3893. Microfilm. Perkins Library, Duke University.

U.S. Bureau of the Census. *Tenth Census (1880)*. Vol. 2, *Manufacturing*. Washington, D.C.: Government Printing Office, 1883.

———. *Tenth Census (1880)*. *Population Schedule, Pennsylvania: Mifflin Township*. Vol. 4, pt. 3. Microfilm T-9, roll 1090. National Archives. Washington, D.C.

———. *Eleventh Census (1890)*. Vol. 1, *Population*, pt. 1; vol. 6, *Manufacturing*, pt. 3. Washington, D.C.: Government Printing Office, 1892–97.

U.S. Commissioner of Corporations. *Report on the Steel Industry*. 3 vols. Washington, D.C.: Government Printing Office, 1911–13.

U.S. Commissioner of Labor. *Eleventh Special Report of the Commissioner of Labor, Regulation and Restriction of Output*. Washington, D.C.: Government Printing Office, 1904.

U.S. Congress. House. *Hearings before the Special Committee to Investigate the Taylor and Other Systems of Shop Management*. Washington, D.C.: Government Printing Office, 1911.

———. *Investigation By a Select Committee of the House of Representatives Relative to the Causes of the General Depression in Labor and Business*. 45th Cong., 3d sess. Misc. Doc. no. 29. Washington, D.C.: Government Printing Office, 1879.

———. *Labor in Europe*. 48th Cong., 2d sess. Washington, D.C.: Government Printing Office, 1884.

———. Committee on the Judiciary. *Report 2447: Investigation of Homestead Troubles*, 52d Cong., 2d sess., 1892–93. Washington, D.C.: Government Printing Office, 1893. Cited in the notes as U.S. House, *Report 2447*.

U.S. Congress. Senate. *Report of the Committee of the Senate upon the Relations between Labor and Capital*. 3 vols. Washington, D.C.: Government Printing Office, 1885.

———. *Report on the Conditions of Employment in the Iron and Steel Industry*. 62d Cong., 1st sess. Washington, D.C.: Government Printing Office, 1913. Vol. 1. *Wages and Hours of Labor*. Vol. 3. *Working Conditions and the Relations of Employers and Employees*.

———. *Reports of the United States Commissioners to the Paris Universal Exposition, 1867*. Washington, D.C.: Government Printing Office, 1870.

———. Committee on Finance. *Wholesale Prices, Wages, and Transportation, Report by Mr. Aldrich*. 4 vols. Senate Report 1394. 52d Cong., 2d sess., 1893.

———. Committee on Labor and Education. *Report 1280: Investigation in Relation to the Employment for Private Purposes of Armed Bodies of Men, or Detectives, in Connection with Differences between Workmen and Employers. 52 Cong., 2d sess., 1892–93. Washington, D.C.: Government Printing Office, 1893. Cited in the notes as U.S. Senate, *Report 1280.*

U.S. Department of Commerce and Labor. *Bulletin of the Bureau of Labor* 51. Washington, D.C.: Government Printing Office, 1904.

U.S. Department of Labor. Bureau of Labor Statistics. *History of Wages in the United States from Colonial Times to 1928.* Bulletin no. 604. Washington: Government Printing Office, 1934.

———. *Wages and Hours of Labor in the Iron and Steel Industry, 1907–1913.* Bulletin no. 168. Washington, D.C.: Government Printing Office, 1915.

———. *Wages and Hours of Labor in the Iron and Steel Industry, 1907–1915.* Bulletin no. 218. Washington, D.C.: Government Printing Office, 1917.

U.S. Immigration Commission. *Reports on Immigrants in Industries, Iron and Steel Manufacturing.* Vols. 8–9. Washington, D.C.: Government Printing Office, 1911.

U.S. Industrial Commission. *Reports.* Vols. 1, 7, 13. Washington, D.C.: Government Printing Office, 1899–1901.

NEWSPAPERS, TRADE PUBLICATIONS, AND UNION PROCEEDINGS

Amalgamated Association of Iron and Steel Workers. *Constitution, By-Laws and Rules of Order of the National Association and Subordinate Lodges.* Columbus, Ohio: Paul and Thrall, 1876.

Amalgamated Association of Iron and Steel Workers. *Constitution, By-Laws and Rules of Order of the National Association and Subordinate Lodges.* Pittsburgh: Herald Printing Co., 1878.

Amalgamated Association of Iron and Steel Workers. *Revised Constitution.* Pittsburgh: Herald Printing Co., 1882.

Amalgamated Association of Iron and Steel Workers. *Revised Constitution.* Pittsburgh: Amalgamated Association of Iron and Steel Workers, 1890.

Amalgamated Journal. 27 August 1942.

American Manufacturer and Iron World. 1880–92.

Amerikansky Russki Viestnik (Pittsburgh). 1894–1900.

Braddock Tribune. 1889–93.

Bulletin of the American Iron and Steel Association. 1866–82, 1888–92.

Chicago Daily News. 1889, 1892.

Chicago Tribune. 1889, 1892.

Commoner and American Glassworker. 1887–89.

Duquesne Times. 1889.

Elizabeth Herald. 1889–93.

Engineering and Mining Journal. 1866–82.

Homestead Eagle. 1888.

Homestead Local News. 1884–92.

Homestead Mirror. 1881–82.

Homestead Times. 1881–83.

Irish Pennsylvanian and Catholic News. 1891–92.

Irish World and American Industrial Liberator. 1879–82.

Iron Age. 1882, 1889, 1892.

John Swinton's Paper. 1883–88.

Journal of United Labor. 1880–89.

Knights of Labor, District Assembly 3. *Proceedings of the Second Quarterly Meeting, April 1888.* Pittsburgh: Snowden & Harrison, 1888.

———. *Proceedings for the First Quarterly Meeting, January 1889.* Pittsburgh: Devine & Co., 1889.

———. *Proceedings for the Second Quarterly Meeting, April 1889.* Pittsburgh: Devine & Co., 1889.

———. *Proceedings for the Third Quarterly Meeting, July 1889.* Pittsburgh: Homer L. McGaw, 1889.

———. *Proceedings for the First Quarterly Meeting, January 1890.* Pittsburgh: Devine & Co., 1890.

Knights of Labor, District Assembly 9. *Proceedings, January 1882.* Pittsburgh: J. H. Barrows & Co., 1882.

———. *Proceedings, July 1882.* Pittsburgh: J. H. Barrows & Co., 1882.

Knights of Labor, Local Assembly 300. *Report of the Fifth National Convention.* Pittsburgh: Herald Printing Co., 1889.

Národnie noviny (Martin, Slovakia). 1890–92.

National Labor Tribune. 1874–92.

New York Herald. 1889, 1892.

New York Sun. 1889, 1892.

New York Times. 1877, 1889, 1892.

New York Tribune. 1889, 1892.

New York World. 1889, 1890, 1892.

Ohio Valley Budget. 1888.

Pittsburgh Bulletin. 1 April 1911.

Pittsburgh Catholic. 1882–92.

Pittsburgh Chronicle Telegraph. 1882, 1889, 1890, 1892.

Pittsburgh Commercial-Gazette. 1877, 1882, 1889, 1892.

Pittsburgh Commercial. 1865–66, 1875.

Pittsburgh Dispatch. 1890, 1892, 1900.

Pittsburgh Evening Chronicle. 1882.

Pittsburgh Evening Telegraph. 1875, 1882.

Pittsburgh Gazette. 1868, 1871, 1874, 1895.

Pittsburgh Index. 28 March 1914.

Pittsburgh Post. 1865–67, 1877, 1882, 1889–1890, 1892, 1900.

Pittsburgh Press. 1882, 1889, 1892, 1895.

Pittsburgh Times. 1877, 1882, 1889–90, 1892.

Trades Journal (Pittsburgh). 1888–90.

Vulcan Record: Proceedings of the National Forge of the United States United Sons of Vulcan. 1867–75.

Wheeling (W. Va.) Daily Intelligencer. 1889, 1892.

Workingman (Philadelphia). 29 August 1882.

Youngstown (Ohio) Evening Vindicator. 1892.

Youngstown (Ohio) Weekly Telegram. 1892.

CONTEMPORARY ACCOUNTS AND SECONDARY SOURCES

Abelove, Henry, Betsy Blackmar, Peter Dimick, and Jonathan Schneer, eds. *Visions of History.* New York: Pantheon Books, 1983.

Alexander, John K. "The Fort Wilson Incident of 1779: A Case Study of the Revolutionary Crowd." *William and Mary Quarterly,* 3d ser., 31 (October 1974): 589–612.

Alexander, June Granatir. "City Directories as 'Ideal' Censuses: Slovak Immigrants and Pittsburgh's Early Twentieth-Century Directories as a Test Case." *Western Pennsylvania Historical Magazine* 65 (July 1982): 203–20.

———. "Staying Together: Chain Migration and Patterns of Slovak Settlement in Pittsburgh prior to World War I." *Journal of American Ethnic History* 1 (Fall 1981): 56–83.

Alexander, Sylvia June. "The Immigrant Church and Community: The Formation of Pittsburgh's Slovak Religious Institutions, 1880–1914." Ph.D. diss., University of Minnesota, 1980.

Allen, Robert C. "The Peculiar Productivity History of American Blast Furnaces, 1840–1913." *Journal of Economic History* 37 (1977): 605–33.

American Institute of Mining Engineers. "Committee Report on Nomenclature. *Transactions of the American Institute of Mining Engineers* 5 (1876): 19–20.

———. *Memorial of Alexander Lyman Holley.* New York: American Institute of Mining Engineers, 1884.

American Iron and Steel Institute. *A Selected List of Articles, Speeches, and Studies on the Steel Industry.* Washington, D.C.: American Iron and Steel Institute, 1973.

American Society of Mechanical Engineers. *Mechanical Engineers Born prior to 1861: A Biographical Dictionary.* New York: American Society of Mechanical Engineers, 1980.

Amsden, Jon, and Stephen Brier. "Coal Miners on Strike: The Transformation of Strike Demands and the Formation of a National Union." *Journal of Interdisciplinary History* 7 (1977): 583–616.

Anderson, Perry. *Arguments within English Marxism.* London: Verso, 1980.

Andrews, J. Cutler. "The Civil War and Its Aftermath." In *Pittsburgh: The Story of an American City.* Edited by Stefan Lorant, pp. 129–76. Garden City, N.Y.: Doubleday & Co., 1964.

Andrews, John B. "Nationalisation." In *History of Labor in the United States.* 4 vols. Edited by John R. Commons, 2: 3–191. New York: Macmillan Co., 1918–35.

Appleby, Joyce. "One Good Turn Deserves Another: Moving Beyond the Linguistic; A Response to David Harlan." *American Historical Review* 94 (1989): 1326–32.

• Asher, Robert. "Painful Memories: The Historical Consciousness of Steelworkers and the Steel Strike of 1919." *Pennsylvania History* 45 (1978): 61–86.

Asher, Robert, and Charles Stephenson. "American Capitalism, Labor Organization, and the Racial/Ethnic Factor: An Exploration." In *Labor Divided: Race and Ethnicity in United States Labor Struggles, 1835–1960.* Edited by Robert Asher and Charles Stephenson, 3–27. Albany: State University of New York Press, 1990.

Ashton, Thomas S. *Iron and Steel in the Industrial Revolution*. Manchester, England: University of Manchester Press, 1924.

Ashworth, John H. *The Helper and American Trade Unions*. Baltimore: Johns Hopkins Press, 1915.

Aston, James, and Edward B. Storey. *Wrought Iron: Its Manufacture, Characteristics, and Applications*. Pittsburgh: A. M. Byers Co., 1941.

Aurand, Harold. "Social Motivation of the Anthracite Mine Workers, 1901–1920." *Labor History* 18 (1977): 360–65.

Ayers, Phyllis L. "The History of Pennsylvania Sunday Blue Laws." M.A. thesis, University of Pittsburgh, 1952.

Babbage, Charles. *On the Economy of Machinery and Manufactures*. New York: Augustus M. Kelley, 1963 (1832).

Backert, Adolphus Otto, ed. *The ABC of Iron and Steel*. Cleveland, Ohio: Penton Publishing Co., 1925.

Bakhtin, Mikhail. *Rabelais and His World*. Translated by Helene Iswolsky. Cambridge, Mass.: MIT Press, 1968.

Balch, Emily Greene. *Our Slavic Fellow Citizens*. New York: Charities Publication Committee, 1910.

Baldwin, Leland D. *Pittsburgh: The Story of a City*. Pittsburgh: University of Pittsburgh Press, 1937.

Bannister, Robert C. *Social Darwinism: Science and Myth in Anglo-American Social Thought*. Philadelphia: Temple University Press, 1979.

Barnett, George Ernest. *Chapters on Machinery and Labor*. Cambridge, Mass.: Harvard University Press, 1926.

Barton, Josef J. *Peasants and Strangers: Italians, Rumanians, and Slovaks in an American City, 1870–1950*. Cambridge, Mass.: Harvard University Press, 1975.

Bayles, J. C. "The Engineer and the Wage Earner." *Transactions of the American Institute of Mining Engineers* 14 (1885–86): 327–36.

————. "A Tribute to Alexander Lyman Holley." *Transactions of the American Society of Mechanical Engineers* 3 (1882): 34–48.

Beard, Charles A., ed. *Toward Civilization*. New York: Longmans, Green, 1930.

Bell, I. Lowthian. *Notes of a Visit to Coal and Iron Mines and Ironworks in the United States*. 2d ed. Newcastle-on-Tyne: I. Lowthian Bell, 1875.

————. "On the Probable Future of the Manufacture of Iron." *Transactions of the American Institute of Mining Engineers* 19 (1890–91): 834–55.

————. *Principles of the Manufacture of Iron and Steel*. London: George Routledge Sons, 1884.

Bell, Thomas. *Out of This Furnace*. Pittsburgh: University of Pittsburgh Press, 1976 (1941).

Bemis, Edward. "The Homestead Strike." *Journal of Political Economy* 2 (June 1894): 369–96.

Bender, Thomas. "Wholes and Parts: The Need for Synthesis in American History." *Journal of American History* 73 (June 1986): 120–36.

Bennett, John W. "Iron Workers in Woods Run and Johnstown: The Union Era, 1865–95." Ph.D. diss., University of Pittsburgh, 1977.

Bennett, Sari J., and Carville V. Earle. "Labour Power and Locality in the Gilded Age: The Northeastern United States, 1881–94." *Histoire Sociale* 15 (November 1982): 383–405.

Berg, Maxine. *The Machinery Question and the Making of Political Economy, 1815–1848.* Cambridge: Cambridge University Press, 1980.

Berko, John. "Thomas Bell (1903–1961), Slovak-American Novelist. *Slovak Studies* 15 (1975): 143–58.

Berman, Paul. "A Chronology of Hugh O'Donnell at the Homestead Strike of 1892." Manuscript, 1976, author's possession.

———. "Democracy in the Union and in the Mill." Manuscript, 1976, author's possession.

———. "Negotiations." Manuscript, 1976, author's possession.

Berman, Paul, and Stephen Brier. "Homestead File." Manuscript, 1976, author's possession.

Bernstein, Iver. *The New York City Draft Riots: Their Significance for American Society and Politics in the Age of the Civil War.* New York: Oxford University Press, 1990.

Bernstein, Samuel. "American Labor in the Long Depression, 1873–1878." *Science and Society* 20 (Winter 1956): 59–83.

Berthoff, Rowland. *British Immigrants in Industrial America, 1790–1950.* Cambridge, Mass.: Harvard University Press, 1953.

———. "Peasants and Artisans, Puritans and Republicans: Personal Liberty and Communal Equality in American History." *Journal of American History* 69 (1982): 579–98.

———. "Welsh." In *Harvard Encyclopedia of American Ethnic Groups,* edited by Stephan Thernstrom, 1011–17. Cambridge, Mass.: Harvard University Press, 1980.

Bessemer, Henry. *An Autobiography.* London: Offices of *Engineering,* 1905.

Bew, Paul. *Land and the National Question in Ireland, 1858–1882.* Dublin: Gill & Macmillan, 1978.

Bining, Arthur C. *Pennsylvania Iron Manufacture in the Eighteenth Century.* Harrisburg: Pennsylvania Historical Commission, 1938.

———. *Writings on Pennsylvania History: A Bibliography.* Harrisburg: Pennsylvania Historical and Museum Commission, 1946.

Birch, Alan. *The Economic History of the British Iron and Steel Industry, 1784–1879: Essays in Industrial and Economic History with Special Reference to the Development of Technology.* New York: Augustus M. Kelley, 1968.

Blackenburg, Rudolph. "Forty Years in the Wilderness: Or Masters and Rulers of 'The Freemen' of Pennsylvania." *Arena* 33 (1905): 1–10, 113–27, 225–39, 345–60, 457–74, 569–83.

———. "The Ills of Pennsylvania," *Atlantic Monthly* 88 (1901): 558–66.

Blair, William Alan. "A Practical Politician: The Boss Tactics of Matthew Stanley Quay," *Pennsylvania History* 56 (1989): 77–92.

Blake, Casey. "Lewis Mumford: Values over Technique." *democracy* 3, 2 (Spring 1983): 125–37.

Bledstein, Burton. *The Culture of Professionalism: The Middle Class and the Development of Higher Education in America.* New York: W. W. Norton, 1976.

Blum, Jerome. *The End of the Old Order in Rural Europe.* Princeton: Princeton University Press, 1978.

Bodnar, John E. *Immigration and Industrialization: Ethnicity in an American Mill Town, 1870–1940.* Pittsburgh: University of Pittsburgh Press, 1977.

———. "Immigration and Modernization: The Case of Slavic Peasants in America." In *American Working-Class Culture: Explorations in American Labor and Social History.* Edited by Milton Cantor, 333–60. Westport, Conn.: Greenwood Press, 1979.

———. "Immigration, Kinship, and the rise of Workingclass Realism in Industrial America." *Journal of Social History* 14 (1980): 45–65.

———. *The Transplanted: A History of Immigrants in Urban America.* Bloomington: Indiana University Press, 1987.

Bodnar, John, ed. *The Ethnic Experience in Pennsylvania.* Lewisburg, Pa.: Bucknell University Press, 1973.

Bodnar, John E., Roger Simon, and Michael P. Weber. *Lives of Their Own: Blacks, Italians, and Poles in Pittsburgh, 1900–1960.* Urbana: University of Illinois Press, 1981.

Boston, Ray. *British Chartists in America, 1839–1900.* Manchester: Manchester University Press, 1971.

Boucher, John N. *William Kelly: A True History of the So-Called Bessemer Process.* Greensburg, Pa.: John N. Boucher, 1924.

Boyer, Paul. *Urban Masses and Moral Order in America, 1820–1920.* Cambridge, Mass.: Harvard University Press, 1978.

Boyer, Paul, and Stephen Nissenbaum. *Salem Possessed: The Social Origins of Witchcraft.* Cambridge, Mass.: Harvard University Press, 1974.

Braverman, Harry. *Labor and Monopoly Capital: The Degradation of Work in the Twentieth Century.* New York: Monthly Review Press, 1974.

Brecher, Jeremy. *Strike.* Cambridge, Mass.: Straight Arrow Books, 1972.

———, comp. *Brass Valley: The Story of Working People's Lives and Struggles in an American Industrial Region.* Philadelphia: Temple University Press, 1982.

Brecher, Jeremy, and the Work Relations Group. "Uncovering the Hidden History of the American Workplace." *Review of Radical Political Economics* 10 (Winter 1978): 1–23.

Bremner, Robert H. *American Philanthropy.* Chicago: University of Chicago Press, 1960.

Bridge, James H. *The Inside History of the Carnegie Steel Company.* New York: Aldine Book Co., 1903.

Brier, Steven. "Technological Change at Homestead, 1881–1892." Manuscript, 1976, author's possession.

British Iron and Steel Institute. *The Iron and Steel Institute in America in 1890.* London: British Iron and Steel Institute, n.d. (c. 1891).

Brody, David. "Labor." In *Harvard Encyclopedia of American Ethnic Groups,* edited by Stephan Thernstrom, 609–18. Cambridge, Mass.: Harvard University Press, 1980.

———. *Labor in Crisis: The Steel Strike of 1919.* Philadelphia: Lippincott, 1965.

———. "The Old Labor History and the New: In Search of an American Working Class." *Labor History* 20 (1979): 111–26.

———. "The Public World of Late Nineteenth-Century America." In James A. Henretta and others, *America's History,* 619–44. Chicago: The Dorsey Press, 1987.

———. "Rural America." In James A. Henretta and others, *America's History,* 588–618. Chicago: The Dorsey Press, 1987.

————. *Steelworkers in America: The Non-Union Era.* New York: Harper & Row, 1969.

————. *Workers in Industrial America: Essays on the Twentieth-Century Struggle.* New York: Oxford University Press, 1980.

Bruce, Robert V. *1877: Year of Violence.* Indianapolis: Bobbs-Merrill, 1959.

Buck, Peter. "Hard Driving and Efficiency: Iron Production in 1890." *Journal of Economic History* 38 (1978): 879–900.

Bucke, Emory S., and others, eds. *The History of American Methodism.* 3 vols. New York: Abingdon Press, 1964.

Buhle, Mary Jo. *Women and American Socialism, 1870–1920.* Urbana: University of Illinois Press, 1981.

Buhle, Paul. "The Knights of Labor in Rhode Island." *Radical History Review* 17 (1978): 39–73.

Burgoyne, Arthur G. *All Sorts of Pittsburghers, Sketched in Prose and Verse.* Pittsburgh: Leader All Sorts Co., 1892.

————. *The Homestead Strike of 1892.* Pittsburgh: University of Pittsburgh Press, 1979 (1893).

Burke, Peter. *Popular Culture in Early Modern Europe.* New York: Harper Torchbooks, 1978.

Burlingame, Roger. *Engines of Democracy: Inventions and Society in Mature America.* New York: Charles Scribner's Sons, 1940.

————. *March of the Iron Men: A Social History of Union through Invention.* New York: Charles Scribner's Sons, 1938.

Burn, D. L. *The Economic History of Steelmaking, 1867–1939.* Cambridge: Cambridge University Press, 1940.

Butler, Joseph G., Jr. *Fifty Years of Iron and Steel.* Cleveland, Ohio: Penton Press Co., 1922.

Byington, Margaret F. *Homestead: The Households of a Mill Town.* Pittsburgh: University Center for International Studies, 1974 (1910).

Byrn, Edward W. *The Progress of Invention in the Nineteenth Century.* New York: Munn Publishers, 1900.

Calhoun, Daniel H. *The American Civil Engineer: Origins and Conflict.* Cambridge, Mass.: Technology Press, 1960.

Calvert, Monte A. *The Mechanical Engineer in America, 1830–1910.* Baltimore: Johns Hopkins Press, 1967.

Cameron, Richard M. "The Church Divides." In *The History of American Methodism,* 3 vols. Edited by Emory S. Bucke and others, 2: 22–39. New York: Abingdon Press, 1964.

Camp, J. M., and C. B. Francis. *The Making, Shaping, and Treating of Steel.* Pittsburgh: Carnegie Steel Co., 1925.

Campbell, Henry Huse. *The Manufacture and Properties of Iron and Steel.* New York: Engineering and Mining Journal, 1903.

Cantor, Milton, ed. *American Working Class Culture: Explorations in American Labor and Social History.* Westport, Conn.: Greenwood Press, 1979.

Carnegie, Andrew. *Autobiography of Andrew Carnegie.* Boston: Northeastern University Press, 1986 (1920).

————. *Dedication of the Carnegie Library at the Edgar Thomson Steel Rail Works, Braddock: Address to Workingmen.* Pittsburgh: n.p., n.d. (c. 1889).

―――. *The Gospel of Wealth and Other Timely Essays*. New York: Century Co., 1900.

―――. *Triumphant Democracy, Or, Fifty Years' March of the Republic*. New York: Charles Scribner's Sons, 1886.

Carnegie, Brothers, and Company, Ltd. *Edgar Thomson Steel Works and Blast Furnaces*. Pittsburgh: Joseph Eichbaum & Co., 1891.

Carnegie Steel Co. *General Statistics and Special Treatise on the Homestead Steelworks*. Pittsburgh: Carnegie Steel Co., 1921.

Carr, J. C., and W. Taplin. *History of the British Steel Industry*. Cambridge, Mass.: Harvard University Press, 1952.

Cassity, Michael J. "Modernization and Social Crisis: The Knights of Labor and a Midwest Community, 1885–86." *Journal of American History* 66 (June 1979): 41–61.

Casson, Herbert N. *The Romance of Steel*. New York: A. S. Barnes & Co., 1907.

Caye, James, Jr. "Violence in the Nineteenth-Century Community: The Roundhouse Riot, Pittsburgh, 1877." Seminar paper, University of Pittsburgh, 1969.

Chambers, Clarke A. *Paul U. Kellogg and the Survey: Voices for Social Welfare and Social Justice*. Minneapolis: University of Minnesota Press, 1971.

Chandler, Alfred D., Jr. "Anthracite Coal and the Beginnings of the Industrial Revolution in the United States." *Business History Review* 46 (1972): 141–81.

―――. "The Beginnings of 'Big Business' in American Industry." *Business History Review* 33 (1959): 47–58.

―――. *The Visible Hand: The Managerial Revolution in American Business*. Cambridge, Mass.: Harvard University Press, 1977.

Christoph, James B. "Alexander Berkman and American Anarchism." M.A. thesis, University of Minnesota, 1952.

Clark, Sam. "The Social Composition of the Land League." *Irish Historical Studies* 17 (1971): 447–69.

―――. *The Social Origins of the Irish Land War*. Princeton: Princeton University Press, 1978.

Clark, Victor S. *History of Manufactures in the United States*. 3 vols. New York: McGraw-Hill Book Co., 1929.

Clawson, Dan. *Bureaucracy and the Labor Process: The Transformation of United States Industry, 1860–1920*. New York: Monthly Review Press, 1980.

Cohen, Steven R. "From Industrial Democracy to Professional Adjustment: The Development of Industrial Sociology in the United States, 1900–1955." *Theory and Society* 12 (January 1983): 47–67.

―――. "Reconciling Industrial Conflict and Democracy: 'The Pittsburgh Survey' and the Growth of Social Research in the United States." Ph.D. diss., Columbia University, 1981.

―――. "Steelworkers Rethink the Homestead Strike of 1892." *Pennsylvania History* 48 (April 1981): 155–77.

Cole, Arthur H. "An Approach to the Study of Entrepreneurship." *Journal of Economic History* 6, Supplement (1946): 1–15.

Cole, Arthur H., ed. *Facts and Figures in Economic History*. Cambridge, Mass.: Harvard University Press, 1932.

Commons, John R. *Races and Immigrants in America*. London: Macmillan, 1907.

———. "Wage Earners of Pittsburgh." *Charities and the Commons*, 6 March 1909.

Commons, John R., ed. *Trade Unionism and Labor Problems*. Boston: Ginn & Co., 1905.

Commons, John R., and others. *History of Labor in the United States*. 4 vols. New York: Macmillan Co., 1918–35.

Commons, John R., and others, eds. *A Documentary History of American Industrial Society*. Vols. 9–10. Cleveland, Ohio: Arthur H. Clark Co., 1910–11.

Conlin, Joseph R., ed. *The American Radical Press, 1880–1960*. 2 vols. Westport, Conn.: Greenwood Press, 1974.

Conway, Alan, ed. *The Welsh in America: Letters from the Immigrants*. Minneapolis: University of Minnesota Press, 1961.

Cooper, H. C., Jr., Brother, and Company. *Twentieth-Century Bench and Bar of Pennsylvania*. 2 vols. Chicago: H. C. Cooper, Jr., Brother, & Co., 1903.

Cooper, Jerry M. "The Army as Strikebreaker: The Railroad Strikes of 1877 and 1894." *Labor History* 18 (Spring 1977): 179–98.

Corbin, David A. *Life, Work, and Rebellion in the Coal Fields: The Southern West Virginia Coal Mines, 1880–1922*. Urbana: University of Illinois Press, 1981.

Courtheaux, Jean Paul. "Privilèges et misères d'un métier sidèrurgique au XIXe siècle: Le Puddleur." *Revue d'Histoire Economique et Sociale* 37 (1959): 161–84.

Couvares, Francis, G. "Knights, Trade Unionists, and Local Politics in Pittsburgh, 1867–87." Paper presented at the Knights of Labor Centennial Symposium. Newberry Library, Chicago, 17–19 May 1979.

———. *The Remaking of Pittsburgh: Class and Culture in an Industrializing City, 1877–1919*. Albany: State University of New York Press, 1984.

———. "Telling a Story in Context; or, What's Wrong with Social History?" *Theory and Society* 9 (September 1980): 674–76.

———. "Work, Leisure, and Reform in Pittsburgh: The Transformation of an Urban Culture, 1860–1920." Ph.D. diss., University of Michigan, 1980.

Cowles, Karen. "The Industrialization of Duquesne and the Circulation of Elites, 1891–1933." *Western Pennsylvania Historical Magazine* 62 (January 1979): 1–17.

Coxe, Eckley B. "Secondary Technical Education." *Transactions of the American Institute of Mining Engineers* 7 (1879): 217–26.

Crockatt, Richard. "Response to Alan Munslow, 'Andrew Carnegie and the Discourse of Cultural Hegemony.' " *Journal of American Studies* 23 (April 1989): 77–83.

Crooker, Ralph, Jr. "The Development of the American Blooming Mill." *Proceedings of the Engineers' Society of Western Pennsylvania* 13 (1897): 325–39.

Curtis, G. T. "The Homestead Strike: A Constitutional View." *North American Review* 155 (September 1982): 364–70.

Curtis, Gram. "Apparatus for the Manipulation of Iron and Steel Plates During the Process of Finishing." *Transactions of the American Society of Mechanical Engineers* 20 (1891): 347–51.

Dacus, Joseph A. *Annals of the Great Strikes*. Chicago: L. T. Palmer & Co. 1877.

Dalzell, Robert F., Jr. *Enterprising Elite: The Boston Associates and the World They Made*. Cambridge, Mass.: Harvard University Press, 1987.

Darnton, Robert. *The Great Cat Massacre and Other Episodes in French Cultural History*. New York: Vintage Books, 1985.

David, Henry. "Upheaval at Homestead." In *America in Crisis*, edited by Daniel Aaron, 132–70. Hamden, Conn.: Archon Books, 1971 (1952).

Davis, George L. "Greater Pittsburgh's Commercial and Industrial Development, 1850–1900, with Emphasis on the Contributions of Technology." Ph.D. diss., University of Pittsburgh, 1951.

Davis, Horace B. *Labor and Steel*. New York: International Publishers, 1933.

Davis, James J. *The Iron Puddler: My Life in the Rolling Mills and What Came of It*. Indianapolis: Bobbs-Merrill Co., 1922.

Davis, Jerome. *The Russians and Ruthenians in America: Bolsheviks or Brothers?* New York: George H. Doran Co., 1922.

Davis, Pearce. *The Development of the American Glass Industry*. Cambridge, Mass.: Harvard University Press, 1949.

Dawley, Alan. *Class and Community: The Industrial Revolution in Lynn*. Cambridge, Mass.: Harvard University Press, 1976.

Dawson, Andrew. "The Paradox of Dynamic Technological Change and the Labor Aristocracy in the United States, 1880–1914." *Labor History* 20 (Summer 1979): 325–51.

Dawson, Charles T., ed. *Our Fireman: The History of the Pittsburgh Fire Department, from the Village Period Until the Present Time*. Pittsburgh: Henry Fenno, 1889.

Debouzy, Marianne. "Grève et violence de classe aux Etats-Unis en 1877." *Mouvement Social* 102 (1978): 41–66.

———. "Workers' Self-Organization and Resistance in the 1877 Strikes." In *American Labor and Immigration History, 1877–1920s: Recent European Research*. Edited by Dirk Hoerder, 61–77. Urbana: University of Illinois Press, 1983.

Destler, Chester McArthur. *American Radicalism, 1865–1901*. New York: Quadrangle Books: 1966 (1946).

———. "Entrepreneurial Leadership among the 'Robber Barons': A Trial Balance." *Journal of Economic History* 6, Supplement (1946): 28–49.

———. "The Influence of Edward Kellogg upon American Radicalism, 1865–1896." *Journal of Political Economy* 40 (June 1932): 338–65.

Dickerson, Dennis C. "The Black Church in Industrializing Western Pennsylvania." *Western Pennsylvania Historical Magazine* 64 (October 1981): 329–44.

Dickson, Paul. *The Library in America: A Celebration in Words and Pictures*. New York: Facts on File Publications, 1986.

Dickson, William B. *History of Carnegie Veteran Association*. Montclair, N.J.: Mountain Press, 1938.

Diffenbacher, J. F. *Directory of Pittsburgh and Allegheny Cities*. Pittsburgh: J. F. Diffenbacher, 1890.

• Diggins, John Patrick. "Comrades and Citizens: New Mythologies in American Historiography." *American Historical Review* 90 (June 1985): 614–38.

Ditzion, Sidney H. *Arsenals of a Democratic Culture: A Social History of the American Public Library Movement in New England and the Middle Atlantic States from 1850 to 1900*. Chicago: American Library Association, 1947.

Dobson, John M. *America's Ascent: The United States Becomes a World Power, 1880–1914*. DeKalb: Northern Illinois University Press, 1978.

Doeringer, Peter B. "Piece Rate Wage Structures in the Pittsburgh Iron and Steel Industry, 1880–1900." *Labor History* 9 (Spring 1968): 262–74.

Dorko, Nicholas. "The Geographical Background of the Faithful of the Apostolic Exarchate of Pittsburgh." *Slovak Studies* 4 (1964): 217–21.

Douglas, James. "The Characteristics and Conditions of the Technical Progress of the Nineteenth Century." *Transactions of the American Institute of Mining Engineers* 29 (1900): 648–65.

Doyle, David. "The Irish and American Labor, 1880–1929." *Saothar: Journal of the Irish History Society* 1 (1975): 42–53.

Drinnon, Richard. *Rebel in Paradise: A Biography of Emma Goldman.* New York: Bantam Books, 1973.

Dublin, Thomas. *Women at Work: The Transformation of Work and Community in Lowell, Massachusetts, 1826–1860.* New York: Columbia University Press, 1979.

———. "Women, Work, and Protest in the Early Lowell Mills: 'The Oppressing Hand of Avarice Would Enslave Us.' " *Labor History* 16 (Winter 1975): 99–116.

Dubofsky, Melvyn. "The Homestead Strike: Working-Class Protest in an Industrializing Society." Manuscript, 1973, author's possession.

———. *Industrialism and the American Worker, 1865–1920.* Arlington Heights, Ill.: AHM Publishing Corp., 1975.

Duncan, George Sang, comp. *Bibliography of Glass.* London: Dawsons of Pall Mall, 1960.

Durand, William F. *Robert Henry Thurston, A Biography: The Record of a Life of Achievement as Engineer, Educator, and Author.* New York: American Society of Mechanical Engineers, 1929.

Durant, S. W. *History of Allegheny County, Pennsylvania.* Philadelphia: L. H. Everts Co., 1876.

Durbin, Paul T., ed. *A Guide to the Culture of Science, Technology, and Medicine.* New York: Free Press, 1980.

Durfee, William F. "An Account of a Chemical Laboratory Erected at Wyandotte, Michigan, in the Year 1863." *Transactions of the American Institute of Mining Engineers* 12 (1884): 223–38.

———. "The Development of American Industries Since Columbus, Part II: Iron Mills and Puddling Furnaces." *Popular Science Monthly* 38 (November 1890–April 1891): 314–38.

———. "The Development of American Industries Since Columbus, Part VIII: The Manufacture of Steel." *Popular Science Monthly* 39 (October 1891): 729–49; 40 (November 1891): 15–40.

Edwards, P. K. *Strikes in the United States, 1881–1974.* New York: St. Martin's Press, 1981.

Edwards, Richard C. *Contested Terrain: The Transformation of the Workplace in the Twentieth Century.* New York: Basic Books, 1979.

Edwards, Richard C., Michael Reich, and David M. Gordon, eds. *Labor Market Segmentation.* Lexington Mass.: D. C. Heath, 1975.

Eggert, Gerald G. *Steelmasters and Labor Reform, 1886–1923.* Pittsburgh: University of Pittsburgh Press, 1981.

Egleston, T. "The Basic Bessemer Process." *Transactions of the American Society of Mechanical Engineers* 7 (1885): 34–80.

————. "Some Thoughts and Suggestions on Technical Education." *Transactions of the American Institute of Mining Engineers* 16 (1887–88): 623–61.

Ehrlich, Richard L. "Immigrant Strikebeaking Activity: A Sampling of Opinion Expressed in the *National Labor Tribune, 1878–1885.*" *Labor History* 15 (Fall 1974): 529–42.

Ehrlich, Richard L., ed. *Immigrants in Industrial America: Proceedings of a Conference Sponsored by the Balch Institute and the Eleutherian Mills–Hagley Foundation, November 1–3, 1973.* Charlottesville: University of Virginia Press, 1977.

Elbaum, Bernard Louis. "Industrial Relations and Uneven Development: Wage Structure and Industrial Organization in the British and U.S. Iron and Steel Industries, 1870–1970." Ph.D. diss., Harvard University, 1982.

Elbaum, Bernard, William Lazonick, Frank Wilkinson, and Jonathan Zeitlin. "Symposium: The Labour Process, Market Structure, and Marxist Theory." *Cambridge Journal of Economics* 3 (1979): 227–303.

Elbaum, Bernard, and Frank Wilkinson. "Industrial Relations and Uneven Development: A Comparative Study of the American and British Steel Industries." *Cambridge Journal of Economics* 3 (1979): 275–303.

Eley, Geoff, and Keith Nield. "Why Does Social History Ignore Politics?" *Social History* 5 (May 1980): 249–71.

Elsas, Madeleine, ed. *Iron in the Making: Dowlais Iron Co. Letters, 1782–1860.* London: Glamorgan County Council, 1960.

Ely, Richard T. *The Labor Movement in America.* New York: T. Y. Crowell & Co., 1886.

Epstein, James. *The Lion of Freedom: Feargus O'Connor and the Chartist Movement.* London: Croom Helm, 1982.

————. "Rethinking the Categories of Working Class History." *Labour/Le Travail* 18 (1986): 195–208.

Epstein, James, and Dorothy Thompson, eds. *The Chartist Experience: Studies in Working-Class Radicalism and Culture, 1830–1860.* London: Macmillan Press, 1982.

Erickson, Charlotte. *British Industrialists: Steel and Hosiery, 1850–1950.* Cambridge: Cambridge University Press, 1959.

Evans, Chris. *History of the United Mine Workers of America, 1860–1890.* 2 vols. N.p., n.d.

Evans, Cyril James Oswald. *Glamorgan: Its History and Topography.* 2d ed. Cardiff: W. Lewis, 1946.

Evans, James E. *Guide to the "Amerikansky Russky Viestnik," Volume I: 1894–1914.* Fairview, N.J.: Carpatho-Rusyn Research Center, 1979.

Everts, L. H., & Co. *History of Allegheny County, Pennsylvania, with Illustrations Descriptive of Its Scenery, Palatial Residences. . . .* Philadelphia: L. H. Everts & Co., 1876.

Fackanthal, B. F., Jr. "John Fritz, the Ironmaster." *Pennsylvania German Society* 34 (October 1923): 95–112.

Faherty, William B. "The Clergyman and Labor Progress: Cornelious O'Leary and the Knights of Labor." *Labor History* 11 (1970): 175–89.

Faires, Nora. "Ethnicity in Evolution: The German Community in Pittsburgh and Allegheny City, Pennsylvania, 1845–85." Ph.D. diss., University of Pittsburgh, 1981.

————. "Immigrants and Industry: Peopling the 'Iron City'." In *City at the Point: Essays on the Social History of Pittsburgh*. Edited by Samuel P. Hays, 3–31. Pittsburgh: University of Pittsburgh Press, 1989.

Faler, Paul. "Cultural Aspects of the Industrial Revolution: Lynn, Mass., Shoemakers and Industrial Morality, 1826–1860." *Labor History* 15 (Spring 1974): 367–94.

————. *Mechanics and Manufacturers in the Early Industrial Revolution: Lynn, Massachusetts, 1780–1860*. Albany: State University of New York Press, 1981.

————. "Working Class Historiography." *Radical America* 3 (1969): 56–68.

Falzone, Vincent J. *Terrence V. Powderly: Middle-Class Reformer*. Washington, D.C.: University Press of America, 1978.

Farrah, Margaret Ann. "Andrew Carnegie: A Psychohistorical Sketch." D.A. diss., Carnegie-Mellon University, 1982.

Finch, James Kip. *Engineering and Western Civilization*. New York: McGraw Hill, 1951.

————. *The Story of Engineering*. Garden City, N.Y.: Doubleday, 1960.

Fine, Sidney. *Laissez Faire and the General-Welfare State: A Study of Conflict in American Thought, 1865–1901*. Ann Arbor: University of Michigan Press, 1964.

————. *Sit-Down: The General Motors Strike of 1936–1937*. Ann Arbor: University of Michigan Press, 1969.

Fink, Gary, ed. *Biographical Dictionary of American Labor Leaders*. Westport, Conn.: Greenwood Press, 1974.

Fink, Leon. "Class Conflict in the Gilded Age: The Figure and the Phantom." *Radical History Review* (Fall 1975): 56–73.

————. "Gramsci and the Gilded Age: Power, Culture, and the Limits of Consent." Paper presented at the U.S. Working Class History and Contemporary Labor Movement Symposium, Indiana University of Pennsylvania, October 1985.

————. "Labor, Liberty, and the Law: Trade Unionism and the Problem of the American Constitutional Order." In *The Constitution and American Life*, edited by David Thelen, 244–65. Ithaca, N.Y.: Cornell University Press, 1987.

————. "The New Labor History and the Powers of Historical Pessimism: Consensus, Hegemony, and the Case of the Knights of Labor." *Journal of American History* 75 (June 1988): 115–61.

————. *Workingmen's Democracy: The Knights of Labor and American Politics*. Urbana: University of Illinois Press, 1983.

Fisher, Douglas Alan. *The Epic of Steel*. New York: Harper & Row, 1963.

Fitch, John A. "Old Age at Forty." *American Magazine* 71 (March 1911): 655–64.

————. *The Steel Workers*. New York: Russell Sage Foundation, 1910.

Fleming, George T. *History of Pittsburgh and Environs*. 6 vols. New York: American Historical Society, 1922.

Fogel, Robert, and Stanley Engerman. "A Model for the Explanation of Industrial Expansion during the Nineteenth Century: With an Application to the American Iron Industry." *Journal of Political Economy* 77 (1969): 306–28.

Foner, Eric. "Class, Ethnicity, and Radicalism in the Gilded Age: The Land League and Irish America." *Marxist Perspectives* 1 (Summer 1978): 6–55.

Reprinted in his *Politics and Ideology in the Age of the Civil War,* 150–200.

———. *Free Soil, Free Labor, Free Men: The Ideology of the Republican Party before the Civil War.* New York: Oxford University Press, 1970.

———. *Nothing but Freedom: Emancipation and Its Legacy.* Baton Rouge: Louisiana State University Press, 1983.

———. *Politics and Ideology in the Age of the Civil War.* New York: Oxford University Press, 1980.

———. *Reconstruction: America's Unfinished Revolution, 1863–1877.* New York: Harper & Row, 1988).

———. *Tom Paine and Revolutionary America.* New York: Oxford University Press, 1976.

———. "Why Is There No Socialism in the United States?" *History Workshop Journal* 17 (1984): 57–80.

Foner, Philip S. *American Labor Songs of the Nineteenth Century.* Urbana: University of Illinois Press, 1975.

———. *The Great Labor Uprising of 1877.* New York: Monad Press, 1977.

———. *History of the Labor Movement in the United States, Vol. 1: From Colonial Times to the Founding of the American Federation of Labor.* New York: International Publishers, 1978.

Forbath, William E. "The Ambiguities of Free Labor: Labor and the Law in the Gilded Age." *Wisconsin Law Review* (1985): 767–817.

———. "The Shaping of the American Labor Movement." *Harvard Law Review* 102 (1989): 1109–256.

Foster, William Z. *Unionizing Steel.* New York: Workers' Library Publishers, 1936.

Fox, Richard Wightman, and T. J. Jackson Lears, eds. *The Culture of Consumption: Critical Essays in American History, 1880–1980.* New York: Pantheon Books, 1983.

Freifeld, Mary. "The Emergence of the American Working Classes: The Roots of Division, 1865–85." Ph.D. diss., New York University, 1980.

French, John D. "Reaping the Whirlwind: The Origins of the Allegheny County Greenback Labor Party in 1877." *Western Pennsylvania Historical Magazine* 64 (April 1981): 97–119.

Friedman, Morris. *The Pinkerton Labor Spy.* New York: Wilshire Book Co., 1907.

Frisch, Michael H., and Daniel J. Walkowitz, eds. *Working-Class America: Essays on Labor, Community, and American Society.* Urbana: University of Illinois Press, 1983.

Fritz, John. *The Autobiography of John Fritz.* New York: John Wiley & Sons, 1912.

———. "The Progress of the Manufacture of Iron and Steel." *Transactions of the American Society of Mechanical Engineers* 18 (1897): 39–69.

Gale, W. K. V. *Iron and Steel.* London: Longmans, Green & Co., 1969.

Garland, Hamlin. "Homestead and Its Perilous Trades: Impressions of a Visit." *McClure's Magazine* 3 (June 1894): 3–20.

Garlock, Jonathan. "A Structural Analysis of the Knights of Labor." Ph.D. diss., University of Rochester, 1974.

Garlock, Jonathan, ed. *Guide to the Local Assemblies of the Knights of Labor.* Westport, Conn.: Greenwood Press, 1982.

Garlock, Jonathan, and N. C. Builder, eds. "The Knights of Labor Data Bank and Users' Manual and Index to Local Assemblies." Manuscript, University of Rochester, N.Y., n.d.

Garraty, John A. "The U.S. Steel Corporation versus Labor: The Early Years." *Labor History* 1 (1960): 3–38.

Garrett, William. "A Comparison between American and British Rolling Mill Practice." *Journal of the Iron and Steel Institute* 59 (1901): 101–45.

Geertz, Clifford. *The Interpretation of Cultures.* New York: Basic Books, 1973.

Genovese, Eugene D. *Roll, Jordan, Roll: The World the Slaves Made.* New York: Vintage Books, 1976.

Genovese, Eugene D., and Elizabeth Fox-Genovese. "The Political Crisis of Social History: A Marxian Perspective." *Journal of Social History* 10 (1976): 205–20.

———. "The Political Crisis of Social History: Class Struggle as Subject and Object." In their *The Fruits of Merchant Capital: Slavery and Bourgeois Property in the Rise and Expansion of Capitalism*, 179–212. New York: Oxford University Press, 1983.

Gerner, Richard. "The Aesthetics of Engineering." *Van Nostrand's Engineering Magazine* 20 (June 1879): 472g–472j.

Gilfillan, S. S. *The Sociology of Invention.* Chicago: Follett, 1935.

Glab, Caroline. *Immigrant Destinations.* Philadelphia: Temple University Press, 1977.

Glazier, Willard. *Peculiarities of American Cities.* Philadelphia: Hubbard Brothers, 1886.

Gompers, Samuel. *Seventy Years of Life and Labor: An Autobiography.* Ithaca, N.Y.: ILR Press, 1984.

Goodwyn, Lawrence. "The Cooperative Commonwealth and Other Abstractions: In Search of a Democratic Promise." *Marxist Perspectives* 3 (Summer 1980): 8–42.

———. *Democratic Promise.* New York: Oxford University Press, 1976.

———. *The Populist Moment: A Short History of Agrarian Revolt in America.* New York: Oxford University Press, 1978.

Gordon, David M. "Capitalist Efficiency and Socialist Efficiency." *Monthly Review* 28 (1976): 19–39.

Gosiorovsky, Milos. "Contribution to the History of the Slovak Workers' Society in the U.S.A." Translated by Anton Farkas. *Historica* 12–13 (1961–62): 3–40.

Graham, Hugh D., and Ted R. Gurr., eds. *Violence in America: Historical and Comparative Perspectives.* Beverly Hills, Calif.: Sage Publications, 1979.

Gramsci, Antonio. *Selections from the Prison Notebooks of Antonio Gramsci.* Edited and translated by Quintin Hoare and Geoffrey Nowell Smith. New York: International Publishers, 1980.

Graziosi, Andrea. "Common Laborers, Unskilled Workers: 1880–1915." *Labor History* 22 (Fall 1981): 512–44.

Green, James J. "American Catholics and the Irish Land League." *Catholic Historical Review* 35 (1949): 19–42.

Greenberg, Dolores. "Energy, Power, and Perceptions of Social Change in the Early Nineteenth Century." *American Historical Review* 95 (June 1990): 693–714.

Greene, Victor R. *The Slavic Community on Strike: Immigrant Labor in Pennsylvania Anthracite*. Notre Dame, Ind.: University of Notre Dame Press, 1968.

Greenwald, Maurine Weiner. "Women and Class in Pittsburgh, 1850–1920." In *City at the Point: Essays on the Social History of Pittsburgh*. Edited by Samuel P. Hays, 33–67. Pittsburgh: University of Pittsburgh Press, 1989.

Grob, Gerald. "The Railroad Strike of 1877." *Midwest Journal* 6 (Winter 1954–55): 16–34.

———. *Workers and Utopia: A Study of Ideological Conflict in the American Labor Movement, 1865–1900*. Chicago: Quadrangle Books, 1969 [1961].

Grossman, Jonathan. "Co-operative Foundries." *New York History* 24 (1943): 196–210.

———. *William Sylvis, Pioneer of American Labor: A Study of the Labor Movement During the Civil War Era*. Columbia University Studies in History, Economics, and Public Law no. 516. New York, 1945.

Gulovich, Stephen C. "The Rusin Exarchate in the United States." *Eastern Churches Quarterly* 6 (1946): 459–85.

Gutman, Herbert G. "Black Coal Miners and the Greenback-Labor Party in Redeemer, Alabama: 1878–1879." *Labor History* 10 (1969): 506–36.

———. "The Braidwood Lockout of 1874." *Journal of the Illinois State Historical Society* 5 (Spring 1960): 5–68.

———. "An Iron Worker's Strike in the Ohio Valley, 1873–74." *Ohio Historical Quarterly* 68 (October 1959): 353–70.

———. "Joseph P. McDonnell and the Workers' Struggle in Paterson, New Jersey." In *Power and Culture: Essays on the American Working Class*. Edited by Ira Berlin, 93–116. New York: Pantheon, 1987.

———. "Reconstruction in Ohio: Negroes in the Hocking Valley Coal Mines in 1873 and 1874." *Labor History* 3 (Fall 1962): 244–64.

———. Review of *Lockout*, by Leon Wolff. *Pennsylvania Magazine of History and Biography* 90 (1966): 273–76.

———. "Trouble on the Railroads in 1873–74: Prelude to the 1877 Crisis?" *Labor History* 2 (1961): 215–35.

———. *Work, Culture, and Society in Industrializing America: Essays in American Working-Class and Social History*. New York: Vintage, 1977.

———. "The Worker's Search for Power: Labor in the Gilded Age." In *The Gilded Age: A Reappraisal*. Edited by H. Wayne Morgan, 38–68. Syracuse, N.Y.: Syracuse University Press, 1963.

Habakkuk, H. J. *American and British Technology in the Nineteenth Century: The Search for Labor-Saving Inventions*. Cambridge: Cambridge University Press, 1962.

Hahn, Steven. "Common Right and Commonwealth: The Stock-Law Struggle and the Roots of Southern Populism." In *Region, Race and Reconstruction: Essays in Honor of C. Vann Woodward*. Edited by J. Morgan Kousser and James M. McPherson, 51–88. New York: Oxford University Press, 1982.

———. "Herbert Gutman's History." *Socialist Review* 89 (1989): 153–59.

Halich, Wasyl. *Ukrainians in the United States*. Chicago: University of Chicago Press, 1937.

———. "Ukrainians in Western Pennsylvania." *Western Pennsylvania Historical Magazine* 18 (June 1935): 139–46.

Hall, Fred S. *Sympathetic Strikes and Sympathetic Lockouts.* New York: Columbia University Press, 1898.

Hall, John Howe. "Manufacture of Bessemer Steel." In *The ABC of Iron and Steel.* Edited by A. O. Backert, 121–28. Cleveland: Penton Publishing Co., 1925.

Halsey, F. A. "The Premium Plan of Paying for Labor." *Transactions of the American Society of Mechanical Engineers* 12 (1890): 755–80.

Hanagan, Michael P. "Artisan and Skilled Worker: The Problem of Definition." *International Labor and Working Class History* 12 (November 1977): 28–31.

———. *The Logic of Solidarity: Artisans and Industrial Workers in Three French Towns, 1871–1914.* Urbana: University of Illinois Press, 1980.

Hanagan, Michael P., and Charles Stephenson. "The Skilled Worker and Working-Class Protest." *Social Science History* 4 (Winter 1980): 5–13.

Harper, Frank C. *Pittsburgh of Today: Its Resources and People.* 4 vols. New York: American Historical Society, 1931.

Hartman, Edward George. *Americans from Wales.* Boston: Christopher Publishing House, 1967.

Hartog, Hendrik. "The Constitution of Aspiration and 'The Rights That Belong to Us All.' " In *The Constitution and American Life,* edited by David Thelen, 353–74. Ithaca, N.Y.: Cornell University Press, 1987.

Harvey, George. *Henry Clay Frick—The Man.* New York: Charles Scribner's Sons, 1928.

Haupt, Lewis M. "Technical Education." *Transactions of the American Institute of Mining Engineers* 5 (1876–77): 510–15.

Hays, Samuel P. "The Development of Pittsburgh as a Social Order." *Western Pennsylvania Historical Magazine* 57 (October 1974): 431–48.

———. *The Response to Industrialism, 1885–1914.* Chicago: University of Chicago Press, 1957.

Hays, Samuel, ed. *City at the Point: Essays on the Social History of Pittsburgh.* Pittsburgh: University of Pittsburgh Press, 1989.

Hegel, G. W. F. *The Philosophy of Right.* Translated by T. M. Knox. New York: Oxford University Press, 1978.

Heilbroner, Robert L. *The Worldly Philosophers: The Lives, Times, and Ideas of the Great Economic Thinkers.* New York: Simon and Schuster, 1980 (1953).

Hendrick, J. Burton. *The Life of Andrew Carnegie.* 2 vols. New York: Doubleday, Doran & Co., 1932.

Hessen, Robert. *Steel Titan: The Life of Charles M. Schwab.* New York: Oxford University Press, 1975.

Hewitt, Abram S. "Acceptance Speech for the Bessemer Medal." *Transactions of the American Institute of Mining Engineers* 19 (1890–91): 517–22.

———. "A Century of Mining and Metallurgy in the United States." *Transactions of the American Institute of Mining Engineers* 5 (1876–77): 164–96.

———. "Iron and Labor." *Transactions of the American Institute of Mining Engineers* 19 (1890–91): 475–522.

———. "The Production of Iron and Steel in Its Economic and Social Relations." In *Reports of the U.S. Commissioners to the Paris Universal Exposition, 1867,* 1–63. Washington, D.C.: Government Printing Office, 1870.

———. *Selected Writings of Abram S. Hewitt.* Edited by Allan Nevins. New York: Columbia University Press, 1937.

Higham, John. *Strangers in the Land: Patterns of American Nativism, 1860–1925.* New York: Atheneum, 1971.

Hill, Charles. "Fighting the Twelve-Hour Day in the American Steel Industry." *Labor History* 15 (Winter 1974): 19–35.

Hill, Charles, and Steven Cohen. "John A. Fitch and the Pittsburgh Survey." *Western Pennsylvania Historical Magazine* 67 (Jan. 1984): 17–32.

Hill, Christopher. *The World Turned Upside Down: Radical Ideas During the English Revolution.* New York: Penguin Books, 1972.

Hiller, Ernest T. *The Strike: A Study in Collective Action.* Chicago: University of Chicago Press, 1928.

Hirsch, Susan E. *Roots of the American Working Class: The Industrialization of Crafts in Newark, 1800–1860.* Philadelphia: University of Pennsylvania Press, 1978.

Hoagland, H. E. "Trade Unionism in the Iron Industry: A Decadent Organization." *Quarterly Journal of Economics* 31 (1917): 674–89.

Hobsbawm, E. J. *Labouring Men: Studies in the History of Labour.* London: Weidenfeld & Nicolson, 1965.

———. *Workers: Worlds of Labor.* New York, Pantheon Books, 1984.

Hoerder, Dirk, ed. *American Labor and Immigration History, 1877–1920s: Recent European Research.* Urbana: University of Illinois Press, 1983.

———. *"Struggle a Hard Battle": Essays on Working-Class Immigrants.* DeKalb, Ill.: Northern Illinois University Press, 1986.

Hofstadter, Richard. *The American Political Tradition and the Men Who Made It.* New York: Vintage Books, 1974.

———. *Social Darwinism in American Thought, 1860–1915.* Philadelphia: University of Pennsylvania Press, 1944.

Hogan, William T. *Economic History of the Iron and Steel Industry in the United States.* 5 vols. Lexington, Mass.: D. C. Heath & Co., 1971.

Hogg, J. Bernard. "The Homestead Strike of 1892." Ph.D. diss., University of Chicago, 1943.

———. "Public Reaction to Pinkertonism and the Labor Question." *Pennsylvania History* 11 (July 1944): 171–99.

Holley, Alexander L. "An Adaptation of the Bessemer Plant to the Basic Process." *Transactions of the American Society of Mechanical Engineers* 1 (1880): unpaginated.

———. "Bessemer Machinery." *Journal of the Franklin Institute* 44 (1873): 252–65.

———. "Engineering, the Intermediate Power between Nature and Civilization." In *Memorial of Alexander Lyman Holley,* 167–68. New York: American Institute of Mining Engineers, 1884.

———. "The Field of Mechanical Engineering." *Transactions of the American Society of Mechanical Engineers* 1 (1880): 1–6.

———. "The Inadequate Union of Engineering Science and Art." *Transactions of the American Institute of Mining Engineers* 4 (1876): 191–207.

———. "Recent Improvements in Bessemer Machinery." *Transactions of the American Institute of Mining Engineers* 2 (1874): 263–74.

———. "Some Pressing Needs of Our Iron and Steel Manufacturers." *Transactions of the American Institute of Mining Engineers* 4 (1876): 77–99.

———. "What Is Steel." *Transactions of the American Institute of Mining Engineers* 4 (1875–76): 138–49.

————. "Wrought Iron and Steel Manufacture in 1876." *Metallurgical Review* 1 (December 1877): 327–41.

Holmes, Joseph J. "The National Guard of Pennsylvania: Policemen of Industry, 1865–1905." Ph.D. diss., University of Connecticut, 1970.

————. "Red Baiting as Used against Striking Workingmen in the United States, 1871–1920." *Studies in History and Society* 5 (1974): 1–19.

Holt, James. "Trade Unionism in the British and U.S. Steel Industries, 1888–1912: A Comparative Approach. *Labor History* 18 (1977): 5–35.

Hopkins, C. M., and Company. *Atlas of the Cities of Pittsburgh, Allegheny, and Adjoining Boroughs.* Philadelphia: Edward Busch, 1872.

Hopkins, C. M. *Atlas of the County of Allegheny, Pennsylvania.* Philadelphia: C. M. Hopkins, 1876.

————. *Atlas of the Vicinity of the Cities of Pittsburgh and Allegheny, Pennsylvania.* Philadelphia: C. M. Hopkins, 1886.

Horan, James David. *Desperate Men: Revelations from the Sealed Pinkerton Files.* New York: Putnam's Sons, 1949.

Horner, Clare Dahlberg. "Producers' Co-operatives in the United States, 1865–1900." Ph.D. diss., University of Pittsburgh, 1978.

Horowitz, Daniel. "Insight into Industrialization: American Conceptions of Economic Development and Mechanization 1865–1910." Ph.D. diss., Harvard University, 1966.

Howard, N. P. "The Strikes and Lockouts in the Iron Industry and the Formation of the Ironworkers' Unions, 1862–1869." *International Review of Social History* 18 (1973): 396–427.

Howe, Henry M. "The Nomenclature of Iron." *Transactions of the American Institute of Mining Engineers* 5 (1876–77): 515–37.

————. "Notes on the Bessemer Process." *Transactions of the American Society of Mechanical Engineers* 19 (1890–91): 1120–67.

Hunt, R. W. "Discussion: Response to F. A. Halsey's 'The Premium Plan of Paying for Labor.' " *Transactions of the American Society of Mechanical Engineers* 12 (1890): 776–77.

————. "The Evolution of American Rolling Mills." *Transactions of the American Society of Mechanical Engineers* 13 (1891–92): 45–69.

————. "A History of Bessemer Manufacture in America." *Transactions of the American Institute of Mining Engineers* 5 (1876): 201–16.

————. "The Original Bessemer Steel Plant at Troy." *Transactions of the American Society of Mechanical Engineers* 6 (1885): 61–70.

Hunter, Louis C. "Financial Problems of the Early Pittsburgh Iron Manufacturers." *Journal of Economic and Business History* 2 (1930): 520–44.

————. "Influence of the Market upon Technique in the Iron Industry in Western Pennsylvania up to 1860." *Journal of Economic and Business History* 1 (1928–29): 241–81.

Hutton, Frederick Remson. *A History of the American Society of Mechanical Engineers from 1889 to 1915.* New York: American Society of Mechanical Engineers, 1915.

Hyde, Charles. *Technological Change and the British Iron Industry.* Princeton: Princeton University Press, 1977.

Ihde, Don. *Existential Technics.* Albany: State University of New York Press, 1983.

Ingham, John N. "Elite and Upper Class in the Iron and Steel Industry, 1874–95." Ph.D. diss., University of Pittsburgh, 1973.

———. *The Iron Barons: A Social Analysis of an American Urban Elite, 1874–1965.* Westport, Conn.: Greenwood Press, 1978.

———. "Steel City Aristocrats." In *City at the Point: Essays on the Social History of Pittsburgh.* Edited by Samuel P. Hays, 265–94. Pittsburgh: University of Pittsburgh Press, 1989.

Innes, Lowell. *Pittsburgh Glass, 1797–1891: A History and Guide for Collectors.* Boston: Houghton Mifflin & Co., 1976.

Jable, J. Thomas. "Sport, Amusements, and Pennsylvania's Blue Laws, 1682–1973." Ph.D. diss., Pennsylvania State University, 1975.

James, Alfred P. "The First Convention of the AFL, Pittsburgh, Pennsylvania, Nov. 15–18, 1881." *Western Pennsylvania Historical Magazine* 6 (1923): 201–33.

Jansak, Stefan. "The Land Question in Slovakia." *Slavonic Review* 8 (1979): 612–26.

Jarrett, John. "The Story of the Iron Workers." In *The Labor Movement: The Problem of Today.* Edited by George McNeill, pp. 268–311. Boston: A. M. Bridgman Co., 1887.

Jeans, J. Stephen, ed. *American Industrial Conditions and Competition: Reports of Commissioners Appointed by the British Iron Trade Association.* London: Iron and Steel Institute, 1902.

Jelavich, Peter. "Popular Dimensions of Modernist Elite Culture: The Case of Theater in Fin-de-Siècle Munich." In *Modern European Intellectual History: Reappraisals and New Perspectives.* Edited by Dominick LaCapra and Steven L. Kaplan, 220–50. Ithaca: Cornell University Press, 1982.

Jenkins, R. T., and William Rees. *A Bibliography of the History of Wales.* Cardiff: University of Wales Press, 1931.

Jenks, Leland H. "Early Phases of the Management Movement." *Administrative Science Quarterly* 5 (1960): 421–47.

Johnson, Donald Bruce, and Kirk H. Porter, comps. *National Party Platforms, 1840–1872.* Urbana: University of Illinois Press, 1973.

Jones, Gareth Stedman. "Class Expression versus Social Control? A Critique of Recent Trends in the Social History of 'Leisure.' " *History Workshop Journal* 4 (Autumn 1977): 162–70.

———. "Class Struggle and the Industrial Revolution." *New Left Review* 90 (March-April 1975): 35–69.

———. "From Historical Sociology to Theoretical History." *British Journal of Sociology* 27 (September 1976): 295–305.

———. "The Language of Chartism." In *The Chartist Experience: Studies in Working-Class Radicalism and Culture, 1830–1860.* Edited by James Epstein and Dorothy Thompson, 3–58. London: Macmillan, 1982.

———. *Languages of Class: Studies in English Working Class History, 1832–1982.* Cambridge: Cambridge University Press, 1985.

———. "Working Class Culture and Working Class Politics in London, 1870–1900: Notes on the Remaking of the Working Class." *Journal of Social History* 7 (Summer 1974): 460–508.

Jones, W. R. "On the Manufacture of Bessemer Steel and Steel Rails in the United States." *Journal of the Iron and Steel Institute* 1 (1881): 129–45.

———. "Remarks on Steel Rails." *Transactions of the American Institute of Mining Engineers* 7 (1878–79): 407–13.

———. "Supplementary Paper: On the Manufacture of Bessemer Steel and Steel Rails in the United States." *Journal of the Iron and Steel Institute* 2 (1881): 370–72.

Jordan, John W. *Encyclopedia of Pennsylvania Biography.* 2 vols. New York: Lewis Publishing Co., 1914.

———. *Geneological and Personal History of Western Pennsylvania.* 2 vols. New York: Lewis Publishing Co., 1915.

———. *Pittsburgh and Her People.* Pittsburgh: Lewis Publishing Co., 1908.

Josephson, Matthew. *The Politicos, 1865–1896.* New York: Harcourt, Brace & World, Inc., 1938.

———. *The Robber Barons: The Great American Capitalists, 1861–1901.* New York: Harcourt, Brace & World, 1934.

Joyce, Patrick. *Work, Society, and Politics: The Culture of the Factory in Later Victorian England.* New Brunswick, N.J.: Rutgers University Press, 1980.

Joynson, F., ed. *The Iron and Steel Maker.* London: Ward, Lock, Bouden & Co., 1892.

Kalassy, Louis. "The Educational and Religious History of the Hungarian Reformed Church in the United States." Ph.D. diss., University of Pittsburgh, 1939.

Kammen, Michael, ed. *The Past before Us: Contemporary Historical Writing in the United States.* Ithaca, N.Y.: Cornell University Press, 1980.

Kasson, John F. *Civilizing the Machine: Technology and Republican Values in America, 1776–1900.* New York: Penguin Books, 1979.

Katznelson, Ira, and Aristide R. Zolberg, eds. *Working-Class Formation: Nineteenth-Century Patterns in Western Europe and the United States.* Princeton: Princeton University Press, 1986.

Kaylor, Earl Clifford. "The Prohibition Movement in Pennsylvania, 1865–1920." Ph.D. diss., Pennsylvania State University, 1963.

Kazin, Alfred. *On Native Grounds: An Interpretation of Modern American Prose Literature.* New York: Harcourt, Brace Jovanovich, 1982 [1942].

Kazin, Michael. "Struggling with Class Struggle: Marxism and the Search for a Synthesis of U.S. Labor History." *Labor History* 28 (1987): 497–514.

Kealey, Gregory, S. *Toronto Workers Respond to Industrial Capitalism, 1867–92.* Toronto: University of Toronto Press, 1980.

Kealey, Gregory S., and Bryan D. Palmer. *Dreaming of What Might Be: The Knights of Labor in Ontario, 1880–1900.* Cambridge: Cambridge University Press, 1982.

Keeler, Ralph, and Harry Fenn. "The Taking of Pittsburgh." *Every Saturday.* "Part 1: The March," 4 March 1871, 198–99; "Part 2: The Reconnaissance," 11 March 1871, 236–38; "Part 3: Before the Works," 18 March 1871, 260–63; "Part 4: Among the Inhabitants," 25 March 1871, 272–75.

Kehl, James A. *Boss Rule in the Gilded Age: Matt Quay of Pennsylvania.* Pittsburgh: University of Pittsburgh Press, 1981.

Keller, Morton. *Affairs of State: Public Life in Late Nineteenth Century America.* Cambridge, Mass.: Harvard University Press, Belknap Press, 1977.

Kennedy, Julian. "Blast-Furnace Working." *Transactions of the American Institute of Mining Engineers* 8 (1879–80): 348–55.

Kennedy, Paul. *The Rise and Fall of the Great Powers: Economic Change and Military Conflict from 1500 to 2000.* New York: Vintage Books, 1989.

Kent, William. "The Relation of Engineering to Economics." *Scientific American* 40, Supplement (14 September 1895): 16425–26; (21 September 1895): 16451–52.

Kerr, Allen Humphreys. "The Mayors and Recorders of Pittsburgh, 1816–1951: Their Lives and Somewhat of Their Times." Manuscript, nd, Historical Society of Western Pennsylvania, Pittsburgh.

Kidney, Walter C. *Landmark Architecture: Pittsburgh and Allegheny County.* Pittsburgh: Pittsburgh History and Landmarks Foundation, 1985.

Kindl, Fred H. "The Rolling Mill Industry." In *The ABC of Iron and Steel.* Edited by A. O. Backert, 155–82. Cleveland: Penton Publishing Co., 1925.

Kirkland, Edward C. *Dream and Thought in the American Business Community, 1860–1900.* Chicago: Quadrangle Books, 1964 (1956).

———. *Industry Comes of Age. Business, Labor, and Public Policy, 1860–1897.* New York: Holt, Rinehart & Winston, 1961.

Kish-Sklar, Katherine. *Catherine Beecher: A Study in American Domesticity.* New Haven, Conn.: Yale University Press, 1973.

Kitson, James. "British Contributions to the Metallurgy of Iron and Steel." *Transactions of the American Institute of Mining Engineers* 19 (1890–91): 807–34.

———. "Iron and Steel Industries of America: Notes on the Visit of the British Iron and Steel Institute to the United States, 1890." *Contemporary Review* 59 (May 1891): 625–41.

Kleinberg, S. J. *The Shadow of the Mills: Working-Class Families in Pittsburgh, 1870–1907.* Pittsburgh: University of Pittsburgh Press, 1989.

———. "Technocracy's Stepdaughters: The Impact of Industrialization upon Working-Class Women, Pittsburgh, 1865–90." Ph.D. diss., University of Pittsburgh, 1973.

Kleppner, Paul. "Government, Parties, and Voters in Pittsburgh." In *City at the Point: Essays on the Social History of Pittsburgh.* Edited by Samuel P. Hays, 151–80. Pittsburgh: University of Pittsburgh Press, 1989.

———. "The Greenback and Prohibition Parties." In *History of U.S. Political Parties, Vol. II, 1860–1910: The Gilded Age of Politics.* Edited by Arthur M. Schlesinger, Jr., 1549–66. New York: Chelsea House Publishers, 1973.

Klingender, Francis Donald. *Art and the Industrial Revolution.* Edited and revised by Arthur Elton. London: Evelyn, Adams & Mackay, 1968.

Kloman, Andrew. "An Improved Friction Clutch for Reversing Rolls." *Metallurgical Review* 1 (1878): 505–09.

Knight, Edward H. "The First Century of the Republic; Mechanical Progress, II: Iron." *Harper's Magazine* 50 (December 1874–May 1875): 212–32.

Kolko, Gabriel. *Railroads and Regulation, 1877–1916.* Princeton: Princeton University Press, 1965.

———. *The Triumph of Conservatism: A Reinterpretation of American History, 1900–1916.* London: Free Press of Glencoe, 1963.

Korson, George. *Coal Dust on the Fiddle: Songs and Stories of the Bituminous Industry.* Philadelphia: University of Pennsylvania Press, 1943.

———. *Pennsylvania Songs and Legends.* Philadelphia: University of Pennsylvania Press, 1949.

Kramnick, Isaac. "The 'Great National Discussion': The Discourse of Politics in 1787." *William and Mary Quarterly*, 3d Ser., 45 (January 1988): 3–32.

———. "Republican Revisionism Revisited." *American Historical Review* 87 (1982): 629–64.

Krause, Paul. "Labor Republicanism and '*Za Chlebom*': Anglo-American and Slavic Solidarity in Homestead." In *"Struggle a Hard Battle": Essays on Working-Class Immigrants*. Edited by Dirk Hoerder, 143–69. DeKalb, Ill.: Northern Illinois University Press, 1986.

———. "Old Beeswax and the First Strike." *In These Times*, 27 Oct.–2 Nov. 1982.

———. "Patronage and Philanthropy in Industrial America: Andrew Carnegie and the Free Library in Braddock, Pa." *Western Pennsylvania Historical Magazine* 72 (April 1988): 127–47.

Kuritz, Hyman. "The Pennsylvania State Government and Labor Controls from 1865 to 1922." Ph.D. diss., Columbia University, 1953.

Kushner, Jozef A. *Slováci Katolíci Pittsburghského Biskupstva* [Slovak Catholics of the Pittsburgh Diocese]. Passaic, N.J.: Slovensky Katolicky Sokol, 1946.

"L. W." "Homestead as Seen by One of Its Workmen." *McClure's Magazine* 3 (July 1894): 163–69.

LaCapra, Dominick. *Rethinking Intellectual History: Texts, Contexts, Language*. Ithaca, N.Y.: Cornell University Press, 1983.

LaCapra, Dominick, and Steven L. Kaplan, eds. *Modern European Intellectual History: Reappraisals and New Perspectives*. Ithaca, N.Y.: Cornell University Press, 1982.

Lacko, Michael. "A Brief Survey of the History of the Slovak Catholics of the Byzantine-Slavonic Rite." *Slovak Studies* 3 (1963): 199–224.

Ladurie, Emmanuel Le Roy. *Carnival in Romans*. Translated by Mary Feeney. New York: George Braziller, Inc., 1979.

LaFeber, Walter. *The American Age: United States Foreign Policy at Home and Abroad Since 1750*. New York: W. W. Norton & Co., 1989.

———. *Inevitable Revolutions: The United States in Central America*. New York: W. W. Norton & Co., 1984.

LaFeber, Walter. *The New Empire: An Interpretation of American Expansion, 1860–1898*. Ithaca: Cornell University Press, 1968.

Landes, David S. *The Unbound Prometheus: Technological Changes and Industrial Development in Western Europe from 1750 to the Present*. London: Cambridge University Press, 1969.

Langley, Lester D. *The United States and the Caribbean in the Twentieth Century*. Rev. ed. Athens: University of Georgia Press, 1985.

Larner, John William, Jr. "The Glass House Boys: Child Labor Conditions in Pittsburgh's Glass Factories, 1890–1917." *Western Pennsylvania Historical Magazine* 48 (October 1965): 355–64.

Laslett, J. H. M. "The Independent Collier: Some Recent Studies of Nineteenth-Century Coalmining Communities in Britain and the United States." *International Labor and Working Class History* 21 (1982): 18–27.

Lauck, W. Jett. "The Bituminous Coal Miner and Coke Worker of Western Pennsylvania." *Survey* 26 (1911): 41–53.

Laureau, L. G. "A Bessemer Converting House without the Casting Pit." *Transactions of the American Institute of Mining Engineers* 13 (1884–85): 697–708.

Laurie, Bruce. *Artisans into Workers: Labor in Nineteenth-Century America.* New York: The Noonday Press, 1989.

Layton, Edwin T., Jr. "American Ideologies of Science and Engineering." *Technology and Culture* 17 (October 1976): 688–701.

———. "Mirror Image Twins: The Communities of Science and Technology in Nineteenth-Century America." *Technology and Culture* 12 (October 1971): 562–80.

———. *The Revolt of the Engineers.* Cleveland, Ohio: Case Western Reserve University Press, 1971.

———. "Technology as Knowledge." *Technology and Culture* 15 (1974): 31–41.

———. "Veblen and the Engineers." *American Quarterly* 14 (Spring 1962): 64–72. Reprinted as "Engineers in Revolt." In *Technology and Social Change in America.* Edited by Edwin T. Layton, Jr., 147–55.

Layton, Edwin T., Jr., ed. *Technology and Social Change in America.* New York: Harper & Row, 1973.

Lazonick, William H. "Factor Costs and the Diffusion of Ring Spinning in Britain Prior to World War I." *Quarterly Journal of Economics* 96 (February 1981): 89–109.

———. "Production Relations, Labor Productivity, and Choice of Technique: British and United States Cotton Spinning." *Journal of Economic History* 41 (September 1981): 491–516.

Lears, T. J. Jackson. "The Concept of Cultural Hegemony: Problems and Possibilities." *American Historical Review* 90 (June 1985): 567–593.

———. *No Place of Grace: Antimodernism and the Transformation of American Culture, 1880–1920.* New York: Pantheon Books, 1981.

Lens, Sidney. *The Labor Wars: From the Molly Maguires to the Sitdowns.* New York: Doubleday & Co., 1973.

Leonard, Henry B. "Ethnic Cleavage and Industrial Conflict in Late Nineteenth-Century America: The Cleveland Rolling Mill Company Strikes of 1882 and 1885." *Labor History* 20 (Fall 1979): 524–48.

Lesley, John Peter. *The Iron Manufacturer's Guide to the Furnaces, Forges and Rolling Mills of the United States.* New York: John Wiley & Sons, 1859.

Levine, Susan. *Labor's True Woman: Carpet Weavers, Industrialization, and Labor Reform in the Gilded Age.* Philadelphia: Temple University Press, 1984.

———. "Labor's True Woman: Domesticity and Equal Rights in the Knights of Labor." *Journal of American History* 70 (1983): 323–339.

Linaberger, James. "The Rolling Mill Riots of 1850." *Western Pennsylvania Historical Magazine* 47 (Winter 1964): 1–18.

Linebaugh, Peter. "Labour History without Labour Process: A Note on John Gast and His Times." *Social History* 7 (1982): 319–28.

Link, Arthur S. *Woodrow Wilson and the Progressive Era, 1910–1917.* New York: Harper & Row, 1963.

Litterer, Joseph A. "The Emergence of Systematic Management as Indicated by the Literature of Management from 1870 to 1900." Ph.D. diss., University of Illinois, 1959.

————. "Systematic Management: Design for Organization Recoupling in American Manufacturing Firms." *Business History Review* 37 (1963): 369–91.

————. "Systematic Management: The Search for Order and Integration." *Business History Review* 35 (1961): 461–76.

Livesay, Harold C. *Andrew Carnegie and the Rise of Big Business.* Boston: Little, Brown, 1975.

Locke, John. *Second Treatise of Government.* Edited by C. B. Macpherson. Indianapolis: Hackett Publishing Co., Inc. 1980 (1690).

Lorant, Stefan, ed. *Pittsburgh: The Story of an American City.* Garden City, N.Y.: Doubleday & Co., 1964.

Lord, W. M. "The Development of the Bessemer Process in Lancashire, 1856–1900." *Transactions of the Newcomen Society* 25 (1945–47): 163–80.

Lubove, Roy. "Pittsburgh and the Uses of Social Welfare History." In *City at the Point: Essays on the Social History of Pittsburgh.* Edited by Samuel P. Hays, 295–325. Pittsburgh: University of Pittsburgh Press, 1989.

Lubove, Roy, ed. *Pittsburgh.* New York: New Viewpoints, 1976.

Lynd, Staughton. "Communal Rights." *Texas Law Review* 62 (1984): 1417–41.

————. "The Genesis of the Idea of a Community Right to Industrial Property in Youngstown and Pittsburgh, 1977–1987." In *The Constitution and American Life.* Edited by David Thelen, 266–98. Ithaca, N.Y.: Cornell University Press, 1988.

————. *The Intellectual Origins of American Radicalism.* New York: Vintage Books, 1969.

————. "Resisting Plant Shutdowns." *Labor History* 30 (1989): 294–300.

————. "Toward a Not-For-Profit Economy: Public Development Authorities for Acquisition and Operation of Industry." *Harvard Civil Rights/Civil Liberties Law Review* 22 (1987): 13–41.

McBride, John. "Coal Miners." In *The Labor Movement: The Problem of Today.* Edited by George E. McNeill, 241–67. Boston: A. M. Bridgman & Co., 1887.

McCabe, James D. *The History of the Great Riots and of the Molly Maguires.* Philadelphia: National Publishing Co., 1877.

McCagg, William O. "Hungary's 'Feudalized Bourgeoisie.' " *Journal of Modern History* 44 (March 1972): 65–78.

McCloskey, Robert Green. *American Conservatism in the Age of Enterprise, 1865–1910.* New York: Harper Torchboocks, 1964 (1951).

McClymer, John F. "The Pittsburgh Survey, 1907–14: Forging an Ideology in the Steel District." *Pennsylvania History* 41 (April 1974): 169–86.

McCullough, David M. "The Case for Pittsburgh." *Pittsburgh History* 74 (Summer 1991): 62–70.

————. *The Great Bridge.* New York: Simon & Schuster, 1972.

McDonald, Terrence J. *The Parameters of Urban Fiscal Policy: Socioeconomic Change and Political Culture in San Francisco, 1860–1906.* Berkeley & Los Angeles: University of California Press, 1985.

McHugh, Jeanne. *Alexander Holley and the Makers of Steel.* Baltimore: Johns Hopkins University Press, 1980.

McKearin, George S., and Helen McKearin. *American Glass.* New York: Crown Publishers, 1941.

Mackintosh-Hemphill Co. *1803–1924: Over One Hundred and Twenty Years of*

Service—Pioneering, Engineering, Building. Pittsburgh: Mackintosh-Hemphill Co., 1924.

———. *Experience for Sale Since 1803.* Pittsburgh: Mackintosh-Hemphill Co., 1934.

———. *Rolling Mills, Rolls, and Roll Making: A Brief Historical Account of Their Development from the Fifteenth Century to the Present Day.* Pittsburgh: Mackintosh-Hemphill Co., 1953.

McNeill, George, "The Problem of Today." In *The Labor Movement: The Problem of Today.* Edited by George NcNeill, 454–69. Boston: A. M. Bridgman Co., 1887.

McNeill, George, ed. *The Labor Movement: The Problem of Today.* Boston: A. M. Bridgman & Co., 1887.

Macpherson, C. B. *Democratic Theory: Essays in Retrieval.* Oxford: Clarendon Press, 1973.

———. *The Political Theory of Possessive Individualism: Hobbes to Locke.* Oxford: Clarendon Press, 1962.

Magocsi, Paul Robert. "Carpatho-Rusyns." In *Harvard Encyclopedia of American Ethnic Groups,* edited by Stephan Thernstrom, 200–210. Cambridge, Mass.: Harvard University Press, 1980.

———. "Eastern Catholics." In *Harvard Encyclopedia of American Ethnic Groups,* edited by Stephan Thernstrom, 301–02. Cambridge, Mass.: Harvard University Press, 1980.

———. "Immigrants from Eastern Europe: The Carpatho-Rusyn Community of Proctor, Vermont." *Vermont History* 42 (1974): 48–52.

———. *The Shaping of National Identity: Subcarpathian Rus', 1848–1948.* Cambridge, Mass.: Harvard University Press, 1978.

Mann, Henry, ed. *Our Police: A History of the Pittsburgh Police Force, Under the Town and City.* Pittsburgh: Henry Fenno, 1889.

Marchbin, A. A. "Hungarian Activities in Western Pennsylvania." *Western Pennsylvania Historical Magazine* (23 September 1940): 163–74.

Marcus, Irwin. "Working Class Historiography and the Small Industrial Town: Homestead, 1880–1900." Paper presented to the Duquesne History Forum, Pittsburgh, Pa., 1983.

Marcus, Irwin, and others. "The Struggle Continues: People, Power, and Profits in Homestead, 1880–1895." Manuscript, 1984, author's possession.

Marcus, Irwin, Jennie Bullard, and Rob Moore. "Change and Continuity: Steel Workers in Homestead, Pennsylvania, 1889–1895." *Pennsylvania Magazine of History and Biography* 111 (January 1987): 61–75.

———. "The Role of the Populist Party in Homestead." *Western Pennsylvania Historical Magazine* 69 (July 1986): 273–79.

Marcuse, Herbert. "Some Social Implications of Modern Technology." *Studies in Philosophy and Social Science* 9 (1941): 414–39.

Marglin, Stephen A. "What Do Bosses Do? The Origins and Functions of Hierarchy in Capitalist Production." *Review of Radical Political Economics* 6 (Summer 1974): 60–112.

Marks, Gary Wolfe. "Trade Unions in Politics: A Comparison of Trade Union Political Activity and Its Development in Britain, Germany, and the United States in the Nineteenth and Early Twentieth Centuries." Ph.D diss., Stanford University, 1982.

Marsh, John L. "Captain Fred, Co. I., and the Workers of Homestead." *Pennsylvania History* 46 (1979): 291–311.

———. "Colonel Fred: The Handsomest Man in the Pennsylvania National Guard." *Pennsylvania Heritage* 6 (1980): 10–14.

Martin, William. "A Brief History of the Amalgamated Association." *Amalgamated Journal*, 30 August 1906.

Mauss, Marcel. *The Gift: Forms and Functions of Exchange in Archaic Societies.* Translated by Ian Cunnison. New York: W. W. Norton and Co., 1967 (1925).

Mavrinac, Harry C. "Labor Organization in the Iron and Steel Industry in the Pittsburgh District, 1870–90, with Special Reference to William Martin." M.A. thesis, University of Pittsburgh, 1956.

May, Earl Chapin. *Principio to Wheeling, 1715–1945: A Pageant of Iron and Steel.* New York: Harper & Brothers, 1945.

May, Henry F. *Protestant Churches and Industrial America.* New York: Harper Torchboocks, 1967.

Meiksins, Peter. "The 'Revolt of the Engineers' Reconsidered," *Technology and Culture* 29 (April 1988): 219–46.

Mellon, Thomas. *Thomas Mellon and His Times.* New York: Kraus Reprint Co., 1969 (1885).

Merrill, Mike. "Interview with Herbert Gutman." In *Power and Culture: Essays on the American Working Class.* Edited by Ira Berlin, 329–56. New York: Pantheon, 1987.

Merton, Robert K. "The Machine, the Worker, and the Engineer." *Science*, 2d ser., 105 (24 January 1947): 79–87.

Metcalf, William. "Can the Commercial Nomenclature of Iron Be Reconciled to Scientific Definitions of the Terms Used to Distinguish Various Classes." *Transactions of the American Institute of Mining Engineers* 5 (1876–77): 355–65.

Metcalf, William, N. M. McDowell, and Thomas Wickersham. "In Memoriam: James Park, Jr." *Proceedings of the Engineers' Society of Western Pennsylvania* 2 (1882–84): 239–40.

Meyer, B. H. "Fraternal Beneficiary Societies in the United States." *American Journal of Sociology* 6 (1901): 646–61.

Mickelson, Peter. "American Society and the Public Library in the Thought of Andrew Carnegie." *Journal of Library History, Philosophy, and Comparative Librarianship* 10 (1975): 117–38.

Miner, Curtis. " 'The Deserted Parthenon': Class, Culture, and the Carnegie Library of Homestead, 1898–1937." *Pennsylvania History* 57 (April 1990): 107–35.

———. *Homestead: The Story of a Steel Town.* Pittsburgh: Historical Society of Western Pennsylvania, 1989.

Montgomery, David. *Beyond Equality: Labor and the Radical Republicans, 1862–1872.* Urbana: University of Illinois Press, 1981 (1961).

———. *The Fall of the House of Labor: The Workplace, the State, and American Labor Activism, 1865–1925.* New York: Cambridge University Press, 1987.

———. "Gutman's Nineteenth-Century America." *Labor History* 19 (1978): 416–29.

———. "Labor and the Republic in Industrial America: 1860–1920." *Mouvement Social* 3 (1980): 201–15.

————. "On Goodwyn's Populists." *Marxist Perspectives* 1 (1978): 166–73.

————. "Strikes in Nineteenth-Century America." *Social Science History* 4 (1980): 81–104.

————. "The Working Class of the Preindustrial American City, 1780–1830." *Labor History* 9 (1968): 1–22.

————. *Workers' Control in America: Studies in the History of Work, Technology, and Labor Struggles.* New York: Cambridge University Press, 1979.

————. "Workers' Control of Machine Production in the Nineteenth Century." *Labor History* 17 (1976): 485–509.

Moore, Barrington, Jr. *Injustice: The Social Bases of Obedience and Revolt.* White Plains, N.Y.: M. E. Sharpe, 1978.

Morawska, Eva. "The Internal Status Hierarchy in the East European Immigrant Communities of Johnstown, Pennsylvania, 1890–1930s." *Journal of Social History* 16 (Fall 1982): 75–107.

Morgan, Charles H. "Some Landmarks in the History of the Rolling Mill." *Transactions of the American Society of Mechanical Engineers* 22 (1901): 31–64.

Morgan, Edmund S. "Slavery and Freedom: The American Paradox." *Journal of American History* 59 (1972): 5–29.

Morgan, H. Wayne. *The Gilded Age: A Reappraisal.* Syracuse N.Y.: Syracuse University Press, 1963.

Morgan, Kenneth O. *Rebirth of a Nation: Wales, 1880–1980.* New York: Oxford University Press, 1981.

Morton, G. R., and N. Mutton "The Transition to Cort's Puddling Process." *Journal of the Iron and Steel Institute* 205 (1967): 722–28.

Mowry, George E. *The Era of Theodore Roosevelt and the Birth of Modern America, 1900–1912.* New York: Harper & Row, 1958.

Muller, Edward K. "Metropolis and Region: A Framework for Enquiry Into Western Pennsylvania." In *City at the Point: Essays on the Social History of Pittsburgh.* Edited by Samuel P. Hays, 181–211. Pittsburgh: University of Pittsburgh Press, 1989.

Mumford, Lewis. "Authoritarian and Democratic Technics." *Technology and Culture* 5 (Winter 1964): 1–8.

————. *Technics and Civilization.* New York: Harcourt Brace & Co., 1934.

Munro, Dana G. *Intervention and Dollar Diplomacy in the Caribbean, 1900–1921.* Princeton: Princeton University Press, 1964.

• Munslow, Alun. "Andrew Carnegie and the Discourse of Cultural Hegemony." *Journal of American Studies* 22 (August 1988): 213–24.

Musson, A. E., ed. *Science, Technology, and Economic Growth in the Eighteenth Century.* London: Methuen & Co., 1972.

Musson, A. E., and Eric Robinson. *Science and Technology in the Irish Republic.* Toronto: University of Toronto Press, 1969.

Nash, Gary B. "Popular Political Thinking in Late Eighteenth-Century America." Paper presented at a conference entitled "All the Powers Vested: North Carolina and the Federal Constitution, 1780–1800," Duke University, October 1985.

Nash, Michael. *Conflict and Accommodation: Coal Miners, Steel Workers, and Socialism, 1890–1920.* Westport, Conn.: Greenwood Press, 1982.

————. "Conflict and Accommodation: Some Aspects of the Political Behavior of

America's Coal Miners and Steel Workers, 1890–1920." Ph.D. diss., State University of New York at Binghamton, 1975.

National Conference of Catholic Bishops. *Economic Justice for All: Pastoral Letter on Catholic Social Teaching and the U.S. Economy.* Washington, D.C.: National Conference of Catholic Bishops, 1986.

Nelson, Daniel. *F. W. Taylor and the Rise of Scientific Management.* Madison: University of Wisconsin Press, 1980.

———. *Managers and Workers: Origins of the New Factory System in the United States, 1880–1920.* Madison: University of Wisconsin Press, 1975.

———. "Scientific Management, Systematic Management, and Labor, 1880–1915." *Business History Review* 48 (1974): 479–500.

Nevins, Allan. *Abram S. Hewitt, with Some Account of Peter Cooper.* New York: Harper & Brothers, 1935.

Nicholas, Thomas. *The History and Antiquities of Glamorganshire and Its Families.* London: Longmans, Green & Co., 1874.

Nicholson, D. K. "Heating Furnaces." *Transactions of the American Society of Mechanical Engineers* 11 (1890): 896–902.

Nizmansky, Jaraj J., ed., *Dejiny a Pamätnica Národného Slovenského Spolku, 1890–1950* [History and Memorial Album of the National Slovak Society, 1890–1950]. Pittsburgh: National News, 1950.

Noble, David F. *America by Design: Science, Technology, and the Rise of Corporate Capitalism.* New York: Oxford University Press, 1977.

———. "Present Tense Technology." *democracy* 3 (Spring 1983): 8–24; (Summer 1983): 70–82.

Northwestern Historical Association. *Memoirs of Allegheny County.* 2 vols. Madison, Wis.: Northwestern Historical Association, 1904.

Novack, David E., and Richard Perlman. "The Structure of Wages in the American Iron and Steel Industry, 1860–1890." *Journal of Economic History* 22 (September 1962): 334–47.

Novak, Michael. *The Guns of Lattimer. The True Story of a Massacre and a Trial, August 1897–March 1898.* New York: Basic Books, 1978.

Nowlin, William Gerald, Jr. "The Political Thought of Alexander Berkman." Ph.D. diss., Tufts University, 1980.

Nugent, Walter T. K. *Money and American Society, 1865–1900.* New York: Free Press, 1968.

———. *The Money Question during Reconstruction.* New York: W. W. Norton Co., 1967.

Nuwer, Michael. "From Batch to Flow: Production Technology and Work-Force Skills in the Steel Industry, 1880–1920." *Technology and Culture* 29 (October 1988): 808–38.

Oates, W. C. "The Homestead Strike: A Congressional View." *North American Review* 155 (September 1892): 355–64.

O'Connor, Richard. "Cinderheads and Iron Lungs: Window Glassworkers and Their Unions, 1865–1920." Ph.D. diss., University of Pittsburgh, in progress.

Oestreicher, Richard. "Socialism and the Knights of Labor in Detroit, 1877–1889." *Labor History* 22 (Winter 1981): 5–30.

———. *Solidarity and Fragmentation: Working People and Class Consciousness in Detroit, 1875–1900*. Urbana: University of Illinois Press, 1986.

———. "Working-Class Formation, Development, and Consciousness in Pittsburgh, 1790–1960." In *City at the Point: Essays on the Social History of Pittsburgh*. Edited by Samuel P. Hays, 111–50. Pittsburgh: University of Pittsburgh Press, 1989.

Oliver, John W. *History of American Technology*. New York: Ronald Press Co., 1956.

Overman, Frederick. *A Treatise on Metallurgy, Comprising Mining and General and Particular Metallurgical Operations*. New York: D. Appleton, 1854.

Palmer, Bruce. *Man over Money: The Southern Populist Critique of American Capitalism*. Chapel Hill: University of North Carolina Press, 1980.

Palmer, Bryan D., and Gregory S. Kealey. *Dreaming of What Might Be: The Knights of Labor in Ontario, 1880–1900*. New York: Cambridge University Press, 1982.

Palmer, N. D. *The Irish Land League*. New Haven, Conn.: Yale University Press, 1952.

Park, James, Jr., and James Hemphill. "Kloman Eulogy." *Proceedings of the Engineers' Society of Western Pennsylvania* 1 (1880–82): 250–54.

Parsons, A. F. *History and Commerce of Pittsburgh and Environs, Consisting of Allegheny, McKeesport, Braddock, and Homestead, 1893–94*. New York: A. F. Parsons, 1894.

Pennypacker, Isaac. "Quay of Pennsylvania," *American Mercury* 9 (1926): 357–64.

Pepper, Simon. "A Department Store of Learning." *Times Literary Supplement*, 9 May 1986.

Perlman, Selig. *A Theory of the Labor Movement*. New York: MacMillan Co., 1928.

———. "Upheaval and Reorganisation." In *History of Labor in the United States*. 4 vols. Edited by John R. Commons, 2: 195–520. New York: The Macmillan Co., 1918–35.

Perrucci, Robert, and Joel Gerstl, eds. *The Engineers and the Social System*. New York: John Wiley & Sons, 1969.

Peters, Richard, Jr. *Two Centuries of Iron Smelting in Pennsylvania*. Philadelphia: Chester Times Press, 1921.

Phillips, W. B. "Note on the Possible Origin of the Pneumatic Process of Making Steel." *Transactions of the American Institute of Mining Engineers* 28 (1898): 745–46.

Pittsburgh Writers' Club. *Book of Writers*. Pittsburgh: Writers Club of Pittsburgh, 1897.

Pocock, J. G. A. *The Machiavellian Moment: Florentine Political Thought and the Atlantic Republican Tradition*. Princeton: Princeton University Press, 1975.

———. "Machiavelli, Harrington, and English Political Ideologies in the Eighteenth Century." *William and Mary Quarterly* 22 (1965): 549–83.

———. *Politics, Languages and Time: Essays on Political Thought and History*. New York: Atheneum, 1971.

———. *Three British Revolutions: 1641, 1688, and 1776*. Princeton: Princeton University Press, 1980.

———. "Virtue and Commerce in the Eighteenth Century." *Journal of Interdisciplinary History* (1972): 119–34.

Polanyi, Karl. *The Great Transformation: The Political and Economic Origins of Our Time*. New York: Farrar & Rinehart, 1944.

Pollard, Sidney. "Factory Discipline in the Industrial Revolution." *Economic History Review* 16 (1963): 254–71.

———. *The Genesis of Modern Management: A Study of the Industrial Revolution in Great Britain*. Cambridge, Mass.: Harvard University Press, 1965.

———. *History of Labour in Sheffield*. Liverpool: Liverpool University Press, 1959.

Popplewell, Frank. *Some Modern Conditions and Recent Developments in Iron and Steel Production in America*. Manchester, England: University of Manchester Press, 1906.

Potemra, Ladislav A. "Ruthenians in Slovakia and the Greek Catholic Diocese of Presov." *Slovak Studies* 1 (1961): 199–220.

Potter, E. C. "Review of American Blast Furnace Practice." *Transactions of the American Institute of Mining Engineers* 23 (August 1893): 370–82.

Powderly, T. V. "The Homestead Strike: A Knight of Labor's View." *North American Review* 155 (September 1892): 370–75.

———. *The Path I Trod: The Autobiography of Terrence V. Powderly*. Edited by Harry J. Carman, Henry David, and Paul N. Guthrie. New York: Columbia University Press, 1940.

———. *Thirty Years of Labor: 1859–1889*. Columbus, Ohio: Excelsior Publishing House, 1889.

Price, Richard. "The Labour Process and Labour History." *Social History* 8 (1983): 57–75.

Prime, Frederick, "What Steel Is." *Transactions of the American Institute of Mining Engineers* 4 (1875–76): 328–39.

Procko, Bohdan P. "The Establishment of the Ruthenian Church in the United States, 1884–1907." *Pennsylvania History* 42 (1975): 137–54.

Pursell, Carroll W., Jr. "History of Technology." In *A Guide to the Culture of Science, Technology, and Medicine*. Edited by Paul T. Durbin, 70–120. New York: Free Press, 1980.

Rabb, Theodore K., and R. I. Rotberg, eds. *Industrialization and Urbanization: Studies in Interdisciplinary History*. Princeton: Princeton University Press, 1981.

Rachleff, Peter J. *Black Labor in the South: Richmond, Virginia, 1865–1890*. Philadelphia: Temple University Press, 1984.

Rae, John B. "The Engineer as Business Man in American Industry." *Explorations in Entrepreneurial History* 7 (December 1954): 94–104.

———. "The Engineer-Entrepreneur in the American Automobile Industry." *Explorations in Entrepreneurial History* 8 (October 1955): 1–11.

Raymond. R. W. "Biographical Notice of W. R. Jones." *Transactions of the American Society of Mechanical Engineers* 18 (1889–90): 621–24.

Reddy, William M. "The *Batteurs* and the Informer's Eye: A Labor Dispute under the French Second Empire." *History Workshop Journal* 7 (Spring 1979): 30–44.

———. "Letter to the Editorial Collective." *History Workshop Journal* 10 (August 1980): 216–17.

———. *The Rise of Market Culture: The Textile Trade and French Society, 1750–1900*. New York: Cambridge University Press, 1984.

————. "The Textile Trade and the Language of the Crowd at Rouen, 1752–1871." *Past and Present* 74 (1977): 62–89.

Redlich, Fritz. *History of American Business Leaders.* Vol.1. Ann Arbor, Mich.: Edwards Brothers, 1940.

Reeves, Charles E. "Davitt's American Tour of 1882." *Quarterly Journal of Speech* 54 (1968): 357–62.

Reid, Ira de Augustine. "The Negro in the Major Industries and Building Trades in Pittsburgh." M.A. thesis, University of Pittsburgh, 1925.

Reitell, Charles. *Machinery and Its Benefits to Labor in the Crude Iron and Steel Industries.* Menasha, Wis.: George Banta Publishing Co., 1917.

Renkiewicz, Frank, comp. *A Guide to Newspapers and Periodicals: The Carpatho-Ruthenian Microfilm Project.* St. Paul, Minn.: Immigration History Research Center, 1979.

Ricker, Ralph Ross. *The Greenback-Labor Movement in Pennsylvania.* Bellefonte: Pennsylvania Heritage, 1966.

Richards, Miles. "Thomas A. Armstrong: A Forgotten Advocate of Labor." Manuscript, 1983, author's possession.

Ricoeur, Paul. "The Model of the Text: Meaningful Action Considered as Text." *Social Research* 38 (Autumn 1971): 529–62.

Roberts, Percival, Jr. "The Puddling Process, Past and Present. *Transactions of the American Institute of Mining Engineers* 8 (1879–80): 355–62.

Robinson, Jesse S. *The Amalgamated Association of Iron, Steel, and Tin Workers.* Baltimore: Johns Hopkins University Press, 1920.

Rock, Howard B. *Artisans and the New Republic: The Tradesmen of New York City in the Age of Jefferson.* New York: New York University Press, 1979.

Rodechko, James Paul. *Patrick Ford and His Search for America: A Case Study of Irish-American Journalism.* New York: Arno Press, 1976.

Rodgers, Daniel T. "Tradition, Modernity and the American Industrial Worker: Reflections and Critique." *Journal of Interdisciplinary History* 7 (Spring 1977): 655–81.

————. *The Work Ethic in Industrial America, 1850–1920.* Chicago: University of Chicago Press, 1978.

Roediger, David. "Ira Steward and the Anti-Slavery Origins of American Eight-Hour Theory." *Labor History* 27 (Summer 1986): 410–26.

Roney, Frank. *Irish Rebel and California Labor Leader: An Autobiography.* Edited by Ira B. Cross. New York: Arno Press, 1976.

Rose, Carol. "The Comedy of the Commons: Custom, Commerce, and Inherently Public Property." *University of Chicago Law Review* 53 (1986): 711–81.

Rosenberg, David. "Wages versus the Library: The *National Labor Tribune* and Carnegie Library Philanthropy, 1876–1908." Seminar paper, University of Pittsburgh, 1988.

Rosenberg, Nathan. "The Direction of Technological Change: Inducement Mechanisms and Focusing Devices." *Economic Development and Cultural Change* 18 (October 1969): 3–24. Reprinted in his *Perspectives in Technology,* 108–25. Cambridge: Cambridge University Press, 1975.

————. *Inside the Black Box: Technology and Economics.* Cambridge: Cambridge University Press, 1982.

————. *Technology and American Economic Growth.* New York: Harper & Row, 1973.

Rosenberg, Nathan, comp. *The American System of Manufactures: The Report of the Committee on the Machinery of the United States, 1855. . . .* Edinburgh: Edinburgh University Press, 1969.

Ross, Steven J. "Workers on the Edge: Work, Leisure, and Politics in Industrializing Cincinnati." Ph.D. diss., Princeton University, 1980.

———. *Workers on the Edge: Work, Leisure, and Politics in Industrializing Cincinnati, 1788–1890.* New York: Columbia University Press, 1985.

Rossell, Glenora E. *Pennsylvania Newspapers.* 2d ed. Pittsburgh: Pennsylvania Library Association, 1978.

Roy, Andrew. *A History of the Coal Miners of the United States.* Columbus, Ohio: J. L. Trauger Printing Co., 1906.

Rubery, Jill. "Structured Labour Markets, Worker Organization, and Low Pay." *Cambridge Journal of Economics* 2 (March 1978): 17–36.

Rusnak, Michael. "The Religious Customs of the Slovaks of the Byzantine-Slavonic Rite." *Slovak Studies* 3 (1963): 173–77.

Ruttan, V. W. "Usher and Schumpeter on Invention, Innovation, and Technological Change." *Quarterly Journal of Economics* 73 (1959): 596–606.

Ryan, Mary P. *Women in Public: Between Banners and Ballots, 1825–1880.* Baltimore: Johns Hopkins University Press, 1990.

Sabel, Charles F. *Work and Politics: The Division of Labor in Industry.* Cambridge: Cambridge University Press, 1982.

Sabel, Charles, and Jonathan Zeitlin. "Historical Alternatives to Mass Production." *Past and Present* 108 (August 1985): 133–76.

St. Anthony's Church. *Souvenir Booklet of the Golden Jubilee of St. Anthony's Church, Homestead, Pennsylvania.* Pittsburgh: Pittsburgher Publications, 1949.

St. Mary Magdalene Church, Homestead, Pa. *One Hundredth Anniversary: St. Mary Magdalene Church.* Homestead: St. Mary Magdalene Church, 1980.

St. Michael Church, Munhall, Pa. *75th Anniversary.* Pittsburgh: n.p., 1972.

Salisbury, Ruth, ed. *Pennsylvania Newspapers: A Bibliography and Union List.* Pittsburgh: Pennsylvania Library Association, 1969.

Salvatore, Nick. *Eugene V. Debs: Citizen and Socialist.* Urbana: University of Illinois Press, 1982.

———. "Response to Sean Wilentz, 'Against Exceptionalism: Class Consciousness and the American Labor Movement, 1790–1920'." *International Labor and Working Class History* 26 (Fall 1984): 25–30.

———. "Some Thoughts on Class and Citizenship in America in the Late Nineteenth Century." In *A l'ombre de la Statue de la Liberté: Immigrants, ouvriers et citoyens dans la République américaine, 1880–1920.* Edited by Marianne Debouzy, 215–30. Paris: Presses Universitaires de Vincennes, 1988.

Sawyer, John E. "The Social Basis of the American System of Manufacturing." *Journal of Economic History* 14 (1954): 361–79.

Scheiber, Harry. "Public Rights and the Rule of Law in American Legal History." *California Law Review* 72 (1984): 217–50.

Schlatter, Richard. *Private Property: The History of an Idea.* New Brunswick, N. J.: Rutgers University Press, 1951.

Schnapper, Morris B. *American Labor: A Pictorial Social History.* Washington: Public Affairs Press, 1972.

Schneider, Linda. "American Iron and Steel Workers Reinterpret Republicanism, 1870–1920." Manuscript, c. 1984, author's possession.

——. "American Nationality and Workers' Consciousness in Industrial Conflict, 1870–1920: Three Case Studies." Ph.D. diss., Columbia University, 1975.

——. "The Citizen Striker: Workers' Ideology In the Homestead Strike of 1892." *Labor History* 23 (1982): 47–66.

——. "Republicanism Reinterpreted: American Ironworkers, 1860–1892." In *A l'Ombre de la Statue de la Liberté: Immigrants, ouvriers et citoyens dans la République américaine, 1880–1920*, edited by Marianne Debouzy, 199–214. Paris: Presses Universitaires de Vincennes, 1988.

Schneirov, Richard Samuel. "The Knights of Labor in the Chicago Labor Movement and in Municipal Politics, 1877–1887." Ph.D. diss., Northern Illinois University, 1984.

Schooley, M. P., and J. R. Schooley, comps. *Directory of Homestead, 1890*. Homestead: Local News, 1890.

——. *Directory of Homestead, 1891*. Homestead: Local News, 1891.

——. *Directory of Homestead, 1892*. Homestead: Local News, 1892.

Schroeder, Gertrude G. *The Growth of the Major Steel Companies, 1900–1950*. Baltimore: Johns Hopkins Press, 1953.

Schubert, H. R. *History of the British Iron and Steel Industry*. London: Routledge & K. Paul, 1957.

Schumpeter, Joseph A. *Capitalism, Socialism, and Democracy*. 3d ed. New York: Harper & Brothers, 1950.

Scobey, David. "Boycotting the Politics Factory: Labor Radicalism and the New York Mayoral Election of 1886." *Radical History Review* 28–30 (Sept. 1984): 280–325.

Scott, Henry D. *Iron and Steel in Wheeling*. Toledo, Ohio: Caslon Co., 1929.

Scott, Joan W. *The Glassworkers of Carmaux: French Craftsmen and Political Action in a Nineteenth-Century City*. Cambridge, Mass.: Harvard University Press, 1974.

Scoville, Warren C. *Revolution in Glassmaking: Entrepreneurship and Technological Change in the American Industry, 1889–1920*. Cambridge, Mass.: Harvard University Press, 1948.

Scranton, Philip. "The Workplace, Technology, and Theory in American Labor History." *International Labor and Working Class History* 35 (Spring 1989): 3–22.

Seaver, Kenneth. "The Manufacture of Open-Hearth Steel." In *The ABC of Iron and Steel*. Edited by A. O. Backert, 133–54. Cleveland: Penton Publishing Co., 1925.

Seilhamer, George Overcash. *Leslie's History of the Republican Party*. Vol. 2. New York: Judge Publishing Co., [c. 1910].

Senyshyn, Ambrose. "The Ukrainian Catholics in the United States." *Eastern Churches Quarterly* 6 (1946): 439–58.

Serene, Frank Huff. "Immigrant Steelworkers in the Monongahela Valley: Their Communities and the Development of a Labor Class Consciousness." Ph.D. diss., University of Pittsburgh, 1979.

Sewell, William H., Jr. *Work and Revolution in France: The Language of Labor from the Old Regime to 1848*. New York: Cambridge University Press, 1980.

Shand, Gwendolyn V. "The Sociological Aspects of an Industrial Community." M.A. thesis, Carnegie Institute of Technology, 1923.

Sharkey, Robert P. *Money, Class, and Party: An Economic Study of the Civil War and Reconstruction.* Baltimore: Johns Hopkins Press, 1967.

Sheppard, Muriel Earley. *Cloud by Day: The Story of Coal and Coke People.* Chapel Hill: University of North Carolina Press, 1947.

Shefter, Martin. "Trade Unions and Political Machines: The Organization and Disorganization of the American Working Class in the Late Nineteenth Century." In *Working-Class Formation: Nineteenth-Century Patterns in Western Europe and the United States.* Edited by Ira Katzelson and Aristide R. Zolberg, 197–276. Princeton: Princeton University Press, 1986.

Shinn, William P. "Pittsburgh—Its Resources and Surroundings." *Transactions of the American Society of Mechanical Engineers* 8 (1879–80): 11–26.

Sinclair, Bruce. *A Centennial History of the American Society of Mechanical Engineers, 1889–1980.* Toronto: University of Toronto Press, 1980.

Slade, Frederick J. "Bessemer Steel." A special report submitted by Abram S. Hewitt. In *Reports of the U.S. Commissioners to the Paris Universal Exposition, 1867.* Washington, D.C.: Government Printing Office, 1870: 63–84.

Smeltzer, Wallace Guy. *The History of United Methodism in Western Pennsylvania.* Nashville: Parthenon Press, 1975.

———. *Homestead Methodism, 1830–1933.* Pittsburgh: D. K. Murdoch Co., 1933.

———. *Methodism in Western Pennsylvania, 1784–1968.* Little Valley, N.Y.: Straight Publishing Co., 1969.

———. *Methodism on the Headwaters of the Ohio: The History of the Pittsburgh Conference of the Methodist Church.* Nashville: Parthenon Press, 1951.

Smith, Adam. *An Inquiry Into the Nature and Causes of The Wealth of Nations.* New York: The Modern Library, 1937 (1776).

Smith, Cyril Stanley. *A History of Metallography: The Development of Ideas on the Structure of Metals before 1890.* Chicago: University of Chicago Press, 1960.

Smith, Cyril Stanley, ed. *Proceedings of the Sorby Centennial Symposium on the History of Metallurgy.* New York: Gordon & Breach Science Publishers, 1965.

Smith, Merritt Roe. *Harper's Ferry Armory and the New Technology: The Challenge of Change.* Ithaca, N.Y.: Cornell University Press, 1977.

Smith, Percifer F. *Notable Men of Pittsburgh and Vicinity.* Pittsburgh: Pittsburgh Printing Co., 1901.

Smith-Rosenberg, Carroll. "The Female World of Love and Ritual: Relations between Women in Nineteenth-Century America." *Signs* 1 (1975): 1–29.

Sobel, Robert, and John Raino. *Biographical Directory of the Governors of the United States, 1789–1978.* Westport, Conn.: Merkler Books, 1978.

Soderbergh, Peter A. "Theodore Dreiser in Pittsburgh, 1894." *Western Pennsylvania Historical Magazine* 51 (July 1968): 229–42.

Soffer, Benson. "A Theory of Trade Union Development: The Role of the 'Autonomous' Workman." *Labor History* 1 (Spring 1960): 141–63.

Solo, Carolyn S. "Innovation in the Capitalist Process: A Critique of Schumpeterian Theory." *Quarterly Journal of Economics* 65 (1951): 417–28.

Sombart, Werner. *Why Is There No Socialism in the United States?* Translated by Patricia M. Hocking. London: Macmillan, 1976 (1906).

Spahr, Charles B. *America's Working People*. New York: Longmans, Green & Co., 1900.

Stark, David. "Class Struggle and the Transformation of the Labor Process: A Relational Approach." *Theory and Society* 9 (1980): 89–150.

Staudenmaier, John M. "Recent Trends in the History of Technology," *American Historical Review* 95 (June 1990): 715–25.

Steffens, Lincoln. *The Shame of the Cities*. New York: McClure, Phillips & Co. 1904.

Stein, Howard Finn. "An Ethno-Historic Study of Slovak American Identity." Ph.D. diss., University of Pittsburgh, 1972.

Stevens, Sylvester K. "The Hearth of the Nation." In *Pittsburgh: The Story of an American City*. Edited by Stefan Lorant, 177–206. Garden City, N.Y.: Doubleday & Co., 1964.

Stevens, W. F. "The Carnegie Library, Homestead." In Margaret F. Byington, *Homestead: The Households of a Mill Town*, 255–70. Pittsburgh: University Center for International Studies, 1974 (1910).

Stoebuck, William B. "A General Theory of Eminent Domain." *Washington Law Review* 47 (1972): 553–608.

Stolarik, Marian Mark. "Immigration and Urbanization: The Slovak Experience, 1870–1918." Ph.D. diss., University of Minnesota, 1974.

———. "From Field to Factory: The Historiography of Slovak Immigration to the United States." *International Migration Review* 10 (Spring 1976): 81–102.

———. "Slovaks." In *Harvard Encyclopedia of American Ethnic Groups*. Edited by Stephan Thernstrom, 926–34. Cambridge, Mass.: Harvard University Press, 1980.

Stone, Katherine. "The Origins of Job Structures in the Steel Industry." *Review of Radical Political Economics* 6 (1974): 113–73.

Stowell, Myron R. *"Fort Frick," Or the Siege of Homestead*. Pittsburgh: Pittsburgh Printing Co., 1893.

Strassman, W. Paul. *Risk and Technological Innovation: American Manufacturing Methods during the Nineteenth Century*. Ithaca, N.Y.: Cornell University Press, 1959.

Stromquist, Shelton. "Working Class Organization and Industrial Change in Pittsburgh." Seminar paper, University of Pittsburgh, 1973.

Sturm, Theodore Paul. "The Social Gospel in the Methodist Churches of Pittsburgh, 1865–1920." Ph.D. diss., West Virginia University, 1971.

Sullivan, William A. *The Industrial Worker in Pennsylvania, 1800–1840*. Harrisburg: Pennsylvania Historical and Museum Commission, 1955.

Susman, Warren I. *Culture as History: The Transformation of American Society in the Twentieth Century*. New York: Pantheon Books, 1984.

Swank, James M. *The History of the Manufacture of Iron in All Ages*. Philadelphia: American Iron and Steel Association, 1892.

———. "The Manufacture of Iron and Steel Rails in Western Pennsylvania." *Pennsylvania Magazine of History and Biography* 28 (1904): 1–11.

———. *Progressive Pennsylvania*. Philadelphia: J. B. Lippinncott Company, 1908.

Swetnam, George. *Andrew Carnegie*. Boston: Twayne Publishers, 1980.

———. "Labor-Management Relations in Pennsylvania's Steel Industry, 1800–1959." *Western Pennsylvania Historical Magazine* 62 (October 1979): 321–32.

Sykes, Robert. "Early Chartism and Trade Unionism in South-East Lancashire."

In *The Chartist Experience: Studies in Working-Class Radicalism and Culture, 1830–1860*. Edited by James Epstein and Dorothy Thompson, 152–93. London: MacMillan, 1982.

Taft, Philip. *Organized Labor in American History.* New York: Harper & Row, 1964.

Tarr, Joel A. "Infrastructure and City-Building in the Nineteenth and Twentieth Centuries." In *City at the Point: Essays on the Social History of Pittsburgh.* Edited by Samuel P. Hays, 213–63. Pittsburgh: University of Pittsburgh Press, 1989.

———. *Transportation Innovation and Changing Spatial Patterns: Pittsburgh, 1850– 1910.* Pittsburgh: Transportation Research Institute, Carnegie-Mellon University, 1972.

Tawney, R. H. *Religion and the Rise of Capitalism: A Historical Study.* London: J. Murray, 1926.

Taylor, Charles. "Interpretation and the Sciences of Man." In *Interpretive Social Science: A Reader.* Edited by Paul Rabinow and William M. Sullivan, 25–71. Berkeley & Los Angeles: University of California Press, 1979.

Tchneroff, D. K. "Notes on the Manufacture of Bessemer Steel." *Metallurgical Review* 1 (1877–78): 139–52, 283–90, 349–54.

Temin, Peter. *Iron and Steel in Nineteenth-Century America: An Economic Inquiry.* Cambridge, Mass.: MIT Press, 1964.

———. "Labor Scarcity and the Problem of American Industrial Efficiency in the 1850s." *Journal of Economic History* 26 (September 1966): 277–98.

———. "Labor Scarcity in America." *Journal of Interdisciplinary History* 1 (1971): 251–64.

———. "A New Look at Hunter's Hypothesis about the AnteBellum Iron Industry." *American Economic Review, Papers and Proceedings* 59 (1964): 344–51.

Thernstrom, Stephan, ed. *Harvard Encyclopedia of American Ethnic Groups.* Cambridge, Mass.: Harvard University Press, 1980.

Thomas, W. I., and F. Zmaniecki. *The Polish Peasants in Europe and America.* 2 vols. New York: Alfred Knopf, 1927.

Thompson, E. P. *The Making of the English Working Class.* New York: Viking, 1963.

———. "The Moral Economy of the English Crowd in the Eighteenth Century." *Past and Present* 50 (1971): 76–136.

———. "Patrician Society, Plebeian Culture." *Journal of Social History* (Summer 1974): 382–405.

———. *The Poverty of Theory and Other Essays.* New York: Monthly Review Press, 1978.

———. "Time, Work-Discipline, and Industrial Capitalism." *Past and Present* 38 (1967): 56–97.

Thrasher, Eugene C. "The Magee-Flinn Political Machine, 1895–1903." M.A. thesis, University of Pittsburgh, 1951.

Thurston, George H. *Allegheny County's Hundred Years.* Pittsburgh: A. A. Anderson & Son, 1888.

———. *Pittsburgh's Progress, Industries, and Resources.* Pittsburgh: A. A. Anderson & Son, 1886.

Thurston, Robert Henry. "The Mechanical Engineer—His Work and His Policy." *Van Nostrand's Engineering Magazine* 27 (December 1882): 482–99. Reprinted in *Transactions of the American Society of Mechanical Engineers* 4 (1883): 75–105.

————. "Our Progress in Mechanical Engineering." *Van Nostrand's Engineering Magazine* 25 (December 1881): 455–70.

————. "President's Inaugural Address." *Transactions of the American Society of Mechanical Engineers* 1 (1880): 1–15.

Tilly, Charles. "Collective Violence in European Perspective." In *Violence in America: Historical and Comparative Perspectives*. Rev. ed. Edited by Hugh Davis Graham and Ted Robert Gurr, 83–118. Beverly Hills, Calif.: Sage Publications, 1979.

Tilly, Charles, and Louise A. Tilly, eds. *Class Conflict and Collective Action*. Beverly Hills, Calif.: Sage Publications, 1981.

Tilly, Charles, Louise Tilly, and Richard Tilly. *The Rebellious Century, 1830–1930*. Cambridge, Mass.: Harvard University Press, 1975.

Tocqueville, Alexis de. *Democracy in America*. Translated by Henry Reeve and others. New York: The Modern Library, 1981 (1835 and 1840).

Towne, Henry R. "The Engineer as an Economist." *Transactions of the American Society of Mechanical Engineers* 7 (1886): 428–432.

Trachtenberg, Alan. *Brooklyn Bridge: Fact and Symbol*. New York: Oxford University Press, 1965.

————. *The Incorporation of America: Culture and Society in the Gilded Age*. New York: Hill & Wang, 1982.

Trachtenberg, Alexander. *The History of Legislation for the Protection of Coal Miners in Pennsylvania, 1824–1915*. New York: International Publishers, 1942.

Trusilo, Sharon. "The Ironworkers' Case for Amalgamation, 1867–1876." *Western Pennsylvania Historical Magazine* 71 (Jan. 1988): 47–67.

Twain, Mark, and Charles Dudley Warner. *The Gilded Age: A Tale of Today*. New York: Harper & Brothers, 1915 (1873).

Ulman, Lloyd. *The Rise of the National Trade Union: The Development and Significance of Its Structure, Governing Institutions, and Economic Policies*. Cambridge, Mass.: Harvard University Press, 1955.

Unger, Irwin. *The Greenback Era: A Social and Political History of American Finance, 1865–1879*. Princeton: Princeton University Press, 1964.

United States Steel Corporation. *Homestead Works, United States Steel*. Pittsburgh: United States Steel Corporation, n.d., c. 1982.

————. *U.S. Steel's Homestead Works: Into a Second Century*. Pittsburgh: U.S. Steel Corp., 1981.

Urwick, Lyndall. "Management's Debt to Engineers." *Advanced Management* 17 (December 1952): 5–12.

Usher, A. P. *A History of Mechanical Inventions*. Cambridge, Mass.: Harvard University Press, 1954.

Veblen, Thorstein. *The Engineers and the Price System*. New York: B. W. Huebsch, 1921.

————. *The Theory of Business Enterprise*. New York: Charles Scribner's Sons, 1904.

————. *The Theory of the Leisure Class: An Economic Study of Institutions*. New York: Random House, 1934.

Vecoli, Rudolph J. "Contadini in Chicago: A Critique of *The Uprooted*." *Journal of American History* 51 (1964): 404–17.

————. "The Immigrant Experience: New Perspectives and Old Prejudices." *Reviews in American History* 7 (1979): 43–50.

Walker, Joseph E. *Hopewell Village: A Social and Economic History of an Iron-Making Community.* Philadelphia: University of Pennsylvania Press, 1966.

Walker, Samuel. " 'Abolish the Wage System': Terrence V. Powderly and the Rhetoric of Labor Reform." Paper presented to the Knights of Labor Symposium, Newberry Library, Chicago, Ill., 1979.

———. "Terrence V. Powderly, 'Labor Mayor': Workingmen's Politics in Scranton, Pennsylvania, 1870–1884." Ph.D. diss., Ohio State University, 1973.

Walkowitz, Daniel J. *Worker City, Company Town: Iron and Cotton Worker Protest in Troy and Cohoes, New York, 1855–1884.* Urbana: University of Illinois Press, 1978.

Wall, Joseph Frazier. *Andrew Carnegie.* Pittsburgh: University of Pittsburgh Press, 1989 (1970).

Walsh, Victor A. "Class, Culture, and Nationalism: The Irish Catholics of Pittsburgh, 1870–83." Seminar paper, University of Pittsburgh, 1976.

———. " 'A Fanatic Heart': The Cause of Irish-American Nationalism in Pittsburgh during the Gilded Age." *Journal of Social History* 15 (1982): 182–204.

Walsh, William David. *The Diffusion of Technological Change in the Pennsylvania Pig Iron Industry, 1850–70.* New York: Arno Press, 1975.

Walzer, Michael. *Exodus and Revolution.* New York: Basic Books, 1985.

———. "Puritanism as a Revolutionary Ideology." *History and Theory* 3 (1963): 59–90.

Ward, John W. "Violence, Anarchy, and Alexander Berkman." *New York Review of Books,* 5 November 1970, 25–30.

Ware, Norman J. *The Labor Movement in the United States, 1860–95: A Study in Democracy.* New York: Appleton & Co., 1929.

Warner, A., and Company. *History of Allegheny County, Pennsylvania.* 2 vols. Chicago: A. Warner & Company, 1889.

Warren, Kenneth. *The American Steel Industry, 1850–70: A Geographical Interpretation.* Oxford: Clarendon Press, 1973.

———. "The Business Career of Henry Clay Frick." *Pittsburgh History* 73 (Spring 1990): 3–15.

Wartenberg, Thomas E. "Marx, Class Consciousness, and Social Transformation." *Praxis International* 2 (April 1982): 52–69.

Warzeski, Walter C. *Byzantine Rite Rusins in Carpatho-Ruthenia and America.* Pittsburgh: Byzantine Seminary Press, 1971.

Weber, Max. *Economy and Society.* Edited by Guenther Roth and Claus Wittick, and translated by Roth, Wittick, and others. 3 vols. New York: Bedminster Press, 1968.

Weber, Michael P. *Don't Call Me Boss: David L. Lawrence, Pittsburgh's Renaissance Mayor.* Pittsburgh: University of Pittsburgh Press, 1988.

Wedding, Hermann. "The Nomenclature of Iron." *Transactions of the American Institute of Mining Engineers* 5 (1876–77): 309–14.

Weeks, Joseph D. "The Invention of the Bessemer Process." *Transactions of the American Institute of Mining Engineers* 26 (1896): 980–91.

Weitzman, David L. *Traces of the Past: A Field Guide to Industrial Archaeology.* New York: Scribners, 1980.

Wellman, S. T. "The Early History of Open-Hearth Steel Manufacture in the

United States." *Transactions of the American Society of Mechanical Engineers* 23 (1901–02): 78–98.

Welter, Barbara. "The Cult of True Womanhood: 1820–1860." *American Quarterly* 18 (1966): 151–74.

Wertime, Theodore A. *The Coming of the Age of Steel.* Chicago: University of Chicago Press, 1962.

Whitlatch, Lewis Wade. "The Attitude of the Public towards the Homestead Strike." M.A. thesis, Duke University, 1942.

Wieck, Edward A. *The American Miners' Association: A Record of the Origin of Coal Miners' Unions in the United States.* New York: Russell Sage Foundation, 1940.

• Wilentz, Sean. "Against Exceptionalism: Class Consciousness and the American Labor Movement, 1790–1920." *International Labor and Working Class History* 26 (Fall 1984): 1–24.

———. "Artisan Republican Festivals and the Rise of Class Conflict in New York City, 1788–1837." In *Working-Class America, Essays on Labor, Community, and American Society.* Edited by Michael Frisch and Daniel Walkowitz, 37–77. Urbana: University of Illinois Press, 1983.

———. *Chants Democratic: New York City and the Rise of the American Working Class, 1788–1850.* New York: Oxford University Press, 1984.

———. "Industrializing America and the Irish: Towards the New Departure." *Labor History* 20 (1979): 579–95.

———. "A Reply to Criticism." *International Labor and Working Class History* 28 (Fall 1985): 46–55.

Williams, David A. *A History of Modern Wales.* 2d ed. London: John Murray, 1977.

Williams, Glanmor, ed. *Glamorgan County History.* Cardiff: University of Wales Press, 1971.

Williams, John I. "The Danks Furnace at the Millvale Works of Graff, Bennett, and Co., Pittsburgh." *The Metallurgical Review* 1 (September 1877): 37–58.

Williams, Raymond. *The Country and the City.* New York: Oxford University Press, 1973.

———. *Culture and Society, 1780–1850.* New York: Columbia University Press, 1958.

———. *The Long Revolution.* New York: Harper & Row, 1966 (1961).

———. *Marxism and Literature.* Oxford: Oxford University Press, 1977.

Wilson, Erasmus, ed. *Standard History of Pittsburgh, Pennsylvania.* Chicago: H. R. Cornell and Co, 1898.

Wiltshire, David. *The Social and Political Thought of Herbert Spencer.* Oxford: Oxford University Press, 1978.

Winch, Donald. *Adam Smith's Politics: An Essay in Historiographic Revision.* Cambridge: Cambridge University Press, 1978.

Wolff, Leon. *Lockout: The Story of the Homestead Strike of 1892—A Study of Violence, Unionism, and the Carnegie Steel Empire.* New York: Harper & Row, 1965.

Wood, Gordon S. *The Creation of the American Republic, 1776–1787.* New York: W. W. Norton and Co., 1972.

Wood, Peter. *Black Mority: Negroes in Colonial South Carolina from 1670 through the Stono Rebellion.* New York: W. W. Norton & Co., Inc., 1974.

Woodward, C. Vann. *Reunion and Reaction: The Compromise of 1877 and the End of Reconstruction*. Boston: Little & Brown, 1951.

Wright, Carroll D. "The Amalgamated Association of Iron and Steelworkers." *Quarterly Journal of Economics* 7 (July 1893): 400–32.

———. "The National Amalgamated Association of Iron, Steel, and Tin Workers, 1892–1901." *Quarterly Journal of Economics* 16 (1901): 37–68.

Wright, Herbert F. "Knox, Philander Chase." In *Dictionary of American Biography*. Edited by Dumas Malone, 5: 478–80. New York: Charles Scribner's Sons, 1960–61.

———. "Philander Chase Knox." In *The American Secretaries of State and Their Diplomacy*. Edited by Samuel Flagg Bemis, 9: 303–57. New York: Alfred A. Knopf, 1929.

Wymar, Lubomyr, and Anna Wymar. *Encyclopedic Directory of Ethnic Newspapers and Periodicals in the United States*. Little, Colo.: Libraries Unlimited, 1976.

Wymar, Lubomyr Roman. *Encyclopedic Directory of Ethnic Organizations in the United States*. Littleton, Colo.: Libraries Unlimited, 1975.

Yeager, Mary A. "Trade Protection as an International Commodity: The Case of Steel." *Journal of Economic History* 40 (1980): 33–44.

Yellen, Samuel. *American Labor Struggles*. New York: S. A. Russell, 1936.

Yellowitz, Irwin. *Industrialization and the American Labor Movement, 1850–1900*. Port Washington, N. Y.: Kennikat Press, 1977.

Youmans, Edward L., comp. *Herbert Spencer on the Americans and the Americans on Herbert Spencer*. New York: Arno Press, 1973.

Young, Alfred F. "George Robert Twelves Hewes (1742–1840): A Boston Shoemaker and the Memory of the American Revolution." *William and Mary Quarterly*, 3 ser., 38 (1981): 561–623.

Younger, Rina C. "Paintings and Graphic Images of Industry in Nineteenth-Century Pittsburgh: A Study of the Relationship between Art and Industry." Ph.D. diss., University of Pittsburgh, 1991.

Zeitlin, Jonathan. "Social Theory and the History of Work." *Social History* 8 (Oct. 1983): 365–74.

Zimbalist, Andrew, ed. *Case Studies on the Labor Process*. New York: Monthly Review Press, 1979.

Zink, Harold. *City Bosses in the United States: A Study of Twenty Municipal Bosses*. New York: AMS Press, 1968 (1930).

Index

AAISW. *See* Amalgamated Association of Iron and Steel Workers (AAISW)

Abbott, William L., 241, 279, 287

Address of the National Labor Congress to the Workingmen of the United States (coauthored by Armstrong), 84, 96, 113–14

Advisory Committee, 87, 292, 293; address to public of, 347–48, 352–54; and arming of the Homestead workers, 21; control of Homestead by, 311–12; disbanding of, 314; and 1882 strike, 179, 186, 190; and Frick, 355; during Homestead battle, 16–17, 18, 20, 319; and the lockout of 1889, 247, 248; and militia, 336; and O'Donnell, 344, 345, 356; and Pattison, 333, 334, 335; and Pinkertons, 38; and request to be deputized, 313; treason charges against, 26, 271, 331, 348–50. *See also* Amalgamated Association of Iron and Steelworkers

AFL. *See* American Federation of Labor

AIME. *See* American Institute of Mining Engineers

Allegheny Bessemer Steel Works, 94, 209, 270

Amalgamated Association of Iron and Steelworkers (AAISW), 3, 4, 13, 84, 186; and Bessemer steel production, 142, 144–46, 156, 183; and call for sympathy strike, 179, 189; and Carnegie's antiunionism, 159, 234, 242, 286, 287; and Clark, 171–76; conservatism of, 246, 289, 290, 292, 333; creation of, 103, 118; and customary rights, 120; decline in membership of, 199–200; democratic principles of, 292–93, 302; and East European immigrants, 87, 316, 317, 320–21, 332; and Edgar Thomson Works, 76, 141, 234–35; and 1892 contract, 300, 302, 309; and Frick's ultimatum, 303, 304, 305, 306, 307–08, 309, 311; and "Grand Labor Parade," 193, 194, 196–97, 198, 199; and growth of membership in 1892, 332, 475n64; and Homestead Works wage scale, 291; and intercraft rivalry, 119–20, 196–98, 199–200; and internal solidarity, 208–09; and internal dissension, 288–89; and John Elias Jones, 173, 175; and Knights of Labor, 182, 205–07,212, 213–14, 237, 310, 320; McLuckie's leadership of, 86; and mill committees, 293–95; national leadership of, and Homestead battle, 25, 30, 31, 33, 39; and nonunion workers, 308, 309; and pickets, 184; and settlement of 1882 strike, 180, 188, 190, 191; and sliding scale, 241, 248–50; social functions of, 213; and Solar Iron Works strike, 145; support of women for, 319; skilled workers in, 246–47, 248; and unskilled workers, 210, 213, 246–47, 248, 289, 298

American Federation of Labor (AFL), 207, 253, 261, 284, 290, 357

American Flint Glass Workers Union, 210, 319

American Institute of Mining Engineers (AIME), 58–59, 61, 62, 68, 71, 72

American Iron and Steel Association, 270

American Iron Works, 93, 126

American Law Review, 349

American Manufacturer, 164, 197, 288, 354

American Manufacturer and Iron World, 244–45

535

PITTSBURGH SERIES IN SOCIAL AND LABOR HISTORY
Maurine Weiner Greenwald, Editor